WORKSHOPS IN COMPUTING
Series edited by C. J. van Rijsbergen

Joseph M. Morris and Roger C. Shaw (Eds.)

4th Refinement Workshop

Proceedings of the 4th Refinement Workshop, organised by BCS-FACS, 9–11 January 1991, Cambridge

Springer-Verlag London Ltd.

Joseph M. Morris, PhD
Department of Computing Science
University of Glasgow
Glasgow, G12 8QQ, Scotland

Roger C. Shaw
Lloyd's Register of Shipping
Lloyd's Register House
29 Wellesley Road
Croydon, Surrey CR0 2AJ

ISBN 978-3-540-19657-0

British Library Cataloguing in Publication Data
4th refinement workshop, Cambridge 1991.
1. Microcomputers. Software
I. Morris, Joseph M. *1951–* II. Shaw, Roger C. F. III British Computer Society IV. Series
005. 1
ISBN 978-3-540-19657-0 ISBN 978-1-4471-3756-6 (eBook)
DOI 10.1007/978-1-4471-3756-6

Library of Congress Cataloging-in-Publication Data
Refinement Workshop (4th: 1991: Cambridge, England)
4th Refinement Workshop, Cambridge, 1991: proceedings of the 4th Refinement Workshop / organised by BCS-FACS, 9–11 January 1991, Cambridge: Joseph M. Morris and Roger C. Shaw, eds.
p. cm. — (Workshops in computing)
"Published in collaboration with the British Computer Society."
Includes index.
ISBN 978-3-540-19657-0
1. Computer software–Development–Congresses. 2. Computers–Congresses. I. Morris, Joseph M., *1951–* II. Shaw, Roger C., *1945–*
III. British Computer Society. Specialist Group in Formal Aspects of Computing Science. IV. Title. V. Title: Fourth Refinement Workshop, Cambridge, 1991.
VI. Series
QA76.76—D47R44 1991 91-422
005.1–dc20 CIP

34/3830-543210 Printed on acid-free paper

Preface

This volume contains the proceedings of the 4th Refinement Workshop which was organised by the British Computer Society specialist group in Formal Aspects of Computing Science and held in Wolfson College, Cambridge, on 9-11 January, 1991. The term *refinement* embraces the theory and practice of using formal methods for specifying and implementing hardware and software. Most of the achievements to date in the field have been in developing the theoretical framework for mathematical approaches to programming, and on the practical side in formally specifying software, while more recently we have seen the development of practical approaches to deriving programs from their specifications. The workshop gives a fair picture of the state of the art: it presents new theories for reasoning about software and hardware and case studies in applying known theory to interesting small- and medium-scale problems. We hope the book will be of interest both to researchers in formal methods, and to software engineers in industry who want to keep abreast of possible applications of formal methods in industry.

The programme consisted both of invited talks and refereed papers. The invited speakers were Ib Sørensen, Jean-Raymond Abrial, Donald MacKenzie, Ralph Back, Robert Milne, Mike Read, Mike Gordon, and Robert Worden who gave the introductory talk.This is the first refinement workshop that solicited papers for refereeing, and despite a rather late call for papers the response was excellent. Indeed we received more good quality papers than we had room for in the programme, and so the proceedings contains a couple more papers than there were presentations at the workshop.

The organising committee consisted of Rosalind Barden (Logica Cambridge, local arrangements), Stephen Bear (Hewlett-Packard), Bernard Carre (Program Validation Ltd), Tim Denvir (Praxis and DTI, finance), Joseph Morris (Glasgow University, technical programme), Roger Shaw (Lloyds Register, chair), Jim Woodcock (PRG, Oxford), and John Wordsworth (IBM, publicity). We had support from three quarters: Logica Cambridge generously gave financial support; IBM donated a prize for the best presentation (which the participants elected to give to Ken Wood); and an army of referees kindly gave up their time to review the submitted papers without delay. Perhaps it says something for the hope that formal methods may make a real contribution to the development of serious software that so many of these expert reviewers came from industry.

February 1991

Joseph M. Morris
Roger C. Shaw

Contents

The Process of Refinement

Robert Worden

Logica Cambridge Ltd
104 Hills Road
Cambridge CB2 1LQ
United Kingdom

Abstract

Ideas of opportunistic design are related to the process of refinement suggesting that it is not an ordered sequence, but that the designer's attention switches rapidly between different levels. The overall trend may be summarised as a "saw tooth".

An Introductory talk to the 4th Refinement Workshop

Logica Cambridge is Logica's advanced research centre. However, our main aim is not so much to do original research in software engineering, as to take the results of advanced research — in areas such as Formal Methods, Knowledge Based Systems and Speech technology — and introduce them into the mainstream of Logica's work. This mainstream is the development of large, complex computer systems for clients in a broad range of market sectors, such as manufacturing industry, finance, aerospace and defence. Our rôle in Logica is to show by example that the advanced techniques are practicable for use by large teams on multi-million pound projects.

In the past few years, therefore, it has been very gratifying to see formal methods moving from being an academic research topic to practical industrial takeup for at least parts of some major projects — particularly where aspects of system security or safety are critical. In these areas, formal proof as well as formal specification is important. We are also seeing increasing evidence that the use of formal notations simply for system specification, without proofs of implementations, has tremendous value in clarifying requirements and design at an early stage.

However, there is another facet of Logica Cambridge's work which is not so obviously tied to advanced software engineering research. We are also charged with ensuring that the techniques and tools used for the bulk of any large project — structured methods such as Yourdon, CASE tools, estimating and project planning tools — are chosen appropriately for each project and applied effectively. This question is obviously of major concern to Logica, since our profit on a typical large fixed-price contract is a difference between two large numbers; a difference determined by how effectively we apply today's techniques. This other side of Logica Cambridge's work therefore involves the empirical study of how people in project teams actually develop software now; of what goes right and what goes wrong with today's techniques and tools.

I am speaking to you today not as an expert on formal methods and refinement; but as somebody who, from a contact both with advanced formal methods and with the empirical study of how people develop software today , wonders how the two come together. Research on refinement is based on the view (or hope) that in future some software will be developed in a different and better way than the way it is developed now. I should like to compare that view with some recent findings about how software is developed using today's techniques.

How do people develop software ? There have been a number of empirical studies over the years. Some of these have been strongly based on some 'theoretical' view of the process, which has perhaps biassed and limited their findings. I should like to talk only about some more recent work, done at MCC in Texas, which strives hard to avoid theoretical bias and simply to observe the process. The MCC team have studied software development both 'in the large' — observing projects up to many hundreds of staff-years — and in the small. I shall discuss just one study of software design in the small, by Raymonde Guindon [1,2].

Guindon took three experienced software designers, who were rated by their colleagues as being of above average competence, and asked them to solve that old chestnut of computing, the lift control problem. They were given up to two hours to design the software to control M lifts serving N floors with realistic constraints (that the system should give a 'reasonable' service, not leaving any floors unserviced for long periods, and so on). As they solved the problem, they were asked to think out loud; they were videotaped, and the tapes and their notes were subsequently analysed.

One particularly interesting result concerned the movement of their focus of attention — whether at a particular time they were thinking mainly about the general domain of lifts and how they work, or about the specific requirement to control a lift, or about their proposed solution. On the solution side, they might be thinking about the high-level architecture, about the low-level details, or about some mid-level between the two. A graph showing the shift of this attention focus through the design session is shown in Figure 1.

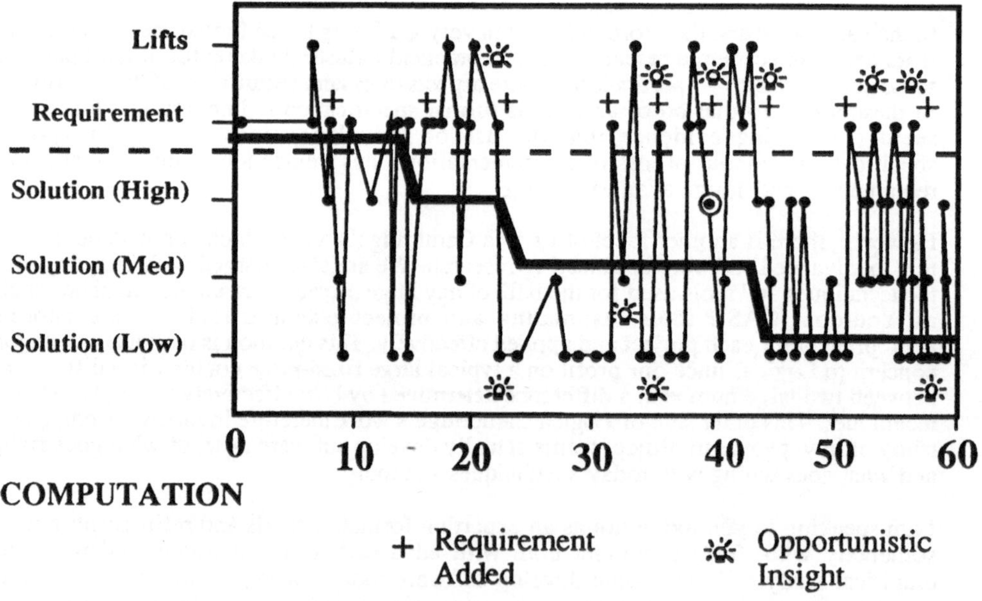

Figure 1 : Shifts of Attention during Design of a Lift Control System (Guindon 1988)

The clear result is that the designer's attention is not following any fixed path, as one would expect if he really were doing the design top-down, or bottom-up, or whatever. Guindon describes the observed design process as **opportunistic**; attention shifts are triggered in an opportunistic manner by many different aspects of the problem or its solution.

Some other features are worth noting. Since design involves bringing together a knowledge of the application domain (lifts) with a knowledge of possible computing solutions, rapid shifts of attention between the two (from top to bottom of the graph) are needed to bring the two together. Second, the "+" signs scattered throughout the process denote moments when the designer's understanding of the **requirement** was amplified and clarified as a result of trying to find a solution; this process of continually clarifying (and perhaps modifying) the requirement seems to be characteristic of software design.

Guindon notes that many of the shifts of attention were driven by the results of a **mental simulation** of the lift operation; designers without the necessary "common sense" knowledge of the domain required to make realistic simulations would be at a severe handicap.

Finally, we should note that the particular designer whose thinking is shown in Figure 1 had been trained in the JSD methodology, and was in fact trying to apply it to this problem. The idealised JSD approach is shown in the thick solid line, moving systematically from an analysis of the application domain through high-level solution to detailed solution. It is clear how different his actual design process was from the process he was trying to follow !

What has this to do with refinement ? The end result of the process — a refinement — is a strict sequence from an abstract high level specification to a detailed implementation. Each step of the sequence must (provably) preserve the meaning of the specification. This sequence starts at the top of figure 1, in abstract knowledge of the application domain, and proceeds towards the bottom, ending in a detailed computing domain. However, if the result is a strict sequence, what about the process which creates it ? Is that process, like the result, a strict sequence, or does it move back and forth like the process in figure 1 ?

Many published papers have presented the process as an ordered sequence. However, the individual steps of the sequence are each quite hard (since they involve making provably correct steps), and are therefore slow. A strict sequence would not allow the designer rapidly to bring together different kinds of knowledge at either end of the application domain/computing domain spectrum; so I suspect that a top-down sequence is not a good way to design software, even by refinement, and that it is not the way refinements are done today. I believe that whatever tools and techniques we give designers, they will still design by rapid and opportunistic shifts of attention as in Figure 1.

My personal guess at how refinements really happen is shown in figure 2.

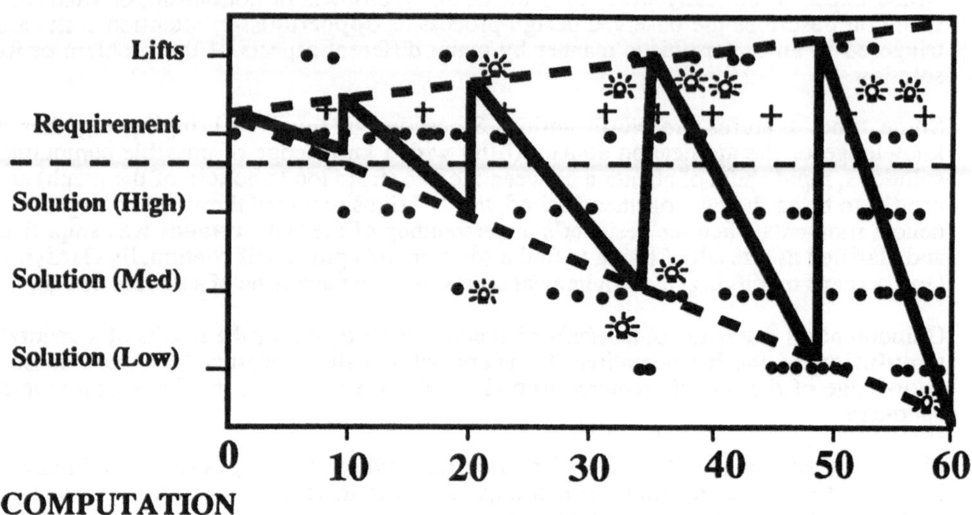

Figure 2 : Suggested Shifts of Attention in a Software Design by Refinement

The designer's focus of attention still moves rapidly between the different levels (small dots and light-bulbs), but the overall trend is summarised by the solid "saw-tooth" line. From an initial specification of the problem, the designer starts to move slowly towards a solution — the first downward slope. This soon stalls, and the designer moves back to a better (perhaps more abstract) statement of the problem — the first upward line of the saw-tooth. From this new specification the next refinement proceeds more rapidly (a steeper slope) and further; but it too eventually stalls leading back to another re-statement of the problem. The process continues, leading to more abstract and elegant statements of the problem (note the upward slope of the upper dashed line), and to more rapid refinements, until on the final descent the full solution is obtained.

What is usually reported, in published papers or in project documentation, is only the last (cleanest) specification and the last descent of the refinement slope— perhaps giving a false impression of a process more elegant and systematic than that which really took place. There is in fact a lot of useful information in the previous traversals of the saw-tooth — for instance, about why certain forms of specification or design were not used — which usually ends up in the waste-paper basket. Only the designer remembers his/her mistakes, and buries them so that others cannot learn from them.This information would be very useful to future developers of the system to explain the rationale for the chosen design, and to help them avoid repeating the mistakes. As the system evolves and as requirements change, it is important to know which altered requirements invalidate which assumptions in the development; some changes might require going back over several peaks of the saw-tooth.

Clearly a 'clean' set of documentation which describes only the chosen solution is most useful for many purposes; but some way of digging beneath the surface of this clean set, to find what lies behind it, is also necessary.

The search for better ways of developing software by refinement is largely a search for mathematical power and elegance. In this search for elegant solutions, we should not forget the less elegant processes which precede them. Our tools and techniques should support those inelegant, opportunistic human processes as much as they support the elegant results.

References

[1] R Guindon, *The knowledge exploited by experts during software system design*, International Journal of Man-Machine Studies 33, pp279 - 304, 1990

[2] R, Guindon, *Designing the design process: Exploiting opportunistic thoughts*, Human Computer Interaction, in press

Engineering Real Software Using Formal Methods

M. K. O. Lee, P. N. Scharbach and I. H. Sørensen

Information Science and Engineering Branch
BP Research
Sunbury Research Centre
Sunbury-on-Thames, Middx TW16 7LN

Abstract

B is a formal method for the incremental development of specifications and their refinements. A prototype set of software tools supporting the method has been developed by J.-R. Abrial and BP Research. The tools support the method in the development of verifiably correct software over the spectrum of activities from early specification to coding. The platform of the toolkit is the B tool, an interactive proof assistant. The process followed using the method and tools is illustrated here in the development of a document management system. We present some early indications of the productivity of the method. It is our ultimate purpose to establish the practicality of fully applying formal techniques at all stages of software development.

1 Introduction

B is a formal method, based on the Abstract Machine Notation [1], [2], for the incremental development of specifications and their refinements. The semantics of the notation is axiomatised by a calculus of Generalised Substitutions, an extension of earlier work by Dijkstra [3]. AMN is a state-based approach in the tradition of VDM [4] and Z [5], and captures both specification and refinement concepts in one notation. A prototype set of computer-aided tools supporting the **B** method has been developed by J.-R. Abrial and BP Research. The tools support the method over the spectrum of development from specification to coding.

The tools are written as rule bases, encoding along with other programming knowledge the calculus of Generalised Substitutions. The toolkit has at its kernel the **B** tool, an interactive proof assistant developed by Abrial [6]. As the **B** tool's central mechanism is that of pattern matching, it can be - and is - used both for generating and discharging the proof obligations incurred in formal software development, and for generating documentation and code through the use of specialised rule bases.

To date, aspects of the method and tools have been demonstrated on a range of applications, from small case studies (see, e.g., [7]) to large-scale industrial real-time systems and information systems. *It is our ultimate purpose to establish the practicality of fully applying formal techniques at all stages of software development.*

In this paper we briefly introduce the method and the tool assistance developed so far. A full development, from an informal specification to a system written in C and providing an X windows interface, is then described using the example of a document management system. Section 2 gives an informal description of the functionality of the required system. Section 3 provides some details of the formal specification, using the Abstract Machine Notation, which was analysed for consistency using the tool **devB**. Section 4 describes how the refinement is carried out by the importation of a reusable Abstract Machine providing low-level file storage and access functions. The tools **genB**, **genC** and **transC** are used in the design and refinement. In Section 5, a user interface to the system is constructed, again through the importation of a standard Abstract Machine. An X windows interface to the document management system was generated by the tool **transX** from the specification of the interface given in this Section. We conclude with some observations on the productivity of the approach based on the present example, and on an industrial application currently under development by BP.

1.1 The Method

The development process used for the application described in this paper consists of the following stages (illustrated in figure 1):

1. The functional requirements for the system are captured in a form (the formal specification) which can be mathematically analysed for consistency.
2. A design of the system is systematically produced by refinement of the formal specification (using reusable design components) in such a way that the design can be formally verified to meet the specification.
3. The required programs are automatically synthesized from the design using rules embedded in code generators which ensure that the delivered software is correct with respect to its specification.

The method is model-oriented. The AMN specification is an abstract model (based on set theory) of the information which needs to be recorded in the system, together with a description of the transformations on the information involved in meeting the various functional requirements concerned. The design is a model of the objects which are used to represent the information within the computer together with a description of the transformations on the objects. These verifiable models are referred to as Abstract Machines.

Essentially there are three views of the model representing a software system. On the one hand, the client focuses on the requirements specification; on the other hand the user's main source of reference is the documentation provided; yet the computer is only concerned with the programs that run on it. The toolkit ensures that the three views are indeed consistent. This consistency is a prerequisite for any claim of high product quality.

1.2 The Toolkit

The practical application of the method exploits a set of suitably integrated tools, covering several stages of software development. The major tools in place at present are:

- **devB**: a specification and refinement development assistant
- **genB, genC**: automatic specification and code generators for reusable design components
- **transC**: a translator for producing C code
- **transX**: a translator for producing an X windows interface program

- **docB: a LaTeX documentation synthesizer**

Figure 2 illustrates the use of the tools in developing software using the method. The specification and refinement development tool automatically isolates out those properties that must be verified for correctness, and helps in performing the verification. The generators produce specifications and corresponding code from a library of reusable designs. The translators produce code automatically from AMN specifications. This includes C code for the main program and a corresponding window interface based on the X window management system. The documentation synthesizer systematizes and automates the production of high quality LaTeX documentation. The basic platform for these tools is the generic interactive theorem proving assistant, the B tool.

The typical sequence of steps followed in developing software using the full range of tools is shown in table 1. Figure 3 illustrates the detailed processes involved and the various information flows within the method.

1.3 The B Proof Assistant

The backbone of the toolkit is the **B** tool, a powerful symbolic manipulator which assumes the dual role of a symbolic interpreter (on which the other tools run) and a rule-based general purpose theorem-proving assistant. The emphasis of the theorem-proving assistant is on providing a convenient environment to assist the user in the ordinary process of formal manipulation by reducing some of the mental and clerical effort required.

The **B** proof assistant is implemented as an interactive program providing an environment in which formal models (e.g. of software) can be built and subsequently refined and tested (e.g. verified) using theorem-proving techniques. By basing the development tools on the **B** tool and exploiting its symbolic interpreter mode, an integrated environment is obtained which facilitates the software development process and helps to bridge the gap between design and verification in practice.

2 Informal User Requirements: a Document Management System

A computer-based system is required for sharing *information* among *people* working in an *organisation*. More specifically, the aim of the system is to allow an individual in an organisation to:

1. publish information in the form of *documents* to particular teams of people

2. access information related to teams to which the individual belongs
3. join and leave teams.

The following characteristics of the system were identified about information and documents:

- *Information* resides in *documents* which are accessible to *team workers* who belong to *teams.*

Concerning teams:

- *Current workers* may be *team members* of more than one team at a time.
- The organisation, known as the *Centre*, is a team to which all workers belong.
- Every current worker forms a *private team* consisting of him/herself only.
- Teams form and disperse. The lifetime of a private team ends when the current worker comprising that team leaves the Centre. However, the Centre itself has an infinite lifetime.
- The Centre team cannot be removed. When a worker leaves, the corresponding private team is removed. All other teams can be removed explicitly.
- The removal of a team results in the removal of the associated team documents.

Concerning publishing and accessing documents:

- Information is published as a document for a particular team; subsequently this document is accessible to members of that team only.
- A publisher is the one person responsible for publishing a document even in the case of joint authors.
- When publishing, the publisher chooses the recipient team. The recipient team can be the entire organisation, in which case the published information is *public information.* The recipient team can be a *private team*, in which case the published information is *private information.* A worker can use his/her own private team to maintain a private record of his/her own documents.

Concerning documents:

- A document is published as a unit. Therefore, if some information contained in it is intended to have a different access restriction, then this part of the document must be published as another unit.

- The document name chosen for a published document must be unique within a team.
- A published document cannot be amended. Either it must be removed, or a second document containing the amended version must be published in which case it must be given a different name e.g. draft1, draft2.
- The authority to remove a published document is given to its owners, that is to any members of the team to whom the document was published.

3 The Specification

In this section the informal requirements outlined above are restated formally. The specification is in three parts: the context, the state and the operations.

3.1 The "DMSCtx" Context

This subsection describes the contextual information for interpreting the model of the state of the Document Management System (DMS).

3.1.1 SETS

The following (finite, non-empty) abstract sets are used in the model of the state of the system:

The set of all possible information, denoted by

$$INFORMATION,$$

the set of all possible documents, denoted by

$$DOCUMENT,$$

the set of all possible people, denoted by

$$PEOPLE,$$

the set of all possible teams, denoted by

$$TEAM,$$

the set of all possible names, denoted by

NAME

3.1.2 CONSTANTS

The constant *Centre* is used in the model as the name of the organisation team:

Centre

3.1.3 PROPERTIES

Centre belongs to the set *NAME*:

$Centre \in NAME$

3.2 Specification of "DMSMachine"

The Abstract Machine model of the DMS system state is given in a number of clauses: the contextual information used in the model of the state; the variables (concepts) used in the model of the state; the invariant conditions which define the allowable states of the system; the initialisation of the state variables; the operations. The DMS Abstract Machine

3.2.1 SEES

the contextual information as described above in

DMSCtx

3.2.2 VARIABLES

Employees, current employees, former employees and employee names are described below using the variables

TeamWorkers, *CurrentWorkers*, *LeftWorkers*, *WorkerName*,

Groups of employees identified as needing access to common information are known as teams. The teams and the team structure are described below using the variables

CCteams, TeamName, TeamMembers, PrivateTeam, CC,

Information in the Centre is organised into documents. The documents and the document-team interrelationships are described below using the variables

CCdocuments, DocumentName, DocInfo, Publisher, TeamDocument

3.2.3 INVARIANT

The invariant conditions listed below define the allowable system state.

The known team workers consist of those workers currently working for the Centre and those workers who have left the Centre. All team workers have names.

$TeamWorkers \subseteq PEOPLE$;
$CurrentWorkers \subseteq PEOPLE$;
$LeftWorkers \subseteq PEOPLE$;
$TeamWorkers = CurrentWorkers \cup LeftWorkers$;
$CurrentWorkers \cap LeftWorkers = \varnothing$;
$WorkerName \in TeamWorkers \rightarrowtail NAME$;

The known team workers are represented by the set *TeamWorkers*, a subset of *PEOPLE*. The workers who are currently working as team workers are represented by the set *CurrentWorkers*. The workers who no longer work as team workers, having left the Centre, are represented by the set *LeftWorkers*. Both sets *CurrentWorkers* and *LeftWorkers* are subsets of *PEOPLE*. The known team workers are all the known current workers and all the known left workers. At any one time, a team worker is either a current worker or a left worker, but not both. All team workers have a uniquely identifiable name associated with them, hence the one-to-one mapping *WorkerName*.

Every team has a name:

$CCteams \subseteq TEAM$;
$TeamName \in CCteams \rightarrowtail NAME$;

The known teams are represented by the set *CCteams*, a subset of *TEAM*. Every team has a unique name, hence the one-to-one mapping *TeamName*.

All current workers are organised into at least one team, namely their own private team.

$TeamMembers \in CCteams \leftrightarrow CurrentWorkers$;
$PrivateTeam \in CurrentWorkers \rightarrowtail CCteams$;
$PrivateTeam^{-1} \subseteq TeamMembers$;
$CurrentWorkers \lhd WorkerName = (PrivateTeam ; TeamName)$;

All known current workers are organised into teams. A team may have several workers and a worker may participate in several teams, hence the many-to-many relationship *TeamMembers*. Moreover, every current worker is at least in the one team that is his/her *PrivateTeam*. Such an individual team consists of that single member. The name of any such private team is the same as the name of the current worker whose individual team it is.

The Centre is a special team, *CC*.

$$
\begin{aligned}
&CC \in CCteams\,;\\
&TeamName(CC) = Centre\,;\\
&\neg\,(CC \in ran\,(PrivateTeam))\,;\\
&CurrentWorkers = TeamMembers[\{CC\}]\,;
\end{aligned}
$$

The Centre, *CC*, is a special team amongst all the teams. The team name of the Centre is simply *Centre*. The current workers are the team members of the Centre.

Centre documents have a name, contain information and have a publisher.

$$
\begin{aligned}
&CCdocuments \subseteq DOCUMENT\,;\\
&DocumentName \in CCdocuments \rightarrow NAME\,;\\
&TeamDocument \in CCdocuments \rightarrow CCteams\,;\\
&\forall\, t\,.\,(t \in CCteams \;\Rightarrow\; TeamDocument^{-1}[\{t\}] \lhd DocumentName\\
&\qquad\quad \in CCdocuments \rightarrowtail\!\!\!\!\rightarrow NAME)\,;\\
&DocInfo \in CCdocuments \rightarrow INFORMATION\,;\\
&Publisher \in CCdocuments \rightarrow TeamWorkers
\end{aligned}
$$

The Centre documents are represented by the set *CCdocuments*, a subset of *DOCUMENT*. A document belongs to one team only. All Centre documents have a uniquely identifiable name within a team and all documents contain information. Centre documents are published by Centre team workers; more precisely, both current and left workers can be recorded publishers of documents. (However, at the time of publication the publisher must be a current worker).

3.2.4 INITIALISATION

The state variables are initialised by:

```
begin
   any  ct  where
      ct ∈ TEAM
   then
      TeamWorkers := ∅ ||
      CurrentWorkers := ∅ ||
      LeftWorkers := ∅ ||
      WorkerName := ∅ ||
      CCteams := {ct} ||
      TeamName := {ct ↦ Centre} ||
      TeamMembers := ∅ ||
      PrivateTeam := ∅ ||
      CCdocuments := ∅ ||
      DocumentName := ∅ ||
      DocInfo := ∅ ||
      Publisher := ∅ ||
      TeamDocument := ∅ ||
      CC := ct
   end
end
```

3.2.5 OPERATIONS

In this document, only the operation of introducing a new worker into the DMS system will be discussed in detail. Two query operations will also be needed in constructing the *CREATE WORKER* option offered by the DMS user interface (Section 5). Their specifications are also given below.

The "CreateNewWorker" Operation

In order for the creation of a new worker and the corresponding private team to take place the name provided must be a new name, it must neither be a name of an existing team nor must it be a name of a worker (current or left).

As a result of the creation of a new worker, the new member joins the Centre team and, therefore, can access all public information and use his/her private team to receive private information.

In what follows, *newworker* denotes an element from the *PEOPLE* set which is not already in the set *TeamWorkers*. *newteam* denotes an element from the *TEAM* set which is not already in the *CCteams* set. *CurrentWorkers* is extended to include *newworker*. *WorkerName* is extended to associate the *newworker* with his/her name. *PrivateTeam* is extended to associate the *newworker* with his/her private *newteam*. *CCteams* is extended to include this private *newteam* and *TeamName* is extended to associate this private *newteam* with the name of *newworker*. *TeamMembers* is extended to make *newworker* a member of the Centre and a member of his/her private team.

```
CreateNewWorker (name) =
  pre
    name ∈ NAME ∧
    ¬ (name ∈ ran (TeamName)) ∧
    ¬ (name ∈ ran (WorkerName))
  then
    any  newworker, newteam  where
      newworker ∈ PEOPLE − TeamWorkers ∧
      newteam ∈ TEAM − CCteams
    then
      CurrentWorkers := CurrentWorkers ∪ {newworker} ||
      WorkerName := WorkerName ∪ {newworker ↦ name} ||
      TeamWorkers := TeamWorkers ∪ {newworker} ||
      PrivateTeam := PrivateTeam ∪ {newworker ↦ newteam} ||
      CCteams := CCteams ∪ {newteam} ||
      TeamName := TeamName ∪ {newteam ↦ name} ||
      TeamMembers := TeamMembers ∪ {CC ↦ newworker, newteam ↦ newworker}
    end
  end;
```

The "getTeamNames" Operation

```
s ⟵ getTeamNames =
  begin
    s := ran (TeamName)
  end;
```

The "getWorkerNames" Operation

```
s ⟵ getWorkerNames =
  begin
    s := ran (WorkerName)
  end
```

3.3 Analysis of the AMN Specification

The tool **devB** may be used to analyse the AMN specification for internal consistency. **devB** parses the input specification and generates a number of proof obligations:

- **That, under the hypothesis of the context, the initialisation establishes the invariant:**

$$ctx(DMSMachine)$$
$$\Rightarrow$$
$$[ini(DMSMachine)]inv(DMSMachine)$$

- **That, under the assumption of the context, the invariant and the precondition of the operation, each operation re-establishes the invariant:**

$$ctx(DMSMachine) \wedge$$
$$inv(DMSMachine) \wedge$$
$$pre(CreateNewWorker(name))$$
$$\Rightarrow$$
$$[CreateNewWorker(name)]inv(DMSMachine)$$

(Here, *ini* denotes the initialisation operation, *ctx* and *inv* denote the context and invariant of the machine, respectively, *pre* denotes the precondition of the operation, and square brackets denote multiple substitution). The calculus of Generalised Substitutions is used by **devB** to reduce each proof obligation to a number of mathematical lemmas, or subgoals, on which its correctness depends. For example, the following two lemmas must be proved in order to verify that the *CreateNewWorker* operation preserves the invariant constraint that *CurrentWorkers* and *LeftWorkers* partition *TeamWorkers* (see Section 3.2.3):

$$ctx(DMSMachine) \wedge$$
$$inv(DMSMachine) \wedge$$
$$pre(CreateNewWorker(name)) \wedge$$
$$newworker \in PEOPLE - TeamWorkers \wedge$$
$$newteam \in TEAM - CCteams$$
$$\Rightarrow$$
$$(CurrentWorkers \cup \{newworker\}) \cap LeftWorkers = \varnothing$$

$$ctx(DMSMachine) \wedge$$
$$inv(DMSMachine) \wedge$$
$$pre(CreateNewWorker(name)) \wedge$$
$$newworker \in PEOPLE - TeamWorkers \wedge$$
$$newteam \in TEAM - CCteams$$
$$\Rightarrow$$
$$TeamWorkers \cup \{newworker\} = (CurrentWorkers \cup \{newworker\}) \cup LeftWorkers$$

The lemmas generated may be discharged by the underlying **B** proof assistant, using standard mathematical laws from theory libraries or input by the user [6].

4 Design and Refinement

The specification is a model of the real world (*what*). Design and refinement model the corresponding representation in the computer (*how*). Both specification and refinement use the same Abstract Machine Notation. Design decisions are based on knowledge about possible implementations and are guided by the characteristics of the implementations, especially with respect to the size of storage they require, and the speed at which they execute. The choice is also guided by knowledge about the frequency with which the specified operations are invoked and their corresponding response requirements. Hence the introduction of redundancy in the design below (Section 4.4.3).

The design intentions for the DMS system are prescribed (using a special-purpose notation for input to the **genB** and **genC** tools) by:

4.1 Design for the "DMSBase" System

$Center \in OBJ(Teams)$;

The "Workers" Database

Mandatory Fields:

$Wname \in STR$;
$WCworkers \in OBJ$

Optional Fields:

$WorkerTeam \in OBJ(Teams)$;
$Wteams \in SET(Teams)$;
$Wpubdoc \in SET(Documents)$;

The "Teams" Database

Mandatory Fields:

$TCteams \in OBJ$

Optional Fields:

$Tname \in STR$;
$Tmembers \in SET(Workers)$;
$Tdoc \in SET(Documents)$;

The "Documents" Database

Mandatory Fields:

$DCdocuments \in OBJ$

Optional Fields:

$Dname \in STR$;
$Dinfo \in STR$;
$Dteam \in OBJ(Teams)$;
$Dpub \in OBJ(Workers)$

The design includes three databases: *Workers*, *Teams* and *Documents*, each modelled as a subset of *OBJECT* (see below). Each data structure has several attributes. Some attributes are mandatory, e.g. *Wname*, in which case the model is a total function. Some attributes are optional, e.g. *Wpubdoc*, in which case the model is a partial function. Attributes can be objects (*OBJ*, e.g. integers, references, bit patterns), strings (*STR*) or sets of objects (*SET*).

The specification generator **genB** produces an AMN specification from the above input system description. This generated Abstract Machine, *DMSBase*, will be imported [7] into the refinement of *DMSMachine*. The *DMSBase* machine, which is not fully given here, consists of a model of the concrete state and a specification of all necessary operations for that model. The model generated by **genB** is

4.2 Specification of "DMSBase"

4.2.1 INVARIANT

Center is the special centre team.

$Center \in Teams$;

The *Workers* database contains the total functions *Wname* and *WCworkers*, the partial function *WorkerTeam* and relations *Wteams* and *Wpubdoc*:

$Workers \in \mathbb{P}\ OBJECT$;
$Wname \in Workers \rightarrow STRING$;
$WCworkers \in Workers \rightarrow OBJECT$;
$WorkerTeam \in Workers \nrightarrow Teams$;
$Wteams \in Workers \leftrightarrow Teams$;
$Wpubdoc \in Workers \leftrightarrow Documents$;

The *Teams* database contains the total function *TCteams*, the partial function *Tname* and relations *Tmembers* and *Tdoc*:

$Teams \in \mathbb{P}\ OBJECT$;
$TCteams \in Teams \rightarrow OBJECT$;
$Tname \in Teams \nrightarrow STRING$;
$Tmembers \in Teams \leftrightarrow Workers$;
$Tdoc \in Teams \leftrightarrow Documents$;

The *Documents* database contains the total function *DCdocuments* and partial functions *Dname*, *Dinfo*, *Dteam* and *Dpub*:

$Documents \in \mathbb{P}\ OBJECT$;
$DCdocuments \in Documents \rightarrow OBJECT$;
$Dname \in Documents \nrightarrow STRING$;
$Dinfo \in Documents \nrightarrow STRING$;
$Dteam \in Documents \nrightarrow Teams$;
$Dpub \in Documents \nrightarrow Workers$

4.2.2 OPERATIONS

The "rangeTname" Operation

The range of the function *Tname* is returned:

$v \longleftarrow rangeTname\ =$
begin
$v := ran\,(Tname)$
end;

The "assignTname" Operation

Sets $Tname(o)$ to a given string:

$assignTname\,(o, t)\ =$
pre
$o \in dom\,(Tname) \wedge$
$t \in STRING$
then
$Tname(o) := t$
end;

The "creTname" Operation

Puts a new element in the domain of *Tname* and sets its image to the empty string:

```
creTname (o)  =
   pre
      o ∈ Teams − dom (Tname)
   then
      Tname(o) := <>
   end;
```

The "addTmembers" Operation

Adds a given maplet to the relation *Tmembers*:

```
addTmembers (o, t)  =
   pre
      o ∈ Teams ∧
      t ∈ Workers
   then
      Tmembers := Tmembers ∪ {o ↦ t}
   end;
```

The "makTeams" Operation

Creates a new element in the *Teams* database, returns an identifier for the new element, and sets its mandatory attribute *TCteams* to a given value:

```
o ⟵ makTeams (a)  =
   pre
      a ∈ OBJECT
   then
      any  oo  where
         oo ∈ OBJECT − Teams
      then
         Teams := Teams ∪ {oo} ||
         TCteams(oo) := a ||
         o := oo
      end
   end;
```

The "rangeWname" Operation

The range of the attribute *Wname* is returned:

$v \longleftarrow rangeWname \;=$
  begin
    $v := ran\,(Wname)$
  end;

The "assignWname" Operation

Sets $Wname(o)$ to a given string:

$assignWname\,(o, t) \;=$
  pre
    $o \in Workers \wedge$
    $t \in STRING$
  then
    $Wname(o) := t$
  end;

The "modWorkerTeam" Operation

Sets $WorkerTeam(o)$ to a given value:

$modWorkerTeam\,(o, v) \;=$
  pre
    $o \in Workers \wedge$
    $v \in Teams$
  then
    $WorkerTeam(o) := v$
  end;

The "addWteams" Operation

Adds a given maplet to the relation *Wteams*:

```
addWteams (o, t)  =
   pre
      o ∈ Workers ∧
      t ∈ Teams
   then
      Wteams := Wteams ∪ {o ↦ t}
   end;
```

The "makWorkers" Operation

Creates a new element in the *Workers* database, returns an identifier for the new element, and sets its mandatory attribute *WCworkers* to a given value and its mandatory attribute *Wname* to the empty string:

```
o ⟵ makWorkers (a)  =
   pre
      a ∈ OBJECT
   then
      any  oo  where
         oo ∈ OBJECT − Workers
      then
         Workers := Workers ∪ {oo} ||
         WCworkers(oo) := a ||
         Wname(oo) := <> ||
         o := oo
      end
   end;
```

The "valCenter" Operation

The value of the variable *Center* is returned:

```
s ⟵ valCenter  =
   begin
      s := Center
   end
```

4.3 The "DMSRefCtx" Context

The decisions on how to represent concretely the abstract sets of the *DMSMachine* specification are documented in this context.

4.3.1 CONSTANTS

Two constants are introduced as status flags in the refinement (Section 4.4.3):

yes, no

4.3.2 PROPERTIES

Some abstract sets are represented as sets of objects:

$DOCUMENT = OBJECT$;
$PEOPLE = OBJECT$;
$TEAM = OBJECT$;

Some abstract sets are represented as sets of strings:

$NAME = STRING$;
$INFORMATION = STRING$;

The constant *yes* is represented as an object:

$yes \in OBJECT$;

The constant *no* is represented as an object:

$no \in OBJECT$;

yes and *no* are distinct:

$\neg\ (yes = no)$;

The name of the Centre team is represented by the string *CIT*:

$Centre = CIT$

4.4 Refinement of "DMSMachine"

4.4.1 SEES

DMSRefCtx,
ObjectsRefCtx

ObjectsRefCtx is further concrete contextual information generated by **genB**, and is not reproduced here.

4.4.2 IMPORTS

DMSBase

The abstract machine generated by **genB** is imported in the refinement of *DMS-Machine*. A simultaneous operation and data refinement will be carried out in one step.

4.4.3 CHANGE

Some of the abstract state variables are directly represented by concrete state variables:

$TeamWorkers = Workers\,;$
$WorkerName = Wname\,;$
$TeamName = Tname\,;$
$TeamMembers = Tmembers\,;$
$PrivateTeam = WorkerTeam\,;$
$DocumentName = Dname\,;$
$DocInfo = Dinfo\,;$
$Publisher = Dpub\,;$
$TeamDocument = Dteam\,;$
$CC = Center\,;$

A change to a concrete variable, involving a status flag, is used for partitioned abstract variables:

$CurrentWorkers = dom\,(WCworkers \rhd \{yes\})\,;$
$LeftWorkers = dom\,(WCworkers \rhd \{no\})\,;$
$CCteams = dom\,(TCteams \rhd \{yes\})\,;$
$CCdocuments = dom\,(DCdocuments \rhd \{yes\})\,;$

We shall want the DMS system to be able, for example, not only to find the members of a given team, but also the teams to which a given worker belongs. To improve the performance of searching, redundant concrete variables are introduced, which are inverses of concrete variables already introduced:

$TeamMembers = Wteams^{-1}\,;$
$Publisher = Wpubdoc^{-1}\,;$
$TeamDocument = Tdoc^{-1}$

4.4.4 INITIALISATION

The initialisation is not reproduced here.

4.4.5 OPERATIONS

The "CreateNewWorker" Operation

The refined operation is written as a sequence of operations from the imported machine:

```
CreateNewWorker (name) =
   var  w, t, c  in
      w ←— makWorkers(yes);
      assignWname(w, name);
      c ←— valCenter;
      addWteams(w, c);
      addTmembers(c, w);
      t ←— makTeams(yes);
      modWorkerTeam(w, t);
      creTname(t);
      assignTname(t, name);
      addWteams(w, t);
      addTmembers(t, w)
   end;
```

The "getTeamNames" Operation

The specification of the interface requires the following refinements:

```
s ←— getTeamNames  =
   begin
      s ←— rangeTname
   end;
```

The "getWorkerNames" Operation

```
s ←— getWorkerNames  =
   begin
      s ←— rangeWname
   end
```

4.5 Analysis of the Refinement

The tool **devB** is able, on the basis of an input proposed refinement, to generate the proof obligations which must be discharged to verify that the proposal correctly refines the specification [2]. The process followed is similar to that of verifying specification consistency (Section 3.3). A proof obligation is produced for the initialisation and for each of the operations. In the present case, the initialisation refinement proof obligation is

$$ctx(DMSMachine)$$
$$\Rightarrow$$
$$[ini(DMSMachine_2)]not([ini(DMSMachine_1)]not(inv(DMSMachine_{21})))$$

where $ctx(DMSMachine)$ denotes the context of the machine, $ini(DMSMachine_1)$ and $ini(DMSMachine_2)$ denote the initialisations of the specification and refinement respectively, and $inv(DMSMachine_{21})$ denotes the change of variable between the concrete and abstract variables.

For the *CreateNewWorker* operation, for example, the proof obligation generated is

$$ctx(DMSMachine) \wedge$$
$$inv(DMSMachine_2) \wedge$$
$$pre(CreateNewWorker_1(name))$$
$$\Rightarrow$$
$$[CreateNewWorker_2(name)]not([CreateNewWorker_1(name)]not(inv(DMSMachine_{21})))$$

Here, $inv(DMSMachine_2)$ denotes the conjunction of the invariant of the specification, the change of variable, and the invariant of the imported *DMSBase* machine. Labels 1 and 2 on variables and operation names refer to the specification and refinement, respectively. $inv(DMSMachine_{21})$ denotes the change of variable predicate.

As in the case of the specification analysis, (Section 3.3), **devB** reduces each refinement proof obligation to a set of mathematical subgoals on which the correctness proof depends. The B tool may be used to prove the subgoals.

5 The User Interface

The DMS interface, i.e. the code which allows the end user to invoke the operations of the system, supply the correct parameters and read the results, is also specified as an Abstract Machine. The specification takes the form of the design of an algorithm for the invocation of the operations, within their specified preconditions, of the underlying *DMSMachine*.

A library of reusable AMN specifications for read and display operations (some of which are parametrised) is used in the specification. This library is implemented within the window generator tool transX. Only that part of the interface specification relevant to the creation of a new worker is presented below.

5.1 The "DMS" Interface

5.1.1 IMPORTS

DMSMachine

The *DMS* interface imports the Abstract Machine *DMSMachine* (and, implicitly, a standard input/output Abstract Machine).

5.1.2 INVARIANT

$allTeamNames \in SET$;
$allWorkerNames \in SET$;
$newName \in STRING$

5.1.3 OPERATIONS

The "CREATE WORKER" Operation

The *CREATE WORKER* operation requests the user to input a worker's name (*newName*). Provided it does not already exist as a worker name or as a team name in the system, a worker is created with the *newName*.

getTeamNames, *getWorkerNames* and *CreateNewWorker* are operations specified, refined and implemented as part of the imported *DMSMachine*. *readString* is a parametrised, reusable operation imported from a standard i/o Machine.

CREATE WORKER =

begin
allTeamNames ⟵ *getTeamNames*;
allWorkerNames ⟵ *getWorkerNames*;
newName ⟵ *readString*(" *What is the workers name?*" *WHERE*
¬ (*newName* ∈ *allTeamNames*) ∧ ¬ (*newName* ∈ *allWorkerNames*));
CreateNewWorker(*newName*)
end

The interface specification serves two purposes:

1. Given specifications of the reusable input/output operations, e.g. *readString*, and the specifications of the operations of *DMSMachine*, it can be verified that all operations are in fact invoked within their preconditions (future versions of **devB** will automatically generate the relevant proof obligations).
2. The code generator **transX** generates, from the interface specification, all necessary code modules for a simple X windows-based interface. This interface allows the user to select DMS operations from a menu, and to input parameters either directly or by mouse selection. Directives to the code generator are included in the interface specification, e.g. the *readString* operation prompts the user with the message *What is the workers name?*, and will accept only an input *newName* string satisfying the predicate appearing in the *WHERE* clause of the operation. The specification of $a \longleftarrow readString(b \ WHERE \ P(a))$ is:

```
pre
   b ∈ STRING
then
   any  c  where
      c ∈ STRING ∧ P(c)
   then
      prompt := b ||
      a := c
   end
end
```

6 Conclusions

A prototype document management system was formally developed from an Abstract Machine specification, using the **B** toolkit. The system governs the creation and dissemination of information to users under a defined access policy. The refinement makes use of reusable low-level storage and access components, and interface operations, all available as off-the-shelf Abstract Machines. The resulting DMS system, consisting of 2300 lines of code, is written in C and presents an X windows user interface. All code was generated by **B** rule bases.

But does the approach scale up to the production of industrial-size systems? Projects undertaken with the **B** method at BP and elsewhere indicate that this is indeed the case. For example, we are now engaged in an effort to develop a large generic graphical system with underlying applications. A team spent approximately four man-months formally specifying the system taking a broad-based business requirements statement and an informal functional specification as a starting point. The entire AMN specification can be proved mathematically correct. To date, only parts of this specification have been proved. Design and coding was done in two separate parts - a central module and a graphical user interface based on a windows toolkit. The module was built entirely within the B method. The interaction with the windowing toolkit was done by hand, and followed the B method closely. The module took two man-months to design formally and approximately one man-month to generate the code; the windows took six man-months to design and handcode. To give a rough estimate to the split in the final system between these two aspects, approximately 28,000 lines of final code make up the central module and 17,000 lines of code make up the windows aspect of the system. The rate of code production suggests that the effort in specification and design greatly simplified the work during this stage of the project.

Our experience provides an example of how the method includes maintainability in the design. A more elegant and maintainable design for the central module emerged. The module was then redesigned and reimplemented, taking only two man-months. There was no change to the windows code, since the specification remained the same. This is attributable to the separation of concerns encouraged by the Abstract Machine approach.

References

[1] Abrial, J.-R. A Formal Approach to Large Software Construction, in *Mathematics of Program Construction* (ed. J. L. A. van de Snepscheut). Springer Verlag, 1989.

[2] Abrial, J.-R. *Assigning Programs to Meanings.* To be published, 1991.

[3] Dijkstra, E. W. *A Discipline of Programming.* Prentice Hall, 1976.

[4] Jones, C. B. *Systematic Software Development Using VDM.* Prentice Hall International, 1988.

[5] Spivey, J. M. *The Z Notation - a Reference Manual.* Prentice Hall International, 1989.

[6] Abrial, J.-R. *B Reference Manual.* Draft report, 1990.

[7] Abrial, J.-R. *A Refinement Case Study*, these Proceedings.

Action	Result
1. Specify the System in B	Formal System Specification
2. Invoke devB on the result of 1	Proof Obligations for Specification Consistency automatically generated
3. Use B Proof-Assistant to discharge result of 2	Specification Proved Consistent
4. Select reusable components from the library, invoke genB to generate specification of selected components	Specification of design components
5. Design the System using the selected components of 4	System Design Specification
6. Invoke devB on the results of 1 and 5	Proof Obligations for Design correctness automatically generated
7. Use B Proof-Assistant to discharge result of 6	Design Proved Correct
8. Specify Interface Dialogue	Interface Specification
9. Invoke transX on the result of 8	Interface Code
10. Invoke transC on the result of 5	High-Level Access Code
11. Invoke genC on the resuable components of 4	File/Storage Access Code
12. Invoke docB on the results of 1 and 5	Documentation produced

Note: the results of procedures 9, 10 and 11 together constitute the required operational programs.

Table 1 Typical Steps in the "B" Development Method

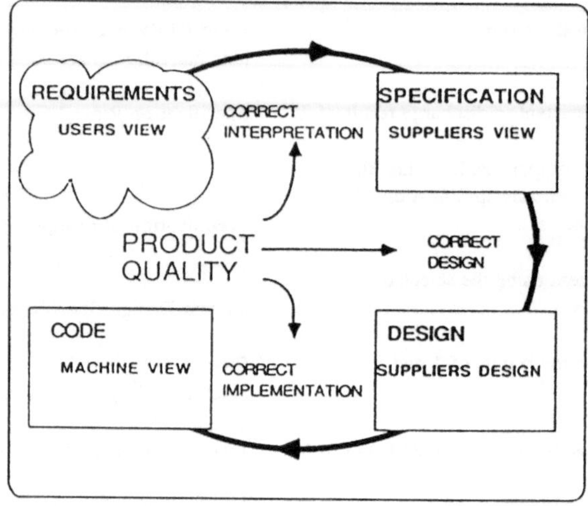

FIGURE 1

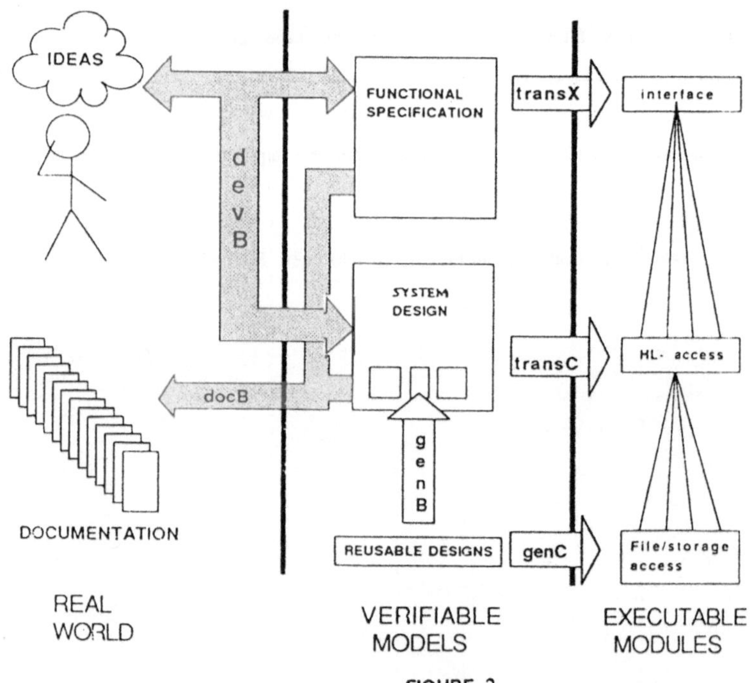

FIGURE 2

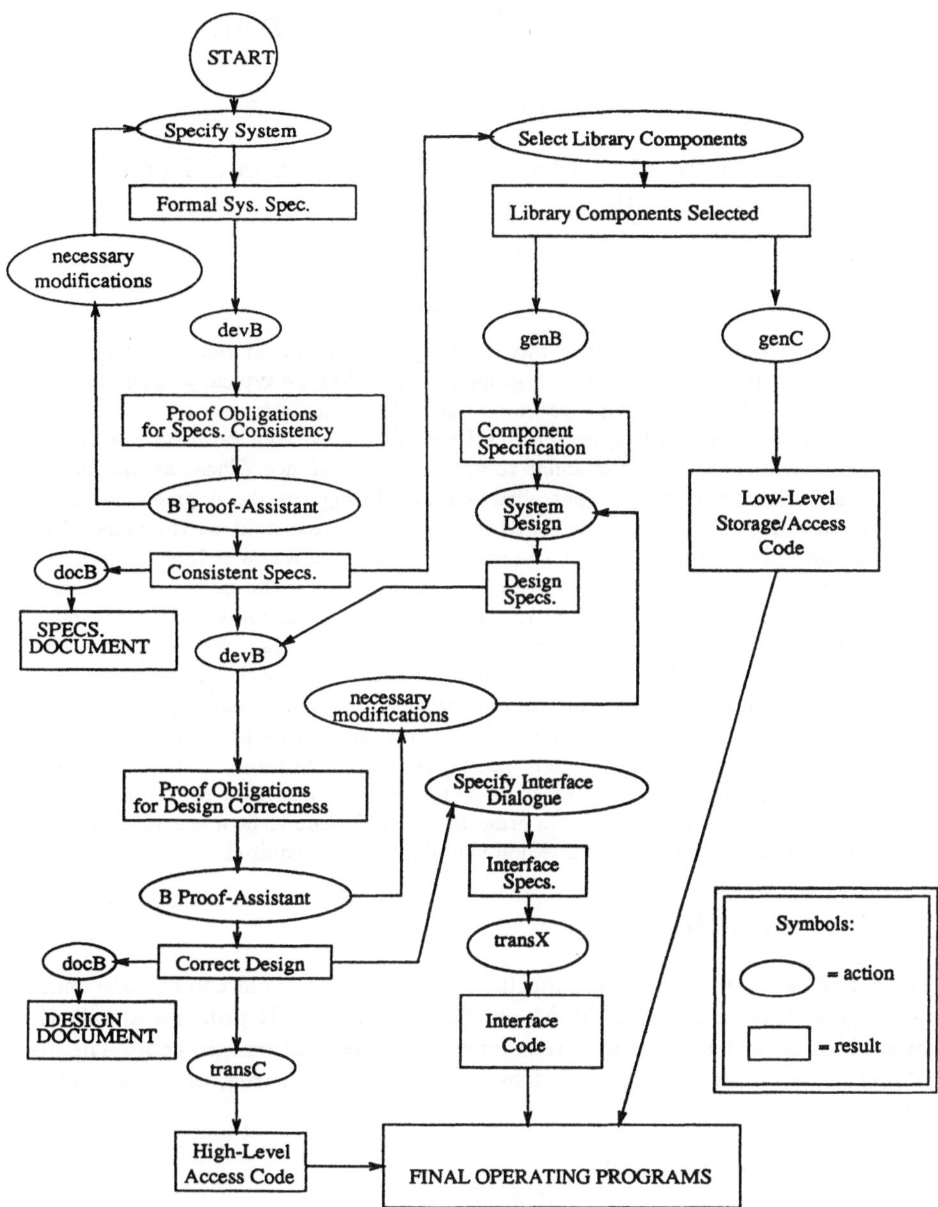

Fig. 3 THE "B" SOFTWARE DEVELOPMENT PROCESS

Specialising Abstract Programs

Andrew Gravell

Department of Electronics and Computer Science
University of Southampton

Abstract

Stepwise refinement is a way of designing families of related programs. The refinement calculus formalises design steps that are typically taken during stepwise refinement. One technique that helps in designing program families is to begin with a very general specification of the problem, omitting assumptions that are particular to one problem instance. These assumptions can be introduced in a controlled manner during the development, at the point where they are needed, rather than all at once right at the start. To support this approach within the refinement calculus, a new refinement step is needed, namely specialisation, which means introducing the extra assumptions. This paper uses specialisation to derive a family of related search programs, including binary search, and shows how binary search can also be specialised to give programs that divide, and find the square root of, binary numbers. It is hoped that, by developing many programs at once, the effort per program is reduced. To a certain extent, the derivations in this paper support that view. It appears however that specialised programs often contain complex expressions, which usually must be simplified before further refinements can be made. This suggests that, in order for specialisation to be a practical design technique, a mechanical expression simplifier is also required.

1 Introduction

The refinement calculus unifies specifications and executable code in one combined language of programs [Back 80, Morris 87, Morgan 88]. It provides a collection of laws which permit the stepwise refinement of a specification into code. The history of such a development is recorded by a list, or rather a tree, of refinement steps, each written:

$$program1 \sqsubseteq program2$$

A benefit of composing programs by stepwise refinement is that at each stage of development the refined program represents a family of possible solutions to the original problem: some design decisions have been made, while others have yet to be considered. Since the designer makes the choices explicit by selecting an appropriate refinement step, he or she is more aware of the range of possible solutions. Furthermore, by going back to some earlier point of the tree, redesigns can be carried out in a controlled way.

Another approach that is made possible by deriving programs in this way is to make use of design steps in the development of many different programs. Reuse of existing programs or designs is not, however, widely practiced, largely because it is rare to find programs or designs that fulfill exactly the desired objective of a new development. Object oriented programming supports reuse because it divides programs into small separable pieces. This contrasts with mathematics which supports reuse through abstraction and generality.

It is possible to use the refinement calculus to derive programs at a high level of abstraction, for example, programs operating on data types such as sets of abstract values. It is not possible in general to execute such programs efficiently. However, if more detail is given about the kinds of values (say, they are numbers between 1 and 8), or about the kinds of sets (say, they have at most 2 members), then more efficient implementations can be derived that exploit the particular circumstances. Usually, a representation of the data type is selected that exploits the extra assumptions. However, much of the design is independent of the assumptions, just as it is independent of the representation that the assumptions permit. It is suggested here that greater generality (and thus possibility for reuse) is achieved by carrying out the early part of the refinement at the higher level of abstraction, and without the extra assumptions being available. Only when it is important to exploit them do they need to be introduced.

Using this approach the development proceeds in two phases:

$$General\ Specification \sqsubseteq Abstract\ Program$$

$$Abstract\ Program \wedge Extra\ Assumptions \sqsubseteq Concrete\ Code$$

The first phase can be thought of as an abstract refinement. The second phase is the specialisation phase. Extra assumptions are added and exploited in a further series of refinement steps. The process may continue with the later addition of other assumptions.

From the two refinements above, it can be inferred that:

$$General\ Specification \wedge Extra\ Assumptions \sqsubseteq Concrete\ Code$$

In the examples we will be considering, the extra assumptions will simply be extra constraints on the input values. They correspond to stronger pre-conditions. The soundness of this inference then follows from the monotonicity of refinement. In particular, letting A be the extra assumption(s):

$$\begin{array}{lll} & P1 \sqsubseteq P2 & \\ \Rightarrow & S; P1 \sqsubseteq S; P2 & \text{for any statement S} \\ \Rightarrow & [true, A]; P1 \sqsubseteq [true, A]; P2 & \text{taking S as [true, A]} \\ \Rightarrow & \{A\}P1 \sqsubseteq \{A\}P2 & \text{by definition of assumption} \end{array}$$

Specialisation is the step of adding the assumption to both specification and implementation. It differs from pure refinement steps in that the specification changes as well as the implementation.

The argument above shows that specialisation is sound. Of course it is possible to add assumptions which make the augmented specification infeasible: this can, as usual, be checked for explicitly, or diagnosed through failure to reach executable code. An example of the technique is given, starting with a simple abstract search program. This is then specialised to give linear and binary searches, and, perhaps more surprisingly, some binary arithmetic algorithms, including square root.

The algorithms here are not new, nor is their derivation through formal techniques (for example see chapter 9 of Morgan's book [Morgan 90]). The purpose of this paper is to show how abstraction and specialisation permit concise, well structured refinements of families of algorithms. A number of related searching methods are covered, though only in simple forms: the intention is to cover a variety of different algorithms in a short space, and to highlight the similarities between them.

The notation used is that a mixture of Morgan's refinement calculus, used for defining algorithms, and the Z notation [Spivey 89], used for defining data.

2 The Search Problem

The binary search algorithm is well known. It is thoroughly explored by Knuth, and by Bentley in his entertaining Programming Pearls [Knuth 73, Bentley 86]. However, as Dijkstra points out, even experienced programmers frequently err in coding it. This is typically because they remember the trick for choosing the middle point, but forget the other essential details.

In a letter to Bentley, Bill McKeeman demonstrates an abstract algorithm for binary search [Bentley 84], which is more succinct, and hopefully more memorable, than the final concrete program. Here I will start with an even simpler abstract algorithm. First, let us specify the problem.

2.1 The Abstract Specification

A general search problem can be specified as follows. There is some domain of data D, with a subset of interesting items I. A program is required which will find and return a datum d which is one of the items of interest. To simplify the development we will assume that the set I is non-empty, so that there is always some such datum to be found. This description can be formalised:

$[D]$
var $I : \mathcal{P}\ D$
$d : D \bullet$
$d : [I \neq \{\}, d \in I] \quad \triangleleft$

This specification is both abstract and general. In a sense, it describes just about any programming problem. As the design unfolds, we will compromise this generality in order to obtain an efficient solution.

To help you keep track of the development, the following dependency graph shows how the algorithms are related:

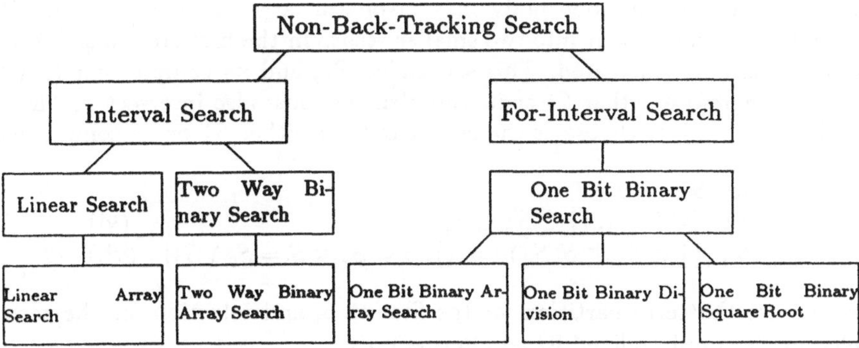

2.2 An Abstract Algorithm

In this section we will derive an abstract program that contains the essence of a particular search strategy. Later sections will take this abstract program, add extra assumptions, and derive a variety of different concrete programs.

A general search strategy involves choosing some subset S of possible candidate items. The search set S must contain at least some items of interest. If it is known that the search set has only one element, that element can be assigned to d. For simplicity, we will assume it is possible to choose a finite search set initially. A suitable strategy is therefore to start with a finite search set, to reduce its size till it has only one element, and to pick that element as the final answer.

$$\begin{array}{ll} \sqsubseteq \text{var } S : \mathcal{P}\, D \bullet & \\ \quad S : [I \neq \{\}, S \cap I \neq \{\} \wedge S \text{ finite}]; & \text{(i)} \\ \quad S : [S \text{ finite}, S \cap I \neq \{\}, \#S = 1]; & \text{(ii)} \\ \quad d : [\#S = 1, d \in S] & \text{(iii)} \end{array}$$

The middle statement is simply refined by a loop.

$$\begin{array}{lll} \text{(ii)} & \sqsubseteq & \text{do } \#S > 1 \rightarrow \\ & & \quad S : [\#S > 1, S \cap I \neq \{\}, 0 < \#S < \#S_0] \quad \text{(iv)} \\ & & \text{od} \end{array}$$

A smaller search set can be found by picking a strict subset.

$$\text{(iv)} \sqsubseteq S : [\#S > 1, S \cap I \neq \{\}, S \subset S_0] \quad \text{(v)}$$

Progress is made by choosing successively smaller search sets, until a singleton set is reached, so that only one item remains. This process is guaranteed to terminate provided since S is always finite. A diagram may help to visualise the technique.

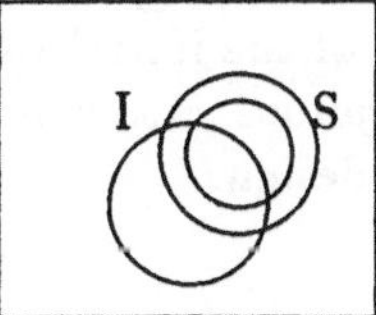

The single step in the loop body may involve a large amount of work. It is perhaps helpful to separate it into two smaller steps. In the first step, a strict, non-empty subset of S is calculated. This set, called $S1$, and its complement $(S \setminus S1)$ partition S. Therefore, either $S1$ or its complement must also intersect I. Thus, in the second step, we just choose as the new search set either $S1$ or its complement.

$$\begin{array}{lll} \text{(v)} \sqsubseteq & \text{var } S1 : \mathcal{P}\, D\bullet & \\ & S1 : [\#S > 1, \{\} \subset S1 \subset S]; & \text{(vi)} \\ & S : [\{\} \subset S1 \subset S, S \cap I \neq \{\}, S = S1 \vee S = S_0 \setminus S1] & \text{(vii)} \end{array}$$

We will use the term partition for the first step, and selection for the second. The selection is simply refined by an alternation:

$$\begin{array}{ll} \text{(vii)} \sqsubseteq & \text{if } S1 \cap I \neq \{\} \rightarrow S := S1 \\ & [] S1 \cap I = \{\} \rightarrow S := S \setminus S1 \\ & \text{fi} \qquad\qquad\qquad\qquad \text{(viii)} \end{array}$$

Note that the alternation adopted here is biased toward the first subset in the partition.

The following diagram illustrates this approach.

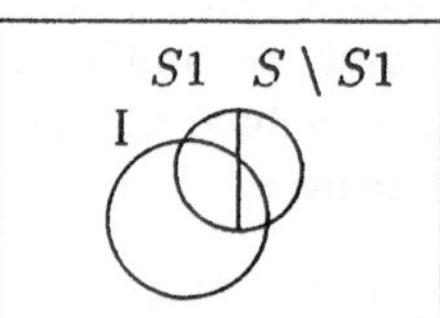

This concludes the abstract refinement. We have derived a non-back-tracking search program. At each stage, the program divides the search space in two. This feature will enable us to develop some binary search programs.

$$\begin{array}{l} S : [I \neq \{\}, S \cap I \neq \{\} \wedge S \text{ finite}]; \\ \text{do } \#S > 1 \rightarrow \\ \quad \text{var } S1 : \mathcal{P}\, D\bullet \\ \quad S1 : [\#S > 1, \{\} \subset S1 \subset S]; \\ \quad \text{if } S1 \cap I \neq \{\} \rightarrow S := S1 \\ \quad [] S1 \cap I = \{\} \rightarrow S := S \setminus S1 \\ \quad \text{fi} \\ \text{od} \\ d : [\#S = 1, d \in S] \end{array}$$

Non-Back-Tracking Search

The invariant we used to construct this abstract program is $S \cap I \neq \{\}$. In fact there are many other invariants, for example, that S is a subset of the initial value assigned to it by command (i). This particular one is a *serendipitous invariant*; it happened by chance, but then is found to be useful later in the design.

2.3 Specialising the Abstract Program

At this point, we make our first assumptions. We will require that the data type D is in fact the type of integers, and that the set of interest I is finite, or equivalently, that there are known bounds within which candidate solutions may be found. This permits the loop initialisation to be refined.

$$\text{(i)} \sqsubseteq \text{“given } D = \mathcal{Z}; M, N : \mathcal{Z}; I \subseteq M..N\text{”} \\ S := M..N$$

This initialisation also suggests a convenient representation for S, as a pair of integer variables, lo and hi, with the coupling invariant $S = lo..hi$. This implies that, at each stage, S must be a contiguous sub-range of the integers, and similarly for $S1$, and $S \setminus S1$. If $S \setminus S1$ is to be an integer sub-range, then $S1$ must have either the same start point, or the same end point as S. For simplicity, we will assume that S and $S1$ share the start point lo. We can therefore represent $S1$ by the sub-range $lo..hi1$ where $hi1$ is a new variable. The complement of $S1$ will then be $hi1 + 1..hi$.

This *data refinement* requires the entire program developed above to be transformed. In this data refinement the search set S is replaced by two new (integer valued) variables lo, hi and $S1$ by $hi1$. The coupling invariants are $S = lo..hi$, and $S1 = lo..hi1$.

Original Program	Refined Program	
$S := M..N;$	$lo, hi := M, N$	
do $\#S > 1 \rightarrow$	do $\#lo..hi > 1 \rightarrow$	
var $S1 : \mathcal{P}\ D\bullet$	var $hi1 : \mathcal{Z}\bullet$	
$S1 : [\#S > 1,$	$hi1 : [\#lo..hi > 1,$	
$\{\} \subset S1 \subset S];$	$\{\} \subset lo..hi1 \subset lo..hi];$	(ix)
if $S1 \cap I \neq \{\} \rightarrow$	if $lo..hi1 \cap I \neq \{\} \rightarrow$	
$S := S1$	$lo, hi := lo, hi1$	
$[]S1 \cap I = \{\} \rightarrow$	$[]lo..hi1 \cap I = \{\} \rightarrow$	
$S := S \setminus S1$	$lo, hi = hi1 + 1, hi$	
fi	fi	(x)
od;	od;	
$d : [\#S = 1, d \in S]$	$d : [\#lo..hi = 1, d \in lo..hi]$	(xi)
Non-Back-Tracking Search	Interval Search	

Since the abstract variables are determined by the concrete ones, the data refinement above can be performed simply by substituting the appropriate expression for each of the abstract variables.

As it stands, this is hardly an executable program. However many of the expressions can be simplified using the laws of integer arithmetic. Much of this simplification could be performed mechanically. For example, consider the loop guard $(\#lo..hi) > 1$.

$$\begin{aligned} &\#lo..hi > 1 \\ &\quad \Longleftrightarrow hi + 1 - lo > 1 \\ &\quad \Longleftrightarrow lo < hi \end{aligned}$$

The loop finalisation simplifies as follows:

$$\begin{array}{lll} (\text{xi}) & = & [lo = hi, d \in lo..lo] \\ & = & [lo = hi, d = lo] \\ & \sqsubseteq & d := lo \end{array}$$

The partition can also be simplified:

$$(\text{ix}) = hi1 : [lo < hi, lo \leq hi1 < hi]$$

The only choice is what value to assign to $hi1$. From above, we can see that the value must be at least lo, and less than hi. An obvious and correct choice is lo.

$$(\text{ix}) \sqsubseteq hi1 := lo$$

This leads to a linear time search.

As is well known, to do better, we should divide the search space into two subsets of roughly equal size at each stage. This requires some more manipulation of inequalities. Since this is the key step in developing binary search, it is worth examining in detail. The inequalities below involve *real-valued* quantities, as / stands for *real-valued* division.

$$\begin{array}{ll} lo < hi & \\ \quad \Rightarrow (lo + lo)/2 < (lo + hi)/2 < (hi + hi)/2 & \\ \quad \Rightarrow lo < (lo + hi)/2 < hi & \\ \quad \Rightarrow lo \leq \lfloor (lo + hi)/2) \rfloor < hi & \text{since } hi \text{ and } lo \text{ are integers} \\ \quad \Rightarrow lo \leq (lo + hi) \div 2 < hi & \text{by definition of integer division} \end{array}$$

Thus, another correct way to split the search space is:

$$(\text{ix}) \sqsubseteq hi1 := (lo + hi) \div 2$$

You may doubt that integer division in your favourite programming language satisfies the defining identity $x \div 2 = \lfloor x/2 \rfloor$, specifically when x is negative. In that case, make sure you only use the more efficient expression $(lo + hi) \div 2$ in situations where you are confident that $lo + hi$ is positive.

We have now derived a general interval search algorithm, and two particular versions of it, a linear search, and a binary search. There are a number of variations on binary search, so I will call this particular one a two way binary search, since at each step it divides the search space in two.

So far, we have made no assumptions about what we are searching for; all we have assumed is that I is a finite set of integers. To be able to refine the program into executable code, we will need to know more. Notice however that we have already performed most of the development without introducing such details.

2.4 Searching Arrays

The algorithm developed above can now be specialised by giving more details of the problem. For example, consider searching for some value v in an array ar with indices ranging from M to N. In this case, the items of interest are those *indices* at which the value v is found. From this point of view, the program is searching for a satisfactory index rather than the value v. In this section we will assume the extra declarations:

$$
\begin{array}{l}
[V] \\
ar : M..N \rightarrow V \\
v : V \\
I = \{n : M..N \mid ar(n) = v\}
\end{array}
$$

We can now refine the selection command. This means simplifying the guard:

$$
\begin{array}{l}
S1 \cap \{n : M..N \mid ar(n) = v\} \neq \{\} \\
\quad \iff \{n : S1 \cap M..N \mid ar(n) = v\} \neq \{\} \\
\quad \iff v \in ar(\!|\ S1\ |\!)
\end{array}
$$

The notation $ar(\!|\ S1\ |\!)$ stands for the set of array values whose indices are in the set $S1$.

In the linear search, we know that, at the point of selection, $hi1 = lo$. This allows to simplify the guard in context:

$$
\begin{array}{ll}
v \in ar(\!|\ lo..hi1\ |\!) & \\
\quad \iff v \in ar(\!|\ lo..lo\ |\!) & \text{since } hi1 = lo \\
\quad \iff v \in \{ar(lo)\} & \\
\quad \iff v = ar(lo) &
\end{array}
$$

This (finally) gives us executable code for the linear array search. Displaying the full program allows us to see that it can easily be simplified, by eliminating the variable $hi1$.

```
Specialisation              Simplification

lo, hi := M, N;             lo, hi := M, N
do lo < hi →                do lo < hi →
   var h1 : Z•
   hi1 := lo;
   if v = ar(lo) →             if v = ar(lo) →
      hi := hi1                   hi := lo
   []v ≠ ar(lo) →              []v ≠ ar(lo) →
      lo := hi1 + 1               lo := lo + 1
   fi                          fi
od;                         od;
d := lo                     d := lo
```

Linear Array Search

It is the nature of such optimisations that they can only be performed in the context of the whole program. Further refinements can be used to optimise the program. For example, the variable hi can be replaced by a flag *found* using the coupling invariant ($found = \text{true} \iff hi = lo$). Since our main concern in this paper is with binary search, we will not develop the linear search code further.

To be able to use the binary search, we need a cheap way to determine whether the value is in the left sub-range, or not. The traditional way to achieve this is by requiring the array to be sorted. We must assume both that the data type V is ordered, and that the array is in order. This is usually expressed:

$$\forall i, j : M..N \bullet i < j \Rightarrow ar(i) < ar(j)$$

Writing $<$ and $\leq$ for these inequalities promoted to sets of values, we can follow Morgan [Morgan 90] and use instead an equivalent form of the assumption:

$$\forall S1, S2 : \mathcal{P}\, M..N \bullet S1 < S2 \Rightarrow ar(\!|\ S1\ |\!) < ar(\!|\ S2\ |\!)$$

In particular, we can infer the following inequality by instantiating the universal quantification above with the sub-ranges $lo..hi1 - 1$ for $S1$ and $hi1..hi1$ for $S2$.

$$\Rightarrow ar(\!|\ lo..hi1 - 1\ |\!) < ar(\!|\ hi1..hi1\ |\!)$$
$$\Rightarrow ar(\!|\ lo..hi1\ |\!) \leq ar(\!|\ hi1..hi1\ |\!) = ar(\!|\ \{hi1\}\ |\!) = \{ar(hi1)\}$$

The selection guard can then be further simplified as follows:

$v \in ar(\!|\ lo..hi1\ |\!)$
$\Rightarrow \{v\} \leq \{ar(hi1)\}$ from the argument above
$\Rightarrow v \leq ar(hi1)$
$\Rightarrow v \in ar(\!|\ lo..hi1\ |\!)$ as $v \in ar(\!|\ lo..hi\ |\!)$ is invariant

Thus $lo..hi1 \cap I \neq \{\} \iff v \in ar(\!|\ lo..hi1\ |\!) \iff v \leq ar(hi1)$, and the selection can be refined:

(x) $\sqsubseteq$ "assuming the array is sorted"
if $v \leq ar(hi1) \rightarrow hi := hi1$
$[]v > ar(hi1) \rightarrow lo := hi1 + 1$
fi

Note that the superficially plausible refinement below is *wrong* (since the sub-range $lo..hi$ may become empty).

(x) $\not\sqsubseteq$ "plausible but *wrong* alternative"
if $v \leq ar(hi1) \rightarrow hi := hi1 - 1$
$[]v > ar(hi1) \rightarrow lo := hi1$
fi

The (correct) concrete program is as follows:

```
lo, hi := M, N;
do lo < hi →
   var h1 : Z•
   hi1 := (lo + hi) ÷ 2;
   if v ≤ ar(hi1) → hi := hi1
   []v > ar(hi1) → lo := hi1 + 1
   fi
od;
d := lo
```

Two Way Binary Array Search

You will have realised by now that specialisation often needs to be followed by tricky, low-level simplifications. This is undoubtedly a disadvantage of this approach. However it is clear that in this example, the required manipulations could be accomplished by a formula simplifier of only moderate sophistication. Such a tool would make this, and many other methods of formal refinement, rather more practical.

2.5 One Bit Binary Search

In this section we develop another version of binary search. The idea in this refinement is to choose a slightly different representation for the interval being searched. Rather than a low point and a high point, we represent the interval by a low point and the width of the interval. One advantage of this representation is that it shows in more detail how the the size of the search space changes with each iteration of the loop.

We will choose as our starting point for this data refinement the non-back-tracking search. We replace S with $lo :: wd$, and $S1$ with $lo :: wd1$. The notation $lo :: wd$ is pronounced "low *for* width". It stands for the sub-range of numbers starting at lo and of width wd, so that it is short for $lo..(lo + wd - 1)$.

Original Program	Refined Program	
$S := M..N;$	$lo, wd := M, \#M..N$	
do $\#S > 1 \rightarrow$	do $\#lo :: wd > 1 \rightarrow$	
var $S1 : \mathcal{P}\ D \bullet$	var $wd1 : \mathbb{Z} \bullet$	
$S1 : [\#S > 1,$	$wd1 : [\#lo :: wd > 1,$	
$\{\} \subset S1 \subset S];$	$\{\} \subset lo :: wd1 \subset lo :: wd];$	(xii)
if $S1 \cap I \neq \{\} \rightarrow$	if $lo :: wd1 \cap I \neq \{\} \rightarrow$	
$S := S1$	$lo, wd := lo, wd1$	
$[] S1 \cap I = \{\} \rightarrow$	$[] lo :: wd1 \cap I = \{\} \rightarrow$	
$S := S \setminus S1$	$lo, wd = lo + wd, wd - wd1$	
fi	fi	
od;	od;	
$d : [\#S = 1, d \in S]$	$d : [\#lo :: wd = 1, d \in lo :: wd]$	(xiii)
Non-Backtracking-Search	For-Interval Search	

As usual, much of this program can be simplified. Some useful identies that help with this are:

$$\#M..N = N + 1 - M$$

$$\#lo :: wd = wd$$

$$d \in lo :: 1 \iff d = lo$$

The loop finalisation is simplified and refined as before:

$$\text{(xiii)} \sqsubseteq d := lo$$

The partition can be refined:

$$\text{(xii)} \quad = wd1 : [wd > 1, 0 < wd1 < wd] \sqsubseteq wd1 := wd \div 2$$

It can be seen that if the original width is even, both the two new widths are the same, namely half the original width. If the original width is a power of two, at each step, it will be exactly halved, and will thus remain a power of two. Thus if we add the extra assumption that $\#M..N$ is a power of two, then the predicate "wd is a power 2" becomes another serendipitous invariant. This invariant allows us to simplify the program above still further. In particular, if wd is even, $wd-(wd\div 2) = wd\div 2$. This observation permits the variable $wd1$ to be eliminated.

Original Program	Specialisation and Simplification
	$\{\#M..N$ is a power of $2\}$
$lo, wd := M, N+1-M$	$lo, wd := M, N+1-M$
do $wd > 1 \rightarrow$	do $wd > 1 \rightarrow$
var $wd1 : \mathcal{Z}\bullet$	
$wd1 := wd \div 2;$	$wd := wd \div 2$
if $lo :: wd1 \cap I \neq \{\} \rightarrow$	if $lo :: wd \cap I \neq \{\} \rightarrow$
$wd := wd1$	*skip*
$[]lo :: wd1 \cap I = \{\} \rightarrow$	$[]lo :: wd \cap I = \{\} \rightarrow$
$lo, wd := lo + wd1, wd - wd1$	$lo := lo + wd$
fi	fi (xiv)
od;	od;
d := lo	$d := lo$
For-Interval Search	One Bit Binary Search

For the array search, we require a simple version of the selection guard. Once again, we assume that the array is sorted, so that in particular:

$$ar(\!|\ lo :: wd\ |\!) < ar(\!|\ \{lo + wd\}\ |\!) = \{ar(lo + wd)\}$$

The selection guard can be simplified along the same lines as before:

$$\begin{aligned} & lo :: wd \cap \{n : M..N \mid ar(n) = v\} \neq \{\} \\ \iff & v \in ar(\!|\ lo :: wd\ |\!) \\ \iff & v < ar(lo + wd) \quad \text{since } v \in ar(\!|\ lo :: 2 * wd\ |\!) \text{ is invariant} \end{aligned}$$

Thus the selection command can be refined:

$$\begin{aligned} \text{(xiv)} \sqsubseteq \; & \text{if } v < ar(lo + wd) \rightarrow \text{skip} \\ & []v \geq ar(lo + wd) \rightarrow lo := lo + wd \\ & \text{fi} \end{aligned}$$

This program is interesting because it has a particularly simple pattern of iteration. In particular if the initial value of wd is known at compile time, say it is 32, the loop can be unrolled, and redundant variables removed, to give the surprising and elegant program:

if $v >= ar(lo+16)$ then $lo := lo+16$;
if $v >= ar(lo+8)$ then $lo := lo+8$;
if $v >= ar(lo+4)$ then $lo := lo+4$;
if $v >= ar(lo+2)$ then $lo := lo+2$;
if $v >= ar(lo+1)$ then $lo := lo+1$;

It can be seen that this calculates the offset of the desired value one bit at a time, starting with the high order bit. That is why this version of binary search can sensibly be called one bit binary search.

Even if $\#M..N$ is not a power of two, say the indices range from 1 to 50, the same technique can be exploited. All you need to do is to determine initially whether v is to be found in $ar(\!|\ 1..32\ |\!)$, or in $ar(\!|\ 19..50\ |\!)$, two slices of the array, each of size 32, which cover the whole array. This simply means comparing v with the array element $ar(19)$, and initialising lo to 1 or 19 accordingly. The rest of the search is then performed by the unrolled loop above.

2.6 Tabulating the Specialisations

Rather than write out each specialisation of the abstract program fully as above, it is perhaps more helpful to give the salient details in a table as follows. The specialisations are all solutions to the problem of searching for a value v in an array ar.

Assumptions	Array bounds are $M..N$	and array is sorted	and $\#M..N$ is a power of 2
Representation of S	$lo..hi$	$lo..hi$	$lo :: wd$
Initial value for S	$M..N$	$M..N$	$M :: N+1-M$
Loop guard ($\#S > 1$)	$lo < hi$	$lo < hi$	$wd > 1$
Partition ($S1$)	$lo...lo$	$lo..(lo+hi) \div 2$	$lo :: wd \div 2$
Selection ($S1 \cap I \neq \{\}$)	$v = ar(lo)$	$v \leq ar((lo+hi) \div 2)$	$v < ar(lo + wd \div 2)$
Type of Search	Linear	Two Way Binary	One Bit Binary

2.7 Binary Arithmetic Operations

We can now look at some problems in binary arithmetic. These will be further specialisations of the one bit binary search, which can be thought of as calculating a solution from the high order bits downwards. Both division and square root are operations that can be calculated in this manner (in contrast to addition, subtraction and multiplication where the low order bits are calculated first). For the sake of efficiency we will take as our starting point the simplified one bit binary search above.

For division we have the assumptions:

$$x, y, w : \mathcal{N}$$
$$y \neq 0$$
$$0 \leq x \div y < 2^w$$
$$I = \{i : 0 :: 2^w \mid i = x \div y\}$$

We can simplify the guard of the selection command (xiv) as follows:

$$\begin{aligned} & lo :: wd \cap \{i : 0 :: 2^w \mid i = x \div y\} \neq \{\} \\ \Longleftrightarrow\; & lo \leq x \div y < lo + wd \\ \Longleftrightarrow\; & x \div y < lo + wd \quad \text{since } lo \leq x \div y \text{ is invariant} \\ \Longleftrightarrow\; & x < (lo + wd) * y \end{aligned}$$

For (integer) square root we have the assumptions:

$$x, w : \mathcal{N}$$
$$x > 0$$
$$0 \leq \lfloor\sqrt{x}\rfloor < 2^w$$
$$I = \{i : 0 :: 2^w \mid i = \lfloor\sqrt{x}\rfloor\}$$

Once again, we must simplify the selection guard:

$$\begin{aligned} & lo :: wd \cap \{i : 0 :: 2^w \mid i = \lfloor\sqrt{x}\rfloor\} \neq \{\} \\ \Longleftrightarrow\; & lo \leq \lfloor\sqrt{x}\rfloor < lo + wd \\ \Longleftrightarrow\; & \lfloor\sqrt{x}\rfloor < lo + wd \quad \text{since } lo \leq \lfloor\sqrt{x}\rfloor \text{ is invariant} \\ \Longleftrightarrow\; & x < (lo + wd)^2 \end{aligned}$$

As usual, specialisation leads to correct, but sub-optimal programs. In particular, the multiplication in the guards above leads to less efficient code than we want. The inefficiency can be avoided by strength reduction, which is a particular case of finite differencing [Paige 82]. This involves the addition of extra variables whose values can simplify the selection, so that it can also be viewed as a data refinement.

For the division problem, we re-arrange the guard as follows:

$$\begin{aligned} & x < (lo + wd) * y \\ \Longleftrightarrow\; & x - lo * y < wd * y \end{aligned}$$

Introducing auxiliary variables r (for remainder) and p (for product) to hold these quantities, we arrive at the following refinement of the selection statement:

$$\begin{aligned} & \text{if } x - lo * y < wd * y \rightarrow \text{ skip} \\ & [] x - lo * y \geq wd * y \rightarrow lo := lo + wd \\ & \text{fi} \\ \sqsubseteq\; & \text{“maintaining auxiliary variable } r = x - lo * y\text{”} \\ & \text{if } r < p \rightarrow \text{ skip} \\ & [] r \geq p \rightarrow lo, r := lo + wd, r - p \\ & \text{fi} \end{aligned}$$

The assignment to r is introduced to preserve the coupling invariant $r = x - lo * y$. Similarly, the assignments to wd must be refined:

$$\begin{array}{l} wd := 2^w \\ \sqsubseteq \text{"maintaining auxiliary variable } p = wd * y\text{"} \\ wd, p := 2^w, 2^w * y \end{array}$$

and

$$\begin{array}{l} wd := wd \div 2 \\ \sqsubseteq \text{"maintaining auxiliary variable } p = wd * y\text{"} \\ wd, p := wd \div 2, p \div 2 \end{array}$$

This is well suited to implementing in hardware. The basic operations are simply shifting, addition, subtraction and comparison which are easily and economically performed by standard circuits. It is interesting to see how standard techniques of program derivation and optimisation can lead from the abstract program of section 2.2 to a standard one bit at a time binary division such as the above.

Applying similar techniques to the binary square root algorithm we rearrange the guard:

$$\begin{array}{l} x < (lo + wd)^2 \\ \quad \iff x < lo^2 + 2 * lo * wd + wd^2 \end{array}$$

This prompts us to introduce auxiliary variables $lo2 = lo^2$, $lowd = lo * wd$, and $wd2 = wd^2$. Introducing extra assignments where necessary to preserve these invariants, we arrive at the following efficient program.

```
lo, wd, lo2, lowd, wd2 := 0, 2^w, 0, 0, 2^(2*wd);
do wd > 1 →
   wd, lowd, wd2 := wd ÷ 2, lowd ÷ 2, wd2 ÷ 4;
   if x < lo2 + 2 * lowd + wd2 →skip
   []x ≥ lo2 + 2 * lowd + wd2 → lo, lowd := lo + wd, lowd + wd2
   fi
od;
d := lo
```

This program appears in a paper by Blikle, who attributes it to O. J. Dahl [Blikle 78].

3 Further and Related Work

3.1 Further Developments

Other variations of binary search could also be derived using this approach. For example, you could split the search set three ways into a "middle" element, and two other subsets. This would give rise to the other popular version of binary search. Note however the problem arising from the partition $lo..mid-1$ $mid..mid$ $mid+1..hi$; that it is now possible for the search set to become empty. This means that d may be assigned a value outside the range $M..N$ (of valid indices into the array). Thus the three way binary search leads to more complex code which also has a weaker post-condition.

It would also be interesting to show how binary search trees arise from the abstract program by refining the search sets into search trees.

We have only considered successful search here. This simplifies the derivations. In fact, since the value assigned to d is arbitrary, all that matters is that the programs should terminate when asked to search for a non-existent value. Since it can be seen that the original variant $\#S$ also applies to unsuccessful searches, the programs also satisfy the more general search specification:

$$d : [\text{true}, I \neq \{\} \Rightarrow d \in I]$$

as well as the original one:

$$d : [I \neq \{\}, d \in I]$$

Finally it is worth considering some of the disadvantages of the approach.

There is a significant problem developing several programs at once as we do here, namely that it is easy to lose track of what assumptions are valid at any time in the development. A possible solution to this is to make formal the refinement annotations used to introduce assumptions. Morgan uses formal refinement annotations to introduce new definitions, variables and constants. It seems natural to extend this to introducing new assumptions, and perhaps also the coupling invariants of a data refinement.

Similarly, there is the need to exploit extra invariants that may arise as a result of the extra assumptions, for example that wd remains a power of two in the one bit binary search. These invariants require the designer to back-track to earlier stages in the refinement in order to verify them, which should be avoided in a pure top-down approach.

A final problem that we have seen that the specialised programs can be inefficient and clumsy. Extra simplification seems to be an unavoidable necessity when starting with a general abstract program.

3.2 Related Work

The use of assertions in applicative programs is covered by [Möller 89]. The observation that data refinement can be thought of as transforming both specification and program can be found in [Bjlkle 78]. Program inversion is another example of a technique which changes both specification and program [Dijkstra 78].

Formal refinement techniques have been used to derive and classify a number of sorting algorithms in a functional language [Clarke 78, Darlington 78]. Similar derivations have also been carried out in an imperative context.

In a recent article [Smith 90] on the KIDS interactive program development system, a general schema for search programs is presented. This is used to derive a correct, but inefficient, program for the Queens program. A variety of techniques including simplification, partial evaluation [Sestoft 87] and finite differencing are then used to transform the first solution into a more efficient program. It is encouraging to note that much of the tedious formula manipulation involved in formal design can be automated. The intuition of the designer is still however needed to control the process.

4 Summary and Conclusions

A method of program development is proposed in which the refinement is carried out in a number of distinct phases. In each phase, the design is carried out at a high level of abstraction, with minimal assumptions being made. A new phase begins by introducing extra assumptions, and possibly a more concrete view of the data. Families of similar programs can easily be developed in this way.

The approach also provides a convenient way of structuring the work into separate phases. Each phase has an abstract program (in the sense of the refinement calculus) as input and output. Since assumptions are introduced only when they are needed, each refinement, particularly at the early stages, is quite general, and may be suitable for reuse. These points show that the approach is compatible with good software engineering practices.

A disadvantage of the approach is that the final programs, derived from a general purpose, abstract program, may not be the most efficient. Further improvements in efficiency can be made, either using the refinement calculus, or more general program transformation techniques. Systems such as KIDS demonstrate that such improvements can be mechanically supported, or perhaps even fully automated. The history of a development can then be summarised by listing the key steps in some suitable way. Where many similar developments are being summarised, a table like the one in section 2.6 above acts as a useful documentation aid.

Some readers may feel that concrete programs are easier to read than abstract ones, since it is easier to see what they are doing, and to what. Catalogs of known algorithms, such as Knuth's famous unfinished series, now run into thousands of pages. To help future students of our subject, we must find economical ways of presenting algorithms. Abstraction certainly provides such savings, as one abstract program can, as we have seen, summarise many interesting, and different, concrete programs.

References

[Back 78] *On the Correctness of Refinement Steps in Program Development*, R J-R Back, 1978, Report A-1978-4, Department of Computer Science, University of Helsinki.

[Bentley 84] *Programming Pearls*, July 1984, Communications of the ACM.

[Bentley 86] *Programming Pearls*, J L Bentley, 1986, Addison Wesley.

[Blikle 78] *Specified Programming*, A Blikle, August 1978, in Mathematical Studies of Information Processing, pages 229-251, ed. E K Blum et al, Springer Verlag, LNCS 75.

[Clark 78] *Algorithm Classification Through Synthesis*, K L Clark and J Darlington, 1978, The Computer Journal, vol 23, no 1, pages 61-65.

[Darlington 78] *A Synthesis of Several Sorting Algorithms*, J Darlington, 1978, Acta Informatica, vol 11, pages 1-30.

[Knuth 73] *The Art of Computer Programming, vol 3, Sorting and Searching*, D E Knuth, 1973 and 1975, Addison Wesley.

[Möller 89] *Applicative Assertions*, B Möller, 1989, in Mathematics of Program Construction, ed. J L A van de Snepscheut, LNCS 375, Springer Verlag.

[Morgan 88] *The Refinement Calculus*, C Morgan, K Robinson and P Gardiner, 1988, Oxford University Programming Research Group Monograph 70.

[Morgan 90] *Programming from Specifications*, C Morgan, 1990, Prentice Hall.

[Morris 87] *A Theoretical Basis for Stepwise Refinement and the Programming Calculus*, J M Morris, 1987, Science of Computer Programming, vol 9, no 3, pages 287-306.

[Paige 82] *Formal Differentiation of Set-Theoretic Expressions*, R Paige and S Koenig, 1982, ACM Transactions on Programming Languages and Systems, vol 4, no 3, pages 402-454.

[Sestoft 87] *A Bibliography on Partial Evaluation*, P Sestoft and H Sondergaard, 1987, SIGPLAN Notices, vol 23, no 2, pages 19-27.

[Smith 90] *KIDS: a semi-automatic program development system*, D R Smith, September 1990, IEEE Transactions on Software Engineering, pages 1024-1043.

[Spivey 89] *The Z Notation: a reference manual*, J M Spivey, 1989, Prentice Hall.

A Refinement Case Study (using the Abstract Machine Notation)

J.R. Abrial

Consultant *

January 9, 1991

Abstract

In this paper, we develop *with great details* a classical little example [1] of refinement from initial specification down to final code. We insist on a few methodological points among which are the following:

- the importance of a sound mathematical preamble,
- the systematic usage of data refinement steps based on clear and intuitive technical decisions,
- the reusability of already specified and refined pieces of code.

The exercise is conducted using an homogeneous notational style based on *Abstract Machines* and *Generalized Substitutions* [1].

1 Notations

In the course of this article, we use various notations which we introduce just before their first usage; a few conventions, however, are used systematically throughout so that we present them now.

When we mention a *sequence*, this always means a sequence of natural numbers: the corresponding set is denoted by $\mathsf{seq}(\mathbb{N})$. The empty sequence is denoted by

*26, rue des Plantes 75014 Paris France

[1] The longest upsequence algorithm

[]. Given a sequence s and a natural number v, the construct $s \leftarrow v$ denotes the sequence obtained by appending v to s. Sequences are also understood to be total functions whose domains are *intervals* of the form $1\,..\,n$ where the natural number n is said to be the *size* of the sequence. The ith element of a sequence s is denoted by s_i. Sequences may be written *in extension* by listing their successive elements enclosed in square brackets as in [4, 9, 6, 7].

Functions can be defined on sequences *by recursion*: this means that the value of the function is expressed in the form of two rewriting rules, one yielding the value of the function at the empty sequence, and the other yielding the value of the function at a sequence of the form $s \leftarrow v$, value expressed in terms of v and of the value of the function at s. For example, the function *size* can be defined recursively as follows:

$$\begin{aligned} size([]) &= 0 \\ size(s \leftarrow v) &= size(s) + 1 \end{aligned}$$

Sometimes, we use the construct $append(v)$ (where v is a natural number) which denotes a function from seq(N) to itself such that

$$append(v)(s) = s \leftarrow v$$

The function $append(v)$ is *injective*. We also use the function *last*, a total function from non-empty sequences to natural numbers which is such that:

$$last(s \leftarrow v) = v$$

In order to *totalize* the function *last*, we define the function $last_0$ whose value at the empty sequence is equal to 0, formally we have the following recursive definition:

$$\begin{aligned} last_0([]) &= 0 \\ last_0(s \leftarrow v) &= v \end{aligned}$$

and we obviously have the following property

$$last_0 \circ append(v) = \mathsf{seq}(\mathbb{N}) \times \{v\}$$

In the previous equality, we use the operator $\circ$ which is the traditional *backward* relational composition operator. We also use the *forward* relational composition operator ; which is such that $g \circ f$ is equal to $f\,;g$.

Given a binary relations r with source the set a and with destination the set b, and a subset t of a, the construct $r[t]$ denotes the *image* of t under r. It is defined as the subset of b whose elements are related (through r) with at least one element of t, formally:

$$r[t] = \{y \mid y \in b \ \wedge \ \exists x \cdot (x \in t \ \wedge \ x, y \in r)\}$$

We also use the ***inverse image*** of a subset u of b under r; it is denoted by $r^{-1}[u]$ and is defined as follows:

$$r^{-1}[u] \;=\; \{x \mid x \in a \;\wedge\; \exists y \cdot (y \in u \;\wedge\; x, y \in r)\}$$

For instance, the inverse image of the interval $0 \,..\, v$ under the just defined function $last_0$, that is $last_0^{-1}[0 \,..\, v]$, is thus equal to the set containing the empty sequence as well as all non-empty sequences whose last element is smaller than or equal to v, formally:

$$last_0^{-1}[0 \,..\, v] \;=\; \{s \mid s \in \mathrm{seq}(\mathsf{N}) \;\wedge\; (s = [] \;\vee\; last(s) \leq v)\}$$

We have the following equality

$$\mathrm{seq}(\mathsf{N}) - \{[]\} \;=\; \bigcup v \cdot (v \in \mathsf{N} \mid last^{-1}[\{v\}])$$

In the previous equality, the construct $\bigcup v \cdot (v \in \mathsf{N} \mid last^{-1}[\{v\}])$ denotes the ***generalized union*** of sets of the form $last^{-1}[\{v\}]$ for all values of v such that $v \in \mathsf{N}$.

2 The Problem

Our problem is to construct an algorithm for calculating the ***size of the longest non-decreasing subsequence*** of a ***given*** sequence s. Note that, in this informal definition, we do not make precise how the sequence s is indeed "given": it is left open to the implementer.

More precisely, suppose that we have been able to define ***somehow*** the set $ups(s)$ of all non-decreasing subsequences of s, then our algorithm is to compute the quantity $\max(size[ups(s)])$.

This problem has already been studied by many people among which are the authors of the following books or article: [4], [5], [6], and [7]. We have the impression that the development proposed here is slightly different from that of the others in that it uses systematically a data refinement approach.

3 Formal Explanations

Before proceeding, we have to explain in detail (i.e. formally) what is meant by a non-decreasing subsequence of a sequence s. As we, clearly, have two notions here, we split our explanation into that of two separate notions: first a notion of ***subsequence***, second a notion of ***non-decreasingness.***

A subsequence t of a given sequence s is a sequence made of elements of s occuring in t in the *same order* as they do in s. For example, let s be the following sequence:

$$s = [4, 9, 6, 7]$$

then the following sequence t is a subsequence of s

$$t = [4, 6, 7]$$

The set of all subsequences of s, denoted by the function $subseq(s)$, can be defined recursively as follows:

$$\begin{aligned} subseq([]) &= \{[]\} \\ subseq(s \leftarrow v) &= subseq(s) \cup append(v)[subseq(s)] \end{aligned} \tag{1}$$

A non-decreasing sequence s is either the empty sequence or a non-empty sequence such that any two *successive* elements in it, say s_i and s_{i+1}, are such that $s_i \leq s_{i+1}$. More formally, the set $ndec$ of non-decreasing sequences can be defined as follows:

$$ndec = \{s \mid s \in \text{seq}(\mathbb{N}) \ \wedge \ \forall i \cdot (i \in 1 \,..\, size(s) - 1 \ \Rightarrow \ s_i \leq s_{i+1})\}$$

As this definition is not very manageable, we intend, in what follows, to informally derive a property that will prove to be more practical. The set $ndec \cap last_0^{-1}[0\,..\,v]$ is obviously equal to the set of non-decreasing sequences that are either equal to the empty sequence or to non-empty sequences whose last element are smaller than or equal to v. Clearly, the image of that set under $append(v)$ is a set of non-decreasing sequences whose last element exist and are all equal to v; formally

$$append(v)[ndec \cap last_0^{-1}[0\,..\,v]] \subseteq ndec \cap last^{-1}[\{v\}]$$

Conversely, removing the last element v of every sequence of the set $ndec \cap last^{-1}[\{v\}]$ yields a set, s say, of nondecreasing sequences whose elements (if any) are all smaller than or equal to v; as appending back v to the element of s certainly yields the same set $ndec \cap last^{-1}[\{v\}]$, we obtain the following

$$ndec \cap last^{-1}[\{v\}] \subseteq append(v)[ndec \cap last_0^{-1}[0\,..\,v]]$$

so that we have eventually

$$append(v)[ndec \cap last_0^{-1}[0\,..\,v]] = ndec \cap last^{-1}[\{v\}]$$

As a consequence, we have

$$\bigcup v \cdot (v \in \mathbb{N} \mid append(v)[ndec \cap last_0^{-1}[0..v]])$$
$$=$$
$$\bigcup v \cdot (v \in \mathbb{N} \mid ndec \cap last^{-1}[\{v\}])$$
$$=$$
$$ndec \cap \bigcup v \cdot (v \in \mathbb{N} \mid last^{-1}[\{v\}])$$
$$=$$
$$ndec \cap (\mathrm{seq}(\mathbb{N}) - \{[]\})$$
$$=$$
$$ndec - \{[]\}$$

So that we have the following equality:

$$ndec \;=\; \{[]\} \;\cup\; \bigcup v \cdot (v \in \mathbb{N} \mid append(v)[ndec \cap last_0^{-1}[0..v]])$$

from which we deduce easily:

$$append(v)[subseq(s)] \cap ndec$$
$$= \qquad (2)$$
$$append(v)[subseq(s)] \cap append(v)[ndec \cap last_0^{-1}[0..v]]$$

Now comes our last definition, that of the set $ups(s)$ of non-decreasing subsequences of s; formally we have

$$ups(s) \;=\; subseq(s) \cap ndec \qquad (3)$$

From the previous results, we can derive a recursive definition which is the point of departure of our future algorithmic construction:

$$ups([]) \;=\; \{[]\}$$
$$ups(s \leftarrow v) \;=\; ups(s) \cup append(v)[ups(s) \cap last_0^{-1}[0..v]]$$

Proof of the second rewriting rule

$$ups(s \leftarrow v)$$
$$= \qquad (3)$$
$$subseq(s \leftarrow v) \cap ndec$$
$$= \qquad (1)$$
$$(subseq(s) \cup append(v)[subseq(s)]) \cap ndec$$
$$=$$
$$(subseq(s) \cap ndec) \;\cup\; (append(v)[subseq(s)] \cap ndec)$$
$$= \qquad (2)$$
$$(subseq(s) \cap ndec) \cup$$
$$\quad (append(v)[subseq(s)] \cap append(v)[ndec \cap last_0^{-1}[0..v]])$$
$$=$$
$$(subseq(s) \cap ndec) \;\cup\; append(v)[subseq(s) \cap ndec \cap last_0^{-1}[0..v]]$$
$$= \qquad (3)$$
$$ups(s) \cup append(v)[ups(s) \cap last_0^{-1}[0..v]]$$

The last but one step in this derivation is due to the fact that the image of a set under a relation distributes through intersection when the relation in question is an *injective function.*

Example:

The set $ups([4,\ 9,\ 6,\ 7])$ can be computed as follows:

$$\begin{array}{lcl} ups([]) & = & \{[]\} \\ ups([4]) & = & \{[],\ [4]\} \\ ups([4,\ 9]) & = & \{[],\ [4],\ [9],\ [4,9]\} \\ ups([4,\ 9,\ 6]) & = & \{[],\ [4],\ [9],\ [4,9],\ [6],\ [4,6]\} \\ ups([4,\ 9,\ 6,\ 7]) & = & \{[],\ [4],\ [9],\ [4,9],\ [6],\ [4,6],\ [7],\ [4,7],\ [6,7],\ [4,6,7]\} \end{array}$$

and we have

$$size[ups([4,\ 9,\ 6,\ 7])] \ = \ \{0,\ 1,\ 2,\ 3\}$$

so that we have eventually

$$\mathsf{max}(size[ups([4,\ 9,\ 6,\ 7])]) \ = \ 3$$

4 Methodology

One possible approach to solve the problem at hand is to write an (abstract) algorithm using the various definitions given in the previous sections, formally

---

```
n ⟵ maxsizeups(s)  =
   pre
      s ∈ seq(N)
   then
      n := max(size[ups(s)])
   end
```

In this formulation, the header, $n \longleftarrow maxsizeups(s)$, clearly shows what the input parameter, s, and the output parameter, n, are; the pre clause is to indicate what the *pre-condition* is; and, finally, the **then** clause is to indicate (by means of a *substitution*) what the result is.

We could then derive an implementation by further refining that specification until we reach a level of details allowing us to perform a direct encoding using a traditional imperative programming language.

An alternative approach consists of solving a more general problem: rather than constructing an algorithm with the initial sequence as an input parameter, we, preferably, define an *abstract machine* encapsulating that sequence.

More precisely, our machine has an *initialization* and two *operations* whose semantics are *modeled* according to their effect on the encapsulated sequence; initially, the sequence is empty; the first operation, *insert*(v), appends the natural number v to it; and the second operation $v \longleftarrow$ *result* yields our desired result, that is the size of the longest non-decreasing subsequence of the encapsulated sequence.

From the point of view of its eventual *users*, the machine is a *black box* : we do not know what is inside it; we simply understand what the semantics of the offered initialization and operations are; they may be defined (in first approximation) as follows in terms of a mathematical model based on a *state* made of a single sequence ss:

```
initialization  =
    begin
        ss := []
    end

insert(v)  =
    pre
        v ∈ N
    then
        ss := ss ← v
    end

v ⟵ result  =
    begin
        v := max(size[ups(ss)])
    end
```

The specification of these operations is what is *guaranteed* by the seller of the machine. In other words, as long as the machine behaves in this way then we can use it freely.

For instance, we can write an *external interface* which, in one way or another, will first initialize (turn on) the machine, then perform various *calls* of the operation *insert(v)* for various values of v, then, eventually, perform a final call of the operation $v \longleftarrow$ ***result***. The exact form of that interface, however, is *not* our concern for the moment; we might even consider developing several such interfaces depending on the way we would like the input sequence to be fed into the machine. In section 14 we propose such an interface.

Of course, the *real* machine purchased by the user might *function* in a way that is quite different from what is stipulated by our first abstract model; in particular the encapsulated sequence *might have disappeared* from the eventual implementation which takes the final form of a *concrete module* corresponding to our *abstract model* [2].

More precisely, if the module is a *correct refinement* of the model then our external interface written solely in terms of the model is still valid; this is so because in our writing of the interface we *promise* to only work with the operations of the machine, never with the encapsulated data (in our case, the sequence ss); this very strong discipline is called the *Hiding Principle* [8].

5 Specification

In this section, we present the complete formal specification of our abstract machine; it is expressed in terms of the Abstract Machine Notation (for short, **AMN**) which is part of our development method [1].

```
machine

    upseq(VALUE, maxsize)

variables

    ss

invariant

    ss ∈ seq(VALUE) ∧
    size(ss) ≤ maxsize

initialization

    ss := []

operations

    insert(v)  =
       pre
          v ∈ VALUE  ∧
          size(ss) < maxsize
       then
          ss := ss ← v
       end;

    v ⟵ result  =
       begin
          v := max(size[ups(ss)])
       end

end
```

The machine is called *upseq* and it has two *parameters* called *VALUE* and *maxsize*: the role of the parameters of an abstract machine is to leave open a number of *finite dimensions* of the machine: these parameters are all supposed to be either *finite non-empty intervals* of natural numbers or simple natural number *scalars* [2]

[2] As a convenient lexical convention, abstract machine parameters written with upper case letters only are assumed to be intervals

As already stated, our machine as a single *state variable*, *ss*, subjected to a reasonable *invariant*: *ss* is supposed to be a finite sequence of *VALUE* of size limited by the number *maxsize*.

Our machine is *initialized* with an empty sequence.

Finally, our machine has two *operations* defined in a straightforward manner according to the little mathematical preamble given in the previous sections.

In order to be *consistent*, the machine should be such that: (1) its initialization *establishes* the invariant and (2) its operations *preserves* it. We shall come back in section 7 to these various *proof obligations* which, clearly, are all fulfilled by our proposed machine *upseq*.

We now undertake a number of refinements of this machine, each one of them corresponding, hopefully, to a clear *technical decision* based on some *mathematical properties* and aiming at a final implementation encodable in an imperative programming language.

6 First Refinement

The idea underlying our first refinement is to *replace* the sequence *ss* by a set *uu* which is equal *ups*(*ss*): we can do so because, clearly, we do not need the sequence itself to compute our final result.

Example

$$ss = [4,\ 9,\ 6,\ 7]$$

$$uu = \{[\,],\ [4],\ [9],\ [4,9],\ [6],\ [4,6],\ [7],\ [4,7],\ [6,7],\ [4,6,7]\}$$

At first glance, that refinement step seems to complicate matters since a set of sequences is certainly less simple than a single sequence; what is greatly simplified, however, is our second operation.

As for the specification of the machine in the previous section, we present the refinement, and then we make some comments about its various constituents.

refinement

$upseq(VALUE,\ maxsize)$

variables

uu

change

$uu\ =\ ups(ss)$

initialization

$uu := \{[]\}$

operations

$insert(v)\ =$
begin
$uu := uu\ \cup\ append(v)[uu\ \cap\ last_0^{-1}[0\,..\,v]]$
end;

$v \longleftarrow result\ =$
begin
$v := \max(size[uu])$
end

end

As you can see, a refinement ressembles a machine, the only difference being the fact that the *invariant* clause has disappeared: it has been replaced by a *change* of variables clause linking the *abstract* variable *ss* and the *concrete* variable *uu*.

In the present case, the relationship between the two categories of variables is very peculiar since the concrete variable is *functionally* expressed in terms of the abstract one. When this is so, and provided a number of mathematical properties is met, then the refinement can be derived *automatically* from the specification. We shall develop that topic in next section.

7 Proof Obligations

We suppose that we have an abstract machine and a corresponding refinement defined in general as follows:

machine

M

variables

x

invariant

I

initialization

A

operations

$r \longleftarrow op(z) \;=$
  pre
    P
  then
    K
  end

end

refinement

M

variables

y

change

J

initialization

B

operations

$r \longleftarrow op(z) \;=$
  pre
    Q
  then
    L
  end

end

where I, J, P, and Q are *predicates* and where A, B, K, and L are *generalized substitutions* [1]. In this schematic machine and refinement, we have only one operation with header $r \longleftarrow op(z)$; in practice, machines, of course, have more than one operation which may or may not have parameters, so that there are, in fact, four possible headers, namely $r \longleftarrow op(z)$, $r \longleftarrow op$, $op(z)$, and simply op. The proof obligations we present in what follows correspond to the most general case only (the first case).

The machine is subjected to the following proof obligations [1]:

$[A]I$	initialization *establishes* invariant
$\forall x \cdot (I \wedge P \Rightarrow [K]I)$	operation *preserves* invariant

Note that a construct of the form $[S]R$ where S is a generalized substitution and R is a predicate, denotes the, so-called [3], *weakest pre-condition* for S to *establish* R.

In order to be correct, the refinement is subjected to the following proof obligations [1]:

$[B] \neg [A] \neg J$	initialization
$\forall x, y \cdot (I \wedge P \wedge J \Rightarrow Q \wedge [L'] \neg [K] \neg (J \wedge r = r'))$	operation

In the last proof obligation, the substitution L' denotes the substitution L with variable r replaced by r'.

In the case (which is ours) where the change of variable expresses the fact that the concrete variable is functionally defined in terms of the abstract variable, that is when it has the following form

$$y = h(x)$$

and when the abstract initialization and its concrete implementation have the following respective simple forms

$$x := v$$
$$y := w$$

then the proof obligation for initialization becomes

$$[y := w] \neg [x := v] \neg (y = h(x))$$

that is, quite intuitively

$$w = h(v)$$

[3]by E.W. Dijkstra in [3]

When the abstract operation is of the form

$$\textbf{pre} \quad P \quad \textbf{then} \quad x := f(x) \quad \textbf{end}$$

and the corresponding concrete operation is of the form

$$\textbf{begin} \quad y := g(y) \quad \textbf{end}$$

then the refinement proof obligation becomes

$$\forall x, y \cdot (I \ \wedge \ P \ \wedge \ y = h(x) \ \Rightarrow \ [y := g(y)] \neg [x := f(x)] \neg (y = h(x)))$$
$$\Leftrightarrow$$
$$\forall x, y \cdot (I \ \wedge \ P \ \wedge \ y = h(x) \ \Rightarrow \ g(y) = h(f(x)))$$
$$\Leftrightarrow$$
$$\forall x \cdot (I \ \wedge \ P \Rightarrow \ g(h(x)) = h(f(x)))$$

Finally, when the abstract operation yields a result r as follows:

$$\textbf{begin} \quad r := k(x) \quad \textbf{end}$$

and when the corresponding concrete operation has the following form

$$\textbf{begin} \quad r := l(y) \quad \textbf{end}$$

then our refinement proof obligation becomes

$$\forall x, y \cdot (I \ \wedge \ y = h(x) \ \Rightarrow \ [r' := l(y)] \neg [r := k(x)] \neg (y = h(x) \ \wedge \ r = r'))$$
$$\Leftrightarrow$$
$$\forall x, y \cdot (I \ \wedge \ y = h(x) \ \Rightarrow \ k(x) = l(y))$$
$$\Leftrightarrow$$
$$\forall x \cdot (I \ \Rightarrow \ k(x) = l(h(x)))$$

Conversely, when we have an abstract machine encapsulating a variable x subjected to the invariant I, whose initialization has the form

$$x := v$$

and with two operations such as

$$\textbf{pre} \quad P \quad \textbf{then} \quad x := f(x) \quad \textbf{end}$$
$$\textbf{begin} \quad n := k(x) \quad \textbf{end}$$

then, provided we prove three lemmas of the following forms

$h(v) \ = \ w$	**Lemma A**
$I \wedge P \ \Rightarrow \ h(f(x)) \ = \ g(\underline{h(x)})$	**Lemma B**
$I \ \Rightarrow \ k(x) \ = \ l(\underline{h(x)})$	**Lemma C**

then we can be *sure* that a refinement with concrete initialization

$$y := w$$

and concrete operations

begin $y := g(y)$ **end**
begin $n := l(y)$ **end**

is a correct refinement of our abstract machine together with the change of variable $y = h(x)$.

For example, comming back to our specification of the machine *upseq* (section 5) and since we have (**Lemma A**)

$$ups([]) = \{[]\}$$

and also (**Lemma B**)

$$\begin{array}{l} ss \in \mathrm{seq}(VALUE) \\ size(ss) \leq maxsize \\ v \in VALUE \\ size(ss) < maxsize \\ \Rightarrow \\ ups(ss \leftarrow v) \;=\; \underline{ups(ss)} \cup append(v)[\underline{ups(ss)} \cap last_0^{-1}[0\,..\,v]] \end{array}$$

and finally (**Lemma C**)

$$\begin{array}{l} ss \in \mathrm{seq}(VALUE) \\ size(ss) \leq maxsize \\ \Rightarrow \\ \max(size[ups(ss)]) \;=\; \max(size[\underline{ups(ss)}]) \end{array}$$

then our proposed first refinement (section 6) is indeed correct together with the change of variable $uu = ups(ss)$.

8 Second Refinement

By looking closely at our first refinement, and also at our example valuation of the variable uu, namely

$$uu \;=\; \{[],\ [4],\ [9],\ [4,9],\ [6],\ [4,6],\ [7],\ [4,7],\ [6,7],\ [4,6,7]\}$$

it appears that we can *loose information*: clearly, the *inside* of the various non-decreasing sequences is not needed, only their last element and their size are meaningful; therefore, each non-decreasing subsequence s of uu could be replaced by a *couple* of informations yielding (1) the size of s and (2) the last element of s.

Consequently, a candidate refinement would consist of replacing the set uu by a binary relation rr made of the mentioned couples. The corresponding change of variable is then the following

$$rr = size^{-1} \,;\, (uu \lhd last_0)$$

Example

$$uu = \{[], [4], [9], [4,9], [6], [4,6], [7], [4,7], [6,7], [4,6,7]\}$$

$$rr = \{0 \mapsto 0,\ 1 \mapsto 4,\ 1 \mapsto 9,\ 2 \mapsto 9,\ 1 \mapsto 6,\ 2 \mapsto 6,\ 1 \mapsto 7,\ 2 \mapsto 7,\ 3 \mapsto 7\}$$

As it seems too big a step to swallow, we prefer to split that refinement step into two separate ones; consequently, the technical decision underlying our second refinement consists of replacing the set uu by a function pp which is equal to $uu \lhd last_0$ (that is, the function $last_0$ with domain restricted by the set uu).

Example

$$uu = \{[], [4], [9], [4,9], [6], [4,6], [7], [4,7], [6,7], [4,6,7]\}$$

$$pp = \{[] \mapsto 0,\ [4] \mapsto 4,\ [9] \mapsto 9,\ [4,9] \mapsto 9,\ [6] \mapsto 6,\ [4,6] \mapsto 6,\ [7] \mapsto 7,\ [4,7] \mapsto 7,\ [6,7] \mapsto 7,\ [4,6,7] \mapsto 7\}$$

As the change of variable is functional, we can generate automatically the refinement, provided we prove the following lemmas [4]

Lemma 1

$$\{[]\} \lhd last_0 = \{[] \mapsto 0\}$$

Lemma 2

$$(uu \cup append(v)[uu \cap last_0^{-1}[0..v]]) \lhd last_0$$
$$=$$
$$\underline{uu \lhd last_0} \cup append(v)^{-1} \,;\, \underline{uu \lhd last_0} \,;\, (0..v) \times \{v\}$$

Lemma 3

$$\max(size[uu]) = \max(size[\mathrm{dom}(\underline{uu \lhd last_0})])$$

[4] These lemmas have not exactly the form required by Lemmas A, B, and C of the previous section (typing informations are missing), but they, clearly, are sufficient to prove the required lemmas

We leave the proofs of the first and last lemmas as exercises to the reader. In order to prove **Lemma 2**, we need a few mathematical laws which are the following (for the sake of simplicity, the set-theoretic typing of the variables of these laws is left to the reader)

$$(a \cup b) \lhd r \quad = \quad a \lhd r \;\cup\; b \lhd r \qquad \textbf{Law 1}$$

$$append(v)[s] \lhd last_0 \quad = \quad append(v)[s] \times \{v\} \qquad \textbf{Law 2}$$

$$r[a] \times b \quad = \quad r^{-1};\ (a \times b) \qquad \textbf{Law 3}$$

$$(a \cap b) \times c \quad = \quad a \lhd (b \times c) \qquad \textbf{Law 4}$$

Proof of Lemma 2

$$(uu \;\cup\; append(v)[uu \cap last_0^{-1}[0\,..\,v]]) \lhd last_0$$

$$= \qquad \textbf{Law 1}$$

$$uu \lhd last_0 \;\cup\; append(v)[uu \cap last_0^{-1}[0\,..\,v]]) \lhd last_0$$

$$= \qquad \textbf{Law 2}$$

$$uu \lhd last_0 \;\cup\; append(v)[uu \cap last_0^{-1}[0\,..\,v]] \times \{v\}$$

$$= \qquad \textbf{Law 3}$$

$$uu \lhd last_0 \;\cup\; append(v)^{-1};\ (uu \cap last_0^{-1}[0\,..\,v] \times \{v\})$$

$$= \qquad \textbf{Law 4}$$

$$uu \lhd last_0 \;\cup\; append(v)^{-1};\ uu \lhd (last_0^{-1}[0\,..\,v] \times \{v\})$$

$$= \qquad \textbf{Law 3}$$

$$uu \lhd last_0 \;\cup\; append(v)^{-1};\ uu \lhd last_0;\ (0\,..\,v) \times \{v\}$$

End of Proof

Our second refinement follows then immediately

---

refinement

$upseq(VALUE)$

variables

pp

change

$pp = uu \lhd last_0$

initialization

$pp := \{[] \mapsto 0\}$

operations

$insert(v) \ =$
begin
$pp := pp \ \cup \ append(v)^{-1} ; \ pp ; \ (0 \,..\, v) \times \{v\}$
end;

$v \longleftarrow result \ =$
begin
$v := \max(size[\mathrm{dom}(pp)])$
end

end

---

9 Third Refinement

As already announced at the beginning of the previous section, in this third refinement we replace the function pp by the relation rr which is equal to $size^{-1} ; pp$. Here, definitely, we simplify our data structure which, however, is still not so easy to implement with a traditional programming language since it is a genuine binary relation; in a future refinement, our intention is to replace the relation rr by a function.

Example

$$pp = \{[] \mapsto 0,\ [4] \mapsto 4,\ [9] \mapsto 9,\ [4,9] \mapsto 9,\ [6] \mapsto 6,\ [4,6] \mapsto 6,\ [7] \mapsto 7,\ [4,7] \mapsto 7,\ [6,7] \mapsto 7,\ [4,6,7] \mapsto 7\}$$

$$rr = \{0 \mapsto 0,\ 1 \mapsto 4,\ 1 \mapsto 9,\ 2 \mapsto 9,\ 1 \mapsto 6,\ 2 \mapsto 6,\ 1 \mapsto 7,\ 2 \mapsto 7,\ 3 \mapsto 7\}$$

As for the previous refinements, we need to prove a few lemmas in order to generate our refinement automatically:

Lemma 4

$$size^{-1};\ \{[] \mapsto 0\} = \{0 \mapsto 0\}$$

Lemma 5

$$size^{-1};\ (pp \cup append(v)^{-1};\ pp;\ (0\,..\,v) \times \{v\})$$
$$=$$
$$\underline{size^{-1};pp} \cup succ[(\underline{size^{-1};\ pp})^{-1}[0\,..\,v]] \times \{v\}$$

Lemma 6

$$\max(size[\mathrm{dom}(pp)]) = \max(\mathrm{dom}(\underline{size^{-1};pp}))$$

We leave the proofs of the first and last lemmas as exercises to the reader. In order to prove **Lemma 5**, we need a few more mathematical laws:

$$r;\ (a \cup b) = r;\ a \cup r;\ b \qquad \textbf{Law 5}$$

$$size \circ append(v) = succ \circ size \qquad \textbf{Law 6}$$

Proof of Lemma 5

$$size^{-1};\ (pp \cup append(v)^{-1};\ pp;\ (0\,..\,v) \times \{v\})$$
$$= \qquad \textbf{Law 5}$$
$$size^{-1};pp \cup size^{-1};append(v)^{-1};\ pp;\ (0\,..\,v) \times \{v\}$$
$$= \qquad \textbf{Law 6}$$
$$size^{-1};pp \cup succ^{-1};size^{-1};\ pp;\ (0\,..\,v) \times \{v\}$$
$$= \qquad \textbf{Law 3}$$
$$size^{-1};pp \cup succ[(size^{-1};\ pp)^{-1}[0\,..\,v]] \times \{v\}$$

End of Proof

Our third refinement follows then immediately

---

refinement

upseq(*VALUE*, *maxsize*)

variables

rr

change

$rr \ = \ size^{-1} \, ; \, pp$

initialization

$rr := \{0 \mapsto 0\}$

operations

$insert(v) \ =$
begin
$rr := rr \ \cup \ succ[rr^{-1}[0\,..\,v]] \times \{v\}$
end;

$v \longleftarrow result \ =$
begin
$v := \max(\mathrm{dom}(rr))$
end

end

---

10 Fourth Refinement

The fourth refinement is sligtly different from the previous ones: in fact it is not really a refinement, we rather prove an extra bit of invariant, namely the fact that all sets of the form $rr^{-1}[0..w]$ (where w is a natural number) are *initial* segments of the natural numbers. More formally, we define the predicate *initial*(s) as follows:

$$initial(s) \ \Leftrightarrow \ s \subseteq \mathbb{N} \ \wedge \ s \neq \varnothing \ \wedge \ s = 0\,..\,\max(s)$$

In order to prove the preservation of this invariant by the operation *insert*(v) we, obviously, need the following lemma

Lemma 7

$$\begin{array}{l} initial(rr^{-1}[0\,..\,w]) \\ initial(rr^{-1}[0\,..\,v]) \\ \Rightarrow \\ initial((rr \;\cup\; succ[rr^{-1}[0\,..\,v]] \times \{v\})^{-1}[0\,..\,w]) \end{array}$$

The proof of this lemma is easy provided we have the following mathematical laws

$$(a \cup b)^{-1} \;=\; a^{-1} \cup b^{-1} \qquad \textbf{Law 7}$$

$$(a \cup b)[s] \;=\; a[s] \cup b[s] \qquad \textbf{Law 8}$$

$$initial(s) \wedge initial(t) \;\Rightarrow\; initial(\, s \cup succ[t]\,) \qquad \textbf{Law 9}$$

$$v \leq w \;\Rightarrow\; (s \times \{v\})^{-1}[0\,..\,w] = s \qquad \textbf{Law 10}$$

$$v > w \;\Rightarrow\; (s \times \{v\})^{-1}[0\,..\,w] = \varnothing \qquad \textbf{Law 11}$$

Proof of Lemma 7

We have two hypotheses, namely

$$initial(rr^{-1}[0\,..\,w]) \qquad \textbf{Hyp 1}$$

$$initial(rr^{-1}[0\,..\,v]) \qquad \textbf{Hyp 2}$$

and we have to prove

$$initial((rr \;\cup\; succ[rr^{-1}[0\,..\,v]] \times \{v\})^{-1}[0\,..\,w])$$

We have

$$\begin{array}{ll} (rr \;\cup\; succ[rr^{-1}[0\,..\,v]] \times \{v\})^{-1}[0\,..\,w] & \\ = & \textbf{Law 7} \\ (rr^{-1} \;\cup\; (succ[rr^{-1}[0\,..\,v]] \times \{v\})^{-1})[0\,..\,w] & \\ = & \textbf{Law 8} \\ rr^{-1}[0\,..\,w] \;\cup\; (succ[rr^{-1}[0\,..\,v]] \times \{v\})^{-1}[0\,..\,w] & \end{array}$$

We consider two cases: **(1)** $v \leq w$ and **(2)** $v > w$. In case **(1)**, we have, according to **Law 10**

$$\begin{array}{l} rr^{-1}[0\,..\,w] \;\cup\; (succ[rr^{-1}[0\,..\,v]] \times \{v\})^{-1}[0\,..\,w] \\ = \\ rr^{-1}[0\,..\,w] \;\cup\; succ[rr^{-1}[0\,..\,v]] \end{array}$$

Consequently, the result follows according to **Hyp 1**, **Hyp 2** and **Law 9**.

In case **(2)**, and according to **Law 11**, we have

$$rr^{-1}[0\,..\,w] \;\cup\; (succ[rr^{-1}[0\,..\,v]] \times \{v\})^{-1}[0\,..\,w] \;=\; rr^{-1}[0\,..\,w]$$

Consequently, the result follows according to **Hyp 1**.

End of Proof

Technically, we have a "refinement" with no *variables* clause and with the same *operations* clause as the previous one, yielding

---

refinement

$upseq(VALUE)$

change

$\forall w \cdot (w \in VALUE \;\Rightarrow\; initial(rr^{-1}[0\,..\,w]))$

initialization

$rr := \{0 \mapsto 0\}$

operations

```
insert(v)  =
   begin
      rr := rr ∪ succ[rr⁻¹[0 .. v]] × {v}
   end;


v ⟵ result  =
   begin
      v := max(dom(rr))
   end
```

end

---

11 Fifth Refinement

This refinement corresponds to the key step towards the final implementation: we replace our binary relation *rr* by a function *ff* obtained by *minimizing* our relation.

More precisely, given a binary relation r, the construct $minfnc(r)$ denotes a function linking each element i of the domain of r to the ***smallest*** element of the image of the singleton set $\{i\}$ under r, formally

$$minfnc(r)(i) \;=\; \min(r\,[\{i\}])$$

Example

$$rr \;=\; \{0 \mapsto 0,\; 1 \mapsto 4,\; 1 \mapsto 9,\; 2 \mapsto 9,\; 1 \mapsto 6,\; 2 \mapsto 6,\; 1 \mapsto 7,\; 2 \mapsto 7,\; 3 \mapsto 7\}$$

$$ff \;=\; \{0 \mapsto 0,\; 1 \mapsto 4,\; 2 \mapsto 6,\; 3 \mapsto 7\}$$

In order to generate our refinement automatically, we need our usual three lemmas

Lemma 8

$$minfnc(\{0 \mapsto 0\}) \;=\; \{0 \mapsto 0\}$$

Lemma 9 [5]

$$\begin{array}{l} initial(r^{-1}[0\,..\,v]) \\ \Rightarrow \\ minfnc(r \;\cup\; succ[r^{-1}[0\,..\,v]] \times \{v\}) \;=\; \\ \quad \underline{minfnc(r)} \lhd\!\!\!+ \{\,1 + \max(\underline{minfnc(r)}^{-1}[0\,..\,v]) \mapsto v\,\} \end{array}$$

Lemma 10

$$\max(\mathrm{dom}(r)) \;=\; \max(\mathrm{dom}(\underline{minfnc(r)}))$$

In order to prove **Lemma 9**, we need a few more mathematical laws which are the following

$$initial(s) \;\Rightarrow\; succ[s] \;=\; 1\,..\,1 + \max(s) \qquad \textbf{Law 12}$$

$$(1\,..\,1 + n) \times \{v\} \;=\; (1\,..\,n) \times \{v\} \cup \{1 + n \mapsto v\} \qquad \textbf{Law 13}$$

$$\begin{array}{l} s \;\subseteq\; minfnc(r)^{-1}[0\,..\,v] \\ \Rightarrow \\ minfnc(r \;\cup\; s \times \{v\}) \;=\; minfnc(r) \end{array} \qquad \textbf{Law 14}$$

[5] oparator $\lhd\!\!\!+$ used in this lemma is the relation *overriding* operator

$$j \in \mathrm{dom}(r)$$
$$j \notin \mathit{minfnc}(r)^{-1}[0\,..\,v]$$
$$\Rightarrow \qquad \textbf{Law 15}$$
$$\mathit{minfnc}(r \;\cup\; \{j \mapsto v\}) \;=\; \mathit{minfnc}(f) \lhd\!\!+ \{j \mapsto v\}$$

$$j \notin \mathrm{dom}(r)$$
$$\Rightarrow \qquad \textbf{Law 16}$$
$$\mathit{minfnc}(r \;\cup\; \{j \mapsto v\}) \;=\; \mathit{minfnc}(f) \lhd\!\!+ \{j \mapsto v\}$$

$$r^{-1}[0\,..\,v] \;=\; \mathit{minfnc}(r)^{-1}[0\,..\,v] \qquad \textbf{Law 17}$$

Proof of Lemma 9

We have one hypothesis

$$\mathit{initial}(r^{-1}[0\,..\,v]) \qquad \textbf{Hyp 1}$$

The proof goes as follows:

$$\mathit{minfnc}(r \;\cup\; \mathit{succ}[r^{-1}[0\,..\,v]] \times \{v\})$$
$$= \qquad \textbf{Hyp 1 Law 12}$$
$$\mathit{minfnc}(r \;\cup\; (1\,..\,1 + \max(r^{-1}[0\,..\,v])) \times \{v\})$$
$$= \qquad \textbf{Law 13}$$
$$\mathit{minfnc}(r \;\cup\; (1\,..\,\max(r^{-1}[0\,..\,v])) \times \{v\} \;\cup\; \{1 + \max(r^{-1}[0\,..\,v]) \mapsto v\})$$

At this point, we have to cases to consider: **(1)** $1+\max(r^{-1}[0\,..\,v]) \in \mathit{dom}(r)$, and **(2)** $1+\max(r^{-1}[0\,..\,v]) \notin \mathit{dom}(r)$. In case **(1)**, since clearly $1+\max(r^{-1}[0\,..\,v]) \notin r^{-1}[0\,..\,v]$, then, according to **Law 17** and **Law 15**, we have

$$\mathit{minfnc}(r \;\cup\; (1\,..\,\max(r^{-1}[0\,..\,v])) \times \{v\} \;\cup\; \{1 + \max(r^{-1}[0\,..\,v]) \mapsto v\})$$
$$=$$
$$\mathit{minfnc}(r \;\cup\; (1\,..\,\max(r^{-1}[0\,..\,v])) \times \{v\}) \;\lhd\!\!+\; \{1 + \max(r^{-1}[0\,..\,v]) \mapsto v\}$$

In case **(2)**, we have the same result according to **Law 16**. We may then proceed as follows:

$$\mathit{minfnc}(r \;\cup\; (1\,..\,\max(r^{-1}[0\,..\,v])) \times \{v\}) \;\lhd\!\!+\; \{1 + \max(r^{-1}[0\,..\,v]) \mapsto v\}$$
$$= \qquad \textbf{Hyp 1 Law 17 Law 14}$$
$$\mathit{minfnc}(r) \;\lhd\!\!+\; \{1 + \max(r^{-1}[0\,..\,v]) \mapsto v\}$$
$$= \qquad \textbf{Law 17}$$
$$\mathit{minfnc}(r) \;\lhd\!\!+\; \{1 + \max(\mathit{minfnc}(r)^{-1}[0\,..\,v]) \mapsto v\}$$

End of Proof

Our fifth refinement follows then immediately

---

refinement

$upseq(VALUE,\ maxsize)$

variables

ff

change

$ff\ =\ minfnc(rr)$

initialization

$ff := \{0 \mapsto 0\}$

operations

$insert(v)\ \ =$
begin
$ff(1 + \max(ff^{-1}[0\,..\,v])) := v$
end;

$v \longleftarrow result\ \ =$
begin
$v := \max(\mathrm{dom}(ff))$
end

end

Note that in the operation $insert(v)$ the substitution

$$ff(1 + \max(ff^{-1}[0\,..\,v])) := v$$

is a shorthand for

$$ff := ff \mathbin{\lhd\!\!\!+} \{1 + \max(ff^{-1}[0\,..\,v]) \ \mapsto\ v\}$$

where $\lhd\!\!\!+$ is the relation *overriding* operator.

12 Implementing a Machine on Another one

By looking closely at our last refinement, we realize that our problem is now *quite different* from what it used to be originally: our state variable has become a function whose domain is an interval and our operations correspond to simple manipulations of that function.

The idea is to consider that our operations might be further refined and implemented as *mere external interfaces* of *another* abstract machine; more precisely, our intention is to *code* our operations in terms of *calls* to some operations of a (simpler) abstract machine that we may have at our disposal *off the shelf.*

For example, we can suppose that we have been given an abstract machine offering a number of useful operations on arrays (notice that an *array* is nothing but a function whose domain is a finite interval).

That machine, called *array*, has the same parameters, *VALUE* and *maxsize*, as our previous machine; it encapsulates two variables called *bound* and *table*: the former is a natural number limited to *maxsize*, and the latter is a function whose domain is an interval of the form $1 \,..\, maxsize$. The variable *bound* is initialized to 0, and the variable *table* is initialized to *any*[6] function consistent with its type .

The *array* machine offers three operations:

- The operation $n \longleftarrow maxindex(v)$ computes the *greatest* element n in the domain of *table* (limited by *bound*) such that $table(n)$ is smaller than or equal to v; in the case where such an element does not exist, n is set to 0.
- The operation $enter(i, v)$ modifies *table* in such a way that $table(i)$ becomes equal to v; in the case where the value of i exceeds that of *bound* then *bound* is set to i.
- The operation $v \longleftarrow boundvalue$ yields the value of *bound*

We now present the *array* machine

[6] The operator $:\in$ used in the initialization can be read "becomes a member of"

---

machine

array(*VALUE*, *maxsize*)

variables

bound, *table*

invariant

$bound \in 0 \,..\, maxsize \;\wedge$
$table \in 1 \,..\, maxsize \rightarrow VALUE$

initialization

$bound := 0 \;\;||$
$table :\in 1 \,..\, maxsize \rightarrow VALUE$

operations

```
n ⟵ maxindex(v)  =
   pre
      v ∈ VALUE
   then
      n := max({0} ∪ (1 .. bound ◁ table)⁻¹[0 .. v])
   end;

enter(i, v)  =
   pre
      i ∈ 1 .. maxsize ∧
      v ∈ VALUE
   then
      table(i), bound := v, max({i, bound})
   end;

v ⟵ boundvalue  =
   begin  v := bound  end
```

end

We may now define our sixth refinement as follows:

---

refinement

$upseq(VALUE,\ maxsize)$

imports

$array(VALUE,\ maxsize)$

change

$ff\ =\ \{0 \mapsto 0\}\ \cup\ (1\,..\,bound) \lhd table$

operations

$insert(v)\ \ =$
  var i **in**
    $i \longleftarrow maxindex(v)$;
    $enter(1+i, v)$
  end;

$v \longleftarrow result\ \ =$
  begin
    $v \longleftarrow boundvalue$
  end

end

As you can see, the *variables* and *initialization* clauses have disappeared and we have an extra clause, the *imports* clause, whose role is to put the imported machine (in our case the *array* machine) within the *scope* of our refinement. Practically, this means that the formal refinement proofs should be done after

1. instantiating the imported machine with the *actual parameters* as provided in the imports clause (in our case which is *not* the most general case, the actual parameters are the same as the formal parameters of the importing refinement),

2. incorporating the *variables* of the instantiated imported machine so that they become the genuine variables of our refinement,

3. assuming the *invariant* of the instantiated imported machine,

4. incorporating the *initialization* of the instantiated imported machine,

5. expanding the *called operations* of the instantiated imported machine within the operations of our refinement.

As soon as these steps are accomplished (probably with the help of some automatic tool), then we are in a *normal* refinement situation so that we can proceed by using the general proof obligations as summarized in section 7. For instance, after expanding the various *calls* to the operations of the *array* machine found in our last refinement of the operation *insert*(v), we obtain the following:

$$
\begin{array}{l}
insert(v) \quad = \\
\quad \textbf{var} \;\; i \;\; \textbf{in} \\
\quad\quad \textbf{pre} \\
\quad\quad\quad v \in VALUE \\
\quad\quad \textbf{then} \\
\quad\quad\quad i := \mathsf{max}(\{0\} \cup (1\,..\,bound \lhd table)^{-1}[0\,..\,v]) \\
\quad\quad \textbf{end;} \\
\quad\quad \textbf{pre} \\
\quad\quad\quad 1 + i \in 1\,..\,maxsize \;\; \wedge \\
\quad\quad\quad v \in VALUE \\
\quad\quad \textbf{then} \\
\quad\quad\quad table(1+i),\; bound := v,\; \mathsf{max}(\{1+i,\; bound\}) \\
\quad\quad \textbf{end} \\
\quad \textbf{end}
\end{array}
$$

According to the general refinement conditions of section 7, we have then to prove the following refinement lemma for the operation *insert*(v):

Lemma 11

$$
\begin{array}{l}
ss \in \mathsf{seq}(VALUE) \\
size(ss) \leq maxsize \\
v \in VALUE \\
size(ss) < maxsize \\
uu \;=\; ups(ss) \\
pp \;=\; uu \lhd last_0 \\
rr \;=\; size^{-1} \,;\, pp \\
ff \;=\; minfnc(rr) \\
ff \;=\; \{0 \mapsto 0\} \;\cup\; (1\,..\,bound) \lhd table \\
\Rightarrow \\
[insert(v)] \\
\neg\, [ff(1 + \mathsf{max}(ff^{-1}[0\,..\,v])) := v] \,\neg\, (ff \;=\; \{0 \mapsto 0\} \;\cup\; (1\,..\,bound) \lhd table)
\end{array}
$$

Notice that we accumulate the invariant, the original pre-condition of the operation, and the various changes of variables

Proof of Lemma 11

We assume the following

$ss \in \mathrm{seq}(VALUE)$ **Hypothesis**
$size(ss) \leq maxsize$
$v \in VALUE$
$size(ss) < maxsize$
$uu = ups(ss)$
$pp = uu \lhd last_0$
$rr = size^{-1} ; pp$
$ff = minfnc(rr)$
$ff = \{0 \mapsto 0\} \cup (1 \,..\, bound) \lhd table$

After "performing" the generalized substitutions according to the corresponding Calculus [1] and after doing some simplifications, we remain with the following three statements to prove:

$v \in VALUE$ **Statement 1**

$1 + i \in 1 \,..\, maxsize$ **Statement 2**

$ff \lhd\!\!\!+ \{1 + \max(ff^{-1}[0 \,..\, v]) \mapsto v\}$
$=$ **Statement 3**
$\{0 \mapsto 0\} \cup (1 \,..\, max(\{1 + i,\ bound\}) \lhd (table \lhd\!\!\!+ \{1 + i \mapsto v\})$

where i is such that

$$i = \max(\{0\} \cup (1 \,..\, bound \lhd table)^{-1}[0 \,..\, v])$$

that is, obviously, according to the last **Hypothesis**

$$i = \max(ff^{-1}[0 \,..\, v])$$

As you can see, **Statement 1** and **Statement 2** correspond to the verification that each operation of the *array* machine *is called within its pre-condition.* **Statement 1** is obvious since it is exactly the third **Hypothesis. Statement 2** simplifies to

$$1 + \max(ff^{-1}[0 \,..\, v]) \in 1 \,..\, maxsize$$

which is obvious since we have $\max(ff^{-1}[0 \,..\, v]) \leq \max(\mathrm{dom}(ff))$ and also $\max(\mathrm{dom}(ff)) \leq size(ss)$[7]: **Statement 2** then follows immediately according to

[7]Intuitively, $\max(\mathrm{dom}(ff))$, which is our final result, *cannot exceed* the size of the sequence ss

the fourth **Hypothesis**, that is $size(ss) < maxsize$. Finally, **Statement 3** simplifies to the following:

$$\begin{array}{l}(\{0 \mapsto 0\} \ \cup \ (1\,..\,bound) \lhd table) \ \Leftarrow \{1+i \mapsto v\} \\ = \\ \{0 \mapsto 0\} \ \cup \ (1\,..\,max(\{1+i,\ bound\})) \lhd (table \ \Leftarrow \{1+i \mapsto v\})\end{array}$$

that is, equivalently

$$\begin{array}{l}(1\,..\,bound \lhd table) \ \Leftarrow \{1+i \mapsto v\} \\ = \\ (1\,..\,max(\{1+i,\ bound\})) \lhd (table \ \Leftarrow \{1+i \mapsto v\})\end{array}$$

We have to cases to consider: **(1)** $1+i \le bound$, and **(2)** $1+i > bound$. In case **(1)**, we are left to prove the following which is obvious

$$\begin{array}{l}(1\,..\,bound \lhd table) \ \Leftarrow \{1+i \mapsto v\} \\ = \\ (1\,..\,bound) \lhd (table \ \Leftarrow \{1+i \mapsto v\})\end{array}$$

In case **(2)** and according to the last **Hypothesis** and the definition of i, we have $i = bound$ and we are left to prove the following which is obvious

$$\begin{array}{l}(1\,..\,bound \lhd table) \ \Leftarrow \{1+bound \mapsto v\} \\ = \\ (1\,..\,1+bound) \lhd (table \ \Leftarrow \{1+bound \mapsto v\})\end{array}$$

End of Proof of Lemma 11

We leave the proofs of the refinement of the initialization and that of the second operation as exercises to the reader.

An important consequence of what we have done in this section is that we do not need to *further* refine our *upseq* machine; this is so because any refinement of the *array* machine produces *automatically* a refinement of the *upseq* machine: this is due to the fact that refinement is *monotonic* on all our *generalized substitution* constructs [1].

At this level, we should have the possibility to *code* directly the refinement of our operations by using a traditional programming language[8]. This does not mean, however, that our task is finished: our problem is now to refine the *array* machine unless, of course, we already have one (or several) *ready made* refinement at our disposal for that machine.

[8]this is done in section 15

In this section, we presented the concept of *implementing* the refinement of an abstract machine on the specification of another one: it is definitely a fundamental concept as it allows us to design our system as *layers* of modules with well defined relationships.

It also shows the possibility to *reuse* already specified abstract machines. For that possibility to be fully available, however, we need to generalize a little what is done in the *imports* clause of our sixth refinement.

In some cases, it might happen that we need to import *several time* the *same* machine; for that to be possible, we need to have a simple *renaming mechanism* by which an imported machine might be *repainted*; technically, this is done by prefixing the name of the machine with an identifier; for example, in order to import twice the *array* machine, the content of the corresponding *imports* clause might be the following:

$$first.array(VALUE, maxsize),\ second.array(VALUE, maxsize)$$

Of course, each call to operations of both machines has now to be *qualified* with the same sort of prefixes as shown in the following examples:

$$i \longleftarrow first.maxindex(v) \qquad second.enter(i, v)$$

Consequently, when importing a machine, a renaming phase has to be performed before the five other phases already considered in this section (again, an automatic tool might be of some help here).

13 Refining the Second Machine

As announced in the previous section, we suppose that we have at our disposal the following straightforward refinement of the *array* machine [1].

refinement

array(*VALUE*, *maxsize*)

initialization

bound := 0 ||
table :∈ 1 .. *maxsize* → *VALUE*

operations

```
n ⟵ maxindex(v)  =
   var  l, u  in
      l, u := 0, bound;
      while  l ≠ u  do
         if  table(u) ≤ v  then  l := u  else  u := u − 1  end
      end;
      n := u
   end;

enter(i, v)  =
   begin
      table(i) := v;
      if  i > bound  then  bound := i  end
   end;

v ⟵ boundvalue  =
   begin
      v := bound
   end
```

end

14 Interfaces

It remains now for us to write, as promised, the *interface* allowing us to enter progressively our input sequence into the *upseq* machine.

Formally, an interface is a sort of hybrid construct: like machines or refinements, an interface has a (parameterized) *name*, and it has an *operations* clause; but it has no *variables*, *invariant* and *initialization* clauses; however, like refinements, an interface imports other machines (or other interfaces) so that the operations of an interface are essentially made up of *calls* to operations of the imported machines (or interfaces).

Another way to look at an interface is to consider that it is the refinement of an *implicit machine* with no variable and with operations doing nothing. Consequently, there remains something to prove once you have written an interface: namely, that the mentioned imported operations are called *within their pre-conditions.*

Before proposing our interface, we have to present the semantics of a little *io* machine for reading and writing numbers on some media

---

```
machine

    io(VALUE)

operations

    v ⟵ readvalue  =
       begin
          v :∈ VALUE
       end;


    writevalue(v)  =
       pre
          v ∈ VALUE
       then
          skip
       end

end
```

As you can see, that machine specification is rather minimal (that is, we leave lots of freedom to the implementer): the first operation yields in v any member of the set *VALUE* (it is the *least* assumption we can made about a "read" operation) and, as we are not interested in the exact behaviour of the second operation, we suppose that it does nothing (of interest for a proof) although it has a precondition expressing that the parameter v has to be a member of the interval

VALUE.

We define now our *mainloop* interface in a straightforward manner as follows:

```
interface

    mainloop(VALUE, maxsize)

imports

    upseq(VALUE, maxsize), io(VALUE)

operations

    loop  =
        var  v, c  in
            c := 0;
            while  c < maxsize  do
                v ⟵ readvalue;
                insert(v);
                c := c + 1
            end;
            v ⟵ result;
            writevalue(v)
        end

end
```

Notice that our interface is still parameterized with *VALUE* and *maxsize*; consequently, we still have to fix these parameters: this can be done in the following extra interface

---

interface

mainitf

imports

mainloop(0 .. 10000, 10)

operations

main = **begin** *loop* **end**

end

Consequently the overall structure of our interfaces and machines is the following

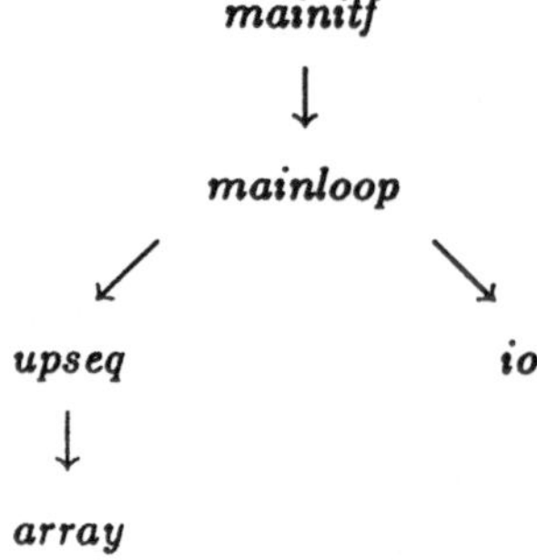

15 Code Generation

We envisage to perform our code generation by using a very simple programming language which is nothing but that part which is *common* to all decent imperative programming languages. It is called **B0**. In what follows, we give a very brief informal description of that language.

The *typing system* of **B0** is more than simplistic: variables can only be either of type *integer* [9] or of type *array* [10].

The *statements* of **B0** are the following:

- skip
- multiple assignment to scalar variables or to array elements
- sequencing
- conditional (**if** ... **then** ... **else** ... **end**)
- case
- loop (**while** ... **do** ... **end**)
- local variable introduction (**var** ... **in** ... **end**)
- operation call

An *operation* may have input parameters and output parameters (mind the plural), so that an operation *header* or an operation *call* may have one of the four following different forms:

- *name*
- *name*(InputList)
- OutputList ⟵ *name*
- OutputList ⟵ *name*(InputList)

In the case of a *header*, the InputList or OutputList are lists of distinct *formal parameters* supposed *implicitely* to be of type *integer* (no *array*).

In the case of a *call*, the InputList is a list of *expressions* of type *integer*, and the OutputList is a list of scalar variables or array elements of the same nature as those found in a *multiple assignment statement*.

Local variables introduced by corresponding statements are also *implicitely* of type *integer* only.

[9] the type *integer* is the interval *minint* .. *maxint* where these two constants are "reasonable" numbers

[10] an *array* is a total function from an interval of *integers* to an *integer* or to another *array*

Arithmetic expressions may be formed, as usual, with the basic arithmetic operators.

Boolean expressions (which are needed in conditional or in loop statements) are formed, as usual, with the basic relational and boolean operators.

Global variables are encapsulated into *modules* containing a number of operations which are the only ones having direct visibility of these variables. Modules may have parameters which are either *intervals of integers* or *integers*.

A module A may *import* one (or several) module B, meaning that within the operations of A you may call operations of B (but not refer to the global variables encapsulated into B). Note that importation may be done with *renaming* in exactly the same way as we presented it in section 12 for abstract machines.

Modules may have a special operation called after the name of the module and whose role is to *initialize* it.

A *system* is made of a number of modules whose *imports* structure should be a tree structure. The root of that tree is a module having an operation without input or output parameters and whose name is *main*.

Clearly, the writing of a translator from **B0** to an imperative programming language is a simple task. Also simple is the organization of such a translator so that each module can be *separately translated*, the final object code being put together eventually at *link edit* time.

The philosophy of **B0** is the same as that underlying the concept of **RISC** machines: simplicity. We do not claim that everything can be programmed in **B0**, but we do believe that most of our systems can be programmed using the simple, easy to learn, and well understood concepts of **B0**, concepts having a *mathematical counterpart* within the Abstract Machine Notation and the Generalized Substitutions Notation [1].

With all this in mind, we can generate a *system* from the development we have done in previous sections. This is done in a very simple way: to each *machine* or *interface*, there corresponds a *module*.

For a machine, the code generation is done by considering the *last refinement*: the module is generated in a straightforward manner, provided each operation of the refinement has reached a form which is *exactly* a **B0** program. For instance, the following module can be generated from the sixth refinement of the *upseq* machine:

```
module

    upseq(VALUE, maxsize)

imports

    array(VALUE, maxsize)

operations

    insert(v)  =
       var  i  in
          i ⟵ maxindex(v);
          enter(1 + i, v)
       end;


    v ⟵ result  =
       begin
          v ⟵ boundvalue
       end

end
```

Likewise, the following module can be generated from the only refinement of the *array* machine:

```
module

    array(VALUE, maxsize)

variables

    bound, table(1 .. maxsize)

operations

    initarray  =
      begin
        bound := 0
      end;

    n ⟵ maxindex(v)  =
      var  l, u  in
        l, u := 0, bound;
        while  l ≠ u  do
          if  table(u) ≤ v  then  l := u  else  u := u − 1  end
        end;
        n := u
      end;

    enter(i, v)  =
      begin
        table(i) := v;
        if  i > bound  then  bound := i  end
      end;

    v ⟵ boundvalue  =
      begin
        v := bound
      end

end
```

For interfaces, the module is generated directly provided each operation of the interface corresponds exactly to a B0 program. For instance, the module generated from our interface *mainloop* is the following:

```
module

    mainloop(VALUE, maxsize)

imports

    upseq(VALUE, maxsize), io(VALUE)

operations

    loop  =
       var  v, c  in
          c := 0;
          while  c < maxsize  do
             v ←— readvalue;
             insert(v);
             c := c + 1
          end;
          v ←— result;
          writevalue(v)
       end

end
```

And, finally, the module generated from the interface *mainitf* is the following:

```
module

    mainitf

imports

    mainloop(0 .. 10000, 10)

operations

    main  =  begin  loop  end

end
```

We have no **B0** module for the *io* machine: this is so because we have no refinement at our disposal: the translation of the *io* machine into code *depends* on our final target language and on its *Input-Output Library*: in fact, the *io* machine is just given to represent a *reasonable model* of the pre-defined operations *readvalue* and *writevalue*. All those parts of a system that cannot be tranlated into **B0** will be handled in this way; it is our belief that it only corresponds to a *very small proportion* of its constituent machines.

16 Maintenance

Maintenance is that activity by which people modify a running system because it does not appear, for various reasons, to work satisfactorily. It is well known to be very dangerous because some of the undertaken modifications, although apparently innocent, may have unforseen consequences.

In this section, we would like to conduct a little maintenance experiment on our example and see how its consequences could be limited *by construction*. The fundamental rule about maintenance is that it should *never* be done on the generated code directly but at the precise level of our development where the modification is to be originated.

For instance, in our case, we may decide to have a closer look at our fifth refinement of section 11. We have the feeling that the variable *ff* which is a function is also a *non-decreasing* function. We would like to improve the running speed of our system by taking advantage of this intuition. The consequence of this modification will probably be a new version of our sixth refinement, itself implemented on a new machine. Looking again at the structure of our interfaces and machines (remember, it is also the structure of our modules)

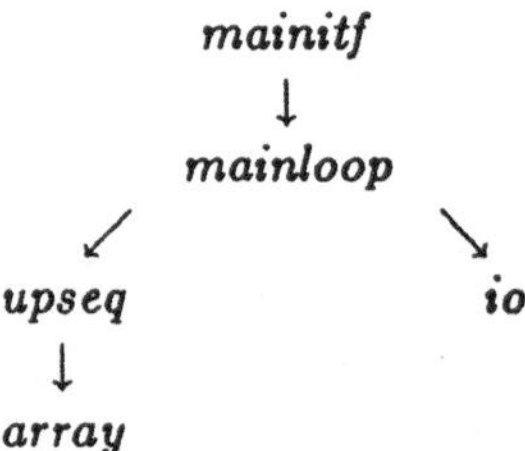

indicates that the *mainitf*, *mainloop*, and *io* modules are all *untouched*, and perhaps, if we are lucky enough, also the *upseq* module itself. The idea is to modify slightly our array machine by imposing that the variable *table*, restricted to the interval 1 .. *bound* is non-decreasing, formally

```
machine

      sortedarray(VALUE, maxsize)

variables

      bound, table

invariant

      bound ∈ 0..maxsize ∧
      table ∈ 1..maxsize → VALUE ∧
      (1..bound ◁ table) ∈ ndec

initialization

      bound := 0  ||
      table :∈ 1..maxsize → VALUE

operations

      n ⟵ maxindex(v)  =
         pre
            v ∈ VALUE
         then
            n := max({0} ∪ (1..bound ◁ table)⁻¹[0..v])
         end;

      enter(i, v)  =
         pre
            bound < maxsize ∧
            i = 1 + max({0} ∪ (1..bound ◁ table)⁻¹[0..v]) ∧
            v ∈ VALUE
         then
            table(i), bound := v, max({i, bound})
         end;

      v ⟵ boundvalue  =
         begin  v := bound  end

end
```

As you can see, the *only* differences between the *array* and the *sortedarray* machines are to be found in the invariant and in the pre-condition of the operation *enter(i,v)*. Consequently, we can be sure that our *upseq* module is also *untouched.*

It remains for us to refine our new *sortedarray* machine. As for the previous case, we may have a ready made refinement implementing the first operation by means of a *binary search* [1] as follows:

```
refinement

      sortedarray(VALUE, maxsize)

initialization

      bound := 0 ||
      table :∈ 1 .. maxsize → VALUE

operations

      n ⟵ maxindex(v)  =
         var  l, u, m  in
            l, u := 0, bound;
            while  l ≠ u  do
               m := (l + u − 1) div 2;
               if  table(m + 1) ≤ v  then  l := m + 1  else  u := m  end
            end;
            n := u
         end;

      enter(i, v)  =
         begin
            table(i) := v;
            if  i > bound  then  bound := i  end
         end;

      v ⟵ boundvalue  =
         begin
            v := bound
         end

end
```

Consequently, we may generate a new *array* module which replaces the previous one in our system

```
module

    array(VALUE, maxsize)

variables

    bound, table(1 .. maxsize)

operations

    initarray  =
       begin
          bound := 0
       end;

    n ←— maxindex(v)  =
       var  l, u, m  in
          l, u := 0, bound;
          while  l ≠ u  do
             m := (l + u − 1) div 2;
             if  table(m + 1) ≤ v  then  l := m + 1  else  u := m  end
          end;
          n := u
       end;

    enter(i, v)  =
       begin
          table(i) := v;
          if  i > bound  then  bound := i  end
       end;

    v ←— boundvalue  =
       begin
          v := bound
       end

end
```

References

[1] J.R. Abrial *Assigning Programs to Meanings* Book to appear.

[2] J.R. Abrial *A Formal Approach to Large Software Construction* 1989.

[3] E.W. Dijkstra *A Discipline of Programming* Prentice Hall 1976.

[4] E.W. Dijkstra and W.H.J. Feijen *A Method of Programming* Addison-Wesley 1988.

[5] R.G. Dromey *How to Solve it by Computer* Prentice Hall International 1982.

[6] D. Gries *The Science of Programming* Springer Verlag 1981.

[7] J. Misra *A Technique of Algorithmic Construction on Sequences* IEEE Transaction on Software Engineering January 1978.

[8] D.L.Parnas *A Technique for Software Module Specification with Examples* CACM 14,5 1972.

Assertional Data Reification Proofs: Survey and Perspective

J. Coenen*
Dept. of Math. and Computing Science
Eindhoven University of Technology
P.O. Box 513
5600 MB Eindhoven, The Netherlands

W.-P. de Roever†
Institut für Informatik und
Praktische Mathematik
Christian-Albrechts-Universität Kiel
D-2300 Kiel, Fed. Rep. Germany

J. Zwiers‡
University of Twente
P.O. Box 217
7500 AE Enschede, The Netherlands

Abstract

In this survey we discuss three methods for program development, which incorporate data reification: VDM, Reynolds' method, and Back's method and develop a modest predicate transformer based framework to relate them. At first we consider partial correctness only, and discuss Reynolds' method and a partial correctness version of VDM. Later we also consider total correctness in order to cover (part of) Back's refinement calculus and the full notion of specification and associated refinement methods in VDM.

1 Introduction

Already in the early seventies it became clear that data reification is a powerful principle in program development [Milner71][Hoare72] [Gerhart75]. It was already present in the methods presented in [Back78][Jones80] and [Reynolds81], which laid the foundations for the program development methods like e.g. VDM [VDM86][VDM89].

In this survey we discuss three methods for program development, which incorporate data reification: VDM, Reynolds' method, and Back's method and develop a modest predicate transformer based framework to relate them. The Vienna Development Method is included, because it has become one of the major design methods. Back's refinement calculus is included as a representative of the class of refinement

*Supported by NWO/SION Project 612-316-022: "Fault Tolerance: Paradigms, Models, Logics, Construction." E-mail: wsinjosc@win.tue.nl

†Partially supported by ESPRIT project 3096: "SPEC." E-mail: wpr@informatik.uni-kiel.dbp.de

‡E-mail: zwiers@utwente.nl

calculi such as [Morgan90] and [Morris89]. Finally, we consider the method advocated by Reynolds in chapter 5 of [Reynolds81], because in our opinion it is the one presented most elegantly along with the best worked out examples.

As mentioned already, besides surveying the above mentioned methods, we also set up a modest theory based on predicate transformers and relations which we use to relate them. At first we consider partial correctness only, and discuss Reynolds' method and a partial correctness version of VDM. Later we extend our theory to total correctness in order to cover Back's refinement calculus and the full notion of refinement in VDM.

Maybe this is the proper place to explain our usage of the term reification instead of refinement. In our opinion *refinement* is best defined by Gardiner and Morgan in [Gardiner90]: "One module is said to be refined by a second if no program using the second module can detect that it is not using the first." As such it can be conceived of as a compositional notion, related to the notion of subdistributivity by Hoare, He and Sanders [Hoare87]. However in actual program development sometimes noncompositional "refinement" techniques occur such as e.g. optimization in compilers. Another example of noncompositional refinement, in the style of Reynolds, is the implementation of the program fragment

$$\textbf{begin new}\, y;\ y := \textit{a member of } U;\ U := U - \{y\}\ \textbf{end}$$

by $b := b - 1$, where the set U is represented by an array segment and b denotes the upper bound of that segment. The statement implements neither of the two abstract operations and is only correct for this particular abstract program fragment. As a last example illustrating a noncompositional aspect of refinement we mention a notion of Abadi and Lamport which is related to the introduction of prophecy variables that add stuttering (cf. section 5.3 of [Abadi88]). To cover both these cases and action refinement we prefer to use the term reification, for want of a better term.

Actually there is multitude of refinement notions in program development:

- **compositional** or **process refinement** exploiting the compositional nature of a formalism, see e.g. [Gries81][Hehner84] [Morgan90][Zwiers89],
- **action refinement** typically applying to the implementation of atomic actions in a concurrent programming environment, see e.g. [Lamport83] [Abadi88], or the many references in [deBdeRRoz90],
- **data refinement**, see e.g. [Hoare72][Gerhart75] [Jones80][Reynolds81][Back88].

We will be concerned with data refinement only in this paper.

The outline of the remainder of this paper is as follows. In section two we discuss refinement within Hoare's logic. Section three is devoted to partial correctness preserving refinement. Total correctness preserving refinement is the subject of section four, and we conclude with a discussion and some ideas for future work.

2 Reification in Hoare's logic

We start with the presentation of a modest theory of relations and predicate transformers. Next, we define the meaning of correctness formulae and specifications. Furthermore, we discuss four simulation notions, and show how these simulations can be used to prove refinement in Hoare's logic. Most of the results are already well known, although they are sometimes presented in a different framework.

Although, in this section, we are mainly concerned with reification in a Hoare-style proof system we set up the theory in such a way that also a concise meaning can be given to our version of partial correctness formulae in VDM.

2.1 Relations and predicate transformers

Relations appear in four ways in our theory. Firstly, programs are interpreted as relations on states, i.e. we use a relational semantics. Therefore, secondly, we also interpret specification as relations. Thirdly, the postconditions in VDM specifications and correctness formulae denote relations on states. For this reason they are often referred to as post-relations. And fourthly, representation invariants, which are used to prove reification steps correct, define relations between states of two possibly different state spaces.

We use the following notations for relations. Throughout this paper p and q denote sets of states, and (indexed) r denotes a relation on states.

$$\begin{aligned}
r^{-1} &\mathrel{\hat{=}} \{(\tau,\sigma) \mid (\sigma,\tau) \in r\} , \\
p \leadsto q &\mathrel{\hat{=}} \{(\sigma,\tau) \mid \sigma \in p \to \tau \in q\} , \\
p \leadsto r &\mathrel{\hat{=}} \{(\sigma,\tau) \mid \sigma \in p \to (\sigma,\tau) \in r\} , \\
p; r &\mathrel{\hat{=}} \{(\sigma,\tau) \mid \sigma \in p \wedge (\sigma,\tau) \in r\} , \\
r_0; r_1 &\mathrel{\hat{=}} \{(\sigma,\tau) \mid \exists_{\sigma'}((\sigma,\sigma') \in r_0 \wedge (\sigma',\tau) \in r_1)\} .
\end{aligned}$$

The symbol $\leadsto$ is pronounced as "leads to", r^{-1} denotes the converse of r, $p; r$ and $r_0; r_1$ respectively denote the sequential composition of a filter and a relation and the sequential composition of two relations.

Furthermore, we use the following notations for sets:

$$\begin{aligned}
\langle r\rangle p &\mathrel{\hat{=}} \{\sigma \mid \exists_\tau((\sigma,\tau) \in r \wedge \tau \in p)\} , \\
[r]p &\mathrel{\hat{=}} \{\sigma \mid \forall_\tau((\sigma,\tau) \in r \to \tau \in p)\} , \\
r(p) &\mathrel{\hat{=}} \{\tau \mid \exists_\sigma((\sigma,\tau) \in r \wedge \sigma \in p)\} .
\end{aligned}$$

These sets correspond with the notions of strongest postcondition ($r(p)$ or $\langle r^{-1}\rangle p$) and weakest precondition ($[r]p$). Lemma 2.1.1 lists some useful properties of the above predicate transformers.

Lemma 2.1.1

$$\begin{aligned}
\langle r^{-1}\rangle p &= r(p) \\
\langle r_0; r_1\rangle p &= \langle r_0\rangle\langle r_1\rangle p \\
[r_0; r_1]p &= [r_0][r_1]p
\end{aligned}$$

□

A relation r is *total* if for every state σ in the domain of r there exists a state τ such that $(\sigma, \tau) \in r$.

Lemma 2.1.2
If, and only if r is total then

$$\begin{array}{lcl} (p \rightsquigarrow q); r^{-1} & = & p \rightsquigarrow (\langle r \rangle q) \\ r; (p \rightsquigarrow q) & = & ([r]p) \rightsquigarrow q \end{array}$$

□

2.2 Specifications and correctness formulae

We assume a syntactic class $\mathcal{E}xpr$ of expressions with occurrences of program variables $x \in \mathcal{V}ar$, a disjoint set of 'hooked' program variables $\overleftarrow{x}$, and another set, disjoint with the previous ones, of logical variables $g \in \mathcal{L}var$. We use Σ for the set of (program) states $\sigma : \mathcal{V}ar \rightarrow \mathcal{V}al$ and Γ for the set of logical states $\gamma : \mathcal{L}var \rightarrow \mathcal{V}al$. Furthermore, we assume that an interpretation function $\mathcal{E}[\![\,.\,]\!] : \mathcal{E}xpr \rightarrow (\Gamma \rightarrow ((\Sigma \times \Sigma) \rightarrow \mathcal{V}al))$ is defined such that

$$\begin{array}{lcl} \mathcal{E}[\![\, x \,]\!]\gamma(\sigma,\tau) & \hat{=} & \tau(x) \\ \mathcal{E}[\![\, \overleftarrow{x} \,]\!]\gamma(\sigma,\tau) & \hat{=} & \sigma(x) \\ \mathcal{E}[\![\, g \,]\!]\gamma(\sigma,\tau) & \hat{=} & \gamma(g) \end{array}$$

The syntactic class $\mathcal{A}ssn$ of assertions, with typical elements χ, is defined by ($e_1, e_2 \in \mathcal{E}xpr$)

$$\chi \ ::= \ \text{true} \mid e_1 = e_2 \mid \neg\chi \mid \chi_1 \rightarrow \chi_2 \mid \exists_g(\chi)$$

We will use the usual abbreviations such as e.g. $\chi_1 \vee \chi_2$. Assertions are interpreted by a truth-valued function $\mathcal{T}[\![\,.\,]\!] : \mathcal{A}ssn \rightarrow (\Gamma \rightarrow ((\Sigma \times \Sigma) \rightarrow \{tt, f\!f\}))$, which defined as follows.

$$\begin{array}{lcl} \mathcal{T}[\![\,\text{true}\,]\!]\gamma(\sigma,\tau) & \hat{=} & tt \\ \mathcal{T}[\![\, e_1 = e_2 \,]\!]\gamma(\sigma,\tau) & \hat{=} & \mathcal{E}[\![\, e_1 \,]\!]\gamma(\sigma,\tau) = \mathcal{E}[\![\, e_2 \,]\!]\gamma(\sigma,\tau) \\ \mathcal{T}[\![\, \neg\chi \,]\!]\gamma(\sigma,\tau) & \hat{=} & \text{not}\, \mathcal{T}[\![\, \chi \,]\!]\gamma(\sigma,\tau) \\ \mathcal{T}[\![\, \chi_1 \rightarrow \chi_2 \,]\!]\gamma(\sigma,\tau) & \hat{=} & \mathcal{T}[\![\, \chi_1 \,]\!]\gamma(\sigma,\tau) \Rightarrow \mathcal{T}[\![\, \chi_2 \,]\!]\gamma(\sigma,\tau) \\ \mathcal{T}[\![\, \exists_g(\chi) \,]\!]\gamma(\sigma,\tau) & \hat{=} & \begin{cases} tt & , \text{ there exists a } v \in \mathcal{V}al \text{ such that} \\ & \quad \mathcal{T}[\![\, \chi \,]\!]\gamma[v/g](\sigma,\tau) \\ f\!f & , \text{ otherwise .} \end{cases} \end{array}$$

Often assertions are interpreted as sets of pairs of states.

$$\begin{array}{l} [\![\,.\,]\!] : \mathcal{A}ssn \rightarrow (\Gamma \rightarrow \mathcal{P}(\Sigma \times \Sigma)) \\ [\![\, \chi \,]\!]\gamma \,\hat{=}\, \{(\sigma,\tau) \mid \mathcal{T}[\![\, \chi \,]\!]\gamma(\sigma,\tau)\} \end{array}$$

We will distinguish three kinds of assertions in $\mathcal{A}ssn$

$\varphi, \psi \in$	$\mathcal{A}ssn_H$	, assertions in which 'hooked' variables do not occur, to be used in Hoare-style correctness formulae.
$\rho \in$	$\mathcal{A}ssn_R$	, assertion without free occurrences of logical variables, but with 'hooked' ones, to be used in post relations of VDM-style correctness formulae.
$\pi \in$	$\mathcal{A}ssn_J$	, assertion in $\mathcal{A}ssn_H \cap \mathcal{A}ssn_R$, to be used as preconditions in VDM-style correctness formulae.

For these assertions the following interpretation functions are defined.

$$[\![.]\!]_H : \mathcal{A}ssn_H \rightarrow (\Gamma \rightarrow \mathcal{P}(\Sigma))$$
$$[\![.]\!]_R : \mathcal{A}ssn_R \rightarrow \mathcal{P}(\Sigma \times \Sigma)$$
$$[\![.]\!]_J : \mathcal{A}ssn_J \rightarrow \mathcal{P}(\Sigma)$$

$$[\![\varphi]\!]_H\gamma \ \hat{=}\ \bigcap_{\sigma}\{\tau \mid \mathcal{T}[\![\varphi]\!]\gamma(\sigma,\tau)\}$$
$$[\![\rho]\!]_R \ \hat{=}\ \bigcap_{\gamma}\{(\sigma,\tau) \mid \mathcal{T}[\![\rho]\!]\gamma(\sigma,\tau)\}$$
$$[\![\pi]\!]_J \ \hat{=}\ \bigcap_{\gamma,\sigma}\{\tau \mid \mathcal{T}[\![\pi]\!]\gamma(\sigma,\tau)\}$$

Let R denote a relation — R possibly stands for a program $S \in \mathcal{L}an$ of some programming language with a relational semantics $\mathcal{R}[\![.]\!] : \mathcal{L}an \rightarrow \mathcal{P}(\Sigma \times \Sigma)$, but not necessarily — then the syntactic class $\mathcal{F}orm$ of correctness formulae is defined by

$$f ::= (\varphi)\ R\ (\psi)_H \mid (\pi)\ R\ (\rho)_J \mid \forall_g(f) \mid f_1 \vee f_2 \mid f_1 \wedge f_2 \mid f_1 \rightarrow f_2$$

We use $\mathcal{F}orm_H$ for the subclass of correctness formulae that are obtained by deleting $(\pi)\ R\ (\rho)_J$ from the above definition, and $\mathcal{F}orm_J$ for the subclass which is obtained by deleting $(\varphi)\ R\ (\psi)_H$ and $\forall_g(f)$ from the above definition. The basic formulae in $\mathcal{F}orm_H$ and in $\mathcal{F}orm_J$ are respectively Hoare correctness formulae and VDM correctness formulae.

The semantics of correctness formulae is defined by the truth-valued function $\mathcal{F}[\![.]\!] : \mathcal{F}orm \rightarrow (\Gamma \rightarrow \{tt, ff\})$:

$$\mathcal{F}[\![(\varphi)\ R\ (\psi)_H]\!]\gamma \ \hat{=}\ [\![R]\!]([\![\varphi]\!]_H\gamma) \subseteq [\![\psi]\!]_H\gamma$$
$$\mathcal{F}[\![(\pi)\ R\ (\rho)_J]\!]\gamma \ \hat{=}\ [\![\pi]\!]_J;\ [\![R]\!] \subseteq [\![\rho]\!]_R$$
$$\mathcal{F}[\![\forall_g(f)]\!]\gamma \ \hat{=}\ \begin{cases} tt & \text{, for all } v \in \mathcal{V}al\ \ \mathcal{F}[\![f]\!]\gamma[v/g] \\ ff & \text{, otherwise .} \end{cases}$$
$$\mathcal{F}[\![f_1 \vee f_2]\!]\gamma \ \hat{=}\ \mathcal{F}[\![f_1]\!]\gamma \text{ or } \mathcal{F}[\![f_2]\!]\gamma$$
$$\mathcal{F}[\![f_1 \wedge f_2]\!]\gamma \ \hat{=}\ \mathcal{F}[\![f_1]\!]\gamma \text{ and } \mathcal{F}[\![f_2]\!]\gamma$$
$$\mathcal{F}[\![f_1 \rightarrow f_2]\!]\gamma \ \hat{=}\ \mathcal{F}[\![f_1]\!]\gamma \Rightarrow \mathcal{F}[\![f_2]\!]\gamma$$

Note that this definition deviates from the standard convention, as e.g. in [Apt81], in that logical variables are not universally quantified in $(\varphi)\ R\ (\psi)_H$, and therefore the truth of this formula is relative to a logical state. As result reasoning over correctness formulae becomes more natural (see [Zwiers89], page 125).

Observe also that VDM correctness formulae are interpreted as partial correctness formulae, which is unlike the total correctness interpretation in e.g. [VDM89]. It is not until we deal with total correctness that we capture the complete total correctness meaning of VDM correctness formulae.

Now, consider a Hoare-style specification $\{\varphi\}$ *name* $\{\psi\}_H$. There are two important differences with a correctness formula $\forall_g((\varphi)\ S\ (\psi)_H)$. The first one is that *name* is just a name for the program that is specified, whereas S is a program. As a consequence, the meaning of the correctness formula depends on S, but the meaning of the specification does not depend on *name*. The second difference is that a correctness formula is either true or false, but a specification defines the set of programs that satisfy that specification.

There is of course also a strong relationship between correctness formulae and specifications that becomes clear if we define what it means if a program satisfies a given specification. Intuitively a program S satisfies the specification $\{\varphi\}$ *name* $\{\psi\}_H$, if the corresponding correctness formula $\forall_g((\varphi)\ S\ (\psi)_H)$ is true. Thus one would like to have a definition of satisfaction such that

$$R \textbf{ sat } \{\varphi\}\ \textit{name}\ \{\psi\}_H \Leftrightarrow \forall_g((\varphi)\ R\ (\psi)_H)\ .$$

Following a similar argument as for Hoare-style specifications, we find the corresponding requirement for the definition for VDM-style (partial correctness) specifications.

$$R \textbf{ sat } \{\pi\}\ \textit{name}\ \{\rho\}_J \Leftrightarrow (\pi)\ R\ (\rho)_J\ .$$

The following lemma about correctness gives a sound basis for the definition of specifications and satisfaction.

Lemma 2.2.1

$$\begin{array}{lll} \forall_g((\varphi)\ R\ (\psi)_H) & \text{if, and only if,} & [\![R]\!] \subseteq \bigcap_\gamma([\![\varphi]\!]_H\gamma \rightsquigarrow [\![\psi]\!]_H\gamma) \\ (\pi)\ R\ (\rho)_J & \text{if, and only if,} & [\![R]\!] \subseteq [\![\pi]\!]_J \rightsquigarrow [\![\rho]\!]_R \end{array}$$

□

Lemma 2.2.1 defines the maximal relation, that satisfies a correctness formula of either type. Because the maximal relation which satisfies a specification characterizes the set of all relations which satisfy that specification, we define the semantics of a specification accordingly.

$$\begin{array}{lll} [\![\{\varphi\}\ \textit{name}\ \{\psi\}_H]\!] & \hat{=} & \bigcap_\gamma([\![\varphi]\!]_H\gamma \rightsquigarrow [\![\psi]\!]_H\gamma) \\ [\![\{\pi\}\ \textit{name}\ \{\rho\}_J]\!] & \hat{=} & [\![\pi]\!]_J \rightsquigarrow [\![\rho]\!]_R \end{array}$$

If specifications denote relations, satisfaction becomes simply inclusion between relations, and can be defined for arbitrary relations.

Definition 2.2.1

R_0 **sat** R_1 if, and only if, $R_0 \subseteq R_1$

□

2.3 Simulation

It is good programming practice to define a representation invariant when replacing an abstract data type by a more concrete one, c.f. [Hoare72]. A representation invariant is a predicate that defines how the abstract data type is related to the concrete one. It typically is conjunction of a characteristic predicate of an abstraction relation and a data invariant of the concrete data type. The abstraction relation relates the abstract variables with the concrete variables and the data invariant defines the allowed states of the concrete data type.

As we already pointed out in the introduction, we say that a concrete program refines an abstract one if no program using the concrete one can detect it is not using the abstract program. This notion of refinement is also used in e.g. [Hoare87]. Let $P(A)$ denote a program P using an abstract data type A and its operations. And, likewise, let $P(C)$ denote the same program P, with the abstract data type and its operations replaced by the concrete data type C and corresponding operations. Let AI and AF be the initialization and the finalization statements of the abstract data type, and CI and CF be the initialization and finalization of the concrete data type. Then, C refines A if, and only if,

$$[\![CI;\ P(C);\ CF]\!] \subseteq [\![AI;\ P(A);\ AF]\!]$$

for all programs P, cf. [Hoare87].

Proving a reification step correct can be done by showing that there exists a simulation relation. For data reification, the simulation relation is the abstraction relation, which is defined by the representation invariant.

There are different kinds of simulation that are used for reification.

Definition 2.3.1
Let $S^A \subseteq \Sigma^A \times \Sigma^A$ be an abstract relation (program) and $S^C \subseteq \Sigma^C \times \Sigma^C$ be a concrete relation, and $\alpha \subseteq \Sigma^C \times \Sigma^A$ an abstraction relation. Then

S^C L-simulates S^A w.r.t. α	if, and only if,	$\alpha^{-1};\ S^C \subseteq S^A;\ \alpha^{-1}$
S^C L^{-1}-simulates S^A w.r.t. α	if, and only if,	$S^C;\ \alpha \subseteq \alpha;\ S^A$
S^C U-simulates S^A w.r.t. α	if, and only if,	$\alpha^{-1};\ S^C;\ \alpha \subseteq S^A$
S^C U^{-1}-simulates S^A w.r.t. α	if, and only if,	$S^C \subseteq \alpha;\ S^A;\ \alpha^{-1}$

□

L-simulation and L^{-1}-simulation are respectively called downward simulation and upward simulation in [Hoare87]. U-simulation is used in [Back88], and U^{-1}-simulation is used in [Lamport83] for concurrent systems.

From the definition above it follows that any two relations simulate each other, because one can choose the empty relation for α. Therefore we demand that the abstraction relation is total on the concrete state space defined by the data invariant of the concrete data type. The requirement that an abstraction relation must be total causes no problems, because one can always choose a sufficiently strong data invariant at the implementation level.

Although the different versions of simulation are in general incomparable — e.g. some refinements can be proven by L^{-1}-simulation but not by L-simulation cf. [Gardiner90], and vice versa — they can be compared if one requires the abstraction relation to be total or functional.

Lemma 2.3.1
If, and only if, α is functional then

$$U^{-1}\text{-simulation} \begin{array}{c} \nearrow \; L\text{-simulation} \; \searrow \\ \searrow \; L^{-1}\text{-simulation} \; \nearrow \end{array} U\text{-simulation}$$

□

This diagram should be read as follows. E.g. if S^C U^{-1}-simulates S^A then S^C also L-simulates S^A.

Lemma 2.3.2
If, and only if, α is total then

$$U\text{-simulation} \begin{array}{c} \nearrow \; L\text{-simulation} \; \searrow \\ \searrow \; L^{-1}\text{-simulation} \; \nearrow \end{array} U^{-1}\text{-simulation}$$

□

In [Hoare87] it was proven that L- and L^{-1}-simulation together are sufficient to prove refinement (see also [He89]). This implies that U^{-1}-simulation is sufficient to prove refinement if only total abstraction relations are used, and U-simulation is sufficient if only abstraction functions are used. However, requiring that the abstraction relation must be functional causes a problem if one allows implementation bias, a notion which can be very useful in practical situations.

A specification is implementation biased if it contains more information than strictly necessary to specify the desired operation. Although, implementation bias can always be avoided it may be used to give a specification that is easier to understand. There is also a practical reason for permitting implementation bias. Suppose you have designed a large and complex system. However, you 're quite unhappy with the inefficiency of some of the operations. Because, you don't want to redesign the complex algorithms used for these operations, you might decide to apply some optimization techniques to the operations instead. This means you consider the implementations of the operations as specifications, thereby introducing implementation bias.

It is tempting to conclude from the above that U^{-1}-simulation is the simulation one should use to prove refinement. This is true if one considers refinement of a single abstract operation, but when refining a large program this is no longer true. Suppose that S_1^C simulates S_1^A and S_2^C simulates S_2^A, and P is a program with statements S_1^A and S_2^A. Then P with S_1^A and S_2^A replaced by S_1^C and S_2^C should also simulate P. This property is called subdistributivity in [Hoare87], where L- and L^{-1}-simulation where shown to be subdistributive. Unfortunately, U- and U^{-1}-simulation are in general not subdistributive, and can therefore not be used to prove refinement of a complete program by proving the refinement of the operations in isolation. The problem is sequential composition. In lemma 2.3.3, sufficient and necessary conditions are given under which these simulations are subdistributive.

Lemma 2.3.3
If S_1^C U-simulates S_1^A and S_2^C U-simulates S_2^A, then

$$S_1^C;\ S_2^C \text{ } U\text{-simulates } S_1^A;\ S_2^A \Leftrightarrow \alpha \text{ is total}$$

If S_1^C U^{-1}-simulates S_1^A and S_2^C U^{-1}-simulates S_2^A, then

$$S_1^C;\ S_2^C \text{ } U^{-1}\text{-simulates } S_1^A;\ S_2^A \Leftrightarrow \alpha \text{ is functional}$$

□

Thus the abstraction relation must be total and functional, if we insist that U- or U^{-1}-simulation is subdistributive and sufficient to prove refinement in the sense of [Hoare87]. A similar problem arises if one uses L-simulation and L^{-1}-simulation for proving reification of different parts of the same program. If S_1^C L-simulates S_1^A and S_2^C L^{-1}-simulates S_2^A, then it is not guaranteed that S_1^C; S_2^C L- or L^{-1}-simulates S_1^A; S_2^A.

2.4 Proving reification

We want to answer the following question. Suppose we are provided with a specification $\{\pi\}$ op^A $\{\psi\}$ of an abstract operation op^A. How should we specify the concrete operation op^C such that every program that satisfies the specification of op^C is a correct implementation op^A w.r.t. a given abstraction relation α? This question is answered in theorem 2.4.1, for each of the simulation notions discussed in section 2.3.

We include $\langle\alpha\rangle\psi$ and $[\alpha]\psi$ in the assertion language $Assn_H$ as abbreviations of respectively $\exists_a(\chi_\alpha \wedge \psi)$ and $\forall_a(\chi_\alpha \rightarrow \psi)$, where χ_α ($\in Assn_I$) denotes the characteristic predicate of α and a is the list of all free abstract variables in this predicate.

Theorem 2.4.1

- *(U-simulation).*

$$\begin{aligned}&\alpha^{-1};\ S;\ \alpha\ \mathbf{sat}\ \{\varphi\}\ op^A\ \{\psi\}_H\\ \Leftrightarrow\ & S\ \mathbf{sat}\ \{\langle\alpha\rangle\varphi\}\ op^C\ \{[\alpha]\psi\}_H\end{aligned}$$

- *(U^{-1}-simulation).* If, and only if, α is total then

$$\begin{aligned}& S\ \mathbf{sat}\ \alpha;\ (\{\varphi\}\ op^A\ \{\psi\}_H);\ \alpha^{-1}\\ \Leftrightarrow\ & S\ \mathbf{sat}\ \{[\alpha]\varphi\}\ op^C\ \{\langle\alpha\rangle\psi\}_H\end{aligned}$$

- *(L-simulation).* If, and only if, α is total then

$$\begin{aligned}&\alpha^{-1};\ S\ \mathbf{sat}\ (\{\varphi\}\ op^A\ \{\psi\}_H);\ \alpha^{-1}\\ \Leftrightarrow\ & S\ \mathbf{sat}\ \{\langle\alpha\rangle\varphi\}\ op^C\ \{\langle\alpha\rangle\psi\}_H\end{aligned}$$

- *(L^{-1}-simulation).* If, and only if, α is total then

$$\begin{aligned}& S;\ \alpha\ \mathbf{sat}\ \alpha;\ (\{\varphi\}\ op^A\ \{\psi\}_H)\\ \Leftrightarrow\ & S\ \mathbf{sat}\ \{[\alpha]\varphi\}\ op^C\ \{[\alpha]\psi\}_H\end{aligned}$$

□

Suppose we want to prove that $S_0;\ S_1$ is an implementation of $\{\varphi_0\}\ op^A\ \{\varphi_2\}_H$ under abstraction relation α. If we use L-simulation it suffices to prove[1] $(\langle\alpha\rangle\varphi_0)\ S_0\ (\langle\alpha\rangle\varphi_1)_H$ and $(\langle\alpha\rangle\varphi_1)\ S_1\ (\langle\alpha\rangle\varphi_2)_H$ for some assertion φ_1. If we use U-simulation we have to find an assertion φ_1 such that $(\langle\alpha\rangle\varphi_0)\ S_0\ ([\alpha]\varphi_1)_H$ and $(\langle\alpha\rangle\varphi_1)\ S_1\ ([\alpha]\varphi_2)_H$ *and* $[\alpha]\varphi_1 \rightarrow \langle\alpha\rangle\varphi_1$. This extra proof obligation is needed because U-simulation is not subdistributive. In case that α is total, and hence U-simulation is subdistributive, $[\alpha]\varphi_1 \rightarrow \langle\alpha\rangle\varphi_1$ is always true. Thus subdistributivity guarantees nice proof rules, but it is not always necessary to require subdistributivity. In a correctness proof one is interested in a particular assertion φ for which $[\alpha]\varphi \rightarrow \langle\alpha\rangle\varphi$ (or $\langle\alpha\rangle\varphi \rightarrow [\alpha]\varphi$) may very well be true.

3 Partial correctness preserving transformations

We will show how the verification conditions for reification in Reynolds' method and in VDM can be derived within the theory of section two.

[1] This is an example where one explicitly reasons over correctness formulae within a given logical state and not about implicitly quantified formulae.

3.1 Reynolds' reification method

Each reification step in Reynolds' method consists of four smaller steps. First, the concrete variables and the representation invariant are introduced. Second, each assignment that affects the representation invariant is augmented with one or more assignments to the concrete variables such that the representation invariant is reestablished (or achieved in case of initialization). Third, expressions that contain abstract variables, but occur outside of an assignment to abstract variables, are replaced by expressions that do not contain abstract variables but are guaranteed by the representation invariant to have a value that could have been the result of the abstract expression. Fourth, the declarations of and the assignments to abstract variables that have become auxiliary by the previous step are eliminated. The second and the third step are the most interesting ones, because they implicitly describe what correctness of a reification step in Reynolds' method means.

According to step two, a simultaneous assignment $a := e^A(a,x)$ is augmented with assignments to concrete variables to reestablish the representation invariant. The assignments to the concrete variables can be contracted into a single simultaneous assignment $c := e^C(c,x)$. Thus, one has to prove that

$$(\chi_\alpha)\ a := e^A(a,x);\ c := e^C(c,x)\ (\chi_\alpha)_H$$

holds, where χ_α denotes the representation invariant. This boils down to proving $\chi_\alpha \rightarrow \chi_\alpha[e^C(c,x)/c][e^A(a,x)/a]$, or because the abstract and concrete variables are disjoint

$$\chi_\alpha \rightarrow \chi_\alpha[e^C(c,x)/c, e^A(a,x)/a]\,.$$

Observe that in this verification condition nothing is said about the pre- and post-condition of the abstract assignment itself. In this respect there is a difference between Reynolds' method and Back's method on one hand and ours and VDM on the other. In VDM operations are characterized by their specifications, whereas Reynolds characterizes them through their semantics. Thus, Reynolds interprets the meaning of an abstract program and this is in principle independent of the proof outline of that program (of course validity of a proof outline does depend on the semantics of the abstract operations).

If we specify the abstract assignment by $\{a = g\}\ op^A\ \{a = e^A(g,x)\}_H$ — with the restriction that assignment to the variables in x is not allowed — we can use the rule for L-simulation to obtain $\{\exists_a(\chi_\alpha \wedge a = g)\}\ op^C\ \{\exists_a(\chi_\alpha \wedge a = e^A(g,x))\}_H$. For a concrete assignment $c := e^C(c,x)$ this means we have to prove

$$\exists_a(\chi_\alpha \wedge a = g) \rightarrow \exists_a(\chi_\alpha[e^C(c,x)/c] \wedge a = e^A(g,x))\,.$$

In Reynolds' method the abstract operation $a := e^A(a,x)$ always terminates, and therefore we have to prove that $\exists_a(\chi_\alpha \wedge a = g) \rightarrow \chi_\alpha[e^C(c,x)/c, e^A(g,x)/a]$, which is equivalent to the verification condition above.

Next, we turn to step three of Reynolds' method. In case that an abstract variable occurs in an expression outside an assignment to an abstract variable, we concentrate on nondeterministic assignments of the form $x := x'.\pi^A(a, x')$. The intended meaning of this statement is that the variable x is assigned a value such that $\pi^A(a, x)$ is true if possible, otherwise it does not terminate. According to step three, proving that $x := x'.\pi^C(c, x')$ is a correct implementation, can be done by verifying that

$$\chi_\alpha \rightarrow (\pi^C(c, x) \rightarrow \exists_a(\chi_\alpha \wedge \pi^A(a, x)))\,.$$

This verification condition can be deduced within our framework. The abstract operation satisfies $\{\text{true}\}\ op^A\ \{\pi^A(a, x)\}_H$, with the restriction that only assignment to x is allowed. The rule for L-simulation requires a proof of

$$(\exists_a(\chi_\alpha))\ x := x'.\pi^C(c, x')\ (\exists_a(\chi_\alpha \wedge \pi^A(a, x)))_H\,.$$

Using the axiom for nondeterministic assignment this generates the following verification condition

$$\exists_a(\chi_\alpha) \rightarrow \forall_g(\pi^C(c, g) \rightarrow \exists_a(\chi_\alpha \wedge \pi^A(a, g)))\,.$$

And this is equivalent with Reynolds' verification condition. The replacement of abstract variables by concrete variables in boolean expressions is completely analogous.

From the considerations in the previous paragraphs one may conclude that Reynolds uses L-simulation to prove reification, and therefore the method of Reynolds is incomplete.

3.2 Reification in VDM: partial correctness

To investigate the relationship between reification in VDM and reification in the other methods we use a translation from VDM specifications to Hoare specifications and a translation the other way around. Of course, the same translations can be applied to correctness formulae.

A VDM specification $\{\pi\}\ op^A\ \{\rho\}_J$ denotes the same relation as the Hoare specification $\{\pi \wedge x = g\}\ op^A\ \{\rho[g/\overleftarrow{x}]\}_H$, where $x = g$ is a freeze predicate that "freezes" the values of all hooked program variables in ρ.

Thus, if logical variables are used then primed variables become superfluous. The opposite is also true. If primed variables are used one does not need logical variables, because a Hoare specification $\{\varphi\}\ op^A\ \{\psi\}_H$ denotes the same relation as $\{\text{true}\}\ op^A\ \{\forall_g(\varphi[\overleftarrow{x}/x] \rightarrow \psi)\}_J$, where g is the list of free logical variables in φ and ψ. In [VDM89], Jones gives two proof rules for reification. One that is used if the abstraction relation is functional, i.e. it is a retrieve function. And, secondly, a proof rule that is used in case that the abstraction relation is not functional, i.e. it is a retrieve relation. In case of a retrieve function, Jones uses U-simulation as a basis for his proof rule, and therefore has a complete proof rule. However the retrieve functions used in [VDM89] are also total and adequate — i.e. for each instance of the abstract datatype there is an instance of the concrete datatype that represents it and vice versa — so that the simulations in section two are equal. For this reason we move directly to the more interesting case of nonfunctional abstraction relations. It is already known, see e.g. [Gardiner90] that the proof rule for retrieve relations expresses L-simulation, but we give a proof of this fact within the theory of section two.

To prove in VDM that $\{\pi^C\}\ op^C\ \{\rho^C\}_J$ specifies a correct implementation of $\{\pi^A\}\ op^A\ \{\rho^A\}_J$ under α, one has to verify that ([VDM89], page 222)

$$\begin{array}{lll} & \chi_\alpha \wedge \pi^A \rightarrow \pi^C & ,\ \textit{domain rule;} \\ \text{and} & \chi_\alpha[\overleftarrow{a}\ /a, \overleftarrow{c}\ /c] \wedge \pi^A[\overleftarrow{a}\ /a] \wedge \rho^C \rightarrow \exists_a(\rho^A \wedge \chi_\alpha) & ,\ \textit{result rule.} \end{array}$$

The above conditions are satisfied if the concrete operation satisfies

$$\{\chi_\alpha \wedge \pi^A\}\ op^C\ \{\exists_a(\rho^A \wedge \chi_\alpha)\}_J\ .$$

This is also the weakest specification that guarantees that the domain rule and result rule are satisfied. This can be explained as follows. From the domain rule it follows that $\chi_\alpha \wedge \pi^A$ is the strongest precondition that is allowed in the specification of op^C. Because,

$$[\![\chi_\alpha[\overleftarrow{a}\ /a, \overleftarrow{c}\ /c] \wedge \pi^A[\overleftarrow{a}\ /a] \rightarrow \exists_a(\rho^A \wedge \chi_\alpha)]\!]_R = [\![\{\chi_\alpha \wedge \pi^A\}\ op\ \{\exists_a(\rho^A \wedge \chi_\alpha)\}_J]\!]$$

it follows that $\exists_a(\rho^A \wedge \chi_\alpha)$ is also the weakest postcondition that is admissible in the specification of the concrete operation.

The specification above can be translated in the Hoare specification

$$\{\chi_\alpha \wedge \pi^A \wedge x = g\}\ op^C\ \{\exists_a(\rho^A[g/\ \overleftarrow{a}] \wedge \chi_\alpha)\}_H\ .$$

Note that the abstract variables a do not occur free in the postcondition, thus we can apply the adaptation rule (see e.g. [Olderog83]) to obtain

$$\{\exists_a(\chi_\alpha \wedge \pi^A \wedge x = g)\}\ op^C\ \{\exists_a(\rho^A[g/\ \overleftarrow{a}] \wedge \chi_\alpha)\}_H\ .$$

To obtain the previous specification again, just apply the consequence rule. And this is exactly what we would have obtained by first translating the abstract specification and then applying the rule for L-simulation. So, also the VDM verification conditions are deducible within our formalism.

4 Total correctness preserving transformations

Although partial correctness preserving refinement is interesting and can be used to illustrate many ideas about refinement, it has the disadvantage that every abstract operation may be implemented by a nonterminating program at the concrete level. Therefore, we will investigate in this section how our theory might be extended to total correctness preserving reification.

A straightforward way to adapt the theory in section two to total correctness, is to introduce a special state $\perp$ to denote divergence, use a strict interpretation —

evaluation of a predicate in $\perp$ yields false — and require that relations are total. To distinguish the correctness formula with the new interpretation from the old ones we add the superscript $\perp$. Thus, the *total* correctness formula $(\varphi)\ S\ (\psi)^{\perp}_{H}$ is only true if for each initial state that satisfies φ the program S will terminate in a state satisfying ψ. Although this is the approach taken in VDM and by Back, we also want to mention an alternative approach.

The approach sketched in the previous paragraph is in a sense an all-or-nothing approach because one cannot specify that a program may not terminate for certain initial states. However, for concurrent systems it is sometimes desirable to specify that a program does not terminate for some initial values [Zwiers90a]. Therefore one may, again, introduce $\perp$ and a special predicate **fin** which is only false in $\perp$. The total correctness formula above and the partial correctness formulae of section two are respectively obtained as the special cases $(\varphi)\ S\ (\textbf{fin} \wedge \psi)_H$ and $(\varphi)\ S\ (\textbf{fin} \rightarrow \psi)_H$. It is also possible to consider correctness formulae with a meaning different from both partial and total correctness. For example, the formula $(x = g)\ S\ (g \neq 0 \leftrightarrow \textbf{fin})_H$ is true if S terminates only if x is initially not zero.

In the remainder of this section we investigate how total correctness preserving refinement is achieved in VDM and Back's refinement calculus, and how this could be applied to the theory of section two.

4.1 Reification in VDM: total correctness

We already discussed partial correctness preserving reification in VDM, so we can be rather brief about total correctness. In VDM the preservation of total correctness in a reification step is guaranteed by the restriction that the implementation of an abstract data type is *adequate*, which means that for each state that satisfies the data invariant at the abstract level there is a state at the concrete level that represents it. Together with the domain rule this is sufficient to ensure that if the precondition of the abstract operation is true for a particular state, then there exists a corresponding state at the concrete level such that the precondition of the concrete operation is true. Because specifications in VDM specify programs that must terminate for states that satisfy the precondition, the concrete program must terminate also. The result rule ensures that the program terminates in a correct state.

Thus to adapt the theory of section two to total correctness, it is sufficient to interpret the correctness formulae as total correctness formulae and add the requirement that abstraction relations are adequate.

4.2 Reification in Back's refinement calculus

Before we proceed with data reification in Back's calculus, we must admit that it is not possible to cover Back's calculus completely with the theory of section two. The reason for this is that Back allows angelic conditional statements of the form $S_1 \diamond S_2$ with a weakest precondition semantics such that $[S_1 \diamond S_2]p \triangleq [S_1]p \vee [S_2]p$. This statement doesn't have a relational semantics, and is therefore not covered by the theory of section two. However, in data refinement angelic nondeterminism is used in a restricted way, which can be handled in a relational framework, indeed.

In the refinement calculus S implements S' if, and only if, $[S']\pi \rightarrow [S]\pi$ for all π ($\in \mathcal{A}ssn_J$). Likewise, S data refines S' w.r.t. abstraction relation α if, and only if [2], $[S']\pi \rightarrow [\alpha^{-1}; S; \bar{\alpha}]\pi$. The statement $\bar{\alpha}$ is a angelic nondeterministic statement whose predicate transformer semantics is defined by $[\bar{\alpha}]\pi \hat{=} \exists_a(\chi_\alpha \wedge \pi)$, cf. [Back90].

If the abstract statement is specified by $\{\varphi\}$ op^A $\{\psi\}^{\perp}_{H}$ an application of the characterization theorem [Back90] results in the following proof obligation for the implementation S^C

$$(\exists_a(\chi_\alpha) \wedge \forall_a(\chi_\alpha \rightarrow \varphi))\ S^C\ (\exists_a(\chi_\alpha \wedge \psi))^{\perp}_{H}\ .$$

To extend the theory of section two to total correctness in the same way as Back, this means that we only have to replace $[\alpha]\varphi$ by $\langle\alpha\rangle\mathrm{true} \wedge [\alpha]\varphi$ in the proof rules of theorem 2.4.1.

5 Conclusions

Three well-known methodologies for proving data refinement for sequential programs, due to Reynolds [Reynolds81], Jones [VDM89], and Back [Back88] have been presented up to now separately in the literature without without mentioning the underlying principles that relate them. We have investigated how the afore mentioned methodologies are related by

1. Developing a modest predicate transformer framework.
2. Relating four known varieties for proving refinement and express them as verification conditions within this framework.
3. Analyzing Reynolds' method and VDM-style refinement proofs, and stating their associated verification conditions for partial correctness, and then, through an extension of our framework to include nontermination, to total correctness.
4. Mentioning how a restricted form [Back88] of Back's general theory can also be characterized within our formalism.

Although we considered data reification in sequential systems, most issues are also relevant for concurrent systems. Back has applied the same techniques used in data reification to refinement of action systems [Back90a]. Also in [Zwiers90] data refinement was used for the implementation of a queue by a dynamic network of processes. Therefore it is worthwhile to have an overview of the main methods and issues in data refinement as a basis for the refinement of distributed systems.

[2]To avoid confusion, readers familiar with Back's notation should be aware that his abstraction relations are defined on $\Sigma^A \times \Sigma^C$, whereas we have defined them on $\Sigma^C \times \Sigma^A$.

Future work, includes the generalization of the results for concurrency possibly using a framework similar to the one in [Zwiers90a]. This would enable us to integrate e.g. Hehner's work on concurrency [Hehner84b].

We want to emphasize that many results, especially concerning predicate transformers, are but variations upon work reported in existing literature, and mention that we especially learned a lot from Gardiner and Morgan [Gardiner90], although our framework was developed independently from theirs. Our sincere thanks go to John Reynolds, Cliff Jones, and Ralph Back for their fine work in this area, whose study continues to be a source of enjoyment and inspiration for us.

References

[Abadi88] M. Abadi & L. Lamport. *The Existence of Refinement Mappings.* Proceedings of the 3rd IEEE Conference on Logic in Computer Science (LICS), pp. 165–175, 1988.

[Apt81] K.R. Apt. *Ten Years of Hoare's Logic: A Survey—Part I.* ACM Transactions on Programming Languages and Systems 4:431–483, 1981.

[Back78] R.J.R. Back. *On the Correctness of Refinement Steps in Program Development.* Report A-1978-4, Dept. of Computer Science, University of Helsinki, 1978.

[Back88] R.J.R. Back. *Data Refinement in the Refinement Calculus.* Reports on computer science & mathematics 68, Åbo Akademi, 1988.

[Back90] R.J.R. Back & J. von Wright. *Refinement Calculus, Part I: Sequential Nondeterministic Programs.* In Stepwise Refinement of Distributed Systems, LNCS 430, pp. 42–66. Springer-Verlag, 1990.

[Back90a] R.J.R. Back. *Refinement Calculus, Part II: Parallel and Reactive Programs.* In Stepwise Refinement of Distributed Systems, LNCS 430, pp. 67–93. Springer-Verlag, 1990.

[deBdeRRoz90] J.W. de Bakker, G. Rozenberg & W.-P. de Roever. *Stepwise Refinement of Distributed Systems: Models, Formalisms, Correctness.* Proceedings of the NFI/REX Workshop, LNCS 430. Springer-Verlag 1990.

[vanDiepen86] N.W.P. van Diepen & W.-P. de Roever. *Program Derivation through Transformations: The Evolution of List-Copying Algorithms.* Science of Computer Programming 6:213–272, 1986.

[Gardiner90] P. Gardiner & C. Morgan. A Single Complete Rule for Data Refinement, submitted to ACM Transactions on Programming Languages and Systems.

[Gerhart75] S.L. Gerhart. *Correctness Preserving Program Transformations.* Proceedings 2nd Symposium on Principles of Programming Languages, pp. 54–66, 1975.

[Gries81] D. Gries. *The Science of Programming.* Springer-Verlag, 1981.

[He89] He Jifeng. *Process Simulation and Refinement.* Formal Aspects of Computing 1:229–241, 1989.

[Hehner84] E.C.R. Hehner. *The Logic of Programming.* Prentice-Hall, 1984.

[Hehner84a] E.C.R. Hehner. *Predicative Programming Part I.* Communications of the ACM 27:134–143, 1984.

[Hehner84b] E.C.R. Hehner. *Predicative Programming Part II.* Communications of the ACM 27:144–151, 1984.

[Hoare72] C.A.R. Hoare. *Proofs of Correctness of Data Representation.* Acta Informatica 1:271–281, 1972.

[Hoare87] C.A.R. Hoare, He Jifeng & J.W. Sanders. *Prespecification in Data Refinement.* Information Processing Letters 25:71–76, 1987.

[Jones80] C.B. Jones. *Software Development: a Rigorous Approach.* Prentice-Hall, 1980.

[Lamport83] L. Lamport. *Specifying Concurrent Program Modules.* ACM Transactions on Programming Languages and Systems 2:190–220, 1983.

[Lee79] S. Lee, W.-P. de Roever & S.L. Gerhart. *The Evolution of List-Copying Algorithms and The Need for Structured Program Verification.* Conf. Rec. 6th Ann. ACM Symp. on Principles of Progr. Languages, pp. 53–67, 1979.

[Milner71] R. Milner. *An Algebraic Definition of Simulation between Programs.* Proceedings of 2nd Int. Joint Conf. on Artificial Intelligence, pp. 481–489, 1971.

[Morgan90] C. Morgan. *Programming from Specifications.* Prentice-Hall, 1990.

[Morris89] J.M. Morris. *Laws of data refinement.* Acta Informatica 26:287–308, 1989.

[Olderog83] E.-R. Olderog. *On the Notion of Expressiveness and the Rule of Adaptation.* Theoretical Computer Science 24:337–347, 1983.

[Reynolds81] J.C. Reynolds. *The Craft of Programming.* Prentice-Hall, 1981.

[VDM86] C.B. Jones. *Systematic Software Development using VDM.* Prentice-Hall, 1986.

[VDM89] C.B. Jones. *Systematic Software Development using VDM*, 2nd edition. Prentice-Hall, 1989.

[Zwiers89] J. Zwiers. *Compositionality, Concurrency and Partial Correctness: Proof Theories for Networks of Processes, and Their Relationship.* LNCS 321, Springer-Verlag, 1989.

[Zwiers90] J. Zwiers. *Predicates, Predicate Transformers and Refinement.* In Stepwise Refinement of Distributed Systems, LNCS 430, pp. 759–776. Springer-Verlag, 1990.

[Zwiers90a] J. Zwiers & W.-P. de Roever. *Predicates are Predicate Transformers: A Unified Compositional Theory for Concurrency.* To appear in the proc. of Principles of Distributed Computing '89.

Formal Methods and the Sociology of Proof

Donald MacKenzie*

Dept. of Sociology
University of Edinburgh
18 Buccleuch Place
Edinburgh EH8 9LN
Scotland

Abstract

This paper begins by asking whether a sociology of mathematical knowledge is possible. Having answered in the affirmative (drawing examples from the history of mathematics), it goes on to discuss the development of a similar analysis of the mathematical aspects of computer science. A brief vignette is presented: the processes of negotiation of the IEEE floating-point arithmetic specifications. Then the discussion moves on to the verification of software and hardware. If the sociology of mathematics is correct, then formal proofs can be seen as social, not just in the processes of their acceptance, as de Millo, Lipton and Perlis [DLP79] have argued, but also in their internal structure. Placed in the context of pressure for formal verification of safety-critical and security-critical systems, this argument led the author and colleagues to the prediction, three years ago, that litigation involving the nature of mathematical proof was bound to occur. That prediction has now been borne out.

1 The sociology of mathematics

Over the last twenty years, the branch of sociology that deals with science has undergone something of a revolution. Its previous form, most closely associated with the name of the great American sociologist, Robert Merton, considered questions such as the norms and ethos of science, the reward system of science, the careers of scientists and so on. Implicitly, and sometimes explicitly, it excluded the content of scientific knowledge from its remit. A sociology of knowledge did exist (its best-known proponent was Karl Mannheim), but it restricted itself to areas of knowledge such as political and religious beliefs and general styles of thought. Physics and mathematics, in particular, were taken to be areas where the sociology of knowledge could not be applied. The knowledge produced by those disciplines had, at least under normal

*The research reported on here was supported by the Economic and Social Research Council under the Programme on Information and Communication Technologies.

circumstances, nothing to do with the social situation of their practitioners. Nothing social, implied Mannheim [Man36], could be said about the proposition $2 * 2 = 4$.

In the last two decades, the content of scientific knowledge has been brought within the remit of the sociology of knowledge. There are now a substantial number of studies showing ways in which the development of scientific knowledge is influenced by social processes. These are primarily processes within the scientific community, but there are several striking instances of influences from the wider society affecting even what we count as "good" science. Though a lot of these latter concern biology, there are several such cases to be found in, for example, the histories of statistics, chemistry and physics [Sha82]. This work by historians and sociologists of science has, of course, built upon philosophical re–evaluation of the nature of scientific knowledge, most famously by T.S. Kuhn [Kuh70].

Interestingly, there has been much less discussion of mathematics from this point of view than there has been of science. One reason is certainly to do with the absence of a figure like Kuhn revolutionizing the philosophy of mathematics. The closest analogue for mathematics is Wittgenstein (to whom Kuhn owed a great deal). But [Wit67] has never received the sort of fame of [Kuh70]. My colleague David Bloor [Blo73, Blo83] has argued, to my mind convincingly, that Wittgenstein provides the necessary basis for a sociology of mathematical knowledge, but Bloor's argument has not been taken up widely.

Not being a Wittgenstein buff, I'll not attempt any rigorous philosophical development of the case for the sociology of mathematics. Instead, I'll restrict myself to the following assertions:

1. **Alternative forms of mathematics are possible:** For example, for us, "one" is a number. For the Ancient Greeks, it was not: "one" was the generator of numbers, not itself a number. ([Blo76] points out that we still retain some traces of that usage in ordinary speech. We would not say "a number of people attended the lecture", if only one person did.) Futhermore, for us, one is odd. For the Greeks, one was both odd and even, because it was the generator of both even and odd numbers.

   Historically, then, different forms of mathematics have existed (see [Blo76] for a much more extensive discussion). It is tempting to see them as partial, incomplete, or erroneous versions of our mathematics, but that seems typically a subtle form of misinterpretation. Nor is it necessary to turn to the Ancient World for examples of alternative mathematics (even though the more recent examples typically concern contentious parts of mathematics rather than the entirety of mathematics). Consider algebraic manipulations that lack clear geometric interpretation: now, of course, unproblematically accepted, but long anathema within much of British, especially Scottish, mathematics [Mac79]. Consider the well-known controversies over non-Euclidean geometry, over transfinite numbers, or over the place of the Axiom of Choice in set theory.

2. **What constitutes a proof is contingent and contestible**: For a nineteenth century mathematician, much of eighteenth century mathematics consisted of interesting results, but not proofs of those results. Procedures involving infinitely large and infinitely small quantities, regarded as legitimate in the eighteenth century, were regarded as illegitimate in the nineteenth [Gra74]. The

early twentieth century was riven by dispute concerning the validity of the law of the excluded middle, the assertion that either P or not-P must be true.

Just as it has always been tempting to believe that the science of the current generation has finally revealed the truth about the natural world, so it has been tempting to believe that the mathematics of the current generation has achieved absolute rigour. At the start of this century, for example, Henri Poincaré proclaimed: "On peut dire qu'aujourd'hui la rigueur absolue est atteinte" [Poi02]. Yet, of course, the notion of proof (and thus of rigour) was to go through many further upheavals in the following decades. Poincaré could appeal to "l'intuition du nombre pur" as part of the basis of absolute rigour. To many mathematicians, even shortly afterwards, that appeal did not seem adequate.

3. **Sometimes, at least, a social explanation can throw light on variations in response to alternative forms of mathematics and the contingent nature of proof:** Sometimes the explanation is historically quite specific, even idiosyncratic. For example:

   (a) the reaction to non-Euclidean geometry in England was conditioned by its perceived philosophical, even religious. significance, the sort of significance indicated by this quotation from the Cambridge mathematician and philosopher Whewell: "The peculiar character of mathematical truth is that it is necessarily and inevitably true: and one of the most important lessons we learn ... [is] that there are such truths, and a familiarity with their form and character" [Ric79].

   (b) religious and mathematical commitments were intertwined in Cantor's work on transfinite numbers. "The Transfinitum ... existed as eternal ideas [in the 'Divine Intellect'] ... Cantor could only be sure of the propriety of his abstractions because they found their ideal representation in the mind of God" [Dau87]: see also [Dau79].

   (c) There are tantalising suggestions that the intuitionist/formalist controversy in twentieth century mathematics (where the issue of the validity of proofs involving the law of the excluded middle was central) was connected to wider philosophical-cum-political disputes in early twentieth century Europe [Mac86].

Alongside this kind of specific explanation, developed by historians of mathematics, Bloor has suggested a more general form of explanation: that there may be systematic connections between, on the one hand, different kinds of cognitive response by mathematicians and, on the other, variations in their social situations. For example, Bloor suggests that attitudes to mathematical symbolism mirror attitudes to the autonomy of the mathematician. Those who have seen symbols as a self-sufficient, autonomous world, have been the mathematical professionalisers - those who wished to sever connections between mathematics and physics, mathematics and philosophy and mathematics and theology, and establish mathematics as a self-sufficient discipline and profession. Those who have opposed symbols being treated in abstraction from any referents, who have wished to maintain the connection of symbol and referent, have been those who have opposed as isolationist that strategy of professional autonomy. While there may be counterexamples, this sort of pattern does, for example, seem to hold in the controversy in eighteenth and nineteenth century Britain between the proponents of abstract algebra and those who wished to maintain an integral link between geometry and algebra [Blo81, Blo83].

2 Computer arithmetic

The general point about alternative mathematics can be applied to computer arithmetic. Alternative forms of computer arithmetic are possible; the characteristics of computer arithmetic have, therefore, to be negotiated (I choose the term, with its connotations of politics, conflicts, strikes, bargaining, even smoke-filled rooms, quite deliberately), rather than deduced from Poincaré's "intuition of pure number".

This characteristic of computer arithmetic is well known to computer scientists. If, however, you suspend, for a moment, that professional knowledge, you will see how surprising and contrary to ordinary intuitions the point is. We ordinarily take arithmetic to be the least negotiable form of knowledge: take Mannheim's comments on $2*2 = 4$. There is no possibility of an alternative arithmetic: deviance is, straightforwardly, error. We ordinarily understand computers and calculators as simply increasing the speed of arithmetic and removing the possibility of error.

Specialists of course know very well what the problem is: real numbers can be represented inside a calculator or computer in general to only a finite degree of precision, and also typically only a finite range of numbers can be represented. Calculations can, for example, overflow (produce a result beyond the range of numbers that can be represented) or underflow (produce a result below that range). Different forms of representation, different ranges of permissible representation, different ways of handling overflow and underflow: all of these can lead to computers and caculators sometimes producing results at variance both with each other and with the results of human arithmetic.

Three aspects of this are of interest:

1. We ordinarily think of arithmetic as the most mechanical, rote, rule-governed form of human activity. The difficulty of mimicking it on a calculator and computer shows **there is more skill and tacit knowledge in arithmetic than we might think**: skill in knowing when and how much to round, skill in cancelling, for example. Even fairly poor human arithmeticians readily compute $(7/11)*11$ to be equal to 7. As you know, it is not a trivial task to ensure that a computer or calculator produces that result. (I draw the example from [Col90], a most interesting discussion of human interaction with "intelligent" machines from pocket calculators to expert systems.)

2. There is a **spectrum of response to what one might call anomalous calculations**: those that yield results different from those of human arithmetic, or different from one machine to another.This ranges from plain indifference; through what we might call "monster barring" (drawing a distinction between "well posed" and "badly posed" problems, and arguing that there will be no anomalies of any seriousness with well-posed problems); to the active search for anomalies as a means of justifying the need for new forms of computer arithmetic. The last of these is what the philosopher Imre Lakatos, who has

written a most interesting paper on response to anomalies in proof procedures, calls the "dialectical" strategy [Lak76]: see also [Blo78].

Perhaps the key figure adopting the "dialectical" strategy has been the Berkeley mathematician and computer scientist, Velvel Kahan. Pressure from him and his students was instrumental in the establishment in 1977 of an IEEE committee to develop a standard for floating-point arithmetic, which led to the 1985 IEEE/American National Standards Institute floating-point arithmetic standard - a standard which seems to be being adopted internationally, not just in the US.

3. An unsociological view of arithmetic might lead one to the conclusion that all this committee would have needed to do would be to contemplate the real numbers, consider the loss of accuracy in various ways of giving them finite representation, and choose the way that caused least error. In fact, very heated debate took place, especially over the topic of underflow (for more detail see [Mac90]). In brief, some argued that an underflowed result should be set to zero. Others, notably Kahan, argued for the use of a special set of "denormalized" numbers smaller than the smallest normally expressible, which would permit "gradual underflow". There were good technical arguments to be made on both sides. Wider-world interests would be affected by the outcome. There was a lot of investment in machines (eg the DEC VAX series) where underflow was handled by set-to-zero; while Intel was on the way to developing a floating-point chip that could implement gradual underflow. As far as I can tell, the positions adopted on the technical virtues of the competing arithmetics had a strong (though not universal) tendency to follow this kind of vested interest. Eventually, gradual underflow, rather than the DEC position, triumphed. This outcome was perhaps helped by the fact that the committee's meetings were almost all in the San Francisco Bay area, close to Intel, other chip makers and Berkeley, and a continent away from DEC's base in Massachusetts. Be that as it may, it does seem clear that **the word "negotiation" (with its political connotation) is apt here, more apt than, say, "deduction"**. The main way "negotiation" misleads is that it perhaps implies compromise. In this case a compromise solution was rejected, and the Kahan-gradual underflow position adopted by two-thirds majority vote of the committee.

3 Formal methods, especially program proof

Had "deduction" rather than "negotiation" been the more apt term, could there have been anything sociological to be said about deduction? This is a topic that takes us to the heart of formal methods, and is what makes formal methods a fascinating subject for the sociologist of knowledge.

Let me explain. As noted above, the sociology of knowledge has been applied far more vigorously to science than to mathematics. It has, therefore, been predominantly a sociology of induction rather than of deduction. Furthermore, the more slender body of empirical material that makes up the sociology of mathematical knowledge is almost entirely drawn from pre-formal mathematics. If deductive reasoning can be described, in the words of Hoare [Hoa69], as the "application of valid rules of inference to valid axioms", there are obviously different degrees of formality possible in regard both to rules of inference and to axioms. The mathematics discussed in the historical studies I have cited, or that discussed in [Lak76], sometimes involved explicit axioms, but almost never an explicit logical calculus. Wittgenstein (quite deliberately, because he wanted to emphasise the role of rote, habit, the customary, the conventional in mathematics) drew most of the examples in [Wit67] from elementary school mathematics.

So does the sociology of knowledge break down when we come to fully formal proof? Is there anything sociological to be said about deduction, once deduction takes the form of the application of an explicit logical calculus to explicit axioms? That is why formal methods in computer science are of interest to me as a sociologist. Here, even more than in modern mathematics (most of which, as actually practised, uses informal proofs), there is an attempt here at wholly formal, rigorous, deduction.

The question of what can be said sociologically about formal proof is not fully answered in the paper in the computer science literature that is most relevant to my concerns [DLP79]. I should perhaps briefly recall the argument of that paper. DeMillo, Lipton and Perlis noted the continuing dominance of informal proof even in modern mathematics. Proof, they suggested, is a social process:

> A proof is not a beautiful abstract object with an independent existence. No mathematician grasps a proof, sits back, and sighs happily at the knowledge that he can now be certain of the truth of his theorem. He runs out into the hall and looks for someone to listen to it. He bursts into a colleague's office and commandeers the blackboard. He throws aside his scheduled topic and regales a seminar with his new idea. He drags his graduate students a way from their dissertations to listen. He gets onto the phone and tells his colleagues in Texas and Toronto ...
>
> That spoken stage is the first filter for a proof. If it generates no excitement or belief among his friends, the wise mathematician reconsiders it.

The authors went on to describe the further processes within the community of mathematicians through which belief in a proof builds up. It is these processes, they argued, that give a proof its credibility. That credibility involves the belief that the theorem could be proven according to the fully formal notion of proof, but "for almost all theorems no such deduction ever took place or ever will". Obversely, such deductions are not granted the status of proofs in abstraction from these social processes. Deductions that are too long and complex to be grasped cannot be assessed by the processes of the community of mathematicians, and will not in practice attain the status of credible proofs.

Hence De Millo, Lipton and Perlis's well-known argument against program verification, especially automated verification of programs of some length:

> Verifications cannot readily be read; a reader can flay himself through one of the shorter ones by dint of heroic effort, but that's not reading. Being unreadable and - literally - unspeakable, verifications cannot be internalized, transformed, generalized, used, connected to other disciplines, and eventually incorporated into a community consciousness. They cannot acquire credibility gradually, as a mathematical theorem does; one either believes them blindly, as a pure act of faith, or not at all.

There are, however, two interrelated problems with the position of [DLP79]:

1. some of the force of the argument rests on a particular condition of the state-of-the-art of program proof. What should we conclude if technical developments make verifications more lucid and more elegant, or if the necessary experience meaningfully to read the output of an automated theorem prover becomes more widespread?

2. the notion of the sociology of mathematics in [DLP79] is a half-way-house between the old and new sociologies of science described above. This is not intended as professional criticism: DeMillo, Lipton and Perlis are much better sociologists than I am a computer scientist! But what they address is the credibility of proof, and they do not answer the question whether proof itself, in its internal structure, is social.

The work of Bloor (especially [Blo83]) can, however, perhaps begin to supply an answer. I have already noted disputes over the validity of the law of the excluded middle as a principle of logic, disputes that touched upon the practice of mathematics, not just the more abstract discussions of metamathematicians. Bloor's examination of the history of formal logic reveals others. The clearest examples are the Lewis principles, named after the logician Clarence Irving Lewis:

1. a contradiction implies any proposition: $(P \wedge \neg P) \Rightarrow Q$.

2. a tautology is implied by any proposition: $P \Rightarrow (Q \vee \neg Q)$.

The Lewis principles follow from intuitively appealing axiomatizations of formal logic, and are very common. For example, the first Lewis principle is amongst the rules of logic in the important Vienna Development Method, or VDM [Jon90]. Earlier this century they were deeply controversial because intuitions as to their validity differed sharply. Can we sensibly deduce "the moon is made of green cheese" from "John is a man and John is not a man". Makinson, in his survey of modern logic [Mak73] notes no consensus. "Different people react in different ways to the Lewis principles. For some they are welcome guests [ie discoveries about valid inference], whilst for others they are strange and suspect".

What the sociology of knowledge teaches us is that if you have alternative possible ways of proceeding - alternative mathematics, alternative rules of logic - <u>and</u> if you have major interests that will be served well if one way is taken, and disserved if another is taken, you have a recipe for controversy, or at least for negotiation. People's location vis-à-vis these interests will affect their views of what is and what is not valid. If that is correct, the social, in this sense, can stretch into the inner core of deductive inference.

Metamathematics and logic have of course moved on since the time of Lewis or of the classic disputes over the excluded middle. This movement has not taken the form of convergence towards "one true logic". Rather, logic has become relativized, with explicit acceptance of the need for different logics for different domains of application. This does lessen the probability of certain forms of controversy. Heated debate over the validity, in isolation, of a particular logical principle such as excluded middle is now unlikely. Yet controversy <u>between systems of logic</u> is far from impossible.

To date, of course, debate between logical systems has been restricted to esoteric communities of metamathematicians and logicians. Disagreement between different formal methods of software development has scarcely spilled into print, although conversation with members of the formal methods community does show such disagreement to exist. Yet formal proof is moving, however slowly, from academic departments into the commercial world of safety-critical and security-critical systems, and thus into the legal world of standards and liability.

Three years ago, colleagues and I argued that it followed from the sociology of knowledge that, as formal proof entered the "real world" in this way, a legal case centring on the nature of mathematical proof was bound to ensue [PFM87]. This prediction has now been borne out. Controversy has arisen over the VIPER microprocessor, developed at the Royal Signals and Radar Establishment "for use in highly safety-critical military and civil systems". Its developers claimed that "throughout, formal mathematical methods have been used to prove that the gate-level realisations conform to a top-level specification" [CP87].

Following reports critical of the extent and nature of the VIPER proofs [Coh89, BH90], Charter Technologies, Ltd., of Worcester, who licensed aspects of the technology from the Royal Signals and Radar Establishment, has issued a writ against the Secretary of State for Defence alleging negligent misrepresentation, inter alia in the claims that VIPER had a proven design. This action may never come to court. Nor, were it do so, is it clear how central the question of the nature of mathematical proof would be, although those who doubt the capacity of the best lawyers to build such questions into effective arguments should read [OWP82], despite its dealing with quite different subject-matter.

Details of the legal action aside, however, it is evident that those involved in the VIPER case have not shared a single, agreed, notion of what constitutes mathematical proof; indeed the lack of a clear, shared understanding is perhaps the fundamental reason why the litigation has arisen. As many as four general types of meaning of "proof" can be found in discussions of VIPER: lay notions [Mal]; engineers' notions; mathematicians' notions; and the most formal metamathematicians' notions. Thus "intelligent exhaustion" was used to provide a "proof of correspondence between the specification of a hardware module and its gate level implementation" [Pyg85], in what might be described (quite unpejoratively) as an engineer's notion of mathematical proof rather than the notion of mathematical proof as the application of an explicit logical calculus to explicit axioms. Furthermore, there may still be room for contention if we move from an engineer's notion of proof to a mathematician's, or even a metamathematician's. For a device like VIPER to be said to be proven, is it necessary to provide an explicit "abstraction function from Boolean words to integers" [BH90]? How much of arithmetic can be assumed, or must proofs be based upon axioms of arithmetic as a metamathematician might insist? If everything must be based upon explicit axioms and an explicit logical calculus, what axioms and what calculus?

It cannot be denied that there are aspects to the history of VIPER that are particular to it, and which cannot be extrapolated to formal methods more generally. However, the VIPER episode is not so idiosyncratic as to be dismissed as a complete aberration. It lends weight to my more abstract argument based upon the sociology of mathematics. As the uses of formal methods become more numerous and more important, the nature of proof will have to be negotiated. When mathematical proof was a matter for academics alone, a range of different meanings could happily co-exist in different, partially disjoint, technical communities. As commercial and regulatory concerns become ever more prominent, that co-existence will not for long remain peaceful. Those involved will have to attend to the sociology of proof, or, sooner rather than later, the lawyers will do it for them.

References

[BH90] B. Brock and W. A. Hunt. Report on the formal specification and partial verification of the VIPER microprocessor. Technical Report 46, Computational Logic Inc, Austin, Texas, 1990.

[Blo73] D. Bloor. Wittgenstein and Mannheim on the sociology of mathematics. *Studies in the History and Philosophy of Science*, 4:173 - 191, 1973.

[Blo76] D. Bloor. *Knowledge and Social Imagery*. Routledge and Kegan Paul, 1976.

[Blo78] D. Bloor. Polyhedra and the abominations of Leviticus. *British Journal for the History of Science*, 11:245–72, 1978.

[Blo81] D. Bloor. Hamilton and Peacock on the essence of algebra. In H. Mehrtens, H. Bos, and I. Schnieder, editors, *Social History of Nineteenth Century Mathematics*. Birkhauser, 1981.

[Blo83] D. Bloor. *Wittgenstein: A Social Theory of Knowledge*. Macmillan, 1983.

[Coh89] A. Cohn. The notion of proof in hardware verification. *Journal of Automated Reasoning*, 5:127–139, 1989.

[Col90] H. M. Collins. *Artificial Experts: Social Knowledge and Intelligent Machines*. MIT Press, 1990.

[CP87] W. J. Cullyer and C. H. Pygott. Application of formal methods to the VIPER microprocessor. *IEE Proceedings*, 134:133–141, 1987.

[Dau79] J. W. Dauben. *Georg Cantor: His Mathematics and Philosophy of the Infinite*. Harvard University Press, 1979.

[Dau87] J. W. Dauben. Georg Cantor and Pope Leo xiii: Mathematics, theology, and the infinite. *Journal of the History of Ideas*, 38:85–108, 1987.

[DLP79] R. DeMillo, R. Lipton, and A. Perlis. Social processes and proofs of theorems and programs. *Communications of the ACM*, 22:271–280, 1979.

[Gra74] J. V. Grabiner. Is mathematical truth time-dependent? *American Mathematical Monthly*, 81:354–365, 1974.

[Hoa69] C.A.R. Hoare. An axiomatic basis for computer programming. *Communications of the ACM*, 12:576–583, 1969.

[Jon90] C. B. Jones. *Systematic Software Development using VDM.* Prentice Hall, 1990.

[Kuh70] T. S. Kuhn. *The Structure of Scientific Revolutions.* Chicago University Press, 1970.

[Lak76] I. Lakatos. *Proofs and Refutations: The Logic of Mathematical Discovery.* Cambridge University Press, 1976.

[Mac79] D. MacKenzie. Scottish mathematics: a sociological exploration. Paper read to the Conference on the Social History of Mathematics, Technische Universität Berlin, 1979.

[Mac86] D. MacKenzie. Why "the social aspects of science and technology" is not just an optional extra. *ACM Computers and Society*, 15:2–6, 1986.

[Mac90] D. MacKenzie. Negotiating arithmetic, deconstructing proof: The sociology of mathematics and information technology. Unpublished, 1990.

[Mak73] D. C. Makinson. *Topics in Modern Logic.* Methuen, 1973.

[Mal] J. Malins. The VIPER microprocesor: A lay comment on the claim, "proven correct". Charter Technologies, Ltd., Worcester.

[Man36] K. Mannheim. *Ideology and Utopia.* Routledge and Kegan Paul, 1936.

[OWP82] J. S. Oteri, M. G. Weinberg, and M. S. Pinales. Cross-examination of chemists in drugs cases. In Barry Barnes and David Edge, editors, *Science in Context: Readings in the Sociology of Science.* Open University Press, 1982.

[PFM87] E. Peláez, J. Fleck, and D. MacKenzie. Social research on software. Paper read to the National Workshop of Programme in Information and Communications Technologies, Manchester. 1987.

[Poi02] H. Poincaré. Du rôle de l'intuition et de la logique en mathématiques. In *Proceedings of the Second International Congress of Mathematicians*, 1902. Paris.

[Pyg85] C. H. Pygott. Formal proof of correspondence between the specification of a hardware module and its gate level implementation. Technical Report 85012, Royal Signals and Radar Establishment, Malvern, Worcs., 1985.

[Ric79] J. L. Richards. The reception of a mathematical theory: Non-Euclidean geometry in England, 1868-1883. In *Natural Order: Historical Studies of Scientific Culture.* Sage, 1979.

[Sha82] S. Shapin. History of science and its sociological reconstructions. *History of Science*, 20:157–211, 1982.

[Wit67] L. Wittgenstein. *Remarks on the Foundations of Mathematics.* Blackwell, 1967.

Refinement Diagrams

R.J.R. Back

Åbo Akademi University
Department of Computer Science
Lemminkäisenkatu 14, SF-20520 Turku, Finland

Abstract

We consider the problem of structuring and managing large program derivations. A graphical way of structuring such derivations, *refinement diagrams*, are proposed. A browsing and outlining facility for refinement diagrams is also described.

1 Introduction

The problem considered here is how to structure large derivations, as well as how to edit and browse such derivations. The use of program derivations for constructing programs has been around for a while [20,9,12,8,6]. Tools and environments for supporting program derivations have also been constructed (see, e.g., [18,15,11,7]). Our concern here is not so much with the mechanisms and logics of program transformation systems, but more with the way we should structure and visualize program derivations. For small program derivations, this is not a particularly important issue. Larger derivations will, however, produce many different successive versions of program components, and the problem of managing this collection and keeping track of what has been done and what remains to be done becomes more demanding.

We consider the question of structuring large program derivations in the context of the *refinement calculus*, originally proposed in [1,2] and further developed in [3,16,17], among others. The approach proposed here can, however, also be applied to other kinds of derivations. The basic idea is to give a graphical representation of a program derivation such that transitivity and monotonicity of program refinement is built into the representation.

In Section 2 we first show how to formalize a program derivation in a mechanized logic such as LCF or HOL. In Section 3 we then show how the structure of the derivation can be visualized graphically using *refinement diagrams.* In Section 4 we show how to turn refinement diagrams into complete user interfaces for constructing program derivations. In Section 5 we propose a simple textually based browsing and editing tool for working with refinement diagrams, which does not require the diagrams to be displayed graphically. In Section 6 we then show how the refinement diagram and the editor can be seen as two extremes of a general outlining tool for browsing and editing program derivations.

2 Program derivations as theories

Refinement calculus is based on Dijkstra's weakest precondition approach [10]. A program S is said to be correctly refined by another program S', denoted $S \leq S'$, if

$$(\forall q.\ \mathrm{wp}(S, q) \Rightarrow \mathrm{wp}(S', q)). \tag{1}$$

This captures the basic idea that S' preserves the correctness of S. More precisely, (1) holds if and only if any total correctness specification (pre- and postcondition pair) that S satisfies is also satisfied by S'.

The refinement relation is reflexive and transitive. If we choose to identify the meaning of a program with its predicate transformer, as is done in [10], then it is also antisymmetric, i.e., the refinement relation is then a partial ordering of program statements.

The usual sequential program constructors are monotonic with respect to the refinement ordering. Thus, if $S \leq S'$ and $T \leq T'$, then $S;\ T \leq S';\ T'$ holds. Moreover, **if** B**then** S **else** $T \leq$ **if** B **then** S' **else** T' and **while** B **do** $S \leq$ **while** B **do** S' also hold.

The transitivity property is used to model stepwise refinement of programs: If $S_0 \leq S_1 \leq \ldots \leq S_n$, then by transitivity $S_0 \leq S_n$. The monotonicity property is again used to model top-down program construction: If $S(T)$ is a program with subcomponent T, then $T \leq T'$ implies that $S(T) \leq S(T')$, i.e., we may always replace a subcomponent with its refinement without loosing correctness of the whole program.

A *theory* in a mechanized logic such as LCF [14,19] or HOL[13] includes, besides constants and axioms, also the definitions that have been made and the theorems that have been proved. In this it differs from the logician's concept of a theory, which is determined solely by its constants and axioms. This difference stems from the fact that in a mechanized logic, one is not only talking about what is definable or provable, but about what has in fact been defined or proved.

The refinement calculus can be formalized as a theory in a mechanized logic such as HOL [4]. No additional axioms are needed for this, it is sufficient to define refinement as a relation between statements as above, and then prove reflexivity, transitivity antisymmetry, as well as monotonicity of the basic program constructors. Based on this, one can then prove a number of derived theorems about program refinements, as well as theorems about refinement of specific program constructs. One can also build a number of inference rules in the calculus, by which new program refinements can be inferred from given ones.

Given a formalization of the refinement calculus in a mechanized logic, a *program derivation* in this calculus can be seen as a new theory built on top of the refinement calculus theory. This theory may also have other ancestor theories, which are needed to formalize the properties of the data types used in the derivation. The derivation consists of a list of theorems

$$\vdash S_1 \leq S_1'$$

$$\ldots$$

$$\vdash S_m \leq S_m',$$

where $S_1, \ldots, S_m, S'_1, \ldots, S'_m$ are the program components introduced in the derivation and $\vdash S_i \leq S'_i$ states that $S_i \leq S_i$ has been proved.

These theorems have been derived using inference rules in the refinement calculus, including the partial ordering and monotonicity rules. The inference rules and derivation rules usually have assumptions that need to be satisfied for the result of applying them to be valid theorems. Thus, their conclusions are only valid under certain assumptions and hence are of the form $A \vdash t \leq t'$, where A is a list of assumptions about the underlying domains. These assumptions are verified separately, using appropriate theories about the underlying domains.

A program component need not necessarily be a program statement, it can also be a higher order construct such as $\lambda X.S(X)$, where X varies over program statements. Applying this to an ordinary program statement T gives a program statement $S(T)$ with T as a subcomponent. Refinement is extended to such higher order constructs by pointwise extension, so that, e.g., $\lambda X.S(X) \leq \lambda X.S'(X)$ holds iff $(\forall X.\ S(X) \leq S'(X))$.

Besides refinement theorems, a derivation theory may also have a list of definitions, whereby names are given to program components (i.e., they are defined as constants):

$$\begin{array}{l} \textit{define } c_1 = S_1 \\ \ldots \\ \textit{define } c_n = S_n, \end{array}$$

where $c_1, \ldots, c_n$ are constant names and $S_1, \ldots, S_n$ are program statements. By using constants we can avoid writing down the program terms explicitly in theorems. Program terms are quite large, so theorems are difficult to read and cumbersome to manipulate if they are written out in full. Definitions can be used also for other purposes, such as naming loop invariants, pre- or postconditions etc.

3 Refinement diagrams

The above shows that there is a rather straightforward way in which we can regard a program derivation in the refinement calculus as a theory in the sense of a mechanized logic such as HOL. However, the structure of the derivation is lost if we just look at the derivation as a list of refinement theorems $\vdash s \leq s'$. In practice, derivations tend to be constructed as long sequences of successive versions of program components, as well as nested derivations. We will here describe an approach to displaying this structure graphically. We refer to such a graphical description of a derivation as a *refinement diagram.*

The refinement diagrams are not restricted to just to program derivations. We will emphasize their generality by talking about general (lambda) terms and components of terms in the sequel, rather than about programs and program components.

We assume that a theory in higher order logic is fixed. We assume that we have defined an ordering $\leq$ between terms in this theory which is

reflexive, i.e., $u \leq u$,

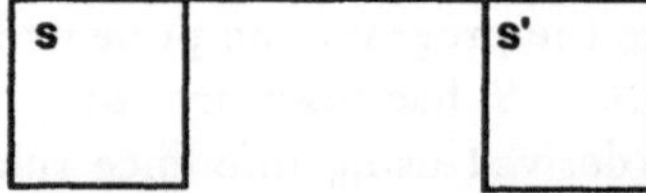

Figure 1: Refinement of program components

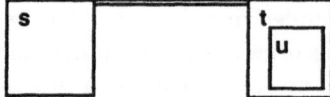

Figure 2: Subcomponents

transitive, i.e., $u \leq v \wedge v \leq w \Rightarrow u \leq w$, and

monotonic, i.e., $u \leq u' \wedge v \leq v' \Rightarrow u\ v \leq u'\ v'$.

We will call this ordering ***refinement***, although it need not be the specific refinement ordering between program statements that we described above. Application is denoted by juxtaposition. The *induced equivalence* between terms is $u \equiv v$, which holds if and only if $u \leq v \wedge v \leq u$.

Let

$$L \quad = \quad \vdash s_1 \leq s_1', \ldots, \vdash s_m \leq s_m'$$

be a list of theorems in this theory. We refer to $s_1, \ldots, s_m, s_1', \ldots, s_m'$ as the *identified components* in L. The rules for constructing a refinement diagram corresponding to L are as follows:

(i) Each *identified component* of L is shown as a box in the diagram. If $\vdash s \leq s'$ has been established, then a line connects the box s to the box s' (Figure 1). Equivalence is shown as a double line between s and s', as in Figure 2.

(ii) An identified component s may have another identified component as *subcomponent*, $s \equiv t\ u$, where $t = (\lambda X.t')$. In that case, we show s as a nested box, with u nested within t (Figure 2). We can have many subcomponents of a given component, either non-overlapping or nested. As an example, $s \equiv t\ (u\ v, w)$ would be shown as in Figure 3.

(iii) A refinement r of a component $t\ u$ is potentially ambiguous in this notation: is r a refinement of the whole term, only of t or only of u. We resolve this ambiguity by drawing the line from the top of the box if the whole term is refined, but otherwise drawing the line somewhere else on the border of the intended box (Figure 4).

(iv) Lines that are deducible by transitivity and monotonicity are omitted in the diagram (Figure 5). Figure 5 shows the omitted lines that can be induced by transitivity and by monotonicity as dashed.

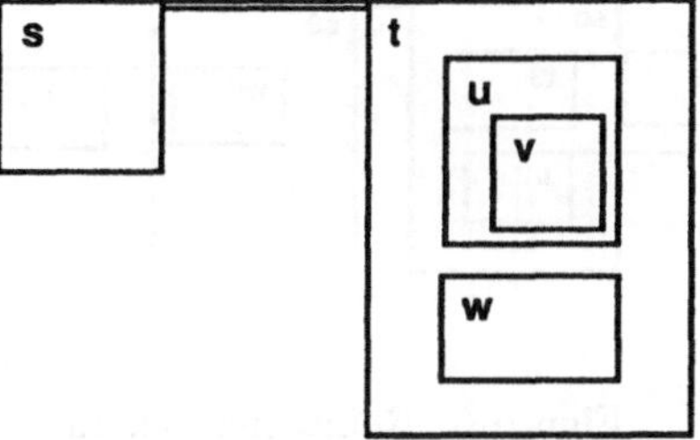

Figure 3: Nested subcomponents

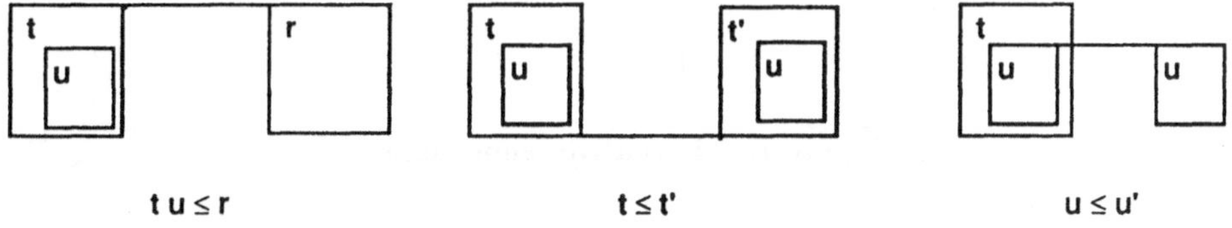

Figure 4: Component refinement

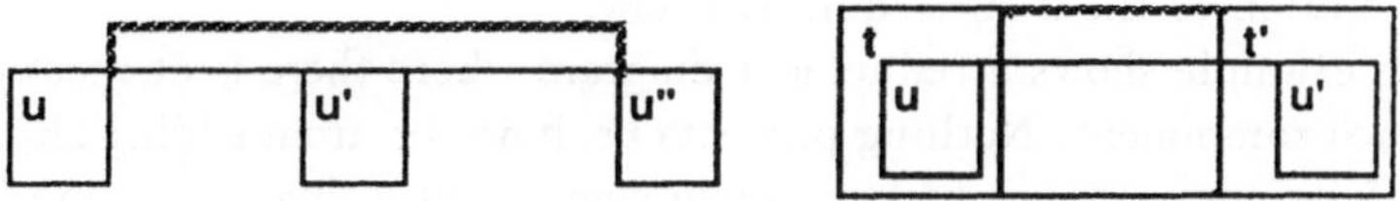

Figure 5: Omitted transitivity and monotonicity lines

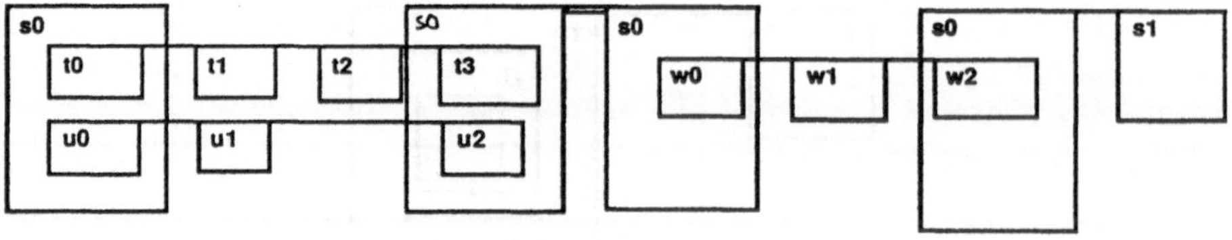

Figure 6: Refinement chain

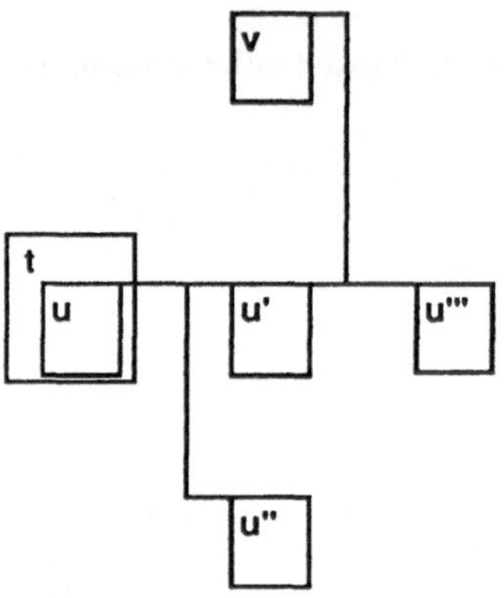

Figure 7: Alternative refinements

Using this approach, quite large derivations can be describe graphically. An example is shown in Figure 6. The derivation starts with a component $s0$ that has two subcomponents, $t0$ and $u0$. These are refined by a sequence of refinement steps, leading to versions $t3$ and $u2$. Then a new component, $w0$, is identified in $s0$, and this is further refined via $w1$ to $w2$, giving version $s0\ w2$. Finally, this is refined to $s1$.

The refinement relations induced by transitivity and monotonicity are not shown here. From transitivity follows, e.g., that $t0 \leq t2$, $t0 \leq t3$, etc. Similarly, from monotonicity follows that $s0\ (t0, u0) \leq s0\ (t3, u2)$. All together, transitivity would add 8 refinement lines and monotonicity would add 2 refinement lines to this specific diagram, in addition to the 9 lines indicated now.

The above example shows a refinement diagram where there is at most one refinement of each component. Nothing prevents us, however, from adding alternative refinements of a component, or to have some component refine two or more other components. This is illustrated in the diagram of Figure 7. Here u is refined by both u' and u'', while u''' is a refinement of both u' and of v. Hence, one can show alternative derivations in the same refinement diagram. The diagram will show explicitly which parts of alternative derivations are shared and which are different, as well as the places where the derivations fork or join.

```
BEGIN
   VAR j: integer, found: boolean;
   j, found:= 0, false;
   DO  j < N & not found -->
          j:= j+1;
          IF safe K j & (E W': solution K|j|W')) -->
                Q:= K|j|W'. solution K|j|W';
                found:= true
          [] not (safe K j & (E W': solution K|j|W')) -->
                SKIP
          FI
   OD
END
```

Figure 8: Example program component

4 A graphical front end

A refinement diagram as described above shows only the structure of a derivation. It is, however, easily turned into a full graphical front end for program derivations. In that case, we choose to write the text of the program component in the boxes. The text can be written in a standard programming language notation, and can be automatically parsed into a term in the logic that denotes the program component. In the other direction, any new program component generated by a transformation rule can be displayed in a box, pretty printing it in the programming language syntax used (an example is shown in Figure 8). The refinement diagram now functions as a store for the program text, while at the same time permitting easy editing, creation and deletion of program components.

Rather than associating the theorem $\vdash s \leq s'$ with a line between s and s', we may associate the *proof* of this fact with the line. In systems like LCF and HOL this proof is itself a term which evaluates to the theorem. Proofs have a fixed textual (and quite concise) syntax. This makes it possible to recreate the derivation theory from the diagram when needed. In this way the refinement diagram also fulfills the role of make files in HOL.

To recreate the derivation theory from the refinement diagram, it may be necessary to indicate in what order the refinement theorems associated with the lines should be proved. One way to do this is to number refinement line successively as they are created by proving the associated theorems. When recreating the theory, the associated theorems are proved in that same order. Note that in this approach, one may also need to number refinement lines that are induced by transitivity or by monotonicity, so that these results can be used in proofs of theorems.

Other kind of information may also be associated with the refinement diagram. For instance, illustrations, motivating text or intuitive descriptions can be quite useful as explanations for the derivation. This information may be associated either with the boxes or the lines of the diagram, and can be stored and accessed in a hypertext like fashion.

5 Diagram editor

The refinement diagrams described above provide an overall view of a program derivation, as well as permitting detailed inspection of selected parts of these. However, large derivations may require extensive scrolling of the diagram. Zooming facilities for reducing the size of the derivation (so that more of it fits on the screen) as well as for blowing up some part of the derivation for more detailed work on a specific part of it can make it easier to work with a diagram. However, this is not sufficient, and a more textually based tool is also be needed. Below we will describe such a tool, which we refer to as a *diagram editor*.

The simplest version of the diagram editor will show only one program component at a time, together with all its subcomponents. The editor is always focused on one specific program component in the refinement diagram. Besides the text of the component, there is also an indication of whether there is a previous version of the program component in the derivation diagram, as well as whether there is a successive version. The same holds for all the subcomponents of this program component. The screen thus shows a snapshot of the refinement diagram. An example is shown in Figure 9, where the initial program component of the refinement diagram in Figure 6 is shown.

The fact that there is a next version of components $t0$, $u0$ and $s0$ is indicated by refinement lines going to the right. We can ask the editor to replace one of these components by its successor. Depending on which one we replace, we get one of the results shown in Figure 10. In the first case, the text of component $t0$ has been replaced by the text of component $t1$. Lines from $t1$ go both left and right, showing that there are both previous and successive refinements of this component. In the second case, the text of component $u0$ has been replaced by the text of component $u1$, with the refinement lines again updated appropriately. In the third case, the whole program component $s0(t0, u0)$ has been replaced. In this case, the next explicitly version of this component in the refinement diagram is shown, $s0(t3, u2)$. The refinement lines have been updated, indicating that there are both previous and successive versions of the whole component, while for the subcomponents, we show that both are last versions in the diagram.

In this way, we can browse through the whole refinement diagram, displaying all the program versions that we are interested in. Besides browsing, the editor can also be used to construct a new (sub)component version, or to edit or delete some existing version.

For refinement diagrams with no alternative derivations, it is sufficient to ask for the next or the previous program component version. With alternative derivations, we may have more than one possible successor or predecessor of a program component. In that case, one needs to indicate which specific alternative should replace the present subcomponent. A possible way of doing this is to combine the

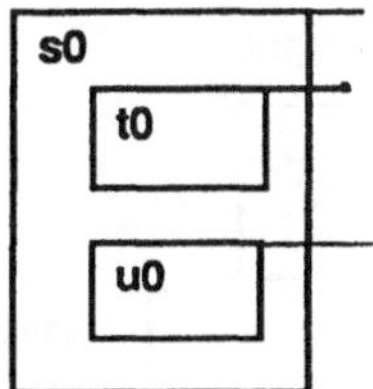

Figure 9: Initial component

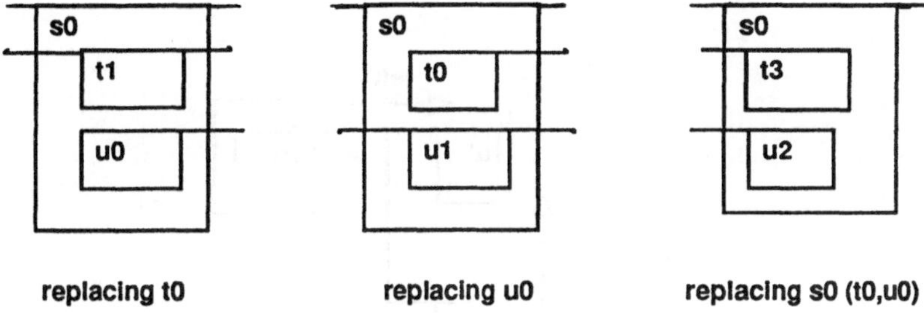

Figure 10: Different replacements

next/previous version replacement with a next/previous alternative. Thus, after having selected a next refinement of a subcomponent, one could replace this with an alternative refinement of the same original subcomponent. Similarly, one could look at previous versions, and alternatives of these. Moving between alternative refinements of a program component u is described in Figure 11, while Figure 12 shows how to move between alternative predecessors of a program component u.

Typical operations for browsing and editing a refinement diagram could, e.g., include the following:

right/left: Replace a selected subcomponent by its next/previous version.

down/up: Replace a selected subcomponent by its next/previous alternative subcomponent.

add/delete/edit: Add/delete/edit a component in a selected direction (next/previous version, next/previous alternative).

extend/shrink: The context that is shown around the selected component may be extended or shrunk.

These are just a few of the possible operations that one would probably find useful in a diagram editor.

It should be clear that the diagram editor can be used even when there is no graphical representation of the diagram. In that case, the refinement diagram func-

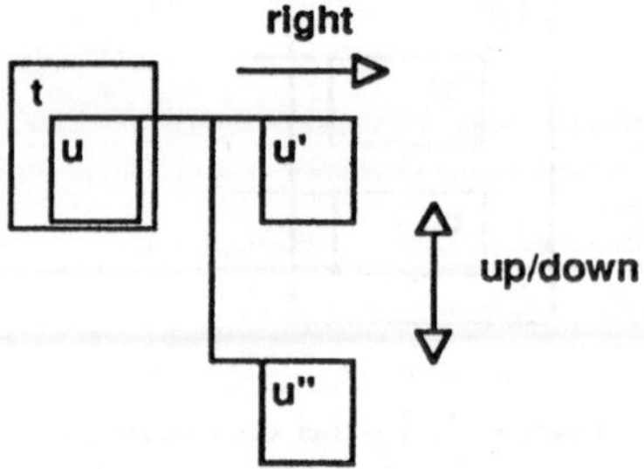

Figure 11: Moving to next version, between alternatives

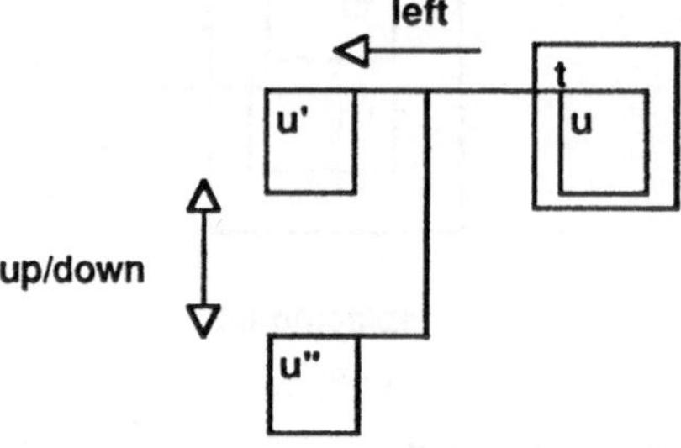

Figure 12: Moving to previous version, between alternatives

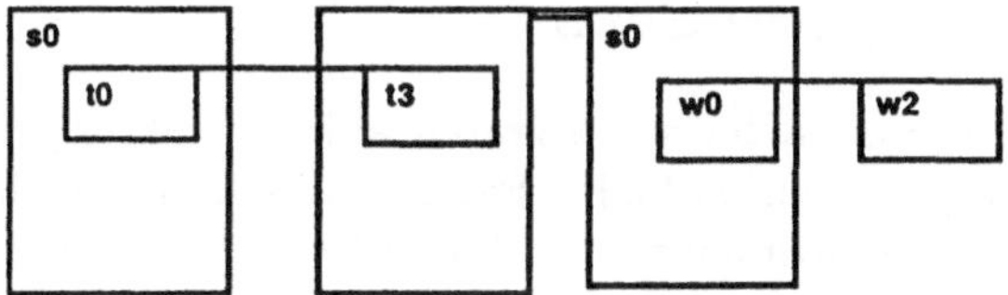

Figure 13: Collapsed diagram

tions as a conceptual model for the structure that the diagram editor is browsing over.

6 Outlining refinement diagrams

The diagram editor can be seen as a collapsed form of the full graphical representation: exactly one program component is shown, with all its subcomponents. More generally, we could choose to show any collection of program components and their refinement relationships simultaneously. This will give us an *outliner* for refinement diagrams.

Starting from the full refinement diagram, one can select the components to be displayed. The other components are then hidden and only the non-redundant refinement lines between the visible components are shown. The latter are constructed as follows. First compute all the induced refinement lines. Then delete all refinement lines that connect to a hidden component. After this, only refinement lines between visible components remain. Of these, delete all those that can be derived from other refinement lines by transitivity and monotonicity.

This procedure will guarantee that a refinement line is shown between two components, if such a line could be inferred in the original diagram, even in the case when the intermediate steps in the refinement are hidden.

The diagram editor can be used for selectively showing more or less of this graph, as well as adding, deleting and modifying parts of the graph. For instance, one can choose to show the next refinement of a program component, side by side with the original component. Or, one can also show the whole subderivations associated with this specific refinement. One can also choose to show a derivation down to a certain level only, hiding all lower level derivation.

The full refinement diagram and the diagram editor are two extreme cases of an outlining tool for editing refinement diagrams: the first one shows a completely expanded diagram, while the second shows a maximally collapsed diagram.

Outlining the refinement diagram can be combined with outlining of the program component text. Thus, one may choose to hide the internal structure of a program component if it is not relevant for the intended refinement step and only show the name of the component. Figure 13 shows a collapsed version of the example derivation in Figure 6.

7 Concluding remarks

We have described a proposal for how a graphical front end for program derivations using refinement calculus can be built. Parts of this front end have already been built, in the Centipede environment at Abo Akademi. Refinement diagrams as described here have been implemented using Prolog, with a syntax directed editor for program entry and editing. A simple prototype of the diagram editor was built by customizing an existing outliner for the Macintosh (More 3.0). A formalization of the refinement calculus in HOL has been done [5].

It should be evident that the refinement diagrams and the editor/outliner tool for manipulating them are general concepts not restricted to the refinement calculus. Any kind of structure with the same kind of transitivity and monotonicity properties is a potential candidate for description using these diagrams. On a more general level, the refinement diagrams provide one possible conceptual model and editing tool for the difficult problem of version control in software engineering.

Acknowledgements

I want to thank Jukka-Pekka Hekanaho and Patrick Waxlax for their contribution in implementing the refinement diagrams, and the members of IFIP WG 2.3 for valuable discussions on the ideas presented here. The work reported here was supported by the FINSOFT III program sponsored by the Technology Development Centre of Finland.

References

[1] R. J. R. Back. *On the Correctness of Refinement Steps in Program Development.* PhD thesis, Department of Computer Science, University of Helsinki, Helsinki, 1978. Report A–1978–4.

[2] R. J. R. Back. *Correctness Preserving Program Refinements: Proof Theory and Applications*, volume 131 of *Mathematical Center Tracts.* Mathematical Centre, Amsterdam, 1980.

[3] R. J. R. Back. A calculus of refinements for program derivations. *Acta Informatica*, 25:593–624, 1988.

[4] R. J. R. Back and J. von Wright. Refinement concepts formalized in higher order logic. Reports on computer science and mathematics 85, Åbo Akademi, 1989.

[5] R. J. R. Back and J. von Wright. Refinement concepts formalized in higher order logic. In *IFIP TC2 Working Conference*, Sea of Galilei, Israel, 1990.

[6] F. L. Bauer and al. *The Munich project CIP*, volume 183 of *Lecture Notes in Computer Science.* Springer-Verlag, 1985.

[7] F. L. Bauer, B. Moller, H. Partsch, and P. Pepper. Formal program construction by transformations – computer-aided, intuition guided programming. *IEEE Transactions on Software Engineering*, 15(2):165–180, 1989.

[8] R. M. Burstall and J. Darlington. Some transformations for developing recursive programs. *J. ACM*, 24(1):44–67, 1977.

[9] E. W. Dijkstra. Notes on structured programming. In E. D. Dahl, O.J. and C. Hoare, editors, *Structured Programming.* Academic Press, 1971.

[10] E. W. Dijkstra. *A Discipline of Programming.* Prentice–Hall International, 1976.

[11] M. S. Feather. A survey and classification of some program transformation approaches and techniques. In L. G. L. T. Meertens, editor, *Program Specification and Transformation*, pages 165–198. North-Holland, 1987.

[12] S. L. Gerhart. Correctness preserving program transformations. In *Proc. 2nd ACM Conference of Principles of Programming Languages*, pages 54–66, 1975.

[13] M. J. Gordon. Hol: A proof generating system for higher order logic. In G. Birtwistle and P. Subrahmanyam, editors, *VLSI Specification, Verification and Synthesis*, pages 73–128. Kluwer Academic Publishers, 1988.

[14] M. J. Gordon, A. J. Milner, and C. P. Wadsworth. *Edinburgh LCF*, volume 78 of *Lecture Notes in Computer Science.* Springer-Verlag, 1979.

[15] P. Lee, F. Pfenning, G. Rollins, and W. Scherlis. The Ergo support system: An integrated set of tools for prototyping integrated environments. In *Third ACM SIGSOFT Symposium on Software Development Environments*, 1988.

[16] C. C. Morgan. *Programming from Specifications.* Prentice–Hall, 1990.

[17] J. M. Morris. A theoretical basis for stepwise refinement and the programming calculus. *Science of Computer Programming*, 9:287–306, 1987.

[18] H. Partsch and R. Steinbrugge. Program transformation systems. *ACM Computing Surveys*, 15:199–236, 1983.

[19] L. C. Paulson. *Logic and Computation: Interactive Proof with Cambridge LCF.* Cambridge University Press, 1987.

[20] N. Wirth. Program development by stepwise refinement. *Communications of the ACM*, 14:221–227, 1971.

A Case Study in Timed Refinement: A Central Heater

Brendan Mahony
Ian Hayes
University of Queensland
St. Lucia, 4072
Australia

January 23, 1991

Abstract

The refinement calculus is proving a useful tool for the specification and refinement of sequential processes. In this paper we contend that it is also useful in the timed case. This paper displays the use of the refinement calculus for a small embedded system.

1 Introduction

The refinement calculus [5, 4, 1, 6] extends Dijkstra's weakest precondition program semantics to the realm of specifications. This provides a uniform notation for the entire refinement process. We assume that the reader is familiar with the notion of weakest precondition semantics for programs. Some familiarity with the refinement calculus and real functions will be useful.

The Z notation [2, 8] is used for expressing predicates on states, but a knowledge of Z is not essential to the reading of this paper. Those not familiar with Z may view the schema boxes as a convenient way of naming and expressing predicates. The schema consists of two sections, the first serving merely to introduce the variables discused in the predicate, appearing in the second section.

For sequential processes the refinement calculus sees programs in terms of the state of a system prior to execution and the state after execution of the program. The suitability of this approach relies on three assumptions about the nature of sequential processes.

1 Sequential processes terminate.

2 Sequential processes have sole access to program variables so there can be no interference from other processes.

3 Sequential processes have no timing obligations other than termination.

We are interested in investigating the usefulness of the refinement calculus where these assumptions break down. Our special interest lies in the realm of non-terminating real-time processes, but the process view we describe is equally applicable wherever these assumptions do not apply.

Specification of processes in terms of their initial and final states is not suitable for discussing non-sequential processes, since there may be no final state or intermediate states may be important. We propose two changes to the way in which predicate transformers are understood.

Firstly, the state of a system should be its behaviour over all time. It is essential whenever any of the above assumptions fail that the initial and final state paradigm is replaced by a state history paradigm. Since our interest is in non-terminating processes and we are also interested in real-time, we adopt a history model in which the time domain is represented by the positive real numbers.

Secondly we observe that the initial/final state paradigm is in fact a degenerate case of the history paradigm. A history in which only two state observations are made. Viewed in this light we can see that the the refinement calculus is in fact dealing with the relationship between the structure induced on the system by the process (the postcondition involving initial and final states) and the structure inherent in the system (the precondition involving only the initial states). Thus the process is actually viewed in terms of how it transforms the behaviour of a system that it acts upon. We contend that the natural generalisation of the sequential refinement calculus is based on mapping the desired behaviour of system plus process, the *effect* of the process, to the known behaviour of the system in isolation, the *assumptions* the process may make about the system. We generalise the weakest precondition semantics for sequential processes to a *weakest assumption* semantics for non-sequential processes.

A full justification for the above decisions and a derivation of the resulting non-sequential refinement calculus may be found in [3]. Here we give give only informal motivations for and explanations of the notation we use. The purpose here is to demonstrate the practical usefulness of the techniques.

2 Central Heating

We consider a household central heating system. The intention of the central heater is to maintain the temperature of a house around a certain minimum temperature

$$tmin : TEMP.$$

We represent the domain of temperatures, *TEMP*, by the positive real numbers, $\mathbb{R}_+$, being the temperature measured in degree Kelvin.

2.1 Functionality

The house may be modelled as a simple thermodynamic system attached to a heat sink (the cold cold snow) and a heat source (the heater). The state of the house may then be represented by its temperature, and the rates at which heat is going out and coming into the house. The history of the temperature and heat loss and heat gain may be represented as functions over all time. To avoid pathological, and unrealistic, cases we restrict consideration to topologically continuous functions. A function is topologically continuous if it respects open sets. Formally, the preimage of an open set in the range must be open in the domain. We write $X \twoheadrightarrow Y$ for the total continuous functions from X to Y and $X \nrightarrow Y$ for the partial ones. Strictly speaking, these definitions should be made with respect to particular topologies, but we will assume that each domain has a default topology and omit explicit reference to them. For instance, in the standard topology for the reals, $\mathcal{T}_R$, the open sets are constructed from arbitrary unions of open intervals. An open interval $(x \dots y)$ is the set of points $\{z : \mathbb{R} \mid x < z < y\}$. $\mathcal{I}_R$ is the set of all open intervals.

The temperature of the house at any time depends on the amount of heat that is flowing into and out of the house.

$$
\begin{array}{|l}
\textit{House} \\
\hline
\theta : \mathit{TIME} \twoheadrightarrow \mathit{TEMP} \\
\mathit{Hin}, \mathit{Hout} : \mathit{TIME} \twoheadrightarrow \mathit{TEMP}\ \mathbf{per}\ \mathit{TIME} \\
\hline
\forall t_1, t_2 : \mathit{TIME} \bullet \\
\qquad \theta(t_2) = \theta(t_1) + \int_{t_1}^{t_2} \mathit{Hin}(s) - \mathit{Hout}(s) \bullet ds \\
\hline
\end{array}
$$

The heat flows are modelled as temperature flows so that the specific heat of the house need not be considered explicitly. The time domain, *TIME*, and the rates of temperature change, *TEMP* **per** *TIME*, are represented by positive reals.

The purpose of the central heater is to regulate the temperature of the house. The temperature must be prevented from falling below *tmin* for periods longer than

$$\delta : \mathit{TIME}.$$

The standard topology for the reals, $\mathcal{T}_R$, has the useful property that any open set may be covered by a countable[1] disjoint union of open intervals [7]. It is thus possible to uniquely define a function,

$$
\begin{array}{|l}
\mathit{OpenCover} : \mathcal{T}_R \rightarrow \mathbf{P}_\omega \mathcal{I}_R \\
\hline
\forall \mathcal{O} : \mathcal{T}_R \bullet \\
\qquad \bigcup \mathit{OpenCover}(\mathcal{O}) = \mathcal{O} \\
\qquad \forall \Delta, \Delta' : \mathit{OpenCover}(\mathcal{O}) \bullet \Delta \neq \Delta' \Rightarrow \Delta \cap \Delta' = \{\}
\end{array}
$$

which decomposes every open set into a countable set of maximal open intervals. In essence any open set of real numbers may be viewed as a (possibly infinite) sequence of intervals.

Using *OpenCover* we are able to concisely express the requirements for the heater in terms of the length of the time intervals for which the temperature is too low. The times for which the temperature is too low are in the pre-image of the temperature region $(0 \ldots \mathit{tmin})$ under the temperature function

[1]We extend the Z notation, using $\mathbf{P}_\omega X$ to represent the countable subsets of X.

θ, i.e. $\theta^{-1}(\!|(0 \ldots tmin)|\!)$. Using the continuity of θ we know this pre-image is an open set, so *OpenCover* may be used to find the maximal intervals of time for which the temperature falls below *tmin*.

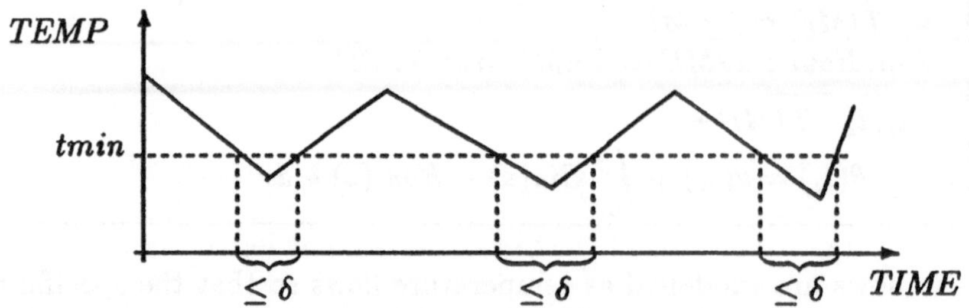

Each such interval, Δ, must have duration, $|\Delta|$, less than δ.

```
┌─ WarmHouse ─────────────────────────────
│ House
├──────────────
│ ∀Δ : OpenCover(θ⁻¹⦇(0 ... tmin)⦈) • |Δ| ≤ δ
└─────────────────────────────────────────
```

This ability to decompose time regions into sets of time intervals adds great expressive power to our specifications.

The question now arises of under what condition can we reasonably expect a central heater to be able to do this. Whether it chooses to keep the house warm by restricting the outflow of heat (improved insulation) or by increasing the inflow of heat, the efforts of the heater will be finite in scope. We cannot expect it to be able to compensate for arbitrary rates of heat loss. Therefore we require that there be a bound

$$Insul : TEMP \text{ per } TIME$$

on the rate at which heat flows out of the house.

For similar reasons to above we cannot expect the heater to heat the house within time δ from an arbitrary starting temperature. Consequently we will assume that the temperature begins in the required range. If desired a terminating process can be used to heat the room up, before turning it over to the standard central heating process.

Consequently we will allow the central heater to assume the house satisfies

$$
\begin{array}{|l}
\hline
\textit{InsulatedHouse} \\
\textit{House} \\
\hline
\theta(0) \geq \textit{tmin} \\
\forall t : \textit{TIME} \bullet \textit{Hout}(t) \leq \textit{Insul} \\
\hline
\end{array}
$$

Our specification is then that the heater must cause the house to satisfy *WarmHouse* as long as the house is known to be an *InsulatedHouse*. We write the specification

$$CentralHeater \mathrel{\widehat{=}} [InsulatedHouse, WarmHouse].$$

This notation mimics the specification statements of Morgan [4]. We also adopt the term specification statement for such constructs. In [4] the first predicate is called the precondition and the second predicate the postcondition. The terms 'precondition' and 'postcondition' are not suitable in the context of non-terminating processes. Instead, we adopt the terms *assumption* and *effect* respectively.

The specification *CentralHeater* is interpreted as: if the environment in isolation satisfies the first predicate (assumption *CentralHeater*), applying the *CentralHeater* process to it will cause it to satisfy the further conditions expressed in the second predicate (effect *CentralHeater*).

2.2 The Heater

The central heating system will be implemented using a heating element, with minimum output

$$Output : TEMP \ \mathbf{per} \ TIME$$

that may be turned on and off to control the house's temperature.

$$
\begin{array}{|l}
\hline
\textit{Heater} \\
\textit{Element} : \textit{TIME} \twoheadrightarrow \{on, off\} \\
\hline
\end{array}
$$

The *Element* function cannot be both continuous and total. Continuous functions into discrete domains must be step functions, with periods of non-definedness between steps. This is a good representation for digital quantities that remain constant until acted on by an event, during the action of which they are undefined.

The heater must act as the heat source of the house.

$$
\begin{array}{|l}
\textit{InstalledHeater} \\
\hline
\textit{House} \\
\textit{Heater} \\
\hline
\textbf{true} \\
\hline
\forall t : \operatorname{dom} \textit{Element} \bullet \\
\qquad \textit{Element}(t) = \textit{on} \Rightarrow \textit{Hin}(t) \geq \textit{Output} \\
\hline
\end{array}
$$

Here the specification statement appears in a vertical format which is more convenient when the process assumptions are trivial. The syntactic format is inspired by the Z schema, with the first section declaring the process' state variables and their types, the second displaying the assumptions predicate, and the third the effects predicate. The invariants expressed in *House* and *Heater* become invariants that are preserved by the process.

When the temperature falls below *tmin* the heater control reacts by turning on the heater until the temperature has again risen above *tmin*. The heater is turned on within

$$r : \textit{TIME}$$

of the temperature becoming too low.

$$
\begin{array}{|l}
\textit{ControlHeater} \\
\hline
\textit{House} \\
\textit{Heater} \\
\hline
\textbf{true} \\
\hline
\forall \Delta : \textit{OpenCover}(\theta^{-1} (\!| (0 \ldots \textit{tmin}) |\!)) \bullet \\
\qquad (\inf \Delta + r \ldots \sup \Delta) \subseteq \textit{Element}^{-1} (\!| \{\textit{on}\} |\!) \\
\hline
\end{array}
$$

The heater will restore the temperature in time as long as

$$\delta.\textit{Insul} \leq (\delta - r).\textit{Output}.$$

So we add the assumption

$$Output \geq \frac{\delta}{\delta - r}.Insul$$

These two processes will implement *CentralHeater* if they are run in parallel. The parallel operator for specification statements [3] is defined

$$[\text{assumption}_1, \text{effect}_1] \mid\mid [\text{assumption}_2, \text{effect}_2] \mathrel{\widehat{=}} \\ \quad [\text{assumption}_1 \wedge \text{assumption}_2, \text{effect}_1 \wedge \text{effect}_2]$$

The design for the central heating system is then

$$CentralHeater_1 \mathrel{\widehat{=}} (InstalledHeater \mid\mid ControlHeater).$$

Theorem 1

$$CentralHeater \sqsubseteq CentralHeater_1$$

Proof

The definition of refinement for specification statements [4, 3] means we must show that

$$\text{assumption } CentralHeater \Rightarrow \\ \quad \text{assumption } CentralHeater_1 \wedge \\ \quad \text{effect } CentralHeater_1 \Rightarrow \text{effect } CentralHeater$$

Since assumption $CentralHeater_1$ is **true** this reduces to

$$\text{assumption } CentralHeater \wedge \text{effect } CentralHeater_1 \Rightarrow \\ \quad \text{effect } CentralHeater$$

Writing this out in full, we find that we must show that

$$\forall t : TIME \bullet \qquad (InsulatedHouse) \\ \quad Hout(t) \leq Insul \\ \quad \theta(0) \geq tmin \\ \forall t : TIME \bullet \qquad (\text{effect } InstalledHeater) \\ \quad Element(t) = on \Rightarrow Hin \geq Output$$

$$\forall \Delta : OpenCover(\theta^{-1}(\!|(0 \dots tmin)|\!)) \bullet \qquad \text{(effect } ControlHeater\text{)}$$
$$(\inf \Delta + r \dots \sup \Delta) \subseteq Element^{-1}(\!|\{on\}|\!)$$
$$\Rightarrow$$
$$\forall \Delta : OpenCover(\theta^{-1}(\!|(0 \dots tmin)|\!)) \bullet$$
$$|\Delta| \leq \delta \qquad (WarmHouse)$$

Case Δ finite

Suppose $\Delta \in OpenCover(\theta^{-1}(\!|(0, tmin)|\!))$ is finite in length, then as θ is continuous and $\theta(0) \geq tmin$

$$\theta(\inf \Delta) = \theta(\sup \Delta) = tmin,$$

so from the invariant on *House*,

$$0 = \int_{\inf \Delta}^{\sup \Delta} Hin(s) - Hout(s) \bullet ds.$$

Using the hypotheses about the heater and the maximum heat loss this gives

$$\int_{\inf \Delta}^{\sup \Delta} Insul \bullet ds$$
$$\geq \int_{\inf \Delta}^{\sup \Delta} Hout(s) \bullet ds \qquad \text{(insulation hypothesis)}$$
$$= \int_{\inf \Delta}^{\sup \Delta} Hin(s) \bullet ds$$
$$\geq \int_{\inf \Delta + r}^{\sup \Delta} Output \bullet ds \qquad \text{(element hypothesis)}$$
$$\geq \int_{\inf \Delta + r}^{\sup \Delta} \frac{\delta}{\delta - r} Insul \bullet ds$$

Thus

$$|\Delta| \, .Insul \geq (|\Delta| - r).\frac{\delta}{\delta - r}.Insul$$
$$\text{i.e. } (\delta - r).\, |\Delta| \geq (|\Delta| - r).\delta$$
$$\text{i.e. } \delta.\, |\Delta| - r.\, |\Delta| \geq |\Delta| .\delta - r.\delta$$
$$\text{i.e. } \delta \geq |\Delta|$$

as required.

Case Δ infinite
A similar proof will show that Δ must be finite.
□
The specification *InstalledHeater* can be implemented by the simple expedient of placing the heating element inside the house. All control logic may therefore be restricted to the process *ControlHeater*, and we can restrict further consideration to that process.

2.3 Avoiding Rapid Oscillations

It would be undesirable if the heater were to turn off immediately the temperature climbed to *tmin*, since this would mean the temperature was usually below *tmin*. To avoid this we strengthen *ControlHeater* to ensure that the heater remains on until the temperature reaches $tmax : TEMP$, where $tmax > tmin$.

ControlHeater₁

House
Heater

---

true

$$\begin{array}{l} \forall \Delta : OpenCover(\theta^{-1} (\!|(0 \ldots tmin)|\!)) \bullet \\ \quad \exists \Delta' : OpenCover(\theta^{-1} (\!|(0 \ldots tmax)|\!)) \bullet \\ \quad\quad \Delta \subseteq \Delta' \wedge \\ \quad\quad (\inf \Delta + r \ldots \sup \Delta') \subseteq Element^{-1} (\!|\{on\}|\!) \end{array}$$

Since $ControlHeater_1$ is gained by strengthening of the effect of *ControlHeater* it is clear that it is a refinement thereof.

Theorem 2

$$ControlHeater \sqsubseteq ControlHeater_1$$

The parallel operator is monotonic with respect to refinement [3]. This means that refining one of the sub-specifications yields a refinement of the combined specification.

Corollary 3

$$CentralHeater \sqsubseteq (InstalledHeater \| ControlHeater_1)$$

3 Conclusion

We have demonstrated that non-terminating real-time processes may be developed using rigorous specification and refinement techniques. The techniques in this paper decompose specifications into assumptions a process may make and the effect required of it. In this way non-terminating processes can also be associated with a predicate transformer semantics. We have demonstrated that notions from the sequential refinement calculus, such as refinment (Theorems 1,2) and monotonic specification combinators (Corollary 3) are applicable to real-time, non-terminating and parallel processes. Whilst our case study lies in the realm of embedded, real-time systems, the techniques demonstrated are applicable to arbitrary non-sequential processes.

Further the techniques we have demonstrated are a generalisation of the refinement calculus for sequential processes. Sequential processes may be considered as a special case in the assumption/effect view of processes. The predicate transformer calculus derived in [1] remains the theoretical grounding for our non-sequential refinement calculus.

Acknowledgements

This paper is the result of work begun while I was visiting the Programming Research Group, Oxford University, under funding from the Australian Commonwealth Postgraduate Research Award Scheme. I would like to thank the Programming Research Group for their hospitality.

I am in debt to Carroll Morgan for his inspiring work.

Lastly I would like to acknowledge the contribution of the English weather in motivating this case study.

References

[1] R. J. R. Back and J. von Wright. Refinement calculus, part I: Sequential nondeterministic programs. Technical Report Ser. A, No 92, Institute för Informationsbehandling, Lemminkäinengatan, 1989.

[2] I. J. Hayes, editor. *Specification Case Studies.* Prentice Hall International, 1987.

[3] B. P. Mahony and I. J. Hayes. Generalising the specification statement to real-time. Department of Computer Science, University of Queensland, 1990.

[4] C. C. Morgan, K. A. Robinson, and P. Gardiner. On the refinement calculus. Technical Monograph PRG-70, Oxford University Programming Research Laboratory, 1988.

[5] C.C. Morgan. The specification statement. *ACM Trans. Prog. Lang. and Sys.*, 10(3), July 1988. Reprinted in [4].

[6] J. M. Morris. A theoretical basis for stepwise refinement and the programming calculus. *Science of Computer Programming*, 9, 1987.

[7] H. L. Royden. *Real Analysis.* Macmillan Publishing Co., Inc., second edition, 1968.

[8] J. M. Spivey. *The Z Notation: A Reference Manual.* Prentice Hall International, 1989.

Object Oriented Specification and Refinement

P J Whysall
J A McDermid

Department of Computer Science
University of York

ABSTRACT

The increasing demand for high integrity and safety critical systems is giving the development of formal methods for software production a high priority. A large number of different approaches to specifying, developing and implementing systems have been devised, however, despite this widespread (but mainly academic) research, formal methods are still very rarely used in industrial practice. This failure can be attributed to a number of causes, among them the inability of the techniques to scale easily to industrial sized problems.

This paper proposes an approach to specification that helps alleviate the problems of scalability by providing a strong separation between parts of a specification, allowing their independent refinement, and hence allowing refinements of the total specification to be produced relatively cheaply. The separation is provided by producing specifications as a set of objects, each of which is described by two specifications, an algebraic export specification and a model oriented body specification. The export describes the object to those who will use it, while the body specification will form the basis of subsequent refinement and implementation.

This approach to specification provides a framework within which to specify and develop software. We describe relationships within this framework for which we must be able to derive and discharge relevant proof obligations in order to verify the specifications. In particular we describe the refinement relation between the object's export and body specifications, the substitution relation implied when we use one object within another, and the composition relation which allows us to correctly combine a set of objects to form a complete system.

1. Introduction

The use of computers is becoming increasingly widespread, and in particular computers are now being used in many safety critical applications† – applications where failure of the system could lead to loss of life or serious injury. The ability to guarantee properties about such systems – correctness, safety, and so on – requires a formal understanding of that system. This formal understanding will typically be based upon a formal specification of what the system is supposed to do, and a formal development process which enforces a relationship between the specification and implementation.

Over a number of years much research effort has been invested in the area of formal methods and formal refinement, by both industry and academia. Despite this effort the techniques are still not widely used in practice. There are a number of reasons, both technical and non-technical, why this is still the case. These reasons include:

Non-technical

- Lack of evidence that the techniques will achieve improvements in practice.
- Lack of suitably trained personnel to apply the techniques on real projects.

Technical

- Inability to deal with most non-functional requirements, e.g. timing, fault tolerance.
- Inability to deal fully with certain classes of functional requirement, e.g. aspects of concurrency.
- Inability to scale easily to realistic sized problems.

This paper is concerned primarily with technical issues.

We believe that the most serious current technical limitation of specification and refinement techniques is simply their inability to scale easily to realistic sized problems. Refinement techniques have been applied successfully to many small example specifications, but when applied to larger specifications they soon become unmanageable. The biggest system we know that was developed using formal refinement is an editor produced by Neilson for his thesis.[1] This produced a C program of some 5000 lines, but even then some corners were cut during the formal development.

These techniques, particularly those based on Z,‡ suffer from a lack of structure in the specifications, and hence composition of large specifications becomes

† The use of safety critical systems provides a motivation for formal methods research, but this paper in fact deals only with 'standard' formal techniques.

‡ This approach to specification and refinement is based entirely on the Z notation. This notation was chosen because of its widespread use in both industry and academia, and because of the expertise already available in this area. However the general approach we propose is not tied to the Z notation, and in fact in some cases problems caused by the limitations of Z might have been avoided in other notations.

difficult. For example Z provides no high level structuring apart from direct combination of schemas using the schema calculus. The result of this is that it is difficult to compose separate parts of a specification together to form a system specification. If such a system specification is produced using the schema calculus then the separate parts are not composed, but physically combined and the original separation is lost. This causes problems if it is necessary to perform further manipulation of the specification, for example to carry out refinement and proofs. These operations must now access the whole combined specification, rather than accessing separate parts by appropriate interfaces to them. In particular this means that there is no real simplification achieved by dividing a system into separate parts, and composing the total system from them.

The aim of our work is to introduce extra structuring into the specification technique, providing a mechanism to specify parts of a system, and then to compose them. This allows access to the components via an appropriate interface, and hence maintains stronger separation between different parts of a system. Within such a framework refinement can be carried out on the separate parts of the system, thus replacing one large refinement by a number of smaller independent refinements. Additionally we must prove that the separate objects can be successfully composed to achieve the overall specification, but again this is relatively simple compared to the original proof.

Section 2 describes the basic specifications, based on the object oriented paradigm, and introduces the notion of separate export and body specifications. Section 3 describes the basic refinement relation introduced by the approach, that between an object's body and export specifications. Section 4 extends this basic refinement relation to include the more general case involving the use of auxiliary objects.

The object oriented paradigm is usually portrayed as including a notion of inheritance. We do not in fact treat the notion of inheritance explicitly in this approach, but rather include the more general notion of substitution.† In section 5 we describe the notion of a view, and discuss why it might be desirable to interface to an object via such a view, only later substituting a particular object which satisfies this view. We then go on to describe the substitution relation formally, and show how an object can indeed be substituted into such a view.

Finally section 6 looks at extensions to the basic approach described in the earlier sections. We consider essentially three issues. Firstly we look at the issue of first class and shared objects, and show how the properties of such objects can only be proved when the objects are composed together into particular systems. This is used as the motivation for an approach to system composition based on the notion of rely and guarantee conditions between objects. Secondly we look at how the object specifications are produced, and propose a modification to the basic notation used in the object export specifications which can make such specifications simpler, and also consider the implications this change has for the overall approach.

† See Atkins[2] and section 5 for further discussion of why inheritance is subsumed by the more general notion of substitution.

Finally we consider the further refinement to implementation of the object body specifications, and show how this task can be performed using a standard approach to refinement, for example Morgan's[3] refinement calculus.

2. Basic specifications

Part of the aim of this work is thus to produce specifications that are better structured than those usually produced using Z. In particular it was required that parts of a specification could be grouped together to form *units*, and that these units could be used by 'higher level' parts of the specification, and could be used without knowledge of details of the unit such as state information. Essentially some form of module notation was required which would support information hiding and abstraction. It is worth noting that introducing some sort of module structure into specifications gives additional advantages over and above those that can be gained by using a module structure in implementation, specifically it should simplify proofs and specification composition.

Given that a module structure would be desirable, the requirement to be able to use the units easily without knowledge of how their constituent operations achieved their aim suggested that an object based approach would be appropriate, in the specifications as well as in the implementation, for the state common to these operations could then be truly hidden from the unit's user. Hence it was decided to investigate the possibility of producing object oriented specifications in Z. This decision was (initially) taken without the knowledge that others were working in the same area[4,5,6] but the different motivation for this work has in any case led to the development of a rather different approach. Clearly this approach is most obviously attractive where the implementation will also be object oriented, but we believe the approach has more general applicability. It is additionally recognised that the advantages of encapsulation are not as clear cut in the presence of sharing. This issue is addressed in part in section 6.1.

Before proceeding further with discussion of our approach it is worth first explaining the notion of object that we will be using. This is not intended to be a motivation or explanation of this notion, but merely a description. The interested reader is referred to Atkins.[2] We consider an object to be a set of named methods, possibly acting on some encapsulated (hidden) state. These named methods are all that is visible to the object user. We will consider these objects to have three basic properties, identity, dynamic lifetime, and substitutability. Object identity implies that the objects have some constant notion of existence independent of any value they might have. This is essential to deal with any but the simplest systems, for example systems involving shared objects. We consider the objects to be dynamic in nature, so that a system does not consist simply of a fixed set of objects, which would again limit the range of applicability. Finally the objects should be substitutable, allowing one object to be substituted in place of another if it is compatible – essentially if the first refines the second. Our approach will be to define classes of objects having certain behaviours, and then to create objects themselves which are instances of these classes.

In the context of refinement the specification of an object will serve two tasks. Firstly it will form the starting point for its own refinement, against which putative refinements must be verified. Secondly, it will be used to help in the proof of properties of higher level objects. For example, if a higher level object A uses this object B, then object A's verification, will be very likely to utilise some properties of object B, as described by object B's specification.

In fact, the specification will be used in significantly different ways in these two contexts, and the requirements on the nature of the specification will be correspondingly different. In carrying out refinement, the interest will be in the behaviour of each of the individual methods, and their influence on the object's state. In particular a refinement must be provided for each of the object's methods. At the higher level it is necessary to reason about the behaviour of the whole object, without considering its state, and details of how the methods modify it. It is thus argued that these uses are sufficiently different to warrant the production of two separate specifications of each object, referred to as an export and a body. The body specifications will be described briefly below, but most attention will be focussed on the more novel export specifications.

The object body specification must provide a detailed description of the state of the object, and of each method that operates on it. This notion of state and state changing operations is very similar to the standard Z approach to specification. We can hence describe all of these parts of the object using schemas in the usual way, and use these schemas as the basis for refinement. The only difference between these and standard schemas is that we might use some of the lower level objects in order to help define a method. Producing a body specification like this does not however make very clear which schemas in fact describe a particular object body. This deficiency is not in fact important at this level, but this could be solved by using an approach like Queensland's Object-Z to specify the bodies, effectively grouping the schemas which define methods together with a state definition and initialisation to give a single 'schema' defining the whole object.

2.1. Export specifications

The only interaction that takes place with an object is the invocation of its methods with particular parameters. Given that this is true, any understanding of an object's behaviour sought outside that object should be expressed solely in terms of those methods. In particular this means that if the full trace of methods invoked on an object is known, then it should be possible to determine exactly the result of any subsequent invocation, up to any residual non-determinism.

The export specifications described here are produced with this property in mind, expressing the behaviour of a method as a function of the trace of that object thus far. This leads to the production of an algebraic description of the overall behaviour of the object. Such an algebraic specification satisfies the aim of describing the interaction of the methods independent of their individual descriptions and the state they act on, and has other advantages, for example being amenable to 'execution' using rewrite techniques common to many algebraic approaches. This notion of a trace based specification is similar to Parnas's traces for modules[7] and more recent 'object like' modules with state[8] although the work is totally independent.

2.1.1. Trace based specification

The aim of the specification is thus to describe the object behaviour by means of a number of equations each expressing properties about the trace of the object. In order to produce such specifications (in Z) a notation must first be sought that is suitable for describing the traces themselves.† These traces can then form the basis of an object specification.

A method is some kind of function which takes as input some state (which will of course be hidden), and yields as a result a new value of the state, and an output value. Such a definition of course restricts methods to be deterministic. The approach described here can be generalised to allow the specification of non-deterministic methods, but for simplicity of exposition we restrict ourselves here to consider only deterministic methods. A method can thus be represented by a function with the following type:

$$\text{Method [res, state]} == \text{state} \rightarrowtail\!\!\!\!\!+ \ (\text{res} \times \text{state})$$

A method is in general a partial function, for it may not be defined for all possible states of the object. Some methods also take parameters: these will be represented by functions which yield methods as their results. They can be represented as follows (where input represents the type of any parameters to the method):

$$\text{input} \longrightarrow \text{Method}_{[\text{res,state}]}$$

The aim here will be to be able to apply sequences of these methods to an object in order to form a trace. A sequencing operator ' ; ' will thus be required which can be applied as shown below (the *resultant* is essentially the hidden internal state of the object which is of course what the each method acts on):

$$\text{resultant ; method1 ; method2}$$

In order for this sort of sequencing to work the sequencing operator must have a type of the form:

$$\text{Resultant} \times \text{Method} \longrightarrow \text{Resultant}$$

Given that the output of each method is a result and state pair, perhaps the most obvious type for the Resultant‡ would thus be:

† Arguably the specification of traces in Z is the least natural aspect of our specification approach. Traces are easier to treat in an algebraic or process algebraic framework. However we need to be able to represent traces in Z in order to manage the refinement to the model oriented body specifications within the same formalism. One of Z's strengths is that it is possible to do this.

‡ We use the term resultant here because entities of this type are in fact the result of each method invocation. Additionally the connotations implied by the physics notion of a resultant are also appropriate, for each invocation of a method modifies the resultant, to give a final resultant which is based on the whole trace of such invocations.

$$Resultant\ [res, state] == (res \times state)$$

This would mean that methods (in our approach) yield these Resultants directly, and the sequencing operator will be a relatively simple composition operator. The Resultant itself contains both the object state and the latest result that can be seen by an object user. We will also think of this as the type of a trace – strictly it is the type not of the trace, but of the result of the trace (a Resultant), but as we will not normally produce real instances of this type it is convenient to consider the traces that produce them to be elements of the type. Finally, by way of preparation, functions can be defined which take such Resultants apart, yielding the 'state' of the Resultant, and an external 'view' of it, being the result of the last method invocation.

$$view\ [X, Y] == first_{[X, Y]}$$

$$state\ [X, Y] == second_{[X, Y]}$$

The sequencing operator for traces can now be defined formally. This operator will combine sequences of method invocations to an object, hiding the internal state between them.[†] Note that the sequencing operator is a partial function, for it attempts to apply a method (also partial) to a general object state, and hence may sometimes be undefined.

[v, r, st]

$$(\_;\_)\ 1 : (Resultant_{[v, st]} \times Method_{[r, st]}) \longrightarrow Resultant_{[r, st]}$$

$$\forall o : Resultant_{[v, st]};\ m : Method_{[r, st]} \bullet o ; m = m\ (state\ o)$$

Application of a method thus modifies an object state. A trace can be defined by applying a sequence of such methods to an initial object state. These traces will form the basis of the object export specifications. In order to produce export specifications it will be necessary to express equivalences between traces, and to express properties about the results of such traces. Firstly an observational equivalence between traces will be defined – two traces are equivalent if no future method invocation can distinguish them. This is the correct equivalence because the object user will only be able to distinguish them by invoking their methods.[‡]

† An alternative choice here would have been to make a Resultant a special kind of method, so that sequencing had the more natural type:

$$Method \times Method \longrightarrow Method$$

We choose not to do this because it blurs the distinction between the object state (part of the Resultant) and methods acting on it, which is useful in defining the other operators.

‡ This formal definition is not yet quite what we want, for it is generic in the result types of the methods, rather than being true for any such result types.

$$
\begin{array}{l}
[r, r1, r2, st] \\
\hline
\_ \equiv \_ : \mathrm{Resultant}_{[r,\, st]} \leftrightarrow \mathrm{Resultant}_{[r1,\, st]} \\
\hline
\forall\, i : \mathrm{Resultant}_{[r,\, st]};\ j : \mathrm{Resultant}_{[r1,\, st]} \bullet \\
\quad (\forall\, s : \mathrm{Method}_{[r2,\, st]} \bullet \mathrm{view}\ (i\, ;s) = \mathrm{view}\ (j\, ; s)) \Leftrightarrow i \equiv j
\end{array}
$$

This equivalence is defined over all the Resultants with a particular state type (st), and by reference to any method applicable to that type. Implicitly it is thought of as being defined only over applications of methods defined by that object, and hence it is assumed that no other object can have methods defined with this same type.† Additionally the equivalence is only defined with reference to a single method invocation. However it is assumed that the methods themselves can be composed, and hence this single method does generalise to any finite sequence of composed methods. Such a composition operator could be defined as follows.

$$
\begin{array}{l}
[r, r1, st] \\
\hline
(\_ \otimes \_)\ 1 : (\mathrm{Method}_{[r,\, st]} \times \mathrm{Method}_{[r1,\, st]}) \longrightarrow \mathrm{Method}_{[r1,\, st]} \\
\hline
\forall\, m : \mathrm{Method}_{[r,\, st]};\ n : \mathrm{Method}_{[r1,\, st]} \bullet \\
\quad m \otimes n = n \circ \mathrm{state} \circ m
\end{array}
$$

Finally a result operation is defined which allows the specification of the result of a trace, the final output observed when applying the sequence of methods. In fact it is defined as a relationship between traces and result values, a trace being related to exactly the value that it will produce.

$$
\begin{array}{l}
[r, st] \\
\hline
\_ \rightarrow \_ : \mathrm{Resultant}_{[r,\, st]} \leftrightarrow r \\
\hline
\forall\, i : \mathrm{Resultant}_{[r,\, st]};\ e : r \bullet \mathrm{first}\ i = e \Rightarrow i \rightarrow e
\end{array}
$$

This solution to the problem of specifying equivalence is not entirely satisfactory technically, but the definition has so far been satisfactory in practice. An alternative formulation which facilitates an improved definition of equivalence is under development.

These operators can be used to specify the exported properties of an object.

† Technically this is perhaps somewhat unsatisfactory for it does not yet capture quite the required relationship, but, in practice, it does not cause any difficulties.

2.1.2. A simple stack example

The definition of a simple stack as an object will be considered. Firstly definitions are given for a void type (a type with only one value, hence carrying no information) and a boolean type which will be used in the main definition given below.

[Void]

Bool ::= True | False

STACK [State, Elem]

$\text{empty} : \text{Resultant}_{[\text{Elem, State}]}$
$\text{pop} : \text{Method}_{[\text{Elem, State}]}$
$\text{push} : \text{Elem} \longrightarrow \text{Method}_{[\text{Void, State}]}$
$\text{top} : \text{Method}_{[\text{Elem, State}]}$
$\text{isempty} : \text{Method}_{[\text{Bool, State}]}$

$$
\begin{array}{l}
\exists\, \text{error} : \text{Elem} \bullet \\
\quad \forall\, i : \text{Resultant}_{[\text{Elem, State}]};\ e : \text{Elem} \bullet \\
\qquad i;\text{push } e;\text{pop} \to e \wedge i;\text{push } e;\text{top} \to e \wedge \\
\qquad i;\text{push } e;\text{isempty} \to \text{False} \wedge \\
\qquad \text{empty};\text{isempty} \to \text{True} \wedge \text{empty};\text{pop} \to \text{error} \wedge \\
\qquad \text{empty};\text{top} \to \text{error} \wedge i;\text{top} \equiv i \wedge i;\text{isempty} \equiv i \wedge \\
\qquad i;\text{push } e;\text{pop} \equiv i \wedge \text{empty};\text{pop} \equiv \text{empty}
\end{array}
$$

The declaration part of this schema defines the methods that the object is going to export. There are two different types of method defined, those (like empty) which define a known initial state of the object, and those (like push and pop) which define state changing methods on the object. The predicate part of the schema also contains two sorts of expression, some defining equivalences between traces, and others defining the results of traces. For example, taking the first expression, i ; push e ; pop $\to$ e, if the stack is in some arbitrary state i, and a value e is pushed onto it, and then the pop method is invoked, then the value returned will be that same value e. This represents an exported property of the stack, defining a property of a particular trace of the stack. Similarly, considering the equation i ; push e ; pop $\equiv$ e, we see that after completion of these methods the object will be in a state equivalent to that before either method was invoked. If complete, then these expressions allow the results output by any method when applied to any possible trace to be deduced.†

An object thus defined can be used elsewhere in a specification. The schema in effect defines a class of objects, and it is hence possible to create instances of

† As indicated earlier this is very similar to the way in which we would define an ADT in an algebraic specification language.

that class. In Z an instance is simply produced by creating an entity of the class type:

$$obj : STACK_{[State,\ Elem]}$$

The methods of such an object can then be utilised in standard object oriented fashion, for example:

obj.push
obj.pop

Higher level objects in a system can hence create instances of such objects, and use expressions like these to utilise the methods of the lower level objects in order to evaluate some higher level results. A larger example of this will be seen in a later section, however as a trivial example we can utilise the stack in a simple swap method:

```
SWAP [Elem]
  x?, y?, x!, y! : Elem
  st : STACK[State, Elem]
  ────────────────
  ∃ ist : Resultant[Elem, State] •
      ist ≡ st.empty; st.push x?; st.push y?; st.pop → x! ∧
      ist; st.pop → y!
```

This is of course not the export specification of swap but rather the body specification of a particular method which has been designed to perform the swap using a stack. In practice we would (probably) never represent swap like this, but it is useful as a simple example. At a later stage when properties of the SWAP operation are to be proved the STACK export specification can be used to aid in the proof.

For completeness it is worth giving part of the corresponding body specification for such a stack object. First the state of the stack is defined:

```
STACK_STATE [Elem]
  stack : seq Elem
```

Methods that operate on the stack object can then be defined as delta operations on this state. The body specifications for the PUSH and POP operations can now be defined as follows:

```
┌─ PUSH [Elem] ─────────────────
│ ΔSTACK_STATE[Elem]
│ elem? : Elem
├──────────
│ stack' = ⟨elem?⟩ ⁀ stack
└───────────────────────────────
```

$$\text{PUSH [Elem]}: \Delta STACK\_STATE_{[Elem]};\ elem? : Elem \mid stack' = \langle elem? \rangle \frown stack$$

```
┌─ POP [Elem] ──────────────────
│ ΔSTACK_STATE[Elem]
│ res! : Elem
├──────────
│ ∃ error : Elem •
│     #stack = 0 ∧ (res! = error ∧ stack' = stack) ∨
│     stack = ⟨res!⟩ ⁀ stack'
└───────────────────────────────
```

Other methods of the stack would be defined in a similar manner. This completes a relatively simple example of the way in which these object specifications are produced.

This section has established the basic approach advocated for specifying objects in Z. In a formal framework the specification of each object will typically be used for different purposes: as the basis for further development, and as the basic description of the object for use in higher level proofs. It is thus appropriate to have two specifications for each object, each specification being tailored to its particular use. Introducing the notion of two specifications for each object of course introduces an additional burden of proof – that the two specifications are compatible, or more particularly, that the body specification refines the export. This is not in fact a serious problem, for the two specifications are both useful, and in the context of refinement such multiple specifications and corresponding proof obligations are already necessary.

In the next section the relationship between the export and body specifications is considered more formally.

3. Basic Refinement Relation

The previous section described a basic approach to specifying objects using Z. It in fact advocated the production of two such specifications for each object. This approach of course introduces an additional proof obligation, for it is necessary to prove that the two specifications really are two different specifications of the same object. We will discuss first the general principles involved, ignoring the problems of representing the relations in Z, and then go on to consider this representation in Z later.

3.1. Refinement of objects

In general it is necessary to show that a refinement relation holds between the two objects – any user requiring an object which behaved like the export would be satisfied by one which behaved like the body. We will derive a refinement relation first ignoring the state of the object, and then extend it to include refinement of that state. For a given object† o we require:

$$\text{export}_o \sqsubseteq \text{body}_o$$

This notion of refinement between objects is not clearly defined, however it is possible to define the relationship required in terms of the more standard notion of refinement between operations:[9]

$$\begin{array}{l} \text{AOP} \sqsubseteq \text{COP} \\ \text{iff} \\ \text{preAOP} \Rightarrow \text{preCOP} \wedge \\ \text{preAOP} \wedge \text{postCOP} \Rightarrow \text{postAOP} \end{array}$$

A concrete operation COP refines an abstract operation AOP if it is applicable in at least the same states (the pre-condition of AOP implies the pre-condition of COP), and when it is applicable it yields the same results (the post-condition of COP implies the post-condition of AOP). Note that in this simple statement we ignore any necessary refinements between states.

The sort of relationship required for the whole object is something of the form:

$$\begin{array}{l} \text{A} \sqsubseteq \text{B} \\ \text{iff} \\ \forall\, \text{method} \in \text{A} \bullet \\ \qquad \exists\, \text{method}' \in \text{B} \bullet \text{method} \sqsubseteq \text{method}' \end{array}$$

An object A is refined by a second object B, if for every method in A there is a corresponding method in object B which refines it. This essentially generalises the refinement operator to be over a whole set of methods. In particular object B may have extra methods which don't correspond to methods of A, but must at least have one method for each in A. The term *method* here refers to a full state changing operation, which takes parameters, returns results, and additionally may modify the internal state of the object. The approach we define ensures that such a refinement maintains the correct interrelationship between the methods – the post-conditions of individual methods may be strengthened, and the pre-conditions weakened, but the refinement relation will ensure that when the methods are applicable they will yield the same results.

Clearly if we are to use the objects as we intend, refining them independently, and composing them, it is essential that the refinement relation used is monotonic. We have not proved this property, but we believe it to hold at least in a useful subset of cases, if not in the general case.

† We discuss the refinement relation here between individual objects although the same notion can also be used to express the refinement relation between the object classes.

Additionally it is necessary to consider refinements which modify the representation of the internal state of the object. An easy way to do this is to consider each method to consist of two separate parts, one which calculates the result, and a second which performs the state change:[†]

method == (ch_state × mk_result)

The refinement of data typically involves the production of refine and retrieve operations, which turn an abstract value into a corresponding concrete value, and vice versa. For simplicity here it will be assumed that these operations are functions, although they could be generalised to relations without difficulty.

We can now go on to consider refinement of state. The refinement of an operation which uses this data must now satisfy the following relation:

$$\text{refine} \circ \text{abstractOP} \circ \text{retrieve} \sqsubseteq \text{concreteOP}$$

The concrete operation must be a refinement of the operation produced by composing the abstract operation with the refine and retrieve operations – it does the same thing when applied to the corresponding data. Using this notion the refinement relation for the whole object can be generalised similarly:

$$\begin{array}{l} A \sqsubseteq B \\ \text{iff} \\ \exists\, \text{refine} : \text{state}(A) \longrightarrow \text{state}(B); \\ \text{retrieve} : \text{state}(B) \longrightarrow \text{state}(A) \mid \text{retrieve} \circ \text{refine} = \text{id} \;\bullet \\ \qquad \forall\, (\text{ch\_state}, \text{mk\_result}) \in A \;\bullet \\ \qquad\qquad \exists\, (\text{ch\_state}', \text{mk\_result}') \in B \;\bullet \\ \qquad\qquad\qquad \text{refine} \circ \text{ch\_state} \circ \text{retrieve} \sqsubseteq \text{ch\_state}' \\ \qquad\qquad\qquad\qquad \text{mk\_result} \circ \text{retrieve} \sqsubseteq \text{mk\_result}' \end{array}$$

In general an object A is refined by an object B if there exist functions that map between the state representations of the two objects, and the methods of the two objects satisfy an enhanced relation using these functions.

For the two functions we require the property $\text{retrieve} \circ \text{refine} = \text{id}$ (where id is the identity function) to be true in order to make sure that the concrete state is an *adequate* representation of the abstract state. If this were not the case then two abstract values would correspond to the same concrete value, and hence they could not be distinguished by any concrete operations. Note that we do not require the reverse composition to be the identity, for it is perfectly acceptable for two concrete values to represent the same abstract one. In particular the concrete state may include extra information not in the abstract which could hence distinguish them

† We can do this without loss of generality, because in the worse case we could simply duplicate the whole method, and in each case throw away the information that is not needed. Note that we could also have made this separation in the first rule above:

$$\begin{array}{l} \text{method} \sqsubseteq \text{method}' \\ \text{iff} \\ \text{ch\_state} \sqsubseteq \text{ch\_state}' \wedge \\ \text{mk\_result} \sqsubseteq \text{mk\_result}' \end{array}$$

only at the concrete level.

Given the two functions above, we can now define the relationship which must hold between the methods. Each method in the abstract object A must still have a corresponding method in the concrete object B which essentially refines it, but the formal relationship is now as follows. The state changing part of the method in B must refine the corresponding part of the method in A when it is nested within the refine and retrieve operations – that is B refines the behaviour of A applied to concrete values via the refine and retrieve functions. Similarly, the result creating part of B's method must refine what the corresponding part of A's method would have done to a concrete value when turned into a abstract value using retrieve.

Note that if refine and retrieve were true relations, and not functions then all the same properties would still be true. The only difference would be that the properties would be expressed differently, for example using relational imaging or a relational composition instead of functional composition. We have not restricted ourselves to functions to simplify the basic problem, but merely to simplify the notation used to represent it.

3.2. Refinement between exports and bodies

This defines a general notion of refinement between objects. In the particular case of a refinement between an export and body specification in the style of the last section, things are slightly different. It is still necessary to prove this basic relation, but the way this is achieved is now changed. The methods of the export are not defined explicitly, but are defined in terms of their relation to other methods. In particular there is no explicit notion of pre and post condition expressed in the export, and hence the standard notion of refinement cannot be applied directly. Instead the equations implicitly define the 'strongest pre-conditions' and 'weakest post-conditions' that the methods are allowed to have. We must hence find a different way to discharge the proof obligation.

Intuitively the way to prove that the body specification does indeed satisfy the export is to prove that the methods of the body satisfy the equations of the export, considered as a set of axioms. In fact we can show that such a set of proofs is equivalent to the general refinement relation above, and hence that such a proof is satisfactory. We will verify this semi-formally below.

Method refinement

The equations in the export essentially come in two forms, those that define equivalences between states, and those that define the results of particular methods. These two types of equation can be thought of as supplying information about the two separate aspects of each method – the ch_state and mk_result parts.

Considering first the equations defining results, and neglecting the issue of refine/retrieve functions, it can be seen that each such equation defines the result that such a method will give if invoked when the object is in a particular state (that is following a particular sequence of method invocations). Each equation thus defines a state in which the method must be applicable, (part of its pre-condition), and the result that must be given in that state (part of its post-condition). If all these equations are satisfied, then each of the body methods must be applicable in at least as many states as the export methods, and when applicable must give the same results. This corresponds exactly to the standard notion of refinement for operations described above.

Note that the results of some methods may not be defined (constrained) by the equations in the export. However, if this is the case, then the result remains undefined, and the post-condition is true. Any mk_result method would satisfy such a post-condition, and hence no proof is necessary for the results of such operations.

The ch_state part of each method is defined in two ways by the export. Both types of equation in the export are defined in terms of traces. If these traces are to be well formed, then the post-condition of each method in a trace must imply the pre-condition of the next. The construction of these traces thus defines part of the pre- and post-conditions of each of the methods, and these relationships are satisfied if we can correctly construct the same traces using the body methods. Additionally the export contains equations defining equivalences between traces (essentially defining equivalences between states). These equivalences enforce extra properties on the ch_state methods. The definition used for equivalence states that two such traces are equivalent if no subsequent method invocations can distinguish them. This essentially means that there must be a logical equivalence between any parts of the post-conditions of these methods that are assumed by the pre-conditions of other methods. (In general we might assume that all such parts are necessary, and hence say that the whole of the post-condition of the methods in that trace must be equivalent.) The equations thus describe the strongest pre-condition and weakest post-condition for the ch_state part of the methods, so that any set of methods satisfying these equations must have weak enough pre-conditions, and strong enough post-conditions, and hence be a refinement of the exported methods.

In the preceding discussion we suggest that the export implicitly defines the pre- and post-conditions for each of its methods. Solving such a set of export equations to deduce these conditions would, in practice, be extremely difficult, and in general there might be no unique solution. However, what has been shown is that any set of methods which satisfy the equations of the export must be a refinement of that export in the traditional sense. (This is unsurprising as what we have done is analogous to an algebraic specification, where any model of the algebra will serve as a refinement.)

State refinement

The result above suggests that we have carried out a refinement of an object, including data refinement, without defining the relevant refine and retrieve functions. This is of course fortunate, for the export state was never explicitly defined, and hence such relations could not be defined in terms of them! However it is useful to notice why these relations were not in fact necessary, and to consider the implications of this for the rest of the refinement.

Strictly, if refining both the data and the operations on that data, then the refinements which must be proved are of the form:†

$$\text{refine} \circ \text{method}_{\text{exp}} \circ \text{retrieve} \sqsubseteq \text{method}_{\text{body}}$$

This means that the methods of the body must in fact be refinements of these export methods nested within the data refinement relations, and must hence satisfy any properties expected of these. The properties that are defined in the export are however properties simply in terms of the exported methods themselves. In order to perform the relevant verification it is thus necessary to deduce the equivalent properties of these 'nested' methods that correspond to the original properties. In fact we will show that exactly the same properties are required.

Each property defined in the export consists mainly of sequence of methods in a trace of the form:

$$\cdots \ ; \ \text{methodA} \ ; \ \text{methodB} \ ; \ \cdots$$

Now if the data refinement is to produce an adequate concrete representation of the abstract state, then the following property must hold,[9] (where id is the identity function):

$$\text{retrieve} \circ \text{refine} = \text{id}$$

We can insert the identity function into the trace at any point (since it is essentially a sequence of compose functions), and can hence similarly insert this retrieve ∘ refine composition at arbitrary positions in the trace. Even if the functions are generalised to relations they must still compose to give the identity if the representation is to be adequate, and we can thus carry out the same modification to the trace. Using the associativity of functional composition (∘) we can rearrange the compositions to give:

$$\cdots \ ; \ \text{refine} \circ \text{methodA} \circ \text{retrieve} \ ; \ \text{refine} \circ \text{methodB} \circ \text{retrieve} \ ; \ \cdots$$

This expansion essentially replaces every method in a trace by its data refined equivalent, except for methods at the beginning and end of each trace. At the beginning of each such trace will be an abstract state (ultimately the initial state of the exported object (class), e.g. empty in the stack example). The expanded trace is thus of the form:

$$\text{refine} \circ \text{init} \ ; \ \text{refine} \circ \text{methodB} \circ \text{retrieve} \ ; \ \cdots$$

However the refined version of the initial state is just the concrete initial state of the object, and hence the abstract state has been replaced by the concrete in this expanded equation.

Each trace is used either to define its result, or to state its equivalence to other traces. In the first case the last method is being used only to evaluate its result

† This is simply a specific instance of the relations defined by the commutativity diagram for refinement.[9]

(mk_result), and its final state ignored, and hence this final state need not be refined. Such a trace can thus be represented as follows:

$$\cdots \ ; \ \text{refine} \circ \text{methodA} \circ \text{retrieve} \ ; \ \text{mk\_result} \circ \text{retrieve}$$

This last term (mk_result ∘ retrieve) is, as was seen earlier, the data refined version of the result operation, and hence again an abstract operation has been replaced by its data refined counterpart.

A general equivalence between traces takes the following form:

$$\cdots \ ; \ \text{methodA} \circ \text{retrieve} \equiv \ \cdots \ ; \ \text{methodB} \circ \text{retrieve}$$

The methods at the end of the traces have not been replaced by their data refined counterparts. However equivalence is formally defined in terms of the results returned by the application of more methods, and hence each such method would allow the insertion of the retrieve ∘ refine identity again replacing the two methods by their data refined counterparts. (In general proof of equivalence in this way is often avoided – if two states are identical we know that methods cannot distinguish them, and they must be equivalent. We thus instead try to show:

$$\cdots \ ; \ \text{methodA} \circ \text{retrieve} = \ \cdots \ ; \ \text{methodB} \circ \text{retrieve}$$

As the refine mapping is a function it can safely be applied to both sides of the equation without altering the equality, performing the necessary change to the final methods in the traces. Hence we deduce that identity at the concrete level is a valid test for equivalence.)

These manipulations have enabled us to see that the way we use the methods means that the properties of the abstract methods are true exactly when the properties of their data refined counterparts are true, hence proving one is equivalent to proving the other. Hence we deduce that if it can be shown that the body methods satisfy the equations defined in the export, then the body specification is a genuine refinement of the export.

3.3. The refinement relation in practice

The object export specification purports to be a description of how its object's methods behave if they are composed, hiding the intervening state. The last section has shown that if actual methods (as described in the body specification) are composed and satisfy these properties, then that body is indeed a refinement of the export. We now show how to construct and discharge the proof obligations in practice. This involves us in some minor notational extensions to Z.

We have two choices here, in terms of representation in Z, either we can compose the operations together directly, as schemas, or we can first turn these schemas into true functions, and compose these. If we compose the schemas together directly, then we will have to specify each of the required properties individually based on the appropriate composed schemas, and moreover we would have to actually derive the properties required, since the export specification would not express these properties in the correct format. Alternately, if we could transform the schemas into functions, then the properties required would be expressible directly – we need merely extract then from the export specification.

Extracting functions from schemas

One of the failings of Z is that having defined a function or operation using the schema notation (with appropriate decorations) it is not possible to use this function or operation directly in other schemas – we can only access it via schema inclusion. It would be useful to have an operator within Z which allowed us to perform this conversion. In particular we would want to be able to do something like this:

```
[Input, Output]

┌─ SCHEMA_FUN ──┐
│ i? : Input
│ o! : Output
├──────
│ ...
└───────────────┘

schema_fun == fun SCHEMA_FUN
```

In this *fun* is our new operator, and *schema_fun* is a new global function, produced using the operator, of type Input ⟶ Output. We cannot in fact define the general operator fun in Z, although we can define specific instances of it relevant to any particular schema. In general we would want it to take the following form:

```
┌═ [S] ═══════════════════════════════════
│ fun S ==
│     λx1?, x2?, xm? : Input •
│         μy1!, y2!, yn! : Output | θS ∈ S • (y1!, y2!, yn!)
│
```

where x1?,..,xm? is the characteristic tuple of input variables of S, and y1!,..,yn! its output variables. Evaluating fun S we thus obtain a function from a set of input variables x to a unique set of output variables y, such that this binding of the variables satisfies the predicate of the schema S. Although we cannot define fun in Z, we can produce the particular functions we require given the schemas that describe them. Additionally it would be possible to define a relatively simple extension to Z which would allow the description of the correct semantics for fun. Such extensions are currently under development.

Similarly we would want to have an operator which allows us to extract a functional representation of a schema operation, that is to do the following:

```
[State]
```

```
SCHEMA_OP
i? : Input
o! : Output
s, s' : State
```

schema_op == op SCHEMA_OP

Defining schema_op to be a new global function of the appropriate type. What type to choose here is a difficult question, and might depend on the circumstances, although it must of course include the types of i?, o!, s and s', if it is to capture all of the information in the schema. The solution we have adopted is to use the type:

$$\text{Input} \longrightarrow \text{State} \longrightarrow (\text{Output} \times \text{State})$$

This separates the input and output so that (in principle) they need not be supplied together, and also gives them the same type as the methods defined earlier. Again we cannot define this operator directly in Z, although in general it would take the following form:

```
[S]
op S ==
    λx1?, x2?, xm? : Input •
        λs1, s2, sp : State •
            μy1!, y2!, ym! : Output; s1', s2', sp' : State |
             θS ∈ S • ((y1!, y2!, ym!), (s1', s2', sp'))
```

Given a set of inputs x, and an initial state s, we return a unique set of outputs y, and final state s' so that the predicate of the schema S is satisfied. Similarly, although we cannot define op in Z, we can define the particular functional representations of thee schemas that we require.

We can now use this notation to represent each of the body methods of an object as a new function. For example for the stack example we have:

pop == op POP
push == op PUSH

etc.

These are a set of global functions that represent the same operations as those described by the schemas representing the body of the object. We will now want to prove that these functions satisfy the properties defined for them in the object export specification. This export specification describes the operations that the object will perform, and also the set of properties that these methods must obey. In particular, as a schema, we can interpret this export specification as a set, the set of all possible instances of the methods, such that the relevant properties hold. We will thus want to prove that a particular instantiation of these methods (as described by the object body) is a member of this set. In particular we will want to combine the particular set of functions into a single entity, and show that it is in the relevant set. The global functions created above are the particular instances of the methods that we want to combine and verify. The θ operator in Z when applied to a schema forms a binding (essentially an entity of a schema type) using the current values defined for the identifiers in that schema. Continuing the stack example, θSTACK will form a binding using the global functions created above, and will hence create a structure combining these separate methods. We will thus want to prove:

$$\vdash \theta STACK \in STACK$$

This represents the property that the current implementation of operations defined in the STACK export schema is a member of the set of possible implementations of those operations, that is that the operations satisfy the export specification. This simple statement thus captures a complex set of proof obligations which must be discharged in order to prove that the correct relationship holds between the objects export and body specifications.

3.4. Discharging the proof obligations

The last section derived a very simple expression of the property which must hold if the appropriate refinement relation is to hold between the body and export specifications. We can now consider how (part of) such a proof obligation might be discharged. We will consider the proof of the refinement of the stack:

$$\vdash \theta STACK \in STACK$$

In order to verify this refinement it is necessary to prove that each of the properties expressed in the schema STACK hold over the functions pop, push and so on, bound by the θSTACK. We will consider the proof of the two properties defining the normal operation of the pop method. The first part that needs proving is that the pop operation yields the correct result. We extract the appropriate property directly from the STACK export schema, in the context of the appropriate quantification. We take the property direct from that schema, but will prove that it is satisfied by the body functions, for they are the functions bound by the θ term.

$$\forall i : Object_{[State,Elem]}; e : Elem \bullet i ; push\ e ; pop \rightarrow e$$

Using the definition of the viewing operator ($\rightarrow$) as an application of the first function we can replace this by the following, (neglecting the quantification from now on):

$$first(i ; push\ e ; pop) = e$$

Sequencing is defined to be the application of the method on the right of the operator to the state part of the object on the left. Unfolding the highest priority application of the sequencing operator (the last one) we obtain:

$$\text{first(pop(state(i ; push e)))} = e$$

Doing the same for the other application of the seqnecing operator ' ; ' yields the following:

$$\text{first(pop(state(push e(state i))))} = e$$

We can now expand the definition of push, given by the definition op PUSH. The expression op PUSH is equivalent to the lambda function:

$$\lambda \text{elem?} \bullet \lambda \text{stack} \bullet \mu \text{res!,stack}' \bullet \theta \text{PUSH} \in \text{PUSH}$$

Hence expanding push and applying the lambda function to the arguments we obtain the following:

$$\text{first(pop(state(}\mu\text{res!,stack}' \mid \theta\text{PUSH} \in \text{PUSH)))} = e$$

The θ binding can now be expanded to show the values that will be bound, and which must hence satisfy the properties of the PUSH schema (using a hopefully obvious notation to indicate the relationship between the values in the binding and the values in the enclosing scope):

$$\begin{array}{l} \text{first(pop(state(}\mu\text{res!,stack}' \mid \\ \langle\!| \text{elem?} \rightarrow e ; \text{stack} \rightarrow \text{state i} ; \text{stack}' \rightarrow \text{stack}' ; \text{res!} \rightarrow \text{res!} |\!\rangle \in \text{PUSH)))} = e \end{array}$$

Substituting the values in this binding into the predicates of the PUSH schema, we can obtain the exact properties that must hold for the membership test to be successful:

$$\text{first(pop(state(}\mu\text{res!,stack}' \mid \text{stack}' = \langle e \rangle \frown \text{state i} \wedge \text{res!} = \text{ok)))} = e$$

This equation can be solved simply (essentially by unification) to give values to the unknown variables res! and stack':

$$\text{first(pop(state(ok,}\langle e \rangle \frown \text{state i)))} = e$$

The state operation throws away the result part of an object, and hence gives the following:

$$\text{first(pop(}\langle e \rangle \frown \text{state i))} = e$$

The definition of pop can now be expanded in the same way as push above, to yield the following binding and membership test in order to satisfy the operation:

$$\begin{array}{l} \text{first(}\mu\text{res!,stack}' \mid \\ \qquad \langle\!| \text{stack} \rightarrow \langle e \rangle \frown \text{state i} ; \text{stack}' \rightarrow \text{stack}' ; \text{res!} \rightarrow \text{res!} |\!\rangle \in \text{POP)} = e \end{array}$$

The values in the binding can now be substituted into the definition of the POP operation in order to obtain:

$$\begin{array}{l} \text{first(}\mu\text{res!,stack}' \mid \exists \text{ error : Elem} \bullet \\ \qquad (\text{length(}\langle e \rangle \frown \text{state i)} = 0 \Rightarrow \text{res!} = \text{error} \wedge \text{stack}' = \langle e \rangle \frown \text{state i)} \vee \\ \qquad (\langle e \rangle \frown \text{state i} = \langle \text{res!} \rangle \frown \text{stack}') = e \end{array}$$

By definition the length of a sequence containing an element is not zero, and hence we can select the second clause of the definition, and simplify the expression:

$$\text{first}(\mu \text{res!}, \text{stack}' \mid (\langle e \rangle \frown \text{state } i = \langle \text{res!} \rangle \frown \text{stack}') = e$$

Solving the equality, again by unifying the unknown variables, simplifies the expression further to just:

$$\text{first}(e, \text{state } i) = e$$

Applying the first operation to the object created simply returns the result part:

$$e = e$$

This final equation is trivially solved to yield true, and hence discharge this obligation.

□

A similar obligation must be discharged to show that the state returned from this operation is also correct. The property, as expressed in the STACK export is as follows:

$$\forall i : \text{Object}_{[\text{State},\text{Elem}]}; e : \text{Elem} \bullet i \,;\, \text{push}e \,;\, \text{pop} \equiv i$$

Using information from the proof above we can substitute the entire left hand side of the equivalence for it is the same trace as was evaluated before. We thus simplify the equivalence to:

$$(e, \text{state } i) \equiv i$$

Applying the definition of the equivalence operator ($\equiv$) we deduce that the following set of proofs must be discharged, considering the invocation of possible subsequent methods:

$$\forall m : \text{Method}_{[\text{Res},\text{State}]} \bullet \text{view}((e, \text{state } i) \,;\, m) = \text{view}(i \,;\, m)$$

Using the definition of the sequencing operator (;) this equation can be simplied to the following:

$$\text{view}(m(\text{state}(e, \text{state } i))) = \text{view}(m(\text{state } i))$$

The definition of state (equivalent to the second operator on pairs) simplifies this further, to just:

$$\text{view}(m(\text{state } i))) = \text{view}(m(\text{state } i))$$

The two states that the subsequent methods must be applied to are now identical, and as was noted earlier, this is one way to prove the required equivalence. Hence the states are equivalent, and the obligation is discharged.

□

We have now discharged two of the ten obligations which must be proved to verify the refinement relation between the STACK export and body. The other obligations can be proved in a similar way. Hopefully this should have illustrated the practicality of performing such proofs, the steps being essentially the same in each case. The only potentially difficult part is solving the sets of equations necessary to show the correct application of each method. (These were solved by relatively simple unification in the example above.) The nature of the proofs suggests that it would be relatively easy to extract these important obligations directly from the definitions, because the rest of the proof can be followed through fairly mechanically.

We have now seen how the basic refinement relation between the export and body can be expressed in a relatively straightforward way, and have seen how the proof obligations involved in such refinement relations can be discharged. The subsequent sections will look more briefly at extensions to this basic relationship necessary to deal with more complicated use and composition of these objects.

4. The *use* relation

The previous section described the basic refinement relation which must hold between the export and body specifications of an object. The aim of producing the separate object specifications was that they might later be composed together to form larger specifications. The simplest form of composition, and the only one that will be addressed in detail in this paper, is the 'use' relation, whereby one object uses another. Essentially the object body of one object contains calls to the methods of the second object.

Writing a body specification which includes the use of a subsidiary object is not very different to writing any other body specifications – a very simple example, SWAP, was seen earlier. The methods of the subsidiary object are simply used to help express the post-condition of the method which uses it. The export of the *using* object makes no reference to such subsidiary objects.†

The change caused by this extension comes when we try to prove the refinement relation between the export and body specifications. The body is no longer defined just in terms of simple functions and data, but using subsidiary objects. Hence when the obligation is to be discharged it is necessary to utilise information about that subsidiary object – in particular its export. The basic refinement relation is hence extended to the following:

$$\text{export}_{\text{used}} \vdash \text{export}_{\text{user}} \sqsubseteq \text{body}_{\text{user}}$$

The important fact to note here is that only the export of the used object is available to aid in the proof. This is the basis of the strong separation for refinement which was described earlier. Once the export of an object has been specified this provides the only description of the object visible to other objects, and forms the basis of all subsequent composition relations.

In the context of our approach, this extension does not change the nature of the basic obligation which must be discharged. This obligation can still be represented by something of the form:

† Except if the objects are used as arguments or results. This more complicated object usage is discussed in section 6.

θOBJ ∈ OBJ

The export of the used object does not get mentioned explicitly, because such objects will be declared to have the type of the export (e.g. s : STACK), and hence will already be constrained to satisfy the exported properties. A difference does occur in the way the proof is carried out. When it is necessary to solve some equations involving the use of the subsidiary object it is no longer necessary to expand the definition of the construction operators (→ , ≡ ,‘ ; ’), and the methods themselves, instead the properties in the export can be used directly. The exported methods are constrained to satisfy the properties in their export specifications, and hence we need merely match (essentially unify) a particular application against the applications in the export in order to simplify or solve the equations. We prove that the body of the used object satisfies the export once, and afterwards need never consider the definition of these methods again, but instead interpret their behaviour directly from the export.

Hopefully a simple example will clarify this. For simplicity we will not define a new object, but instead we will consider the refinement of the single SWAP method as a rather contrived object. This should illustrate the principle involved, which can equally successfully be applied to larger and more realistic examples.

The basic SWAP method is defined as follows:

[Elem]

```
┌ SWAP ─────────────────────────────────────────────
│ x?, y?, x!, y! : Elem
│ st : STACK[State, Elem]
├───────────────────────
│ ∃ ist : Resultant[Elem, State] •
│     ist ≡ st.empty; st.push x?; st.push y?; st.pop → x! ∧
│     ist; st.pop → y!
└───────────────────────────────────────────────────
```

The export of a trivial object which includes just this method can be defined as follows:

```
┌ OBJ ──────────────────────────────────
│ swap : (Elem × Elem) ⟶ (Elem × Elem)
├──────────────────
│ ∀ x, y : Elem • swap (x, y) = (y, x)
└───────────────────────────────────────
```

We can then go on to express the refinement relation as follows. Note that we use the fun operation to functionalise the schema SWAP, for it does not have any state.

$$swap == fun\ SWAP$$

$$\vdash \theta OBJ \in OBJ$$

The proof obligation can then be discharged relatively simply. The only equation we need to discharge is the following, which we have extracted from schema OBJ:

$$\forall x,y : Elem \bullet swap(x,y) = (y,x)$$

We must prove that property is true for the definition of swap bound by the θ term. This definition is fun SWAP which expands to the lambda function:

$$\lambda x?,y? \bullet \mu x!,y! \bullet \theta SWAP \in SWAP$$

Expanding the definition of swap in the proof, and applying the lambda function to the arguments (x,y) we get:

$$(\mu x!,y! : Elem \mid \theta SWAP \in SWAP) = (y,x)$$

Instantiating the theta binding with the values bound in the current scope, and substituting them into the definition of the schema SWAP we obtain the following equation:

$$(\mu x!,y! : Elem \mid \exists\, ist \bullet ist \equiv s.create ; s.push\ x ; s.push\ y ; s.pop \rightarrow x!$$
$$ist ; s.pop \rightarrow y!) = (y,x)$$

Separating the use of the two relations, ≡ and → in the predicate we obtain:

$$(\mu x!,y! : Elem \mid \exists\, ist \bullet ist \equiv s.create ; s.push\ x ; s.push\ y ; s.pop \wedge$$
$$s.create ; s.push\ x ; s.push\ y ; s.pop \rightarrow x! \wedge$$
$$ist ; s.pop \rightarrow y!) = (y,x)$$

The first line directly matches an equivalence from the export, and can be simplified accordingly. If the variable x! is unified with the value y then the second line also matches a property from the export. We thus simplify the whole second line to the simple equality x! = y – the two expressions are logically equivalent.

$$(\mu x!,y! : Elem \mid \exists\, ist \bullet ist \equiv s.create ; s.push\ x \wedge$$
$$x! = y \wedge$$
$$ist ; s.pop \rightarrow y!) = (y,x)$$

The new value of ist can be substituted into the last line in order to help simplify it. (We can then ignore the first line, since ist is no longer used elsewhere.)

$$(\mu x!,y! : Elem \mid x! = y \wedge$$
$$s.create ; s.push\ x ; s.pop \rightarrow y!) = (y,x)$$

We can then simplify this last line by unifying the variable y! with x, and matching the trace with one from the export, thus again leaving only the equality expressing the unification:

$$(\mu x!,y! : Elem \mid x! = y \wedge$$
$$y! = x) = (y,x)$$

This finally allows us to evaluate the result of the μ expression and obtain a simple equality which can be trivially discharged.

$$(y,x) = (y,x)$$

□

This section has shown how the basic refinement relation described earlier can be extended to deal with object use. In particular in discharging such proofs we can utilise the exports of subsidiary objects, and hence achieve the aim of enforcing a logical separation between (the specifications of) different objects, and simplifying subsequent proofs about those objects. The next section will take this separation a step further.

5. Object views and substitution

The previous section described a technique for allowing objects, once defined, to be used within other objects, and went on to show how the export specification of such an object could be used to verify that the method invocations achieved the desired result. However this approach to object use is fairly rigid – we must define the export of an object before we can use it;[†] and having chosen to use a particular object cannot instead use any other object.

The object oriented paradigm is often associated with a notion of inheritance. This allows new objects to be defined as extensions of previous objects, inheriting their behaviour. In particular the new object can still be used anywhere that the old object could, in addition to having new uses of its own. Formally we can substitute the new object in place of the old. In fact this substitution is the more general notion, inheritance is just one mechanism which facilitates the policy of allowing substitution. If we have a mechanism for extending objects (i.e. defining some new object including part of the behaviour of an existing object), and a notion of substitution, then we can represent the standard notion of inheritance, but can also do more. In particular we can carry out substitution (when appropriate) without defining the new object in terms of the old, and can also carry out extensions to existing objects that do not satisfy the substitution relation. In our approach we will thus consider primarily this notion of substitution although, as we will see below, inheritance can be carried out within the framework, and will typically make the proof of substitutability simpler.

5.1. Views

We define first the notion of a *view*. A view will describe the behaviour that an object wants to use independent of any object that might ultimately provide that behaviour. It will typically be written in such a way as to define just the behaviour required by the user, and in such a way as to make its own refinement (that the user's body satisfies its export) easy. Structurally such a view will look like an object export specification, describing a set of methods and some properties of those methods. However such a specification is not an export, for it is not (and will

† This is significant when considering top down design as a way of handling the complexity of large systems. Unless we can defer definition of lower level (used) objects we cannot support a top-down approach.

never be) associated with a particular object which supplies that behaviour. The refinement of the using object will thus now take the form:

$$\text{view} \vdash \text{export} \sqsubseteq \text{body}$$

Later, of course it will necessary to prove that there is some object(s) capable of satisfying this view, and to substitute them into the using object.

Using a view in this way has several particular advantages. Firstly, the behaviour required can be expressed directly and in the manner most appropriate, without any reference to how this behaviour will be provided. Secondly, the view need not correspond exactly to the object that will eventually provide the behaviour – the view may hide information from the viewer. In a simple case this may just give a restricted view of the object which hides some of the methods available; thus the approach can be used to represent access control limitations, for example the connections between ports and windows recommended by MASCOT3. More generally it might hide some complex internal structure, for example a distributed network of interconnected objects; thus the method facilitates specification of distributed systems without requiring knowledge about distribution when describing particular objects. Finally of course the view might not always be an interface to the same object, different objects can be substituted at different times, as long as they satisfy the view; thus the mechanism facilitates specification of systems which can be reconfigured dynamically.

5.2. Substitution

As was hinted above we must at some stage provide some real behaviour to instantiate the view, and must prove that this behaviour satisfies the view. Substitution in object oriented languages usually involves showing that the correct methods are available, and in the case of strongly typed languages that these methods have the right type. In the case of substitution based on inheritance these properties follow automatically (providing the changes are purely extensions), and hence no checking need be carried out. In a formal specification we must show not only that the types of the methods are the same, but also that the behaviour they provide is the same, or substitution cannot safely be carried out. We must show that the export of the substituted object satisfies the view, or more particularly that it refines the view:

$$\text{view} \sqsubseteq \text{export}$$

Often it will be simplest to implement an object that provides exactly the behaviour described by the view,† and we will have the equality:

$$\text{view} = \text{export}$$

and hence the refinement is trivially proved. More generally, however, there will not be an equality, and the export will be a genuine refinement of the view. Assuming for the moment that the export supplies exactly the methods required by the view, then we need merely prove that any such set of methods which satisfy the

† This doesn't render the approach nugatory – it still assists us in top-down design.

export also satisfy the view. Recalling that the export and view in fact represent the sets of possible objects satisfying their behaviour (this is just the semantics of schemas), we require the export to be a subset of the view.

$$\text{export} \subseteq \text{view}$$

More generally the specification will not describe the same methods, and such a predicate would be type incorrect. However we can say:

$$\forall x \in \text{export} \bullet f(x) \in \text{view}$$

For some function f which extracts the appropriate part of the object to give that required in the view. Generally this function f will simply throw away the unnecessary methods, and we can represent the whole predicate as follows, because the θ term has the same effect of discarding the methods not in the view.

$$\forall \text{export} \bullet \theta\text{view} \in \text{view}$$

For any set of methods which satisfy the export, those visible to the view must satisfy the predicates defined in the view. This expresses the general property that must be proved to show that a substitution is valid. The discharge of such obligations is similar in nature to the proof of use in the last section (essentially matching traces in the view against those of the export), and we do not consider an example here.

Having established that a substitution is valid we will then need to perform the substitution, essentially putting something of the export type where something of the view type is expected. In objected oriented languages this transformation is typically unnecessary, the type rules being sufficiently powerful to allow the substitution directly. In Z such entities are in fact type incompatible, and we must define the function f above explicitly.

$$f = \lambda e : \text{export} \bullet \mu\text{export} \mid \theta\text{export}{=}e \bullet \theta\text{view}$$

In general f may be more complex requiring method renaming or method composition so that the substituted object satisfies the view. We do not consider such possibilities further here.

5.3. Inheritance

As we noted earlier substitution in views provides a more general mechanism than that of inheritance. However there is an obvious notation for inheritance in our approach and it seems worth commenting briefly on this, and its relation to the substitution above. If when defining the export of an object we include the (schema defining the) export of another object, then we introduce all the methods of that object, along with the properties defined for them – essentially we inherit the behaviour of that object.

```
┌─ EXT_STACK [State, Elem] ─────────────────────────────
│ STACK[State, Elem]
│ size : Method[ℕ, State]
├──────────────────
│ ∀ i : Resultant[Elem, State]; x : Elem •
│     i ; push x ; size → 1 + view (i ; size) ∧ empty ; size → 0 ∧
│     i ≡ i ; size
└───────────────────────────────────────────────────────
```

If we wish to use this extended object in place of the simpler one, then we must prove the substitution relation discussed above. It is only if this property is proved that the extension corresponds to inheritance in the standard sense. However it is worth noting that this 'standard' view of inheritance is not necessarily appropriate for specifications, for it would always allow the substitution to take place, even if the new object did not satisfy the specification of the old.

$$\vdash \forall\, EXT\_STACK \bullet \theta STACK \in STACK$$

This will typically be trivial unless new predicates have been introduced which weaken or contradict the original ones. (This will become manifest as some of the initial traces will no longer be valid.)

Additionally we will need to define the body of the new object. In order to do this it is necessary to do three things. Firstly we must define the state of the new object. This will in general be an extension to the old state.

```
┌─ New_State ──────
│ Old_State
│ new_value : Type
└──────────────────
```

Secondly we must extend the old methods to operate on the new state. In fact this can be achieved without modifying those definitions, but by giving a new definition of the ΔOld_State schema which they all use.

```
┌─ ΔOld_State ──────
│ ΔNew_State
├──────────
│ new_value' = new_value
└───────────────────
```

Finally, of course, we need to define the bodies of the new methods themselves. Having defined the body of the new operation we must verify that this body satisfies the extended export. Clearly we have to discharge any obligations involving the new methods, however it is also necessary to ensure that the new methods do not affect the validity of the previous predicates. This will usually only happen if either the new predicates weaken or contradict the old, or if one of the new methods can distinguish values of the old state which the original methods could not (thereby invalidating a supposed equivalence).

This section has described how the notion of 'object use' can be extended by introducing an extra specification called a *view* as an 'insulation' between an object and the objects it uses. This mechanism does not cost anything if it is not needed, for the view and export which satisfies it can be the same but, more generally we can allow these to differ to give more flexibility in the way objects can be composed. Additionally we saw how such substitutions can be verified within our approach, and how the same basic notion of substitution could be used to allow inheritance in the standard object oriented fashion.

6. Extensions to the basic approach

The previous sections have, out of necessity, given only an introduction to the basic approach we advocate. The approach has been extended and modified beyond what has been discussed so far, and it is these extensions and modifications which will be discussed briefly in this section.

6.1. System specifications

The previous two sections discussed notions of object use. However they considered only a simple tree-like structure of object use in which each object may use a number of objects lower than it in the tree. This is often not sufficient to represent real systems, which may have more complex structure, for instance allowing shared object use, and to allow dynamic changing of the structure, for instance by passing around 'first class' objects.

Allowing object sharing makes the problem of proof about object usage much more complex. In particular, the advantages provided by encapsulation are not so clear cut, and the relationships between the objects more complex. In the earlier discussion it was always implicitly assumed that the object user would have full knowledge of the trace of objects that it used, and hence given any subsequent method invocation it was possible to determine the result of that method, and hence prove properties about the objects. If the object is shared this is no longer true, for other users may invoke methods on the object, and hence change its state and subsequent behaviour. The relationship between the objects thus becomes more complex, and we must make explicit information that was previously implicit.

When proving properties about the use of an object, we typically make use of two sorts of information – information about how the methods interact with each other, the export, and secondly information about the current state of the object, its trace so far. We can weaken either the export or the trace to represent different kinds of system containing shared objects.

Weakening just the state information implies that when a method is invoked it will not know the initial state of any objects it uses as they may have changed since that object last used them. However the using object can rely on the export of any used objects to determine their subsequent behaviour, in other words the using object can rely on the properties of the traces of the used objects, but will not know all the history of these objects, their full trace. This means that objects are shared, but methods that use them are executed without interference from other users. This can be thought of as a form of ***sequential*** sharing, and is what we would expect if the system utilised shared objects, but allowed at most a single thread of control in each object. This corresponds to a wide class of systems.

In general then we can no longer assume that the state of a shared object remains unchanged between method invocations. However we introduce the notion of a ***rely*** condition[10] which allows the object to assume extra properties about the objects it uses, for example that the objects do in fact remain unchanged, or that certain methods are not used. Correspondingly each object has a ***guarantee*** condition which states what this object is prepared to guarantee to other objects, for example, that it does, or does not, use certain methods at certain times (in certain states). The notion of refinement for such an object is therefore extended to include these extra properties. As before the behaviour of the ***user*** must be proved with respect to the view it has of the objects it uses.

$$\text{view}_{\text{user}} \vdash \text{export}_{\text{user}} \sqsubseteq \text{body}_{\text{user}}$$

However the view is now based on more information, because the user now relies explicitly on extra information about the objects it uses. Hence we must find an object o which satisfies the view as follows:

$$\text{export}_{\text{o}} \wedge \text{rely}_{\text{user}} \Rightarrow \text{view}_{\text{user}}$$

However this is not sufficient, for we must also prove that the rely condition of the user is consistent with the other objects that use o. In particular, introducing the notion of an access relation,† we must prove that:

$$(\forall\ \text{user}' \mid \text{access}(\text{user}',\text{o}) \bullet \text{guar}_{\text{user}'}) \Rightarrow \text{rely}_{\text{user}}$$

That is, the conjunction of all the guarantee conditions of the other users implies the rely condition of this object. This will be discussed further below.

If we additionally weaken the export then a calling object cannot assume that invoking two methods in sequence on a used object will always yield the same result. In essence this means that we admit some form of concurrency and hence two methods supposedly invoked sequentially on a used object may in fact be separated by invocations, of other methods of the same used object, by other users. In other words the using object can no longer rely on the properties of the trace defined in the export. All we can rely on from the object's export is that the result will be one of the possible results for that method – we cannot predict which of the possibilities will eventually arrive.

We can always extend the minimum export by relying on additional properties, but of course we must prove that these properties are guaranteed by the other objects. The change in the relation above is thus to 'minimise' the export in the way described:

† The notion of access can easily be formalised but we do not do so here.

$$\text{min(export}_o) \wedge \text{rely}_{user} \Rightarrow \text{view}_{user}$$

This corresponds to another wide class of systems. The third possibility, weakening just the export and not the trace does not appear to correspond to any such set of systems.

As we noted above, in order to verify the properties of such a system involving sharing it is necessary to prove that properties relied on by one user are indeed guaranteed by other object users. Unfortunately this cannot be done until the system of objects is formally defined – until this is done it cannot be known whether objects will be introduced which violate these conditions. Our approach has hence been extended to allow such rely and guarantee conditions to be expressed, and to include a notion of system specification in which framework the proof obligations relating rely and guarantee conditions can be discharged. Such a framework also allows an overall behaviour to be described for such a system based on the set of objects which comprise it. This extension will be described elsewhere.

6.2. Explicit abstract states

An object is often portrayed as a set of methods which provide an interface to a hidden state. The object does indeed hide details of the state and its representation, but it does not completely hide the state. In particular it is possible to deduce an abstract notion of the state from the interactions that are possible with the object. This is of course exactly the notion of equivalence between object (traces) defined earlier – 'if it is impossible to distinguish between two such objects by invoking methods on them then they are in the same abstract state. The equivalence classes over traces defined by the equivalence relation hence correspond to different abstract states.

Typically an object user relies on this notion of abstract state in order to understand the behaviour of the object. In fact an obvious analogy to use is that of a finite state machine. An object starts in some initial state and, as its methods are invoked, it changes state so that after the change different methods are available, and they are liable to return different results. Some objects will consist of a complex network of many states, while others may have very few, or even just one basic state. Additionally, many objects could be viewed as finite state machines in several different ways, depending on the complexity perceived for each individual state.

As an example of a finite state machine representation of an object, consider a simple binary semaphore. This can be thought of as a two-state machine with methods to move between the two states.

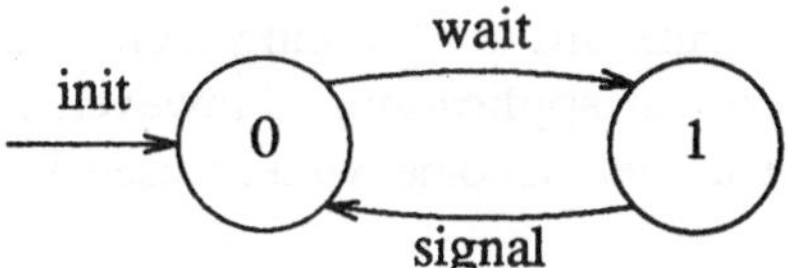

We believe it is beneficial to make this notion of abstract state explicit, and introduce it into the formal specifications. This approach has two advantages. Firstly it makes it easier for the engineer to produce and understand the specification, for the specification can be thought of directly in terms of the (abstract) state changes brought about by the methods, rather than having to consider the effect of a method on an arbitrary set of traces. Secondly this approach has a simplifying effect on the specification itself, for it now contains equations relating these simple named states, rather than complex method sequences.

However this approach makes the subsequent refinement more difficult, for we no longer have properties described in terms of the full trace, but in terms of these abstract states. In order to carry out proofs we must therefore add some additional information. Either we must explicitly define the refine and retrieve relations between the abstract and concrete states, or we must essentially define the *constructive* methods of the object, so that given an abstract state we can deduce some canonical trace to which it is equivalent. The first choice is undesirable, for the intention is still to think of the behaviour in terms of its traces and the abstract states are used merely as a convenient abbreviation for the traces they represent. The second approach thus seems more appropriate.

An extension to the basic specification technique has been defined which allows the use of such abstract states. Work is currently underway to extend the refinement notion to this new approach, and hence to compare and contrast the two approaches. If this change proves successful then it would allow objects to be developed (more) easily, by first expressing them informally using a finite state machine, and then to translate them into formal object exports for further development.

6.3. Refinement to code

The work described so far represents an approach to structuring specifications, hopefully so as to simplify their further development. We have shown how a system can be divided into separate objects, and how the appropriate relationships between these derived and proven. However it is still necessary to refine the individual objects into code. Such separate objects should be amenable to refinement using the standard refinement techniques, and without regard for other objects in the system.

For example Morgan[3] describes an approach to the refinement of modules. We believe that our 'body' specifications could be translated into Morgan's module specifications relatively simply, and hence his refinement calculus would provide a suitable approach for the refinement to code.

7. Conclusions

Formal techniques of specification and refinement are becoming increasingly important as the value of formalism is becoming more widely appreciated, particularly in so-called safety critical applications. However, for a number of reasons, such techniques have not as yet become widely used in industrial practice. We believe that the main technical problem limiting the use of the techniques is simply their inability to scale easily to realistic sized systems, and it is this problem which we set out to address.

We isolated lack of structure in specifications as one of the limiting factors in such scalability, and hence proposed an object oriented structuring notion for Z. We derived an approach to specification based on the notion of giving each object a separate export and body specification, and then composing them based on their export specifications. We extended these ideas by introducing rely and guarantee conditions for objects in order to be able to describe the properties of shared objects, and described the relationships which must hold between these. For each of the relationships we introduced, both between body and export, and in the composition of objects, we have given the formal (refinement) relation which must hold and shown how the relevant proof obligations can be derived and discharged. Given such a structure, objects can then be refined independently into code, and we believe it is possible to do this using existing approaches. It is worth noting here that the approach would seem to be applicable outside the realm of standard object oriented design and programming, for the specifications produced are amenable to standard refinement into other languages, for example Ada packages and tasks.

Work on the technique is still ongoing. In particular extensions have been proposed which make export specification simpler, but which complicate subsequent refinement. We are currently investigating standard ways to deal with this extra complexity, hence making the new approach more similar to the old, and hence more practical. Additionally the technique is being applied to more examples. So far the approach has only been applied to a number of relatively small examples, most of which have been produced by the authors. The largest such example is a small but real example of a 'tokenless block system', a system for ensuring that trains cannot collide while involved in single track working. The technique is also being used for the specification of a realistic example in the realm of security.

The approach to specification described here is an attempt to solve a practical problem in the application of formal methods. Technically the approach addresses a number of issues (e.g. object sharing) which are not adequately addressed by other approaches, and appears to allow the specification of a wide class of systems. In particular we have showed that the derivation and discharge of proof obligations to verify the correctness of such specifications is tractable, if not trivial. Clearly the practicality of the approach has not yet been demonstrated and this will remain the case until we have been able to try out the techniques on realistically sized examples. We do however believe that the approach will prove practical, and we will continue to apply it to more and larger examples in order to try to validate the concepts and the detail of the method.

8. Acknowledgements

This work is funded by a SERC/CASE award in conjunction with Roke Manor Research. We would also like to thank Barry Sowerbutts of Roke Manor for his comments on the work, and Ian Toyn of York for his invaluable CADiZ Z tools without which the Z in this paper would certainly not have been type correct.

9. References

1. D Neilson, "From Z to C: A Rigorous Refinement Method for Z.", D.Phil. Thesis, Programming Research Group, Oxford University (1990).
2. M C Atkins, *Implementation Techniques for Object Oriented Systems*, DPhil Thesis, University of York (1989).
3. C Morgan, *Programming from Specifications*, Prentice Hall International (1990).
4. Carrington D, Duke D, Duke R, King P, Rose G and Smith G, *Object-Z: An Object-Oriented Extension to Z*, FORTE.89 (December 1989).
5. A Hall, "Using Z as a Specification Calculus for Object Oriented Sytems", in *Proceedings of VDM-90*, Springer-Verlag (1990).
6. Schuman S A and Pitt D H, "Object Oriented Subsystem Specification", pp. 313-341 in *Program Specification and Transformation*, ed. Meertens L G L T, North Holland (1985).
7. Bartussek W and Parnas D, "Using Assertions About Traces to Write Abstract Specifications fo Software Modules", pp. 111-130 in *Software Specification Techniques*, ed. Gehani N and McGettrick A D (1985).
8. Parnas D L and Wang Y, "The Trace Assertion Method of Module Interface Specification", Technical Report 89-261, Queen's University, Ontario (1989).
9. D Neilson, "Hierarchical Refinement of A Z Specification", in *The Theory and Practice of Refinement*, ed. J A McDermid, Butterworth Scientific (1989).
10. C B Jones, "Development Methods for Computer Programs including a Notion of Interference", D.Phil. Thesis, Programming Research Group, Oxford University (1981).

The Ecology of Class Refinement

Cecily Bailes *Roger Duke*

Key Centre for Software Technology
Department of Computer Science
University of Queensland

Abstract

The behaviour of an object depends not only upon its class but also upon the environment within which it operates: the class specifies all possible behaviour; the environment determines a framework for behaviour. An object's behaviour must fall within the framework set by the environment but subject to the possibilities determined by its class. Intuitively, class refinement will lead to some kind of behavioural compatibility; hence a theory of class refinement must take account of the environment and its effect upon behaviour. In this paper we construct formal models for class and environment and unify them into a coherent theory of class refinement. This unified view incorporates existing refinement theories as special cases.

1 Introduction

Fundamental to the construction of any software system is the stepwise refinement of a high-level specification of the system's functionality into an executable program. Stepwise refinement has been extensively studied [1, 5, 15, 17, 21] (see [8] for an overview of current work) from a variety of points of view. Two aspects of refinement in particular, namely, process refinement[14, 18] and procedural refinement[17, 21] have been recognised.

Our particular concern in this paper is with the refinement of classes within object-oriented systems. At first glance, classes would seem to have nothing new to offer the study of stepwise refinement. However, none of the standard approaches to refinement is able to capture entirely the transformation of an object-oriented system specification to an implementation. At a specification level, e.g. using an object-oriented specification language such as Object-Z[7], classes often model reactive systems[2, 4, 12], and process refinement may be appropriate. At an implementation level, e.g. using object-oriented programming languages such as C++[23] or Eiffel[19], classes usually specify abstract data types, and procedural refinement may be appropriate. Neither process nor procedural refinement is completely adequate to describe the refinement of classes; the aim of this paper is to present a unified theory of class refinement within which process refinement and procedural refinement can be considered as special cases.

The key to a unified theory is to take an ecological view of objects and study not just the classes to which they belong but also the environments in which they operate. An object's class specifies the complete set of its possible behaviours, while the environment imposes behavioural constraints. Any particular object, therefore, must behave within the constraints of the environment whilst conforming with its class specification. The role of the environment in refinement has been widely recognised and discussed: Abadi and Lamport[1] and Hoare[16] consider the environment as a separate entity reacting with any given system. We have found it helpful to abstract away from this view and consider the environment as being determined by the effect it has upon objects. Existing theories usually consider the environment as fixed throughout any refinement. In our approach, however, the environment itself can also be refined as part of the refinement of the overall system.

In order to amalgamate the concepts of class and environment, we develop an abstract model of both. An environment is modelled as offering events in which an object may participate. The object may then select one of the offered events, subject to the restrictions imposed by its class. An environment offering only one compatible event at each stage corresponds to the object being directed (programmed). An environment offering several events at each stage corresponds to a reactive system.

A class together with an environment is refined by a new class together with a new environment if the behaviour of any object of the new class within the new environment is compatible (consistent) with the behaviour of an object of the original class within the original environment.

To illustrate this point, consider the two classes *Queue* and *OneQueue*. The class *Queue* has two operations *Join* and *Leave* and has no upper bound placed upon the number of items it contains. The class *OneQueue* has the same operations but contains at most one item. Consider the environment which offers both *Join* and *Leave* at each stage. Within this environment an object can choose either operation provided it is enabled (i.e. the performance of the operation is consistent with the class specification). In this environment *Queue* is refined by *OneQueue* as any behaviour of an object of *OneQueue* is a possible behaviour for an object of *Queue*. Notice that this is neither process nor procedural refinement. Now consider a second environment which offers the (single) operation *Join* and the (single) operation *Leave* alternately. The class *Queue* within the original environment is refined by the class *Queue* within this new environment. (Indeed, *Queue* within the new environment is behaviourally equivalent to *OneQueue* within the original environment.) In this case the class has remained fixed but the environment has been refined.

In Section 2 we present our most abstract model of environment and define ecological refinement. A more specific view of class and environment is developed in Section 3: classes are related to their failures model, and environments to the sets of events offered at each stage.

In Sections 4 and 5 we show how process refinement and procedural refinement respectively can be realised as special cases of ecological refinement. In Section 6, by taking a simple example we consider the refinement of systems composed of objects. Within such systems, the environment of a component object is determined by the rest of the system. Refinement of the object relative to this environment leads to a refinement of the overall system.

In Section 7 we discuss and compare our work with related work.

The meta-notation chosen for our models is the Z specification language[13, 22] based on sets and first-order predicate logic. For readers not familiar with Z we have added parenthetical comments as required.

2 An Abstract View of Class and Environment

In order to formally discuss class refinement within an environment, we need to construct abstract models for classes and environments and examine the interplay between them.

Intuitively, a class represents potential for behaviour, where individual behaviours are represented by a trace, or sequence of events. Each object is associated with a unique class and exhibits some specific behaviour, or history, consistent with the potential behaviour of its class, and the environment in which it operates.

Let *Class* denote the set of all classes, and *Event* the set of all events. At this level of abstraction these concepts are not further specified; in Section 3 we shall be more specific. We define

$$Trace == \operatorname{seq} Event$$

('==' denotes definition; 'seq' denotes the set of finite sequences—it will be sufficient for our purposes to restrict attention to environments in which behaviour is finite).

An environment can be modelled as a relation between classes and traces.

$$Environ == \{e : Class \leftrightarrow Trace \mid \operatorname{dom} e = Class\}$$

If $e \in Environ$ and $c \in Class$ then $e(c)$ will denote the non-empty set of traces corresponding to all possible behaviours for objects of class c operating within environment e. The 'non-empty' condition on $e(c)$ captures the notion that even if an object is placed within an entirely incompatible environment some behaviour (perhaps only the empty trace, $\langle\rangle$) is always possible.

If *Object* is the set of all objects then we have a function

$$class : Object \rightarrow Class$$

which associates a unique class with each object. A given object within a given environment will have a specific (complete) history.

$$hist : Object \times Environ \rightarrow Trace$$
$$\forall ob : Object;\ e : Environ \bullet hist(ob, e) \in e(class(ob))$$

Ecology is the study of how species (i.e. classes) behave within their environment. We define

$$Ecology == Class \times Environ$$

and view refinement as a relation on *Ecology*: an ecology (c_1, e_1) is refined by another ecology (c_2, e_2) (written $(c_1, e_1) \sqsubseteq (c_2, e_2)$) if the behaviour of any object of class c_2 within environment e_2 is a possible behaviour of an object of class c_1 within environment e_1. That is, ecological refinement is defined by

$$\begin{array}{|l}
\sqsubseteq : Ecology \leftrightarrow Ecology \\
\hline
\forall c_1, c_2 : Class;\ e_1, e_2 : Environ \bullet \\
\quad (c_1, e_1) \sqsubseteq (c_2, e_2) \ \Leftrightarrow\ e_1(c_1) \supseteq e_2(c_2)
\end{array}$$

Notice that the relation $\sqsubseteq$ on *Ecology* is transitive and reflexive.

In the special case when refinement takes place within the same environment, the 'refined by' relation on *Ecology* simplifies to a relation on *Class*. For any $e : Environ$ let $\underset{e}{\sqsubseteq}$ denote the relation:

$$\begin{array}{|l}
\underset{e}{\sqsubseteq} : Class \leftrightarrow Class \\
\hline
\forall c_1, c_2 : Class \bullet \\
\quad c_1 \underset{e}{\sqsubseteq} c_2 \ \Leftrightarrow\ (c_1, e) \sqsubseteq (c_2, e)
\end{array}$$

As we shall see, the most commonly studied refinement theories can be expressed using $\underset{f}{\sqsubseteq}$; however, as discussed in the introduction, in general the refinement of classes cannot be restricted to unchanging environments.

3 Specifying Class and Selecting Environment

In order to give specific illustrations of ecological refinement, we now extend our notion of class and environment to consider an external view of object behaviour. Let *Name* denote the set of (visible) names for events, and *In* and *Out* the set of all possible (visible) inputs and outputs to events.

In this model, events are characterised externally by input, output and name, and it is with respect to such external behaviour that refinement is defined. Any notion of internal state, or of internal (non-visible) operations affecting only this internal state, is important for a complete description of object behaviour, but is not needed for the examples of refinement we wish to consider. We define

$$Event == Name \times In \times Out$$

(We assume a special 'null' character in both *In* and *Out* to allow for events that have no input or no output (or both).)

To capture a concrete view of object behaviour we associate a failures model [6] with each class. We define

$$Failure == Trace \times \mathbb{P}\, Event$$

and define the relation *fail* which associates with each class a subset of *Failure*.

$$\begin{array}{|l}
fail : Class \leftrightarrow Failure \\
\hline
\forall c : Class \bullet \text{let } F == fail(c) \bullet \\
\quad (\langle\rangle, \varnothing) \in F \\
\quad \forall s, t : Trace;\ ev : Event;\ X, Y : \mathbb{P}\, Event \bullet \\
\qquad (s \frown t, \varnothing) \in F \ \Rightarrow\ (s, \varnothing) \in F \\
\qquad (s, X) \in F \wedge Y \subseteq X \ \Rightarrow\ (s, Y) \in F \\
\qquad (s, X) \in F \wedge (s \frown \langle ev \rangle, \varnothing) \notin F \ \Rightarrow \\
\qquad\qquad (s, X \cup \{ev\}) \in F
\end{array}$$

The predicate of *fail* is based on the set of axioms for the failures model given by Brookes et al[6].

To capture a particular concrete view of a possible environment we define

$$Selection == \mathrm{seq}(\mathbf{P}_1\ Event)$$

('$\mathbf{P}_1$' denotes the set of non-empty subsets).

Intuitively, *Selection* denotes the set of possible sequences of sets of events that may be offered an object. In fact, offering any particular selection determines an environment, i.e. we can be specific about the relation between classes and traces. Hence we have

$$\begin{array}{l}
offer : Selection \rightarrow Environ \\
\hline
\forall select : Selection;\ c : Class;\ t : Trace \bullet \\
\quad t \in offer(select)(c) \ \Leftrightarrow \\
\qquad (t, \varnothing) \in fail(c) \\
\qquad \#t \leqslant \#select \\
\qquad \forall i : \mathrm{dom}\, t \bullet t(i) \in select(i) \\
\qquad \#t < \#select \ \Rightarrow \ (t, select(1 + \#t)) \in fail(c)
\end{array}$$

That is, the environment determined by a particular *select* is such that given any class c, the set of potential histories of an object of c within this environment is precisely the set of traces that can be obtained from the failures model for c subject to the condition that the event selected by the object at each stage is one of those offered by the environment at that stage. (The determination of an environment in terms of the offering of events involving both input and output would seem to indicate that the environment is determining the output of events. If we wish to consider an environment which supplies inputs but cannot influence outputs, the associated selection will consist of all events with the given input and each possible output. In general, however, we are often interested in modelling systems which act angelically with an environment not necessarily willing to accept any output. An example of this is given in Section 6.)

We emphasise that not all environments can be obtained by application of the *offer* function to *Selection*. For example, environments where the set of events offered at each stage depends upon the earlier choices made by the object do not fall within this offer-selection viewpoint. Such reactive environments arise when we wish for fairness between event selection and can be defined within the abstract view of Section 2.

4 Process Refinement

A process[16, 20] may be specified by a class; from this point of view process refinement is relevant[14, 18]. Hence we follow [6] and define the relation of 'process-refined by' as

$$\begin{array}{|l}
\underset{(psr)}{\sqsubseteq} : Class \leftrightarrow Class \\
\hline
\forall c_1, c_2 : Class \bullet \\
\qquad c_1 \underset{(psr)}{\sqsubseteq} c_2 \;\Leftrightarrow\; fail(c_1) \supseteq fail(c_2)
\end{array}$$

The following theorem shows that the notion of process refinement can be expressed equivalently in terms of ecological refinement: process refinement is equivalent to ecological refinement holding in all environments specified by the selections of Section 3.

Theorem

$$\begin{array}{l}
\forall c_1, c_2 : Class \bullet c_1 \underset{(psr)}{\sqsubseteq} c_2 \Leftrightarrow \\
\qquad \forall select : Selection \bullet \textbf{let } e == offer(select) \bullet c_1 \underset{e}{\sqsubseteq} c_2
\end{array}$$

Proof
Suppose $c_1 \underset{(psr)}{\sqsubseteq} c_2$. Then $fail(c_1) \supseteq fail(c_2)$.
Suppose $select : Selection$ and $e = offer(select)$. Consider any trace $t \in e(c_2)$. Then (by definition of $offer$) $(t, \varnothing) \in fail(c_2)$; hence $(t, \varnothing) \in fail(c_1)$ and so $t \in e(c_1)$. Hence $e(c_1) \supseteq e(c_2)$ and so $c_1 \underset{e}{\sqsubseteq} c_2$.
Conversely, suppose $\forall select : Selection \bullet c_1 \underset{e}{\sqsubseteq} c_2$ where $e = offer(select)$.
Suppose $(t, X) \in fail(c_2)$. Let $select : Selection$ be such that

$$\begin{array}{l}
\#select \geqslant \#t \\
\forall i : \mathrm{dom}\, t \bullet select(i) = \{t(i)\} \\
X \neq \varnothing \;\Rightarrow\; \#select > \#t \;\wedge\; select(1 + \#t) = X
\end{array}$$

Then (by definition of $offer$) $t \in e(c_2)$ where $e = offer(select)$;
hence $t \in e(c_1)$ and so $(t, X) \in fail(c_1)$. Hence $fail(c_1) \supseteq fail(c_2)$ and so $c_1 \underset{(psr)}{\sqsubseteq} c_2$.
□

5 Procedural Refinement

A class may be used to specify an abstract data type; from this point of view procedural refinement is relevant[17, 21]. Traditionally, a class c_1 is procedural-refined by a class c_2 if given any program, the behaviour of an object of c_2 operated under this program is consistent with the possible behaviour of an object of c_1 operated under the same program. In our context we interpret 'program' to refer to an environment which offers precisely one event at each stage, and where the result is chaotic (i.e. unspecified) if that offered event is not enabled. Hence we define the relation 'procedural-refined by' as

$$\begin{array}{|l}
\underset{(plr)}{\sqsubseteq} : Class \leftrightarrow Class \\
\hline
\forall c_1, c_2 : Class \bullet c_1 \underset{(plr)}{\sqsubseteq} c_2 \Leftrightarrow \\
\quad \forall t : Trace \bullet (t, \varnothing) \in fail(c_2) \Rightarrow \\
\quad\quad (t, \varnothing) \in fail(c_1) \\
\quad\quad \vee \\
\quad\quad \exists s : Trace \bullet s \subset t \wedge (s, \{t(1 + \#s)\}) \in fail(c_1)
\end{array}$$

Notice an immediate consequence of this definition is that

$$\forall c_1, c_2 : Class \bullet c_1 \underset{(psr)}{\sqsubseteq} c_2 \Rightarrow c_1 \underset{(plr)}{\sqsubseteq} c_2.$$

In this section we shall show how this notion of procedural refinement can be expressed equivalently in terms of ecological refinement. Define

$$SimpleSelection == \operatorname{seq} Event.$$

Notice that there is a natural embedding $SimpleSelection \rightarrow Selection$ where any $s = \langle e_1, e_2, \ldots \rangle$ in *SimpleSelection* is mapped to $\langle \{e_1\}, \{e_2\} \ldots \rangle$ in *Selection*. With this embedding in mind we shall think of *SimpleSelection* as a subset of *Selection*. The relation *safe* associates with each class those selections in *SimpleSelection* which cannot lead to a deadlocked trace within the failures model.

$$\begin{array}{|l}
safe : Class \leftrightarrow SimpleSelection \\
\hline
\forall c : Class; select : SimpleSelection \bullet \\
\quad select \in safe(c) \Leftrightarrow \\
\quad\quad \forall t : offer(select)(c) \bullet \\
\quad\quad\quad \#t = \#select
\end{array}$$

Procedural refinement is equivalent to ecological refinement where the environment is restricted to safe selections.

Theorem

$$\forall c_1, c_2 : Class \bullet c_1 \underset{(plr)}{\sqsubseteq} c_2 \Leftrightarrow$$
$$\forall select : safe(c_1) \bullet \textbf{let } e == offer(select) \bullet c_1 \underset{e}{\sqsubseteq} c_2$$

Proof
Suppose $c_1 \underset{(plr)}{\sqsubseteq} c_2$.
Now suppose $select : safe(c_1)$ and $e = offer(select)$.
Consider any trace $t \in e(c_2)$; then (by definition of *offer*) $(t, \varnothing) \in fail(c_2)$ and $\#t < \#select$. By the definition of $\underset{(plr)}{\sqsubseteq}$, either

(a) $(t, \varnothing) \in fail(c_1)$, in which case $t \in e(c_1)$, or

(b) $\exists s : Trace \bullet s \subset t \ \land \ (s, \{t(1 + \#s)\}) \in fail(c_1)$.
But as $t(i) = select(i)$ for all i, this contradicts $select \in safe(c_1)$.

Hence $e(c_1) \supseteq e(c_2)$ and so $c_1 \underset{e}{\sqsubseteq} c_2$.

Conversely, suppose $\forall select : safe(c_1) \bullet c_1 \underset{e}{\sqsubseteq} c_2$ where $e = offer(select)$.
Suppose $(t, \varnothing) \in fail(c_2)$.
Define $select : safe(c_1)$ to be the unique sequence satisfying

$$\#select \leqslant \#t$$
$$\forall i : \mathrm{dom}\, select \bullet select(i) = t(i)$$
$$\#select < \#t \Rightarrow select \frown \langle t(1 + \#select)\rangle \notin safe(c_1).$$

Let $e = offer(select)$.

(a) If $\#select = \#t$ then $t \in e(c_2)$ so $t \in e(c_1)$ (by supposition).
Hence $(t, \varnothing) \in fail(c_1)$.

(b) If $\#select < \#t$, let $s : Trace$ be such that $s \subset t$ and $\#s = \#select$.
Then $s \in e(c_2)$ so $s \in e(c_1)$;
but $(s, \{t(1 + \#s)\}) \in fail(c_1)$ (by construction of $select$).

Hence the conditions ensuring $c_1 \underset{(plr)}{\sqsubseteq} c_2$ are satisfied.

□

Those classes where no trace deadlock is possible, and hence where all simple selections are safe, constitute an important subset of *Class*. Hence we define

$$DeadlockFreeClass ==$$
$$\{c : Class \mid \forall t : Trace;\ X : \mathbb{P}\, Event \bullet (t, X) \in fail(c) \Rightarrow X = \varnothing\}$$

The following theorem shows that for such classes the notions of process and procedural refinement coincide.

Theorem

$$\forall c_1, c_2 : DeadlockFreeClass \bullet c_1 \underset{(psr)}{\sqsubseteq} c_2 \ \Leftrightarrow\ c_1 \underset{(plr)}{\sqsubseteq} c_2$$

Proof
We have already observed that process refinement implies procedural refinement.
Suppose that $c_1 \underset{(plr)}{\sqsubseteq} c_2$.
The condition defining procedural refinement in the case of both classes being deadlock free becomes

$$\forall t : Trace \bullet (t, \varnothing) \in fail(c_2) \Rightarrow (t, \varnothing) \in fail(c_1).$$

But for such classes this is precisely the condition $fail(c_1) \supseteq fail(c_2)$.
Hence $c_1 \underset{(psr)}{\sqsubseteq} c_2$.

□

As a corollary of the last theorem, we get an alternative equivalence between process refinement and ecological refinement for deadlock-free classes: we need only consider refinement within environments determined by simple selection.

Corollary

$$\forall c_1, c_2 : \mathit{DeadlockFreeClass} \bullet c_1 \underset{(\mathit{par})}{\sqsubseteq} c_2 \Leftrightarrow$$
$$\forall \mathit{select} : \mathit{SimpleSelection} \bullet \mathbf{let}\ e == \mathit{offer}(\mathit{select}) \bullet c_1 \underset{e}{\sqsubseteq} c_2$$

Proof
We simply observe that for any $c : \mathit{DeadlockFreeClass}$

$$\mathit{select} \in \mathit{SimpleSelection} \quad \Leftrightarrow \quad \mathit{select} \in \mathit{safe}(c).$$

□

6 Composing Objects

An object-oriented system is often composed of a collection of communicating objects. In refining such a system we would hope that the component objects can be refined separately, so that the composition of the refined objects gives a refinement of the original system. In this section we illustrate with an example that for this hope to be realised, it is in general necessary to take into account the environment of a component object when considering refinement, i.e. ecological refinement is relevant. The environment of a component object is determined by the rest of the system.

Consider a closed system composed of two objects A and B. Object A has one operation, named α, which requires the number 3 as input and non-deterministically outputs the number 4 or 5. Object B has one operation, also named α, which requires the number 4 as input and non-deterministically outputs the number 2 or 3. Within the system, A and B are composed angelically with the output of A becoming the input of B and vice-versa. That is, the system also has one operation named α, and the external behaviour of the system is the sequence

$$\langle \alpha, \alpha, \ldots \rangle.$$

There are no inputs or outputs from the system as all message passing between A and B is internal.

In this case, the environment of object A is determined by object B, i.e. A is offered the set

$$\{(\alpha, 2, 4), (\alpha, 3, 4)\}$$

of events at each stage. The only possible behaviour of A within this environment is

$$\langle (\alpha, 3, 4), (\alpha, 3, 4) \ldots \rangle.$$

Consider now refining A by removing the non-determinism. Suppose object A' has one operation named α which requires the number 3 as input and outputs the number 4, and object A'' has one operation named α which requires the number 3 as input and outputs the number 5. Both A' and A'' are process or procedural refinements of A. However, the system with A' and B composed angelically is a refinement of the original system, but the system with A'' and B composed angelically is not. This is because A' is a refinement of A in the environment determined by B, but A'' is not.

In general, any component object within a system can be replaced by an object which is an ecological refinement of the original object (the environment being determined by the rest of the system) and it will lead to a new system which refines the original system.

7 Discussion and Conclusions

This paper developed out of work on the formal specification of object-oriented systems[7, 11]; such work is related to the modular specification of reactive systems[2, 12]. In attempting to refine such specifications into an object-oriented executable program it became clear that the role of the environment is crucial.

Abadi and Lamport[1] discuss the role of the environment and consider specifications of the form $E \Rightarrow M$ where M denotes a system's overall functionality and E specifies assumptions about the environment.

Our approach has been to define refinement in terms of externally visible behaviour and to abstract away from the notion of internal state. This approach is similar to the action systems of Milner[20] and compares to the state-based approaches[1, 14, 18, 9]. We do not consider internal events[16] or stuttering[1].

In our most abstract model, the notion of class is left unspecified and the environment is defined in terms of the effect it has upon the objects of a class. As an illustration, a semantic model for classes is developed based upon the failures model of Brookes et al[6]. If, alternatively, a class were defined in terms of methods (operations) applied to an internal state[7], the transformation to a failures model would be straightforward[10].

Our results could be expressed within the context of labelled transition systems[9]. However, it is our view that it is the changing role of the environment within object-oriented systems that makes the class the appropriate setting. Furthermore, class refinement is intimately connected with the concept of subtyping in object-oriented systems[3, 24]. Subtyping allows objects from different, but related, classes to be treated as equivalent in certain contexts (typically to allow operations to be applied polymorphically). It is our view that the methods of this paper, i.e. incorporating the environment into the class model, allow a unified view of subtyping to be achieved.

In this paper we demonstrate that process and procedural refinement can be considered as special cases within a general theory of refinement that incorporates environment. Other aspects of refinement (see De Nicola[9] for a survey) can also be incorporated within our framework. We can also extend the particular kinds of environments discussed in Section 3 to consider more specific situations. For example, an environment that cycles through the possible operations and offers an object the next one enabled can be treated within our model; such an environment may be incorporated within a system so as to ensure the fair performance of operations.

References

[1] M. Abadi and L. Lamport. Composing specifications. In J.W. de Bakker, W.-P. de Roever, and G.Rozenberg, editors, *Proc. REX Workshop on Stepwise Refinement of Distributed Systems*, volume 430 of *Lect. Notes in Comput. Sci.*, pages 1–41. Springer-Verlag, 1990.

[2] M. Abadi, L. Lamport, and P. Wolper. Realizable and unrealizable specifications of reactive systems. In G. Ausiello, M. Dezani-Ciancaglini, and S. Ronchi Della Rocca, editors, *Proc. 16th Intl. Colloquium on Automata, Languages and Programming (ICALP'89)*, volume 372 of *Lect. Notes in Comput. Sci.*, pages 1–17. Springer-Verlag, 1989.

[3] P. America. Inheritance and subtyping in a parallel object-oriented language. In J. Bézivin, J.-M. Hullot, P. Cointe, and H. Lieberman, editors, *Proc. European Conf. on Object-Oriented Programming (ECOOP'87)*, volume 276 of *Lect. Notes in Comput. Sci.*, pages 234–242. Springer-Verlag, 1987.

[4] R.J.R. Back. Refinement calculus, Part II: Parallel and reactive programs. In J.W. de Bakker, W.-P. de Roever, and G. Rozenberg, editors, *Proc. REX Workshop on Stepwise Refinement of Distributed Systems*, volume 430 of *Lect. Notes in Comput. Sci.*, pages 67–93. Springer-Verlag, 1990.

[5] R.J.R. Back and J. von Wright. Refinement calculus, Part I: Sequential nondeterministic programs. In J.W. de Bakker, W.-P. de Roever, and G. Rozenberg, editors, *Proc. REX Workshop on Stepwise Refinement of Distributed Systems*, volume 430 of *Lect. Notes in Comput. Sci.*, pages 42–66. Springer-Verlag, 1990.

[6] S.D. Brookes, C.A.R. Hoare, and A.W. Roscoe. A theory of communicating sequential processes. *J. ACM*, 31(7):560–599, 1984.

[7] D. Carrington, D. Duke, R. Duke, P. King, G. Rose, and G. Smith. Object-Z: An object-oriented extension to Z. In S. Vuong, editor, *Formal Description Techniques, II (FORTE'89)*, pages 281–296. North-Holland, 1990.

[8] J.W. de Bakker, W.-P. de Roever, and G. Rozenberg, editors. *Proc. REX Workshop on Stepwise Refinement of Distributed Systems*, volume 430 of *Lect. Notes in Comput. Sci.* Springer-Verlag, Mook, The Netherlands, 1990.

[9] R. De Nicola. Extensional equivalences for transition systems. *Acta Informatica*, 24:211–237, 1987.

[10] D. Duke and R. Duke. Towards a semantics for Object-Z. In D. Bjørner, C.A.R. Hoare, and H. Langmaack, editors, *VDM'90: VDM and Z!*, volume 428 of *Lect. Notes in Comput. Sci.*, pages 242–262. Springer-Verlag, 1990.

[11] R. Duke, G. Rose, and A. Lee. Object-oriented protocol specification. In L. Logrippo, R.L. Probert, and H. Ural, editors, *Protocol Specification, Testing, and Verification, X*, pages 325–338. North-Holland, 1990.

[12] D. Harel and A. Pnueli. On the development of reactive systems. In K. Apt, editor, *Proc. NATO Advanced Course on Logics and Models of Concurrent Systems*, pages 477–499. Springer-Verlag, 1985.

[13] I. Hayes, editor. *Specification Case Studies.* International Series in Computer Science. Prentice-Hall, 1987.

[14] J. He. Process simulation and refinement. *Formal Aspects of Computing*, 1:229–241, 1989.

[15] J. He, C.A.R. Hoare, and J. Sanders. Data refinement refined. In B. Robinet and R. Wilhelm, editors, *European Symp. on Programming (ESOP'86)*, volume 213 of *Lect. Notes in Comput. Sci.*, pages 187–196, 1986.

[16] C.A.R. Hoare. *Communicating Sequential Processes.* International Series in Computer Science. Prentice-Hall, 1985.

[17] C. Jones. *Systematic Software Development Using VDM.* International Series in Computer Science. Prentice-Hall, 1986.

[18] M. Josephs. A state-based approach to communicating processes. *Distributed Computing*, 3:9–18, 1988.

[19] B. Meyer. *Object-Oriented Software Construction.* International Series in Computer Science. Prentice-Hall, 1988.

[20] R. Milner. *A Calculus of Communicating Systems*, volume 92 of *Lect. Notes in Comput. Sci.* Springer-Verlag, 1980.

[21] C. Morgan. *Programming from Specifications.* International Series in Computer Science. Prentice-Hall, 1990.

[22] J.M. Spivey. *The Z Notation: A Reference Manual.* International Series in Computer Science. Prentice-Hall, UK, 1989.

[23] B. Stroustrup. *The C++ Programming Language.* Addison-Wesley, 1986.

[24] P. Wegner. The object-oriented classification paradigm. In B. Shriver and P. Wegner, editors, *Research Directions in Object-Oriented Programming*, pages 479–560. MIT Press, 1987.

Transforming axioms for data types into sequential programs

Robert Milne*

Cambridge University Computer Laboratory
New Museums Site, Pembroke Street
Cambridge, CB2 3QG
United Kingdom

Abstract

A process is proposed for refining specifications of abstract data types into efficient sequential implementations. The process needs little manual intervention. It is split into three stages, not all of which need always be carried out. The three stages entail interpreting equalities as behavioural equivalences, converting functions into procedures, and replacing axioms by programs. The stages can be performed as automatic transformations which are certain to produce results that meet the specifications, provided that simple conditions hold. These conditions describe the adequacy of the specifications, the freedom from interference between the procedures, and the mode of construction of the procedures. Sufficient versions of these conditions can be checked automatically. Varying the conditions could produce implementations for different classes of specification. Though the transformations could be automated, the intermediate results, in styles of specification which cover both functions and procedures, have interest in their own right and may be particularly appropriate to object-oriented design.

*This work was partly supported by a Royal Society / SERC Industrial Fellowship held on leave from STC Technology Ltd, London Road, Harlow, Essex, CM17 9NA, United Kingdom.

1 Introduction

1.1 Scope

Most work on specifying data types abstractly emphasises applicative constructs, without any notion of store. Most work on implementing software emphasises imperative constructs; for instance, informal structured analysis and design methods use data stores instead of parameters, and programming methods use object classes instead of abstract data types. There are both cultural and technical reasons for this difference of emphasis: applicative constructs are regarded by their supporters as being easier to understand and to manipulate formally, whilst imperative constructs are regarded by their supporters as being easier to write and to execute efficiently. Indeed, to people accustomed to data stores and object classes, the benefits offered by applicative constructs are rarely self-evident. The work in this paper explores ways of reducing this difference between theory and practice. The ways involve providing imperative specifications of software, relating applicative and imperative specifications, and converting specifications into implementations systematically; here an 'applicative specification' is one which specifies applicative functions, whilst an 'imperative specification' is one which specifies imperative procedures.

This work contributes to the assembly of techniques for developing specifications by stages into implementations that guarantee correctness by construction. The implementations are adequately efficient for conventional computers and readily expressible in commonplace programming languages, such as C and C++. They could nonetheless be generated automatically for a very wide range of specifications. The stages of development are distinguished from one another partly so that alternative implementations may be devised if necessary and partly so that the corresponding stages of maintenance, which in practice often involve moving from implementations to specifications, may be understood more fully.

This work also assists with the validation of specifications, by identifying conditions which specifications must meet in order to be acceptable for abstract data types. These conditions could be checked automatically.

In this paper the techniques discussed allow equalities to be interpreted as equivalences of observable behaviour, applicative functions to be converted into imperative procedures, and axioms to be replaced by programs using assignable store. Each of these three techniques requires that specifications be validated against some associated conditions. These conditions ensure that the functions in applicative specifications are adequately defined (and, in particular, are sufficiently complete), that the procedures in imperative specifications do not interfere with one another, and that the functions or procedures are constructed in certain ways. The first and second of these conditions could reasonably be imposed on specifications of all abstract data types. The third is specific to a particular technique for replacing axioms by programs and to a particular class of abstract data types; other techniques and classes are also important and should be considered.

The emphasis in the paper is on sequential implementations. Some work has been done on handling concurrent implementations in a similar manner [11], but more needs to be done to provide techniques for such implementations which satisfy enough compositionality conditions.

In order to convey the ideas, the presentation in this paper is fairly informal; the formal definitions, assumptions, and proofs should appear elsewhere.

1.2 Structure

As motivation, in §2 there is a simple application of the techniques, an argument for the correctness of the application, a discussion of the limitations of the application, and an outline of how the techniques are generalised to circumvent the limitations. The notation used by the imperative specifications is explained in §3; it is very closely related to that for the RAISE specification language. The concepts used for the applicative specifications are discussed in §4, but some of them are not used until much later in the paper. The separate stages of the general techniques are described in some detail in §5, §6 and §7; they are illustrated using modest extensions of the simple example, but the stages have been tested on several realistic abstract data types. For ease of reference, the specifications considered are collected together, in §8.

2 Motivation

2.1 Survey

The techniques considered in this paper permit applicative specifications to be transformed into imperative implementations. To demonstrate the techniques in their simplest forms the obvious example (of lists or stacks) is discussed in 2.2. An argument for the correctness of the techniques in this case is sketched in 2.3. The reasons why the simplest forms cannot be generalised immediately are given in 2.4. The appropriately general techniques are outlined in 2.5.

2.2 A simple illustration

In 8.1 there is an applicative specification of 'List' which largely takes a familiar form. The axioms in it consist of equations and an induction rule. The equations are actually *unconditional*, in that they hold irrespective of any pre-conditions; in other specifications the equations may need to be *conditional*. The induction rule quantifies over predicates, which are treated as functions having result type **Bool** (as is usual in systems based on higher order logic). (Many languages provide short ways of writing induction rules, but in this paper the long way exhibited in 8.1 is adopted, in order to expose the concepts more clearly.) In the specification in 8.1 (and in every other specification in this paper) 'Element' is taken to be a type which is given in advance; it might be **Bool** or **Int**, for instance. The general forms of types and specifications are analysed in 4.1 and 4.3.

An intuitive conversion of this applicative specification into an imperative specification is given in 8.2, using notation which is explained in 3.1, 3.2, 3.3 and 3.4. (Again the notation is not shortened, in order to expose the concepts.) Among the axioms are ones asserting that 'empty ( )' and 'add (e)' are always 'deterministically convergent' in the sense discussed in 3.4. The presence of these particular axioms is justified informally because the types of 'empty' and 'add' convey less information in 8.2 than in 8.1 and formally because such axioms are needed for the argument in 2.3.

Before the imperative procedures can be compared directly with the applicative functions their names must be changed to avoid clashes. A specification which changes the names is provided by 8.3. It has the same properties as the specification in 8.2, except that it uses the names 'empty_', 'add_', 'head_', 'tail_' and 'is_empty_' instead of 'empty', 'add', 'head', 'tail' and 'is_empty'.

The imperative specification in 8.2 does not mention the type 'List' and is not immediately susceptible to being proved correct using abstraction functions [7] or simulation relations [13]. To establish that it is correct, versions of 'List' and the applicative functions acting on lists are defined in terms of the imperative procedures by extending the specification in 8.3 without giving the procedures new properties. The relevant definitions are given in 8.4. These definitions are examined at some length in 2.3, which sketches an argument that they have the properties laid down in 8.1. This argument relies heavily on the notation explained in 3.1, 3.2, 3.3 and 3.4. It demonstrates that the specification in 8.4 is a 'refinement' of that in 8.1, in the sense discussed in 4.2; this particular refinement effectively uses an abstraction function which is the identity.

It is straightforward to implement the procedures specified in 8.2 by defining them fully. This is done in the specification in 8.5, on the assumption that the implementation language provides variables capable of holding finite lists. The procedures in 8.5 evidently have the properties laid down in 8.2, so they can be interpreted as in 8.4 to provide functions having the properties laid down in 8.1.

2.3 The correctness of the illustration

In 8.4 the members of 'List' are taken to be procedures; the application of one of these procedures terminates with a store which embodies the fact that 'add_' has been applied some number of times since the most recent application of 'empty_'. Consequently,

$$\lambda\ (\ )\ \bullet\ \text{empty\_}\ (\ )$$

must be such a procedure, and if 'l' is such a procedure then

$$\lambda\ (\ )\ \bullet\ \text{l}\ (\ )\ ;\ \text{add\_}\ (\ \text{e}\ )$$

(which signifies what happens when an application of 'l' is followed by one of 'add_') must also be such a procedure. However, not every member of the type

$$\textbf{Unit} \overset{\sim}{\rightarrow} \textbf{write any Unit}$$

can be a member of 'List': to be so, it must represent a sequence of applications of 'empty_' and 'add_'. There is therefore a representation invariant which restricts attention to the subtype of

$$\textbf{Unit} \overset{\sim}{\rightarrow} \textbf{write any Unit}$$

comprising members of 'List'. This representation invariant is provided by the predicate 'is_list'. It could be defined by primitive recursion; however, in practice it is more convenient to ignore 'is_list' and use instead an induction rule to describe all the possible members of 'List', as in 8.4. This induction rule is in fact that provided in 8.1, but relies on the definitions

$$\text{empty} = \lambda\ (\ )\ \bullet\ \text{empty\_}\ (\ )$$

and

$$\text{add}\ (\ \text{e}\ ,\ \text{l}\ ) = \lambda\ (\ )\ \bullet\ \text{l}\ (\ )\ ;\ \text{add\_}\ (\ \text{e}\ )$$

Here 'add' is defined to be a function which, when applied to an element and a procedure representing a list, returns a procedure representing a list. It is therefore a higher order function.

Similarly 'tail' is defined to be a function which, when applied to a procedure representing a list, returns a procedure representing a list. It satisfies

$$\text{tail}\ (\ \text{l}\ ) = \lambda\ (\ )\ \bullet\ \text{l}\ (\ )\ ;\ \text{tail\_}\ (\ )$$

When it is applied to non-empty lists, 'tail' cannot construct any lists that cannot already be constructed using 'empty' and 'add', owing to the assertion

$$\Box\ (\ \text{add\_}\ (\ \text{e}\ )\ ;\ \text{tail\_}\ (\ )\equiv (\ )\ )$$

inherited by the specification in 8.4 from the specification in 8.3 which changes the names of the procedures in 8.2. This assertion ensures that given the functions in 8.4, for every element 'e' and for every list 'l',

$$\begin{array}{l} \text{tail (add (e , l))} = \\ (\ \lambda\ (\ )\ \bullet\ \text{add (e , l) ( ) ; tail\_ ( ))} = \\ (\ \lambda\ (\ )\ \bullet\ \text{l ( ) ; add\_ (e) ( ) ; tail\_ ( ))} = \\ (\ \lambda\ (\ )\ \bullet\ \text{l ( ) ; ( ))} = \\ (\ \lambda\ (\ )\ \bullet\ \text{l ( ))} = \\ \text{l} \end{array}$$

However, 'head' is applied to lists but does not return lists. In effect it must execute a procedure representing a list and then execute 'head_' in order to extract information from the store. The information extracted should depend only on the list; in other words, it should depend only on the effect of executing, in any store, the procedure representing the list. Consequently 'head' should satisfy the assertion

$$\square\ (\ \text{head (l)} \equiv \textbf{result}\ \text{(l ( ) ; head\_ ( )))}$$

It is not immediately obvious that this assertion is appropriate, because it is not immediately apparent that

$$\textbf{result}\ \text{(l ( ) ; head\_ ( ))}$$

represents the element at the head of the list independently of the store. Indeed, if 'l' is 'empty' then nothing in the axioms of 8.2 ensures that this is so; also, if the execution of 'l ( )' did not terminate then

$$\textbf{result}\ \text{(l ( ) ; head\_ ( ))}$$

could be defined arbitrarily. However, there is no need for 'head (l)' to be useful for every 'l'; all that is necessary is that it be useful for non-empty lists. In fact induction demonstrates that 'l ( )' is always deterministically convergent for every list 'l', because the specification in 8.4 inherits the assertions

$$\square\ \textbf{definite}\ \text{empty\_ ( )}$$

and

$$\square\ \textbf{definite}\ \text{add\_ (e)}$$

from the specification in 8.3. Furthermore, as 'l ( )' is deterministically convergent, the inherited assertion

$$\square\ (\ \text{add\_ (e) ; head\_ ( )} \equiv \text{add\_ (e) ; e)}$$

for every element 'e' guarantees that

$$\begin{array}{l} \text{head (add (e , l))} \equiv \\ \textbf{result}\ \text{(add (e , l) ( ) ; head\_ ( ))} \equiv \\ \textbf{result}\ \text{(l ( ) ; add\_ (e) ; head\_ ( ))} \equiv \\ \textbf{result}\ \text{(l ( ) ; add\_ (e) ; e)} \equiv \\ \textbf{result}\ \text{e} \equiv \\ \text{e} \end{array}$$

The connection between 'is_empty' and 'is_empty_' is similar to that between 'head' and 'head_'.

2.4 The limitations of the illustration

The transformation of an applicative specification of lists into an imperative one illustrated in 2.2 appears simple. However, it cannot instantly be formalised in a way which covers types other than lists as specified in 8.1. The reason for this is that these lists are subject to various limitations and treating them offers no hints about how to deal with the following problems.

Equalities satisfied only as behavioural equivalences

The proof that

$$\text{tail} (\text{add} (\text{e} , \text{l})) = \text{l}$$

for the specification in 8.4 depends crucially on the assertion

$$\Box (\text{add\_} (\text{e}) ; \text{tail\_} ( ) \equiv ( ))$$

However, this assertion may be invalid: in an implementation an application of 'add_' may modify the store in a way which is not reversed by 'tail_' but which is irrelevant to the observable behaviour of lists. If this happens, the correctness proof outlined in 2.3 breaks down. This can happen in an implementation of lists like that in 8.12 which, by contrast with that in 8.5, does not assume that lists are available as members of a concrete data type which can be held in single variables.

Specifications containing inadequately defined functions

The proof that

$$\text{head} (\text{add} (\text{e} , \text{l})) = \text{e}$$

for the specification in 8.4 depends crucially on the fact that an application of 'head_' returns a result which is independent of the store, provided that, immediately before, a procedure representing a non-empty list is executed; as 'add_ (e)' is always deterministically convergent this fact is evidently ensured by the assertion

$$\Box (\text{add\_} (\text{e}) ; \text{head\_} ( ) \equiv \text{add\_} (\text{e}) ; \text{e})$$

If now the specification in 8.1 is extended with the declaration

$$\text{unhead} : \text{List} \xrightarrow{\sim} \text{Element}$$

and the assertion

$$\sim (\text{unhead} (\text{add} (\text{e} , \text{l})) = \text{e})$$

(with the intention, perhaps, that 'unhead' is a choice function of some kind when 'Element' contains at least two members), then the specification in 8.2 must be extended in a corresponding manner, which when inherited in turn by the specifications in 8.3 and 8.4 gives the declaration

$$\text{unhead\_} : \textbf{Unit} \xrightarrow{\sim} \textbf{read any} \ \text{Element}$$

and the assertion

$$\Box \sim (\ \text{add\_}(\ e\ )\ ;\ \text{unhead\_}(\ )\equiv \text{add\_}(\ e\ )\ ;\ e\ )$$

This assertion does not at all guarantee that an application of 'unhead_' ever returns a result which is independent of the store. The problem arises not because of the use of '$\sim$' but because in a certain sense 'unhead' is inadequately defined. Realistic examples where the problem arises are provided by name generators and hash tables (both of which allow hitherto unused names to be generated when a particular function is applied) and, in a less troublesome manner, by queues (which allow elements to be added at their feet and examined at their heads).

Assertions about more than one object

The specification in 8.2 relies on the restriction that only one list need ever be identified in any of the assertions in 8.1: none of the functions acting on lists ever acts on more than one list at once. This restriction in the specifications is quite common and is ruthlessly exploited in object-oriented programming languages, which typically declare the procedures acting on the objects in a class alongside the variables private to an object. However, sometimes the restriction is violated; for example, the specification in 8.1 might be extended with the declaration

$$\text{join} : (\ \text{List} \times \text{List}\ ) \stackrel{\sim}{\rightarrow} \text{List}$$

and with assertions which mention more than one list, such as

$$\text{join}\ (\ \text{add}\ (\ e\ ,\ l_1\ )\ ,\ l_2\ ) = \text{add}\ (\ e\ ,\ \text{join}\ (\ l_1\ ,\ l_2\ )\ )$$

When a class definition must consider more than one object in the class at once, object-oriented programming languages typically resort to a syntactic device (**self** or **this**) to indicate the instance with which the procedures are associated. This device is both ugly and irrelevant to the issue for specifications, which involves finding ways of providing imperative implementations for functions like 'join'. Other examples where the issue manifests itself are provided by trees (as a tree is usually constructed from more than one tree at once) and by equality functions which are intended to be implemented by equality procedures; this latter case is the one handled in the specification in 8.9.

Relations between constructed values

The specification in 8.1 contains an induction rule which indicates that all the members of 'List' can be constructed using 'empty' and 'add'. However, it contains no axioms relating an application of 'add' to another application of 'add' or to 'empty': the equations in it just define functions ('head', 'tail' and 'is_empty') in terms of 'empty' and 'add'. A specification concerned with sets instead of lists might contain axioms relating applications of 'constructor' functions like 'add'. The first and second of the transformation techniques discussed in this paper do deal with such axioms. The third does not do so, at least in the form presented here.

2.5 The general techniques

In order to handle the problems mentioned in 2.4, it is necessary to impose constraints on the specifications to be transformed and to introduce extra functions. The resulting process is sketched below. It is split into three stages, involving different transformation techniques, because departing from the process at some stages can allow implementations to be optimised or specifications to be implemented despite violating the assumptions underlying subsequent stages. The stages are discussed in more detail in §5, §6 and §7.

Interpreting equalities as behavioural equivalences

When verifying that a refinement of a specification is correct, '=' in the specification may need to be interpreted as ***behavioural equivalence*** (equality of observable behaviour) rather than as equality in the refined specification. To achieve this, given the view of refinement outlined in 4.2, the specification must be transformed so that '=' is replaced by a conventional operation. If it is to embody behavioural equivalence, this operation should distinguish between the values of two expressions if and only if observations of behaviour can distinguish between the expressions. In order to make sure that this operation is definable in simple terms conditions must be imposed on the applicative specification; these ensure that the functions are adequately defined, in that (in a certain sense) they depend only on the construction of their parameters. The transformation of the equalities into equivalences, and a sufficient check on the adequacy of the definitions of the functions, could be automated.

Converting functions into procedures

An applicative specification can be transformed into an imperative specification, provided that the functions in the applicative specification are adequately defined; if the functions are adequately defined the procedures in the imperative specification are influenced only by relevant aspects of objects. If the functions in the applicative specification depend on more than one member of the types to be implemented, then the procedures must satisfy conditions which ensure that they do not interfere with each other when they act on different objects; only if this is so does the imperative specification give rise to a 'refinement' of the applicative one, in the sense discussed in 4.2. The transformation of the functions into procedures, and a sufficient check that the procedures in a pre-existing specification do not interfere with one another, could be automated.

Replacing axioms by programs

The axioms in a specification can be replaced by programs, using a technique which is specific to a given class of abstract data types; the class considered in this paper is quite wide. The transformation of the axioms into programs, and a sufficient check that a given abstract data type is in this class, could be automated.

3 Notation

3.1 Functions and procedures

For types 't_1' and 't_2',

$$t_1 \stackrel{\sim}{\rightarrow} t_2$$

signifies the type of applicative partial functions which take members of the parameter type, 't_1', as parameters and which may return members of the result type, 't_2', as results. By contrast,

$$t_1 \stackrel{\sim}{\rightarrow} \textbf{write any } t_2$$

signifies the type of imperative partial procedures which take members of 't_1' as parameters, which may read from or write to any accessible variable, and which may return members of 't_2' as results. In addition,

$$t_1 \stackrel{\sim}{\rightarrow} \textbf{read any } t_2$$

signifies the subtype of this type of procedures comprising those procedures which may read from, but not write to, any accessible variable.

If types 't_1' and 't_2' have subtypes 't_3' and 't_4' respectively then

$$t_3 \stackrel{\sim}{\rightarrow} t_4$$

consists of those applicative partial functions ('f', say) in

$$t_1 \stackrel{\sim}{\rightarrow} t_2$$

such that when the execution of an application of 'f' to a parameter in 't_3' terminates then the result is in 't_4'; in other words,

$$\begin{array}{l} t_3 \stackrel{\sim}{\rightarrow} t_4 = \\ \{ f \mid \\ \quad f : t_1 \stackrel{\sim}{\rightarrow} t_2 \bullet \\ \qquad \forall x_3 : t_3 \bullet (\exists x_2 : t_2 \bullet x_2 = f (x_3)) \Rightarrow (\exists x_4 : t_4 \bullet x_4 = f (x_3)) \} \end{array}$$

3.2 Units

The type **Unit** has a unique (trivial) member. Accordingly,

$$t_1 \stackrel{\sim}{\rightarrow} \textbf{write any Unit}$$

is the type of procedures which take members of the type 't_1' as parameters, which may read from or write to any accessible variable, and which may return trivial results; such procedures are effectively "without results" and are used only because they modify the store. Also,

Unit $\tilde{\rightarrow}$ **write any** t_2

is the type of procedures which take trivial parameters, which may read from or write to any accessible variable, and which may return members of the type 't_2' as results; such procedures are effectively "without parameters".

The unique member of **Unit** can be written as '( )'. The application of a function or procedure ('f', say) to a parameter of type **Unit** can be shortened to 'f ( )'. A function abstraction 'λ x : **Unit** • e' such that 'x' is not mentioned in 'e' can be shortened to 'λ ( ) • e'.

3.3 Specifying the effects of expressions

For any expression 'e' having type **Bool**

$$\Box\ e$$

indicates that 'e' is equal to **true** for every store, no matter what values have been written to the variables.

For any expressions 'e_1' and 'e_2' with the same types evaluating the equivalence

$$e_1 \equiv e_2$$

returns **true** for the current store if and only if the executions of 'e_1' and 'e_2' in the current store have identical effects. These effects may be to modify the store and to return results. The evaluation of the equivalence itself does not modify the store; it merely returns a member of **Bool** by comparing the modifications to the store and the results returned. Moreover, the executions of 'e_1' and 'e_2' do not have to terminate in order to make the evaluation of the equivalence return **true**; hence a specification which relies on '$\equiv$' (as opposed to one which relies on '=') typically needs to include explicit assertions to ensure that executions terminate.

As with '$\forall$' and 'λ' in higher order logic,

$$(\Box (e_1 \equiv e_2)) =$$
$$((\lambda ( ) \cdot e_1) = (\lambda ( ) \cdot e_2))$$

For example, the assertion

$$\text{empty} = \lambda ( ) \cdot \text{empty\_} ( )$$

in 8.4 is equivalent with

$$\Box (\text{empty} ( ) \equiv \text{empty\_} ( ))$$

or indeed with

$$\text{empty} = \text{empty\_}$$

In this paper '$\Box$' is given the same precedence as the quantifiers (which are given higher precedence than implication and conjunction). Also, '$\equiv$' is given higher precedence than ';'.

3.4 Describing the results of expressions

For any expression 'e' without input and output, the assertion that in the current store 'e' is ***deterministically convergent***, in that its execution terminates with a unique store and with a unique result, is written in this paper as

definite e

In the RAISE specification language this is

e **post true**

The result returned by the execution of 'e' is signified by

result e

Provided that 'e' is deterministically convergent, in the RAISE specification language this is

let i : t • (e ≡ (e ; i)) **in** i **end**

Here executing the expression 'e ; i' involves executing 'e', discarding its result, and executing 'i' (which simply returns as its result the (value denoted by the) constant 'i').

Much as with 'ι' and '∃!', '**result** e' is usable if '**definite** e' evaluates to **true**:

definite e ⇒ ∃! i : t • (e ≡ (e ; i))

For example, in the imperative specification in 8.2 if the assertion

□ **definite** add (e)

holds, then

□ (add (e) ; head ( ) ≡ add (e) ; e)

is equivalent with

□ **definite** (add (e) ; head ( )) ∧ (**result** (add (e) ; head ( )) ≡ e)

or indeed with

□ **definite** head (add (e)) ∧ (**result** head (add (e)) ≡ e)

In 2.3 and elsewhere it is necessary to require that the sequential composition of deterministically convergent expressions be deterministically convergent and that the results of the expressions be properly related; in other words, for all expressions 'e_1' and 'e_2',

(**definite** e_1 ∧ (**result** (e_1 ; **definite** e_2) ≡ **true**)) ⇒
(**definite** (e_1 , e_2) ∧
(**result** (e_1 , e_2) ≡ (**result** e_1 , **result** (e_1 ; **result** e_2))))

If there are non-deterministic constructs in the language, this requirement is not met just by demanding that the results of the expressions be unique; they must also modify the store in ways that are deterministic. As an illustration of this, in the RAISE specification language

(n := 0 $\sqcap$ n := 1) ; n

does not have a unique result, though both

(n := 0 $\sqcap$ n := 1)

and

n

do have unique results.

Both **definite and result** have precedence no higher than the precedence of '$\equiv$'.

4 Concepts

4.1 The form of types

The types declared in a specification may be either *sorts* or abbreviations for other types. Sorts are not interpreted further in the specification but may be constrained by axioms. Types may be pre-defined types (such as **Bool**), sorts or composite types composed by applying pre-defined operators (such as $\times$) to other types.

A *flat* type is one that can be composed without the use of function type operators like those in 3.1.

A subset of a type may be a type. Hence possible declarations of types include

List

and, when 'is_list' is a predicate defined on members of 'List_',

List = { l | l : List_ • is_list (l) }

The range of types permitted allows specifications to be either model-oriented (as in VDM [9]) or property-oriented (as in OBJ [1]). However, the only types that may be refined are sorts. Where a type is expected to be refined, it should be treated as a sort; a concrete data type can be used to model this sort by introducing an 'observer' function which has the concrete data type as its result type. An example of this is provided by extending the specification of lists in 8.1 with the declaration

gather : List $\xrightarrow{\sim}$ Element-**list**

and the assertions

$$\text{gather (empty)} = \langle\, \rangle\ ,$$
$$\text{gather (add (e , l))} = \langle\, \text{e}\, \rangle \frown \text{gather (l)}$$

In fact, for all 'l_1' in 'List' and for all 'l_2' in 'List',

$$\text{gather} (l_1) = \text{gather} (l_2) \Rightarrow l_1 = l_2$$

but 'List' is not identified with 'Element-**list**', just as an abstract data type of trees is not identified with the set of encodings of trees as lists.

Behavioural abstraction requires that the members of a sort can be distinguished from one another by observations. It therefore requires the selection of certain *observable* types; all other types are *unobservable*. The observable types are those composed from pre-defined types and observable sorts by applying pre-defined operators. A sort which is regarded as observable at one stage in a development may be regarded as unobservable at a subsequent stage.

4.2 The nature of refinement

In this paper, a refinement of a specification is another specification which allows one to make the same assertions (and possibly more besides). This view of refinement (as theory extension) seems common to HOL [2], Larch [3] and RAISE [11] (though the emphasis on refinement, and the underlying logic, differ between the cases cited). It requires behavioural abstraction from model-oriented specifications to be treated explicitly (as exemplified in 4.1). A more general view, adopted for Extended ML [14], permits behavioural abstraction to be treated more succinctly but needs reasoning about model classes when there are no suitable proof rules; such proof rules are beginning to emerge, but they are of little help if the equivalence induced by the behavioural abstraction is itself intended to be implemented.

Here, as for the RAISE specification language, a specification can contain declarations (of types, constants and functions, among other things) and axioms, and refining a specification can involve turning sorts into abbreviations for other types, adding extra declarations or adding extra axioms.

4.3 The form of specifications

Applicative specifications are often expressed as conditional equations plus induction rules. Each conditional equation may have ***quantified names***, which are named members of types bound by universal quantifiers, a ***premise***, which is a finite conjunction of equations between expressions having observable types, and a ***consequence***, which is a finite conjunction of equations between expressions having observable or unobservable types. Each induction rule takes a standard form, with a finite conjunction of *hypotheses* that themselves have quantified names, premises and consequences; the premises help to indicate when the functions occurring subsequently in the premises or the consequences are applicable. In order to let behavioural equivalences take simple forms, either premises should be allowed to include universal quantifiers binding members of observable types or types consisting of finite sets (or lists) of members of observable types should be observable.

In practice certain abbreviations to conditional equations are permitted. For instance, an equation taking the form 'e = **false**' may be shortened to '$\sim$ e'.

It is not a severe practical restriction to require that applicative specifications of abstract data types rely on conditional equations and induction rules. In particular, specifications of applicative functions using pre-conditions and total correctness post-conditions, as in VDM, are equivalent with ones using conditional equations. For instance,

$$\text{add} (\text{e} , \text{l}) \ \textbf{as} \ \text{l}' \ \textbf{post} \ (\text{head} (\text{l}') = \text{e} \wedge \text{tail} (\text{l}') = \text{l})$$

is equivalent with

$$\text{head} (\text{e} , \text{add} (\text{e} , \text{l})) = \text{e} \wedge \text{tail} (\text{e} , \text{add} (\text{e} , \text{l})) = \text{l}$$

In fact specifications of imperative procedures using pre-conditions and total correctness post-conditions can also be turned into things akin to conditional equations by using '$\equiv$' and **definite** (discussed in 3.3 and 3.4).

Hereafter the definitions assume that applicative specifications are expressed as conditional equations plus induction rules.

4.4 Constructors, inspectors and observers

The functions in applicative specifications can usually be defined in terms of *constructor* constants and functions, *inspector* functions and *observer* functions. The types of the constants, and the parameter and result types of the functions, are flat. (In the specification of lists in 8.1, 'empty' and 'add' are constructors, 'tail' is an inspector, and 'head' and 'is_empty' are observers.)

The constructors are the constants and functions used in the (consequences of hypotheses in the) induction rules: every consequence applies a predicate to a constructor constant or function. Each constructor constant has an unobservable type and each constructor function has an unobservable result type. (A stronger version of this assumption, to the effect that the types are actually sorts, would preclude treating procedures which both return results and have effects on the store.) Though in principle this use of the term 'constructor' is different from that in term rewriting theory [8], in practice it is very similar.

The inspectors and observers are the functions used to distinguish between different members of sorts. An inspector function serves to extract other members of an unobservable sort from a given member, so it has an unobservable result type. An observer function serves to observe the members of an unobservable sort, so it has an observable result type.

These terms need to be generalised somewhat (though the generalisation can largely be ignored in the reading of this paper). Loosely, a ***generalised*** constructor is defined using conditional equations formed from suitable expressions using constructors; a generalised inspector or observer is defined using conditional equations formed from suitable expressions using inspectors and observers (in such a way that the result type is unobservable for an inspector and observable for an observer). A ***suitable*** expression is a constant, a quantified name, an application of a function to a suitable expression, a product of suitable expressions, or a component of a product. (For the specification of lists in 8.1, 'λ l : List • (head (l) , tail (l))' is a generalised inspector.)

In any application of a generalised constructor function there is a greatest depth of nesting of constructor functions. As the constructors constitute the constants and functions used in the induction rules, every member of an unobservable sort can be expressed in terms of them (though the means of expressing it may not be apparent in the absence of extra conditions). The *construction level* of a member of an unobservable type is the greatest depth of nesting of constructor functions needed by the "shallowest" means of constructing the member by applying generalised constructor functions to generalised constructor constants.

4.5 Applicability functions

Associated with every generalised constructor, inspector or observer function ('f', say) there is its ***applicability*** function, '*applicable*⟦f⟧'. This is a generalised observer which provides the pre-condition indicating when 'f' is applicable in the conditional equations and induction rules; it is a total function. If 'f' has type '$t_1 \tilde{\rightarrow} t_2$' then '*applicable*⟦f⟧' has type '$t_1 \tilde{\rightarrow}$ **Bool**'. The applicability function for 'f' can (for the present) be any total function which, when applied to any parameter to which 'f' is applied in the specification, evaluates to **true**. (In fact the applicability functions used in this paper can be devised by a systematic process, the details of which are omitted.)

4.6 Destructors

Associated with a constructor function ('c', say) there may be a *destructor* function, '*destructor*⟦c⟧'. This is a generalised inspector which acts as a left inverse for 'c' when 'c' is applicable. If 'c' has type '$t_1 \xrightarrow{\sim} t_2$' then when '*destructor*⟦c⟧' exists it has type '$t_2 \xrightarrow{\sim} t_1$' and

$$\forall\, x_1 : t_1 \bullet \\ \quad \mathit{applicable}[\![c]\!] (x_1) \Rightarrow \\ \quad \mathit{destructor}[\![c]\!] (c (x_1)) = x_1$$

For example, for the lists specified in 8.1, 'λ l : List • (head (l) , tail (l))' is a destructor function for 'add'. There may not be any destructor functions: a specification of sets, for instance, would not have them (because set union is commutative) but could have inspectors and observers.

4.7 Discrimination functions

Associated with a constructor constant ('k', say) there may be a *discrimination* function, '*discriminant*⟦k⟧'. This is a generalised observer which indicates when something must be 'k'; it is a total function. If 'k' has type 't_2' then when '*discriminant*⟦k⟧' exists it has type '$t_2 \xrightarrow{\sim}$ **Bool**' and, for every generalised constructor function 'f' of type '$t_3 \xrightarrow{\sim} t_2$' such that 'k' is not mentioned in 'f' but another constructor is mentioned in 'f',

$$\forall\, x_3 : t_3 \bullet \\ \quad \mathit{applicable}[\![f]\!] (x_3) \Rightarrow \\ \quad \mathit{discriminant}[\![k]\!] (k) \wedge \sim \mathit{discriminant}[\![k]\!] (f (x_3))$$

For example, for the lists specified in 8.1, 'is_empty' is a discrimination function for 'empty'.

Associated with a constructor function ('c', say) there may be a discrimination function, '*discriminant*⟦c⟧'. This is a generalised observer which indicates when something can only be constructed by an application of 'c'; it is a total function. If 'c' has type '$t_1 \xrightarrow{\sim} t_2$' then '*discriminant*⟦c⟧' has type '$t_2 \xrightarrow{\sim}$ **Bool**' and, for every generalised constructor function 'f' of type '$t_3 \xrightarrow{\sim} t_2$' such that 'c' is not mentioned in 'f' but another constructor is mentioned in 'f',

$$\forall\, x_1 : t_1 ,\, x_3 : t_3 \bullet \\ \quad \mathit{applicable}[\![c]\!] (x_1) \wedge \mathit{applicable}[\![f]\!] (x_3) \Rightarrow \\ \quad \mathit{discriminant}[\![c]\!] (c (x_1)) \wedge \sim \mathit{discriminant}[\![c]\!] (f (x_3))$$

For example, for the lists specified in 8.1, 'λ l : List • ~ is_empty (l)' is a discrimination function for 'add'. There may not be any discrimination functions: an assertion such as

$$\text{join} (\text{add} (e , l_1) , l_2) = \text{add} (e , \text{join} (l_1 , l_2))$$

(which is discussed in 2.4) precludes 'add' and 'join' from having discrimination functions if both 'add' and 'join' are classified as constructors. (However, in the case discussed in 2.4, 'join' would be not be classified as a constructor, because the induction rule would use only 'empty' and 'add'.)

5 Interpreting equalities as behavioural equivalences

5.1 Survey

The first stage in refining applicative specifications into imperative implementations entails interpreting equalities as behavioural equivalences. The technique needed replaces tests for equality between the members of unobservable types by applications of functions having result type **Bool**. The specification must obey conditions which ensure that no implicit uses of equality in it cannot be made explicit. These conditions are rather weaker than 'stability' requirements [15], which also prohibit the use of set and map operators involving abstract data types.

The technique is described in 5.2 and illustrated in 5.3. Assumptions that it requires are mentioned in 5.4. Variants of it are discussed in 5.5. The main assumption about the applicative specification is formalised in 5.6.

5.2 Tasks

5.2.1 Transforming the specification to interpret equality

- For each unobservable sort with name 'S', a function

  $$\mathrm{eq\_s} : (\mathrm{S} \times \mathrm{S}) \stackrel{\sim}{\to} \mathbf{Bool}$$

  is introduced. This function is intended to replace '=' for 'S'.

- For each such 'S', 'eq_s' is postulated to be an equivalence (which is reflexive, symmetric and transitive). In fact this amounts to asserting that 'eq_s' is symmetric and is a congruence for the function 'eq_s', in the sense that when two members of 'S' are related by 'eq_s' then one may be substituted for the other in parameters of the function.

- The explicit uses of '=' in the specification are replaced by uses of 'eq_s' (with appropriate modifications when the types of the left and right hand sides of the equality are not unobservable sorts).

- The implicit uses of '=' which exploit cardinality assertions are replaced by uses of 'eq_s'. For example,

  $$\exists!\ \mathrm{i} : \mathrm{t} \bullet \mathrm{e}$$

  needs to be regarded as

  $$(\ \exists\, \mathrm{i} : \mathrm{t} \bullet \mathrm{e}\ ) \wedge (\ \forall\, \mathrm{i}_1 : \mathrm{t}\ ,\ \mathrm{i}_2 : \mathrm{t} \bullet (\ \mathrm{e}[\mathrm{i}_1/\mathrm{i}] \wedge \mathrm{e}[\mathrm{i}_2/\mathrm{i}]\ ) \Rightarrow \mathrm{i}_1 = \mathrm{i}_2\ )$$

  Cardinality assertions also arise from size functions (such as **card** for sets).

- The implicit uses of '=' which exploit congruence properties are replaced by uses of 'eq_s'. The congruence properties of '=' are used in the application of functions to parameters, so there must be assertions to ensure that 'eq_s' is a congruence for all the functions declared in the specification (including the functions which are used as predicates in the induction rules); for instance, if 'f' is a function having type 'S $\tilde{\rightarrow}$ S' then it must satisfy

  $$\forall\, s_1 : S\,,\ s_2 : S \bullet$$
  $$\quad \text{eq\_s}\,(\,s_1\,,\ s_2\,) \Rightarrow \text{eq\_s}\,(\,f\,(\,s_1\,)\,,\ f\,(\,s_2\,)\,)$$

  This style of assertion can be used whatever the parameter and result types of the function may be.

- Given that the functions introduced in the specification satisfy the conditions outlined in 5.6, there is no need to postulate that 'eq_s' is an equivalence and a congruence for all the functions declared in the specification. Indeed, 'eq_s' can be defined as a total function using just the observers and inspectors, applied when their applicability functions permit; for instance, if there is only one inspector function 'i' and only one observer function 'o' and if they both have 'S' as parameter type then 'eq_s' can satisfy

  $$\forall\, s_1 : S\,,\ s_2 : S \bullet$$
  $$\quad \text{eq\_s}\,(\,s_1\,,\ s_2\,) =$$
  $$\quad (\,(\,\textit{applicable}[\![i]\!]\,(\,s_1\,) \wedge \textit{applicable}[\![i]\!]\,(\,s_2\,) \Rightarrow$$
  $$\qquad \text{eq\_s}\,(\,i\,(\,s_1\,)\,,\ i\,(\,s_2\,)\,)\,) \wedge$$
  $$\quad\ (\,\textit{applicable}[\![o]\!]\,(\,s_1\,) \wedge \textit{applicable}[\![o]\!]\,(\,s_2\,) \Rightarrow$$
  $$\qquad o\,(\,s_1\,) = o\,(\,s_2\,)\,)\,)$$

  This style of definition can be used whenever the parameter types of the inspector and observer functions each contain at most one occurrence of an unobservable sort; however, when these types are not sorts, the premises in a specification must include universal quantifiers binding members of observable types if the definition is to be turned into conditional equations.

5.2.2 Renaming the specification to distinguish names

- The specification, thus transformed, is subject to renaming by changing the names declared in it to avoid clashes with the names declared in the original specification. (Below, the name of an unobservable sort 'S' is taken to be changed by this means to 'S_'.)

5.2.3 Extending the specification to show refinement

- For each hitherto unobservable sort with name 'S', the declaration

  $$S =$$
  $$\quad \{\, s \mid$$
  $$\qquad s : \textbf{S\_-infset} \bullet$$
  $$\qquad\quad s \neq \{\,\} \wedge$$
  $$\qquad\quad \forall\, s_{\_1} : S\_\,,\ s_{\_2} : S\_ \bullet s_{\_1} \in s \Rightarrow \text{eq\_s}\,(\,s_{\_1}\,,\ s_{\_2}\,) = (\,s_{\_2} \in s\,)\,\}$$

is provided. The type 'S' comprises the equivalence classes of members of 'S_' with respect to 'eq_s', so '=' for it is the equality between equivalence classes.

- For each such 'S', functions

  $$\text{abs\_s} : \text{S\_} \xrightarrow{\sim} \text{S} \ ,$$
  $$\text{rep\_s} : \text{S} \xrightarrow{\sim} \text{S\_}$$

  are introduced. These functions constitute the main use of abstraction and representation functions required by the view of refinement adopted in this paper.

- For each such 'S', 'abs_s' and 'rep_s' are made to satisfy

  $$\forall \text{ s\_1} : \text{S\_} \bullet \text{abs\_s} (\text{s\_1}) = \{ \text{s\_2} \mid \text{s\_2} : \text{S\_} \bullet \text{eq\_s} (\text{s\_1} , \text{s\_2}) \} \ ,$$
  $$\forall \text{ s} : \text{S} \bullet \text{rep\_s} (\text{s}) \in \text{s}$$

  Consequently

  $$\forall \text{ s\_1} : \text{S\_} \bullet \text{eq\_s} (\text{s\_1} , \text{rep\_s} (\text{abs\_s} (\text{s\_1}))) \ ,$$
  $$\forall \text{ s} : \text{S} \bullet \text{s} = \text{abs\_s} (\text{rep\_s} (\text{s}))$$

  Here the abstraction function, 'abs_s', maps the members of equivalence classes to the equivalence classes, and the representation function, 'rep_s', maps the equivalence classes to representative members.

- Versions of the constants and functions declared in the original specification are defined using 'abs_s' and 'rep_s' according to the usual 'homomorphic' approach; for instance, if 'f_' is a function having type 'S_ $\xrightarrow{\sim}$ S_' then the defined function 'f' must satisfy

  $$\forall \text{ s} : \text{S} \bullet \text{f} (\text{s}) = \text{abs\_s} (\text{f\_} (\text{rep\_s} (\text{s})))$$

  This style of definition can be used whatever the parameter and result types of the function may be.

- Given that the functions introduced in the specification satisfy the conditions outlined in 5.6, there must be induction rules. In this situation the constructor constants and functions can construct all the members of each unobservable sort, so the specification thus extended provides a refinement of the original specification in which '=' is replaced by a function which can be implemented further.

5.3 Example

5.3.1 Transforming the specification to interpret equality

The applicative specification of 'List' given in 8.1 can be transformed by applying the technique described in 5.2. The outcome of doing so is presented in 8.6.

5.3.2 Renaming the specification to distinguish names

The type, constant and functions declared in 8.6 must have their names changed before they can be compared directly with those in 8.1. This is done in 8.7.

5.3.3 Extending the specification to show refinement

To establish that the specification in 8.6 is an appropriate transformation of that in 8.1, versions of the type, constant and functions declared in the specification in 8.1 are defined by extending the specification in 8.7. The outcome of doing so is presented in 8.8.

5.4 Assumptions

In order to exploit the explicit construction of 'eq_s' in terms of inspectors and observers, the applicative specification must take the form described in 4.3 and the functions introduced in it must satisfy the conditions outlined in 5.6.

The parameter type of each inspector or observer function must contain only one occurrence of an unobservable sort. (This assumption is not merely convenient; it is central to defining 'eq_s'.)

In this situation induction on construction levels can demonstrate that 'eq_s', defined according to the scheme in 5.2, is a total function, an equivalence and a congruence for all the functions (including the constructors); accordingly it is sufficient to define 'eq_s', as is done in 8.6, and it is unnecessary to postulate that 'eq_s' is an equivalence and a congruence for the functions. In fact 'eq_s' is the interpretation of '=' which distinguishes between two members of 'S' if and only if they can be distinguished using applicable observations. (However, 'eq_s' depends on the applicability functions, which can be devised in various ways.)

The specification must contain no constructs that may read from or write to variables having unobservable types.

Every construct in the specification which implicitly makes a cardinality assertion must be capable of being rewritten to make the assertion explicit through the use of '='. In particular, if the language provides 'ι' it must provide 'ϵ' also.

Every construct in the specification which implicitly exploits a congruence property of '=' must be capable of being rewritten to make the property explicit through the use of '='. In particular, if the language provides types which are not flat then it must provide subtypes also.

5.5 Variants

The technique described in 5.2 is applicable even when the conditions outlined in 5.6 are not satisfied. When this happens, it is necessary to postulate that the constructor constants and functions can construct all the members of each unobservable sort (perhaps owing to induction rules) and that 'eq_s' is an equivalence and a congruence for all the functions. (For lists this is done in 8.13; the specification in 8.13 can be related to the specification in 8.1 by the same renamings and extensions as are adopted in 5.3 for the specification in 8.6.) It may still be necessary to ensure separately that 'eq_s' distinguishes members of 'S' only if they can be distinguished using observations.

The technique can be specialised as well as generalised. When the functions satisfy the conditions outlined in 5.6 and for each constructor function there is a corresponding destructor function, the only generalised inspectors that need be considered are the destructors. In particular, the scheme for the definition of equality in 5.2 need mention only the destructors instead of the inspectors. This can be established by induction on construction levels.

5.6 The adequacy of the definitions

The functions declared in a specification can be related in varied ways. However, they generally obey conditions that enable them to induce behavioural equivalences that can even be used in imperative specifications. These conditions ensure that applications of functions to parameters produce results which are determined solely by the way in which their parameters are constructed; they thereby facilitate induction on construction levels.

Induction on construction levels, as practiced in this paper, requires essentially that for any inspector 'i' and for any appropriate parameter 'x' the construction level of 'i (x)' is less than that of 'x'. To bring this about it is necessary to impose conditions on the constructors, inspectors and observers. The condition for the inspectors and observers is that they all be adequately defined, in a sense to be clarified below. The condition for the constructors is that no constructor function can produce a constructor constant as a result; in other words for any generalised constructor constant 'k' with type 't_2' (and with greatest depth of nesting of constructor functions 0) and for any generalised constructor function 'c' with type '$t_1 \tilde{\rightarrow} t_2$' (and with greatest depth of nesting of constructor functions 1) there must be a generalised observer 'o' with type '$t_2 \tilde{\rightarrow}$ **Bool**' such that

$$\forall\, x_1 : t_1 \bullet \quad \mathit{applicable}[\![c]\!]\,(\,x_1\,) \Rightarrow \quad o\,(\,k\,) \wedge \sim o\,(\,c\,(\,x_1\,)\,)$$

An inspector 'i', with type '$t_2 \tilde{\rightarrow} t_3$', is ***adequately defined*** by a specification if the following conditions hold:

- for any generalised constructor constant 'k' with type 't_2' (and with greatest depth of nesting of constructor functions 0) it is the case that

  $$\sim \textit{applicable}[\![i]\!] (k)$$

  so a constructor constant is never extracted by applying an inspector function, just as it is not constructed by applying a constructor function;

- for any generalised constructor function 'c' with type '$t_1 \tilde{\rightarrow} t_2$' (and with greatest depth of nesting of constructor functions 1) there can be inferred $m \geq 0$ conditional equations, each with the form

  $$\begin{array}{l} \forall\ x_1 : t_1 \bullet \\ \quad \textit{applicable}[\![c]\!] (x_1) \wedge p_l (x_1) = q_l (x_1) \Rightarrow \\ \quad i (c (x_1)) = c_l (i_l (x_1)) \end{array}$$

  where

  $$\begin{array}{l} \forall\ x_1 : t_1 \bullet \\ \quad \textit{applicable}[\![c]\!] (x_1) \wedge \textit{applicable}[\![i]\!] (c (x_1)) \Rightarrow \\ \quad p_1 (x_1) = q_1 (x_1) \vee \ldots \vee p_m (x_1) = q_m (x_1) \end{array}$$

  and where (for all l having $m \geq l \geq 0$) 'p_l' is a generalised observer function, 'q_l' is a generalised observer function, 'c_l' is a generalised constructor function and 'i_l' is a generalised inspector function such that the greatest depth of nesting of constructor functions in 'c_l' is no more than the least depth of nesting of inspector functions in 'i_l'.

For example, for the lists specified in 8.1, if

$$\sim \textit{applicable}[\![\text{tail}]\!] (\text{empty})$$

'tail' is adequately defined as, for all 'e' in 'Element' and for all 'l' in 'List',

$$\text{tail} (e , \text{add} (e , l)) = l$$

An observer 'o', with type '$t_2 \tilde{\rightarrow} t_3$', is ***adequately defined*** by a specification if the following conditions hold:

- for any generalised constructor constant 'k' with type 't_2' (and with greatest depth of nesting of constructor functions 0) there can be inferred an equation with the form

  $$\textit{applicable}[\![o]\!] (k) \Rightarrow o (k) = b$$

  where 'b' is a constant which has an observable type and which can be defined without mentioning members of unobservable types;

- for any generalised constructor function 'c' with type '$t_1 \tilde{\rightarrow} t_2$' (and with greatest depth of nesting of constructor functions 1) there can be inferred $m \geq 0$ conditional equations, each with the form

$$\forall\, x_1 : t_1 \bullet$$
$$\quad applicable[\![c]\!] \,(\, x_1 \,) \wedge p_l \,(\, x_1 \,) = q_l \,(\, x_1 \,) \Rightarrow$$
$$\quad o \,(\, c \,(\, x_1 \,)\,) = f_l \,(\, o_l \,(\, c_l \,(\, i_l \,(\, x_1 \,)\,)\,)\,)$$

where

$$\forall\, x_1 : t_1 \bullet$$
$$\quad applicable[\![c]\!] \,(\, x_1 \,) \wedge applicable[\![o]\!] \,(\, c \,(\, x_1 \,)\,) \Rightarrow$$
$$\quad p_1 \,(\, x_1 \,) = q_1 \,(\, x_1 \,) \vee \ldots \vee p_m \,(\, x_1 \,) = q_m \,(\, x_1 \,)$$

and where (for all l having $m \geq l \geq 0$) 'f_l' is a function which has observable parameter and result types and which can be defined without mentioning members of unobservable types, 'p_l' is a generalised observer function, 'q_l' is a generalised observer function, 'o_l' is a generalised observer function, 'c_l' is a generalised constructor function and 'i_l' is a generalised inspector function such that the greatest depth of nesting of constructor functions in 'c_l' is no more than the least depth of nesting of inspector functions in 'i_l'.

For example, for the lists specified in 8.1, if

$$\sim applicable[\![head]\!] \,(\, empty \,)$$

'head' is adequately defined as, for all 'e' in 'Element' and for all 'l' in 'List',

$$head \,(\, e \,,\, add \,(\, e \,,\, l \,)\,) = e$$

However, an assertion such as

$$\sim (\, unhead \,(\, add \,(\, e \,,\, l \,)\,) = e \,)$$

(which is discussed in 2.4) is not enough to make 'unhead' adequately defined, even when it appears as the more orthodox conditional equation

$$unhead \,(\, add \,(\, e \,,\, l \,)\,) = e \Rightarrow \mathbf{true} = \mathbf{false}$$

The function 'unhead' could be made adequately defined in several ways; the simplest of them, which ensures that 'unhead (add (e , l))' depends only on 'e', entails introducing the declaration

$$reject : Element \xrightarrow{\sim} Element$$

and the assertions

$$unhead \,(\, add \,(\, e \,,\, l \,)\,) = reject \,(\, e \,) \,,$$
$$\sim (\, reject \,(\, e \,) = e \,)$$

In order to ensure that members of unobservable types are not used in the definitions of the constants like 'b' and the functions like 'f_l' used above these constants and functions can be taken to be *fully defined* in a different specification.

A specification may introduce other functions beside the constructors, inspectors and observers; for instance, the function 'join' described in 2.4 is likely not to be a constructor or an inspector, at least if it is being defined for lists. These *primitively defined* functions are all taken to be 'primitive recursive', in that if 'f' is such a function having type '$t_1 \xrightarrow{\sim} t_2$' it must satisfy equations taking the general form

$$\forall\, x_1 : t_1 \bullet \\ p_l (x_1) = q_l (x_1) \Rightarrow \\ f (x_1) = g_l (f_l (i_l (x_1)))$$

where

$$\forall\, x_1 : t_1 \bullet \\ \textit{applicable}[\![f]\!] (x_1) \Rightarrow \\ p_1 (x_1) = q_1 (x_1) \vee \ldots \vee p_m (x_1) = q_m (x_1)$$

and where (for all l having $m \geq l \geq 0$) 'p_l' is a generalised observer function, 'q_l' is a generalised observer function, 'g_l' is a generalised constructor, inspector or observer function, 'f_l' is a generalised primitively defined function and 'i_l' is a generalised inspector function such that the greatest depth of nesting of primitively defined functions in 'f_l' is no more than both 1 and the least depth of nesting of inspector functions in 'i_l'. (In fact this condition can be weakened.) Here a generalised primitively defined function is defined by conditional equations formed from suitable expressions using primitively defined functions.

Induction on construction levels can demonstrate that, if the observer and inspector functions in the specification are adequately defined and the functions other than the constructor, inspector and observer functions are primitively defined, then the specification is *sufficiently complete*: every suitable expression in which there are no occurrences of quantified names and in which the functions are applied only to parameters which satisfy their applicability functions can be reduced to a term which does not mention observer or inspector functions. (This notion of sufficient completeness is the counterpart for partial functions of the notion for total functions [3].)

6 Converting functions into procedures

6.1 Survey

The second stage in refining applicative specifications into imperative implementations entails converting functions into procedures. The technique needed turns declarations of, and assertions about, functions into declarations of, and assertions about, procedures. The functions must be defined so adequately that the procedures are influenced only by relevant aspects of the objects on which they act. Moreover, if the functions depend on more than one member of the types being implemented, then the procedures acting on different objects must not interfere with one another.

The technique is described in 6.2 and illustrated in 6.3. Assumptions that it requires are mentioned in 6.4. Variants of it are discussed in 6.5. The main constraint on the imperative specifications is formalised in 6.6.

6.2 Tasks

6.2.1 Transforming the specification to convert functions

- Any function having an unobservable parameter type is given the right to read from any accessible variable. Any function having an unobservable result type is given the right to read from or write to any accessible variable; however, any such function which is used in the definition of a function having an observable result type (such as 'eq_s') may only be given the right to read from variables, not to write to them. The functions are thereby replaced by procedures.

- For each unobservable sort with name 'S', a procedure

  has_s : S $\tilde{\rightarrow}$ **read any Bool**

  is introduced. This procedure is intended to provide a test that in a given store a member of a type with name 'S' gives access through the store to a representation of a member of the unobservable sort 'S'.

- For each such 'S', 'has_s' is postulated to be deterministically convergent for every store and for every parameter.

- For each such 'S', 'has_s' is postulated to return the result **true** when applied to a constructor constant.

- For each such 'S', 'has_s' is postulated to provide results that are not interfered with by the application of any procedure declared in the specification for every store and for every parameter which satisfy both the applicability procedure and 'has_s' (with appropriate modifications when the parameter type or the result type is not an unobservable sort); for instance, if 'f' is a procedure having type 'S $\tilde{\rightarrow}$ **write any** S' then it must satisfy

  $\forall\, s_1 : S\ ,\ s_2 : S \bullet$
  $\quad applicable[\![f]\!]\ (\ s_1\ ) \wedge \mathrm{has\_s}\ (\ s_1\ ) \wedge \mathrm{has\_s}\ (\ s_2\ ) \Rightarrow$
  $\quad (\ \mathbf{result}\ (\ f(\ s_1\ )\ ;\ \mathrm{has\_s}\ (\ s_2\ )\ ) \equiv \mathbf{true}\ )$

  This style of assertion can be used whenever the parameter types of the procedures are flat.

- After every universal quantifier binding members of unobservable types, '□' is inserted and an extra premise is added, to test that each quantified name of sort 'S' satisfies 'has_s' (with appropriate modifications when the types of the quantified names are not unobservable sorts).

- Any equation '$e_1 = e_2$' is treated as follows. If 'e_1' and 'e_2' have unobservable sorts the equation is replaced by '$e_1 \equiv e_2$'. If 'e_1' and 'e_2' have observable types the equation is replaced by '**result** $e_1 \equiv$ **result** e_2' (though '$\equiv$' is used instead of '$=$' purely for clarity). If 'e_1' and 'e_2' have unobservable types that are not sorts the equation is regarded as a conjunction of equations between the components of 'e_1' and 'e_2'.

- Each procedure declared in the specification is postulated to be deterministically convergent and to provide results that satisfy 'has_s' for every store and for every parameter which satisfies both its applicability procedure and 'has_s' (with appropriate modifications when the parameter type or the result type is not an unobservable sort).
- Each inspector or observer procedure (or, if there are equations between expressions having unobservable types, each constructor procedure) is postulated to provide results that are not interfered with by the application of any declared in the specification for every store and for all parameters which satisfy both the applicability procedures and 'has_s' (with appropriate modifications when the parameter type or the result type is not an unobservable sort). The nature of the postulates depends on the forms taken by the conditional equations in the specification and is discussed in 6.6.
- The induction rules are removed.

6.2.2 Renaming the specification to distinguish names

- The specification, thus transformed, is subject to renaming by changing the names declared in it to avoid clashes with the names declared in the original specification. (Below, the name of an unobservable sort 'S' is taken to be changed by this means to 'S_'.)

6.2.3 Extending the specification to show refinement

- For each hitherto unobservable sort with name 'S', the declaration

  S = { s | s : **Unit** $\stackrel{\sim}{\rightarrow}$ **write any** S_ • is_s (s) }

  is provided. The type 'S' comprises procedures members of 'S_' with respect to 'eq_s', which may read from or write to any accessible variable and which may return members of 'S_'.
- For each such 'S', a function

  is_s : (**Unit** $\stackrel{\sim}{\rightarrow}$ **write any** S_) $\stackrel{\sim}{\rightarrow}$ **Bool**

  is introduced. This function is used merely to indicate that 'S' may not comprise all the members of '**Unit** $\stackrel{\sim}{\rightarrow}$ **write any** S_'.
- The induction rules are added from the original specification to delimit 'S'.
- Versions of the constants and functions declared in the original specification are defined; for instance, if 'k_' is a constant having type 'S_' then the defined constant 'k' must satisfy

  k = λ ( ) • k_

if 'f_' is a procedure having type '**Bool** $\stackrel{\sim}{\rightarrow}$ **write any** S_' then the defined function 'f' must satisfy

$$\forall \text{b} : \textbf{Bool} \bullet \text{f}(\text{b}) = \lambda(\,) \bullet \text{f\_}(\text{b})$$

if 'f_' is a procedure having type 'S_ $\stackrel{\sim}{\rightarrow}$ **write any** S_' then the defined function 'f' must satisfy

$$\forall \text{s} : \text{S} \bullet \text{f}(\text{s}) = \lambda(\,) \bullet \text{f\_}(\text{s}(\,))$$

and if 'f_' is a procedure having type 'S_ $\stackrel{\sim}{\rightarrow}$ **read any Bool**' then the defined function 'f' must satisfy

$$\forall \text{s} : \text{S} \bullet \Box(\text{f}(\text{s}) \equiv \textbf{result}\ \text{f\_}(\text{s}(\,)))$$

This style of definition can be used whenever the types of the constants and the parameter and result types of the procedures are flat and the types of the constants and the result types of the procedures each contain at most one occurrence of an unobservable sort.

- Given that the functions introduced in the specification satisfy the conditions outlined in 5.6, the specification thus extended provides a refinement of the original specification in which functions are interpreted as acting on procedures.

6.3 Example

6.3.1 Transforming the specification to convert functions

The applicative specification of 'List' given in 8.6 can be transformed by applying the technique described in 6.2. The outcome of doing so is presented in 8.9.

6.3.2 Renaming the specification to distinguish names

The type, constant and functions declared in 8.9 must have their names changed before they can be compared directly with those in 8.6. This is done in 8.10.

6.3.3 Extending the specification to show refinement

To establish that the specification in 8.9 is an appropriate transformation of that in 8.6, versions of the type, constant and functions declared in the specification in 8.6 are defined by extending the specification in 8.10. The outcome of doing so is presented in 8.11.

6.4 Assumptions

The applicative specification must take the form described in 4.3 and the inspectors and observers must satisfy the conditions outlined in 5.6.

The type of each constructor constant and the result type of each constructor or inspector function must contain only one occurrence of an unobservable sort. (This assumption is not merely convenient; it is central to demonstrating that the transformation provides a refinement of the original specification.)

In any equation '$e_1 = e_2$' the expressions 'e_1' and 'e_2' must be 'suitable' in the sense explained in 4.4.

An observer can be used in a parameter of a function only if the function has observable parameter and result types. This precludes having assertions such as

add (head (l) , tail (l)) = l

Functions must be able to take procedures as parameters.

6.5 Variants

Very often the applicative specification which is to be transformed does not make assertions about more than one object (where the term 'object' is used in the sense of object-oriented programming). This is so if every equation in the applicative specification satisfies the following:

- no product of expressions in the equation contains more than one expression which has an unobservable type and is not a constant;
- the expressions equated by the equation have observable types if there is a quantified name having an unobservable type which is mentioned in one expression but not in the other expression.

For instance, the specification in 8.1 satisfies these conditions, but that in 8.6 does not (because the assertion about 'eq_list' depends on two members of the sort 'List').

When the applicative specification satisfies these conditions, the technique given in 6.2 can be modified to produce less intricate imperative specifications. Doing this involves:

- replacing in the applicative specification each constructor constant, having type 't', by a constructor function having type '**Unit** $\tilde{\rightarrow}$ t', so that when its type is altered by the transformation it is given the right to read from or write to any accessible variable;

- taking 'has_s' in the imperative specification to be 'λ ( ) • **true**' (or omitting its declaration entirely);
- taking 'S' in the imperative specification to be **Unit** (or omitting its declaration entirely);
- removing superfluous components of type **Unit** from the parameters and results of procedures in the imperative specification;
- omitting the assertions about freedom from interference from the imperative specification.

The specification in 8.2 results from applying this modified transformation to the specification in 8.1, so the modified transformation formalises the process described in 2.2.

The trick of replacing each constructor constant by a constructor function can be employed quite generally, whenever creating a member of an abstract data type ought to have an effect on the store. It is usually appropriate if the abstract data type is implemented using static storage allocation and is frequently appropriate if the abstract data type is implemented using dynamic storage allocation.

6.6 Freedom from interference between procedures

In order to make sure that the procedures in imperative specifications do not interfere with one another, it is necessary to introduce certain conditions into the specifications. The form of these conditions is influenced by the form of the specifications; in the interests of simplicity the versions presented here are fairly insensitive to the form of the specifications.

If, in some equation '$e_1 = e_2$' either 'e_1' or 'e_2' contains a product of expressions more than one of which has an unobservable type and is not a constant, then 'commutativity' assertions are added. If 'e_1' and 'e_2' have unobservable types, then the commutativity assertions take the following form: if 'f' is a constructor procedure (or any procedure used in the product of expressions) having type '$t_1 \xrightarrow{\sim}$ **write any** t_3' and if 'c' is a constructor procedure having type '$t_2 \xrightarrow{\sim}$ **write any** t_4', then

$$\begin{array}{l} \forall\, x_1 : t_1 ,\, x_2 : t_2 \bullet \\ \quad \mathit{applicable}[\![f]\!] (x_1) \wedge \mathit{applicable}[\![c]\!] (x_2) \Rightarrow \\ \quad (\mathbf{let}\ x_3 = f (x_1)\ \mathbf{in}\ \mathbf{let}\ x_4 = c (x_2)\ \mathbf{in}\ (x_3 , x_4)\ \mathbf{end}\ \mathbf{end} \equiv \\ \quad\quad \mathbf{let}\ x_4 = c (x_2)\ \mathbf{in}\ \mathbf{let}\ x_3 = f (x_1)\ \mathbf{in}\ (x_3 , x_4)\ \mathbf{end}\ \mathbf{end}) \end{array}$$

If 'e_1' and 'e_2' have observable types, then the commutativity assertions are typified by the following: if 'f_1' is a constructor procedure (or any other procedure used in the product of expressions) having type 'S $\xrightarrow{\sim}$ **write any** t_1' and if 'f_2' is an inspector or observer procedure having type 'S $\xrightarrow{\sim}$ **write any** t_2', then

$$\begin{array}{l} \forall\, s_1 : S ,\, s_2 : S \bullet \\ \quad \textit{applicable}[\![f_1]\!] (s_1) \wedge \text{has\_s} (s_1) \wedge \textit{applicable}[\![f_2]\!] (s_2) \wedge \text{has\_s} (s_2) \Rightarrow \\ \quad (\textbf{let } x_3 = f_1 (s_1) \textbf{ in let } x_4 = f_2 (s_2) \textbf{ in } (x_3 , x_4) \textbf{ end end} \equiv \\ \qquad \textbf{let } x_4 = f_2 (s_2) \textbf{ in let } x_3 = f_1 (s_1) \textbf{ in } (x_3 , x_4) \textbf{ end end}) \end{array}$$

(with appropriate modifications when a parameter type is not an unobservable sort). The second assertion is implied by the first. It can be omitted when 'f_2' is not needed in the characterisation of behavioural equivalence (in other words, in the definition of 'eq_s') and can be reduced to

$$\begin{array}{l} \forall\, s_1 : S ,\, s_2 : S \bullet \\ \quad \textit{applicable}[\![f_1]\!] (s_1) \wedge \text{has\_s} (s_1) \wedge \textit{applicable}[\![f_2]\!] (s_2) \wedge \text{has\_s} (s_2) \Rightarrow \\ \quad (\textbf{result} (f_1 (s_1) ; f_2 (s_2)) \equiv f_2 (s_2)) \end{array}$$

when 'f_2' is an inspector or observer having type '$S \xrightarrow{\sim} \textbf{read any } t_2$'. This reduced form of the second assertion is essentially the form taken by the condition imposed on 'has_s' in 6.2.

If, in some equation '$e_1 = e_2$' either 'e_1' or 'e_2' mentions more than once some quantified name having an unobservable type, then 'idempotence' assertions may be needed. If 'e_1' and 'e_2' have unobservable types, then the idempotence assertions take the following form: if 'c' is a constructor procedure having type '$t_1 \xrightarrow{\sim} \textbf{write any } t_2$', then

$$\begin{array}{l} \forall\, x_1 : t_1 \bullet \\ \quad \textit{applicable}[\![c]\!] (x_1) \Rightarrow \\ \quad (c (x_1) ; c (x_1) \equiv c (x_1)) \end{array}$$

If 'e_1' and 'e_2' have observable types, then the idempotence assertions are unnecessary, because the commutativity assertions are needed anyway and are enough already.

If, in some equation '$e_1 = e_2$' only one of 'e_1' and 'e_2' mentions some quantified name having an unobservable type, then 'absorption' assertions may be needed. If 'e_1' and 'e_2' have unobservable types, then the absorption assertions take the following form: if 'c' is a constructor procedure having type '$t_1 \xrightarrow{\sim} \textbf{write any } t_3$' and if 'f' is a procedure used in the expression that does not mention the quantified name and having type '$t_2 \xrightarrow{\sim} \textbf{write any } t_4$', then

$$\begin{array}{l} \forall\, x_1 : t_1 ,\, x_2 : t_2 \bullet \\ \quad \textit{applicable}[\![c]\!] (x_1) \wedge \textit{applicable}[\![f]\!] (x_2) \Rightarrow \\ \quad (c (x_1) ; f (x_2) \equiv f (x_2)) \end{array}$$

If 'e_1' and 'e_2' have observable types, then the absorption assertions are unnecessary, because the use of **result** in the equations ensures that the effects on the store are disregarded.

In an implementation it is difficult to reconcile the commutativity and absorption assertions needed by equations between expressions having unobservable types. Hence all such equations tend to be replaced by behavioural equivalences using 'eq_s'.

7 Replacing axioms by programs

7.1 Survey

The third stage in refining applicative specifications into imperative implementations entails replacing axioms by programs. The technique needed supplies the procedures declared in a specification with executable definitions. The specification must obey conditions which ensure that no member of the sorts can be constructed in two distinct ways by using constructors alone. These conditions therefore allow lists and queues, but not sets and maps, to be implemented using this technique. In fact they permit many of the flat "recursive" types that can be defined briefly in RAISE [6] and all of those that can be defined briefly in Standard ML [5], HOL [10] and Z [16].

The technique is described in 7.2 and illustrated in 7.3. Assumptions that it requires are mentioned in 7.4. Variants of it are discussed in 7.5.

7.2 Tasks

7.2.1 Transforming the specification to replace axioms

- For each hitherto unobservable sort with name 'S', the declaration

  S = **Int**

  is provided. The type 'S' comprises the possible indexes into an array. It induces a representation of the members of any flat, hitherto unobservable, type. (If the induction rules indicate that there is a bound on the permitted depth of constructor functions, then a finite range of integers can be used instead of **Int**; this range must contain one entry per constructor constant and one entry per permitted depth of nesting.)

- For each such 'S', an index variable

  index_s : S

  is introduced. This index variable is intended to indicate where unused array elements lie.

- For each such 'S', an array object

  array_s : ...

  is introduced. An element of this array is brought into use by the application of a constructor procedure; it must be capable of storing information which can identify the constructor procedure and represent the parameter in the application of the constructor procedure. Consequently the array object must provide, for every possible index, a finite collection of variables which suffices to store both a tag (drawn from an observable type in which every constructor procedure is allocated a distinct tag) and the representation of any parameter in a constructor procedure application. The tag can be omitted if there is only one constructor procedure.

- For each such 'S', each application of 'has_s' tests whether its integer parameter lies between the value most recently written to the index variable and the lowest representation of a constructor constant. (A more modular treatment would combine the array, the index and the definition of 'has_s' in the implementation of a name generator; it is omitted from this paper in order to concentrate on the systematic development of just one module.)

- For each such 'S', each constructor constant is represented by a different integer; the representations are arranged consecutively.

- For each such 'S', each application of a constructor procedure increments the value in 'index_s' (making sure that it is above the highest representation of a constructor constant) and stores in the corresponding element of 'array_s' the information noted above.

- For each such 'S', each application of a destructor procedure uses its parameter to determine an array element from which it then extracts the representation of the parameter in a constructor procedure application.

- For each such 'S', each application of a discrimination procedure checks whether its parameter is a constructor constant; if so, it checks which constructor constant is its parameter, but, if not so, it uses its parameter to determine an array element which identifies a constructor procedure.

- Given that the procedures introduced in the specification are derivable from functions which satisfy the conditions outlined in 5.6, the remaining procedures are defined recursively in terms of the constructor procedures, the destructor procedures, the discrimination procedures, and the observations on the constructor constants: some of the axioms are replaced by definitions, in which first the discrimination procedures and then the appropriate constructor, inspector and observer procedures are applied.

- Any axioms that are not replaced in the above manner should be proved to be consequences of the definitions of the procedures. If they are proved to be consequences, they can be deleted from the specification; if they are not proved to be consequences, they must be retained in the specification (which may well be inconsistent).

7.3 Example

7.3.1 Transforming the specification to replace axioms

The imperative specification of 'List' given in 8.6 can be transformed by applying the technique described in 7.2. The outcome of doing so is presented in 8.12. No renaming or extending is needed in order to establish refinement: the procedures in 8.12 have already all the properties specified for those in 8.9.

7.4 Assumptions

The imperative specification must be derivable by applying the transformation described in 6.2 to an applicative specification satisfying the conditions in 6.4.

For each constructor function in the applicative specification there must be destructor and discrimination functions obeying the rules in 4.6 and 4.7. There is then a unique way of constructing each member of a sort using constructors alone.

For every observable type which can appear as part of the parameter type for a constructor function there must be a way of declaring a finite collection of variables which can hold any member of the type.

7.5 Variants

An extension to the technique considered in 7.2 allows certain inspector procedures to be implemented without the use of constructor procedures (which write to variables) and destructor procedures (which need to be applied recursively). It applies if there is a unique constructor constant 'k' and if for all constructor and inspector functions ('c' and 'i' respectively), in the notation of 5.6,

$$\begin{array}{l} \forall\ x_1 : t_1 \bullet \\ \quad \textit{applicable}[\![c]\!]\ (\ x_1\ ) \wedge \textit{applicable}[\![i]\!]\ (\ c\ (\ x_1\ )\ ) \Rightarrow \\ \quad i\ (\ c\ (\ x_1\ )\ ) = k \vee i\ (\ c\ (\ x_1\ )\ ) = c\ (\ i\ (\ x_1\ )\ ) \end{array}$$

In this case, each array element must store, besides the information noted in 7.2, an "upwards-pointing" array index indicating which array element (if any) is constructed from the given one; also, the representation of a member of 'S' must provide, beside the array index for its "latest" constructor, array indexes for the results of applying the inspector procedures.

This extension to the technique can be used to implement queues for which applications of the inspector procedures produce results in constant time (whereas the technique as described in 7.2 requires time linear in the lengths of the queues).

8 Specifications

8.1 First applicative specification

```
FIRST_APPLICATIVE_LIST =
  class
    type
      List
    value
      empty : List ,
      add : ( Element × List ) ~→ List ,
      head : List ~→ Element ,
      tail : List ~→ List ,
      is_empty : List ~→ Bool
    axiom forall e : Element , l : List •
      is_empty ( empty ) = true ,
      head ( add ( e , l ) ) = e ,
      tail ( add ( e , l ) ) = l ,
      is_empty ( add ( e , l ) ) = false ,
    axiom forall p : List ~→ Bool •
      ( p ( empty ) ∧
        ( ∀ e : Element , l : List • p ( l ) ⇒ p ( add ( e , l ) ) ) ) ⇒
      ( ∀ l : List • p ( l ) )
  end
```

8.2 First imperative specification

```
FIRST_IMPERATIVE_LIST =
  class
    value
      empty : Unit ~→ write any Unit ,
      add : Element ~→ write any Unit ,
      head : Unit ~→ read any Element ,
      tail : Unit ~→ write any Unit ,
      is_empty : Unit ~→ read any Bool
    axiom forall e : Element •
      □ definite empty ( ) ,
      □ ( empty ( ) ; is_empty ( ) ≡ empty ( ) ; true ) ,
      □ definite add ( e ) ,
      □ ( add ( e ) ; head ( ) ≡ add ( e ) ; e ) ,
      □ ( add ( e ) ; tail ( ) ≡ ( ) ) ,
      □ ( add ( e ) ; is_empty ( ) ≡ add ( e ) ; false )
  end
```

8.3 Renamed first imperative specification

```
RENAMED_FIRST_IMPERATIVE_LIST =
  use
    empty_ for empty ,
    add_ for add ,
    head_ for head ,
    tail_ for tail ,
    is_empty_ for is_empty
  in FIRST_IMPERATIVE_LIST
```

8.4 Extended renamed first imperative specification

```
EXTENDED_RENAMED_FIRST_IMPERATIVE_LIST =
  extend RENAMED_FIRST_IMPERATIVE_LIST with
  class
    type
      List = { l | l : Unit ~→ write any Unit • is_list ( l ) }
    value
      empty : List ,
      add : ( Element × List ) ~→ List ,
      head : List ~→ Element ,
      tail : List ~→ List ,
      is_empty : List ~→ Bool
    value
      is_list : ( Unit ~→ write any Unit ) ~→ Bool
    axiom forall e : Element , l : List •
      empty = λ ( ) • empty_ ( ) ,
      add ( e , l ) = λ ( ) • l ( ) ; add_ ( e ) ,
      □ ( head ( l ) ≡ result ( l ( ) ; head_ ( ) ) ) ,
      tail ( l ) = λ ( ) • l ( ) ; tail_ ( ) ,
      □ ( is_empty ( l ) ≡ result ( l ( ) ; is_empty_ ( ) ) )
    axiom forall p : List ~→ Bool •
      ( p ( empty ) ∧
        ( ∀ e : Element , l : List • p ( l ) ⇒ p ( add ( e , l ) ) ) ) ⇒
      ( ∀ l : List • p ( l ) )
  end
```

8.5 Completed imperative specification

```
COMPLETED_IMPERATIVE_LIST =
  class
    value
      empty : Unit ~→ write any Unit ,
      add : Element ~→ write any Unit ,
      head : Unit ~→ read any Element ,
      tail : Unit ~→ write any Unit ,
      is_empty : Unit ~→ read any Bool
    variable
      list : Element-list
    axiom
      empty = λ ( ) • list := ⟨ ⟩ ,
      add = λ e : Element • list := ⟨ e ⟩ ^ list ,
      head = λ ( ) • hd list ,
      tail = λ ( ) • tl list ,
      is_empty = λ ( ) • list = ⟨ ⟩
  end
```

8.6 Second applicative specification

```
SECOND_APPLICATIVE_LIST =
  class
    type
      List
    value
      empty : List ,
      add : ( Element × List ) ~→ List ,
      head : List ~→ Element ,
      tail : List ~→ List ,
      is_empty : List ~→ Bool
    value
      eq_list : ( List × List ) ~→ Bool
    axiom forall e : Element , l : List •
      is_empty ( empty ) = true ,
      head ( add ( e , l ) ) = e ,
      eq_list ( tail ( add ( e , l ) ) , l ) = true ,
      is_empty ( add ( e , l ) ) = false
    axiom forall p : List ~→ Bool •
      ( ∀ l1 : List , l2 : List • eq_list ( l1 , l2 ) ⇒ p ( l1 ) = p ( l2 ) ) ⇒
      ( p ( empty ) ∧
        ( ∀ e : Element , l : List • p ( l ) ⇒ p ( add ( e , l ) ) ) ) ⇒
      ( ∀ l : List • p ( l ) )
    axiom forall l1 : List , l2 : List •
      eq_list ( l1 , l2 ) =
      ( is_empty ( l1 ) = is_empty ( l2 ) ∧
        ( ~ is_empty ( l1 ) ∧ ~ is_empty ( l2 ) ⇒
          head ( l1 ) = head ( l2 ) ∧ eq_list ( tail ( l1 ) , tail ( l2 ) ) ) )
  end
```

8.7 Renamed second applicative specification

```
RENAMED_SECOND_APPLICATIVE_LIST =
  use
    List_ for List ,
    empty_ for empty ,
    add_ for add ,
    head_ for head ,
    tail_ for tail ,
    is_empty_ for is_empty
  in SECOND_APPLICATIVE_LIST
```

8.8 Extended renamed second applicative specification

```
EXTENDED_RENAMED_SECOND_APPLICATIVE_LIST =
  extend RENAMED_SECOND_APPLICATIVE_LIST with
  class
    type
      List =
        { l |
          l : List_-infset •
            l ≠ { } ∧
            ∀ l_1 : List_ , l_2 : List_ • l_1 ∈ l ⇒ eq_list ( l_1 , l_2 ) = ( l_2 ∈ l ) }
    value
      empty : List ,
      add : ( List × List ) ~→ List ,
      head : List ~→ Element ,
      tail : List ~→ List ,
      is_empty : List ~→ Bool
    value
      abs_list : List_ ~→ List ,
      rep_list : List ~→ List_
    axiom forall e : Element , l : List , l : List •
      empty = abs_list ( empty_ ) ,
      add ( e , l ) = abs_list ( add_ ( e , rep_list ( l ) ) ) ,
      head ( l ) = head_ ( rep_list ( l ) ) ,
      tail ( l ) = abs_list ( tail_ ( rep_list ( l ) ) ) ,
      is_empty ( l ) = is_empty_ ( rep_list ( l ) )
    axiom forall l : List , l_1 : List_ •
      abs_list ( l_1 ) = { l_2 | l_2 : List_ • eq_list ( l_1 , l_2 ) } ,
      rep_list ( l ) ∈ l
  end
```

8.9 Enriched imperative specification

```
SECOND_IMPERATIVE_LIST =
  class
    type
      List
    value
      empty : List ,
      add : ( Element × List ) ~→ write any List ,
      head : List ~→ read any Element ,
      tail : List ~→ read any List ,
      is_empty : List ~→ read any Bool
```

```
  value
    eq_list : ( List × List ) ~→ read any Bool
  value
    has_list : List ~→ read any Bool
  axiom forall e : Element , l : List •
    □ has_list ( empty ) ,
    □ definite is_empty ( empty ) ∧
      ( result is_empty ( empty ) ≡ true ) ,
    □ has_list ( l ) ⇒
      definite add ( e , l ) ∧
    □ has_list ( l ) ⇒
      definite head ( add ( e , l ) ) ∧
      ( result head ( add ( e , l ) ) ≡ e ) ,
    □ has_list ( l ) ⇒
      definite tail ( add ( e , l ) ) ∧
      ( result has_list ( tail ( add ( e , l ) ) ) ≡ true ) ∧
      ( result eq_list ( tail ( add ( e , l ) ) , l ) ≡ true ) ,
    □ has_list ( l ) ⇒
      definite is_empty ( add ( e , l ) ) ∧
      ( result is_empty ( add ( e , l ) ) ≡ false )
  axiom forall l : List •
    □ has_list ( l1 ) ∧ has_list ( l2 ) ⇒
      ( eq_list ( l1 , l2 ) =
        ( is_empty ( l1 ) = is_empty ( l2 ) ∧
          ( ~ is_empty ( l1 ) ∧ ~ is_empty ( l2 ) ⇒
            head ( l1 ) = head ( l2 ) ∧ eq_list ( tail ( l1 ) , tail ( l2 ) ) ) ) ) )
  axiom forall l : List •
    □ definite has_list ( l )
  axiom forall e : Element , l1 : List , l2 : List •
    □ has_list ( l1 ) ∧ has_list ( l2 ) ⇒
      ( result ( add ( e , l1 ) ; has_list ( l2 ) ) ≡ has_list ( l2 ) )
  axiom forall e : Element , l1 : List , l2 : List •
    □ has_list ( l1 ) ∧ has_list ( l2 ) ⇒
      ( result ( add ( e , l1 ) ; head ( l2 ) ) ≡ head ( l2 ) ) ,
    □ has_list ( l1 ) ∧ has_list ( l2 ) ⇒
      ( result ( add ( e , l1 ) ; tail ( l2 ) ) ≡ tail ( l2 ) ) ,
    □ has_list ( l1 ) ∧ has_list ( l2 ) ⇒
      ( result ( add ( e , l1 ) ; is_empty ( l2 ) ) ≡ is_empty ( l2 ) )
end
```

8.10 Renamed second imperative specification

```
RENAMED_SECOND_IMPERATIVE_LIST =
  use
    List_ for List ,
    empty_ for empty ,
    add_ for add ,
    head_ for head ,
    tail_ for tail ,
    is_empty_ for is_empty ,
    eq_list_ for eq_list
  in SECOND_IMPERATIVE_LIST
```

8.11 Extended renamed second imperative specification

```
EXTENDED_RENAMED_SECOND_IMPERATIVE_LIST =
  extend RENAMED_SECOND_IMPERATIVE_LIST with
  class
    type
      List = { l | l : Unit ~→ write any List_ • is_list ( l ) }
    value
      empty : List ,
      add : ( Element × List ) ~→ List ,
      head : List ~→ Element ,
      tail : List ~→ List ,
      is_empty : List ~→ Bool
    value
      eq_list : List × List ~→ Bool
    value
      is_list : ( Unit ~→ write any List_ ) ~→ Bool
    axiom forall e : Element , l : List •
      empty = λ ( ) • empty_ ,
      add ( e , l ) = λ ( ) • add_ ( e , l ( ) ) ,
      □ ( head ( l ) ≡ result head_ ( l ( ) ) ) ,
      tail ( l ) = λ ( ) • tail_ ( l ( ) ) ,
      □ ( is_empty ( l ) ≡ result is_empty_ ( l ( ) ) )
    axiom forall p : List ~→ Bool •
      ( ∀ l1 : List , l2 : List • eq_list ( l1 , l2 ) ⇒ p ( l1 ) = p ( l2 ) ) ⇒
      ( p ( empty ) ∧
        ( ∀ e : Element , l : List • p ( l ) ⇒ p ( add ( e , l ) ) ) ) ⇒
      ( ∀ l : List • p ( l ) )
    axiom forall l1 : List , l2 : List •
      □ ( eq_list ( l1 , l2 ) ≡ result eq_list_ ( l1 ( ) , l2 ( ) ) )
  end
```

8.12 Completed second imperative specification

```
COMPLETED_SECOND_IMPERATIVE_LIST =
  class
    type
      List = Int
    value
      empty : List ,
      add : ( Element × List ) ~→ write any List ,
      head : List ~→ read any Element ,
      tail : List ~→ read any List ,
      is_empty : List ~→ read any Bool
    value
      eq_list : ( List × List ) ~→ read any Bool
    value
      has_list : List ~→ read any Bool
    variable
      index_list : Int
    object
      array_list [ l : List ] : class variable h : Element , t : List end
    axiom
      empty = 0 ,
      add =
      λ ( e , l₁ ) : Element × List •
        if 0 ≥ index_list =
        then index_list := 1
        else index_list := index_list + 1
        end ;
        let l₂ = index_list =
        in array_list [ l₂ ] . h := e ; array_list [ l₂ ] . t := l₁ ; l₂
        end ,
      head = λ l : List • array_list [ l ] . h ,
      tail = λ l : List • array_list [ l ] . t ,
      is_empty = λ l : List • array_list [ l ] . t = empty
    axiom
      eq_list =
      λ ( l₁ , l₂ ) : List × List •
        is_empty ( l₁ ) = is_empty ( l₂ ) ∧
        ( ~ is_empty ( l₁ ) ∧ ~ is_empty ( l₂ ) ⇒
          head ( l₁ ) = head ( l₂ ) ∧ eq_list ( tail ( l₁ ) , tail ( l₂ ) ) )
    axiom
      has_list = λ l : List • index_list ≥ l ∧ l ≥ 0
  end
```

8.13 Third applicative specification

```
THIRD_APPLICATIVE_LIST =
  class
    type
      List
    value
      empty : List ,
      add : ( Element × List ) ~→ List ,
      head : List ~→ Element ,
      tail : List ~→ List ,
      is_empty : List ~→ Bool
    value
      eq_list : ( List × List ) ~→ Bool
    axiom forall e : Element , l : List •
      is_empty ( empty ) = true ,
      head ( add ( e , l ) ) = e ,
      eq_list ( tail ( add ( e , l ) ) , l ) = true ,
      is_empty ( add ( e , l ) ) = false
    axiom forall p : List ~→ Bool •
      ( ∀ l1 : List , l2 : List • eq_list ( l1 , l2 ) ⇒ p ( l1 ) = p ( l2 ) ) ⇒
      ( p ( empty ) ∧
        ( ∀ e : Element , l : List • p ( l ) ⇒ p ( add ( e , l ) ) ) ) ⇒
      ( ∀ l : List • p ( l ) )
    axiom forall l1 : List , l2 : List , l3 : List •
      eq_list ( l1 , l1 ) ,
      eq_list ( l1 , l2 ) ⇒ eq_list ( l2 , l1 ) ,
      eq_list ( l1 , l2 ) ∧ eq_list ( l2 , l3 ) ⇒ eq_list ( l1 , l3 )
    axiom forall e1 : Element , e2 : Element , l1 : List , l2 : List •
      eq_list ( empty , empty ) ,
      e1 = e2 ∧ eq_list ( l1 , l2 ) ⇒
      eq_list ( add ( e1 , l1 ) , add ( e2 , l2 ) ) ,
      eq_list ( l1 , l2 ) ∧ ~ is_empty ( l1 ) ∧ ~ is_empty ( l2 ) ⇒
      head ( l1 ) = head ( l2 ) ,
      eq_list ( l1 , l2 ) ∧ ~ is_empty ( l1 ) ∧ ~ is_empty ( l2 ) ⇒
      eq_list ( tail ( l1 ) , tail ( l2 ) )',
      eq_list ( l1 , l2 ) ⇒
      is_empty ( l1 ) = is_empty ( l2 )
  end
```

9 References

[1] Goguen, J.A., and Winkler, T., *Introducing OBJ3*, Report SRI-CSL-88-9, SRI International (1988).

[2] Gordon, M.J.C., *HOL: A Proof Generating System for Higher-Order Logic*, in **VLSI Specification, Verification and Synthesis**, edited by Birtwistle, G., and Subrahmanyam, P.A., (Kluwer, 1988) 73-128.

[3] Guttag, J.V., and Horning, J.J., *The Algebraic Specification of Abstract Data Types*, **Acta Informatica**, 10 (1978), 27-52.

[4] Guttag, J.V., Horning, J.J., and Wing, J.M., *Larch in Five Easy Pieces*, Report 5, DEC System Research Center (1985).

[5] Harper, R., Milner, A.J.R.G., and Tofte, M., *The Definition of Standard ML*, Report ECS-LFCS-88-62, Laboratory for Foundations of Computer Science, Department of Computer Science, University of Edinburgh (1988).

[6] Havelund, K., *An RSL Tutorial*, Report LACOS/CRI/DOC/1/V3, Computer Resources International A/S (1991).

[7] Hoare, C.A.R., *Proof of Correctness of Data Representations*, **Acta Informatica**, 1 (1972), 271-281.

[8] Huet, G., and Hullot, J.-M., *Proofs by induction in equational theories with constructors*, **Journal of Computer and System Sciences**, 25, 2 (October 1982), 239-266.

[9] Jones, C.B., **Software Development: A Rigorous Approach** (Prentice-Hall, 1980).

[10] Melham, T.F., *Automating Recursive Type Definitions in Higher Order Logic*, in **Current Trends in Hardware Verification and Automated Theorem Proving**, edited by Birtwistle, G., and Subrahmanyam, P.A., (Springer, 1989) 341-386.

[11] Milne, R.E., *The proof theory for the RAISE specification language*, Report RAISE/STC/REM/12/V3, STC Technology Limited (1990).

[12] Milne, R.E., *Specifying and refining concurrent systems*, Report RAISE/STC/REM/13/V1, STC Technology Limited (1990).

[13] Milner, A.J.R.G., *An Algebraic Definition of Simulation Between Programs*, **Proceedings of the Second Joint International Conference on Artificial Intelligence** (British Computer Society, 1971) 481-489.

[14] Sannella, D., and Tarlecki, A., *Toward formal development of ML programs: foundations and methodology*, Report ECS-LFCS-89-71, Laboratory for Foundations of Computer Science, Department of Computer Science, University of Edinburgh (1989).

[15] Schoett, O., *Data Abstraction and the Correctness of Modular Programming*, Report ECS-LFCS-87-19, Laboratory for Foundations of Computer Science, Department of Computer Science, University of Edinburgh (1987).

[16] Spivey, J.M., **Understanding Z** (Cambridge University Press, 1988).

Refinement of two graph problems

D.A. Carrington
Key Centre for Software Technology
Department of Computer Science
University of Queensland
Australia
davec@uqcspe.cs.uq.oz.au

K.A. Robinson
School of Computer Science and Engineering
University of New South Wales
Australia
kenr@spectrum.cs.unsw.oz.au

Abstract

This paper provides a case study demonstrating how both data and algorithmic refinement can be performed in a uniform manner using the specification statement and the refinement calculus. The problems chosen to illustrate these techniques are taken from graph theory. The choice was motivated by a desire to expand the set of example refinements and to show how algorithms in this area may be formally derived from their specifications. The ultimate algorithms are not novel; the emphasis in the paper is on illustrating the use of the refinement calculus.

Introduction

Formal specification in a mathematical specification language, such as Z [4], allows us to capture the essential behavioural characteristics of a system or algorithm without concern for the implementation. Having produced a specification that is considered to be "correct", we want to be able to *refine* the specification by changing the data structures and introducing programming language constructs until we have an executable version of the initial specification. The aim of a formal refinement methodology is to ensure that at all times the refined version is in some essential way *consistent* with the initial specification.

The refinement calculus

The refinement calculus developed by Morgan and Robinson [9] provides a formal technique for deriving an executable program from an abstract specification. The technique ensures that the resulting program is a satisfactory implementation and is based on extending a programming language with the specification statement [8]. The refinement calculus uses Dijkstra's weakest pre-condition semantics [2].

The specification statement captures the essential behaviour of a program or part of a program, without concern for implementation issues. It is denoted

$$\vec{w} : \left[Pre \;/\; Post \right]$$

and denotes a program that, executed in a state satisfying *Pre*, will terminate in a state satisfying *Post* while modifying only variables in $\vec{w}$ (where $\vec{w}$ is a subset of the program variables $\vec{v}$). *Pre* is a predicate in $\vec{v}$ while *Post* is a predicate in $\vec{v}$ and $\vec{v}_0$ where the decorated variables $\vec{v}_0$ refer to the corresponding values in the initial state.

With the refinement calculus, the development of a program is a process of replacing specification statements by other programming constructs using the rules of the calculus to perform the transformations. To ensure that the resulting program is a valid implementation of the initial specification, we require an ordering between specifications that captures the idea that one specification (S_i) may be replaced by another (S_j) in any context. This ordering is denoted $S_i \sqsubseteq S_j$. If in all initial states in which S_i does not abort, the set of final states of S_j is contained in the set of final states of S_i, then we say S_i is refined by S_j. The formal definition uses weakest pre-conditions:

$$S_i \sqsubseteq S_j \text{ iff } (S_i\ R) \Rightarrow (S_j\ R) \text{ for all } \textit{predicates } R$$

Note that we use functional application of a specification S to a predicate R to denote the weakest pre-condition of S with respect to R, *i.e.* $S\ R = wp(S, R)$.

The ordering $\sqsubseteq$ is a partial ordering over specifications and defines a complete lattice.

The rules of the refinement calculus express valid transformations of specifications. Many of the rules have an associated applicability condition that specifies when the rule may be used. Use of a rule requires that any applicability condition be verified. A thorough introduction to the refinement calculus and a substantial set of rules can be found in [7].

Whereas procedural refinement introduces sequential control information into a program, data refinement replaces one set of local variables by another to provide a more efficient representation of data. The concept of data refinement is certainly not new [3, 5, 6], but the refinement calculus provides a unified and constructive approach to this aspect of program design. The refinement calculus gives us a set of rules to transform an abstract program (or program fragment) into a concrete equivalent. We need to supply a set of concrete variables to replace the abstract ones and an invariant that relates the concrete variables to the abstract ones. A detailed exposition is provided in [10].

Specifying Graphs

We begin by defining an abstract representation for a directed graph using a Z schema. We introduce the vertices as a basic set for this specification.

$$[\,VERTEX\,]$$

Our graph representation is the traditional one using a set of vertices and a set of edges (expressed in Z as a relation over the vertices).

$$\begin{array}{|l}
\textit{Graph} \\
\hline
v : \mathbb{P}\ \textit{VERTEX} \\
e : \textit{VERTEX} \leftrightarrow \textit{VERTEX} \\
\hline
\operatorname{dom} e \subseteq v \\
\operatorname{ran} e \subseteq v \\
\hline
\end{array}$$

We extend the standard Z operators to define subgraphs ($\subseteq$), induced subgraphs with respect to some set of vertices ($\lhd$), and the size of a graph ($\#$).

$$\begin{array}{|l}
\hline
_ \subseteq _ : \textit{Graph} \leftrightarrow \textit{Graph} \\
_ \lhd _ : \mathbb{P}\ \textit{VERTEX} \times \textit{Graph} \rightarrow \textit{Graph} \\
\#_ : \textit{Graph} \rightarrow \mathbb{N} \\
\hline
\forall g, h : \textit{Graph};\ s : \mathbb{P}\ \textit{VERTEX} \bullet \\
\quad h \subseteq g \Leftrightarrow h.v \subseteq g.v \land h.e \subseteq g.e \\
\quad s \lhd g = h \Leftrightarrow (h.v = g.v \cap s \land h.e = s \lhd g.e \rhd s) \\
\quad \#g \doteq \#g.v \\
\hline
\end{array}$$

The sink problem

This is a relatively simple problem intended to illustrate the details of the refinement process using the refinement calculus: given a non-empty graph, determine which vertex (if any) is the sink. A vertex k is the sink of a graph g iff there exist edges from all other vertices in g to k and there are no edges from k to any other vertex in g. [1]

$$sink(g, k) \quad \triangleq \quad k \in g.v \land \forall \left(u : g.v \mid u \neq k \bullet \begin{array}{l} (u,k) \in g.e \\ (k,u) \notin g.e \end{array} \right)$$

We can formulate the problem (for a non-empty graph) as a Z schema:

$$\begin{array}{|l}
\textit{FindSink} \\
\hline
g? : \textit{Graph} \\
k! : \textit{VERTEX} \\
result! : \textit{BOOLEAN} \\
\hline
g?.v \neq \{\} \\
\exists \left(u : g?.v \bullet sink(g?, u) \right) \Leftrightarrow result! \\
result! \Rightarrow sink(g?, k!) \\
\hline
\end{array}$$

Note that the operation *FindSink* is total in the sense that one of two outcomes must hold for any graph: either it has a sink or it does not.

[1] This problem is also known as the Celebrity problem; a variant can be defined in terms of paths instead of edges to the sink vertex but this is equivalent to the edge problem applied to the transitive closure of the original graph.

Let us translate the specification into the equivalent specification statement and then refine it towards an algorithmic solution.

$$k, \textit{result}\colon \left[g.v \neq \{\} \;/\; R \right] \qquad [1]$$

$$\text{where } R \;\triangleq\; \begin{pmatrix} \exists \left(u : g.v \bullet \textit{sink}(g,u) \right) \Leftrightarrow \textit{result} \\ \textit{result} \Rightarrow \textit{sink}(g,k) \end{pmatrix}$$

We proceed by realising that only one vertex can be the sink and adopting the strategy of first attempting to identify a candidate vertex and then confirming whether the candidate is really the sink. The first stage both identifies a candidate and rules out all other vertices as possible candidates.

$$\textit{candidate}(g,k) \;\triangleq\; k \in g.v \wedge \exists \left(u : g.v \bullet \textit{sink}(g,u) \right) \Rightarrow \textit{sink}(g,k)$$

Thus we can refine our original specification statement [1] to

$$\underbrace{k\colon \left[g.v \neq \{\} \;/\; \textit{candidate}(g,k) \right]}_{[2A]}; \; \underbrace{\textit{result}\colon \left[\textit{candidate}(g,k) \;/\; R \right]}_{[2B]}$$

Refinement of the first component [2A]

Concentrating on component [2A], we refine this to a block.

$$\begin{array}{ll} [\![\; \textbf{var } t : \textit{Graph} \bullet & \\ \quad t, k\colon \left[g.v \neq \{\} \;/\; t \subseteq g \wedge \textit{candidate}(t,k) \right]; & [3A] \\ \quad t, k\colon \left[t \subseteq g \wedge \textit{candidate}(t,k) \;/\; \textit{candidate}(g,k) \right] & [3B] \\ ]\!] & \end{array}$$

Specification [3A] will be satisfied by $t, k\colon \left[g.v \neq \{\} \;/\; k \in g.v \wedge t = \{k\} \lhd g \right]$ *i.e.* choosing any vertex and the associated single vertex subgraph.

Using a shorthand for specifications that contain an invariant

$$\vec{w}\colon \left[\textit{Pre} \;/\; \textit{Inv} \;/\; \textit{Post} \right] \;\triangleq\; \vec{w}\colon \left[\begin{matrix} \textit{Pre} \\ \textit{Inv} \end{matrix} \;/\; \begin{matrix} \textit{Inv} \\ \textit{Post} \end{matrix} \right]$$

specification [3B] can be rewritten as

$$t, k\colon \left[\textsf{true} \;/\; \begin{matrix} \textit{candidate}(t,k) \\ t \subseteq g \end{matrix} \;/\; t = g \right]$$

which permits a refinement to

$$\textbf{do } t \neq g \rightarrow \underbrace{t, k\colon \left[t \neq g \;/\; \begin{matrix} \textit{candidate}(t,k) \\ t \subseteq g \end{matrix} \;/\; \#t > \#t_0 \right]}_{[4]} \textbf{od}$$

based on the variant function $\#g - \#t$.

The guarded specification [4] now becomes the focus of attention. The task is to extend the subgraph t keeping track of the (only) sink candidate for the subgraph.

$$[4] \sqsubseteq \llbracket \text{ var } x : VERTEX \bullet$$

$$x\colon \left[t \subset g \;/\; x \in g.v - t.v \right]; \qquad [5A]$$

$$t, k\colon \left[x \in g.v - t.v \;\middle/\; \begin{matrix} candidate(t,k) \\ t \subseteq g \end{matrix} \;\middle/\; \#t > \#t_0 \right] \qquad [5B]$$

$$\rrbracket$$

Since we are planning to extend the subgraph t by adding the new vertex x, we can use the weakest pre-specification rule to refine the second component of this block.

$$[5B] \sqsubseteq k\colon \left[\begin{matrix} x \in g.v - t.v \\ candidate(t,k) \end{matrix} \;\middle/\; candidate((t.v \cup \{x\}) \lhd g, k) \right]; \qquad [6A]$$

$$t\colon \left[t = (t_0.v \cup \{x\}) \lhd g \right] \qquad [6B]$$

Our concern is now updating k. We use two guarded refinements to refine [5A] and since the guards are complementary, we can compose an if statement.

$$[6A] \sqsubseteq \textbf{if}$$

$$(k,x) \in g.e \rightarrow k := x$$

$$\talloblong$$

$$(k,x) \notin g.e \rightarrow \textbf{skip}$$

$$\textbf{fi}$$

Refinement of the second component [2B]

Specification [2B] describes the task of checking whether a given vertex is actually the sink now that we have eliminated all other possible candidates.

$$result\colon \left[candidate(g,k) \;/\; R \right]$$

$$\sqsubseteq$$

$$\llbracket \text{ var } s : Graph \bullet$$

$$s, result\colon \left[candidate(g,k) \;/\; I \right]; \qquad [7A]$$

$$s, result\colon \left[I \;/\; R \right] \qquad [7B]$$

$$\rrbracket$$

$$\text{where } I \;\triangleq\; candidate(g,k) \wedge s \subseteq g \wedge R_{[g \backslash s]}$$

The predicate I is established by

$$s, result := \{k\} \lhd g, \mathsf{true}$$

We now refine specification [7B] within the block with the objective of expanding the subgraph s for which k is the sink.

$$[7B] \sqsubseteq \quad s, \mathit{result}\colon \left[\mathsf{true} \;/\; I \;/\; s = g\right]$$

$$\sqsubseteq \quad \mathbf{do}\ s \neq g \rightarrow \underbrace{s, \mathit{result}\colon \left[s \neq g \;/\; I \;/\; \#s > \#s_0\right]}_{[8]}\ \mathbf{od}$$

with the variant $\#g - \#s$.

The loop body [8] is refined to a block

$$[8] \sqsubseteq$$

$$[\![\ \mathrm{var}\ x : \mathit{VERTEX} \bullet$$

$$x\colon \left[s \neq g \;/\; x \in g.v - s.v\right]; \qquad [9A]$$

$$s, \mathit{result}\colon \left[x \in g.v - s.v \;/\; I \;/\; \#s > \#s_0\right] \qquad [9B]$$

$$]\!]$$

Specification [9A] is a simple (non-deterministic) choice of a remaining vertex. To achieve the specification [9B], we consider when the vertex x may be added to the subgraph s while maintaining the invariant. The status of k as the sink is unchanged if some other vertex has an edge to k but no edge from k. This leads to a refinement to a guarded command

$$[9B] \sqsubseteq (x,k) \in g.e \land (k,x) \notin g.e \rightarrow s := (s.v \cup \{x\}) \lhd g$$

Investigating the complementary guard (with a view to creating an if command) we realise that the guard will only be true when k is not the sink for the graph $(s.v \cup \{x\}) \lhd g$. If k is not the sink for some subgraph of g, then it cannot be the sink for the complete graph.

$$[9B] \sqsubseteq \neg\left((x,k) \in g.e \land (k,x) \notin g.e\right) \rightarrow \mathit{result}, s := \mathsf{false}, g$$

The complete abstract algorithm may now be assembled from the leaves of the refinement tree.

```
[ var t : Graph •                                              [10]
    t, k: [k ∈ g.v ∧ t = {k} ◁ g];
    do t ≠ g →
        [ var x : VERTEX •                                     [10A]
            x: [t ⊂ g / x ∈ g.v − t.v];
            if
                (k, x) ∈ g.e → k := x
            []
                (k, x) ∉ g.e → skip
            fi;
            t := (t.v ∪ {x}) ◁ g
        ]
    od
];
[ var s : Graph •                                              [11]
    s, result := {k} ◁ g, true;
    do s ≠ g →
        [ var x : VERTEX •                                     [11A]
            x: [s ≠ g / x ∈ g.v − s.v];
            if
                (x, k) ∈ g.e ∧ (k, x) ∉ g.e → s := (s.v ∪ {x}) ◁ g
            []
                ¬ ((x, k) ∈ g.e ∧ (k, x) ∉ g.e) → result, s := false, g
            fi
        ]
    od
]
```

Our next task is to investigate data refinement of the algorithm.

Data Refinement

The abstract variables in our sink problem are the graph g and the vertex k. There is no need to transform the *result* variable as we can directly represent that in our concrete program. We choose to represent the graph by mapping the vertices onto a subrange of the natural numbers and by mapping the edges onto a two dimensional array (the traditional adjacency matrix [2]). Our concrete variables are:

N — the number of vertices in the graph
A — the adjacency matrix
K — the number corresponding to the sink vertex

[2]this is the appropriate representation for this algorithm — using adjacency lists would be difficult

The abstraction invariant is:

$$AI \quad \triangleq \quad \begin{array}{c} N = \# g.v \\ vmap \in 0 \,..\, N-1 \rightarrowtail\!\!\!\!\twoheadrightarrow g.v \\ A \in 0 \,..\, N-1 \times 0 \,..\, N-1 \rightarrow BOOLEAN \\ \forall \left(i, j : 0 \,..\, N-1 \bullet A(i,j) \Leftrightarrow (vmap(i), vmap(j)) \in g.e\right) \\ k = vmap(K) \end{array}$$

For the initialisation, we have

$$\exists \left(g, k \bullet \begin{array}{c} g \in Graph \\ g.v \neq \{\} \\ k \in VERTEX \\ AI \end{array} \right)$$

$$= \left(\begin{array}{c} N \in \mathbf{N}_1 \\ A \in \textbf{array}[0 \,..\, N-1, 0 \,..\, N-1] \textbf{ of } BOOLEAN \\ K \in 0 \,..\, N-1 \end{array} \right)$$

Each block that introduces new variables that require data refinement will require an additional abstraction invariant to be conjoined to the current one. For block [10] that introduces $t : graph$, the corresponding concrete variable is T and the additional abstraction invariant is:

$$AI_1 \quad \triangleq \quad \left(\begin{array}{c} 1 \leq T \leq N \\ t = vmap(\!| 0 \,..\, T-1 |\!) \lhd g \end{array} \right)$$

Our refinement task is made easier by the choice of functional abstraction invariants (*i.e.* for each concrete state there is at most one corresponding abstract state); AI_1 is a functional abstraction. We can now refine the specification statement $t, k\!: \left[g.v \neq \{\} \;/\; k \in g.v \wedge t = \{k\} \lhd g \right]$ to

$$K, T\!: \left[vmap(\!| 0 \,..\, N-1 |\!) \neq \{\} \;\Big/\; \begin{array}{c} vmap(K) \in vmap(\!| 0 \,..\, N-1 |\!) \\ vmap(\!| 0 \,..\, T-1 |\!) \lhd g = \{vmap(K)\} \lhd g \end{array} \right]$$

$$=$$

$$K, T\!: \left[N \neq 0 \;/\; K \in 0 \,..\, N-1 \wedge 0 \,..\, T-1 = \{K\} \right]$$

$$\sqsubseteq$$

$$K, T := 0, 1$$

The guard $t \neq g$ becomes $vmap(\!| 0 \,..\, T-1 |\!) \lhd g \neq g$ which is just $T \neq N$ (as $g = vmap(\!| 0 \,..\, N-1 |\!) \lhd g$).

For the inner block [10A], our additional invariant is:

$$AI_{1.1} \quad \triangleq \quad x = vmap(X) \wedge 0 \leq X < N$$

The initialization $x\!: \left[t \subset g \;/\; x \in g.v - t.v \right]$ is equivalent to

$$X\!: \left[X \in (0 \,..\, N-1) - (0 \,..\, T-1) \right]$$

and we choose to refine that to $X := T$.

We can separately refine the guards of the if statement, subject to the constraint that we must not weaken the disjunction of the guards. Formally, each guard G is refined to

$$\forall\left(k, x, t \bullet AI \wedge AI_1 \wedge AI_{1.1} \Rightarrow G\right)$$

Our guards are very simple and it is easy to see that $(k, x) \in g.e$ refines to $A[K, X]$, and $(k, x) \notin g.e$ refines to $\neg\ A[K, X]$. Similarly, the guarded statements S_i are separately refined with $k := x$ being transformed into $K := X$.

The statement $t := (t.v \cup \{x\}) \lhd g$ is refined to

$$T\!:\left[\begin{array}{l} AI \\ AI_1 \\ AI_{1.1} \end{array} \Big/ \left(t := (t.v \cup \{x\}) \lhd g\right) \begin{array}{r} AI \\ AI_1 \\ AI_{1.1} \end{array}\right]$$

$$=$$

$$T\!:\left[t = vmap(\!|\, 0 \,..\, T-1 \,|\!) \lhd g \;\Big/\; t.v \cup \{x\} = vmap(\!|\, 0 \,..\, T-1 \,|\!)\right]$$

The only practical refinement of this is $T\!:\left[\,T = T_0 + 1\,\right]$, requiring $X = T$, which is already satisfied. We have now completed the data refinement of the first block which now looks like this:

$$
\begin{array}{l}
\big[\!\big[\ \mathbf{var}\ T : \mathbb{N}_1\ \bullet \\
\quad K, T := 0, 1; \\
\quad \mathbf{do}\ T \neq N \rightarrow \\
\qquad\quad \big[\!\big[\ \mathbf{var}\ X : \mathbb{N}\ \bullet \\
\qquad\qquad X := T; \\
\qquad\qquad \mathbf{if} \\
\qquad\qquad\qquad A[K, X] \rightarrow K := X \\
\qquad\qquad [\!] \\
\qquad\qquad\qquad \neg\ A[K, X] \rightarrow \mathbf{skip} \\
\qquad\qquad \mathbf{fi}; \\
\qquad\qquad T := T + 1 \\
\qquad\quad \big]\!\big] \\
\quad \mathbf{od} \\
\big]\!\big]
\end{array}
$$

The variable X can be removed by a simple optimization of the inner block.

Data refinement of the second block [11]

Refinement of block [11] is similar but not identical to that for [10] so we will concentrate on the differences. We need to consider each vertex in turn except for k. To simplify the selection process, we choose a slightly more complicated abstraction invariant: s is related to the concrete S by

$$AI_2 \;\triangleq\; s = vmap(\!|\, K \circlearrowleft_N S \,|\!) \lhd g \wedge 1 \leq S \leq N$$

where

$\_ \circlearrowleft_N \_ : \mathbb{N} \times \mathbb{N} \rightarrow \mathbb{P}\mathbb{N}$
$\forall a, b : 0 \mathrel{..} N \bullet a \circlearrowleft_N b = \mathrm{mod}_N (\!| a \mathrel{..} a + b - 1 |\!)$

The $a \circlearrowleft_N b$ function generates a set of b numbers starting from a, all modulo N.

This allows us to consider the vertices starting from K in a modulo sequence. The initialisation of s becomes $S := 1$ and the guard $s \neq g$ becomes $S \neq N$. Note that the assignment to *result* is unchanged since it is not involved in the data refinement.

The inner block [11A] uses the invariant

$$AI_{2.1} \quad \triangleq \quad x = vmap(X) \wedge 0 \leq X < N$$

to describe the relationship between x and X. The initialisation of x is required to satisfy $x \in g.v - s.v$, a condition that transforms to $X \in (0 \mathrel{..} N - 1) - (K \circlearrowleft_N S)$. Our chosen refinement is $X := (K + S) \bmod N$.

Transformation of the remainder of the block is straight forward, leading to the final version:

$$
\begin{array}{l}
[\![\ \mathbf{var}\ S : \mathbb{N} \bullet \\
\quad S, \mathit{result} := 1, \mathsf{true}; \\
\quad \mathbf{do}\ S \neq N \rightarrow \\
\qquad\quad [\![\ \mathbf{var}\ X : \mathbb{N} \bullet \\
\qquad\qquad X := (K + S) \bmod N; \\
\qquad\qquad \mathbf{if} \\
\qquad\qquad\qquad A[X, K] \wedge \neg A[K, X] \rightarrow S := S + 1 \\
\qquad\qquad [\,] \\
\qquad\qquad\qquad \neg (A[X, K] \wedge \neg A[K, X]) \rightarrow \mathit{result}, S := \mathsf{false}, N \\
\qquad\qquad \mathbf{fi} \\
\qquad\quad]\!] \\
\quad \mathbf{od} \\
]\!]
\end{array}
$$

Test for an acyclic graph

Many graph algorithms require directed acyclic graphs (DAGs) so we now investigate the specification and refinement of an algorithm for checking whether a given graph is acyclic. We start by defining some necessary concepts. Using the transitive closure of the edge relation, we can define a reachable relation for a graph.

$$\mathit{reachable}(g) \quad \triangleq \quad g.e^{+}$$

An acyclic graph is simply one with no vertex reachable from itself.

$$\mathit{nocycles}(g) \quad \triangleq \quad \mathit{reachable}(g) \cap \mathrm{id}\, g.v = \varnothing$$

so our specification can be written as

$$ac\colon \left[\, ac \Leftrightarrow \mathit{nocycles}(g) \,\right] \qquad [12]$$

A naive approach would be to generate the *reachable* relation and then check for cycles. Instead, we use the *depth-first* graph traversal strategy which identifies a cycle as an attempt to visit a node already on the current path. We define a path in a graph as a sequence of vertices connected by edges and hence the set of all paths for a graph as

$$paths(g) \quad \triangleq \quad \left\{ s : \mathrm{seq}\ VERTEX \mid \begin{array}{c} \mathrm{ran}\ s \subseteq g.v \\ \forall i : 1 \mathrel{..} \#s - 1 \bullet s(i) \mapsto s(i+1) \in g.e \end{array} \right\}$$

To keep track of those nodes we have completed visiting, we introduce the variable *visited*, a subset of the graph's vertices, and refine [12] as follows:

$$[12] \sqsubseteq I \quad \triangleq \quad \left(\begin{array}{c} visited \subseteq g.v \\ ac \Leftrightarrow nocycles(visited \lhd g) \\ \forall p : paths(g) \mid p(1) \in visited \bullet \mathrm{ran}\ p \subseteq visited \end{array} \right) \bullet$$

$$\begin{array}{ll} [\![\ \mathbf{var}\ visited : \mathbb{P}\ VERTEX \bullet & \\ \quad visited, ac\text{:} \left[\mathsf{true}\ \middle/\ I \right]; & [13A] \\ \quad visited, ac\text{:} \left[I\ \middle/\ ac \Leftrightarrow nocycles(g) \right] & [13B] \\ ]\!] & \end{array}$$

Specification [13A] can be refined to

$$visited, ac := \{\}, \mathsf{true}$$

Now refine [13B] to a loop (with variant $\#(g.v - visited)$)

$$\mathbf{do}\ visited \neq g.v \rightarrow \underbrace{visited, ac\text{:} \left[visited \neq g.v \ / \ I \ / \ \#visited > \#visited_0 \right]}_{[14]} \mathbf{od}$$

Concentrating on the inner specification [14], we choose some arbitrary vertex x not yet visited with the intention of adding it to the visited set.

$$\begin{array}{ll} [14] \sqsubseteq [\![\ \mathbf{var}\ x : VERTEX \bullet & \\ \quad x\text{:} \left[visited \neq g.v \ / \ I \ / \ x \in g.v - visited \right]; & [15A] \\ \quad visited, ac\text{:} \left[x \in g.v - visited \ / \ I \ / \ \#visited > \#visited_0 \right] & \\ & [15B] \\ ]\!] & \end{array}$$

We define a procedure *Dfs* for the specification [15B], after first introducing a substitution by value in preparation for a value parameter.

$$\begin{array}{l} visited, ac\text{:} \left[x \in g.v - visited \ / \ I \ / \ \#visited > \#visited_0 \right] \\ \quad \sqsubseteq [\mathbf{value}\ y \backslash x] \bullet \\ \qquad visited, ac\text{:} \left[y \in g.v - visited \ / \ I \ / \ \#visited > \#visited_0 \right] \\ \quad \sqsubseteq \mathbf{procedure}\ Dfs \ \triangleq \\ \qquad\quad visited, ac\text{:} \left[y \in g.v - visited \ / \ I \ / \ \#visited > \#visited_0 \right] \bullet \\ \qquad Dfs \end{array}$$

Summarising our progress so far, our refinement can be collected and arranged (using conventional parameter notation) as

$$
\begin{array}{l}
[\![\ \textbf{var}\ visited : \mathbb{P}\ VERTEX;\\
\quad \textbf{procedure}\ Dfs(\textbf{value}\ y : VERTEX)\ \hat{=}\\
\qquad visited, ac\text{:}\left[\, y \in g.v - visited \;/\; I \;/\; \#visited > \#visited_0 \,\right] \bullet\\
\quad visited, ac := \{\}, \textbf{true};\\
\quad \textbf{do}\ visited \neq g.v \rightarrow\\
\qquad [\![\ \textbf{var}\ x : VERTEX \bullet\\
\qquad\quad x\text{:}\left[\, visited \neq g.v \;/\; I \;/\; x \in g.v - visited \,\right];\\
\qquad\quad Dfs(x)\\
\qquad]\!]\\
\quad \textbf{od}\\
]\!]
\end{array}
\qquad [16]
$$

Focusing on the procedure *Dfs*, and following our approach of keeping track of the visited vertices, we refine the procedure body.

$$
\begin{array}{ll}
visited, ac\text{:}\left[\, y \in g.v - visited \;/\; I \;/\; \#visited > \#visited_0 \,\right] & \\
\quad \sqsubseteq\ visited, ac\text{:}\left[\begin{array}{c} y \in g.v - visited \\ I \end{array} \;\Big/\; I_{[visited \setminus visited \cup \{y\}]} \right]; & [17A]\\
\qquad visited := visited \cup \{y\} & [17B]
\end{array}
$$

where the post-condition of [17A] requires that the visited graph extended by the vertex y is also acyclic. To maintain the invariant I, we need to add all nodes reachable from y to *visited* before adding y. The following restructuring suggests a basis for a recursive solution.

$$
\begin{array}{l}
g.e^{+}(\!|\ \{y\}\ |\!)\\
\quad = g.e^{*}(\!|\ g.e(\!|\ \{y\}\ |\!)\ |\!)\\
\quad = \text{“}adj \mathrel{\hat{=}} g.e(\!|\ \{y\}\ |\!)\text{”}\\
\qquad g.e^{+}(\!|\ adj\ |\!) \cup adj\\
\quad = \bigcup_{x \in adj} (g.e^{+}(\!|\ \{x\}\ |\!) \cup \{x\})
\end{array}
$$

The refinement of [17A] below is based on the invariant

$$J \mathrel{\hat{=}} g.e^{+}(\!|\ \{y\}\ |\!) - g.e^{*}(\!|\ adj\ |\!) \subseteq visited$$

and the variant function $\#adj$.

$$
\begin{array}{l}
[17A] \sqsubseteq \llbracket\ \mathbf{var}\ adj : \mathbb{P}\ Vertex \bullet \\
\quad adj := g.e(\!|\ \{y\}\ |\!); \\
\quad \mathbf{do}\ adj \neq \{\} \rightarrow \\
\quad\quad \llbracket\ \mathbf{var}\ x : VERTEX \bullet \\
\quad\quad\quad x, adj\mathbf{:} \left[adj \neq \{\} \ \middle/ \ x \in adj_0 \wedge adj = adj_0 - \{x\} \right]; \quad [18A] \\
\quad\quad\quad visited, ac, adj\mathbf{:} \left[I \wedge J_{[adj \setminus adj \cup \{x\}]} \ \middle/ \ I \wedge J \right] \quad [18B] \\
\quad\quad \rrbracket \\
\quad \mathbf{od} \\
\rrbracket
\end{array}
$$

A simple refinement of [18B] is

$x \in visited \rightarrow \mathbf{skip}$

So far the derivation has been driven by considering the graph traversal. We also need to consider that part of the invariant that is concerned with cycles. For $x \notin visited$ we have prepared the way for a recursive invocation of *Dfs*, but this should only happen if x is not part of a cycle. To check this, we need to ensure that x is not an element of its own reachable image, *i.e.*

$x \notin g.e^{+}(\!|\ \{x\}\ |\!)$.

One way to do this is to check that there is no pending addition of x to the *visited* set (*i.e.* that x is not an element of the current path being traversed). This check can be made conveniently by making the set of nodes forming the current path a parameter to *Dfs*. Then[3]

$x \in path \rightarrow ac := \mathsf{false}$

and

$x \notin path \wedge x \notin visited \rightarrow Dfs(x, path \cup \{x\})$

The variant function $\#(g.v - path)$ ensures termination of the recursion. The initial call to *Dfs* is augmented with the singleton set $\{x\}$ as the *path* parameter.

[3]with a different invariant this assignment can be supplemented to force immediate termination if required.

We now bring all the pieces of *Dfs* together.

$$
\begin{array}{l}
\textbf{procedure } \mathit{Dfs}(\textbf{value } y : \mathit{VERTEX};\ \textbf{value } \mathit{path} : \mathbb{P}\ \mathit{VERTEX}) \quad \triangleq \\
\quad [\![\textbf{ var } \mathit{adj} : \mathbb{P}\ \mathit{Vertex} \bullet \\
\qquad \mathit{adj} := g.e(\![\{y\}]\!); \\
\qquad \textbf{do } \mathit{adj} \neq \{\} \rightarrow \\
\qquad\quad [\![\textbf{ var } x : \mathit{VERTEX} \bullet \\
\qquad\qquad x, \mathit{adj}\!: \left[\mathit{adj} \neq \{\} \ / \ x \in \mathit{adj}_0 \wedge \mathit{adj} = \mathit{adj}_0 - \{x\} \right]; \\
\qquad\qquad \textbf{if} \\
\qquad\qquad\quad x \in \mathit{path} \rightarrow \mathit{ac} := \mathsf{false} \\
\qquad\qquad [\!] \\
\qquad\qquad\quad x \in \mathit{visited} \rightarrow \textbf{skip} \\
\qquad\qquad [\!] \\
\qquad\qquad\quad x \notin \mathit{path} \wedge x \notin \mathit{visited} \rightarrow \mathit{Dfs}(x, \mathit{path} \cup \{x\}) \\
\qquad\qquad \textbf{fi} \\
\qquad\quad]\!] \\
\qquad \textbf{od} \\
\quad]\!]; \\
\quad \mathit{visited} := \mathit{visited} \cup \{y\}
\end{array}
$$

Data refinement

For simplicity we choose the concrete representation for our graph used in the earlier problem although the graph representation only affects the refinement of the *Dfs* procedure.

$$
AI \quad \triangleq \quad \left(\begin{array}{c}
N = \# g.v \\
\mathit{vmap} \in 0 \mathinner{..} N-1 \rightarrowtail\!\!\!\!\twoheadrightarrow g.v \\
A \in 0 \mathinner{..} N-1 \times 0 \mathinner{..} N-1 \rightarrow \mathit{BOOLEAN} \\
\forall i, j : 0 \mathinner{..} N-1 \bullet A(i,j) \Leftrightarrow (\mathit{vmap}(i), \mathit{vmap}(j)) \in g.e
\end{array} \right)
$$

In the first block, we need a concrete representation for *visited*. We choose to do so via a concrete array *Vstate* with an element corresponding to each vertex. The value of these elements is based on the observation that the set of vertices is partitioned by three sets, the visited set, the unvisited set and the path set. This representation removes the need for a second parameter to *Dfs* and is equivalent to using a global variable for the same purpose. Thus each array element has a value from the set $\{U, P, V\}$.

$$
AI_1 \quad \triangleq \quad \left(\begin{array}{c}
\mathit{Vstate} \in 0 \mathinner{..} N-1 \rightarrow \{U, P, V\} \\
\mathit{path} = \mathit{vmap}(\![\{i : 0 \mathinner{..} N-1 \mid \mathit{Vstate}[i] = P\}]\!) \\
\mathit{visited} = \mathit{vmap}(\![\{i : 0 \mathinner{..} N-1 \mid \mathit{Vstate}[i] = V\}]\!)
\end{array} \right)
$$

The establishment of the predicate I requires a loop rather than the abstract assignment to assign each element of *Vstate* to the value U. More difficult to handle is the refinement of the loop guard $\mathit{visited} \neq g.v$ and the selection of x. To make things easier, we augment the concrete state by the variable T that always indexes an unvisited vertex, if any remain. The state is augmented by the invariant AI_{1a}.

$$AI_{1a} \triangleq \begin{pmatrix} T \neq N \Rightarrow Vstate[T] = U \\ g.v - visited \subseteq vmap(\!| T \mathinner{..} N-1 |\!) \end{pmatrix}$$

We can now refine the body of the loop in [16], noting that

$$T = N \Rightarrow g.v = visited$$

```
[ var Vstate : array[0 .. N − 1] of (U, P, V);
      T : N;
      procedure Dfs(value y : VERTEX)  ≜  ... •
      [ var I : N • I := 0; do I ≠ N → Vstate[I] := U od];
      T := 0;
      ac := true;
      do T ≠ N →
         Dfs(T);
         do T ≠ N ∧ Vstate[T] ≠ U → T := T + 1 od
      od
]
```

where the local variable x is identified with T and can therefore be eliminated.

Turning to the data refinement of *Dfs*, a difficulty arises with the representation of the set *adj*. If we had chosen an adjacency list representation for the graph, the loop would become a simple list traversal but the adjacency matrix representation is not so convenient[4]. We choose to represent *adj* with a concrete variable *Adj* according to the abstraction invariant

$$AI_{Dfs} \triangleq adj \subseteq vmap(\!| Adj \mathinner{..} N |\!)$$

[4]This suggests that the adjacency list would suit the algorithm better, an issue not pursued here.

Based on this invariant, the procedure *Dfs* is refined as follows:

```
procedure Dfs(value Y : 0 .. N − 1)  ≙
    Vstate[Y] := P;
    [[ var Adj : 0 .. N •
        Adj := 0;
        do
            Adj ≠ N ∧ A[Y, Adj] →
                [[ var X : 0 .. N − 1 •
                    X, Adj := Adj, Adj + 1;
                    if
                        Vstate[X] = P → ac := false
                    []
                        Vstate[X] = V → skip
                    []
                        Vstate[X] = U → Dfs(X)
                    fi
                ]]
        []
            Adj ≠ N ∧ ¬ A[Y, Adj] → Adj := Adj + 1
        od
    ]];
    Vstate[Y] := V
```

Note that

1. the path parameter has been replaced by an assignment at the beginning of the procedure to the global variable *Vstate*;
2. we are forced to refine the single guarded command of the **do** command to two guarded commands, each of whose guards is stronger.

Aside: the algorithm can be adapted to generate a topological ordering of the graph by constructing a sequence as the graph is traversed. As each node is added to the visited set, it is prepended to the topsort sequence.

Conclusions

Using the refinement calculus, we have shown how an abstract specification can be refined, with respect to both the algorithmic and the data components. The development of an algorithm is at least as important as the final executable algorithm itself, since it serves to document the design process and provides a method of checking the correctness of the algorithm (with respect to the initial specification). The use of the refinement calculus means that the algorithm will be correct if each refinement step is correct; that is each step is applicable and is correctly performed. We are currently investigating tools to assist the application of the refinement calculus [1]. Such tools are intended to record the development steps and assist with correctly applying the refinement calculus including developing the necessary proofs associated with some refinement laws.

Acknowledgements

We gratefully acknowledge the influence and inspiration of the specification research at the Programming Research Group, Oxford University. Special thanks are owed to Carroll Morgan for his original contributions to the development of the refinement calculus. We would also like to thank Ian Hayes for identifying some problems in an earlier version of this paper. The comments of the referees were also of considerable assistance in improving the paper.

This research is partially supported by an Australian Research Council grant.

References

[1] D.A. Carrington and K.A. Robinson. A prototype program refinement editor. In *Australian Software Engineering Conference*, pages 45–63. ACS, 1988.

[2] Edsgar W. Dijkstra. *A Discipline of Programming.* Prentice-Hall, 1976.

[3] I.J. Hayes. Correctness of data representations. In *Australian Software Engineering Conference*, pages 75–86. I.E.Aust, May 1987.

[4] I.J. Hayes, editor. *Specification Case Studies.* Prentice-Hall, 1987.

[5] C.A.R. Hoare. Proof of correctness of data representation. *Acta Informatica*, 1:271–281, 1972.

[6] C.A.R. Hoare, J.F. He, and J.W. Sanders. Prespecification in data refinement. *Inf. Proc. Lett.*, 25(2):71–76, May 1987.

[7] C. Morgan. *Programming from Specifications.* Prentice-Hall, 1990.

[8] C.C. Morgan. The specification statement. *ACM Transactions on Programming Languages and Systems*, 10(3):403–419, July 1988.

[9] C.C. Morgan and K.A. Robinson. Specification statements and refinement. *IBM Journal of Research and Development*, 31(5):546–555, September 1987.

[10] C.C. Morgan, K.A. Robinson, and P. Gardiner. On the refinement calculus. Technical Report PRG-70, Programming Research Group, 8-11 Keble Road, Oxford OX1 3QD, UK, 1988.

CSP and Timewise Refinement

G.M. Reed, A.W. Roscoe, and S.A. Schneider *

Programming Research Group
Oxford University Computing Laboratory
11 Keble Road
Oxford OX1 3QD
England
{awr,gmr,sas} @ uk.ac.oxford.prg

Abstract

In recent years, G. M. Reed and A. W. Roscoe have developed a hierarchy of untimed and timed models for *CSP*. This mathematical hierarchy allows one to reason about concurrent processes in a uniform fashion by a series of refinements between models, where at each step the specification and verification techniques of the relevant model are appropriate to the complexity of the design decision. S. A. Schneider has exploited the links between the untimed and timed models to create an elegant, systematic theory of *timewise refinement*. In this paper, the authors outline this theory, discuss its mathematical foundations, and utilise it to prove the correctness of timing constraints on well-known protocols such as the alternating bit protocol.

Our goal is to provide a gentle introduction to the complex theory of CSP (both timed and untimed), and to illustrate the theory of timewise refinement. We shall keep the mathematical content to a minimum. Technical details are available in the referenced publications.

*The work reported in this paper was supported by the U.S. Office of Naval Research, Esprit BRA SPEC, and SERC.

1 Introduction

Over the past five years, G. M. Reed and A. W. Roscoe have reformulated and extended work on untimed CSP: earlier CSP models and new ones have been analysed and developed into a consistent hierarchy capturing the full complexity of untimed CSP. They have then extended this hierarchy to include corresponding real-time models. The links between the various untimed and timed models in the hierarchy have been well established and there is currently a large group of academic staff, research staff, and graduate students at Oxford University exploring the use of this hierarchy in the design and specification of real-time processes.

The addition of communication to the models in the hierarchy and the introduction of piping operators with application to the specification and verification of communication protocols with timing constraints has been accomplished by S. A. Schneider. J. W. Davies and Schneider have together developed high level proof systems for efficient reasoning within the timed models. D. M. Jackson, a current graduate student at Oxford (under the sponsorship of Rolls Royce), has developed a temporal logic compatible with the semantics of Timed CSP, i.e., temporal formulae are mapped onto set-theoretic predicates.

Schneider has also formalised the notion of timewise refinement within the context of our hierarchy of models for CSP. This theory relates timed processes to untimed ones, and supports the mapping of correctness results from one model to another. It allows us to restrict timed analysis to parts of a development where it is really necessary. For example, if an untimed process is deadlock-free, then any timewise refinement of it is deadlock-free. Since timewise refinement is preserved by the parallel operator when its argument processes are well-behaved, it supports the verification that networks of well-behaved processes are deadlock-free: it is only necessary to establish this of a corresponding network of untimed components that are individually refined by the timed components.

The above results have now been applied successfully in several large case studies involving industrial participation, e.g., [aircraft engine control (D. M. Jackson - Rolls-Royce)], [telephone switching (A. Kay and J. N. Reed - Greek telephone network, Esprit Rex Project)], [robotics (B. Scattergood - BP)], [robotics (R. Stamper - GEC Turtle, an AGV)].

The paper is organised as follows: In section 2, we give a brief discussion of the crucial issues involved in the study of concurrency and of the CSP/occam approach to these issues. In section 3, we illustrate untimed CSP through a discussion of buffers and protocols. In particular, we consider the specification and verification of the alternating bit protocol in CSP. In section 4, we discuss the complexity of timing constraints on concurrent processes. We illustrate the theory of timewise refinement by implementing the alternating bit protocol in Timed CSP and deriving aspects of its correctness via the links between the untimed and timed models. In section 5, we discuss future work.

2 Concurrency

Parallel computers are starting to become common, thanks to developing technology and our seemingly insatiable demands for computing power. They provide the most obvious examples of concurrent systems, which can be characterised as computer systems where there are a number of different activities being carried out at the same time. But there are others: at one extreme we have loosely coupled networks of workstations, perhaps sharing some common fileserver; and at the other we have a single VLSI circuit, whose internal activity will generally be concurrent. What all examples have in common is a number of separate components which need to communicate with each other. The theory of concurrency is about the study of such communicating systems and applies equally to all these examples and more.

Concurrent systems are more difficult to understand than sequential ones for various reasons. Perhaps the most obvious is that, whereas a sequential program is only 'at' one line at a time, in a concurrent system all the different components are in some (more or less) independent state and it is necessary to understand which combinations of states can arise and the consequences of each. This same observation means that there simply are more states to worry about in parallel code, because the total number of states grows exponentially (with the number of components) rather than linearly (in the length of code) for sequential code. Aside from this state explosion there are a number of more specific misbehaviours which all create their own difficulties.

Nondeterminism A system exhibits *nondeterminism* if two different copies of it may behave differently when given exactly the same inputs. Parallel systems often behave in this way because of contention for communication: if there are three subprocesses P, Q and R where P and Q are competing to be the first to communicate with R, which in turn bases its future behaviour upon which wins the race, then the whole system may veer one way or the other in a manner that is uncontrollable and unobservable from the outside.

Nondeterministic systems are in principle untestable, since however many times one behaves correctly on the test bed with a given set of data, it is impossible to be sure that it will still do so in the field (probably in subtly different conditions). Formal methods are the only way one can hope to establish any property of such a system, since they analyse all possible behaviours. Where possible and desirable, formal methods can also be used to construct programs that are deterministic (i.e., free of nondeterminism).

However one should not think that a nondeterministic system is necessarily incorrect, for it may be that all of its possible behaviours are satisfactory. What is vitally important is that nondeterminism is understood and reconciled with a formal specification.

Deadlock A concurrent system is *deadlocked* if no component can make any progress, generally because each is waiting for communication with others. The most famous example of a deadlocked system is the 'five dining philosophers', where the five philosophers are seated at a round table with a single fork between each pair. But each philosopher requires both neighbouring forks to eat, so if all get hungry simultaneously and pick up their right-hand fork then they deadlock and starve to death. This example is fairly typical, but the possible causes and configurations of deadlock are legion.

Deadlock seems to be the ill that many parallel programmers fear most. Of course a system may nondeterministically deadlock or not, so it is impossible to be sure informally that a system is deadlock free.

Formal methods allow one to prove deadlock freedom or develop a network in such a way that deadlock freedom is guaranteed. Using techniques developed by A.W. Roscoe, N. Dathi and others it is now possible to do this is ways which use only local analysis and hence avoid becoming bogged down by the state explosion mentioned earlier.

Livelock All programmers are used to programs that go into infinite loops, never to interact with their environments again. In addition to the usual causes of this type of behaviour – properly called divergence, where a program performs an infinite unbroken sequence of internal actions – parallel systems can *livelock*. This occurs when a network communicates infinitely internally without any component communicating externally. As far as the user is concerned a livelocked system looks similar to a deadlocked one, though perhaps worse since the user may be able to observe the presence of internal activity and so hope eternally that some output would emerge eventually. However it is operationally very different and so requires different analytic techniques. Fortunately there are fairly straightforward formal techniques that are usually enough to establish freedom from livelock.

CSP and occam There are a number of different models of concurrent systems, all of which contain these problems in one form or another. One cannot in general hope to eliminate them simply by choice of notation, but choosing the right development language can make reasoning about these and other issues much easier. The notations we generally use are CSP, which is a 'blackboard' programming language and occam, a practical language implemented on the inmos Transputer.

CSP was developed by C.A.R. Hoare, whose book [Hoa85] provides an excellent introduction. It contains the constructs necessary for describing parallel systems – plus additional ones which permit us to study nondeterminism in isolation. It is based on the idea that processes communicate only by handshaken communication – which takes place in all participants simultaneously. A CSP process is completely characterised by its possible patterns of communication.

Essentially CSP is a specification language in which to describe the communicating behaviour of proposed implementations. Quite deliberately it includes a number of features which are useful to the developer but usually impractical to implement (for example output guards and multi-way handshaking) with the idea that they can be refined away in the process of implementation. For simplicity it leaves out many of the features of an ordinary programming languages such as assignment.

It is usually possible to describe a system more clearly and concisely using CSP than when an implementation language is used. Languages such as CSP are becoming widely used in industry, mainly for this reason.

There is also a rich mathematical theory underlying CSP which allows us to specify abstract properties, such as deadlock freedom, and prove that processes meet them. This theory breaks into two strands with rather different applications. One, the timed theory, allows us to reason about the precise timing details of systems. The other, untimed theory, deliberately abstracts away from this, recording only the relative order of events, not their speed. Analysis in the untimed theory is generally easier.

Occam was designed as an implementation of CSP, though it restricts us to an 'efficient subset' and brings in additional features to handle the more traditional aspects of programming. This relationship means both that it is possible to begin a development in CSP and refine it into an occam implementation, and that occam has an elegant mathematical theory of its own (closely related to that of CSP [Ros85]) allowing formal development directly in occam.

It can be said that the theory of occam is like the cartesian product of that of CSP and that of a simple sequential language. The latter component is necessary because occam contains features, such as declaration and assignment, which create and manipulate *state*. Its mathematical models are those of CSP with additions to cope with the change of state between a program being terminated and it terminating. Everything that was said of CSP above holds good for occam, and in addition conventional sequential techniques (e.g., Hoare logics) can be applied to the sequential parts of a program. In particular the deadlock and livelock avoidance techniques developed for CSP apply equally to occam.

Like CSP, occam has a complete set of algebraic laws for establishing the equivalence of programs [RH88]. These have been used as the basis of the Occam Transformation System [GR86] , which allows its user to carry out a wide variety of semantic-preserving transformations varying from ones which analyse a program for such things as nondeterminism and deadlock to ones which configure a logical network of processes onto a physical one with different topology. (This transformation system was used in the development of the IMS T800.)

3 Untimed CSP

Real-time specification and analysis are generally detailed and time-consuming. Sometimes they are certainly necessary, but both from the point of view of generality and simplicity it is as well to avoid them whenever possible. In fact the untimed theory predates the timed one, and to a large extent one could say that the concepts (such as handshaken communication and no-shared-memory) behind languages like CSP and occam evolved to allow us to forget about timing details as much as possible.

Both the timed and untimed theories are based on mathematical models where processes are identified with the set of all their possible behaviours. These behaviours give a natural language for stating correctness conditions: a process is correct if all its behaviours are. The models can also be used to establish algebraic laws for proving equivalences between processes and refinement rules for developing processes in ways which reduce nondeterminism.

The theory of CSP There is an extensive literature on the theory of concurrency and it is impossible to convey very much in a small space, but the following gives a flavour of our approach.

The behaviours used by the untimed theory are all based on the communications which a process might make. With each process P we associate a set αP (its *alphabet*) which consists of all events which P may use. The behaviours are:
(i) *Traces*, the finite sequences of communications that a process can perform.
(ii) *Refusals*, the sets of communications which a process might refuse if offered. We usually record which refusals X are possible after each trace s. Such a pair (s, X) is called a *failure*.
(iii) *Divergences*, the traces after which a process can livelock or diverge in some other way.
(iv) Where necessary, *infinite traces*, which are essential for capturing particularly subtle forms of nondeterminism.

These behaviours easily capture all of the misbehaviours described in 'Formal Methods for Concurrent Systems'. A process P can deadlock after trace s if it cannot refuse all possible events, i.e., $(s, \alpha P)$ is a failure. Thus it is deadlock free if it contains no such failures.

A process is divergence (and hence livelock) free if it has no divergences. The way divergence is treated by the untimed theory means that establishing its absence is usually the first part of proofs.

Nondeterminism is present when it is possible both for a process to have both the failure $(s, \{a\})$ and the trace $s\langle a\rangle$: namely, when a process may have the choice whether or not to communicate an event if offered it. A process is deterministic if this never happens (for any s and $\{a\}$).

It is only necessary to consider infinite traces when particularly subtle nondeterminism is allowed so that the possible infinite behaviours are not deducible from the finite ones. It is often natural to specify processes in terms of their infinite traces, for these allow us to state abstract properties not obtainable from finite behaviours. Typically, as in Example 1 below, these properties take the form of asserting that some event happens *eventually* without placing a bound on when.

Applications This theory can be applied directly in the specification, development and proof of concurrent systems: Example 1 below illustrates this. There has also been a lot of work devoted to building formal methods on top of the theory in such a way as to hide the mathematical details; the following paragraphs describe a few of these.

The theory gives a clear definition of what it means for two processes to be the same, and gives a wide range of algebraic laws for proving processes equivalent. Indeed there are enough laws to characterise the theory completely. Laws can be used to develop code by transforming one program into another. They can also be used systematically to prove processes equivalent.

As we have already seen, deadlock and divergence are represented simply in the theory. A number of simple local techniques have been developed for proving them absent from networks. Here, *local* means that they work by examining small parts of a system, so avoiding the exponential growth in the global state-space. For example, suppose processes of a network are divergence-free and can be ordered $P_1, P_2, \ldots, P_n$ in such a way that no P_i ever communicates infinitely often with larger neighbours (P_j with $j > i$) without either communicating with the outside world or a smaller neighbour. Then the network (where all internal communication is hidden) is divergence-free.

There are simple (and very general) conditions which ensure that a tree network (one with no cycles) is deadlock-free. And there are several useful techniques for extending these to networks with cycles. Several are based on similar ordering ideas to the one in the last paragraph.

Example 1 The following is a small example of the way in which the constituents of the untimed theory are used to specify and prove processes. It is a good small example of how abstract concepts such as traces and refusals combine to give a natural language for describing concurrent systems.

First we will specify two different communication services. We might well want: a *buffer* which accepts communications from channel *in* and outputs them on channel *out* in the same order without loss. This is specified in (B1) below. It is, however allowed to accept as many communications as it likes. It can never refuse to input when empty (B2) and cannot refuse to output when it contains a message (B3). All this can be specified by defining $\alpha P = in.T \cup out.T$ (where T is the set of all possible messages); specifying that $divergences(P)$ is empty; and saying that whenever (s, X) is in $failures(P)$ then

B1. $s\downarrow out \leq s\downarrow in$

B2. $s\downarrow out = s\downarrow in \;\Rightarrow\; X \cap in.T = \emptyset$

B3. $s\downarrow out < s\downarrow in \;\Rightarrow\; out.T \not\subseteq X$

Here $s \leq t$ means that the trace s is an initial subsequence of t, and $s\downarrow in$ means the sequence of values communicated over channel in in s: e.g., $\langle in.2, in.3, out.2, in.3\rangle\downarrow in = \langle 2, 3, 3\rangle$. We will define $Buff_{(in,out)}(P)$ to mean that P satisfies these conditions.

There are a large number of CSP processes which satisfy this predicate. We can illustrate a little of the notation of CSP by describing one of them. We will define B_2, a two place buffer, and $B_2(x)$ (for each $x \in T$), a two place buffer containing x.

$$B_2 = in?x \rightarrow B_2(x)$$

$$\begin{aligned} B_2(x) &= in?y \rightarrow out!x \rightarrow B_2(y) \\ &\quad \Box\; out!x \rightarrow B_2 \end{aligned}$$

If P is a process and a is a communication, then $a \rightarrow P$ is the process that communicates a and then acts like P. Thus B_2 is a process which inputs x on channel *in* and then behaves like $B_2(x)$. $P \Box Q$ offers the choice of the first communications of the processes P and Q, and behaves like the one which is chosen. Thus $B_2(x)$ gives its user the choice of making the buffer input one more item – whereupon it is full and must output x – or of making it output x and so becoming empty. Note that these processes have been defined recursively, i.e., in terms of themselves.

There are convenient methods for proving that processes (such as B_2) meet trace/refusal specifications (such as *Buff*). One (sat) is described in Hoare's book on CSP.

We might want to implement such a service between two distant points but only have unreliable channels available. In order to deal with an unreliable channel it is necessary to state what assumptions we are making about it, so again suppose it transmits information from channel *in* to channel *out*. Let us suppose that it can lose messages but does not change the order of or corrupt messages it transmits (L1). (Regarding corruption, the channel might have been constructed using an encoding method which detects corrupted messages and throws them away.) Since it is usually no longer possible to say whether it contains any messages the 'liveness' condition simply states that it is always either able to input or output (L2).

A correct implementation of the specification to date would be a channel that accepts inputs and throws them all away – not very useful. The least we can expect of our channel is that it cannot accept infinitely many inputs without transmitting any of them. This condition is best expressed using infinite traces (see [Ros90]) (L3) – finite traces could only approximate it, for example by saying that the channel never throws away K consecutive communications (where K is any integer).

These conditions can be formalised by again stipulating that $\alpha P = in.T \cup out.T$ and that *divergences*(P) is empty, and that whenever $(s, X) \in$ *failures*(P) and u is an infinite traces of P then

L1. $s{\downarrow}out \preceq s{\downarrow}in$
L2. $X \cap in.T = \emptyset \vee out.T \not\subseteq X$
L3. $u{\downarrow}out$ is infinite

Here $s \preceq t$ means that s is any subsequence of t (not necessarily initial). We will define $LChan_{(in,out)}(P)$ to mean that P satisfies these conditions. (*LChan* stands for 'leaky channel'.)

There are many theorems one can prove about processes satisfying *Buff* and *LChan*. For example, if $Buff_{(a,b)}(P)$ and $Buff_{(b,c)}(Q)$, then the process

$$(P \| Q) \backslash b$$

satisfies $Buff_{(a,c)}$. The effect of this combination is to place P and Q in parallel ($\|$) and to conceal the communications on their common channel ($\backslash b$). Exactly the same result holds if we replace '*Buff*' by '*LChan*'. It is possible to implement a buffer using a pair $C1$, $C2$ of leaky channels by the well-known alternating bit protocol. The network used is illustrated below.

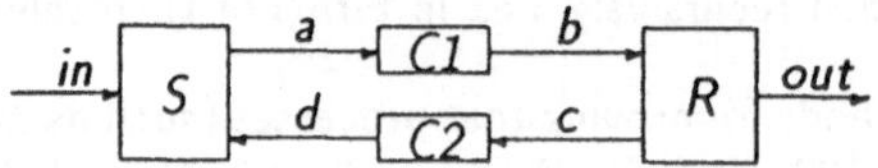

The basic idea is to add an extra bit to each of the messages sent along the leaky channels which alternates between 0 and 1. The sending process sends multiple copies of each message until it is acknowledged. As soon as the receiving process gets a new message it sends repeated acknowledgements of it until the next message arrives. The two ends can always spot a new message or acknowledgement because of the alternating bit.

This is usually described using real-time features such as time-outs, but in fact with a little care it is possible to construct a version whose correctness is independent of timing details. Below we present sender (S) and receiver (R) processes which can readily be proved to work, in the sense that, if $LChan_{(a,b)}(C1)$ and $LChan_{(c,d)}C2$, then

$$(S \| C1 \| C2 \| R) \backslash \{a, b, c, d\}$$

satisfies $Buff_{(in,out)}$.

$R = R(0)$ and $S = S(0)$, where for $s \in \{0,1\}$ and x in the set of messages we define

$$\begin{array}{rcl} S(s) & = & in?x \rightarrow S'(s,x) \\ \\ S'(s,x) & = & a!(s,x) \rightarrow S'(s,x) \\ & & \Box d?s \rightarrow S(\overline{s}) \\ & & \Box d?\overline{s} \rightarrow a!(s,x) \rightarrow S'(s,x) \\ \\ R(s) & = & b?(s,x) \rightarrow out!x \rightarrow R(\overline{s}) \\ & & \Box b?(\overline{s},x) \rightarrow R(s) \\ & & \Box c!\overline{s} \rightarrow R(s) \end{array}$$

In this case the proof breaks down into three parts. The first is show that livelock is impossible – this essentially follows from the assumption that the channels do not lose an infinite sequence of consecutive messages. The second is to prove deadlock freedom, which is easy because all of the component processes are (by construction or specification), and the receiver process never refuses to communicate with either channel unless it is willing to communicate with the environment. Finally we prove partial correctness, namely that, for all traces s,

$$\text{P.} \quad s{\downarrow}out \le s{\downarrow}in' \wedge \#(s{\downarrow}in) \le (s{\downarrow}out) + 1$$

Here, $\#s$ denotes the length of a trace s. Notice that this says both that (B1) holds and that the system never contains more than one item. The proof of (P) is achieved by proving suitable partial correctness results about S and R, combining these with the truth of (L1) for the two channels.

The partial correctness result (P) together with deadlock and livelock freedom actually imply that the system satisfies (B2) and (B3). This is because after any trace it can only input *or* output, never both. In fact we have proved that the system is equivalent to the simple, deterministic process

$$COPY = in?x \rightarrow out!x \rightarrow COPY$$

even though it is built out of unreliable and nondeterministic parts.

By proving this untimed system correct we have in fact proved that a wide variety of timed ones are. The timed and untimed theories of CSP are closely linked. This means that where one is relying on timed behaviour inside some subcomponent to make it satisfy an untimed specification it is possible to restrict timed analysis to the subcomponent. Also for a wide range of timed specifications S it is possible first to use the untimed theory to develop a process meeting the untimed version of S and later use refinement rules to develop it into one which meets the whole of S.

4 Timed CSP

Both the timed and untimed theories are based on mathematical models where processes are identified with the set of all their possible behaviours. These behaviours give a natural language for stating correctness conditions: a process is correct if all its behaviours are. The models can also be used to establish algebraic laws for proving equivalences between processes and refinement rules for developing processes in ways which reduce nondeterminism.

The theory of timed CSP The behaviours used by the timed theory are all based on the communications which a process might make and the times at which such communications are made. With each process P we associate a set αP (its *alphabet*) which consists of all events which P may use. The behaviours are:
(i) *Timed traces*, finite sequences of timed communications (i.e., (t, a) where a is a communication observed at time t) that a process can perform.
(ii) *Timed refusals*, the sets of communications which a process might refuse if offered at specified times (e.g., $\aleph = ([2,3) \times \{a, b\}) \cup ([5,7) \times \{c\})$). We usually record which timed refusals $\aleph$ are possible throughout each timed trace s. Such a pair $(s, \aleph)$ is called a *timed failure*.
(iii) *Timed stability values*, the times after which a process is guaranteed to be stable once a given timed failure has been observed. We encode all this behavioural information in the triple $(s, \sigma, \aleph)$.

As with the untimed theory, these behaviours capture all of the misbehaviours described earlier. Furthermore, the addition of time to our semantics offers the opportunity for a much more subtle analysis of process behaviour than is possible in the untimed models. We can specify not only the eventual refusal behaviour of a process on a given trace, but also what it may refuse at any given instant. For example, we can specify that a process P may not be 'deadlocked' at a particular moment t on the trace s by asserting that for every $t_1 > t$, $(s, [t, t_1) \times \alpha P)$ is not a behaviour of P. The untimed definition of deadlock, which is that the process may come into a state where it will never be able to communicate again, is best expressed in a timed situation as follows. A timed process P can deadlock after a trace s if there exists a time $t_1 \geq end(s)$ such that $(s, [t_1, t_2) \times \alpha P)$ is a failure of P for all $t_2 \geq t_1$, where $end(s)$ denotes the timed component of the last timed communication in s.

Another example of the finer distinctions made possible in the timed models is in the treatment of divergence. We model divergence by consideration of stability. If $(s, \sigma, \aleph)$ is a behaviour of the process P and $\sigma < \infty$, then the next observable event in the life of the process following s may occur at any time on or after time σ at the discretion of the environment, and the set of possible next events must be the same at all such times after stability. A process P is said to be *stable* (and hence livelock free) if for all behaviours $(s, \sigma, \aleph)$ of P, $\sigma < \infty$. Of course, not all livelock-free processes are stable. Timed processes which alternate their refusal behaviour periodically are certainly not stable, but such processes are of interest and are not considered divergent. A timed process P is said to *diverge* after a trace s only when there exists a time $t > end(s)$ such that for all $t_1 > t$, $(s, \infty, [t, t_1) \times \alpha P)$ is a behaviour of P. Even then, unlike the case in untimed CSP we are now not forced to equate a process that can diverge with one that must. Notice that a process which is capable either of deadlocking or of livelocking in the future may for a specified period of time be unable to refuse certain communications.

Nondeterminism is treated by the obvious analogy with its treatment in the untimed case.

Syntax of timed CSP The elegance of timed CSP is that it uses exactly the same syntax as untimed CSP with the addition of one simple primitive, $WAIT\ t$. Whereas $SKIP$ is the process which is willing to terminate immediately at the discretion of the environment, $WAIT\ t$ refuses all communications up to time t when it then is willing to participate in termination. Hence, $WAIT\ t\ ; P$ is a process that after time t will behave exactly as P, but before t will refuse all communications.

A variety of useful time-related operators can then be derived. For example, (given $a \notin \alpha P$) the process

$$P \overset{t}{\triangleright} Q = (P \Box WAIT\ t\ ; a \rightarrow Q) \setminus a$$

gives the environment the choice of communicating with P until time t, then if no such communication has taken place, control is passed to process Q. This is the *time-out* operator. Similar constructions allow us to define, for example, an interrupt operator:

$$P \underset{i}{\nabla} Q$$

behaves like P until i occurs and then behaves like Q. This is an interesting example of an operator which, although its written description does not involve time, can only be defined properly using *Timed* CSP.

A hierarchy of models Although the semantics of the *Timed Failures-Stability Model* for CSP described by G. M. Reed and A. W. Roscoe in [RR87], where behaviours are expressed as above by $(s, \sigma, \aleph)$, is now well understood, it is by necessity so complex as to be a model of last resort. Furthermore, even in the analysis of time-critical systems, we often do not need the full expressive power of the Timed Failures-Stability Model. Hence, we have developed a hierarchy of CSP models (both untimed and timed) with well-defined links between models [Ree90] which allows us analyse the behaviour of a concurrent system by using at each stage only the relevant model appropriate to the complexity of the design decision at that stage. It is possible to use timed analysis to establish that part of a network meets its untimed specification, thereby localising use of the more complex models. It is also possible to infer correctness in a more complex model by analysing only simpler ones.

We will later present a case study where we meet some of the ways in which the timed and untimed theories can be used together.

The models in our hierarchy are all closely related to natural languages for specifying process at their own level of detail. The untimed models are the *Trace Model* with trace behaviours s, the *Stability Model* with behaviours (s, σ), where $\sigma = 0$ if the process cannot diverge after s and $\sigma = \infty$, otherwise, the *Failures Model* with refusal behaviours (s, X), and the *Failures-Stability Model* with behaviours (s, σ, X). The analogous timed models are then constructed with timed traces, continuous stability values over the reals, and timed refusals.

The verification of a CSP process is simply a demonstration that all its possible behaviours meets a proposed specification, expressed as a predicate over the behaviours characterising the semantics of the model concerned. Even with a large number of derived laws relating processes to predicates on behaviours, the construction of verification proofs directly from the semantics in the timed models is often extremely difficult and laborious. Fortunately, through the work of two recent D.Phil. students at Oxford, J. W. Davies and S. A. Schneider (see [DS90], [Dav91] and [Sch90]) we now have a complete set of inference rules for translating a proof obligation on a timed process into proof obligations on its syntactic subcomponents.

An alternative approach to the description of timed systems is the use of temporal logics for specification. Such logics will typically include at least an 'eventually' operator which asserts that some expression will hold at some time in the future, such as 'eventually the system responds'; and a 'continually' operator, which holds for properties that are true at all future times. D.M. Jackson has developed a proof system [Jac91] which supports the application of a temporal logic to Timed CSP, for a logical language that is expressive enough to capture any reasonable requirement of a system, permitting verifications that requirements expressed in that specification language hold of Timed CSP processes.

Schneider has also developed a theory of *timewise refinement*, a relatively easy to use method for exploiting the links between the timed and untimed models in the hierarchy. For Q to be a timewise refinement of P means that if we observe the Timed CSP process Q as though it were an untimed process, then it is – ignoring any requirement for Q to be stable – more deterministic than the untimed process P. Since this depends on timed interactions *within* Q, even if Q were stable this would not be the same as saying that the untimed interpretation of Q is more deterministic than P.

There are two main ways in which we can use timewise refinement. First, if Q is a *stable* timewise refinement of P then one can replace P by Q in any system which has been proved correct using the untimed theory. This allows us to use timing properties within Q either to achieve the refinement or to satisfy some external constraint (such as responsiveness in Q's interface with the external environment).

Secondly, for suitable timed specifications T, we can find an untimed specification S such that, if P can be shown to satisfy S and Q is a timewise refinement of P, then Q satisfies T. Even where the specification T we have does not have a corresponding S which is satisfiable, it may well be possible to write $T = T_1 \wedge T_2$ where T_1 does have such an S and T_2 is considerably easier to establish than T (perhaps in the Timed Traces model). Both these styles of reasoning using timewise refinement are illustrated in the case study below.

We believe these models, algebraic laws, proof systems, and methods of timewise refinement in our hierarchy provide the most powerful mechanism currently available for the analysis of real-time concurrency.

Areas of application Timed CSP is appropriate in many areas where either system correctness depends on low-level timing details, or where it is critical that systems meet detailed timing constraints. The following are some of these:

(i) embedded systems which have to control complex objects (e.g., robots, aircraft and medical equipment) in real-time;

(ii) telecommunications applications such as protocols and switching;

(iii) operating systems (for example process scheduling and interrupts).

And of course it is needed in any application which requires timed constructs such as timeouts.

Case Study The following pages show how Example 1 of can be extended using Timed CSP.

Timed buffers In Timed CSP one can specify various things about a process' timed behaviour. Two of the most useful are *promptness* and *non-retraction* as described below.

A *prompt* process is one which will always become ready to communicate an event within a given time or not at all. There is a bound on the length of time a user must wait for a given event – if it has not been performed by this time, the user knows that it never will be. This may be captured by stipulating that the following property holds (we hope that the meaning of the notation can be deduced from the description that follows).

$$([T, T+t) \times \{a\}) \subseteq \aleph \wedge (s \uparrow (T, T+t) = \langle\rangle) \\ \Rightarrow \ \mathit{first}(s \upharpoonright (T+t)) \neq a$$

This states that if the event a has been refused over an interval of length t, during which no other events have occurred, then the event a will not be the next event. We say that a process which satisfies this specification is t-prompt.

A *non-retracting* process is one which persists in offering events - once it offers to perform an event then it will not retract that offer. This is captured by the following condition on process P:

$$(s, [\mathit{end}(s), t) \times Y) \notin \mathit{failures}(P) \\ \Rightarrow \ (s, [t_1, t) \times Y) \notin \mathit{failures}(P)$$

This condition states that if the set of events Y could not have been refused continuously over the interval between the last observed event and time t, then P cannot have refused Y at the end of that interval. The inability to refuse Y during an interval means that some event from the set must have been offered during it. The condition thus defines non-retraction since it says that, if a message was offered during the course of an interval, then it must still be on offer at the end.

We showed earlier how to specify an untimed buffer: what communications it can perform and what it is obliged to communicate. The finer distinctions possible in Timed

CSP allow one far greater flexibility in specifying a buffer's behaviour. For example, consider the offers of input (when empty) and output (when nonempty) that it must make. Different definitions of a buffer might stipulate

(i) that it must make these offers for some non-zero time, but may subsequently withdraw them for ever,

(ii) the same except that instead of withdrawing the offers for ever, they may only be withdrawn for finite intervals, or

(iii) that the offers eventually become open continuously (until some communication occurs).

Notice that these three versions represent successively stronger specifications, but that a non-retracting process satisfying (i) or (ii) automatically satisfies (iii). A stable process satisfying (ii) must satisfy (iii).

Condition (ii) is the natural condition that relates, under timewise refinement, to the untimed buffer specification. If we wished to prove that some Timed CSP process Q actually satisfied (iii), then a natural route would be to establish (a) that it was the timewise refinement of some untimed buffer P and (b) that it was either stable or non-retracting. Notice how this exactly follows the approach set out under our earlier discussion of timewise refinement: we have decomposed our target timed specification into two parts, one of which can be proved using timewise refinement.

Consider the case where the output channel of one buffer is connected to the input channel of another. This may be modelled (as in the untimed case) by running a buffer P (with inputs on a and outputs on b) in parallel with a buffer Q (with inputs on b and outputs on c), and concealing their common channel: $(P \parallel Q) \setminus b$. Both P and Q synchronise on communications on channel b, so the output of P is fed into the input of Q. If we allow the situation described in (i) or (ii), then there may be no time at which both P and Q are prepared to synchronise on their mutual channel. For example, if P is only prepared to output on even seconds, and Q is only prepared to input on odd seconds, then synchronisation is not possible. Thus the combination could never transmit a message, and so would not be a buffer. However, if one (say P) was non-retracting on b, then if the other satisfied (ii) we could guarantee synchronisation would occur – since the non-retracting process would wait for the other. There is little hope of a useful general result for type (i) buffers, since if, for example, P were one, then it might make its offer to output to Q while Q was full (and unable, temporarily, to input).

Henceforth, by saying that a process is a buffer we will mean that it satisfies condition (iii).

Saying that a process is a buffer yields little timing information about it. A buffer may impose an arbitrary delay between input and output, since it is only committed to outputting eventually. A useful class of buffers is those that are prompt, since this imposes a bound on the possible delay between input and output. Two prompt buffers will produce a buffer when combined, but it need not be prompt since they could fail to synchronise on their common channel until the time (not governed by promptness) when one of them is continuously able to communicate on it. However if, additionally, one of the buffers is non-retracting on the connecting channel, then their combination will be prompt.

Alternating bit protocol We will consider a timewise refinement of the alternating bit protocol described earlier. First, we will show how the component processes S and R can be refined to reflect particular timing strategies. We will discuss later what this establishes about the overall system.

In the untimed treatment of this example, the receiving process R was defined as the parallel composition of $R(0)$ and a constraint process Q which prevents it from performing an infinite number of communications on either b or c to the exclusion of the other. It is most natural to refine this to a sequential process (as discussed there) *before* carrying out any timewise refinement. Specifically we will start our refinement with a process R which, after inputting a message on channel b, may send between 1 and n acknowledgements on c before inputting another.

We will also adapt the definition of the sender process S, though in this case to one which is (in the untimed theory) provably equivalent to the old one, and is more suggestive of a timing strategy. Thus our untimed starting points are as defined below:

$$\begin{aligned}
\widehat{S}(s) &= in?x \to \widehat{S}_1(s,x) \\
\widehat{S}_1(s,x) &= a!(s,x) \to go \to \widehat{S}_2(s,x) \\
&\quad \Box\ d?s \to \widehat{S}(\overline{s}) \\
&\quad \Box\ d?\overline{s} \to \widehat{S}_1(s,x) \\
\widehat{S}_2(s,x) &= timeout \to \widehat{S}_1(s,x) \\
&\quad \Box\ d?s \to \widehat{S}(\overline{s}) \\
&\quad \Box\ d?\overline{s} \to \widehat{S}_2(s,x) \\
CON &= go \to (CON \ \Box\ timeout \to CON)
\end{aligned}$$

$$
\begin{aligned}
S &= (\widehat{S}(0) \parallel CON) \setminus \{go, timeout\} \\
\widehat{R}_0(s) &= b?(s,x) \rightarrow out!x \rightarrow c!s \rightarrow \widehat{R}_{n-1}(\overline{s}) \\
&\quad \Box\, b?(\overline{s},x) \rightarrow c!\overline{s} \rightarrow \widehat{R}_{n-1}(s) \\
\widehat{R}_{m+1}(s) &= b?(s,x) \rightarrow out!x \rightarrow c!s \rightarrow \widehat{R}_{n-1}(\overline{s}) \\
&\quad \Box\, b?(\overline{s},x) \rightarrow c!\overline{s} \rightarrow \widehat{R}_{n-1}(s) \\
&\quad \Box\, c!\overline{s} \rightarrow \widehat{R}_m(s) \\
R &= \widehat{R}_{n-1}(0)
\end{aligned}
$$

When S is in state $\widehat{S}_1$, then after it sends a message along channel a, it starts the timer CON by sending go, and then its state changes to $\widehat{S}_2$, where it may only receive acknowledgements, or perform the timeout event and return to state $\widehat{S}_1$. In the absence of timing information we have no control over when the timeout may happen - we know only that S cannot repeat a message along a until the timeout occurs. It is always possible that the correct acknowledgement will arrive before the timeout is ready to trip, and hence that S will wish to send a new message along a. In this case, the timer will be started again before the occurrence of the timeout.

In Timed CSP we have more control over the occurrence of the timeout. If sending messages is expensive, then we may wish to wait at least until the time the acknowledgement message would arrive if the message was passed successfully, since a second message in that case would be wasted. If T is the time a successful acknowledgement would arrive after a successful message is sent, then we would wish our timeout controller to prevent the sending of a second message within T of the first one. We implement this by altering the timeout controller so that it will not time out over that interval:

$$
CON = go \rightarrow \left(\begin{array}{l} CON \Box \\ WAIT\ T\ ;\ timeout \rightarrow CON \end{array} \right)
$$

The timed controller in its initial state is prepared to be started. Once the timer has been started, it is unable to time out for length of time T (although it may be restarted during that period). In the absence of a correct acknowledgement this forces S to wait for time T before it times out and retransmits its message.

If we wish to force a delay between successive acknowledgements sent by the receiver process, we may simply refine the description of R by inserting an appropriate delay of length t. This is accomplished by rewriting the last line of the definition of $\widehat{R}_{m+1}$ to read

$$
\Box\, WAIT\ t\ ;\ c!\overline{s} \rightarrow \widehat{R}_m(s)
$$

so that the option $c!\overline{s}$ is not possible for time t.

It is easy to establish that the refined versions of R and S are stable, and are non-retracting on *in* and *out*. We must now examine the implications of these refinements for the system as a whole. Depending on what we know about the channels $C1$ and $C2$, we can follow either of the approaches discussed earlier when we introduced the idea of timewise refinement. If we can continue to rely on the untimed specification *LChan* of leaky channels, then we have already done enough (thanks to the first approach) to ensure that the overall system still satisfies the untimed buffer specification – for we may substitute the new versions of R and S and preserve correctness.

On the other hand it may be that $C1$ and $C2$ do not satisfy *LChan*, but do satisfy an analogous but weaker timed specification. They may be unstable and only make offers of communication intermittently in a way corresponding to buffer specification (ii) above. (They do, however, satisfy timed versions of the other constraints from *LChan*, including one strong enough to prevent an infinite sequence of inputs without an output.) Then the fact that S and R are stable processes is enough to guarantee that the whole system

$$(S \| C1 \| C2 \| R) \setminus \{a, b, c, d\}$$

is a timewise refinement of the old one. Since the old one was a buffer, it follows that the new one is a type (ii) timed buffer. Moreover, it is non-retracting on *in* and *out*, which shows it is a type (iii) buffer as we might have hoped.

The specifications we have discussed for the channels $C1$ and $C2$ are not strong enough to ensure that there is a bound on the delay between the input of a message into the protocol and its output. This is for two reasons: first, they say nothing about the length of time it takes a single message to pass through a channel, and secondly there is no bound on the number of messages that may be lost by a channel. Consequently, although the protocol is still a buffer, it is not necessarily prompt.

By placing additional timing constraints on $C1$ and $C2$ we could guarantee that the protocol is prompt. We would first require that the channels be prompt, so that it is possible to tell in a bounded time whether they have lost their message. We would also place a bound on the number of consecutive messages that a channel can lose, so that after a certain number of inputs we know that at least one of them will have been output. Careful analysis of these strengthened specifications and the properties of R and S would reveal a t such that the whole system was t-prompt.

5 Future research

Our immediate goal is the publication of two volumes on Timed CSP during 1991-92. The first of these volumes will give the mathematical foundations of our models, proof systems, and refinement techniques. The second will contain a variety of large-scale case studies.

Areas of current and planned research are as follows:

Simulated time The current timed models do not support the synchrony hypothesis — the principle that the internal progress of a system is infinitely fast whereas external progress takes time. This is a useful abstraction in cases where the speed requirements for a particular machine can be separated from its functionality requirements. This assumption underlies the Esterel programming language, and the computation model of StateCharts. It is also valuable in reasoning about other languages such as occam, and is implicit in the standard untimed semantics of CSP.

By treating delays as orthogonal to functionality we simplify the analysis of complex systems by isolating the timing behaviour.

This research would involve the construction of a model in which simultaneous events may be causally related. Two events occurring at the same time may therefore have one causally prior to the other. Such a model will support both instantaneous prefixing and immediate recursion. The only programming construct which takes time to execute is the explicit delay operator; all other constructors operate in zero time. Among the issues raised by attempts to capture this form of behaviour is the difficulty of defining fixed points, since the domain of processes may not be a complete partial order, and the functions defining fixed points do not correspond to contraction mappings in the standard metric space.

This model will support the laws of the current Timed CSP models as well as some additional laws, which for example allow the parallelism to be removed from a process description.

Specification languages If formal system development techniques are to gain wide acceptance, we must find an acceptable interface to mathematical models such as the Timed CSP semantics. A suitable specification language will allow requirements to be captured in an intuitive and straightforward manner, and should also facilitate both manual and machine-assisted proof.

Among the formalisms which we intend to investigate are:

- First order logics with explicit time variables, possibly including links to the work of Jahanian & Mok, and Hooman.
- Temporal logics - Soundness and completeness of logical systems, decidability of specifications, and levels of expressiveness.
- Duration calculus

Tools The complexity inherent in timed systems increases the need for computer assisted verification of systems. Past research has shown that mechanical proof assistants can be used in correctness proofs of CSP programs, but the large scale practical value of these techniques to timed and untimed CSP has yet to be investigated. During the past year this has been in the planning stage. Needs which have been identified include:

- An agreed CSP syntax. As a blackboard language, the syntax of CSP can be, and has been, more flexible than can be allowed in one which is to be the subject of machine support. The lack of such a syntax has long been the main obstacle to the development of tools.
- A transformation system for untimed CSP akin to the occam transformation system. This should provide support for exploring state-spaces (model-checking).
- Proof-checkers (based on a generic tool such as the B-tool) tailored to behavioural specifications as they appear and are used in both timed and untimed CSP.
- Support for timewise refinement.
- A proof-checker for the temporal logic of Timed CSP, which must be closely linked to that for timed behavioural specifications set out above.
- Mechanization of the transformation of abstract CSP designs from the simulated time model to implementation-oriented languages such as Esterel and occam.

Models To fully exploit both the theories of temporal logic and timewise refinement, we now recognise the need to add a timed model to our hierarchy which adequately models *infinite* behaviours. Such a model, based on infinite timed traces and refusal sets over all future time, is needed to model the eventually operator and to analyse unbounded nondeterminacy. The development of such a model is nontrivial. Only recently has an infinite trace model been constructed by A. W. Roscoe for untimed CSP, and this construction requires quite sophisticated use of higher mathematics. In particular, to create a timed version, we will need a new theory of fixpoints on our domains, and congruent operational semantics for our present timed models.

Not only is the above direction of research the natural extension of our work thus far, it also now appears to be a necessary stage in our plans to develop models for probabilistic behaviour. We believe that the infinite behavioural timed models will be the best starting point from which to analyse probability and fairness.

Finally, we propose to complete our work towards a unified theory of concurrency by adding real-time probability to the models in our hierarchy. We would then have as our comprehensive model, a model in which safety, liveness, and fairness could be adequately expressed. This would facilitate the comparison and unification of the many different methods presently used to reason about concurrent systems, and promote a far deeper understanding of concurrency in general.

Such models would allow a proper universal measure of fairness, i.e, "Within 3.75 milliseconds, there is a 93.7% chance that the process will respond." Much of the current work in protocol design is driven by the need to overcome the unreliability of transport media. However, when using formal methods to verify a protocol, one is forced to make unrealistic assumptions about transport media since the possibility of failure is not quantifiable. Correct reasoning about such designs will only be achieved by a model that encompasses probability.

Bibliography

Dav91 J.W. Davies. *Specification and proof in real-time systems.* D.Phil Thesis, Oxford University, 1991.

DS89 J.W. Davies and S.A. Schneider. *An introduction to Timed CSP.* PRG Monograph 75, Oxford University, 1989.

DS90 J.W. Davies and S.A. Schneider. *Factorizing proofs in Timed CSP.* LNCS 442, pp 129–159, 1990.

GR86 M.H. Goldsmith and A.W. Roscoe. *Transforming occam programs.* in The Design and Application of Parallel Digital Processors (IEE Conference Publication 298), 1986.

Hoa85 C.A.R. Hoare. *Communicating Sequential Processes.* Prentice-Hall, 1985.

Jac89 D.M. Jackson. *The specification of aircraft engine control software using Timed CSP.* M.Sc. Thesis, Oxford University, 1989.

Jac91 D.M. Jackson. *A Temporal Logic Proof System for Timed CSP.* PRG Technical Report TR 91-2, Oxford University 1991.

KR90 A. Kay and J.N. Reed. *A specification of a telephone exchange in Timed CSP.* PRG Technical Report TR 19-90

RB90 A.W. Roscoe and G. Barrett. *Unbounded nondeterminism in CSP.* LNCS 442, pp 160–193, 1990.

Ree88 G.M. Reed. *A uniform mathematical theory for real-time distributed computing.* D.Phil Thesis, Oxford University, 1988.

Ree90 G.M. Reed. *A hierarchy of domains for real-time distributed computing.* LNCS 442, pp80–128, 1990.

RH88 A.W. Roscoe and C.A.R. Hoare. *The laws of occam programming.* Theoretical Computer Science 60, pp177–229, 1988.

Ros85 A.W. Roscoe. *Denotational semantics for occam.* LNCS 197, pp 306–329, 1985.

RR86 G.M. Reed and A.W. Roscoe. *A timed model for communicating sequential processes.* LNCS 226, pp314–323, 1986; Theoretical Computer Science 58, pp 249–261, 1988.

RR87 G.M. Reed and A.W. Roscoe. *Metric spaces as models for real-time concurrency.* LNCS 298, pp331–343, 1987.

Sca90 B.S. Scattergood *An application of Timed CSP to robot control software.* M.Sc Thesis, Oxford University, 1990.

Sch90 S.A. Schneider. *Correctness and communication in real-time systems.* D.Phil Thesis, Oxford University, 1990.

Sta90 R. Stamper. *The specification of AGV control software using Timed CSP.* M.Sc. Thesis, Oxford University, 1990.

The Elusive Software Refinery: a case study in program development

Kenneth R. Wood
Programming Research Group
Oxford University Computing Laboratory
11 Keble Road
Oxford OX1 3QD

krw@uk.ac.oxford.prg

Abstract. In this study we develop a three-valued digital logic simulator using a combination of the Z specification language and Morgan's refinement calculus. This development is illuminating in several ways. First, the simulator—which has been implemented in Occam and used as the basis of a distributed simulator—is a reasonably complex, self-contained program whose formal development reflects the application of refinement to a "real-world" programming task. Second, in the course of our development we demonstrate the benefits of using a subset of the Z notation within the refinement calculus to provide compound types and functions to help structure the specification. This approach allows a natural style of program development to be made mathematically rigorous. Third, we demonstrate the ability to prove useful properties about programs that have been developed using refinement techniques. In our case, we calculate an upper bound on the size of the simulator's event queue and prove our calculation correct. In total, our development indicates that current specification and refinement techniques can provide a very powerful tool for the practising software engineer.

1 Introduction

When we decide to use formal mathematical methods to develop a computer program, it is easy to be lulled into the false supposition that the mathematics will take over the hard parts of the development. It is tempting to believe that we can simply compose a high-level specification of the problem, put the specification through a software refinery of some sort—perhaps pushing a button or oiling a gear or two along the way, but no more than that—and eventually see a pure, correct and efficient program which solves the problem emerge from the refinery. This is, unfortunately, a belief unlikely to be confirmed in practice. However, if we believe instead that current techniques of formal specification and refinement can be used in collaboration with the ingenuity and skill of the software engineer, we find that such collaboration is not only possible but also very fruitful.

Using formal techniques certainly changes the nature of the programmer's task, but does not typically lessen its difficulty. In the first place, arriving at a suitable specification can sometimes be more difficult than informally developing a prototype program straight away. And only after an appropriate and consistent specification has been constructed can the refinement towards executable code begin.

Now, it is true that the mathematical structure of the specification and of intermediate refinement steps will often suggest one or more options for the next refinement. At some points during the refinement process it may even be that a particular refinement step is obviously the most desirable in a way that can be determined heuristically. Thus—as in other branches of engineering—the automation of some stages of the development process is likely possible. However, there will almost invariably be many steps where some problem-related insight is required to devise an appropriate refinement or to choose between two refinements suggested by the mathematical structure. The software engineer's construction of these refinement steps makes up his post-specification development effort, and the effort and ingenuity required is unlikely to be less than that required to develop the program using more traditional methods.

But having exerted the effort and ingenuity required to develop his program formally, the software engineer has the advantage of his more mainstream colleagues in many ways:

- the method ensures the existence of a precise specification of the program's behaviour, something which is often vital but which is equally often missing when informal methods are used.
- the stepwise mathematical nature of the method ensures that the engineer can claim with a very high degree of confidence that the final program meets its specification. Furthermore, this claim can be independently checked by others in a systematic fashion. Neither of these properties holds for programs developed informally, even when a precise specification of the program exists.
- the mathematical structure arising from specification and refinement can be used to prove important program properties much more easily than such properties could be proven for programs developed informally.
- modifications to the desired behaviour of the program can be specified precisely and by following these modifications through the refinement process, correctly modified code can be obtained systematically. This is a vast improvement over traditional hit-and-miss methods of code modification.

The refinement techniques to which we refer in this paper have their roots in Hoare's seminal paper [Hoa69]. They were further developed and applied by Dijkstra [Dij76], and given a thorough exposition by Gries [Gri81]. Recently these techniques have been extended and given a calculational framework by Back [Bac88], Morris [Mor87], and Morgan [MRG88, Mor90]. [Mor90] is particularly noteworthy in that it codifies the extended refinement techniques in a comprehensive set of laws for calculating refinements. Using these laws together with the Z notation [Spi89] which similarly codifies the mathematics of state-based specification, the programmer-in-the-street has at his disposal—perhaps for the first time—a very powerful toolset with which he can apply formal specification and refinement techniques to real problems in software engineering and thereby gain the advantages outlined above. We attempt to illustrate this here by developing a gate-level digital logic simulator using Z and Morgan's refinement laws.

2 Background

The simulator which we develop here is a second incarnation of SEQSIM, a simulator originally presented in [Wood89] where it was used as the basis of a distributed logic simulator. The original version was specified somewhat loosely and at a very low level in Z and implemented in Occam with hand-waving assertions that the implementation met the specification. Z was very useful for describing the simulator's data structures, but had no real provision for algorithmic refinement. Hence the loose specification.

In [Wood90] SEQSIM was again used as the basis of a distributed logic simulator, this time with a slightly novel distributed simulation technique. In order to prove formally the correctness of this technique—something which we have yet to do—we must be able to reason formally about the properties of SEQSIM. In addition, eventually we would like to increase the complexity of SEQSIM's timing model and a precise specification of SEQSIM's behaviour is essential if this is to be done correctly.

These considerations have led us to redevelop SEQSIM using much more rigorous specification and refinement techniques. The refinement laws of [Mor90]—especially the laws surrounding the specification statement—provide the framework for the rigour which is missing from our earlier development.

3 The Problem

An informal statement of our task is that we wish to simulate digital circuits at the gate level. For our purposes, a digital circuit is therefore a collection of gates interconnected by wires, certain of which are identifiable as input wires. (See Figure 1.) We are required to determine the behaviour of the entire circuit over time based on given behaviour of the input wires over time.

It is immediately apparent that virtually every aspect of our informal statement requires clarification before we can hope to begin writing a program to solve the problem. It is natural and probably preferable to proceed in a bottom-up fashion in this clarification—that is, to formalize smaller or subsidiary concepts (e.g. "wire", "gate") before larger or global ones (e.g. "circuit","behaviour"). It is also crucial to realize that at this stage our goal is strictly to state the problem as clearly as we possibly can. We should not yet be concerned with how we might solve it.

3.1 Circuit Structure

A wire will remain an abstract notion. Thus, we introduce *Wire* as a basic type using the Z notation:

Figure 1: A small circuit (2–4 line decoder)

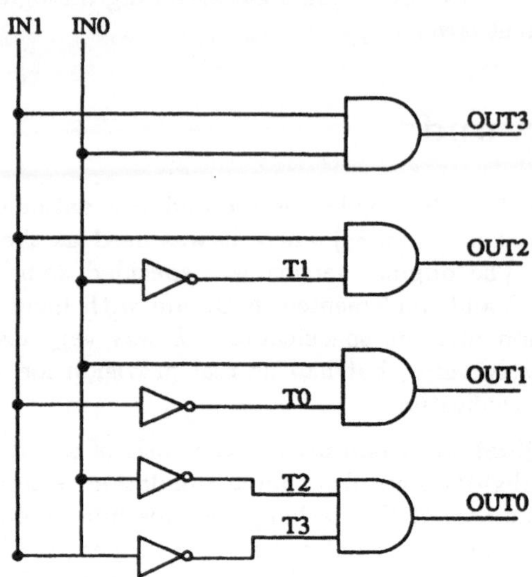

[*Wire*]

Our simulator is to be three-valued. Thus, a wire is always in one of three states: 0,1, or X. State 0 refers to a voltage on the wire which represents a binary 0, state 1 refers to a voltage on the wire which represents a binary 1, and state X refers to an indeterminate state which may be 0 or 1. We therefore introduce the type:

$$\begin{aligned} \mathit{LogicValue} ::= & \ \mathit{Logic}0 \\ | & \ \mathit{Logic}1 \\ | & \ \mathit{LogicX} \end{aligned}$$

together with a collection of functions each of which corresponds to the operation of a primitive gate within a circuit. In the interest of brevity and with no loss of generality, we include here only two of the seven primitive gate functions found in SEQSIM: the inverter and the and-gate. We use a standard three-valued logic in which an indeterminate value is propagated from an input to the output only when other inputs do not make the indeterminate input irrelevant. More specifically, we define the following two logic functions:

$$\begin{array}{|l} \mathit{Inv} : \mathit{LogicValue} \rightarrow \mathit{LogicValue} \\ \hline \mathit{Inv}\ \mathit{Logic}1 = \mathit{Logic}0 \\ \mathit{Inv}\ \mathit{Logic}0 = \mathit{Logic}1 \\ \mathit{Inv}\ \mathit{LogicX} = \mathit{LogicX} \end{array}$$

$$\begin{array}{|l}
And : LogicValue \times LogicValue \rightarrow LogicValue \\
\hline
And\ (Logic0, Logic0) = Logic0 \\
And\ (Logic0, Logic1) = Logic0 \\
And\ (Logic0, LogicX) = Logic0 \\
And\ (Logic1, Logic0) = Logic0 \\
And\ (Logic1, Logic1) = Logic1 \\
And\ (Logic1, LogicX) = LogicX \\
And\ (LogicX, Logic0) = Logic0 \\
And\ (LogicX, Logic1) = LogicX \\
And\ (LogicX, LogicX) = LogicX
\end{array}$$

Furthermore, because we do not want to restrict ourselves to two-input and-gates, we define a multiple-input version of the *And* function which we call *mAnd*. Any binary function which is associative and has a unit can be extended to take an arbitrary number of inputs in this way.

$$\begin{array}{|l}
mAnd : \mathbb{F}\ LogicValue \rightarrow LogicValue \\
\hline
\forall v : LogicValue;\ vs : \mathbb{F}\ LogicValue \bullet \\
\quad mAnd\ \varnothing = Logic1 \\
\quad mAnd\ (\{v\} \cup vs) = And(v, mAnd\ vs)
\end{array}$$

Central to our notion of the behaviour of a circuit is the concept of a wire's changing value over time. We will assume that for any particular circuit and associated input behaviour there is a minimum time between such changes in value. In other words, any wire which changes from value v_1 to value v_2 will remain at value v_1 for some minimum amount of time, say δ, before taking on value v_2. With this (very reasonable) assumption, it is sufficient to model time with the natural numbers since we can take a value equal to or smaller than δ as our unit of time. Hence,

$$Time \mathrel{\widehat=} \mathbb{N}$$

When a wire takes on a particular value at a particular time, we will say that an *event* has occurred. Thus, we define:

$$\begin{array}{|l}
\hline
\textit{Event} \\
wire : Wire \\
value : LogicValue \\
time : Time \\
\hline
\end{array}$$

It may appear that we are slanting our specification of the problem in the direction of a particular solution, namely a discrete-event simulator. Perhaps we are somehow sullying our pure, mathematical specification with dirty implementation-linked details which we should scrap, looking for a more abstract level at which to specify the problem.

But this is not the case. What we are doing here is elucidating our operational understanding of circuit behaviour in mathematical terms. That our formalization of this behaviour reminds us of known techniques for its simulation should not come as a surprise. Indeed, we are modelling the circuit as a discrete system, so any simulator we derive from our specification *must* be a discrete-event simulator. The important point is that careful mathematical description of circuit operation followed by the application of software refinement techniques will yield a simulator about whose correctness with respect to that description we can be highly confident. While it is important to state the problem abstractly, it is not necessary to go to great lengths to ensure that the specification seems entirely removed from any possible implementation.

A gate is a device with one or more input wires and exactly one output wire. It operates continuously such that after some fixed time delay the value of its output wire reflects a logical function of the values of its input wires. We need to pick a certain number of primitive gate types, each of which implements a particular logical function. As mentioned above, we include here only two of the seven primitive gate types found in SEQSIM—the inverter and the and-gate:

$$\begin{aligned} \mathit{GateType} ::= {} & \mathit{InvGate} \\ \mid {} & \mathit{AndGate} \end{aligned}$$

Our formal notion of a gate is given by the following Z schema. Note that we make explicit various natural constraints on a gate: it must have at least one input and cannot have infinitely many, its output wire cannot also be one of its input wires, and it must have a positive delay. For the inverter, we insist that it have exactly one input.

Gate

$$\begin{array}{|l} \mathit{type} : \mathit{GateType} \\ \mathit{inputs} : \mathbb{F}\ \mathit{Wire} \\ \mathit{output} : \mathit{Wire} \\ \mathit{delay} : \mathit{Time} \\ \hline \#\mathit{inputs} \geq 1 \\ \mathit{type} = \mathit{InvGate} \Rightarrow \#\mathit{inputs} = 1 \\ \mathit{output} \notin \mathit{inputs} \\ \mathit{delay} > 0 \end{array}$$

A circuit, as we have said, is a collection of gates interconnected by wires. We can now be much more specific:

$$
\begin{array}{|l}
\multicolumn{1}{l}{\textit{Circuit}} \\
\hline
gates : \mathbb{F}\ Gate \\
wires : \mathbb{F}\ Wire \\
fanout : Wire \rightarrow \mathbb{F}\ Gate \\
primaryInputs : \mathbb{F}\ Wire \\
\hline
wires = \{w : Wire \mid \exists\, g : gates \bullet w \in g.inputs \lor w = g.output\} \\
\forall\, w : wires \bullet (fanout\ w) \subseteq gates \\
\forall\, g : gates;\ w : wires \bullet g \in (fanout\ w) \Leftrightarrow w \in g.inputs \\
\forall\, w : Wire \mid w \notin wires \bullet (fanout\ w) = \varnothing \\
\forall\, g1, g2 : gates \bullet g1 \neq g2 \Rightarrow g1.output \neq g2.output \\
primaryInputs = \{w : wires \mid \nexists\, g : gates \bullet g.output = w\} \\
\hline
\end{array}
$$

The first equation in the *Circuit* schema simply states that all wires connected to a gate in the circuit (and only such wires) appear in the set of wires associated with the circuit. The next three predicates define formally the term *fanout*. (Note that although this term usually denotes the *number* of gates to which another gate's output is an input, for our purposes fanout will be a property of a wire and will represent the *set* of gates within the circuit to which that wire is an input.) The next predicate precludes short circuits by ensuring that no two gates can output to the same wire, and the last equation in the schema indicates that the primary inputs of the circuit are just those wires which appear as an output of no gate in the circuit.

Note that we make *fanout* a total function on *Wire* because total functions are generally easier to reason about than partial functions. We can always refine it to a partial function later. (In fact, we originally made *fanout* a partial function, but found that later reasoning would be easier if it were total. Refinement techniques do not eliminate backtracking!)

It is worth noting here that our circuit model does not distinguish between gate terminals and the wires in the circuit to which the terminals are connected. The most striking consequence of this fact is that we cannot have gates with non-interchangeable inputs (e.g. flip-flops) as primitive gate types. We can, of course, still represent (and therefore simulate) such gates by constructing them from the primitive gate types which we do have. This approach is in fact preferable for our work on distributed simulation as it makes it easier to construct circuits with high gate-counts and complex connection networks which are needed to put the distributed simulator through its paces. In any case, we may augment our model later to allow primitive gates with non-interchangeable inputs as this would make a good case study of the modification of a formally developed program.

3.2 Circuit Behaviour

We now turn to the behaviour of the circuit. Informally, we perceive that a circuit runs as follows:

- input stimuli of the form "wire w goes to value v at time t" are applied to the primary inputs of the circuit. These stimuli can be characterized by a set of events acting on the circuit's primary input wires.
- the stimuli events cause changes at later times in the values of the output wires of various gates. Each such change can be characterized by an event which can in turn act as a stimulus causing more changes at yet later times in the values of output wires.
- this process continues as changes in the value of each wire are triggered by earlier changes in the values of other wires. Depending on the topology of circuit, when the stimuli are exhausted the circuit wires may stop changing value after some finite time or they may continue to change forever.

Thus, we see that a set of events can completely characterize the behaviour of a circuit. In order to formalize this idea, we need to define a few preliminary structures. First, we define a *State* to be a particular assignment of values to wires, again using a total function for simplicity of reasoning,

$$State \mathrel{\widehat{=}} Wire \rightarrow LogicValue$$

and then we note that a set of events gives rise to a unique state, namely the state in which the value of each wire is the value of the most recent event which occurred for that wire or *LogicX* if the set contains no event for that wire. We call the state corresponding to a set of events a *Snapshot*:

$$Snapshot : \mathbb{F}\ Event \rightarrow State$$

$$\begin{array}{l} \forall\, es : \mathbb{F}\ Event \bullet \\ \quad Snapshot\ es = \\ \quad\quad (\lambda\, w : Wire \bullet LogicX) \oplus \\ \quad\quad \{(w, v) : Wire \times LogicValue \mid \\ \quad\quad\quad (\exists\, ev : es \bullet \\ \quad\quad\quad\quad (ev.wire = w \wedge ev.value = v) \wedge \\ \quad\quad\quad\quad (\nexists\, ev' : es \bullet ev'.wire = w \wedge ev'.time > ev.time))\} \end{array}$$

Given a state and a gate, we can compute the value of the gate's output consistent with the values of its inputs in the given state:

$$GateValue : Gate \rightarrow State \rightarrow LogicValue$$

$$\begin{array}{l} \forall\, g : Gate;\ s : State \bullet \\ \quad (g.type = InvGate) \Rightarrow (g.inputs = \{w\}) \wedge (GateValue\ g\ s = Inv(s\ w)) \\ \quad (g.type = AndGate) \Rightarrow GateValue\ g\ s = mAnd\ s(\!|g.inputs|\!) \end{array}$$

Our operational notion of circuit behaviour tells us that when an event occurs, it spawns a set of future events based on the gates to which the event's wire is an input. Formally, we define:

$$
\begin{array}{l}
Spawn : (Circuit \times Event \times State) \rightarrow \mathbb{F}\ Event \\
\hline
\forall c : Circuit;\ e : Event;\ s : State \bullet \\
\quad \#(Spawn\ c\ e\ s) = \#(c.fanout\ e.wire) \\
\quad \forall g : (c.fanout\ e.wire) \bullet \\
\qquad \exists ev : (Spawn\ c\ e\ s) \bullet \\
\qquad\quad ev.wire = g.output\ \wedge \\
\qquad\quad ev.value = GateValue\ g\ s\ \wedge \\
\qquad\quad ev.time = e.time + g.delay
\end{array}
$$

For a set of events to comprise valid stimuli for a given circuit, certain properties must hold. Each event must act on a wire which is a primary input of the circuit, no two events for the same wire should happen at the same time, and no event should happen at time 0. The latter restriction was later found to be necessary in order to allow easy initialization of the simulator. We express these properties as follows:

$$
\begin{array}{l}
ValidStimuli : Circuit \rightarrow \mathbb{P}\ \mathbb{F}\ Event \\
\hline
\forall c : Circuit;\ es : \mathbb{F}\ Event \bullet \\
\qquad es \in ValidStimuli\ c \\
\quad \Leftrightarrow \\
\qquad \{e : es \bullet e.wire\} \subseteq c.primaryInputs\ \wedge \\
\qquad (\forall e1, e2 : es \bullet e1.wire = e2.wire \Leftrightarrow e1.time \neq e2.time)\ \wedge \\
\qquad (\forall e : es \bullet e.time > 0)
\end{array}
$$

These preliminary structures can now be used to describe formally our notion of the behaviour of a circuit. We define the set of *Past* events which completely characterizes the behaviour of a circuit up to a given time upon application of given input stimuli:

$$
\begin{array}{l}
Past : (Circuit \times \mathbb{F}\ Event \times Time) \rightarrow \mathbb{F}\ Event \\
\hline
\forall C : Circuit;\ S : \mathbb{F}\ Event;\ t : Time;\ e : Event \mid S \in ValidStimuli\ C \bullet \\
\qquad e \in Past(C, S, t) \\
\quad \Leftrightarrow \\
\qquad e.time \leq t\ \wedge \\
\qquad (e \in S\ \vee \\
\qquad\quad \exists ev : Past(C, S, t) \bullet \\
\qquad\qquad e \in Spawn(C, ev, Snapshot\ Past(C, S, ev.time)))
\end{array}
$$

This recursive definition of *Past* captures mathematically our intuitive notion of circuit behaviour: any event which occurs in the circuit at or before time t must either be a stimulus event or must have been spawned by some earlier event. Of course, before we proceed to develop a program from our specification, we should prove that *Past* is well-defined. More generally, having constructed a mathematical specification we should always investigate many properties of the specification to ensure that it captures our intentions and that it is mathematically consistent. In this case we would want to show—in addition to the fact that *Past* is well-defined—that *Snapshot* always yields a function, that *Past* yields no two events for the same wire at the same time, and so on.

Here we will not prove all the things we should. However, Appendix A does contain proofs of some of the more desirable properties of our specification such as Theorem 1:

$$\forall C : Circuit;\ S : \mathbb{F}\ Event;\ t, T : Time \mid S \in ValidStimuli\ C \bullet \\ t < T \Rightarrow Past(C, S, t) \subseteq Past(C, S, T)$$

We would be describing very unusual circuits indeed if this were not true! In fact, many of the important proofs necessary for our later refinements rely on this result, so its proof was essential.

However, whether or not we carry out the proof for every property we can think of is irrelevant. The key point is that because we have made our specification mathematically precise, we *can* carry out these proofs if and when they are required. During our refinement we may find that we need to prove X and then discover that X is in fact false, indicating that we have made an error or that our specification did not capture exactly what we had hoped. The mathematics will likely give us a hint at the problem, and we can alter the specification, adjust any affected refinement steps and continue with a better understanding of the problem. Such rigorous analysis is not possible with less formal development methods.

4 The Solution

We are now in a position to write an abstract program to perform the simulation we want. The program is:

$$\begin{array}{l} \textbf{var}\ P, S : \mathbb{F}\ Event; \\ \quad C : Circuit; \\ \quad E : Time; \\ \quad \textbf{and}\ S \in ValidStimuli\ C \bullet \\ P : [true\ ,\ P = Past(C, S, E)] \end{array}$$

This is our starting point for the development of a concrete implementation of a simulator using the refinement laws enumerated in [Mor90]. Note that the program will work for any values of the program variables which satisfy the invariant. We assume that appropriate initial values of C,E, and S are somehow input by the user but here we ignore the details of the input process.

On the natural assumption that we will somehow build up the circuit's *Past* incrementally, our first refinement step is as follows:

$$\sqsubseteq \quad \{\ \text{Add variable } (CI \mathrel{\hat=} true), \text{Law 17.2; Strengthen postcondition, Law 1.1}\ \}$$

$$\begin{array}{l} \textbf{var}\ P, S : \mathbb{F}\ Event; \\ \quad C : Circuit; \\ \quad E, t : Time; \\ \quad \textbf{and}\ S \in ValidStimuli\ C \bullet \\ P, t : [true\ ,\ t = E \wedge P = Past(C, S, t)] \end{array}$$

A few more refinement steps made it apparent that a slight relaxation of our specification would make later refinement steps less cumbersome. (Again we see that although refinement is a powerful tool, it is only a tool and hence must rely on its operator for guidance.) The relaxation of our specification is based upon the observation (a direct result of Theorem 2 in Appendix A) that for $t, T : \mathit{Time}$, and $P = \mathit{Past}(C, S, T)$:

$$T > t \Rightarrow \mathit{Past}(C, S, t) = P \setminus \{ev : P \mid ev.time > t\}$$

Thus, we can always recover $\mathit{Past}(C, S, t)$ from $\mathit{Past}(C, S, T)$ when $T > t$ and we can therefore safely relax our specification to:

$$P, t : [\mathit{true}\ ,\ t \geq E \land P = \mathit{Past}(C, S, t)]$$

We could, of course, make this relaxation into a *bona fide* refinement step by introducing a shadow set of frame variables:

$\sqsubseteq$ { Add variable ($CI \mathrel{\hat=} \mathit{true}$),Law 17.2; Strengthen postcondition,Law 1.1 }

$$P, P', t, t' : [\mathit{true}\ ,\ t' \geq E \land P' = \mathit{Past}(C, S, t') \land \\ P = P' \setminus \{ev : P' \mid ev.time > E\} \land t = E]$$

However, we will accept the possibly more comprehensive *Past* given by P' above and therefore will resume our development with the following program:

var $P, S : \mathbb{F}\ \mathit{Event};$
$C : \mathit{Circuit};$
$E, t : \mathit{Time};$
and $S \in \mathit{ValidStimuli}\ C$ •

$$P, t : [\mathit{true}\ ,\ t \geq E \land P = \mathit{Past}(C, S, t)]$$

Pursuing our notion of the incremental calculation of *Past*, we carry out the following sequence of refinements, omitting the variable and invariant declarations since they do not change:

$\sqsubseteq$ { Sequential composition, Law 4.2 }

$$P, t : [\mathit{true}\ ,\ P = \mathit{Past}(C, S, t)]; \\ P, t : [P = \mathit{Past}(C, S, t)\ ,\ t \geq E \land P = \mathit{Past}(C, S, t)]$$

$\sqsubseteq$ { Strengthen postcondition, Law 1.1; fact that $\mathit{Past}(C, S, 0) = \varnothing$ }

$$P, t : [\mathit{true}\ ,\ t = 0 \land P = \varnothing]; \\ P, t : [P = \mathit{Past}(C, S, t)\ ,\ t \geq E \land P = \mathit{Past}(C, S, t)]$$

For the preceding step we needed the fact that $\mathit{Past}(C, S, 0) = \varnothing$, and it was this that led to the restriction imposed by the function *ValidStimuli* that stimulus events must have $\mathit{time} > 0$.

$\sqsubseteq$ { Assignment, Law 1.3 }

$$P, t := \varnothing, 0; \\ P, t : [P = \mathit{Past}(C, S, t)\ ,\ t \geq E \land P = \mathit{Past}(C, S, t)]$$

$$\sqsubseteq \quad \{\text{ Iteration single guard, Law B.3; Invariant: } P = Past(C,S,t)$$
$$\text{Variant: } V(t) = E - t, \text{ if } t \leq E$$
$$= 0, \quad \text{if } t > E \ \}$$

$P, t := \varnothing, 0;$
do $t < E \rightarrow$
$\quad P, t : [t < E \ , \ P = Past(C,S,t) \ , \ 0 \leq V(t) < V(t_0)]$
od

Note that we cannot use the simple variant $(E - t)$ because it is not bounded below. Our slightly more complicated variant rectifies this problem and ensures the correctness of the refinement step.

$\sqsubseteq$ { Arithmetic; fact that $E > 0$ within the loop body }

$P, t := \varnothing, 0;$
do $t < E \rightarrow$
$\quad P, t : [t < E \ , \ P = Past(C,S,t) \ , \ t > t_0]$ $\quad \triangleleft$**A**
od

Looking at the loop body, marked **A** above, we see the essence of our incremental calculation of *Past*: given the past up to a certain time, we must compute the past up to some greater time. Since as time progresses the circuit's future becomes its past, it will likely be helpful to formalize the concept of the "known future behaviour" of the circuit—i.e., the set of events which have not yet happened but whose occurrence is predicted on the basis of past events. We can describe this set of future events very much like we described *Past*:

$$Future : (Circuit \times \mathbb{F}\ Event \times Time) \rightarrow \mathbb{F}\ Event$$

$$\forall C : Circuit;\ S : \mathbb{F}\ Event;\ t : Time;\ e : Event \mid S \in ValidStimuli\ C \bullet$$
$$e \in Future(C,S,t)$$
$$\Leftrightarrow$$
$$e.time > t \land$$
$$(e \in S \lor$$
$$\exists\ ev : Past(C,S,t) \bullet$$
$$e \in Spawn(C, ev, Snapshot\ Past(C,S,ev.time)))$$

As with the rest of our specification, we should check that this definition of *Future* is consistent and that it does embody our notion of "known future behaviour". In Appendix A we prove the following two properties of *Future* (Theorem 3 and Theorem 4):

$$\forall C : Circuit;\ S : \mathbb{F}\ Event;\ t, T : Time \mid S \in ValidStimuli\ C \bullet$$
$$Future(C,S,t) = \varnothing \Rightarrow$$
$$(T > t \Rightarrow Past(C,S,T) = Past(C,S,t))$$
$$Future(C,S,t) = \varnothing \Rightarrow$$
$$(T > t \Rightarrow Future(C,S,T) = Future(C,S,t) = \varnothing)$$

We now introduce a variable to keep track of the future. We present the entire program because the new variable is global:

$\sqsubseteq$ { Add variable ($CI \mathrel{\hat=} F = Future(C,S,t)$), Laws 17.2 17.3 17.4; fact that $S = Future(C,S,0)$ }

$$\begin{array}{l}
\mathbf{var}\ P,S,F : \mathbb{F}\ Event;\\
\quad C : Circuit;\\
\quad E,t : Time;\\
\quad \mathbf{and}\ S \in ValidStimuli\ C \bullet\\
\\
P,t,F := \varnothing,0,S;\\
\mathbf{do}\ t < E \ \rightarrow\\
\quad P,t,F : [t < E\ ,\\
\qquad\qquad P = Past(C,S,t) \land F = Future(C,S,t)\ ,\\
\qquad\qquad t > t_0] \qquad\qquad\qquad \lhd\mathbf{B}\\
\mathbf{od}
\end{array}$$

An obvious refinement could be made at this point by replacing $t > t_0$ with $t = t_0 + 1$ in the postcondition of the loop body. However, it is equally obvious that this refinement will lead us to a so-called *time-mapping* simulator [RS89]. We would prefer to use the *next-event* approach as it usually results in a much simpler simulation algorithm. This is a case where an obvious refinement is not the one desired and where problem-related insight leads us to investigate other less obvious possibilities. Looking therefore at the definition of *Future*, we note that the following holds:

$$\begin{array}{l}
(Future(C,S,t) = \varnothing)\\
\lor\\
(Future(C,S,t) \neq \varnothing) \land (\min\{ev : Future(C,S,t) \bullet ev.time\} > t)
\end{array}$$

We can interpret this as saying that either (a) there are no future events after time t in which case (by Theorem 3) $Past(C,S,t)$ must describe the behaviour of the circuit at all times greater than or equal to t, or (b) there are some future events after time t and the earliest of these (as one would expect) occur at a time later than t. This leads us to the following refinement of the loop body, marked **B** above:

$\sqsubseteq$ { Strengthen postcondition, Law 1.1; Above property of *Future*; Theorem 3 }

$$\begin{array}{l}
P,t,F : [t < E\ ,\\
\qquad P = Past(C,S,t) \land F = Future(C,S,t)\ ,\\
\qquad (Future(C,S,t_0) = \varnothing \land t = E) \lor\\
\qquad (Future(C,S,t_0) \neq \varnothing \land\\
\qquad\ t = \min\{ev : Future(C,S,t_0) \bullet ev.time\})]
\end{array}$$

$\sqsubseteq$ { Fact that $F_0 = Future(C,S,t_0)$ }

$$\begin{array}{l}
P,t,F : [t < E\ ,\\
\qquad P = Past(C,S,t) \land F = Future(C,S,t)\ ,\\
\qquad (F_0 = \varnothing \land t = E) \lor\\
\qquad (F_0 \neq \varnothing \land t = \min\{ev : F_0 \bullet ev.time\})]
\end{array}$$

$\sqsubseteq$ { Alternation, Law 5.1 }

$$\mathbf{if}\ F = \varnothing \rightarrow P,t,F : [t < E \land F = \varnothing\ ,$$

$$
\begin{array}{l}
\qquad\qquad P = Past(C,S,t) \wedge F = Future(C,S,t)\ , \\
\qquad\qquad (F_0 = \varnothing \wedge t = E) \vee \\
\qquad\qquad (F_0 \neq \varnothing \wedge t = \min\{ev : F_0 \bullet ev.time\})] \\
\Box\ F \neq \varnothing \rightarrow P,t,F : [t < E \wedge F \neq \varnothing\ , \\
\qquad\qquad P = Past(C,S,t) \wedge F = Future(C,S,t)\ , \\
\qquad\qquad (F_0 = \varnothing \wedge t = E) \vee \\
\qquad\qquad (F_0 \neq \varnothing \wedge t = \min\{ev : F_0 \bullet ev.time\})] \\
\textbf{fi}
\end{array}
$$

$\sqsubseteq$ { Strengthen postcondition, Law 1.1 (twice) }

$$
\begin{array}{ll}
\textbf{if}\ F = \varnothing \rightarrow P,t,F : [t < E \wedge F = \varnothing\ , & \\
\qquad\qquad P = Past(C,S,t) \wedge F = Future(C,S,t)\ , & \\
\qquad\qquad F_0 = \varnothing \wedge t = E] & \triangleleft \mathbf{C} \\
\Box\ F \neq \varnothing \rightarrow P,t,F : [t < E \wedge F \neq \varnothing\ , & \\
\qquad\qquad P = Past(C,S,t) \wedge F = Future(C,S,t)\ , & \\
\qquad\qquad F_0 \neq \varnothing \wedge t = \min\{ev : F_0 \bullet ev.time\}] & \triangleleft \mathbf{D} \\
\textbf{fi} &
\end{array}
$$

We now consider separately the two branches of the alternation (marked **C** and **D** above). For branch **C**, we can immediately verify:

$\sqsubseteq$ { Assignment, Law 1.3; Theorem 3 and Theorem 4 }

$t := E$

Branch **D** is a little more interesting:

$\sqsubseteq$ { Specification invariant, Abbreviation 8.1 }

$$
\begin{array}{l}
P,t,F : [t < E \wedge F \neq \varnothing \wedge P = Past(C,S,t) \wedge F = Future(C,S,t)\ , \\
\qquad F_0 \neq \varnothing \wedge t = \min\{ev : F_0 \bullet ev.time\} \wedge \\
\qquad P = Past(C,S,t) \wedge F = Future(C,S,t)]
\end{array}
$$

$\sqsubseteq$ { Initial variable, Abbreviation 6.1; Remove true conjunct from postcondition }

$$
\begin{array}{l}
P,t,F : [t < E \wedge F \neq \varnothing \wedge P = Past(C,S,t) \wedge F = Future(C,S,t)\ , \\
\qquad t = \min\{ev : F_0 \bullet ev.time\} \wedge \\
\qquad P = Past(C,S,t) \wedge F = Future(C,S,t)]
\end{array}
$$

$\sqsubseteq$ { Substitution }

$$
\begin{array}{l}
P,t,F : [t < E \wedge F \neq \varnothing \wedge P = Past(C,S,t) \wedge F = Future(C,S,t)\ , \\
\qquad t = \min\{ev : F_0 \bullet ev.time\} \wedge \\
\qquad P = Past(C,S,\min\{ev : F_0 \bullet ev.time\}) \wedge \\
\qquad F = Future(C,S,\min\{ev : F_0 \bullet ev.time\})]
\end{array}
$$

$\sqsubseteq$ { Introduce local block, Law 3.2; Leading assignment, Law 13.1 }

$$
\begin{array}{l}
|[\ \textbf{var}\ T : Time \bullet \\
\quad T := \min\{ev : F \bullet ev.time\}; \\
\quad P,t,F,T : [t < E \wedge F \neq \varnothing \wedge \\
\qquad\qquad P = Past(C,S,t) \wedge F = Future(C,S,t)\ , \\
\qquad\qquad t = T_0 \wedge \\
\qquad\qquad P = Past(C,S,T_0) \wedge
\end{array}
$$

$$F = \mathit{Future}(C, S, T_0)]$$

$]|$

$\sqsubseteq$ { Contract frame, Law 6.10; Weaken precondition, Law 1.2 }

$$\begin{array}{l} |[\ \mathbf{var}\ T : \mathit{Time} \bullet \\ \quad T := \min\{ev : F \bullet ev.time\}; \\ \quad P, t, F : [t < E \wedge P = \mathit{Past}(C, S, t) \wedge F = \mathit{Future}(C, S, t)\ , \\ \qquad\qquad t = T \wedge P = \mathit{Past}(C, S, T) \wedge F = \mathit{Future}(C, S, T)] \\ ]| \end{array}$$

$\sqsubseteq$ { Following assignment, Law 4.4; Propositional calculus }

$$\begin{array}{l} |[\ \mathbf{var}\ T : \mathit{Time} \bullet \\ \quad T := \min\{ev : F \bullet ev.time\}; \\ \quad P, t, F : [t < E \wedge P = \mathit{Past}(C, S, t) \wedge F = \mathit{Future}(C, S, t)\ , \\ \qquad\qquad P = \mathit{Past}(C, S, T) \wedge F = \mathit{Future}(C, S, T)]; \\ \quad t := T \\ ]| \end{array}$$

$\sqsubseteq$ { Contract frame, Law 6.10; Weaken precondition, Law 1.2 }

$$\begin{array}{l} |[\ \mathbf{var}\ T : \mathit{Time} \bullet \\ \quad T := \min\{ev : F \bullet ev.time\}; \\ \quad P, F : [P = \mathit{Past}(C, S, t) \wedge F = \mathit{Future}(C, S, t)\ , \\ \qquad\qquad P = \mathit{Past}(C, S, T) \wedge F = \mathit{Future}(C, S, T)]; \\ \quad t := T \\ ]| \end{array}$$

$\sqsubseteq$ { Sequential composition, Law B.1; Contract frame, Law 6.10 (twice) }

$$\begin{array}{ll} |[\ \mathbf{var}\ T : \mathit{Time} \bullet & \\ \quad T := \min\{ev : F \bullet ev.time\}; & \\ \quad P : [P = \mathit{Past}(C, S, t) \wedge F = \mathit{Future}(C, S, t)\ , & \\ \qquad P = \mathit{Past}(C, S, T) \wedge F = \mathit{Future}(C, S, t)]; & \lhd \mathbf{E} \\ \quad F : [P = \mathit{Past}(C, S, T) \wedge F = \mathit{Future}(C, S, t)\ , & \\ \qquad P = \mathit{Past}(C, S, T) \wedge F = \mathit{Future}(C, S, T)]; & \lhd \mathbf{F} \\ \quad t := T & \\ ]| & \end{array}$$

The refinement of the specification statements marked with **E** and **F** above—together with our earlier choice of method for increasing t—is the crux of our development. We pick assignment statements which refine these specifications based on our intuition of discrete-event simulation strategies, and the assignment law tells us what we must prove in order to ensure that these refinements are correct. The required proofs, cited below as Theorem 9 and Theorem 10 are, found in Appendix A.

Specification statement **E** is refined as follows:

$\sqsubseteq$ { Assignment, Law 1.3; Theorem 9 }

$$P := P \cup \{ev : F \mid ev.time = T\}$$

and specification statement **F** is refined as follows:

$\sqsubseteq$ { Assignment, Law 1.3; Theorem 10 }

$$F := F \setminus \{ev : F \mid ev.time = T\} \cup \bigcup_{e \in \{ev:F \mid ev.time = T\}} Spawn(C, e, Snapshot\ P)$$

It is perhaps conceivable that we might have calculated these assignments rather than presenting them and proving the refinement steps correct. However, such calculation would have been extremely difficult, and based on our experience with simulation we already had a good idea of the result. Thus, it was in our best interest to proceed as we did: propose our solution and use the tools of the refinement calculus to ensure its correctness. Pursuing the mathematics in isolation from our knowledge about the problem—although it can sometimes provide new insight—is not always the right approach. We must remember that refinement is a programmer's *tool*, not a programmer!

Collecting together the statements of branch **D**, we have:

$$\begin{array}{l}
[\![\ \mathbf{var}\ T : Time \bullet \\
\quad T := \min\{ev : F \bullet ev.time\}; \\
\quad P := P \cup \{ev : F \mid ev.time = T\}; \\
\quad F := F \setminus \{ev : F \mid ev.time = T\} \cup \\
\qquad\qquad \bigcup_{e \in \{ev:F \mid ev.time = T\}} Spawn(C, e, Snapshot\ P); \\
\quad t := T \\
]\!]
\end{array}$$

Since for typical simulations P will be quite large, we would like to eliminate the dependence on P for the calculation of F. Then we could output P incrementally and save storage. We thus require an ongoing record of *Snapshot* P and we introduce a variable σ accordingly, noting for justification that we can easily show:

$$\begin{array}{l}
(\sigma = Snapshot\ P) \Rightarrow \\
\quad \sigma \oplus \{ev : F \mid ev.time = T \bullet (ev.wire, ev.value)\} = \\
\quad Snapshot\ (P \cup \{ev : F \mid ev.time = T\})
\end{array}$$

Because σ is a global variable, we must introduce it to the entire program developed thus far:

$$\begin{array}{ll}
\sqsubseteq & \{ \text{Add variable } (CI \mathrel{\widehat{=}} \sigma = Snapshot\ P), \text{ Laws 17.3 17.4} \} \\
& \mathbf{var}\ P, S, F : \mathbb{F}\ Event; \\
& \qquad C : Circuit; \\
& \qquad E, t : Time; \\
& \qquad \sigma : State; \\
& \qquad \mathbf{and}\ S \in ValidStimuli\ C \bullet \\
& \\
& P, t, F, \sigma := \varnothing, 0, S, (\lambda\, w : Wire \bullet LogicX); \\
& \mathbf{do}\ t < E \rightarrow \\
& \quad \mathbf{if}\ F = \varnothing \rightarrow \\
& \qquad t := E \\
& \quad \Box\ F \neq \varnothing \rightarrow \\
& \qquad [\![\ \mathbf{var}\ T : Time \bullet
\end{array}$$

$$
\begin{array}{l}
\qquad\qquad T := \min\{ev : F \bullet ev.time\}; \\
\qquad\qquad P, \sigma := P \cup \{ev : F \mid ev.time = T\}\ , \\
\qquad\qquad\qquad \sigma \oplus \{ev : F \mid ev.time = T \bullet (ev.wire, ev.value)\}; \\
\qquad\qquad F := F \setminus \{ev : F \mid ev.time = T\} \cup \bigcup_{e \in \{ev : F \mid ev.time = T\}} Spawn(C, e, \sigma); \\
\qquad\qquad t := T \\
\qquad]| \\
\quad \mathbf{fi} \\
\mathbf{od}
\end{array}
$$

5 Data Refinements

We have now reached the point where we have a fairly concrete program over somewhat abstract data types. Thus, the remainder of the development will be a series of data refinements which will bring the data types closer to those found in typical programming languages. For instance, we will refine P to an output sequence of events; σ to a partial function and then to an array; *Event* and *Gate* to record types of some sort; *Wire* to a subset of $\mathbb{N}$; and so on. Here we present only the most interesting of the many data refinements, namely that of F.

Because we use the set of minimum-time events from F throughout the program, and because sets typically must be represented as sequences in programming languages, it makes sense to refine F to a time-ordered sequence of events. Since S is directly related to F, we will refine it in the same way at the same time. We therefore introduce

$$Q, I : \operatorname{seq} Event$$

with the coupling invariant

$$CI \mathrel{\widehat{=}} \operatorname{ran} Q = F \wedge \operatorname{ran} I = S \wedge \operatorname{ordered} Q \wedge \operatorname{ordered} I$$

where we define

$$
\begin{array}{|l}
OrderedEvents : \mathbb{P} \operatorname{seq} Event \\
\hline
\forall es : \operatorname{seq} Event \bullet \\
\qquad es \in OrderedEvents \\
\quad \Leftrightarrow \\
\qquad (\forall i, j : \operatorname{dom} es \bullet i \leq j \Rightarrow (es\ i).time \leq (es\ j).time)
\end{array}
$$

together with the abbreviation

$$\operatorname{ordered} s \mathrel{\widehat{=}} s \in OrderedEvents$$

We now apply the data refinement laws of [Mor90, Chapter 17] to each affected part of our program. We first strengthen the variable invariant which becomes:

and $\text{ran}\, I \in \mathit{ValidStimuli}\ C \wedge \text{ordered}\, I$

We then use Law 17.3 to augment the initial assignment with:

$$P, t, F, \sigma, Q := \varnothing, 0, S, (\lambda\, w : \mathit{Wire} \bullet \mathit{LogicX}), I$$

and Law 17.4 to replace the guards of the **if** statement with $Q = \langle\rangle$ and $Q \neq \langle\rangle$. It remains to refine the first three assignments of the second **if** branch. For the first assignment, we have:

$\sqsubseteq$ { Simple specification, Law 8.9 }

$T : [\mathit{true}\ ,\ T = \min\{ev : F_0 \bullet ev.\mathit{time}\}]$

$\sqsubseteq$ { Augment specification, Law 17.2 }

$T : [\mathit{CI}\ ,\ \mathit{CI} \wedge T = \min\{ev : F_0 \bullet ev.\mathit{time}\}]$

$\sqsubseteq$ { Definition of CI; Substitution }

$T : [\mathit{CI}\ ,\ \mathit{CI} \wedge T = \min\{ev : \text{ran}\, Q_0 \bullet ev.\mathit{time}\}]$

$\sqsubseteq$ { Facts that ordered Q_0 and $Q_0 \neq \langle\rangle$ by guard }

$T : [\mathit{CI}\ ,\ \mathit{CI} \wedge T = (\text{head}\, Q_0).\mathit{time}]$

$\sqsubseteq$ { Remove invariant, Law 8.10 }

$T : [\mathit{true}\ ,\ T = (\text{head}\, Q_0).\mathit{time}]$

$\sqsubseteq$ { Simple specification, Law 8.9 }

$T := (\text{head}\, Q).\mathit{time}$

For the second assignment we use exactly the same unfold-substitute-refold process to obtain:

$\sqsubseteq$ { Reasoning similar to that for first assignment }

$$\begin{aligned} P, \sigma := & P \cup \{ev : \text{ran}\, Q \mid ev.\mathit{time} = T\}, \\ & \sigma \oplus \{ev : \text{ran}\, Q \mid ev.\mathit{time} = T \bullet (ev.\mathit{wire}, ev.\mathit{value})\} \end{aligned}$$

The third assignment is the most complex and the most interesting. We refine it as follows:

$$F := F \setminus \{ev : F \mid ev.\mathit{time} = T\} \cup \bigcup_{e \in \{ev : F \mid ev.\mathit{time} = T\}} \mathit{Spawn}(C, e, \sigma)$$

$\sqsubseteq$ { Simple specification, Law 8.9; Augment specification, Law 17.2 }

$$\begin{aligned} F, Q : [&\mathit{CI}\ , \\ &\mathit{CI} \wedge \\ &F = F_0 \setminus \{ev : F_0 \mid ev.\mathit{time} = T\} \cup \bigcup_{e \in \{ev : F_0 \mid ev.\mathit{time} = T\}} \mathit{Spawn}(C, e, \sigma)] \end{aligned}$$

$\sqsubseteq$ { Substitution from CI; Fix initial value, Law 6.3; Initial variable, Abbreviation 6.1 }

$|[\ \textbf{con}\ \mathcal{R} : \mathbb{F}\ \mathit{Event} \bullet$

$\quad F, Q : [\mathit{CI} \wedge \mathcal{R} = \text{ran}\, Q\ ,$

$$
\begin{array}{l}
\qquad CI \wedge \\
\qquad \operatorname{ran} Q = \mathcal{R} \setminus \{ ev : \mathcal{R} \mid ev.time = T \} \cup \\
\qquad\qquad \bigcup_{e \in \{ ev : \mathcal{R} \mid ev.time = T \}} Spawn(C, e, \sigma)] \\
]|
\end{array}
$$

$\sqsubseteq$ { Introduce local block, Law 3.2; Strengthen postcondition, Law 1.1 }

$$
\begin{array}{l}
|[\ \mathbf{con}\ \mathcal{R} : \mathbb{F}\ Event; \\
\quad \mathbf{var}\ G : \mathbb{F}\ Event \bullet \\
\quad F, Q, G : [CI \wedge \mathcal{R} = \operatorname{ran} Q\ , \\
\qquad\qquad CI \wedge \\
\qquad\qquad (G \cup \{ ev : \operatorname{ran} Q \mid ev.time = T \}) \\
\qquad\qquad\quad = \{ ev : \mathcal{R} \mid ev.time = T \} \wedge \\
\qquad\qquad \operatorname{ran} Q = \mathcal{R} \setminus G \cup \bigcup_{e \in G} Spawn(C, e, \sigma) \wedge \\
\qquad\qquad \{ ev : \operatorname{ran} Q \mid ev.time = T \} = \emptyset] \\
]|
\end{array}
$$

For brevity, we omit the **var** and **con** declarations in subsequent refinements.

$\sqsubseteq$ { Initialised iteration, Law B.2; Invariant: *in loop body below*
Variant: $\#\{ ev : \operatorname{ran} Q \mid ev.time = T \}$ }

$$
\begin{array}{l}
F, Q, G : [CI \wedge \mathcal{R} = \operatorname{ran} Q\ , \\
\qquad\qquad CI \wedge \\
\qquad\qquad (G \cup \{ ev : \operatorname{ran} Q \mid ev.time = T \}) \\
\qquad\qquad\quad = \{ ev : \mathcal{R} \mid ev.time = T \} \wedge \\
\qquad\qquad \operatorname{ran} Q = \mathcal{R} \setminus G \cup \bigcup_{e \in G} Spawn(C, e, \sigma)]; \\
\mathbf{do}\ \{ ev : \operatorname{ran} Q \mid ev.time = T \} \neq \emptyset \rightarrow \\
\quad F, Q, G : [\{ ev : \operatorname{ran} Q \mid ev.time = T \} \neq \emptyset\ , \\
\qquad\qquad CI \wedge \\
\qquad\qquad (G \cup \{ ev : \operatorname{ran} Q \mid ev.time = T \}) \\
\qquad\qquad\quad = \{ ev : \mathcal{R} \mid ev.time = T \} \wedge \\
\qquad\qquad \operatorname{ran} Q = \mathcal{R} \setminus G \cup \bigcup_{e \in G} Spawn(C, e, \sigma)\ , \\
\qquad\qquad 0 \leq \#\{ ev : \operatorname{ran} Q \mid ev.time = T \} \wedge \\
\qquad\qquad \#\{ ev : \operatorname{ran} Q \mid ev.time = T \} < \#\{ ev : \operatorname{ran} Q_0 \mid ev.time = T \}] \\
\mathbf{od}
\end{array}
$$

$\sqsubseteq$ { Strengthen postcondition, Law 6.5 }

$$
\begin{array}{l}
F, Q, G : [CI \wedge \mathcal{R} = \operatorname{ran} Q\ ,\ G = 0]; \\
\mathbf{do}\ \{ ev : \operatorname{ran} Q \mid ev.time = T \} \neq \emptyset \rightarrow \\
\quad F, Q, G : [\{ ev : \operatorname{ran} Q \mid ev.time = T \} \neq \emptyset\ , \\
\qquad\qquad CI \wedge \\
\qquad\qquad (G \cup \{ ev : \operatorname{ran} Q \mid ev.time = T \}) \\
\qquad\qquad\quad = \{ ev : \mathcal{R} \mid ev.time = T \} \wedge \\
\qquad\qquad \operatorname{ran} Q = \mathcal{R} \setminus G \cup \bigcup_{e \in G} Spawn(C, e, \sigma)\ , \\
\qquad\qquad 0 \leq \#\{ ev : \operatorname{ran} Q \mid ev.time = T \} \wedge \\
\qquad\qquad \#\{ ev : \operatorname{ran} Q \mid ev.time = T \} < \#\{ ev : \operatorname{ran} Q_0 \mid ev.time = T \}]
\end{array}
$$

od

$\sqsubseteq$ { Assignment, Law 1.3 }

$F, Q, G : [CI \wedge \mathcal{R} = \text{ran}\, Q \ ,\ G = 0];$
do $\{ev : \text{ran}\, Q \mid ev.time = T\} \neq \varnothing \rightarrow$
$\quad Q, G := \text{tail}\, Q \oslash Spawn(C, \text{head}\, Q, \sigma)\ ,\ G \cup \{\text{head}\, Q\}$
od

where we define $\oslash$ as follows:

$$
\begin{array}{|l}
\_ \oslash \_ : \text{seq}\, Event \times \mathbb{F}\, Event \rightarrow \text{seq}\, Event \\
\hline
\forall\, es : \text{seq}\, Event \mid \text{ordered}\, es \bullet \\
\quad \forall\, E : \mathbb{F}\, Event \bullet \\
\quad\quad \text{ran}(es \oslash E) = (\text{ran}\, es) \cup E \wedge \\
\quad\quad \text{ordered}(es \oslash E)
\end{array}
$$

The refinement continues:

$\sqsubseteq$ { Augment guard, Law 17.4; **cand** connective borrowed from [Gri81]; recall that $T = \min\{ev : \mathcal{R} \bullet ev.time\}$ }

$F, Q, G : [CI \wedge \mathcal{R} = \text{ran}\, Q \ ,\ G = 0];$
do $Q \neq \langle\rangle$ **cand** $(\text{head}\, Q).time = T \rightarrow$
$\quad Q, G := \text{tail}\, Q \oslash Spawn(C, \text{head}\, Q, \sigma)\ ,\ G \cup \{\text{head}\, Q\}$
od

$\sqsubseteq$ { Weaken precondition, Law 1.2; Simple specification, Law 8.9; Remove logical constant, Law 6.4 }

$G := 0;$
do $Q \neq \langle\rangle$ **cand** $(\text{head}\, Q).time = T \rightarrow$
$\quad Q, G := \text{tail}\, Q \oslash Spawn(C, \text{head}\, Q, \sigma)\ ,\ G \cup \{\text{head}\, Q\}$
od

$\sqsubseteq$ { G is auxiliary; Diminish assignment, Law 17.8 (twice) }

do $Q \neq \langle\rangle$ **cand** $(\text{head}\, Q).time = T \rightarrow$
$\quad Q := \text{tail}\, Q \oslash Spawn(C, \text{head}\, Q, \sigma);$
od

Note that the last two steps have eliminated the declaration and use of $\mathcal{R}$ and G. Collecting together our data refinements and applying Law 17.8 to remove variables F and S which are now auxiliary, our simulator program SEQSIM now looks like this:

var $P : \mathbb{F}\, Event;$
$\quad Q, I : \text{seq}\, Event;$
$\quad C : Circuit;$
$\quad E, t : Time;$
$\quad \sigma : State;$

$\quad$ **and** $\text{ran}\, I \in ValidStimuli\ C \wedge \text{ordered}\, I \bullet$

$P, t, Q, \sigma := \varnothing, 0, I, (\lambda\, w : Wire \bullet LogicX);$

```
do t < E →
   if Q = ⟨⟩ →
      t := E
   □ Q ≠ ⟨⟩ →
      |[ var T : Time •
         T := (head Q).time;
         P, σ := P ∪ {ev : ran Q | ev.time = T} ,
                 σ ⊕ {ev : ran Q | ev.time = T • (ev.wire, ev.value)};
         do Q ≠ ⟨⟩ cand (head Q).time = T →
             Q := tail Q ⊘ Spawn(C, head Q, σ);
         od;
         t := T
      ]|
   fi
od
```

It is clear that further data refinements could produce code in a real programming language. We intend to carry out such refinements to yield an implementation of SEQSIM in Occam and we are confident that this version of SEQSIM will present fewer problems upon trial than did the original version. It may not be entirely bug-free, however, since one can make mistakes in constructing mathematical specifications and proofs just as easily as in writing Occam programs from scratch. But the stepwise nature of the development does lessen the likelihood of making a gross error, and the mathematical structure inherent in the process gives us the ability to reason precisely about anything which does happen to go wrong.

6 A Program Property

The mathematical structure arising from the formal specification and refinement process can be used to reason precisely about the developed program. In this way it is possible to prove certain properties of the program which might otherwise be taken on faith, on informal argument, or not be known at all. In our case, we will show that the size of the event queue, Q, is bounded above by a particular value. Such a bound is a very useful thing to have, as it allows us to guarantee that a given simulation will terminate correctly without running out of memory (or, if our computer has less memory available to Q than the bound requires, guarantee that it might not!)

Claim: At all times during the execution of SEQSIM,

$$\#Q \leq \#I + D \cdot n$$

where

$$D = \max\{g : C.gates \bullet g.delay\}$$

$$n = \#C.gates$$

Proof: We first note that because of the coupling invariant used to data refine F into Q, we can equivalently show

$$\#F \leq \#S + D \cdot n$$

and because of the nature of the refinement relation, we can use any intermediate abstract programs developed along the way for our proof. First consider the intermediate program at the end of Section 4.

Let t_i be the value of variable t after the ith iteration, F_i the value of F after the ith iteration, and SP_i the set

$$\bigcup_{e \in \{ev:F \mid ev.time = T\}} Spawn(C, e, \sigma)$$

which is added to F on the ith iteration. (Here "iteration" is equivalent to "execution of the second branch of the **if** statement" since it is easy to show that this branch comprises the complete execution of every loop iteration, expect possibly the last which might instead be the simple assignment $t := E$.) We omit subscripts on F and T in the definition of SP_i because they are not required for the proof.

Assume that at the start of the kth iteration, $\#F > 0$ and $\min\{ev : F \bullet ev.time\} = \tau$.

LEMMA 1: $(\forall ev : SP_k \bullet ev.time \leq \tau + D)$

PROOF: Under our assumption,

$$SP_k = \bigcup_{e \in \{ev:F \mid ev.time = \tau\}} Spawn(C, e, \sigma)$$

Thus,

$$
\begin{aligned}
& ev \in SP_k \\
\Rightarrow \quad & \{ \text{ property of union } \} \\
& (\exists\, e : F \bullet e.time = \tau \wedge ev \in Spawn(C, e, \sigma)) \\
\Rightarrow \quad & \{ \text{ defn } Spawn \ \} \\
& (\exists\, g : Gate \bullet ev.time = \tau + g.delay) \\
\Rightarrow \quad & \{ \text{ defn } D \ \} \\
& ev.time \leq \tau + D
\end{aligned}
$$

□

LEMMA 2: $(\forall j : \mathbb{N} \bullet t_{k+j} \geq \tau + j)$

PROOF: By induction on j.

From our development, we know that the second branch of the **if** statement refines the specification

$$P,t,F : [t < E \wedge F \neq \varnothing \wedge P = Past(C,S,t) \wedge F = Future(C,S,t) \ , \\ F_0 \neq \varnothing \wedge t = \min\{ev : F_0 \bullet ev.time\} \wedge \\ P = Past(C,S,t) \wedge F = Future(C,S,t)]$$

Thus, by our definition of τ, $t_k = \tau$, whence $t_k \geq \tau + 0$ and our hypothesis holds for $j = 0$.

Assume the hypothesis holds for j. From our development, we also know that the loop body refines

$$P,t : [t < E \ , \ P = Past(C,S,t) \ , \ t > t_0]$$

Therefore, beginning with our induction hypothesis:

$$t_{k+j} \geq \tau + j$$

$\Rightarrow$ { above specification of loop body }

$$t_{k+(j+1)} > \tau + j$$

$\Rightarrow$ { property of $\mathbb{N}$ }

$$t_{k+(j+1)} \geq \tau + (j+1)$$

Thus, if the hypothesis holds for j it also holds for $j+1$. The lemma is therefore proved by induction. □

LEMMA 3: $(\forall i : \mathbb{N} \bullet \#SP_i \leq n)$

PROOF: We defined SP_i to be

$$\bigcup_{e \in \{ev:F | ev.time = T\}} Spawn(C,e,\sigma)$$

during the ith iteration. Now,

$$ev \in SP_i$$

$\Rightarrow$ { property of union }

$$\exists\, e : F \bullet e.time = T \wedge ev \in Spawn(C,e,\sigma)$$

$\Rightarrow$ { defn $Spawn$ }

$$\exists\, g : C.gates \bullet ev.wire = g.output \wedge \\ ev.value = GateValue\ g\ \sigma \wedge \\ ev.time = T + g.delay$$

We will label this property $\mathcal{S}_1$. Assume that $e1, e2 \in SP_i$. Therefore, by $\mathcal{S}_1$ we must have $g1, g2 \in C.gates$ where

$$e1.wire = g1.output \wedge e2.wire = g2.output \wedge \\ e1.value = GateValue\ g1\ \sigma \wedge e2.value = GateValue\ g2\ \sigma \wedge \\ e1.time = T + g1.delay \wedge e2.time = T + g2.delay$$

Whence,

$$\begin{array}{ll} & e1.wire = e2.wire \\ \Rightarrow & \{ \text{ propositional calculus } \} \\ & g1.output = g2.output \\ \Rightarrow & \{ \text{ contrapositive of “no short circuit” clause of } \mathit{Circuit} \} \\ & g1 = g2 \\ \Rightarrow & \{ \text{ above relationship among } e1, e2, g1, g2 \} \\ & e1 = e2 \end{array}$$

So therefore, for all $e1, e2$ in SP_i,

$$\begin{array}{ll} & e1 \neq e2 \\ \Rightarrow & \{ \text{ contrapositive of preceding result } \} \\ & e1.wire \neq e2.wire \\ \Rightarrow & \{ \text{ property } \mathcal{S}_1\text{; propositional calculus } \} \\ & \exists\, g1, g2 : C.gates \bullet g1.output \neq g2.output \\ \Rightarrow & \{ \text{ propositional calculus } \} \\ & \exists\, g1, g2 : C.gates \bullet g1 \neq g2 \end{array}$$

From this we can easily deduce

$$\begin{array}{l} \forall\, es\colon \mathbb{F}\ Event \bullet \\ \quad es \subseteq SP_i \Rightarrow (\exists\, gs : \mathbb{F}\ C.gates \bullet \#gs = \#es) \end{array}$$

But

$$\begin{array}{ll} & \#es > n \\ \Rightarrow & \{ \text{ property of finite sets (recall that } n = \#C.gates) \} \\ & \nexists\, gs : \mathbb{F}\ C.gates \bullet \#gs = \#es \\ \Rightarrow & \{ \text{ contrapositive of preceding result } \} \\ & es \not\subseteq SP_i \end{array}$$

A final application of the contrapositive law gives us

$$\begin{array}{ll} & es \subseteq SP_i \Rightarrow \#es \leq n \\ \Rightarrow & \{ \text{ property of sets } \} \\ & \#SP_i \leq n \end{array}$$

□

The proof of our main claim is now straightforward. From the definition of *Future* together with the fact that $F = \mathit{Future}(C, S, t)$, we have:

$$\forall i : \mathbb{N};\ e : F_i \bullet e.time > t_i$$

$\Rightarrow$ { particular case of $i = k + D$ }

$$\forall e : F_{k+D} \bullet e.time > t_{k+D}$$

$\Rightarrow$ { Lemma 2 }

$$\forall e : F_{k+D} \bullet e.time > t_{k+D} \geq \tau + D$$

$\Rightarrow$ { property of $\mathbb{N}$ }

$$\forall e : F_{k+D} \bullet e.time > \tau + D$$

$\Rightarrow$ { Lemma 1 }

$$\forall e : Event \bullet e \in SP_k \Rightarrow e \notin F_{k+D}$$

Events are added to F only by the union of successive SP_is. From the preceding result we can easily infer that at any particular time, F can contain the events of at most D SP_is. Thus, by Lemma 3 and the fact that initially $\#F = \#S$, we have

$$\#F \leq \#S + D \cdot n$$

□

We should note that it is possible (and desirable) to refine SEQSIM such that the events from S are not initially placed in F, but instead are fed into the program separately as an input sequence. In this case, the bound on $\#F$ (and hence $\#Q$) would be simply $D \cdot n$.

We also note that in either case this is not a particularly tight bound on $\#F$ since (a) it ignores the fact that at least one event is removed from F each time an SP_i is added, and (b) it applies to *all* circuits realizable in our model, many of which are pathological cases which would not occur in practice (e.g. a circuit in which the output of each gate is an input to every other gate). Nonetheless, it can be very useful to have a known upper bound on memory usage. Furthermore, the reasoning we have used to arrive at our bound might help us construct a tighter bound based on a realistically restricted circuit topology.

Our proof of this bound is another good recommendation for the use of formal techniques. A bit of drawing and calculating on the back of an envelope originally led us to believe that a bound on $\#F$ (when S is made an input sequence as explained above) was given by

$$\left\lceil \frac{D}{d} \right\rceil \cdot n$$

where $d = \min\{g : C.gates \bullet g.delay\}$. It was only in constructing the proof that we realized our mistake and derived the correct, looser bound.

7 Conclusion

The ideal software refinery is likely to elude us for some time to come. However, as this case study reveals, current software refinement techniques can be used effectively in the development of substantial programs. The resulting product will typically be far better documented and far more reliable than the corresponding product of mainstream development methods. Furthermore, the mathematical structure arising from the specification and refinement process allows the programmer to derive and/or prove desirable properties of his program. Refinement is clearly a tool which warrants wider application in the software engineering community and with specification and refinement techniques codified in books such as [Spi89] and [Mor90], the foundation for such wider application has been laid.

8 Future Work

There are several issues arising from this study which we would like to address. A relatively simple one is the use of Z within the refinement calculus. In this study we made a point of using Z schemas only to define compound types. We used Z axiomatic functions to describe all of the operational (and some of the static) aspects of the problem domain and thereby avoided the use of schemas to describe state changes. This approach did not seem to stifle our creativity or reduce our expressive power at all and it allowed for a clean transition from Z to the refinement calculus. It appears, therefore, to be a good development methodology. However, we would like to study this methodology in more detail and in the context of a variety of different problem domains before drawing any general conclusions.

Because our development of SEQSIM here ignored the input process, we have another problem domain close to hand. It would be interesting to specify and refine the program which creates valid instances of SEQSIM's input variables from a textual description. Such a program would be very different to SEQSIM and would therefore likely provide new insights into the practicalities of refinement in general and of our methodology in particular.

Of more immediate interest to us is the problem of extending our methodology to include a notion of concurrency. We would like to incorporate an existing process algebra (likely CSP) into the methodology and we intend to use our distributed simulator as a vehicle to investigate various ways of doing this.

We would also like to investigate the process of modifying a program which has been developed with a formal methodology. This is an extremely important area, since the bulk of programming man-hours is spent modifying and/or maintaining programs. To this end, we intend to modify SEQSIM by adding to its timing model a component for inertial delay [BF77] and by extending its gate model to allow primitive gates with non-interchangeable inputs.

Finally, it is clear from this case study that the refinement process could benefit from partial automation of some sort. In particular, it would be interesting to look at the idea of a refinement-based CASE tool which might, among other things, maintain a database of refinement laws which one could browse, augment with derived laws, and so on. If it effectively incorporated a theorem-prover or proof-assistant, such a CASE tool could be extremely powerful.

Acknowledgements

The author would like to thank Tony Hoare, Ian Page, and the workshop referees for their very helpful comments on an earlier draft of this paper.

References

[Bac88] R.J.R. Back. A calculus of refinements for program derivations. *Acta Informatica*, 25:593–624, 1988.

[BF77] Melvin A. Breuer and Arthur D. Friedman. *Diagnosis and Reliable Design of Digital Systems.* Pitman, 1977.

[Dij76] E.W. Dijkstra. *A Discipline of Programming.* Prentice-Hall, 1976.

[Gri81] David Gries. *The Science of Programming.* Springer-Verlag, 1981.

[Hoa69] C.A.R. Hoare. An axiomatic basis for computer programming. *Communications of the ACM*, 12(10):576–580,583, Oct. 1969.

[Mor87] Joseph M. Morris. A theoretical basis for stepwise refinement and the programming calculus. *Science of Computer Programming*, 9:287–306, 1987.

[Mor90] Carroll Morgan. *Programming from Specifications.* Prentice-Hall, 1990.

[MRG88] Carroll Morgan, Ken Robinson, and Paul Gardiner. On the refinement calculus. Technical Monograph PRG-70, Programming Research Group, Oxford University Computing Laboratory, Oct. 1988.

[RS89] Gordon Russell and Ian L. Sayers. *Advanced Simulation and Test Methodology for VLSI design.* Van Nostrand Reinhold, 1989.

[Spi89] J.M. Spivey. *The Z Notation: A Reference Manual.* Prentice-Hall, 1989.

[Wood89] Kenneth R. Wood. Accelerated simulation of digital circuits using distributed discrete-event techniques. M.Sc. Thesis, Oxford University, 1989.

[Wood90] Kenneth R. Wood. Distributing gate-level digital timing simulation over arrays of transputers. In D.J. Pritchard and C.J. Scott, editors, *Applications of Transputers 2 (Proceedings of the Second International Conference on the Applications of Transputers)*, pages 565–572. IOS Press, 1990.

A Proofs

It may appear unnecessary to include the full text of these proofs here. However, such proofs are a vital component of any formal software development process, and in a case study such as this we would be remiss to sweep the details of such an important component quietly under the rug.

Theorem 1

$$\begin{array}{l}\forall\, C : \mathit{Circuit};\; S : \mathbb{F}\,\mathit{Event};\; t, T : \mathit{Time} \mid S \in \mathit{ValidStimuli}\ C \bullet \\ \quad t < T \Rightarrow \mathit{Past}(C, S, t) \subseteq \mathit{Past}(C, S, T)\end{array}$$

Proof:

If we define the following abbreviations,

$$\begin{array}{rcl}\sigma_{ev} & \mathrel{\widehat=} & \mathit{Snapshot}\ \mathit{Past}(C, S, ev.time) \\ S_t & \mathrel{\widehat=} & \{e : S \mid e.time \leq t\} \\ \mathit{Spawn}_t(c, e, \sigma) & \mathrel{\widehat=} & \{e : \mathit{Spawn}(c, e, \sigma) \mid e.time \leq t\}\end{array}$$

we can rewrite the definition of *Past* as:

$$\begin{array}{|l}\mathit{Past} : (\mathit{Circuit} \times \mathbb{F}\,\mathit{Event} \times \mathit{Time}) \rightarrow \mathbb{F}\,\mathit{Event} \\ \hline \forall\, C : \mathit{Circuit};\; S : \mathbb{F}\,\mathit{Event};\; t : \mathit{Time};\; e : \mathit{Event} \mid S \in \mathit{ValidStimuli}\ C \bullet \\ \qquad e \in \mathit{Past}(C, S, t) \\ \quad \Leftrightarrow \\ \qquad e \in S_t \vee \\ \qquad \exists\, ev : \mathit{Past}(C, S, t) \bullet e \in \mathit{Spawn}_t(C, ev, \sigma_{ev})\end{array}$$

We now look separately at the forward and backward components of the equivalence. The forward component (with appropriate universal quantifications assumed) is:

$$\begin{array}{l}e \in \mathit{Past}(C, S, t) \Rightarrow e \in S_t \vee \\ \qquad\qquad \exists\, ev : \mathit{Past}(C, S, t) \bullet e \in \mathit{Spawn}_t(C, ev, \sigma_{ev})\end{array} \tag{1}$$

By the definition of *Spawn* and the fact that $(\forall\, g : \mathit{Gate} \bullet g.delay > 0)$ it is easy to establish that

$$e \in \mathit{Spawn}_t(C, ev, \sigma_{ev}) \Rightarrow ev.time < e.time$$

Therefore, from formula (1) above we can derive:

$$\begin{array}{l}e \in \mathit{Past}(C, S, t) \Rightarrow \\ \quad e \in S_t \vee \\ \quad \exists\, ev : \mathit{Past}(C, S, t) \mid ev.time < e.time \bullet e \in \mathit{Spawn}_t(C, ev, \sigma_{ev})\end{array} \tag{1'}$$

The backward component of the equivalence (with appropriate universal quantifications assumed) is:

$$(e \in S_t \vee \exists\, ev : \mathit{Past}(C, S, t) \bullet e \in \mathit{Spawn}_t(C, ev, \sigma_{ev})) \Rightarrow e \in \mathit{Past}(C, S, t)$$

$$\Leftrightarrow \quad \{ \text{ Propositional logic } \}$$
$$e \in S_t \Rightarrow e \in \mathit{Past}(C,S,t) \wedge$$
$$(\exists\, ev : \mathit{Past}(C,S,t) \bullet e \in \mathit{Spawn}_t(C, ev, \sigma_{ev})) \Rightarrow e \in \mathit{Past}(C,S,t)$$

We label the first conjunct,

$$e \in S_t \Rightarrow e \in \mathit{Past}(C,S,t) \tag{2}$$

and we further evaluate and label the second conjunct:

$$(\exists\, ev : \mathit{Past}(C,S,t) \bullet e \in \mathit{Spawn}_t(C, ev, \sigma_{ev})) \Rightarrow e \in \mathit{Past}(C,S,t)$$
$$\Leftrightarrow \quad \{ \text{ Propositional logic } \}$$
$$\forall\, ev : \mathit{Past}(C,S,t) \bullet (e \in \mathit{Spawn}_t(C, ev, \sigma_{ev}) \Rightarrow e \in \mathit{Past}(C,S,t))$$
$$\Leftrightarrow \quad \{ \text{ Defn subset } \}$$
$$\forall\, ev : \mathit{Past}(C,S,t) \bullet \mathit{Spawn}_t(C, ev, \sigma_{ev}) \subseteq \mathit{Past}(C,S,t) \tag{3}$$

With the necessary consequences of our definitions established and labelled, we turn now to the proof of the theorem.

Let t, T : *Time* with $t < T$. By the definitions of S_t and Spawn_t, we have immediately that

$$S_t \subseteq S_T \tag{4}$$

and

$$\forall\, c : \mathit{Circuit};\ e : \mathit{Event};\ \sigma : \mathit{State} \bullet \mathit{Spawn}_t(c, e, \sigma) \subseteq \mathit{Spawn}_T(c, e, \sigma) \tag{5}$$

We consider an arbitrary event e_0 in $\mathit{Past}(C,S,t)$:

$$e_0 \in \mathit{Past}(C,S,t)$$
$$\Rightarrow \quad \{ \text{ Formula } (1') \}$$
$$e_0 \in S_t \vee$$
$$\exists\, e_1 : \mathit{Past}(C,S,t) \mid e_1.\mathit{time} < e_0.\mathit{time} \bullet e_0 \in \mathit{Spawn}_t(C, e_1, \sigma_{e_1})$$

$\Rightarrow$ { *Time* $\widehat{=}$ $\mathbb{N}$; any sequence of natural numbers strictly descending from a particular natural number must be finite }

$$\exists\, n : \mathbb{N};\ e_0, e_1, \ldots, e_n : \mathit{Past}(C,S,t) \bullet$$
$$(\forall\, i : \mathbb{N} \mid 0 \leq i < n \bullet$$
$$e_i \in \mathit{Spawn}_t(C, e_{i+1}, \sigma_{e_{i+1}}) \wedge e_{i+1}.\mathit{time} < e_i.\mathit{time}) \wedge$$
$$e_n \in S_t$$

This result says that for any event e_0 in $\mathit{Past}(C,S,t)$ there is in $\mathit{Past}(C,S,t)$ a finite chain of $n+1$ events, $e_0, e_1, \ldots, e_n$, whose event times are strictly decreasing and whose last element, e_n, is in S_t.

Now, for $i > 0$ and e_i, e_{i-1} in this chain,

$$e_i \in \mathit{Past}(C,S,T)$$

$$\Rightarrow \quad \{ \text{ Formula (3) } \}$$
$$Spawn_T(C, e_i, \sigma_{e_i}) \subseteq Past(C, S, T)$$
$$\Rightarrow \quad \{ \; e_{i-1} \in Spawn_t(C, e_i, \sigma_{e_i}); \text{ Formula (5); defn subset } \}$$
$$e_{i-1} \in Past(C, S, T)$$

Furthermore,

$$e_n \in S_t$$
$$\Rightarrow \quad \{ \text{ Formula (4) } \}$$
$$e_n \in S_T$$
$$\Rightarrow \quad \{ \text{ Formula (2) } \}$$
$$e_n \in Past(C, S, T)$$

Thus, we can conclude by induction that

$$\forall i : \mathbb{N} \mid 0 \leq i \leq n \bullet e_i \in Past(C, S, T)$$

and in particular that $e_0 \in Past(C, S, T)$.

Thus, under our assumption that $t < T$ we conclude that

$$e_0 \in Past(C, S, t) \Rightarrow e_0 \in Past(C, S, T)$$

whence we have

$$t < T \Rightarrow Past(C, S, t) \subseteq Past(C, S, T)$$

as required. □

Theorem 2

$$\forall C : Circuit; \; S : \mathbb{F}\, Event; \; t, T : Time \mid S \in ValidStimuli\ C \bullet$$
$$t < T \Rightarrow Past(C, S, t) = \{ev : Past(C, S, T) \mid ev.time \leq t\}$$

Proof:

This theorem is really a strengthening of Theorem 1 and therefore in its proof we will appeal to Theorem 1 both directly and indirectly. First we note that (assuming $t < T$)

$$e \in Past(C, S, t)$$
$$\Rightarrow \quad \{ \text{ Theorem 1 } \}$$
$$e \in Past(C, S, T)$$
$$\Rightarrow \quad \{ \text{ property of } Past(C, S, t); \wedge\text{-introduction } \}$$
$$e \in Past(C, S, T) \wedge e.time \leq t$$

$$\Rightarrow \quad \{ \text{ set comprehension } \}$$
$$e \in \{ev : Past(C, S, T) \mid ev.time \leq t\}$$

Thus, we have

$$Past(C, S, t) \subseteq \{ev : Past(C, S, T) \mid ev.time \leq t\}$$

It remains for us to show that

$$e \in \{ev : Past(C, S, T) \mid ev.time \leq t\} \Rightarrow e \in Past(C, S, t)$$

Let $P \mathrel{\widehat{=}} \{ev : Past(C, S, T) \mid ev.time \leq t\}$. Then as in the proof of Theorem 1, we consider an arbitrary event e_0 in P:

$$e_0 \in P$$

$$\Rightarrow \quad \{ \text{ Formula } (1'); \text{ defn } P \ \}$$
$$(e_0 \in S_T \wedge e_0.time \leq t \vee$$
$$\exists\, e_1 : Past(C, S, T) \mid e_1.time < e_0.time \leq t \bullet e_0 \in Spawn_T(C, e_1, \sigma_{e_1})$$

$$\Rightarrow \quad \{ \ t < T; \text{ set comprehension } \}$$
$$e_0 \in S_t \vee$$
$$\exists\, e_1 : P \mid e_1.time < e_0.time \leq t \bullet e_0 \in Spawn_t(C, e_1, \sigma_{e_1})$$

$\Rightarrow$ { $Time \mathrel{\widehat{=}} \mathbb{N}$; any sequence of natural numbers strictly descending from a particular natural number must be finite }

$$\exists\, n : \mathbb{N};\ e_0, e_1, \ldots, e_n : P \bullet$$
$$(\forall i : \mathbb{N} \mid 0 \leq i < n \bullet$$
$$e_i \in Spawn_t(C, e_{i+1}, \sigma_{e_{i+1}}) \wedge e_{i+1}.time < e_i.time \leq t) \wedge$$
$$e_n \in S_t$$

Now,

$$e_n \in S_t$$

$$\Rightarrow \quad \{ \text{ defn } Past(C, S, t) \ \}$$
$$e_n \in Past(C, S, t)$$

and an induction similar to that in the proof of Theorem 1 yields

$$e_0 \in Past(C, S, t)$$

Thus, under our assumption that $t < T$ we conclude that

$$e_0 \in P \Rightarrow e_0 \in Past(C, S, t)$$

whence we have

$$t < T \Rightarrow \{ev : Past(C, S, T) \mid ev.time \leq t\} \subseteq Past(C, S, t)$$

Since we have already established that

$$t < T \Rightarrow Past(C,S,t) \subseteq \{ev : Past(C,S,T) \mid ev.time \leq t\}$$

we have

$$t < T \Rightarrow Past(C,S,t) = \{ev : Past(C,S,T) \mid ev.time \leq t\}$$

as required. □

Theorem 3

$$\begin{array}{l} \forall\, C : Circuit;\ S : \mathbb{F}\ Event;\ t, T : Time \mid S \in ValidStimuli\ C\ \bullet \\ \quad Future(C,S,t) = \varnothing \Rightarrow \\ \qquad (T > t \Rightarrow Past(C,S,T) = Past(C,S,t)) \end{array}$$

Proof:

We will again use the abbreviations σ_{ev}, S_t, and $Spawn_t$ introduced in the proof of Theorem 1. In addition, we introduce the abbreviations:

$$\begin{array}{rcl} S^t & \widehat{=} & \{e : S \mid e.time > t\} \\ Spawn^t(c,e,\sigma) & \widehat{=} & \{e : Spawn(c,e,\sigma) \mid e.time > t\} \end{array}$$

We can immediately establish the following properties:

$$S = S_t \cup S^t \tag{6}$$

$$Spawn(c,e,\sigma) = Spawn_t(c,e,\sigma) \cup Spawn^t(c,e,\sigma) \tag{7}$$

Using our abbreviations, we can rewrite the definition of *Future* as:

$$\begin{array}{|l} Future : (Circuit \times \mathbb{F}\ Event \times Time) \to \mathbb{F}\ Event \\ \hline \forall\, C : Circuit;\ S : \mathbb{F}\ Event;\ t : Time;\ e : Event \mid S \in ValidStimuli\ C\ \bullet \\ \qquad e \in Future(C,S,t) \\ \quad \Leftrightarrow \\ \qquad e \in S^t \lor \\ \qquad \exists\, ev : Past(C,S,t) \bullet e \in Spawn^t(C,ev,\sigma_{ev}) \end{array}$$

Assume that $Future(C,S,t) = \varnothing$. By the definition of *Future* we have therefore:

$$\begin{array}{l} \forall\, e : Event \bullet e \notin S^t \land \\ \qquad \nexists\, ev : Past(C,S,t) \bullet e \in Spawn^t(C,ev,\sigma_{ev}) \end{array}$$

and we can break this up into the two properties:

$$\forall e : Event \bullet e \notin S^t \tag{8}$$
$$\forall e : Event \bullet \nexists\, ev : Past(C, S, t) \bullet e \in Spawn^t(C, ev, \sigma_{ev}) \tag{9}$$

Now,

$$\begin{array}{ll}
& e \in (Past(C,S,T) \setminus Past(C,S,t)) \\
\Rightarrow & \{ \text{ defn of set difference } \} \\
& e \in Past(C,S,T) \wedge e \notin Past(C,S,t) \\
\Rightarrow & \{ \text{ abbreviated defn of } Past \text{ from Theorem 1 } \} \\
& (e \in S_T \vee \exists\, ev : Past(C,S,T) \bullet e \in Spawn_T(C, ev, \sigma_{ev})) \wedge \\
& (e \notin S_t \wedge \nexists\, ev : Past(C,S,t) \bullet e \in Spawn_t(C, ev, \sigma_{ev})) \\
\Rightarrow & \{ \text{ Formula 6, Formula 7, Formula 8, Formula 9; sets } \} \\
& (e \in S_T \vee \exists\, ev : Past(C,S,T) \bullet e \in Spawn_T(C, ev, \sigma_{ev})) \wedge \\
& (e \notin S \wedge \nexists\, ev : Past(C,S,t) \bullet e \in Spawn(C, ev, \sigma_{ev})) \\
\Rightarrow & \{ \text{ Formula 6; sets; prop. logic } \} \\
& (\exists\, ev : Past(C,S,T) \bullet e \in Spawn_T(C, ev, \sigma_{ev})) \wedge \\
& (\nexists\, ev : Past(C,S,t) \bullet e \in Spawn(C, ev, \sigma_{ev})) \\
\Rightarrow & \{ \text{ Formula 7 } \} \\
& (\exists\, ev : Past(C,S,T) \bullet e \in Spawn_T(C, ev, \sigma_{ev})) \wedge \\
& (\nexists\, ev : Past(C,S,t) \bullet e \in Spawn_T(C, ev, \sigma_{ev})) \\
\Rightarrow & \{ \text{ sets; prop. logic } \} \\
& \exists\, ev : (Past(C,S,T) \setminus Past(C,S,t)) \bullet e \in Spawn_T(C, ev, \sigma_{ev}) \\
\Rightarrow & \{ \text{ property of } Spawn \text{ } \} \\
& \exists\, ev : (Past(C,S,T) \setminus Past(C,S,t)) \bullet ev.time < e.time
\end{array}$$

Thus, we have shown that assuming $Future(C, S, t) = \varnothing$,

$$\begin{array}{ll}
& e \in (Past(C,S,T) \setminus Past(C,S,t)) \\
\Rightarrow & \\
& \exists\, ev : (Past(C,S,T) \setminus Past(C,S,t)) \bullet ev.time < e.time
\end{array}$$

But this implies the existence of an infinite chain of events with strictly decreasing times which is impossible since $Time \mathrel{\widehat{=}} \mathbb{N}$. Thus, under our assumption we must have

$$Past(C,S,T) \setminus Past(C,S,t) = \varnothing$$

whence

$$Past(C,S,T) \subseteq Past(C,S,t)$$

Under the added assumption that $T > t$, we have by Theorem 1

$$Past(C, S, t) \subseteq Past(C, S, T)$$

yielding by mutual inclusion

$$Future(C, S, t) = \varnothing \Rightarrow (T > t \Rightarrow Past(C, S, T) = Past(C, S, t))$$

as required. □

Theorem 4

$$\begin{array}{l} \forall C : Circuit;\ S : \mathbb{F}\ Event;\ t, T : Time \mid S \in ValidStimuli\ C \bullet \\ \quad Future(C, S, t) = \varnothing \Rightarrow \\ \qquad (T > t \Rightarrow Future(C, S, T) = Future(C, S, t) = \varnothing) \end{array}$$

Proof:

Assume that $Future(C, S, t) = \varnothing$ and $T > t$. Thus, Formula 8 and Formula 9 from Theorem 3 hold again here.

Now,

$$\begin{array}{ll} & e \in Future(C, S, T) \\ \Rightarrow & \{\ \text{abbreviated defn of } Future \text{ from Theorem 3}\ \} \\ & e \in S^T \lor \exists\, ev : Past(C, S, T) \bullet e \in Spawn^T(C, ev, \sigma_{ev}) \\ \Rightarrow & \{\ \text{Formula 8; fact that } S^T \subseteq S^t\text{; prop. logic}\ \} \\ & \exists\, ev : Past(C, S, T) \bullet e \in Spawn^T(C, ev, \sigma_{ev}) \\ \Rightarrow & \{\ \text{Formula 9; sets}\ \} \\ & \exists\, ev : (Past(C, S, T) \setminus Past(C, S, t)) \bullet e \in Spawn^T(C, ev, \sigma_{ev}) \\ \Rightarrow & \{\ \text{Theorem 3}\ \} \\ & \exists\, ev : \varnothing \bullet e \in Spawn^T(C, ev, \sigma_{ev}) \\ \Rightarrow & \{\ \varnothing \text{ contains no elements}\ \} \\ & false \end{array}$$

Thus,

$$\nexists\, e : Event \bullet e \in Future(C, S, T)$$

and so

$$Future(C, S, T) = \varnothing = Future(C, S, t)$$

as required. □

Theorem 5

$$\forall C : \mathit{Circuit};\ S : \mathbb{F}\ \mathit{Event};\ t, T : \mathit{Time} \mid S \in \mathit{ValidStimuli}\ C \bullet$$
$$(T = \min\{ev : \mathit{Future}(C,S,t) \bullet ev.\mathit{time}\} \wedge$$
$$e \in \mathit{Past}(C,S,T) \wedge e.\mathit{time} > t) \Rightarrow e.\mathit{time} = T$$

Proof:

We will use here the abbreviations defined in the proofs of Theorem 1 and Theorem 3 and the associated definitions of *Past* and *Future*.

Assume $T = \min\{ev : \mathit{Future}(C,S,t) \bullet ev.\mathit{time}\}$. Then,

$$e_0 \in (\mathit{Past}(C,S,T) \wedge e_0.\mathit{time} > t$$

$\Rightarrow$ { abbreviated defn of *Past* from Theorem 1 }

$$(e_0 \in S_T \wedge e_0.\mathit{time} > t) \vee$$
$$(\exists\, e_1 : \mathit{Past}(C,S,T) \bullet e_0 \in \mathit{Spawn}_T(C, e_1, \sigma_{e_1}) \wedge e_0.\mathit{time} > t)$$

$\Rightarrow$ { defns of S_t, S^t, Spawn_t, Spawn^t; arithmetic }

$$(e_0 \in S^t \wedge e_0.\mathit{time} \leq T) \vee$$
$$(\exists\, e_1 : \mathit{Past}(C,S,T) \bullet e_0 \in \mathit{Spawn}^t(C, e_1, \sigma_{e_1}) \wedge e_0.\mathit{time} \leq T)$$

We now proceed by case exhaustion on the two disjuncts.

Case 1:

$$e_0 \in S^t \wedge e_0.\mathit{time} \leq T$$

$\Rightarrow$ { defn of *Future* }

$$e_0 \in \mathit{Future}(C,S,t) \wedge e_0.\mathit{time} \leq T$$

$\Rightarrow$ { assumption about T; property of min }

$$e_0.\mathit{time} = T$$

Case 2:

$$\exists\, e_1 : \mathit{Past}(C,S,T) \bullet e_0 \in \mathit{Spawn}^t(C, e_1, \sigma_{e_1}) \wedge e_0.\mathit{time} \leq T$$

$\Rightarrow$ { By defn of *Spawn* we know, $e_1.\mathit{time} < e_0.\mathit{time}$ and hence $e_1.\mathit{time} < T$ so Case 1 cannot apply to e_1 or beyond; a bounded interval on $\mathbb{N}$ is finite }

$$\exists\, n : \mathbb{N} \mid n > 0 \bullet$$
$$\exists\, e_1, e_2, \ldots, e_n : \mathit{Past}(C,S,T) \bullet$$
$$e_0 \in \mathit{Spawn}^t(C, e_1, \sigma_{e_1}) \wedge e_0.\mathit{time} \leq T \wedge$$
$$(\forall\, i : 2 \ldots n \bullet e_{i-1} \in \mathit{Spawn}_t(C, e_i, \sigma_{e_i}) \wedge e_{i-1}.\mathit{time} < T) \wedge$$
$$e_n.\mathit{time} \leq t$$

$\Rightarrow$ { Theorem 2 }

$$\exists\, n : \mathbb{N} \mid n > 0 \bullet$$
$$\exists\, e_1, e_2, \ldots, e_n : \mathit{Past}(C,S,T) \bullet$$
$$e_0 \in \mathit{Spawn}^t(C, e_1, \sigma_{e_1}) \wedge e_0.\mathit{time} \leq T \wedge$$
$$(\forall\, i : 2 \ldots n \bullet e_{i-1} \in \mathit{Spawn}^t(C, e_i, \sigma_{e_i}) \wedge e_{i-1}.\mathit{time} < T) \wedge$$

$$e_n \in Past(C, S, t) \tag{10}$$

Now,

$$n \neq 1$$

$\Rightarrow$ { Formula (10) above }

$$\exists\, e_{n-1} : Past(C, S, T);\ e_n : Past(C, S, t) \bullet e_{n-1} \in Spawn^t(C, e_n, \sigma_{e_n}) \land e_{n-1}.time < T$$

$\Rightarrow$ { defn of *Future* }

$$\exists\, e_{n-1} : Past(C, S, T);\ e_n : Past(C, S, t) \bullet e_{n-1} \in Future(C, S, t) \land e_{n-1}.time < T$$

$\Rightarrow$ { defn of T; no element of a set in $\mathbb{P}\,\mathbb{N}$ can be strictly less than that set's minimum }

false

Thus by contradiction we have $n = 1$ in Formula (10) above, whence:

$$\exists\, e_1 : Past(C, S, t) \bullet e_0 \in Spawn^t(C, e_1, \sigma_{e_1}) \land e_0.time \leq T$$

$\Rightarrow$ { defn of *Future* }

$$e_0 \in Future(C, S, t) \land e_0.time \leq T$$

$\Rightarrow$ { assumption about T; property of min }

$$e_0.time = T$$

We have exhausted the cases, so we have

$$(T = \min\{ev : Future(C, S, t) \bullet ev.time\} \land e \in Past(C, S, T) \land e.time > t) \Rightarrow e.time = T$$

as required. □

Corollary 6

$$\forall\, C : Circuit;\ S : \mathbb{F}\, Event;\ t, T : Time \mid S \in ValidStimuli\ C \bullet (T = \min\{ev : Future(C, S, t) \bullet ev.time\} \land e \in Past(C, S, T) \land e.time \neq T) \Rightarrow e.time \leq t$$

Simple predicate calculus yields this corollary to Theorem 5.

Corollary 7

$$\forall\, C : Circuit;\ S : \mathbb{F}\, Event;\ t, T : Time \mid S \in ValidStimuli\ C \bullet (T = \min\{ev : Future(C, S, t) \bullet ev.time\} \land e \in (Past(C, S, T) \setminus Past(C, S, t))) \Rightarrow e.time = T$$

Simple predicate calculus and set theory together with Theorem 2 yield this corollary to Theorem 5.

Theorem 8

$$\forall C : Circuit;\ S : \mathbb{F}\ Event;\ t, T : Time \mid S \in ValidStimuli\ C \bullet$$
$$T = \min\{ev : Future(C, S, t) \bullet ev.time\} \Rightarrow$$
$$\{ev : Future(C, S, t) \mid ev.time = T\}$$
$$= \{ev : Past(C, S, T) \mid ev.time = T\}$$

Proof:

We will establish the desired equality by mutual inclusion under the assumption that $T = \min\{ev : Future(C, S, t) \bullet ev.time\}$.

$$e \in \{ev : Future(C, S, t) \mid ev.time = T\}$$

$\Rightarrow$ { Sets; defn T; property of *Future* }

$$e \in Future(C, S, t) \wedge$$
$$e.time = T \wedge T > t$$

$\Rightarrow$ { defn of *Future* }

$$(e \in S \vee$$
$$\exists\, ev : Past(C, S, t) \bullet e \in Spawn(C, ev, Snapshot\ Past(C, S, ev.time))) \wedge$$
$$e.time = T \wedge T > t$$

$\Rightarrow$ { Theorem 1 }

$$(e \in S \vee$$
$$\exists\, ev : Past(C, S, T) \bullet e \in Spawn(C, ev, Snapshot\ Past(C, S, ev.time))) \wedge$$
$$e.time = T \wedge T > t$$

$\Rightarrow$ { defn *Past* }

$$e \in Past(C, S, T) \wedge$$
$$e.time = T \wedge T > t$$

$\Rightarrow$ { Sets }

$$e \in \{ev : Past(C, S, T) \mid ev.time = T\}$$

Thus, we have established the forward inclusion. Now,

$$e \in \{ev : Past(C, S, T) \mid ev.time = T\}$$

$\Rightarrow$ { Sets; defn *Past* }

$$e.time = T \wedge$$
$$(e \in S \vee$$
$$\exists\, ev : Past(C, S, T) \bullet e \in Spawn(C, ev, Snapshot\ Past(C, S, ev.time)))$$

$\Rightarrow$ { defn *Spawn* }

$$e.time = T \wedge$$
$$(e \in S \vee$$

$$\exists\, ev : Past(C,S,T) \mid ev.time < T \bullet$$
$$\quad e \in Spawn(C, ev, Snapshot\ Past(C,S,ev.time)))$$

$\Rightarrow$ { Corollary 6; Theorem 2 }

$$e.time = T \wedge$$
$$(e \in S \vee$$
$$\exists\, ev : Past(C,S,t) \mid ev.time < T \bullet$$
$$\quad e \in Spawn(C, ev, Snapshot\ Past(C,S,ev.time)))$$

$\Rightarrow$ { defn *Future* (recall that $T > t$) }

$$e.time = T \wedge$$
$$e \in Future(C,S,t)$$

$\Rightarrow$ { Sets }

$$e \in \{ev : Future(C,S,t) \mid ev.time = T\}$$

This establishes the reverse inclusion, so we have

$$\{ev : Future(C,S,t) \mid ev.time = T\} = \{ev : Past(C,S,T) \mid ev.time = T\}$$

as required. □

Theorem 9

$$T = \min\{ev : F \bullet ev.time\} \wedge t < T \wedge$$
$$P = Past(C,S,t) \wedge F = Future(C,S,t)$$
$$\Rightarrow$$
$$(P = Past(C,S,T) \wedge F = Future(C,S,t))$$
$$\quad [P \leftarrow (P \cup \{ev : F \mid ev.time = T\})]$$

Note that because elsewhere we use '\' in its Z sense of "set difference", we use '←' above to denote substitution. (Morgan uses '\' for substitution.) Note also that the first two conjuncts above come from the context of the refinement step for which this theorem is a justification. Appropriate universal quantifications are assumed.

Proof:

Let *LHS* denote the proposition to the left of the "⇒" in the theorem. Then performing the substitution, we see that we must show:

$$LHS$$
$$\Rightarrow$$
$$(P \cup \{ev : F \mid ev.time = T\}) = Past(C,S,T) \wedge$$
$$F = Future(C,S,t)$$

Simple $\wedge$-elimination yields $F = Future(C,S,t)$ so it remains to show:

$$LHS \Rightarrow (P \cup \{ev : F \mid ev.time = T\}) = Past(C,S,T)$$

We will proceed by showing mutual inclusion of the two sets under the assumption of *LHS*. First the forward inclusion:

$$e \in (P \cup \{ev : F \mid ev.time = T\})$$

$\Rightarrow$ { defn set union }

$$e \in P \vee e \in \{ev : F \mid ev.time = T\}$$

Case F1:

$$e \in P$$

$\Rightarrow$ { *LHS* }

$$e \in Past(C, S, t)$$

$\Rightarrow$ { Theorem 1; $t < T$ }

$$e \in Past(C, S, T)$$

Case F2:

$$e \in \{ev : F \mid ev.time = T\}$$

$\Rightarrow$ { *LHS* }

$$e \in Future(C, S, t) \wedge e.time = T$$

$\Rightarrow$ { abbreviated defn of *Future* from Theorem 3 }

$$(e \in S^t \vee \\ \exists\, ev : Past(C, S, t) \bullet e \in Spawn^t(C, ev, \sigma_{ev})) \wedge \\ e.time = T$$

$\Rightarrow$ { Theorem 1; $t < T$ }

$$(e \in S^t \vee \\ \exists\, ev : Past(C, S, T) \bullet e \in Spawn^t(C, ev, \sigma_{ev})) \wedge \\ e.time = T$$

$\Rightarrow$ { prop. logic }

$$(e \in S^t \wedge e.time = T) \vee \\ (\exists\, ev : Past(C, S, T) \bullet e \in Spawn^t(C, ev, \sigma_{ev}) \wedge e.time = T)$$

$\Rightarrow$ { defns S_t,S^t,$Spawn_t$,$Spawn^t$; $t < T$ }

$$e \in S_T \vee \\ \exists\, ev : Past(C, S, T) \bullet e \in Spawn_T(C, ev, \sigma_{ev})$$

$\Rightarrow$ { defn *Past* }

$$e \in Past(C, S, T)$$

We have exhausted the two cases of the forward inclusion and have therefore established

$$(P \cup \{ev : F \mid ev.time = T\}) \subseteq Past(C, S, T)$$

We now turn to the reverse inclusion:

$$e \in Past(C, S, T)$$

$\Rightarrow$ { $t < T$; Theorem 1; property of subsets }

$$e \in Past(C, S, t) \vee e \in (Past(C, S, T) \setminus Past(C, S, t))$$

Case R1:

$$\begin{array}{ll} & e \in Past(C,S,t) \\ \Rightarrow & \{ \; LHS \; \} \\ & e \in P \\ \Rightarrow & \{ \text{ set union } \} \\ & e \in (P \cup \{ev : F \mid ev.time = T\}) \end{array}$$

Case R2:

$$\begin{array}{ll} & e \in (Past(C,S,T) \setminus Past(C,S,t)) \\ \Rightarrow & \{ \text{ Theorem 2; set comprehension } \} \\ & e \in \{ev : Past(C,S,T) \mid ev.time > t\} \\ \Rightarrow & \{ \text{ abbreviated defn of } Past \text{ from Theorem 1 } \} \\ & (e \in S_T \wedge e.time > t) \vee \\ & (\exists\, ev : Past(C,S,T) \bullet e \in Spawn_T(C,ev,\sigma_{ev}) \wedge e.time > t) \\ \Rightarrow & \{ \text{ defns } S_t, S^t, Spawn_t, Spawn^t;\ t < T \ \} \\ & (e \in S^t \wedge e.time \leq T) \vee \\ & (\exists\, ev : Past(C,S,T) \bullet e \in Spawn^t(C,ev,\sigma_{ev}) \wedge e.time \leq T) \\ \Rightarrow & \{ \text{ defn } Spawn \ \} \\ & (e \in S^t \wedge e.time \leq T) \vee \\ & (\exists\, ev : Past(C,S,T) \mid ev.time < e.time \bullet \\ & \qquad e \in Spawn^t(C,ev,\sigma_{ev}) \wedge e.time \leq T) \\ \Rightarrow & \{ \text{ Corollary 6; Theorem 2 } \} \\ & (e \in S^t \wedge e.time \leq T) \vee \\ & (\exists\, ev : Past(C,S,t) \bullet e \in Spawn^t(C,ev,\sigma_{ev}) \wedge e.time \leq T) \\ \Rightarrow & \{ \text{ abbreviated defn of } Future \text{ from Theorem 3 } \} \\ & e \in Future(C,S,t) \wedge e.time \leq T \\ \Rightarrow & \{ \; LHS \; \} \\ & e \in F \wedge e.time \leq \min\{ev : F \mid ev.time\} \\ \Rightarrow & \{ \text{ property of min } \} \\ & e \in F \wedge e.time = \min\{ev : F \mid ev.time\} \\ \Rightarrow & \{ \; LHS \; \} \\ & e \in F \wedge e.time = T \\ \Rightarrow & \{ \text{ set comprehension } \} \\ & e \in \{ev : F \mid ev.time = T\} \\ \Rightarrow & \{ \text{ set union } \} \\ & e \in (P \cup \{ev : F \mid ev.time = T\}) \end{array}$$

We have now also exhausted the two cases of the reverse inclusion and have therefore established

$$Past(C, S, T) \subseteq (P \cup \{ev : F \mid ev.time = T\})$$

Thus, by mutual inclusion we have

$$Past(C, S, T) = (P \cup \{ev : F \mid ev.time = T\})$$

as required. □

Theorem 10

$$\begin{array}{l} \quad T = \min\{ev : F \bullet ev.time\} \land t < T \land \\ \quad P = Past(C, S, T) \land F = Future(C, S, t) \\ \Rightarrow \\ \quad (P = Past(C, S, T) \land F = Future(C, S, T)) \\ \qquad [F \leftarrow \\ \qquad (F \setminus \{ev : F \mid ev.time = T\} \cup \bigcup_{f \in \{ev:F \mid ev.time=T\}} Spawn(C, f, Snapshot\ P))] \end{array}$$

As in Theorem 9, we use '$\leftarrow$' for substitution in order to avoid confusion with the Z "set difference" operator. The first two conjuncts again come from the context of the refinement step for which this theorem is a justification and appropriate universal quantifications are assumed.

Proof:

Let *LHS* denote the proposition to the left of the "$\Rightarrow$" in the theorem. Then performing the substitution, we see that we must show:

$$\begin{array}{l} \quad LHS \\ \Rightarrow \\ \quad P = Past(C, S, T) \land \\ \quad (F \setminus \{ev : F \mid ev.time = T\} \cup \bigcup_{f \in \{ev:F \mid ev.time=T\}} Spawn(C, f, Snapshot\ P)) \\ \qquad = Future(C, S, T) \end{array}$$

Simple $\land$-elimination yields $P = Past(C, S, T)$ so it remains to show:

$$\begin{array}{l} \quad LHS \\ \Rightarrow \\ \quad (F \setminus \{ev : F \mid ev.time = T\} \cup \bigcup_{f \in \{ev:F \mid ev.time=T\}} Spawn(C, f, Snapshot\ P)) \\ \qquad = Future(C, S, T) \end{array}$$

We will proceed by showing mutual inclusion of the two sets under the assumption of *LHS*. First the forward inclusion:

$$e \in (F \setminus \{ev : F \mid ev.time = T\} \cup \bigcup_{f \in \{ev:F \mid ev.time=T\}} Spawn(C, f, Snapshot\ P))$$

$\Rightarrow$ { set difference; set union; defn T; property of min }
$(e \in F \wedge e.time > T) \vee$
$(\exists\, ev : F \mid ev.time = T \bullet e \in Spawn(C, ev, Snapshot\ P))$

Case F1:

$(e \in F \wedge e.time > T)$

$\Rightarrow$ { defn *Future*; $T > t$ }
$e.time > T \wedge$
$(e \in S \vee$
$\exists\, ev : Past(C, S, t) \bullet$
$e \in Spawn(C, ev, Snapshot\ Past(C, S, ev.time)))$

$\Rightarrow$ { $T > t$; Theorem 1 }
$e.time > T \wedge$
$(e \in S \vee$
$\exists\, ev : Past(C, S, T) \bullet$
$e \in Spawn(C, ev, Snapshot\ Past(C, S, ev.time)))$

$\Rightarrow$ { defn *Future* }
$e \in Future(C, S, T)$

Case F2:

$\exists\, ev : F \mid ev.time = T \bullet e \in Spawn(C, ev, Snapshot\ P)$

$\Rightarrow$ { *LHS* }
$\exists\, ev : Future(C, S, t) \mid ev.time = T \bullet$
$e \in Spawn(C, ev, Snapshot\ Past(C, S, T))$

$\Rightarrow$ { substitution; property of *Spawn* }
$(\exists\, ev : Future(C, S, t) \mid ev.time = T \bullet$
$e \in Spawn(C, ev, Snapshot\ Past(C, S, ev.time))) \wedge$
$e.time > T$

$\Rightarrow$ { Theorem 8; propositional logic }
$(\exists\, ev : Past(C, S, T) \bullet$
$e \in Spawn(C, ev, Snapshot\ Past(C, S, ev.time))) \wedge$
$e.time > T$

$\Rightarrow$ { defn *Future* }
$e \in Future(C, S, T)$

We have exhausted the two cases of the forward inclusion and have therefore established

$$(F \setminus \{ev : F \mid ev.time = T\} \cup \bigcup_{f \in \{ev : F \mid ev.time = T\}} Spawn(C, f, Snapshot\ P)) \subseteq Future(C, S, T)$$

We now turn to the reverse inclusion:

$$e \in \mathit{Future}(C, S, T)$$

$\Rightarrow$ { defn *Future* }

$$\begin{array}{l} e.time > T \wedge \\ (e \in S \vee \\ \exists\, ev : Past(C,S,T) \bullet e \in Spawn(C, ev, Snapshot\ Past(C,S,ev.time))) \end{array}$$

$\Rightarrow$ { excluded middle; unit of $\wedge$ }

$$\begin{array}{l} (e \in Future(C,S,t) \vee e \notin Future(C,S,t)) \wedge \\ e.time > T \wedge \\ (e \in S \vee \\ \exists\, ev : Past(C,S,T) \bullet e \in Spawn(C, ev, Snapshot\ Past(C,S,ev.time))) \end{array}$$

$\Rightarrow$ { propositional logic }

$$\begin{array}{l} (e \in Future(C,S,t) \wedge e.time > T \wedge \\ (e \in S \vee \\ \exists\, ev : Past(C,S,T) \bullet e \in Spawn(C, ev, Snapshot\ Past(C,S,ev.time)))) \\ \vee \\ (e \notin Future(C,S,t) \wedge e.time > T \wedge \\ (e \in S \vee \\ \exists\, ev : Past(C,S,T) \bullet e \in Spawn(C, ev, Snapshot\ Past(C,S,ev.time)))) \end{array}$$

Case R1:

$$\begin{array}{l} e \in Future(C,S,t) \wedge e.time > T \wedge \\ (e \in S \vee \\ \exists\, ev : Past(C,S,T) \bullet \\ \qquad e \in Spawn(C, ev, Snapshot\ Past(C,S,ev.time))) \end{array}$$

$\Rightarrow$ { $\wedge$-elimination }

$$e \in Future(C,S,t) \wedge e.time > T$$

$\Rightarrow$ { *LHS* }

$$e \in F \wedge e.time > T$$

$\Rightarrow$ { defn T; property of min; set difference }

$$e \in (F \setminus \{ev : F \mid ev.time = T\})$$

$\Rightarrow$ { set union }

$$e \in (F \setminus \{ev : F \mid ev.time = T\} \cup \bigcup_{f \in \{ev:F \mid ev.time = T\}} Spawn(C, f, Snapshot\ P))$$

Case R2:

$$\begin{array}{l} e \notin Future(C,S,t) \wedge e.time > T \wedge \\ (e \in S \vee \\ \exists\, ev : Past(C,S,T) \bullet \\ \qquad e \in Spawn(C, ev, Snapshot\ Past(C,S,ev.time))) \end{array}$$

Case R2.1:

$$e \notin Future(C,S,t) \wedge e.time > T \wedge e \in S$$

$\Rightarrow$ { abbreviated defn of *Future* from Theorem 3 }

$$e.time > T \wedge e \in S \wedge (e \notin S^t \wedge \nexists\, ev : Past(C,S,t) \bullet e \in Spawn^t(C, ev, Snapshot\ Past(C,S,ev.time)))$$

$\Rightarrow$ { set comprehension; defn S^t }

$$e \in \{ev : S \mid e.time > T\} \wedge e \notin \{ev : S \mid e.time > t\}$$

$\Rightarrow$ { $t < T$; property of subset }

false

$\Rightarrow$ { false antecedent }

$$e \in (F \setminus \{ev : F \mid ev.time = T\} \cup \bigcup_{f \in \{ev:F \mid ev.time = T\}} Spawn(C, f, Snapshot\ P))$$

Case R2.2:

$$e \notin Future(C,S,t) \wedge e.time > T \wedge \exists\, ev : Past(C,S,T) \bullet e \in Spawn(C, ev, Snapshot\ Past(C,S,ev.time))$$

$\Rightarrow$ { defn *Future* }

$$(e.time \leq t \vee (e \notin S \wedge \nexists\, ev : Past(C,S,t) \bullet e \in Spawn(C, ev, Snapshot\ Past(C,S,ev.time)))) \wedge e.time > T \wedge \exists\, ev : Past(C,S,T) \bullet e \in Spawn(C, ev, Snapshot\ Past(C,S,ev.time))$$

$\Rightarrow$ { $t < T$; propositional logic }

$$e.time > T \wedge e \notin S \wedge \exists\, ev : Past(C,S,T) \bullet e \in Spawn(C, ev, Snapshot\ Past(C,S,ev.time)) \wedge \nexists\, ev : Past(C,S,t) \bullet e \in Spawn(C, ev, Snapshot\ Past(C,S,ev.time))$$

$\Rightarrow$ { propositional logic; set difference }

$$\exists\, ev : (Past(C,S,T) \setminus Past(C,S,t)) \bullet e \in Spawn(C, ev, Snapshot\ Past(C,S,ev.time))$$

$\Rightarrow$ { Corollary 7 }

$$\exists\, ev : Past(C,S,T) \mid ev.time = T \bullet e \in Spawn(C, ev, Snapshot\ Past(C,S,ev.time))$$

$\Rightarrow$ { Theorem 8 }

$$\exists\, ev : Future(C,S,t) \mid ev.time = T \bullet e \in Spawn(C, ev, Snapshot\ Past(C,S,ev.time))$$

$$\Rightarrow \quad \{ \; LHS; \text{set comprehension; set union} \; \}$$
$$e \in \bigcup_{f \in \{ev:F \mid ev.time = T\}} Spawn(C, f, Snapshot\ Past(C, S, f.time))$$
$$\Rightarrow \quad \{ \; \text{substitution} \; \}$$
$$e \in \bigcup_{f \in \{ev:F \mid ev.time = T\}} Spawn(C, f, Snapshot\ Past(C, S, T))$$
$$\Rightarrow \quad \{ \; LHS \; \}$$
$$e \in \bigcup_{f \in \{ev:F \mid ev.time = T\}} Spawn(C, f, Snapshot\ P)$$
$$\Rightarrow \quad \{ \; \text{set union} \; \}$$
$$e \in (F \setminus \{ev : F \mid ev.time = T\} \cup \bigcup_{f \in \{ev:F \mid ev.time = T\}} Spawn(C, f, Snapshot\ P))$$

We have now exhausted all cases of the reverse inclusion and have therefore established

$$Future(C, S, T) \subseteq (F \setminus \{ev : F \mid ev.time = T\} \cup \bigcup_{f \in \{ev:F \mid ev.time = T\}} Spawn(C, f, Snapshot\ P))$$

Thus, by mutual inclusion we have

$$(F \setminus \{ev : F \mid ev.time = T\} \cup \bigcup_{f \in \{ev:F \mid ev.time = T\}} Spawn(C, f, Snapshot\ P)) = Future(C, S, T)$$

as required. □

A Theory of State-based Parallel Programming : Part 1

Xu Qiwen

He Jifeng

Oxford University Computing Laboratory
Programming Research Group
8-11 Keble Road
Oxford OX1 3QD
England
U.K.

January 1991

Abstract

This paper presents the first part of a theory for developing totally correct parallel programs. The emphasis of both specification and program is on the states, rather than actions, of the system. We stress the constructive approach in the development, by means of refinement and decomposition. A compositional proof system is investigated to support decomposition. It is shown to be sound in a computational model. Two examples are included to illustrate the compositionality of the proof system and the use of the methods in constructing an implementation.

1 Introduction

This paper is the first of two companion papers, together they present a theory for developing totally correct parallel programs, where the emphasis of both specification and program is on the states, rather than actions, of the system. It consists of the following three elements.

- A computational model, which provides a semantics to each parallel program and furthermore a formal definition of implementation.
- A specification methodology, which supports constructive design, by means of refinement and decomposition. In order to be able to use decomposition, compositional proof systems are needed.
- A programming language, in this case it is the Owicki-Gries language which is an extension of Dijkstra's Guarded Command. We show programs in this language are subject to a rich and elegant set of laws, just like the sequential programs [Hoare et al 87]. These laws can be used to argue that one program is better than another in the same style as in the traditional algebraic reasoning.

One main feature of our approach is the specification oriented semantics [OH86], that is, we regard that the difference of programs and specifications is not in the kind of semantic properties they define, but in the information they give towards implementation. Both of them describe the relevant properties of the correct implementation. A program is just such a detailed description that it can be immediately executed on a computer. Therefore both programs and specifications are mapped to the same semantic space in the computational model, in which an implementation relation is defined as a partial order. Proof systems bring programs and specifications together syntactically.

1.1 Compositionality and specification

A sequential program is usually described by a relationship between the values of variables before and after the execution. This serves as the starting point of some of the most successful formal methods of program development, although the exact techniques expressing this input-output relation may vary. For example, predicates are used in predicative programming [He84] and Z, pairs of predicates are used in VDM and more recent refinement calculus [Bk88, MRG88]. However, it is obvious that this approach is too simple when subprograms are allowed to run concurrently and access common variables, because we are simply no longer able to derive the behaviors of the whole program from the descriptions of its components, if they are only specified by the input-output relation in the usual way.

This is less a problem in a verification oriented methodology, because we have got all the program code, hence everything we need to know about the system. A number of proof systems, for instance, [OG76, La80, CC89] have existed for some time. Nevertheless, for the following two reasons in a practical methodology we can not wait until a full implementation is constructed and then attempt to verify it. First, the full implementation usually is very complicated and therefore will be very difficult to verify. Second and much more serious reason is that if the verification is not conducted until all the implementation has been completed, an early design error will cause all the rest of the work to be discarded. Therefore in a constructive methodology, a specification is moved gradually, step by step, to its final implementation. We hope each step can be easily checked as soon as it is carried out and the correctness of these steps together guarantees the correctness of whole system, so that when one step does go wrong, we only need to return to the place before this step and start from that, not the very beginning, again. In summary, this is advocated as the *Principle of Reasoning about Specifications* (as against of reasoning about programs) by Hoare, and as the *Principle of Compositionality* by de Roever and Zwiers. It is stated in [Zw89] as,

> The specification of a program should be verified on the basis of specifications of its constituent components, without knowledge of the interior construction of those components.

This idea of hierarchical development is of course not new, but devising a way to specify parallel programs with shared variables supporting this constructive approach has been a challenge. Jones in [Jo81] proposed to describe a parallel program by a quadruple of predicates.

$$(pre,\ rely,\ guar,\ post)$$

where *pre* is the pre-condition–which describes those states in which it is appropriate to invoke the operation; *post* is the post-condition –which describes the effect of the operation; *rely* is the rely-condition –which describes the extent of the interference can be tolerated; *guar* is the guarantee-condition–which describes the extent of the interference it may cause.

Jones' method falls into the category known as *Assumptions-Commitments* or as *Rely-Guarantee*. *pre* and *rely* constitute the assumption part which is about how the program will be used, while *guar* and *post* are about the commitments that the program should make.

A compositional proof system for partial correctness was later studied by Stirling [St88]. However, in general Jones' methodology has received very little attention, and only recently efforts have be taken to apply it in practice [WD88] and to develop proof systems for total correctness [St90].

Stølen [St90] is the first one in this approach to take a deadlock property into specifications, by augmenting Jones' quadruple with another predicate *Wait* which describes the set of states in which the program is allowed to be blocked. We adopt his approach here, but with some minor modification to suit our interpretation. The augmented predicate is renamed as *run*. If the program is blocked, the environment should eventually establish it on the states. A deadlock-free program is one which is able to release itself when blocked, namely one which will not be blocked forever. A terminating program is one which is deadlock-free and will not loop forever. In summary, a specification of a parallel program is now a tuple of these five predicates.

$$(pre,\ rely,\ run,\ guar,\ post)$$

Assume v is the vector of state variables $(v_1, ..., v_n)$, and v' is $(v'_1, ..., v'_n)$, we can be more precise about the predicates in a specification. They should be $pre(v)$, $rely(v,\ v')$, $run(v)$, $guar(v,\ v')$, $post(v,\ v')$, if fully spelled out.

pre, *rely* and *run* are the *Assumptions*-part of specification. It says

- the program will only be invoked in a state which satisfies *pre*.
- any sequence of consecutive environment actions satisfies *rely*, in the sense that the value of $rely(v,\ v')$ is true if v has the values of the variables in the state before this sequence of environment actions and v' has the values of the variables in the state after it.
- the environment will eventually establish *run* if the program is blocked.

guar and *post* belong to the *Commitments*-part of specification. The first commitment from the program is,

- any sequence of consecutive program actions satisfies *guar* in a similar sense as the rely-condition.
- there are only finite number of steps from the program.
- if the computation has stopped, the program should have terminated (rather than being blocked) and the whole computation should satisfy *post*, in the sense that the value of $post(v, v')$ is true if v has the values of the variables in the state before the computation and v' has the values of the variables in the final state.

From this interpretation, *rely* and *guar* obviously should be reflexive and transitive. With this restriction, the above requirement about *rely* and *guar* can be simplified as

- any action from the environment (program) satisfies *rely* (*guar*).

Finally, we observe that Jones' quadruple can be considered as a special case of ours with *run* = *true*.

1.2 Organization of the paper

In section 2, we discuss the computational model in which a computation is represented as a sequence of alternating states and actions. The semantics of a specification or a program is given as a set of these sequences. The implementation relation is simply defined as set inclusion. We show that Jones' proof obligation of refinement between two specifications is sound in our model, but also stronger than needed. A weak proof obligation is then obtained by adding a dynamic invariant to the original one.

In section 3, a transition system from which an operational semantics is derived for an Owicki-Gries programming language, is given in a structured way as in [Pl81].

A proof system for total correctness, which is independent of program structure and can therefore serve as the basis of decomposition, is presented in section 4. Because of the formal model, we are able to state the precise meaning of the rules and furthermore prove them correct. Examples are given to illustrate the development methods.

We prove the soundness of the proof system in section 5.

The algebraic side will be covered by another paper which we are preparing at the moment.

2 Semantic formalism

2.1 Preliminaries

There are two basic concepts about a system, states and actions. State is used to record the relevant information of the system at certain position and in particular which actions are ready to be taken next, while action is responsible for changing from one state to another. A system is run in an environment, for the purposes of this paper we assume that an environment shares the same state space with the system but has different action names. Actually we will use e for the environment action and c for the system action.

An execution of a system in an environment is modeled by a behavior, which is a sequence $s_0\delta_1 s_1, \ldots\delta_n s_n, \ldots$, where each s_i is a state and each δ_i is an action, so it is a sequence of alternating states and actions, beginning with a state. If it is finite, it ends with a state as well. Each action in the behavior is responsible for the change from the state before to the state after it.

This idea of dividing the actions into system and environment ones and taking a sequence of states and actions as observable behavior was first suggested by Aczel as cited in [dR85].

A property G is a set of behaviors satisfying

- for any σ in G, any σ' obtained from σ by adding or removing a 'stuttering' [AL88] (scs) is also in G.

- for any σ in G, any σ' obtained from σ by merging two consecutive c-transition, that is, replacing any $s_1 c s_2 c s_3$ by $s_1 c s_3$, is also in G.

Proposition 1 *If G and H are properties, then $G \cup H$ and $G \cap H$ are properties too.*

Proof. obvious from the definition.

It also follows immediately that property is closed to adding or removing any finite amount of 'stuttering' and merging any finite amount of consecutive c-transition. For any set of behaviors B, we write B^+ for the smallest property containing B. The reason for this complication is to allow abstraction from some unwanted details, in such a way that two programs are regarded equivalent if they only differ in the amount of 'stuttering' they go through, and the program having finer granularity can interfere more often, and is therefore less deterministic. Please refer to the last section for a related discussion on the transitivity of the *guarantee*-condition.

Definition 1 *For any set of behaviors B, its property closure B^+ is the set of behaviors which satisfies*

1. $B \subseteq B^+$
2. B^+ *is a property*
3. *for any property G,* $B \subseteq G \Rightarrow B^+ \subseteq G$

Proposition 2 *For any two sets of behaviors B, C and a property G, the following 1-4 hold.*

1. $B \subseteq C \Rightarrow B^+ \subseteq C^+$

2 $B = C \Rightarrow B^+ = C^+$

3. $B \subseteq G \subseteq B^+ \Rightarrow G = B^+$
4. $G^+ = G$

Proof. The first clause is true from the fact that C^+ is a property, and that $B \subseteq C \subseteq C^+$. The second one follows immediately from 1. The third clause holds by the definition, and the fourth one is a special case of it (with $B = G$).

Proposition 3 *For any two sets of behaviors B and C, we have*

1. $(B^+)^+ = B^+$
2 $(B \cup C)^+ = B^+ \cup C^+$

Proof. The first clause holds from the fact that B^+ is a property, and 4 of the above proposition. For the second one, it is easy to see that $B^+ \cup C^+$ is a property, and $B \cup C \subseteq B^+ \cup C^+ \subseteq (B \cup C)^+$, thus from 3 of the above proposition, we have $(B \cup C)^+ = B^+ \cup C^+$.

Lamport suggested in [La77] to classify properties into two kinds, safety and liveness properties. Informally, safety property says that certain (bad) things will not happen and liveness property says that certain (good) things will eventually happen. Therefore, a safety property is one that is finitely refutable, that is, for every behavior not in a safety property G, there is a finite prefix of it which is not in G; a liveness property G is one that is not finitely refutable, that is, every finite behavior can be extended to a behavior in G.

Definition 2 *A property G is a safety property if for any behavior σ, $\sigma \in G$ iff for any finite behavior σ_1 which is a prefix of σ, $\sigma_1 \in G$.*

Definition 3 *A property G is a liveness property if for any finite behavior σ, there is a behavior σ_1, $\sigma_1 \in G$ and σ is a prefix of it.*

Proposition 4 *If G and H are safety (liveness) properties, then $G \cap H$ is a safety (liveness) property as well.*

Proof. Direct from the definitions of safety and liveness property.

Alpern and Schneider [AS85] studied this classification in a topological setting, by letting safety properties be closed sets and liveness properties be dense sets. By a standard result of topology, every property can be expressed as a conjunction of a safety property and a liveness property. The kind of property (total correctness) we are interested in here is a conjunction of a special safety property (partial correctness) and a special liveness property (termination).

Semantically, a specification is regarded as a definition of the property consisting of all the legal behaviors of the computer system it specifies, and a computer system satisfies a specification if every behavior of the computer system is legal behavior defined by the specification.

As pointed out in [AL89], a system is usually not meant to work in an arbitrary environment, hence, a specification should assert that the system behaves properly if the environment does. They gave a semantic formalism, in which a specification is of the form $E \Rightarrow N$, where E is a set of behaviors, such that in each of these behaviors the environment behaves properly, and N is the set of behaviors in which the system behaves properly, $\Rightarrow$ denotes the set implication. Thus, a legal behavior is either a proper behavior of the system or an improper behavior of the environment.

Definition 4 *A labeled transition system [Ke76] is a structure*

$$(\Sigma,\ \Sigma_0,\ A,\ \rightarrow)$$

where Σ *is the set of configurations,* $\Sigma_0 \subseteq \Sigma$ *is the set of initial configurations,* A *is the action (label) set and* $\rightarrow \subseteq \Sigma \times A \times \Sigma$ *is the transition relation.*

An operational semantics is given by an abstract machine on which the execution of programs is modeled. The labeled transition system used to model the execution of program P is of the form

$$(Prog \times S,\ \{P\} \times S,\ \{c,\ e\},\ \rightarrow)$$

$Prog$, S are the set of programs and states. Therefore a configuration is a pair (Q, s), where Q is the program to be executed, and s is the state from which Q is going to run. In the initial configuration, the program to be executed is P. The transition $(Q, s) \xrightarrow{\delta} (Q', s')$ represents a semantic rule, that is, how the computation can proceed by one step. The label of the transition indicates whether the transition is a computation (system or program) transition or an environment transition, in particular, we say it is a computation transition if it is of the following form

- $(P, s) \xrightarrow{c} (P', s')$

and it is an environment transition if it is of the following form,

- $(P, s) \xrightarrow{e} (P, s')$

It is easy to see that an environment transition does not change the program part of the configuration.

We will give the detail structure of a programming language and its operational semantics in the next section. Before that we are only at the semantic level and deliberately do not involve elements which is dependent on language structure.

We introduce some notations which will be needed later in the paper. $len(\sigma)$ is the *length* of behavior σ. If σ is a finite behavior $s_0\delta_1 s_1, ...\delta_n s_n$, $len(\sigma)\widehat{=}n$, and if σ is a infinite behavior $len(\sigma)\widehat{=}\infty$. For a finite behavior $\sigma = s_0\delta_1 s_1, ...\delta_n s_n$, $first(\sigma)\widehat{=}s_0$ and $last(\sigma)\widehat{=}s_n$ are the first and the last state in the behavior. We write $(P, s) \xrightarrow{\delta}$ for $\exists P', s'. (P, s) \xrightarrow{\delta} (P', s')$. Sometimes we use relation combinators for predicates as well, for instance, for any predicates I, J on $S \times S$, we write $(I; J)(s, s')$ for $\exists s'' I(s, s'') \wedge J(s'', s')$, and define $I_0\widehat{=}(s' = s)$, $I^n\widehat{=}I^{n-1}; I$, $I^*\widehat{=}\bigvee_{n\geq 0} I^n$, etc.

2.2 Computation

We stated that the difference of programs and specification tuples are not in the semantic properties they define, this is substantiated here formally by assigning a set of behaviors to both of them as their semantics. We use *Spec* for the set of all the specifications, and *Obs* for the set of all the properties

$$M : (Prog \cup Spec) \longrightarrow Obs$$

To this end, we need to reveal the structure of a state. For the purpose in this paper, a state records the values of the program variables and the present status of the process, which could be '*running*', '*terminated*', '*blocked*' or '*fail*'. Therefore, a state s is of the form $(v, status)$, where v is a function which maps the program variables to the values they store, and $status \in$ {'*running*', '*terminated*', '*blocked*', '*fail*'}, each indicating whether the process is running, has terminated, has been blocked or resulted in failure. The predicates in the specification tuple, *pre*, *rely* etc are, strictly speaking, defined on the program variables, but we will write *pre*(s), *rely*(s) etc from time to time as well.

For any specification tuple $spec = (pre, rely, run, guar, post)$, we define

$$ES_1(spec) = \{\sigma \mid pre(\sigma_0)\}$$
$$ES_2(spec) = \{\sigma \mid \forall s \xrightarrow{e} \hat{s} \; in \; \sigma \; rely(s, \hat{s})\}$$
$$EL(spec) = \{\sigma \mid (len(\sigma) < \infty \wedge status(last(\sigma)) = \text{`}blocked\text{'}) \Rightarrow run(last(\sigma))\}$$
$$NS(spec) = \{\sigma \mid \forall s \xrightarrow{c} \hat{s} \; in \; \sigma \; guar(s, \hat{s})\}$$
$$NL_1(spec) = \{\sigma \mid \sigma \; has \; only \; finite \; c \; moves\}$$
$$NL_2(spec) = \{\sigma \mid len(\sigma) < \infty \Rightarrow (status(last(\sigma)) = \text{`}terminated\text{'} \wedge post(last(\sigma)))\}$$

Let $E(spec) = ES_1(spec) \cap ES_2(spec) \cap EL(spec)$ and $N(spec) = NS(spec) \cap NL_1(spec) \cap NL_2(spec)$. Now the semantics of a specification $spec$, $M(spec)$, is $E(spec) \Rightarrow N(spec)$. We will drop $spec$ and simply write E, N etc whenever a specific specification $spec$ is understood.

Proposition 5 *ES_1, ES_2 and NS are safety properties, EL, NL_1 and NL_2 are liveness properties.*

Proof: By the definitions of safety and liveness property.

Proposition 6 *$\neg(E(spec))$ is a property.*

Proof: By the definitions of property, note that for any property G, $\neg G$ is not always a property.

Proposition 7 *$M(spec)$ is a property.*

Proof: By proposition 1, 5 and 6.

For every program P, we define $M(P)$ to be $[T(P)]^+$, while $T(P)$ is the smallest set which contains

- $s_0\delta_1 s_1, \ldots \delta_n s_n, \ldots$ which is infinite, if there are programs $P_1, P_2, \ldots, P_n, \ldots$ such that $(P, s_0) \xrightarrow{\delta_1} (P_1, s_1) \ldots \xrightarrow{\delta_n} (P_n, s_n) \xrightarrow{\delta_{n+1}} \ldots$
- $s_0\delta_1 s_1, \ldots \delta_n s_n$ if there are programs $P_1, P_2, \ldots, P_n$, $(P, s_0) \xrightarrow{\delta_1} (P_1, s_1) \ldots \xrightarrow{\delta_n} (P_n, s_n)$ and $\neg(P_n, s_n) \xrightarrow{c}$

Here $status(s_0) = \text{`}running\text{'}$, that is, the initial status of the process is '$running$'. Note by the definition of B^+, the behaviors which have infinite number of c moves in $M(P)$ and $T(P)$ are the same.

2.3 Refinement Order

It is stated before that specifications and programs define properties consisting of all the legal behaviors a correct implementation allowed to produce in execution. Therefore a specification or a program is stronger or better if it gives a more precise definition.

Definition 5 *A program or specification P is refined or implemented by another one Q, writing $P \sqsubseteq Q$, if $M(Q) \subseteq M(P)$.*

Proposition 8 *If P is a specification, then $P \sqsubseteq Q$ if and only if $E(P) \cap M(Q) \subseteq N(P)$.*

Proof. set theory.

Theorem 1 *$\sqsubseteq$ is a pre-order.*

Proof: set theory.
This says that refinement can be carried out stepwisely.

Definition 6 *A program or specification P is equivalent to another one Q, writing $P = Q$, if $P \sqsubseteq Q$ and $Q \sqsubseteq P$.*

Although we map both programs and specification tuples to the same semantic space, and this gives a clear insight of the nature of both programs and specifications, it is difficult to use this definition directly to establish a refinement relation. In practice, a software engineer uses proof obligations and laws to replace a specification by a more stronger one, and a program by a better one. These proof obligations and laws should be studied in the formal semantics, so we can be sure they are sound, and it is often helpful to know if they are complete in certain sense. However, once these things have been established, the proof obligations and laws can be used without further question. It is even desirable to be able to understand, although informally, and furthermore, to use these proof obligations and laws, without a knowledge of the underlying model, so that they can be in the hands of a wide range of software engineers.

There are three possibilities for a refinement relation to hold in a top-down development paradigm, that is, between two specifications, a specification and a program, and finally, two programs. For devising effective proof obligations and laws, it is necessary, or may be just convenient to discuss these cases separately. After all, programs and specification tuples are very different syntactic objects.

2.4 Refining specifications

Here we investigate the conditions for refining specifications. Later we shall discuss the conditions for a program to implement a specification in the framework of a proof system. The refinement of a program by another will be investigated in an algebraic setting in the companion paper.

Let $P = (pre_1,\ rely_1,\ run_1,\ guar_1,\ post_1)$ and $Q = (pre_2,\ rely_2,\ run_2,\ guar_2,\ post_2$

Theorem 2 *$P \sqsubseteq Q$ if*

$$
\begin{array}{l}
pre_1 \Rightarrow pre_2 \\
rely_1 \Rightarrow rely_2 \\
run_1 \Rightarrow run_2 \\
guar_2 \land dinv(P, Q) \Rightarrow guar_1 \\
pre_1 \land post_2 \land dinv(P, Q) \Rightarrow post_1
\end{array}
$$

Here, $dinv(P, Q)$ is predicate on $S \times S$, defined as, $pre_1(s) \land (rely_1 \lor guar_2)^*(s,\ s')$.

Proof: it is easy to show that,

$$
\begin{array}{ll}
ES_1(P) \subseteq ES_1(Q) & \\
ES_2(P) \subseteq ES_2(Q) & (*) \\
EL(P) \subseteq EL(Q) & \\
N(Q) \cap E(P) \subseteq N(P) &
\end{array}
$$

Then we have,

$$
\begin{aligned}
& M(Q) \cap E(P) \\
& = \{\textit{definition of } M(Q)\} \\
& (E(Q) \Rightarrow N(Q)) \cap E(P) \\
& = \{\textit{set theory}\} \\
& (\neg E(Q) \cup N(Q)) \cap E(P) \\
& = \{\textit{definition of } E(Q)\} \\
& (\neg(ES_1(Q) \cap ES_2(Q) \cap EL(Q)) \cup N(Q)) \cap E(P) \\
& = \{\textit{set theory}\} \\
& (\neg ES_1(Q) \cup \neg ES_2(Q) \cup \neg EL(Q) \cup N(Q)) \cap E(P) \\
& = \{\textit{set theory and } (*)\} \\
& N(Q) \cap E(P) \\
& \subseteq \{(*)\} \\
& N(P).
\end{aligned}
$$

The proof obligation given by Jones in [Jo81] is a special case of the one above.

Corollary 1 *(Jones) If*

$$
\begin{aligned}
& pre_1 \Rightarrow pre_2 \\
& rely_1 \Rightarrow rely_2 \\
& guar_2 \Rightarrow guar_1 \\
& pre_1 \wedge post_2 \Rightarrow post_1
\end{aligned}
$$

then $(pre_1,\ rely_1,\ true,\ guar_1,\ post_1) \sqsubseteq (pre_2,\ rely_2,\ true,\ guar_2,\ post_2)$.

However these conditions sometimes are stronger than needed. For example, for the following two specifications P and Q, we have $P \sqsubseteq Q$ in our definition, but not by Jones'.

P:

$$
\begin{aligned}
pre_1 &: \ x = 0 \\
rely_1 &: \ \exists\, n.\ x' = x + n \\
run_1 &: \ true \\
guar_1 &: \ \exists\, n.\ x' = x + n \\
post_1 &: \ x' = 10
\end{aligned}
$$

Q:

$$\begin{aligned}
pre_2 &: \ x = 0 \\
rely_2 &: \ \exists\, n.\ x' = x + n \\
run_2 &: \ true \\
guar_2 &: \ \exists\, n.\ (x \geq 0 \Rightarrow x' = x + n) \wedge (x < 0 \Rightarrow x' = x - n) \\
post_2 &: \ x' = 10 \vee x' = -10
\end{aligned}$$

Here assume n ranges over natural numbers, it is not true that $guar_2 \Rightarrow guar_1$ nor $pre_1 \wedge post_2 \Rightarrow post_1$, thus the refinement is not provable by Jones' definition. This shows an important point that the five elements in a specification tuple are not totally independent, actually the following fact can be used to weaken the *guarantee* and *post* conditions in a specification, although in general they can only be strengthened in the development process.

Corollary 2 $(pre,\ rely,\ run,\ guar,\ post) = (pre,\ rely,\ run,\ guar \wedge dinv,\ post \wedge dinv)$

Here, $dinv$ is defined as $pre(s) \wedge (rely \vee guar)^*(s,\ s')$.

3 An Owicki-Gries language

The language we use in this paper is from [OG76], syntax of which can be partially defined as:

$$\begin{aligned}
S ::= &\quad skip \mid X := E \mid P \mid S_1 \sqcap S_2 \mid S_1 ; S_2 \mid if\ b\ then\ S_1\ else\ S_2 \mid \\
&\quad while\ b\ do\ S \mid await\ b\ then\ S \\
P ::= &\quad pvar\ Y : S \mid P_1 \parallel P_2
\end{aligned}$$

It basically extends the Dijkstra's language by parallel composition and a simple synchronization statement. Our version differs slightly from the original one in [OG76] in that we allow declaration of private variables, which are read-only to the environment. Therefore in $P_1 \parallel P_2$ the set of private variables of P_1 and P_2 must be disjunct, and we further restrict that in the boolean test b of the conditional and iteration statement only the private variables can be used.

As a result, the environment will not change the truth value of the boolean test in the conditional and iteration statement. As noted in [St90], this constraint does not reduce the set of possible algorithms. The advantage is that some proof rules in the proof system become simpler, and moreover, a number of important algebraic laws will only hold with this assumption. A brief explanation of various language structures is as follows.

skip has no effect on any program variables, and terminates promptly. In the assignment statement, X represents a vector of variables $(x_1, ..., x_n)$, and E represents a vector of expressions $(e_1, ..., e_n)$. When executed, the values of $e_1, ..., e_n$ are computed first, and then $x_1, ..., x_n$ are set to the values computed for $e_1, ..., e_n$. $\sqcap$ is the nondeterministic choice, $P \sqcap Q$ behaves either like P or Q. $P; Q$ is executed by executing P first, when P terminates, executing Q. If P is blocked, then $P; Q$ is blocked until P is released. *if b then P else Q* and *while b do P* are the conditional and iteration statements, the evaluation of the boolean test b in the conditional statement is atomic, but the environment can interrupt between the boolean test and first action from P or Q. *pvar* Y : S declares the set of variables Y to be its private ones, that is, they should not be written by the environment, but the computation of itself is just like S.

The above are just sequential structures, the two nonsequential ones are the parallel composition and the *await*-statement. In $P \parallel Q$, P and Q are executed concurrently, with atomic actions from two processes interleaving each other. $P \parallel Q$ is blocked if the two processes are all blocked and released if one of the processes is released. *await b then P* provides a means of synchronization and mutual exclusion, and is the cause of a process to become blocked. When b is true, P will be executed without interruption. If P loops forever, the whole process is led to a failure, while if P terminates, the execution of the statement is atomic. When b is not held, the process is blocked and can only become active again when the environment has set b to true. Since the *await*-body P is intended to be executed without interruption, we stipulate that it can only be a sequential program, that is, a program which does not contain parallel or *await* statements.

The above informal interpretation is captured by the following transition rules.

$(P, v, status) \xrightarrow{c} (P, v', status)$ $status = \text{`}running\text{'} or \text{`}blocked\text{'}$, $v(pvar(P)) = v'(pvar(P))$. Here $pvar(P)$ denotes all the private variables declared in P.

$(skip, v, \text{`}running\text{'}) \xrightarrow{c} (skip, v, \text{`}terminated\text{'})$

$(X := E, v, \text{`}running\text{'}) \xrightarrow{c} (skip, v[E/X], \text{`}running\text{'})$

$(P \sqcap Q, v, \text{`}running\text{'}) \xrightarrow{c} (P, v, \text{`}running\text{'})$

$(P \sqcap Q, v, \text{`}running\text{'}) \xrightarrow{c} (Q, v, \text{`}running\text{'})$

$(P; Q, v, status) \xrightarrow{c} (P'; Q, v', status')$ if $(P, v, status) \xrightarrow{c} (P', v', status')$
$status' \neq \text{`}terminated\text{'}$

$(P; Q, v, status) \xrightarrow{c} (Q, v', \text{`}running\text{'})$ if $(P, v, status) \xrightarrow{c} (P', v', \text{`}terminated\text{'})$

$(if\ b\ then\ P\ else\ Q, v, \text{`}running\text{'}) \xrightarrow{c} (P, v, \text{`}running\text{'})$ if $b(s)$

$(if\ b\ then\ P\ else\ Q, v, \text{`}running\text{'}) \xrightarrow{c} (Q, v, \text{`}running\text{'})$ if $\neg b(s)$

$(while\ b\ do\ P, v, \text{`}running\text{'}) \xrightarrow{c} (P; while\ b\ do\ P, v, \text{`}running\text{'})$ if $b(s)$

$(while\ b\ do\ P, v, \text{`}running\text{'}) \xrightarrow{c} (skip, v, \text{`}running\text{'})$ if $\neg b(s)$

$(pvar\ Y :\ P, v, status) \xrightarrow{c} (pvar\ Y :\ P', v', status')$
if $(P, v, status) \xrightarrow{c} (P', v', status')$

$(P \parallel Q, v, status) \xrightarrow{c} (P' \parallel Q, v', \text{`}running\text{'})$ if $(P, v, status) \xrightarrow{c} (P', v', \text{`}running\text{'})$

$(P \parallel Q, v, status) \xrightarrow{c} (P \parallel Q', v', \text{`}running\text{'})$ if $(Q, v, status) \xrightarrow{c} (Q', v', \text{`}running\text{'})$

$(P \parallel Q, v, status) \xrightarrow{c} (Q, v', \text{`}running\text{'})$ if $(P, v, status) \xrightarrow{c} (P', v', \text{`}terminated\text{'})$

$(P \parallel Q, v, status) \xrightarrow{c} (P, v', \text{'running'})$ if $(Q, v, status) \xrightarrow{c} (Q', v', \text{'terminated'})$

$(P \parallel Q, v, status) \xrightarrow{c} (P \parallel Q, v', \text{'blocked'})$ if $(P, v, status) \xrightarrow{c} (P', v', \text{'blocked'})$ and $(Q, v, status) \xrightarrow{c} (Q', v', \text{'blocked'})$

$(\mathit{await}\ b\ \mathit{then}\ P, v, \text{'running'}) \xrightarrow{c} (\mathit{skip}, v', \text{'running'})$ if $b(s)$ and $\exists\, v_0 = v, \ldots, v_n = v',\ P_0 = P, \ldots, P_n\ \forall 1 \le i \le n-1 (P_{i-1}, v_{i-1}, \text{'running'}) \xrightarrow{c} (P_i, v_i, \text{'running'})$ and $(P_{n-1}, v_{n-1}, \text{'running'}) \xrightarrow{c} (P_n, v_n, \text{'terminated'})$

$(\mathit{await}\ b\ \mathit{then}\ P, v, \text{'running'}) \xrightarrow{c} (\mathit{await}\ b\ \mathit{then}\ P, v, \text{'fail'})$ if $b(s)$ and $\exists\, v_0 = v, \ldots, v_n \ldots,\ P_0 = P, \ldots, P_n \ldots\ \forall i \ge 1\, (P_{i-1}, v_{i-1}, \text{'running'}) \xrightarrow{c} (P_i, v_i, \text{'running'})$

$(\mathit{await}\ b\ \mathit{then}\ P, v, \text{'running'}) \xrightarrow{c} (\mathit{await}\ b\ \mathit{then}\ P, v, \text{'blocked'})$ if $\neg b(s)$

$(\mathit{await}\ b\ \mathit{then}\ P, v, \text{'blocked'}) \xrightarrow{c} (\mathit{await}\ b\ \mathit{then}\ P, v, \text{'running'})$ if $b(s)$

Some people may find the definition of the assignment looks odd, we admit that a more natural one would allow the process to terminate right after the assigning action, namely, $(X := E, v, \text{'running'}) \xrightarrow{c} (\mathit{skip}, v[E/X], \text{'terminated'})$. However, we would like to have $P; \mathit{skip} = P$ as a valid algebraic law. We then have to modify the semantics, allowing the environment actions to appear in the observable behavior even after the process has terminated. This appears strange to us as well, because we like to think that the observation of a process should be able to stop once the process has terminated.

The transition rules are quite concise, we have to do a bit reasoning to find out some properties, such as

If $(P, v, status) \xrightarrow{\delta} (P, v', status')$, *then* $status = \text{'running' or 'blocked'}$

If $(P, v, status) \xrightarrow{c} (P', v', status')$ *and* $v \ne v'$, *then* $status = status' = \text{'running'}$

Theorem 3 *If* $P \sqsubseteq Q$ *and* C *is a program context, then* $C(P) \sqsubseteq C(Q)$.

This says that the semantic formalism is monotonic so we can substitute a program by a better one in any context of use. The proof proceeds by induction on the structure of the language, it is rather tedious and irrelevant to the rest of the paper, hence omitted here.

4 Proof rules

The implementation relation between programs and specifications is usually studied in the form of a proof system, the set of proof rules given below follows from [Jo81]. They are independent of program structure, hence can be used in a top-down methodology. We write $Q\ \underline{imp}\ P$ for $P \sqsubseteq Q$.

Skip

$$\frac{pre\ \underline{stable\ when}\ rely}{Skip\ \ \underline{imp}\ \ (pre,\ rely,\ true,\ (v' = v),\ post)}$$

Here $\forall\, v, v'\, post(v, v') \widehat{=} pre(v')$ and $pre\ \underline{stable\ when}\ rely$ is a shorthand for $\forall\, v,\ v'.\ pre(v) \wedge rely(v,\ v') \Rightarrow pre(v')$. Since we do not assume in the semantics that the first action must be taken by the system, the kind of precondition which can be damaged by the environment is of no use at all.

Nondeterminism

$$\frac{\begin{array}{c} P\ \ \underline{imp}\ \ (pre,\ rely,\ run,\ guar,\ post) \\ Q\ \ \underline{imp}\ \ (pre,\ rely,\ run,\ guar,\ post) \end{array}}{P \sqcap Q\ \ \underline{imp}\ \ (pre,\ rely,\ run,\ guar,\ post)}$$

Assignment

$$\frac{\begin{array}{l} pre \Rightarrow post^{X}_{E} \\ pre\ \underline{stable\ when}\ \ rely \\ post\ \underline{stable\ when}\ \ rely \end{array}}{X := E\ \ \underline{imp}\ \ (pre,\ rely,\ true,\ [X' = E]^{*},\ post)}$$

Here $post\ \underline{stable\ when}\ rely$ is a shorthand for $\forall\, v_1,\ v_2.\ post(v_0, v_1) \wedge rely(v_1,\ v_2) \Rightarrow post(v_0, v_2)$, and $[X' = E] \widehat{=} (X' = E) \wedge \forall\, y \in (v - X)\ y' = y$.

Composition

$$\frac{\begin{array}{l} P \ \underline{imp} \ (pre,\ rely,\ run,\ guar,\ mid) \\ Q \ \underline{imp} \ ((\exists\, v.\ mid)',\ rely,\ run,\ guar,\ post) \end{array}}{P;\ Q \ \underline{imp} \ (pre,\ rely,\ run,\ guar,\ mid;\ post)}$$

For a formula F, which could be a predicate or a function, F' stands for the formula from F with all the unprimed variables in it replaced by the same variables primed, and all the primed variables replaced by the same variables unprimed.

Conditional

$$\frac{\begin{array}{l} P \ \underline{imp} \ (pre \wedge b,\ rely,\ run,\ guar,\ post) \\ Q \ \underline{imp} \ (pre \wedge \neg b,\ rely,\ run,\ guar,\ post) \end{array}}{if\ b\ then\ P\ else\ Q \ \underline{imp} \ (pre,\ rely,\ run,\ guar,\ post)}$$

Iteration

$$\frac{\begin{array}{l} I \ \underline{stable\ when} \ rely \\ E \ \underline{nonincrease\ when} \ rely \\ P \ \underline{imp} \ ((\exists\, v.I)' \wedge b,\ rely,\ run,\ guar,\ I \wedge 0 \leq E' < E) \end{array}}{while\ b\ do\ P \ \underline{imp} \ ((\exists\, v.I)',\ rely,\ run,\ guar,\ I \wedge \neg b)}$$

E is a function from states to a well founded set, with 0 as the minimal member, this is necessary for the total correctness. E $\underline{nonincrease\ when}$ $rely$ is a shorthand for $\forall\, v,\ v'\ rely(v,\ v') \Rightarrow E(v') \leq E(v)$.

Parallel

$$\frac{\begin{array}{l} (post_1 \Rightarrow run_2) \wedge (post_2 \Rightarrow run_1) \wedge (run_1 \vee run_2) \\ (rely \vee guar_1) \Rightarrow rely_2 \\ (rely \vee guar_2) \Rightarrow rely_1 \\ (guar_1 \vee guar_2) \Rightarrow guar \\ P \ \underline{imp} \ (pre,\ rely_1,\ run \wedge run_1,\ guar_1,\ post_1) \\ Q \ \underline{imp} \ (pre,\ rely_2,\ run \wedge run_2,\ guar_2,\ post_2) \end{array}}{P \parallel Q \ \underline{imp} \ (pre,\ rely,\ run,\ guar,\ post_1 \wedge post_2)}$$

Await

$$\frac{\begin{array}{c} pre \ \underline{stable\ when}\ \ rely \\ post\ \underline{stable\ when}\ \ rely \\ P\ \ \underline{imp}\ \ (pre \wedge b,\ v' = v,\ true,\ true,\ post) \end{array}}{await\ b\ then\ P\ \ \underline{imp}\ \ (pre,\ rely,\ pre \Rightarrow b,\ (b \wedge post)^*,\ post)}$$

Private variable

$$\frac{P\ \ \underline{imp}\ \ (pre,\ rely \wedge (Y' = Y),\ run,\ guar,\ post)}{pvar\ Y : P\ \ \underline{imp}\ \ (pre,\ rely,\ run,\ guar,\ post)}$$

Auxiliary variable

$$\frac{P\ \ \underline{imp}\ \ (pre \wedge pre_1,\ rely \wedge rely_1,\ run \wedge run_1,\ guar,\ post)}{P \backslash Y\ \ \underline{imp}\ \ (pre,\ rely,\ run,\ guar,\ post)}$$

Here Y is the set of auxiliary variables which in P only appear in the left hand side of assignment statements. *pre*, *rely*, *guar*, *run* and *post* do not contain free occurrences of y in Y, and pre_1, $rely_1$, run_1 only refer to y in Y. $P \backslash Y$ stands for the program with all the assignments in P to variables $y \in Y$ replaced by $y := y$.

Consequence

$$\frac{\begin{array}{l} P\ \ \underline{imp}\ \ (pre_1,\ rely_1,\ run_1,\ guar_1,\ post_1) \\ (pre_1,\ rely_1,\ run_1,\ guar_1,\ post_1)\ \ \underline{imp}\ \ (pre,\ rely,\ run,\ guar,\ post) \end{array}}{P\ \ \underline{imp}\ \ (pre,\ rely,\ run,\ guar,\ post)}$$

The postulated strengthening rule in [GR89] becomes a special case of the consequence rule.

Postulated strengthening

$$\frac{P\ \ \underline{imp}\ \ (pre,\ rely,\ run,\ guar,\ post)}{P\ \ \underline{imp}\ \ (pre,\ rely,\ run,\ guar,\ pre \wedge (rely \vee guar)^* \wedge post)}$$

It appears to be the right place to offer some explanation of these rules before going on. This system can be regarded as an extension of the proof system in [St88]. Most of the rules are straightforward, so we only mention the ones which seem to be less obvious.

In the iteration rule, a well founded set (which is isomorphic to a ordinal numbers, by a standard result of mathematics), instead of a natural numbers, is used to ensure the termination. This is due to the unbounded nondeterminism from the environment, that is, for a program P and state s, we do not not restrict the number of s' such that $(P, s) \xrightarrow{e} (P, s')$ to be finite, although it is still reasonable to expect them to be countable. It is observed in [St90] that allowing unbounded nondeterminism from the environment makes the specification easy to write. The interference from the environment can be modeled by random assignments. For more discussion on total correctness system, countable nondeterminism and random assignments, see [Ap84] and [AP86].

The most interesting and complicated rule is naturally the parallel rule. Here the program of interest is $P \parallel Q$, suppose it is put together with an overall environment R. Thus, the environment of process P consists of Q and R, and the environment of process Q is made of P and R. Therefore, process P should be able to tolerate the interference from both R and Q, so the best rely-condition P can assume is $rely \vee guar_2$; for the same reason, the best rely-condition Q can assume is $rely \vee guar_1$. We now show that it is not possible for $P \parallel Q$ to deadlock, under the premises of the proof rule. Assume $P \parallel Q$ is deadlocked, then from the interpretation, the overall environment has to establish run. There are two possibilities here, either one of the processes is terminated and the other one is deadlocked, or both of them are deadlocked. We demonstrate neither of the two cases can be true. Suppose P is terminated and Q is deadlocked, then $post_1$ holds, from the premises, this implies run_2 to be true. However, from the specification of Q in the premises, $run \wedge run_2$ should be able to guarantee it to be released, therefore can not be deadlocked. Moreover, P and Q can not be all deadlocked, because either run_1 or run_2 should be true at any time from the premises, then one of them is not deadlocked. It is easy to see a computation action from $P \parallel Q$ is either an action from P or Q, hence it satisfies $guar_1 \vee guar_2$. Finally, both P and Q terminates in the end, as a result, both post-conditions are established for the terminating states.

The *await*-rule is not difficult to understand, the *await*-body P is only executed when b is true, and it is not interrupted. Furthermore, P will not deadlock simply because P does not have any *await*-statements. *await b then P* can only become blocked if b is not true, but from the specification in the conclusion part of the rule, environment will establish $pre \Rightarrow b$ eventually when the program is blocked. This together with the pre-condition *pre* ensures b to be true, thus *await b then P* becomes active again. To the outside, the execution of P in *await b then P* is atomic, therefore the guar-condition is obviously satisfied. Finally, if the post-condition of P is not damaged by the environment, it should hold in the end as well.

Example 1. $x := x + 1 \parallel x := x + 1$.
This extremely simple program has been used many times to test the whether a proof system of a parallel programs is independent of program structure. The trick is to deduce the fact that final value of x is incremented by 2, so say if it is started from initial value 0, value of x would equal to 2 after the execution, not by calculating the semantics of the whole program but through some hierarchical reasoning. This can be done in the same way as in [Ow76] by introducing two auxiliary variables and then hiding them to get the original program.

Let $P1$ to be the program $(x, t_1 := x + 1, t_1 + 1)$, and $P2$ the program $(x, t_2 := x + 1, t_2 + 1)$, then

$P1$ $\underline{imp}$ $(x = t_1 = t_2 = 0, (x' = t_1' + t_2' \wedge t_1' = t_1) \vee I(x, t_1, t_2), (x' = t_1' + t_2' \wedge t_2' = t_2) \vee I(x, t_1, t_2), (x' = t_1' + t_2' \wedge t_1' = 1)$

$P2$ $\underline{imp}$ $(x = t_1 = t_2 = 0, (x' = t_1' + t_2' \wedge t_2' = t_2) \vee I(x, t_1, t_2), (x' = t_1' + t_2' \wedge t_1' = t_1) \vee I(x, t_1, t_2), (x' = t_1' + t_2' \wedge t_2' = 1)$

Here $I(x, t_1, t_2)$ is a shorthand for $x' = x \wedge t_1' = t_1 \wedge t_2' = t_2$. By the parallel rule

$P1 \parallel P2$ $\underline{imp}$ $(x = t_1 = t_2 = 0, I(x, t_1, t_2), (x' = 0 \vee x' = 1 \vee x' = 2), x' = 2)$

By the auxiliary variable rule, we finally get

$$x := x+1 \parallel x := x+1 \ \underline{imp} \ (x = 0, I(x), (x' = 0 \vee x' = 1 \vee x' = 2), x' = 2)$$

Example 2. We now illustrate the use of the techniques discussed so far by developing a concurrent program modeling a bank. The same program appeared in [SA] and was verified (for partial correctness) in their Proof Outline Logic.

Assume the bank manages a collection of accounts

$$acnt[1...n] : money$$

The task is to design a computer program to transfer \$20 from account a to account b ($a \neq b$), and accumulate the bank's total deposits. The top level specification is therefore

$$\begin{aligned} &pre: \ true \\ &rely: \ acnt' = acnt \wedge total' = total \\ &run: \ true \\ &guar: \ true \\ &post: \ (total' = \textstyle\sum_{i=1}^{n} acnt[i]) \wedge (acnt'[a] = acnt[a] - 20) \\ &\quad\quad \wedge (acnt'[b] = acnt[b] + 20) \wedge \forall j \neq a, b\, (acnt'[j] = acnt[j]) \end{aligned}$$

We next split the *post* into two parts, $post_1 = (total' = \sum_{i=1}^{n} acnt[i])$ and $post_2 = (acnt'[a] = acnt[a]-20) \wedge (acnt'[b] = acnt[b]+20) \wedge \forall j \neq a, b\, (acnt'[j] = acnt[j])$. Bearing in mind that in the parallel rule the post-condition is the conjunction of the two, we try to decompose the specification using this rule. Now let us look at $post_1$, it can be transformed to $(total' = \sum_{i=1}^{k-1} acnt[i]) \wedge (k = n + 1)$. Taking $total' = \sum_{i=1}^{k-1} acnt[i]$ as invariant, obviously an iteration structure can be attempted, provided the invariant is maintained by the other process. A sufficient rely-condition is $(total' = total) \wedge (\sum_{i=1}^{k-1} acnt'[i] = \sum_{i=1}^{k-1} acnt[i])$. Obviously this process has no need to change the account, therefore it can easily guarantee that $acnt' = acnt$. At this stage, we write down the following specification for one process.

$$\begin{aligned} &pre_1: \ true \\ &rely_1: \ (total' = total) \wedge (\textstyle\sum_{i=1}^{k-1} acnt'[i] = \sum_{i=1}^{k-1} acnt[i]) \wedge (k' = k) \\ &run_1: \ true \\ &guar_1: \ acnt' = acnt \\ &post_1: \ (total' = \textstyle\sum_{i=1}^{k-1} acnt[i]) \wedge (k = n + 1) \end{aligned}$$

For the other process, its atomic transition must be able to guarantee $rely_1$, while it can not rely more than $guar_1$, we simply take $rely_1$, $guar_1$ respectively as the *guarantee* and *rely* conditions of the other process and write down the specification tentatively as follows.

$$
\begin{aligned}
&pre_2: \ true\\
&rely_2: \ acnt' = acnt\\
&run_2: \ true\\
&guar_2: \ (total' = total) \wedge (\textstyle\sum_{i=1}^{k-1} acnt'[i] = \sum_{i=1}^{k-1} acnt[i]) \wedge (k' = k)\\
&post_2: \ (acnt'[a] = acnt[a] - 20) \wedge (acnt'[b] = acnt[b] + 20)\\
&\qquad \wedge \forall j \neq a, b\, (acnt'[j] = acnt[j])
\end{aligned}
$$

The first specification can be implemented by the following program *Add – deposit*.

$$
\begin{aligned}
&k := 1\\
&while\ k \leq n\ do\\
&\quad begin\ \ total := total + acnt[k];\ \ k := k + 1\ \ end
\end{aligned}
$$

Now we try to implement the second specification, a straightforward program to establish $post_2$ is of course

$$acnt[a],\ acnt[b] := acnt[a] - 20,\ acnt[b] + 20$$

However, a closer look shows that the *guarantee* condition is not satisfied. For example, if $a < b$, then for those k such that $a < k \leq b + 1$, the value of $\sum_{i=1}^{k-1} acnt[i]$ decreases by 20. Nevertheless, let $bool = ((k < a \wedge k < b) \vee (k > a \wedge k > b))$, then the above assignment does guarantee that the value of $\sum_{i=1}^{k-1} acnt[i]$ is unchanged for those k which satisfies *bool*, or formally, it guarantees $bool \Rightarrow guar_2$. This provides the remedy, that is, if the assignment is only executed when *bool* is true, $guar_2$ will then be maintained. To this end, it is obvious the *await* structure,

$$
\begin{aligned}
&await\ ((k < a \wedge k < b) \vee (k > a \wedge k > b))\ then\\
&\quad acnt[a],\ acnt[b] := acnt[a] - 20,\ acnt[b] + 20
\end{aligned}
$$

can be tried. However, this program is still not the correct implementation with respect to the specification, because it can be blocked when *bool* is false, and can therefore only guarantee to terminate successfully in an environment which will finally establish the *run* condition $((k < a \wedge k < b) \vee (k > a \wedge k > b))$. It is easy to see that this condition will be established by the program *Add − deposit*, as it sets k to $n+1$ in the end. We can then simply modify the the second specification by changing run_2 from *true* to $(k > a \wedge k > b)$. In summary, the development steps are recorded as follows.

The top level specification:

$$\begin{array}{l} pre: \ true \\ rely: \ acnt' = acnt \wedge total' = total \\ run: \ true \\ guar: \ true \\ post: \ (total' = \sum_{i=1}^{n} acnt[i]) \wedge (acnt'[a] = acnt[a] - 20) \\ \quad \wedge (acnt'[b] = acnt[b] + 20) \wedge \forall j \neq a, b\, (acnt'[j] = acnt[j]) \end{array}$$

Decomposition by the parallel rule:

$$\begin{array}{l} pre_1: \ true \\ rely_1: \ (total' = total) \wedge (\sum_{i=1}^{k-1} acnt'[i] = \sum_{i=1}^{k-1} acnt[i]) \wedge (k' = k) \\ run_1: \ true \\ guar_1: \ acnt' = acnt \\ post_1: \ (total' = \sum_{i=1}^{k-1} acnt[i]) \wedge (k = n+1) \end{array}$$

$$\begin{array}{l} pre_2: \ true \\ rely_2: \ acnt' = acnt \\ run_2: (k > a \wedge k > b) \\ guar_2: \ (total' = total) \wedge (\sum_{i=1}^{k-1} acnt'[i] = \sum_{i=1}^{k-1} acnt[i]) \wedge (k' = k) \\ post_2: \ (acnt'[a] = acnt[a] - 20) \wedge (acnt'[b] = acnt[b] + 20) \\ \quad \wedge \forall j \neq a, b\, (acnt'[j] = acnt[j]) \end{array}$$

Verification of this decomposition step is to show that the conditions in the premise of the parallel rule are met.

$$\begin{array}{ll} post_1 \Rightarrow run_2 & \{n+1 > a \wedge n+1 > b\} \\ post_2 \Rightarrow run_1 & \{run_1 = true\} \\ run_1 \vee run_2 & \{run_1 = true\} \\ (rely \vee guar_1) \Rightarrow rely_2 & \{guar_1 = rely_2\} \\ (rely \vee guar_2) \Rightarrow rely_1 & \{guar_2 = rely_1\} \\ (guar_1 \vee guar_2) \Rightarrow guar & \{guar = true\} \end{array}$$

Further decomposition and verification is straightforward and therefore omitted here.

5 Soundness

In this section, we study the soundness of the proof system, but due to the limit of space here, we can only include the proof for the parallel rule in this paper, which is of course the most interesting one.

Proposition 9 *For a program P and a specification spec, P imp spec if and only if $T(P) \subseteq M(spec)$.*

Proof: from the fact that $T(P) \subseteq M(P)$ and $[M(spec)]^+ = M(spec)$.

Lemma 1 $\forall \sigma = s_0\delta_1 s_1, \ldots \delta_n s_n, \ldots \in T(P \parallel Q)$, *there exist* $\sigma^1 \in T(P)$ *and* $\sigma^2 \in T(Q)$, *such that they are of the following three cases* $a - c$

a. $\sigma^1 = s_0\delta_1^1 s_1 \ldots \delta_n^1 s_n \ldots$ *and* $\sigma^2 = s_0\delta_1^2 s_1 \ldots \delta_n^2 s_n \ldots$, *both of them are infinite.*
b. $\sigma^1 = s_0\delta_1^1 s_1 \ldots \delta_n^1 \widehat{s}_n$ *and* $\sigma^2 = s_0\delta_1^2 s_1 \ldots \delta_n^2 s_n \ldots$. *Here* σ^1 *is a terminating behavior, and* $v(\widehat{s}_n) = v(s_n)$, $status(\widehat{s}_n) =$ *'terminated'.*
c. $\sigma^1 = s_0\delta_1^1 s_1 \ldots \delta_n^1 s_n \ldots$, $\sigma^2 = s_0\delta_1^2 s_1 \ldots \delta_n^2 \widehat{s}_n$ *and* $v(\widehat{s}_n) = v(s_n)$, $status(\widehat{s}_n) =$ *'terminated'.*

and moreover, the following hold

1. $\forall 1 \leq i \leq min(len(\sigma^1), len(\sigma^2))$

- $\delta_i^1 = c$ *and* $\delta_i^2 = e \Rightarrow \delta_i = c$
- $\delta_i^1 = e$ *and* $\delta_i^2 = c \Rightarrow \delta_i = c$
- $\delta_i^1 = \delta_i^2 = c \Rightarrow \delta_i = c$ *and* $v(s_{i-1}) = v(s_i)$
- $\delta_i^1 = e$ *and* $\delta_i^2 = e \Rightarrow \delta_i = e$

2. $\forall\, min(len(\sigma^1), len(\sigma^2)) < i \leq max(len(\sigma^1), len(\sigma^2))$

- $\delta_i = \delta_i^k$, $k \in \{1, 2\}$ *stands for the longer behavior.*

We say that σ *is from* σ^1 *and* σ^2, *for the above* σ, σ^1 *and* σ^2.

Proof. direct from the transition rules.

Assume in the following,

$$spec = (pre,\ rely,\ run,\ guar,\ post_1 \wedge post_2)$$
$$spec_1 = (pre,\ rely_1,\ run \wedge run_1,\ guar_1,\ post_1)$$
$$spec_2 = (pre,\ rely_2,\ run \wedge run_2,\ guar_2,\ post_2)$$

and moreover

$$P\ \underline{imp}\ spec_1$$
$$Q\ \underline{imp}\ spec_2$$
$$(rely \vee guar_1) \Rightarrow rely_2$$
$$(rely \vee guar_2) \Rightarrow rely_1$$
$$(guar_1 \vee guar_2) \Rightarrow guar$$
$$(post_1 \Rightarrow run_2) \wedge (post_2 \Rightarrow run_1) \wedge (run_1 \vee run_2)$$

Lemma 2 *If $\sigma \in E(spec) \cap T(P \parallel Q)$ and it is from $\sigma^1 \in T(P)$ and $\sigma^2 \in T(Q)$, then each c-transition in σ^1 and σ^2 satisfies $guar_1$ or $guar_2$ respectively.*

Proof. If this is not the case, and assume that the first computation transition which does not satisfy the guarantee condition is from P at step k, thus $\neg guar_1(s_k, s_{k+1})$. The infinite behavior $\widehat{\sigma^1} = s_0\delta_1^1 s_1 \ldots \delta_k^1 s_{k+1} e s_{k+1} \ldots e s_{k+1} \ldots$ belongs to $T(P)$. From lemma 1, each e-transition before step k in this behavior corresponds to a c-transition in σ^2 or a e-transition in σ, therefore it satisfies $rely \vee guar_2$, due to the assumption that the first computation transition which violates the guarantee condition does not happen before k and $\sigma \in E(spec)$. Hence, $\widehat{\sigma^1} \in E(spec_1)$, and this contradicts the fact that $P\ \underline{imp}\ spec_1$, because one c-transition in $\widehat{\sigma^1}$ does not satisfy the guarantee condition.

Lemma 3 *If $\sigma \in E(spec) \cap T(P \parallel Q)$ and it is from $\sigma^1 \in T(P)$ and $\sigma^2 \in T(Q)$, then each e-transition in σ^1 and σ^2 satisfies $rely \vee guar_2$ or $rely \vee guar_1$ respectively.*

Proof. From lemma 1, 2.

Proposition 10 *If $\sigma \in E(spec) \cap T(P \parallel Q)$, then there are only a finite number of c-transition in σ.*

Proof. If this is not the case, that is, there are infinite number of c-transition in σ. From lemma 1, there exist $\sigma^1 \in T(P)$, $\sigma^2 \in T(Q)$ and at least one of them has infinite c-transition, suppose it is σ^1. From lemma 3, each e-transition in it satisfies $rely \vee guar_2$, thus $\sigma^1 \in E(spec_1)$, and this contradicts the fact that P $\underline{imp}$ $spec_1$, because there can only be a finite number of c-transition in σ^1.

Proposition 11 *If* $\sigma \in E(spec) \cap T(P \parallel Q)$ *and* $len(\sigma) < \infty$, *then* $status(last(\sigma))$ *'fail'.*

Proof. By a similar argument as in the proof of the above proposition.

Proposition 12 *If* $\sigma \in E(spec) \cap T(P \parallel Q)$ *and* $len(\sigma) < \infty$, *then* $status(last(\sigma))$ *'blocked'.*

Proof. If this is not the case, that is, the *status* of the final state of σ is '*blocked*' even the environment has established *run* on it. There are two possibilities, either one of P or Q has terminated, or both are blocked. We only prove the case that one of the process has terminated, the other case is more straightforward. Suppose Q has terminated and $len(\sigma) = n$, and assume $\sigma = s_0\delta_1 s_1, \ldots \delta_n s_n$. From lemma 1, there exist $\sigma^1 = s_0\delta_1^1 s_1 \ldots \delta_k^1 s_k \ldots \delta_n^1 s_n \in T(P)$ and $\sigma^2 = s_0\delta_1^2 s_1 \ldots \delta_k^2 \widehat{s}_k \in T(Q)$. From the transition rules, it is easy to see that $\sigma^2 = s_0\delta_1^2 s_1 \ldots e s_k \ldots e s_{n-1} c \widehat{s}_n \in T(Q)$, with $v(\widehat{s}_n) = v(s_n)$. Because Q $\underline{imp}$ $spec_2$, we have $post_2(v(s_n)) = post_2(v(\widehat{s}_n)) = true$, hence $run_1(v(s_n))$ holds. From the assumption, $(run_1 \wedge run)(v(s_n))$ holds, and by P $\underline{imp}$ $spec_1$, we conclude that σ should not be blocked at the final state, this contradicts the assumption.

Proposition 13 *If* $\sigma \in E(spec) \cap T(P \parallel Q)$ *and* $status(last(\sigma)) =$ *'terminated' then* $post_1(last(\sigma)) \wedge post_2(last(\sigma))$.

Proof. Similar to the reasoning above.

From these lemmas and propositions, it is easy to get $E(spec) \cap T(P \parallel Q) \subseteq N(spec)$, and this completes the proof of the soundness of the parallel rule.

6 Discussion

In this paper, we have only considered one situation that a program may fail, namely, when the *await*-body is looping forever. There are, of course, many other possibilities that may lead to a failure, for example, division by zero or using uninitialized variables. It is easy to include these cases, just by adding the appropriate transition rules in the operational semantics, but we prefer to keep this paper as simple as possible to illustrate the main points.

The completeness of a proof system is usually more difficult to establish than the soundness. We have high hope the proof system presented in this paper is complete in the sense of Cook, and following [Ap84] and [AP86], we expect a second order language can be shown to be expressive enough.

Over the last fifteen years, a large amount of research has been done on formal methods of parallel programming, although their relationship has not always been very well studied, nor have them been combined very often. It is our belief that various results can often be put together, in searching for a solution to one particular problem. We are concerned here with developing totally correct state-based parallel programs, and the current research by which the work in this paper has been influenced and is most related to is done by Abadi and Lamport [AL89], and by Stølen [St90].

Abadi and Lamport's work is purely semantic, although the principal concern is the same. The parallel rule here corresponds to their main theorem of composing specifications, but due to the slight different views about the observable behavior, they are not exactly the same.

While the proof system is only part of our theory, Stølen's methodology centres on it. Apart from some obvious difference in certain features, for example, the different interpretation of the third component in the specification and the different use of the auxiliary variables, there is a more subtle difference in the interpretation of the *guarantee*-condition. We have required the *guarantee*-condition to be both reflexive and transitive, while Stølen does not insist that the *guarantee*-condition to be transitive. By doing so, some of his proof rules become a little simpler, but we would prefer to pay this price in the proof system for a specification oriented semantics.

For any two programs, P and Q, the specification oriented semantics requires that for any specification *spec*

$$\textit{If } P \underline{\textit{imp}}\ Q \textit{ and } Q \underline{\textit{imp}}\ \textit{spec}, \textit{ then } P \underline{\textit{imp}}\ \textit{spec}$$

Assume P is the program $x := x + 7$ and Q is the program $x := x + 3; x := x + 4$, then obviously P is more deterministic than Q, because it interferes less, and has less chance to be interfered by. We can indeed show that P is an implementation of Q by calculating the semantics of P and Q, but a more effective way is to use the algebraic reasoning, actually this fact is a special case of one algebraic law in [XH90]. However, without the transitivity of the *guarantee*-condition there are apparently specifications which are satisfied by Q but not P, therefore failing to satisfy the requirement of a specification oriented semantics.

Acknowledgement We are grateful to Ketil Stølen for pointing out a number of mistakes in an early working paper and in the workshop version of this paper, and Cliff Jones for his advice on the state of the art of research in this field. We are also indebted to referees for their comments. For the financial support, the first author would like to thank Sino-British Friendship Scholarship Scheme, and the second author would like to thank the Science and Engineering Research Council of Great Britain and Esprit Basic Research Actions CONCUR and PROCOS.

References

[AL88] M. Abadi and L. Lamport. The existence of refinement mappings. Research report 29, Digital System Research Center 1988.

[AL89] M. Abadi and L. Lamport. Composing specifications Research report, Digital System Research Center 1989.

[Ap84] K.R. Apt. Ten years of Hoare's logic: a survey-part II: nondeterminism. *Theoretical Computer Science* 28 83-109 1984.

[AP86] K.R. Apt and G.D. Plotkin. countable nondeterminism and random assignment. *Journal of the ACM 33* 4 724-767 1986.

[AS85] B. Alpern and F. Schneider. Defining liveness. *Info. Proc. Lett. 21* 181-185.

[Bk88] R.J.R. Back. A calculus of refinement for program derivations. *Acta Informatica 25* 593-624, Springer-Verlag 1988.

[CC89] P. Cousot and R. Cousot. A language independent proof of the soundness and completeness of generalized Hoare logic. *Inform. and Comput. 80* 165-191 1989.

[dR85] W.P. de Roever. The guest for compositionality. in *Proc:IFIP Working Conf. The Role of Abstract Models in Computer Science* North-Holland, 1985.

[GR89] D. Grosvenor and A. Robinson. An evaluation of Rely-Guarantee. draft 1989.

[He84] E.C.R. Hehner. Predicative programming parts 1 and 2. *Commun. ACM 27,* 2 134-151 1984.

[He90] He, Jifeng. A simulation approach to verification of compiling specification of ProCoS level 0 programming language. ESPRIT 3104 ProCoS 1990.

[Hoare et al 87] C.A.R. Hoare et al. Laws of programming. *Commun. ACM 30,* 8 672-686 1987.

[Jo81] C.B. Jones. Development methods for computer programs including a notion of interference. DPhil. Thesis, Oxford University Computing Laboratory, 1981.

[Jo83] C.B. Jones. Tentative steps towards a development method for interfering programs. ACM Trans. Program. Lang. Syst. 5, 4, 596-619 1983.

[Ke76] R.M. Keller. Formal verification of parallel programs. *Commun. ACM 19* 371-384 1976.

[La77] L. Lamport. Proving the correctness of multiprocess programs. *IEEE Trans. on Software Engineering 1* 1977.

[La80] L. Lamport. The Hoare logic of concurrent programming. *Acta Inform. 14* 21-37 1980.

[MRG88] C. Morgan, P.H.B. Gardiner and K. Robinson. *On the Refinement Calculus.* Oxford University Computing Laboratory, Technical Monograph PRG-70, 1988.

[OG76] S. Owicki and D. Gries. An axiomatic proof technique for parallel programs. *Acta Inform. 6* 319-340 Springer-Verlag 1976.

[OH86] E.-R. Olderog and C.A.R. Hoare. Specification-oriented semantics for communicating processes. *Acta Informatica 23* 9-66 Springer-Verlag 1986.

[Ow76] S. Owicki. A consistent and complete deductive system for the verification of parallel programs. *Proceedings of 8th Annual ACM Symposium on Theory of Computing.* Hershey, Pennsylvania, USA 1976.

[Pl81] G.D. Plotkin. A structural approach to operational semantics. Computer Science Department, Aarhus University, Technical Report, DAIMI FN-19,1981.

[SA] F.B. Schneider and G.R. Andrews. Concepts for Concurrent Programming. LNCS, Springer-Verlag

[St88] C. Stirling. A generalization of Owicki-Gries's Hoare logic for a concurrent while language. *Theoretical Computer Science* 58 347-359 1988.

[St90] K. Stølen. *Development of Parallel Programs on Shared Datastructures.* Ph.D Thesis, Computer Science Department, Manchester University, 1990.

[WD88] J.C.P. Woodcock and B. Dickinson. Using VDM with Rely and Guarantee-conditions, experiences from a real project. 2nd VDM-Europe Symposium, Dublin, Ireland, LNCS 328, Springer-Verlag, 1988.

[XH90] Xu Qiwen and He Jifeng. Towards a theory of interfering programs. Draft, Oxford University Computing Laboratory, 1990.

[Zw89] J. Zwiers. *Compositionality, Concurrency and Partial Correctness.* LNCS 321 1989.

Design, verification and documentation of concurrent systems

E. Pascal Gribomont
Philips Research Laboratory
avenue Albert Einstein, 4
B - 1348 Louvain-la-Neuve (Belgium)

Abstract. The concept of invariant is the basis of most formal methods for the design and verification of concurrent systems. It can be noticed that invariants can also be used to give clear and concise *descriptions* of correct programs. As invariants are concerned only with the safety properties of systems, other formal objects have to be used to deal with liveness properties. Unfortunately, the formal objects generally used for liveness properties are somewhat inadequate, especially from the documentation point of view. A new family of formal objects, called *proof graphs*, is introduced. These graphs can be designed together with the corresponding program by stepwise refinement. They turn to be useful for specification, verification and documentation, but only the last point is emphasized in this paper and illustrated by an elementary example.

1 Introduction

Formal tools exist for specifying software, and also for verifying that a program is correct with respect to some specification. Methods have been developed to use these tools and, in principle, programming can be viewed as a mathematical activity. In practice however, very few programs are specified, designed and verified in a formal way; in fact, the mathematical nature of programming is often ignored, probably because a mathematical task is a difficult task.

Many partial solutions have been proposed to this problem, for instance, semi-formal programming methods, or computer-aided programming methods, or semi-automatic program and theorem provers, and so on. Although useful, these partial solutions often fail to bridge the gap between the amount of mathematics needed to formally specify, develop and verify programs, on the one hand, and the mathematical effort a program designer or user is prepared to do within his/her activity, on the other hand. It is therefore interesting to investigate whether formal methods and tools can be used at lower cost.

One can observe that *reading* a (well-written) paper about the formal development of a program is by far easier than *writing* such a paper. This suggests an application: formal documentation should be accepted by program users instead of informal comments, even by those who do not rely on formal methods to design and verify their own programs. This works well in the area of (structured)

This work was partly funded by the Commission of the European Community under the ESPRIT project ICARUS.

sequential programming. It is no longer unrealistic, in the industrial framework, that program designers annotate each loop with an invariant of it, and that program users view invariants as an adequate documentation for programs. (The Esprit project Advanced Techniques for Efficient scientific Software [ATES] has developed this approach.) An invariant can be supplemented with a *terminating expression*, that is, an expression that takes its values in a well-founded set and decreases every time the body of the loop is executed; this provides a termination argument.

This partial success of formal tools is not surprising: the language used to write invariants is more elementary than the languages used to write programs. Furthermore, invariants are often the most efficient way to give insight in algorithms. For instance, let us consider the assertions[1]

$$\text{perm}(A[1:i-1], A_0[1:i-1]) \wedge \text{ordered}(A[1:i-1]) \wedge A[i:n] = A_0[i:n]\,, \quad (1)$$

$$A[1:i-1] = A_1[1:i-1] \wedge \text{perm}(A[i:n], A_1[i:n])\,, \quad (2)$$

where $A[1:n]$ is a linear array ($n > 0$), $A_0[1:n]$ denotes the initial value of A and $A_1[1:n]$ denotes the sorted version of A_0. Assertions (1) and (2), with $1 \leq i \leq n+1$, clearly suggest two distinct iterative ways for sorting a linear array.

Comment. A linear array $A[D]$ is modelled by a function whose domain D is a finite subset of the set $\mathbf{Z}$. The domain D is written as a union of a finite set of non-overlapping intervals. For instance, $D = 1:j-1, j+1:i$ is the set $\{1,\ldots,j-1,j+1,\ldots,i\}$. If $a > b$, then $a:b$ is the empty set; so D reduces to $1:j-1$ if $i \leq j$, and to $j+1:i$ if $j \leq 1$. If a linear array $A[D]$ is defined, subarrays and elements can be noted $A[D']$ and $A[d]$, respectively, where $D' \subset D$ and $d \in D$.
The formula "ordered($A[D]$)" means that $A[d_1] \leq A[d_2]$ for all $d_1, d_2 \in D$ such that $d_1 \leq d_2$. (It is supposed here that the codomain of the function modelling A is an ordered set. The formula reduces to true when D contains 0 or 1 element.)
The formula "perm($A_1[D_1], A_2[D_2]$)" means that a bijection $f: D_1 \rightarrow D_2$ exists such that $A_2[f(d)] = A_1[d]$, for all $d \in D_1$.

Although the need of rigorous documentation is even more critical for concurrent systems, the situation there is less satisfactory. In particular, invariants are not widely accepted as an adequate documentation tool for describing concurrent systems, and many graphical or lexical languages, more or less formal, are used instead. In our opinion, the reasons of this situation is that, in the concurrent framework, invariants do no longer enjoy all the properties accounting for their success in the sequential framework. Section 2 is devoted to the determination of some desirable properties of formal documentation tools, both in sequential and concurrent programming. In the current state of the art, the invariant is still the best tool for dealing with concurrent programs, but it has to be supplemented with specific tools for liveness properties. These tools are briefly reviewed in Section 3,

[1] If a program P is given, an assertion is a formula interpreted on the set Γ_P of program states. An assertion may be viewed as a subset of Γ_P, containing the states for which the assertion is true. In this paper, assertions do not contain temporal operators.

and illustrated in Section 4, with an abstract version of Stenning's data transfer protocol. In Section 5, we introduce proof graphs, as an attempt to gain more of the desirable properties mentioned in Section 2. These objects appear useful to formally document a concurrent system, and also to summarize its development. Some properties of proof graphs are investigated and their use as documentation tool is illustrated with Stenning's protocol.

2 Desirable properties of a documentation object

Our purpose is to determine how by-products of formal proofs can be used to document concurrent systems. A starting point is the situation in structured sequential programming. Annotating each loop with an invariant (and a terminating expression) is a satisfactory way to document sequential programs. Let us try to identify why this is adequate, and then how that can be adapted to concurrent programming. The case of a classical sorting algorithm is considered as an example.

```
i := 1;
{ 1 ≤ i ≤ n+1 ∧ ordered(A[1 : i−1]) ∧
  perm(A[1 : i−1], A0[1 : i−1]) ∧ A[i : n] = A0[i : n] }
while i ≤ n do
    x := A[i];
    j := i;
    { 1 ≤ j ≤ i ≤ n ∧ ordered(A[1 : j−1, j+1 : i]) ∧
      x = A0[i] ∧ ∀k (j ≤ k < i ⇒ x ≤ A[k]) ∧
      perm(A[1 : j−1, j+1 : i], A0[1 : i−1]) ∧ A[i+1 : n] = A0[i+1 : n] }
    while j > 1 ∧ A[j−1] > x do
        A[j] := A[j−1];
        j := j−1
    end;
    A[j] := x;
    i := i+1
end.
```

Let us name I the invariant of the external loop and J the invariant of the internal loop.

Some interesting properties of such an annotation are listed below.

1. Invariants capture the "*algorithmic contents*" of the program. This notion is hardly amenable to a formal definition but, as already mentioned, sorting tactics are best summarized by invariants; this phenomenon is not restricted to sorting, but seems to hold for all problems.

2. The *specification* can be abstracted from the invariants: in the example, the input predicate is $wp[i := 1; I[i/1]]$, that reduces to $A[1:n] = A_0[1:n]$. The output predicate is $I[i/n+1] \wedge i > n$, reducing to
$$i = n+1 \wedge \text{ordered}(A[1:n]) \wedge \text{perm}(A[1:n], A_0[1:n]).$$

3. A *full proof* (full annotation) can be deduced from the invariants in a systematic way, in Floyd's or Hoare's style, using classical programming calculus. The validation of an invariant relies only on classical logic (without temporal operators).

4. A property which is important for large programs is that the annotation system is *modular*. At an abstract level, only the invariant of the external loop might be known. This invariant is clearly a cornerstone in the development of the program. It is a proof of the external loop, and also the basis of the specification of the internal one. A trade-off is possible between conciseness and preciseness.
Comment. Let P be the program
$$\text{while } B \text{ do } [S_1; (\text{while } B' \text{ do } S'); S_2]\,.$$
If I is the invariant of the external loop, then the internal loop is specified by the triple
$$\{sp[(I \wedge B); S_1]\}\ (\text{while } B' \text{ do } S')\ \{wp[S_2; I]\}\,.$$

In our opinion, a formal documentation technique for parallel systems should enjoy these four properties. The sequel of this paper is devoted to see that some adaptation of existing tools is needed to obtain a satisfactory documentation technique.
Comments. In this summary, termination has not be considered, but it will be in the concurrent framework.
In *structured* sequential programming, points 1 and 4 are strongly related, for modules correspond to syntactic components. However, this is usually no longer true in concurrent programming.

3 The concurrent framework: state of the art

There is a wide consensus about using invariants for the formal design and verification of concurrent systems, as far as safety properties are considered. The situation with liveness properties is a bit less clear but most formal liveness proofs can be viewed as proving the validity of some formula in temporal logic. It has been proposed to use graphs to represent such proofs [5,9,7,1].

In this section we will show that, unfortunately, neither invariants nor graphical proofs enjoy all the properties 1, 2, 3 and 4 listed in Section 2.

3.1 Invariant and safety properties

In the concurrency framework, invariants can be represented in two ways. The first way is used when control is left implicit, as in the early work of Owicki and

Gries [8]. A concurrent system is viewed as a set of processes, each of them being annotated by inductive assertions, just as for sequential programs. However, two (interconnected) problems arise. First, the annotation of some process evokes the variables of the other processes (and even auxiliary variables introduced in that purpose) and, second, full annotation is needed; giving loop invariants is not sufficient.

The second way is used when control is made explicit; statements are labelled and place predicates are used. In this case, the invariant appears as a big logical formula, interpreted as a relation between the values of the variables and place predicates of the whole system; this relation is respected by every statement of the program. Once again, the invariant appears here to correspond to the full annotation in the sequential case. Its size is likely to be of the same order as the size of the whole system (and far bigger if the notation has not been carefully chosen).

In both cases, the main problem is the absence of an intermediate level between the formal specification and the formal proof: when concurrency is involved, invariants do no longer enjoy property 4. Properties 2 and 3 are still satisfied, but property 1 is only partially preserved. An invariant still retains the "algorithmic contents" of a concurrent system, but this contents is lost in a lot of technical details about interference between processes.

3.2 Liveness properties, graphical specification and proof

The notion of *proof lattice* (or lattice proof) has proven useful to deal with liveness properties of concurrent programs. It was first suggested in [5] and then formally defined in a more general way in [9]; the elementary version is sufficient for now. A proof lattice is a directed acyclic graph; there is a single entry node and a single exit node and each node is labelled by an assertion. A proof lattice represents a set of temporal formulas. More precisely, a node labelled R whose outgoing edges ends to nodes labelled $R_1, \ldots, R_k$ models the formula $R \mapsto (R_1 \vee \cdots \vee R_k)$.
Comment. Recall that the formula $A \mapsto B$, read "A leads to B", means "if A is true, then B becomes true sooner or later". More formally, a state σ_i satisfying A may occur in a computation $(\sigma_n : n \in \mathbf{N})$ only if there exists $j \geq i$ such that the state σ_j satisfies B.

As documentation tools, proof lattices are attractive for mainly two reasons. First, they model an operator that has both a useful informal meaning and a clear formal semantics; most liveness properties are modelled with the operator *leads-to*. Second, contrary to the invariants, they can be given in several versions, the most condensed corresponding to mere specifications and the most detailed corresponding to a description of the behaviour of the system.

The procedure to get a more abstract proof lattice by suppression of a node N (neither the entry nor the exit node) is elementary: first direct a new arc from the origin of every ingoing arc of N to the extremity of every outgoing arc of N, and afterwards suppress the node N and all arcs connected with N. (If several arcs sharing the same origin and the same extremity exist, then only one of them is maintained.) If the suppression procedure is repeated, the proof lattice reduces to a single arc from the entry node to the exit node, and models the liveness property $(A \mapsto B)$, where A and B respectively label the entry node and the exit node.

Proof lattices may satisfy property 1 and also property 2, for the liveness part of the specification. Unfortunately, there is a problem with property 3: proof lattices usually cannot be verified in a systematic way, even for most detailed versions. The validation of a proof lattice involves additional temporal reasoning and, most of the time, the knowledge of an adequate invariant of the system is also a prerequisite. (See also the comment at the end of Section 4.2.)

The main weakness of proof lattices can be overcome if *proof diagrams* (or diagram proofs) are used instead. Roughly speaking, a proof diagram is like a proof lattice, except that it models the operator *next* instead of the operator *leads-to*. A proof diagram is also acyclic, except that self-loops are allowed.

The formula $(A \Rightarrow \bigcirc B)$, read "if A then next B", means that if formula A is true at some state of some computation, then formula B is true at the next state of this computation. The proof diagram is interpreted as follows. A node labelled by the assertion R whose outgoing edges end to nodes labelled by the assertions $R_1, \ldots, R_k$ models the formula $R \Rightarrow \bigcirc(R_1 \vee \cdots \vee R_k)$. Arcs can be labeled with the name of the process responsible for the move. (This definition slightly departs from the original one, given in [7].)

Proof diagrams can be verified in a mechanical way (as usual in this framework, the valid formulas of classical logic are assumed to be recognized). However, gaining this definite advantage also means losing another one: the node suppression procedure is no longer valid. As a result, proof diagrams enjoy property 3 and also property 2; just as for invariants, property 1 is doubtful, for a proof diagram is a low-level view on an algorithm. Last, property 4 is not satisfied.

There is a great difference between concurrent programming and sequential programming with respect to liveness properties. Indeed, most of the time, the only interesting liveness property of a sequential program is termination. This is no longer true for concurrent systems, which are frequently not intended to terminate. This justifies the use of more complicated objects to specify liveness properties when concurrency is involved. Nevertheless, invariants retain a prominent role in formal design methods.

4 An example: Stenning's protocol

An example is needed to illustrate the formal objects recalled above, and their use as documentation tools. A very abstract version of a data transfer protocol is presented here. As in the language UNITY [1], a concurrent system is viewed as a set of statements. At this abstract level, processes and control flow are not modelled.

4.1 The program and the invariant

The purpose of Stenning's protocol [10] is to transmit a sequence $(X[n] : n \in \mathbf{N})$ of messages. This sequence must be faithfully recorded in $(Y[n] : n \in \mathbf{N})$, in spite of faulty transmission channels; these channels may loose, corrupt and duplicate messages. Corrupted messages are discarded by the receiver, and adequate messages are acknowledged (via a faulty channel).

The set of statements of the abstract version $\mathcal{S}_1$ of Stenning's protocol is:

$$\begin{aligned}
\mathcal{T}_1 = \{&1.\ (HS - LA < W \longrightarrow (HS, Y[HS+1]) := (HS+1, X[HS+1])),\\
&2.\ (HS - LA < W \longrightarrow HS := HS+1),\\
&3.\ (LA < r \leq HS \longrightarrow (Y[r], r) := (X[r], r+1)),\\
&4.\ (LA < r \leq HS \longrightarrow r := r+1),\\
&5.\ (\neg(LA < r \leq HS) \longrightarrow r := LA+1),\\
&6.\ (Y[LR+1] \neq NIL \longrightarrow (LA, LR) := (LR+1, LR+1)),\\
&7.\ (Y[LR+1] \neq NIL \longrightarrow LR := LR+1),\\
&8.\ (Y[LR+1] = NIL \longrightarrow LA := LR),\\
&9.\ (Y[LR+1] = NIL \longrightarrow skip)\}.
\end{aligned}$$

The invariant is

$$\begin{aligned}
I_1 \equiv\ & (LA \leq LR \leq HS \leq LA + W)\ \wedge\\
& \forall s (Y[s] \in \{X[s], NIL\})\ \wedge\\
& \forall s (0 \leq s \leq LR \Rightarrow Y[s] = X[s])\ \wedge\\
& \forall s (HS < s \Rightarrow Y[s] = NIL),
\end{aligned}$$

Messages from $X[0]$ to $X[LA]$ (for Last Acknowledged) have been successfully acknowledged. Messages from $X[0]$ to $X[LR]$ (for Last Received) have been successfully received, but maybe not successfully acknowledged. Messages from $X[0]$ to $X[HS]$ (for Highest Sent) have been sent at least once (but maybe not received). Initially, the common value of the counters LA, LR and HS is -1, and the common value of the $Y[i]$ is NIL. (This value is used both to denote an empty and a corrupted contents.)

In this abstract version, the invariant is a good documentation tool, which summarizes the algorithmic contents. Transitions 1 and 2 correspond to first message transmission. Transitions 3, 4 and 5 implement retransmission of messages lying in the "window"; these messages have not been acknowledged, so maybe they have been lost. The maximal size of the window is a fixed constant $W > 0$. (The case $W = 1$ corresponds to the "Alternate Bit Protocol".) Transitions 6 and 7 correspond to message reception and first acknowledgment, and transitions 8 and 9 implement acknowledgment retransmission.

4.2 Proof lattices

The third line of the invariant I_1 expresses the partial correctness of the system: messages up to index LR have been correctly received. However, nothing guarantees that LR will grow forever, and that will be the required liveness property. It can be expressed as follows:

$$LR = n \mapsto LR > n\,.$$

This corresponds to the abstract proof lattice given in Figure 1.

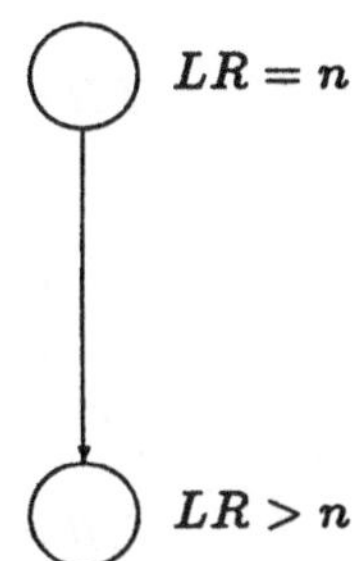

Figure 1: Abstract proof lattice for S_1

This abstract proof lattice is nothing but a graphical version of the specification. A more detailed proof lattice could be obtained by identifying the main steps of the progress from $LR = n$ to $LR > n$. Such a stepping stone can clearly be modelled by the formula $LR = n \wedge Y[LR+1] \neq NIL$. The corresponding proof lattice is given in Figure 2.

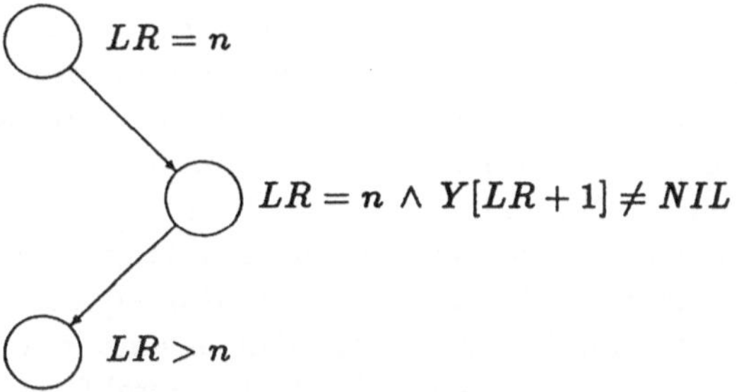

Figure 2: Less abstract proof lattice for S_1

A first problem occurs here: the more abstract proof lattice is a natural step towards the discovery of the less abstract proof lattice, but the former can be validated only after validation of the latter. As a result, a whole sequence of proof lattices have to be found before the beginning of the validation procedure. A single bad choice renders useless all the subsequent lattices (which are the most detailed ones), and such a bad choice cannot be identified just after its production. Furthermore, the validation of even a detailed proof lattice is not an easy matter. (This validation is subject to fairness hypotheses and will not be presented here.)

A second problem happens if we attempt to refine the second proof lattice. The system S_1 may switch from $LR = n$ to $LR = n \wedge Y[LR+1] \neq NIL$ in two ways. Indeed, $Y[LR+1]$ can be assigned (to its correct value $X[LR+1]$) either by transition 1, or by transition 3. This suggests the tentative proof lattice represented in Figure 3.

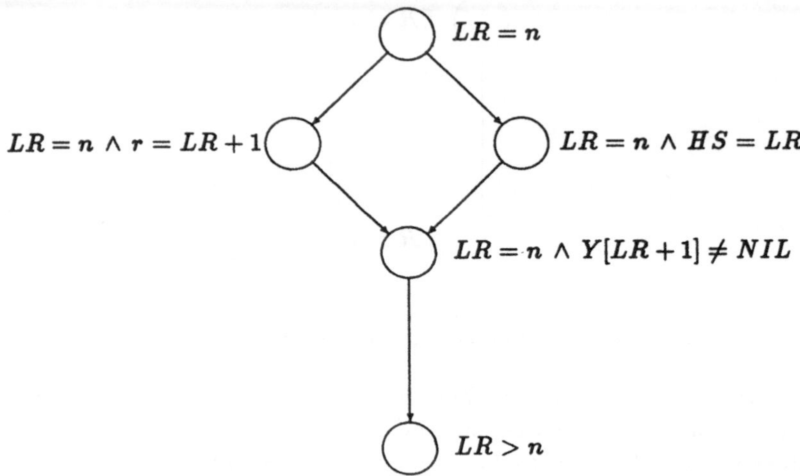

Figure 3: A tentative proof lattice for S_1

Unfortunately, this proof lattice is misleading. When $r = LR + 1$, it is not guaranteed that transition 3 will be executed; transition 4 could be executed instead. A similar unpleasant phenomenon occurs when $HS = LR$; transition 2 could be executed instead of transition 1. In both cases, the "progress" due to reaching a state where $Y[LR+1]$ *can* be assigned simply vanishes.

Comment. This failure does not mean that proof lattices are not fully adequate for proving concurrent systems, but that designing such proofs is rather difficult. The generalized proof lattices introduced in [9] allow to write rather concise proofs of liveness properties, but at the cost of simplicity. Indeed, the nodes of a (generalized) proof lattice are labelled by temporal formulas instead of assertions; besides, reasoning by contradiction is involved. As a result, proof lattices do no longer convey much insight into the concurrent systems whose properties they establish; they are a proof tool and not a documentation tool.

4.3 Proof diagrams

The situation is even worse for proof diagrams. As arrows in such diagrams always correspond to a single move, an unlimited number of nodes may be needed. If for instance the transmission of message $X[LR+1]$ fails, the whole window of messages can be tentatively retransmitted before $X[LR+1]$ gets a new opportunity to be transmitted. As a result, a proof diagram for system S_1 is bound to contain at least W nodes. This prevents us to draw such a diagram, since the value of W is an arbitrary positive integer. Proof diagrams seem to be limited to strict finite-state systems. Nevertheless, proof diagrams are better than proof lattices in the sense that they can be verified easily and, for small finite-state systems, they lead to clear and elegant proofs (see [7] for examples). Besides, as far as only verification is concerned, large proof diagrams can be generated and checked by computer in a rather systematic way; in some cases, concurrent systems involving integer-valued parameters remain accessible with finite-state methods. The first conclusion is that proof diagrams are worth further investigation, and we will consider again Stenning's protocol, in the special case $W = 1$, in order to avoid the problem mentioned above.

Let us call $\mathcal{S}_0$ this restricted version of system $\mathcal{S}_1$. The set of statements is

$$\begin{aligned}
\mathcal{T}_0 = \{ & 1: (LA = HS \longrightarrow (HS, Y[HS+1]) := (HS+1, X[HS+1])), \\
& 2: (LA = HS \longrightarrow HS := HS+1), \\
& 3: (LA < HS \longrightarrow Y[HS] := X[HS]), \\
& 4: (LA < HS \longrightarrow skip), \\
& 5: (Y[LR+1] \neq NIL \longrightarrow (LA, LR) := (LR+1, LR+1)), \\
& 6: (Y[LR+1] \neq NIL \longrightarrow LR := LR+1), \\
& 7: (Y[LR+1] = NIL \longrightarrow LA := LR), \\
& 8: (Y[LR+1] = NIL \longrightarrow skip)\}.
\end{aligned}$$

The invariant I_0 is simply $I_1[W/1]$; it can be rewritten as

$$\begin{aligned}
I_0 \equiv\ & (LA \leq LR \leq HS \leq LA+1) \ \wedge \\
& (Y[HS] = X[HS] \vee Y[HS] = NIL) \ \wedge \\
& \forall s\,(0 \leq s \leq LR \Rightarrow Y[s] = X[s]) \ \wedge \\
& \forall s\,(HS < s \Rightarrow Y[s] = NIL),
\end{aligned}$$

A proof diagram is given in Figure 4 (left part). Notice that arrows are labelled by statements and not by processes (there is no process at this abstract level).

The formulas attached to the nodes are:

$$\begin{aligned}
a_n: &\ LA = LR = HS = n, \\
b_n: &\ LA = LR = n \wedge HS = n+1 \wedge Y[HS] = X[HS], \\
c_n: &\ LA = LR = n \wedge HS = n+1 \wedge Y[HS] = NIL, \\
d_n: &\ LA = n \wedge LR = HS = n+1.
\end{aligned}$$

This proof diagram has two qualities: its verification is simple, and its intuitive meaning is clear. However, one can guess that, even for medium-sized finite-state systems, the size of proof diagrams might be huge.

The size problem can sometimes be overcome by a more careful choice of the formulas labelling nodes. Another, more condensed proof diagram is given in Figure 4 (right part). The formulas attached to the nodes are:

$$\begin{aligned}
A_n: &\ LA + LR + HS = n \wedge Y[LR+1] = NIL, \\
B_n: &\ LA + LR + HS > n, \\
C_n: &\ LA + LR + HS = n \wedge Y[LR+1] = X[LR+1].
\end{aligned}$$

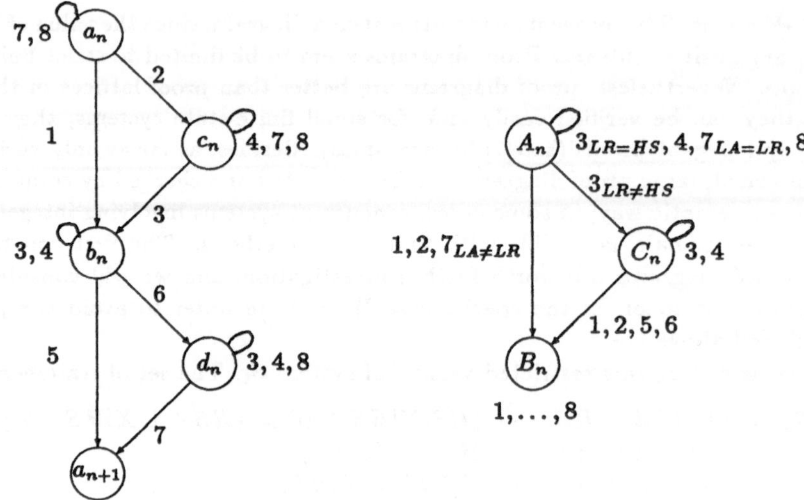

Figure 4: Proof diagrams for system S_0

The idea here is to take into account the invariant. Due to the first line of I_0, the following statements are equivalent:

- all counters LA, LR and HS increase forever;
- at least one of the counters LA, LR and HS increases forever;
- the sum of the counters LA, LR and HS increases forever.

The last formula happens to be "more economical" than the first one, so the second proof diagram is smaller than the first one. However, no formal connection exists between these diagrams.
It was convenient to allow "case-splitting": for instance, transition 7 induces a move when $LA \neq LR$, and no move when $LA = LR$. For this reason, transition 7 gave rise to two *conditional transitions*, respectively noted $7_{LA=LR}$ and $7_{LA \neq LR}$.

The main problem with proof diagrams is that there is no general procedure for reducing their size with preserving (the relevant part of) their semantics, even if impressive reduction can be obtained in some cases [6].

4.4 Some conclusions

The small experiments presented in this section indicate first that invariants remain mandatory both for the verification procedure and for the documentation. For instance, Stenning's "window technique" is adequately summarized into the first line ($LA \leq LR \leq HS \leq LA + W$) of the invariant. Furthermore, the main specification, that is, the partial correctness of the algorithm, is formalized into the third line $\forall s\,(0 \leq s \leq LR \Rightarrow Y[s] = X[s])$. Another point is that the invariant is needed to validate proof lattices, and also most proof diagrams.

As far as only safety properties are concerned, the drawbacks of the invariants in the concurrent framework can be overcome. In particular, it is possible to produce "abstract" versions of invariants, where technicalities about synchronization and interference between processes do not appear [3].

For the liveness properties, it is clear that neither proof lattices nor proof diagrams are fully adequate *documentation* tools, but they seem to be complementary. On the one hand, proof lattices correspond to a high-level temporal operator, therefore allowing the representation of high-level specifications and abstract properties. On the other hand, proof diagrams are based on a low-level temporal operator, therefore allowing the representation of detailed and easily verifiable proofs. This suggests to look for a "hybrid" kind of graph, that would retain the qualities of both lattices and diagrams.

5 Proof graphs

5.1 Towards a definition

The problem of combining proof lattices and proof diagrams becomes simpler if we get back to their temporal interpretation. Proof lattices are associated with the operator "leads-to", and proof diagrams are associated with the operator "next".

This suggests to look for an operator that can be expressed in terms of "next" (to retain property 3, that is, the possibility of systematic validation), and in terms of which "leads-to" can be expressed (in order to preserve properties 1 and 2).
Comment. Property 4 can be investigated only by considering several steps in the development of a program. This will be done in the Section 5.3.

An appropriate candidate is the operator *until*, denoted $\mathcal{U}$. The formula $(A\,\mathcal{U} B)$ means that, in every execution, A remains true until B becomes true; in the "weak" version of until, also called *unless*, B is allowed to remain false forever, provided that A remains true forever.

The formula $(A\;\mathcal{U}\;B)$ (*weak* sense) is valid when the formula $(A \Rightarrow \bigcirc(A \vee B))$ is valid, so the first condition is satisfied. Besides, the operator *leads-to* can be recursively defined from the operator *until* (*strong* sense). The binary relation $(A \mapsto B)$ is the smallest relation which is closed for the inference rules listed below. (The proof is omitted here.)

- $\dfrac{(P\;\mathcal{U}\;Q)}{(P \mapsto Q)}$

- $\dfrac{(P \mapsto R)\,,\;\;(R \mapsto Q)}{(P \mapsto Q)}$

- $\dfrac{(P_m \mapsto Q) \text{ for all } m \in W\,,\;\;(P \Rightarrow \bigvee_{m \in W} P_m)}{(P \mapsto Q)}$

A tentative definition can now be stated. A *proof graph* about a concurrent system S is a connected directed graph, with a single entry node and a single exit node; the nodes are labelled with assertions. Every node but the exit node is interpreted as a temporal formula. More precisely, a node labelled R whose outgoing edges end to nodes labelled $R_1, \ldots, R_k$ models the formula

$$R\,\mathcal{U}\,(R_1 \vee \cdots \vee R_k)\,.$$

(The question whether the operator is used in the weak or in the strong sense is left open for now.)

Until now, this is rather similar to proof lattices and proof diagrams, except that the temporal operator *until* is used instead of *leads-to* or *next*.

In proof diagrams the information was attached not only with nodes but also with arrows; each arrow was labelled with the transition(s) responsible for the corresponding move. This is especially useful, so the same convention will be adopted for proof graphs. Besides, from the documentation point of view, the more complete the proof graph the better, so it is indicated to require that, for each transition τ and for each node N but the exit node, there is an outgoing arrow labelled with τ, except if τ cannot be executed from a state satisfying N.

Every arrow α is interpreted as the Hoare triple

$$\{R\}\,\mathcal{T}\,\{S\}\,, \tag{3}$$

where R and S label respectively the origin and the extremity of α, and where the set $\mathcal{T}$ of conditional transitions labels α itself. The triple (3) means that if a (conditional) transition $\tau_c \in \mathcal{T}$ is executed in a state satisfying R, then the resulting state satisfies S (see [4] for a formal definition).

Proof lattices are acyclic, and so are proof diagrams, except that self-loops are allowed. From the documentation point of view, however, we would like to drop this requirement. Indeed, the intended first role of proof graph is a documentation role, and if a concurrent system may exhibit repetition behaviour (which is frequent), that should be visible in the proof graph.

A proof graph is *valid* when the temporal formulas associated with the nodes and the Hoare triples associated with the arrows are valid. Two results about proof graphs can now be given.

Theorem 1 *The validity of the Hoare triples associated with the arrows implies the validity of the temporal formulas associated with the nodes, provided that the weak sense of until is considered.*

Theorem 2 *The validity of an acyclic proof graph implies the validity of the formula $R \mapsto S$, where the assertions R and S are attached to the entry node and the exit node respectively, provided that the strong sense of until is considered.*

The proofs of these theorems are omitted here. Both weak and strong interpretations of proof graphs appear to be useful. In fact, the weak interpretation corresponds to safety properties, whereas the strong interpretation corresponds to liveness properties.[2]

5.2 Documenting a concurrent system with proof graphs

As mentioned in Section 3, the invariant is the most widely used formal tool for the design and the verification of concurrent systems but, from the documentation point of view, it is not fully satisfactory. The problem addressed in this section is as follows. Given a concurrent system S, an invariant I and a claimed liveness property of S, how can we use proof graphs to document S? This problem is a *representation* problem; we are not concerned here with validation.

Let us consider again the abstract version S_1 of Stenning's protocol introduced in Section 4.1, with its invariant I_1. The claimed liveness property is that the three counters LA, LR and HS keep growing.

The proposed documentation method is to generate an increasing sequence of proof graphs. Each member of the sequence will be less abstract, that is, more detailed, than its predecessor. The formal definition of the ordering relation between proof graphs is omitted here.

Figure 5 presents the most elementary proof graph about system S_1 (top), and a refinement of it, where node A has been split into nodes $A1$ and $A2$. The assertions labelling the nodes are

$$\begin{array}{ll} A: & LA+LR+HS=n\,, \\ A1: & LA+LR+HS=n \,\wedge\, Y[LR+1]=NIL\,, \\ A2: & LA+LR+HS=n \,\wedge\, Y[LR+1]=X[LR+1]\,, \\ B: & LA+LR+HS>n\,. \end{array}$$

Observe that A is equivalent to $(A1 \vee A2)$.

From the safety point of view, the second graph in Figure 5 is hardly more expressive than the first one but, from the documentation point of view, it gives a more detailed description of the behaviour of the system.

Comment. From the liveness point of view, however, there is an essential difference. The first proof graph asserts that progress is guaranteed provided that, e.g., transition 3 does not induce infinite looping. This requirement is indeed to strong, since the second graph shows that, in some cases, transition 3 adds a useful contribution to progress (when $r = LR+1$). As a result, refining proof graphs is useful not only for documentation purposes, but also for proof purposes, as far as liveness properties are concerned.

This can be generalized. Proof graphs are validated with the weak interpretation of until, using Theorem 1, but, for liveness properties, the strong interpretation of until has to be used, according to Theorem 2. This leads us to consider the gap between the weak and the strong interpretation of until as an adequate model for the fairness hypotheses, needed to obtain liveness results.

---

[2]Cycles induce some problems here; the interpretation of proof graphs with cycles will be given in Section 5.3.

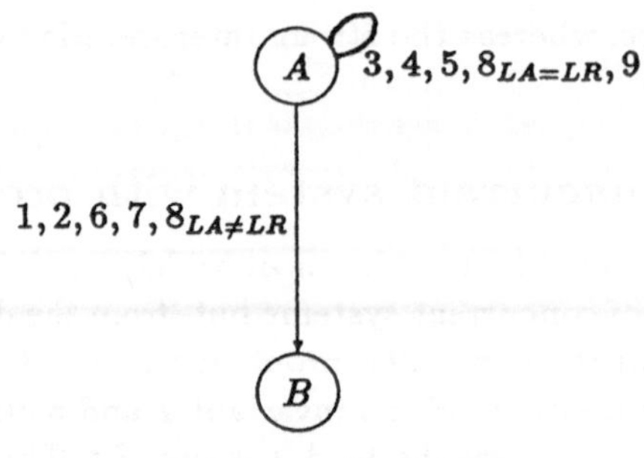

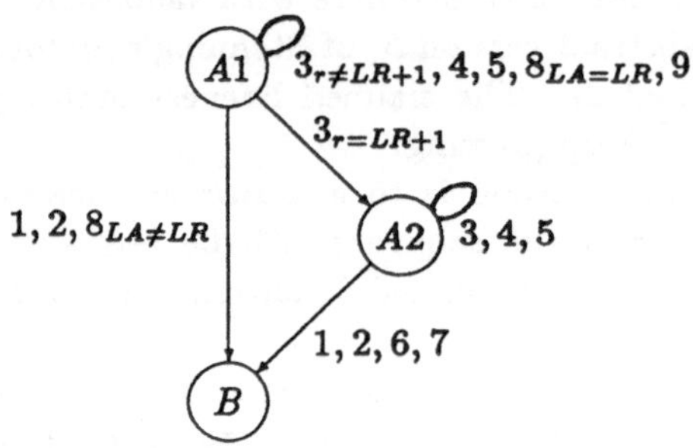

Figure 5: An increasing sequence of proof graphs for $\mathcal{S}_1$

5.3 Refining a sequence of proof graphs

If the system $\mathcal{S}_1$ is refined into a less abstract system $\mathcal{S}_2$, the sequence of proof graphs has to be transformed accordingly. An example of refinement is as follows. System $\mathcal{S}_1$ models message transmission and message reception as synchronous events, jointly modelled by an assignment $Y[s] := X[s]$ (transitions 1 and 4). This is rather unrealistic and, in practice, message transmission and message reception are asynchronous events, that could be respectively represented as $m := X[s]$ and $Y[s] := m$, where m is a transmission buffer.

The asynchronous model is adopted in the refined system $\mathcal{S}_2$; the refinement consists precisely in introducing a buffer memory MB for message transmission (more details appear in [3]). The transitions of the new system are:

$$
\begin{aligned}
\mathcal{T}_2 = \{ & 1:(HS - LA < W \longrightarrow (HS, MB) := (HS+1, (HS+1, X[HS+1]))), \\
& 2:(LA < r \leq HS \longrightarrow (MB, r) := ((r, X[r]), r+1)), \\
& 3:(\neg(LA < r \leq HS) \longrightarrow r := LA+1), \\
& 4:(MB \neq NIL \longrightarrow (Y[MB.1], MB) := (MB.2, NIL)), \\
& 5:(Y[LR+1] \neq NIL \longrightarrow (LA, LR) := (LR+1, LR+1)), \\
& 6:(Y[LR+1] \neq NIL \longrightarrow LR := LR+1), \\
& 7:(Y[LR+1] = NIL \longrightarrow LA := LR), \\
& 8:(Y[LR+1] = NIL \longrightarrow skip), \\
& 9:(MB := NIL)\}.
\end{aligned}
$$

The invariant is easily adapted into:

$$\begin{aligned} I_2 \equiv\ & (LA \leq LR \leq HS \leq LA + W) \ \wedge \\ & \forall s\,(Y[s] \in \{X[s], NIL\}) \ \wedge \\ & \forall s\,(0 \leq s \leq LR \Rightarrow Y[s] = X[s]) \ \wedge \\ & \forall s\,(HS < s \Rightarrow Y[s] = NIL) \ \wedge \\ & (MB = NIL \ \vee \ \exists s\,[(0 \leq s \leq HS) \ \wedge \ MB = (s, X[s])]) \,. \end{aligned}$$

This refinement induces some modification in the sequence of proof graphs. This second kind of proof graph refinement is simpler than the first one, since the *structure* of the graphs is preserved; only the *labelling* might have to be modified. The refined version of the sequence in Figure 5 is given in Figure 6.

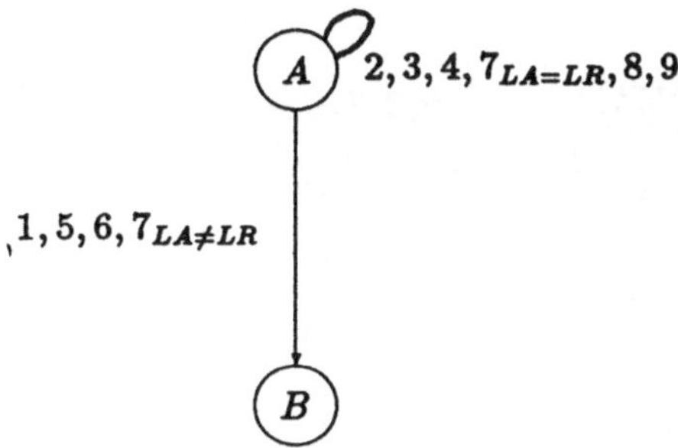

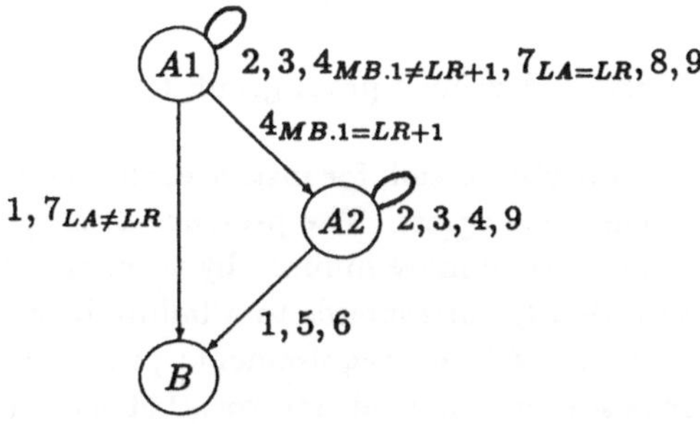

Figure 6: An increasing sequence of proof graphs for $\mathcal{S}_2$

Theorem 1 can be used to check that the proof graphs in Figure 6 are valid.

5.4 A further refinement

A two-element sequence of proof graphs was sufficient for documenting system $\mathcal{S}_1$, but the corresponding sequence for $\mathcal{S}_2$ is no longer satisfactory. From the informal point of view, one can guess that message retransmission (transition 2) has a useful role, since message first transmission (transition 1) may fail. However, from the formal point of view, the second proof graph in Figure 6 indicates that transition 2 induces no useful move, as if useful message transmission was achieved only by transition 1. As a result, this proof graph is not powerful enough to guarantee progress when message first transmission is allowed to fail. This indicates that a further refinement (first kind) has to be performed.

The node (labelled by) $A1$ is split into two new nodes; the corresponding assertions are

$$A11: \; LA + LR + HS = n \wedge Y[LR+1] = NIL \wedge MB.1 \neq LR+1,$$
$$A12: \; LA + LR + HS = n \wedge Y[LR+1] = NIL \wedge MB.1 = LR+1.$$

The refined proof graph is given in Figure 7.

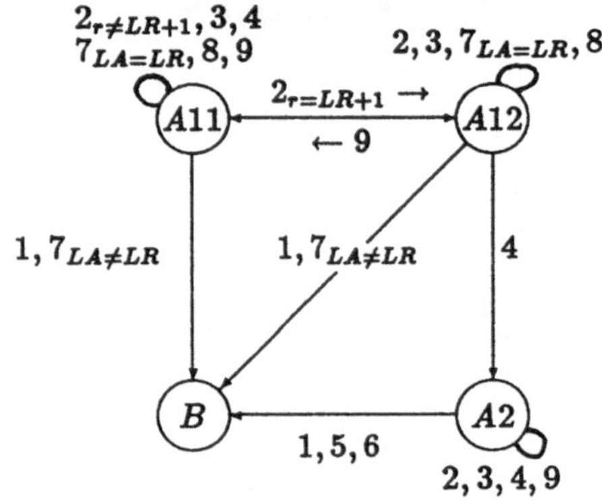

Figure 7: A refined proof graph for S_2

The role of transition 2 is now visible and, for instance, the sequence of transitions $2_{r=LR+1}; 4; 6$ is shown to ensure progress. The presence of a cycle between nodes $A11$ and $A12$ indicates that a useful move induced by transition 2 can be cancelled by transition 9. This cycle clearly corresponds to a failure in message retransmission, and gives rise to an obvious fairness requirement : progress can be guaranteed only if message retransmission does not fail forever. Let us note that systematic failure of message first transmission (transition 1) does not prevent progress.

6 Related work and further work

The concept of proof graph has been derived from the now classical notions of proof lattices and proof diagrams [5,9,7]. As soon as it appeared that the temporal operators *leads-to* and *next* were not fully appropriate for documentation purposes, it was rather natural to try the operator *until* (or *unless*) instead. This was also suggested by the numerous examples of program design given in [1], since many of them demonstrate the usefulness of *until* and *unless*.

It is now standard practice to develop programs by stepwise refinement and, as far as formal methods are used, programs and proofs are better developed simultaneously [2]. Our previous work [3] was an attempt to adapt Dijkstra's method to parallel programming, but it was restricted to safety properties. The present work suggests that an appropriate method for the development of concurrent systems might involve the simultaneous design of programs, invariants and proof graphs. Chandy and Misra have demonstrated [1] that the stepwise refinement approach is adequate not only for programs, but also for specifications in a rather broad sense; in our opinion, this includes proof and documentation objects.

The usual way to deal with fairness in concurrent programming is to adopt a general fairness rule. The most frequent one says that every action which can be executed infinitely often will effectively be executed infinitely often. Proof graphs suggest a more adaptable policy. Each fairness problem appears as a cycle in a proof graph, allowing the designer to see what actions are really important and what actions, however useful, do not endanger progress even in unfair computations. Further work is needed to see if a more flexible policy of fairness is possible and useful in general. Further work is also needed to make the refinement procedure of proof graphs more systematic and more integrated in the design of concurrent systems.

Acknowledgment. We are grateful to the anonymous referees for several helpful comments and suggestions.

References

[1] K.M. CHANDY and J. MISRA, "Parallel Program Design: A Foundation", Addison-Wesley, 1988.

[2] E.W. DIJKSTRA, "A discipline of programming", Prentice Hall, New Jersey, 1976

[3] E.P. GRIBOMONT, "Development of concurrent systems by incremental transformation", Internal report, 30 p.; short version in LNCS, **432**, pp. 161-176, Springer, 1990.

[4] E.P. GRIBOMONT, "A programming logic for formal concurrent systems", LNCS, **458**, pp. 298-313, Springer, 1990.

[5] L. LAMPORT, "Proving the correctness of a multiprocess program", IEEE Trans. on Soft. Eng., **SE-3**, pp. 125-143, 1977.

[6] B.D. LUBACHEVSKY, "Automating the verification of compact parallel coordination of programs I", Acta Informatica, **12**, pp. 125-169, 1984.

[7] Z. MANNA and A. PNUELI, "Adequate proof principles for invariance and liveness properties of concurrent programs", SCP, **4**, pp. 257-289, 1984.

[8] S. OWICKI and D. GRIES, "An axiomatic proof technique for parallel programs", Acta Informatica, **6**, pp. 319-340, 1976.

[9] S. OWICKI and L. LAMPORT, "Proving liveness properties of concurrent programs", ACM Trans. on Prog. Lang. and Syst., **3**, 1982.

[10] N.V. STENNING, "A data transfer protocol", Computer Networks, **1**, pp. 99-110, 1976.

A Formal Method for Hard Real-Time Programming

Mike Gordon

Computer Laboratory
New Museums Site
Pembroke Street
Cambridge CB2 3QG

SRI International
Suite 23
Millers Yard
Cambridge CB2 1RQ

Abstract

A graphical state-transition approach to specifying hard real time reactive systems is described. This is then refined to a formal notation based on sentences called "Non-instantaneous State-transition Assertions" (NSAs). These have a set-theoretic semantics that can be used to justify various laws, which combine aspects of Interval Temporal Logic and Hoare Logic. The semantics of programs can also be represented by sets of NSAs, and then verification is performed by using laws to combine the NSAs from the program to obtain the specification. The derivation of the laws and the mechanization of their use is in progress, but not yet complete.

Warning: It is expected that many of the details in the preliminary work described here will need correcting and elaborating.

1 Introduction

Hard real-time systems are required to meet explicit timing constraints, such as responding to an input within 100 milliseconds of a change. The temporal requirements are an essential part of the required behaviour, not just a desirable property. The work described here aims to combine hardware and software verification techniques to produce a formal method for hard real-time programming. In this method, programs are refined from specifications consisting of a kind of state transition diagram. These diagrams have a precise semantics and the verification that programs implement them is by machine checked formal proof.

A key element of the method is that the program semantics used for verification is determined by what happens when the compiled program runs on the processor being used. This is achieved by defining the semantics via the compiler and processor specification. However, it is hoped eventually to derive a more abstract semantics based on Interval Temporal Logic [3].

The structure of the rest of the paper is as follows.

1. An example is presented informally. This is a device that offers a continuous service for computing a binary operation $\otimes$.

2. A semi-formal specification of the required behaviour of the device is described using a graphical notation.

3. The graphical notation is formalised using "Non-instantaneous State-transition Assertions" (NSAs). These are sentences whose semantics is defined set-theoritically.

4. Proof rules for NSAs are described. These are not axioms, but are derived from the semantics.

5. The example is formally specified using NSAs.

6. A simple programming language is introduced and an implementation of the example is given in it.

7. A simple processor is described and formally specified.

8. A compiler from the programming language to the instruction set of the processor is defined.

9. The derivation of 'atomic' NSAs from machine instructions is discussed.

10. The structure of the verification of the program is discussed.

11. The method is summarized and discussed.

Please note that the work described here is very much 'in progress'. It almost certainly contains errors and the general ideas are still evolving. In particular, the exact semantics of NSAs has not yet stabilized and only a few rules have been formally derived (it may be that deriving new rules will lead to changes of the semantics). Furthermore, the analysis of the main example in this paper has not been completed.

2 Example: OP – a binary operation server

A single 'toy' example will be used in what follows. This is intended to illustrate two aspects of real-time system verification.

1. The detailed analysis of the response time of reactive systems.

2. Formal reasoning about real-time non-terminating programs.

The device OP shown in Figure 1, which is intended to be implemented by a program running on a processor, offers a continuous service for computing a binary operation $\otimes : \mathsf{V} \times \mathsf{V} \rightarrow \mathsf{V}$ where V is some set of values and, for the purposes of this example, $\otimes$ is left unspecified.

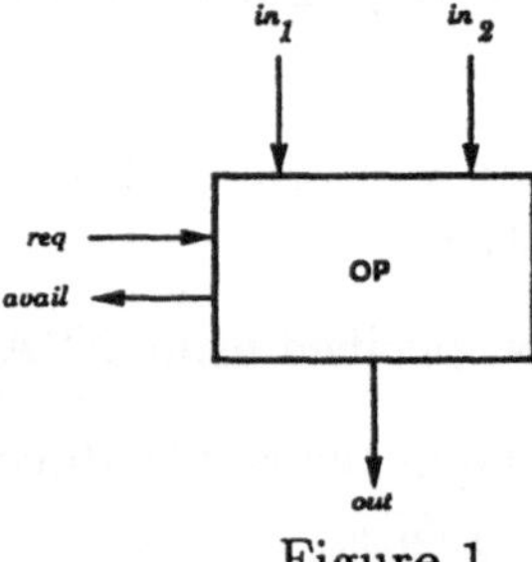

Figure 1

The data inputs in_1 and in_2 carry values from the set V, as does the data output *out*. The control input *req* and the control output *avail* carry single bits (i.e. 1 or 0, which are assumed to be members of V).

The device is said to be "available" whenever the output *avail* has the value 1. It is required to have two properties:

Liveness: it becomes available within δ_1 units of time if *req* is held at 0.

Safety: whenever the device is available, it can be used to compute $in_1 \otimes op_2$ in a predictable amount of time via a four-phase handshake, which is described informally below and in Figure 2.

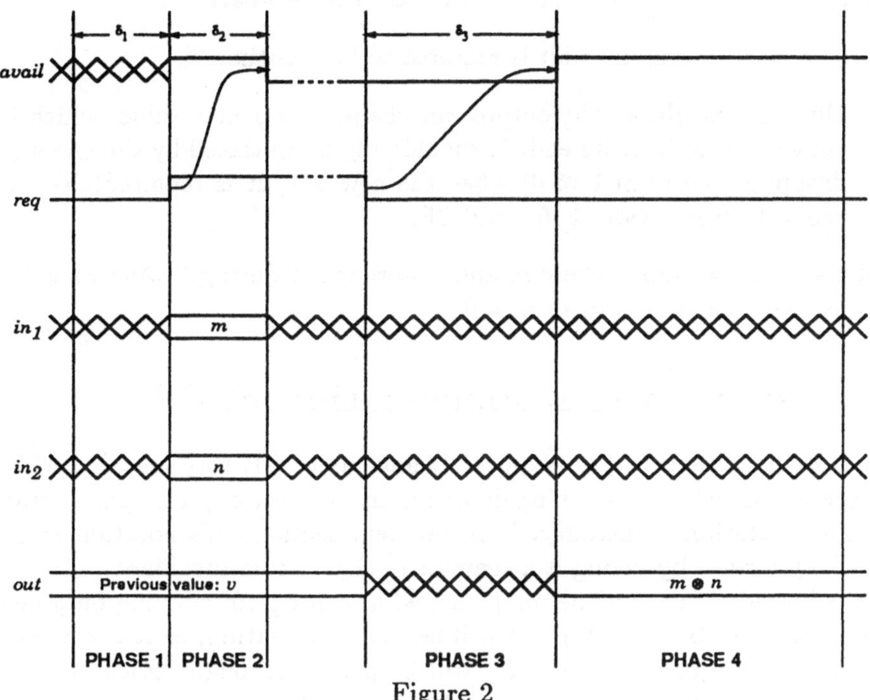

Figure 2

Figure 2 is a timing diagram showing the computation of $m \otimes n$ (where $m, n \in \mathsf{V}$); δ_1, δ_2 and δ_3 are timing constants to be determined by the implementation (in a real example, actual values would be specified). The user of the device will be referred to as the "client".

PHASE 1 : the client keeps $req = 0$ until OP causes $avail = 1$

- The maximum wait is required to be less than δ_1

PHASE 2 : the client holds $req = 1$ and simultaneously $in_1 = m$ and $in_2 = n$ until OP causes $avail = 0$.

- The maximum wait is required to be less than δ_2

During PHASE 1 and PHASE 2 the output *out* stays stable, and will remain so as long as the client keeps $req = 1$.

PHASE 3 : the client holds $req = 0$ until OP causes $avail = 1$.

- The maximum wait is required to be less than δ_3

During this phase, the output *out* changes to a new value, which becomes available at its end. It should only be initiated by the client (by dropping *req* from 1 to 0) when the new output is required. Keeping $req = 1$ after PHASE 2 'freezes' OP.

PHASE 4 : $out = m \otimes n$ (where m and n were input during PHASE 2) as long as the client maintains $req = 0$.

3 A semi-formal specification of OP

In the previous section, the required behaviour of OP was specified with a mixture of English and a timing diagram. In this section, a graphical state-transition notation is introduced. In the next section, this notation will be made fully formal by giving it a semantics relative to a machine.

It is intended that OP be implemented as a program running on a dedicated processor. Such a program will be non-terminating; as it executes an infinite sequence of machine states will be passed through. Each step (i.e. state transition) in this sequence will be the result of executing a single machine instruction; the next state will depend on the current state and the values being input.

It is assumed that inputs (in_1, in_2 and *req* for OP) are supplied asynchronously and that the program can obtain a value from any input line at any time. It is up to the client to ensure that the inputs are valid when they are read. Some inputs will always be valid (e.g. those from sensors), others may only be valid at certain times. If an input is read at the 'wrong' time, an unpredictable value might result – but the read will not block or cause an error. Input just consists in sampling an externally driven line.

Outputs (*avail* and *out* for OP) are written by the program. It is assumed that each output is connected to a register, so that if the program writes this register then the resulting output value will remain stable until the register is updated. In the processor described in Section 8, every program variable is also a possible output port. Output is thus 'memory mapped'; in a real processor only a subset of the memory locations would correspond to outputs. With this model, each machine state determines the value of all the variables and all outputs.

The state transition diagrams below (Figures 3 and 5) consist of nodes joined by arrows. These diagrams are assertions about sequences of state transitions of a machine. For such a sequence of states, a diagram will either be true of the sequence or not. The nodes represent sets of states and the arcs represent transitions between sets of states. These transitions consist of finite sequences of intermediate states and thus have a duration. The formulae written inside the nodes describe the set of states the node represents. The formulae above the arrow are conditions on sequences of inputs that must hold if the transition is to occur. The formulae below the arrow specify properties of the sequence of states making up the transition. Thus the truth of the formulae above the arrow depends on the client (environment), whereas the truth of the formulae below the arrow is determined by the machine.

To make this clearer, consider Figure 3:

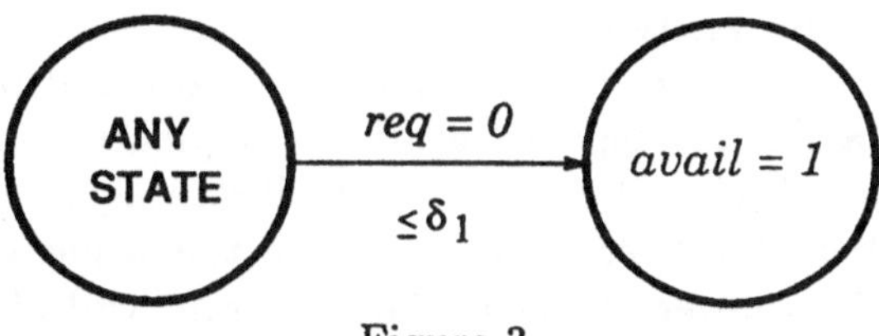

Figure 3

The interpretation of Figure 3 is as an assertion about the behaviour of a machine. This assertion is true if and only if whenever the input *req* is kept equal to 0, then within δ_1 state transitions the output *out* becomes equal to 1. This assertion is false if and only if there is a sequence of inputs $i_1\ i_2\ \ldots\ i_n$, where $n > \delta_1$ and a corresponding sequence of states $s_1\ s_2\ \ldots\ s_n$ such that *req* is 0 in each input $i_1, i_2, \ldots, i_n$ and *avail* is 0 in each state $s_1, s_2, \ldots, s_n$.

The node containing "ANY STATE" represents the set of all states. The node containing $avail = 1$ represents the set of those states in which the output *out* has value 1. The formula $req = 0$ above the arrow is true of any sequence of inputs that keep the value at *req* equal to 0. The formula $\leq\delta_1$ below the arrow is true of any sequence of states of length less than or equal to δ_1.

Consider now Figure 4. This shows the general scheme:

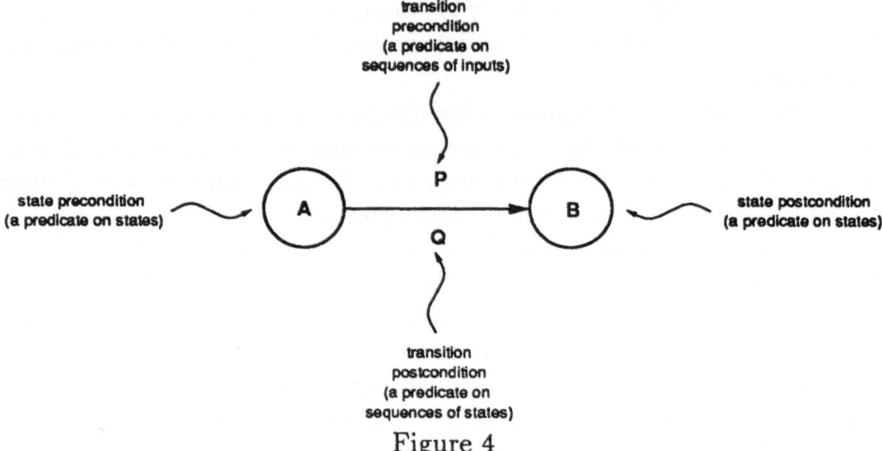

Figure 4

The diagram in Figure 4 is true of a machine if and only if whenever it is in a state statisfying A and a sequence of inputs satisfying P occurs, then eventually a state satisfying B will be reached, and the sequence of intermediate states will satisfy Q.

The diagram will be false, for example, if there is an infinite sequence of inputs $i_1\ i_2\ \ldots$ and a corresponding infinite sequence of states $s_1\ s_2\ \ldots$ such that A is true of s_1 and P is true of all subsequences $i_1\ i_2\ \ldots\ i_n$ (for $n = 1, 2, \ldots$) but B is false for all states in the sequence. In this case a state satisfying B is never reached. The diagram will also be false if a state satisfying B is reached, say B is true of s_m, but there is some sequence $s_1\ s_2\ \ldots\ s_n$, where $n \leq m$, that does not satisfy Q. In this case, although the target state is reached, the sequence of intermediate states does not satisfy the specified condition Q.

The reader should not be worried if he/she finds the preceeding description a bit vague. A formal definition is given in the next section; for the time being only a rough intuitive understanding is needed.

In order to write down predicates on states and state sequences (i.e. transitions) the following notation will be used.

1. If $x = v$ is written in a node then it means that all the states in the set of states corresponding to the node must have value v for the output (or variable) x.

2. If $x = v$ is written above a transition arrow, then it means that x is an input which must have have the constant value v during the transition. Thus, the transition imposes the requirement on the environment that input x be held stable with value v.

3. If $[x = v]$ is written below a transition arrow, then it means that x is an output or program variable and *if* the transition occurs then x will be stable with value v for all states in the transition. The closed interval notation is meant to suggest this meaning. This is an assertion about program behaviour, not (as in the case above) a condition on the environment. To reduce clutter, the square brackets will usually be omitted in diagrams, i.e. $[x = v]$ will be written as just $x = v$.

4. If $[x = v)$ is written below a transition arrow, then it means that x is an output or program variable and *if* the transition occurs then x will be stable with value v for all states in the transition *except the last one*. The half-open interval notation is meant to suggest this meaning. This kind of assertion, like the last one, asserts a property of the program behaviour.

5. If $\leq\delta$ is written below a transition arrow, it means that the transition will contain at most δ states.

6. If $=\delta$ is written below a transition arrow, it means that the transition will contain exactly δ states.

Using this notation, the required behaviour of OP is specified in Figure 5. When there is more than one formula in a node or attached to an arrow, then their conjunction is intended.

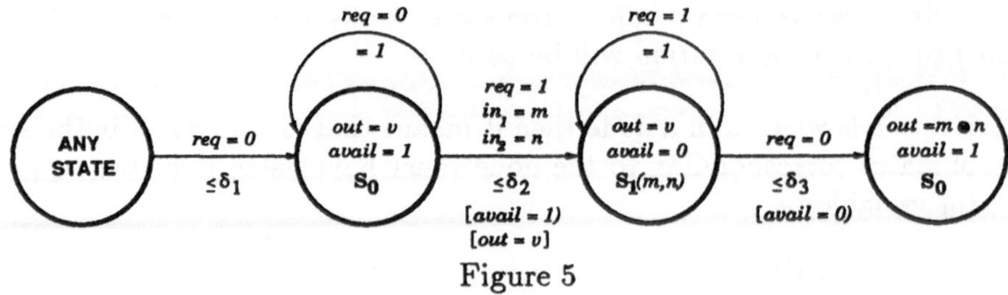

Figure 5

The formulae S_0 and $S_1(m,n)$ occuring in the nodes are predicates that need to be specified in an implementation. Such an implementation will be a machine running a program; it correctly implements the diagram in Figure 5 if interpretations of S_0 and $S_1(m,n)$ (for each m and n) can be found so that the diagram becomes true of the behaviour of the program. In fact, the implementation that is given below defines these predicates in terms of the program counter of the processor. It will turn out (jumping ahead a bit) that S_0 is the predicate that is true of those states for which the program counter's value is a member of $\{3,4,5,6,25\}$ and $S_1(m,n)$ is true of those states for which the program counter's values is a member of $\{13,14,15,16,17\}$ and the variables x, y have values m, n, respectively. As it stands, Figure 5 is a pure specification and S_0 and S_1 are predicates that have the status of free variables. Refining the specification consists of determining interpretations of these variables as predicates on machine states.

Note that the diagram in Figure 5 specifies that if the program is in a state satisfying S_0 and $avail = 1$, then it will stay in a state satisfying these conditions as long as the input *req* is kept at 0. This is the meaning of the curved arrow with $req = 0$ above it and =1 below: keeping $req = 0$ will ensure a return to the node in one step. If S_0 and $avail = 1$ and *out* has some value and the input *req* is held at 1 then a transition towards the next node will start. This will reach the node containing $S_1(m,n)$ as long as the two inputs in_1 and in_2 are held stable, and furthermore the node will be reached in at most δ_2 steps. During the transition the output *out* will be stable with value v and the output *avail* will also be stable with value 1 until the last state of the transition, when it will change to 0. Thus an outside observer can determine when the transition has finished by seeing that *avail* has changed from 1 to 0. The curved arrow going from the node containing $S_1(m,n)$ to itself specifies that as long as the input *req* continues to have value 1 the conditions $S_1(m,n)$ and $avail = 0$ and $out = v$ will continue to hold. If the input *req* is now changed to 0 and kept there, then in less than δ_3 steps the system will reach a state in which S_0 is true again and $avail = 1$ and $out = m \otimes n$. During this transition $avail = 0$ except at the last state. It is not specified when the output *out* changes – all that is specified is that at the end of the transition it has the value $m \otimes n$ (at the beginning it had some, possibly different, value v). Note that the rightmost node in Figure 5 is an 'instance' of the other node containing S_0, with v replaced by $m \otimes n$.

Although the semantics of state transition diagrams have been described as carefully as possible, there are still a number of lurking subtleties. For example, what is the exact status of the free variable v in Figure 5 – is it to be understood as universally or existentially quantified? What precisely does it mean to say that one node is an instance of another with v replaced by $m \otimes n$? To answer these sort of questions it is necessary to give a more formal account of the semantics of state transitions. This is done in the next section. It will become clear that a number of apparently arbitrary decisions have been made. An attempt to justify these is given, but research is still in progress.

4 Machines and their transitions

A machine m is a function $m : \mathsf{I} \times \mathsf{S} \rightarrow \mathsf{S}$, where I is a set of inputs and S is a set of states; $m(i, s)$ is the next state of the machine after s, if the input is i.

The aim of this section is to formally define the conditions for a diagram of the form shown in Figure 4 to be true of a machine m. The notation:

$$m \models \quad A \xrightarrow[Q]{P} B$$

expresses this; it is defined to mean that if m is in a state satisfying A and inputs satisfying P keep arriving, then eventually m will reach a state satisfying B and the sequence of states passed through will satisfy Q; i.e the diagram in Figure 4 is correct for machine m. The notation:

$$A \xrightarrow[Q]{P} B$$

is called a *Non-instantaneous State-transition Assertion*, or NSA for short. The notation "$m \models$ " means "is true for m". Before defining the semantics of NSAs, some auxiliary notions are needed.

A sequence of inputs is a function $i_{seq} : \mathsf{N} \rightarrow \mathsf{I}$, where N is the set of natural numbers. The variable t (for "time") will be used to range over N.

The subsequence of i_{seq} from t to t' is denoted by $i_{seq}[t, t']$, i.e. if $t \leq t'$ then:

$$i_{seq}[t, t'] \quad = \quad i_{seq}(t)\ i_{seq}(t+1)\ \ldots\ i_{seq}(t')$$

If, for any set X, X^* denotes the set of non-empty finite sequences of members of X, then $i_{seq}[t, t'] \in \mathsf{I}^*$

It is routine to define functions StateSeq and FinalState such that:

- $\mathsf{StateSeq}(m, i_{seq}, s, t)$ is the sequence of states of m resulting from the first t inputs of i_{seq} starting from s.

- $\mathsf{FinalState}(m, i_{seq}, s, t)$ is the last state in $\mathsf{StateSeq}(m, i_{seq}, s, t)$.

If X is a set of numbers, then $\mathsf{IsMin}(X, t)$ is true if and only if t is the smallest number in X. Note that if X is non-empty, then there is a unique t such that $\mathsf{IsMin}(X, t)$ is true; however, X may be empty, in which case $\mathsf{IsMin}(X, t)$ is false for all t.

Suppose A, B are predicates on states, P is a predicate on sequences of inputs and Q is a predicate on sequences of states. This means that

$A : \mathsf{S} \rightarrow \mathsf{B}$ (The state precondition)
$B : \mathsf{S} \rightarrow \mathsf{B}$ (The state postcondition)
$P : \mathsf{I}^* \rightarrow \mathsf{B}$ (The transition precondition)
$Q : \mathsf{S}^* \rightarrow \mathsf{B}$ (The transition postcondition)

To help structure the formal statement of the semantics of NSAs, let

$$\mathsf{TranSet}(m, P, B, i_{seq}, s)$$

be the set of those times t such that:

- *if* all initial segments of i_{seq} of length less than or equal to t satisfy P,

- *then* the state of the machine m reached in t steps starting from s and with inputs i_{seq} satisfies B.

Formally:

$$\begin{array}{l}\mathsf{TranSet}(m, P, B, i_{seq}, s) \;=\\ \quad \{t \mid (\forall t' \leq t.\ P(i_{seq}[t, t'])) \Rightarrow B(\mathsf{FinalState}(m, i_{seq}, s, t))\}\end{array}$$

The NSA:

$$A \xrightarrow[Q]{P} B$$

is defined to be true of a machine m, in symbols:

$$m \quad \models \qquad A \xrightarrow[Q]{P} B$$

if and only if the following holds:

$$\begin{array}{l}\forall s \in \mathbf{S}.\ A(s) \Rightarrow \forall i_{seq}.\ \exists t_0.\ \mathsf{IsMin}(\mathsf{TranSet}(m, P, B, i_{seq}, s),\ t_0) \wedge \\ \qquad\qquad\qquad\qquad\qquad\qquad \forall t \leq t_0.\ Q(\mathsf{StateSeq}(m, i_{seq}, s, t))\end{array}$$

This definition is quite subtle and is the result of a surprising amount of experimentation. It may well change as the result of further work. The definition says that if $A(s)$, then the set $\mathsf{TranSet}(m, P, B, i_{seq}, s)$ is non-empty and if t_0 is its least element, then the sequence of t_0 states of m starting from s and with inputs i_{seq} satisfies Q – i.e. the sequence of states making up the transition satisfies Q. To see this observe that $\mathsf{TranSet}(m, P, B, i_{seq}, s)$, i.e.

$$\{t \mid (\forall t' \leq t.\ P(i_{seq}[t, t'])) \Rightarrow B(\mathsf{FinalState}(m, i_{seq}, s, t))\}$$

has the form: $\{t \mid \theta(t) \Rightarrow \psi(t)\}$ and so it will be empty if for all t the formula $\theta(t) \Rightarrow \psi(t)$ is false, which is only the case if $\theta(t)$ is always true and $\psi(t)$ is always false. Applying this observation to the definition of the actual θ and ψ occuring above shows that the set $\mathsf{TranSet}(m, P, B, i_{seq}, s)$ is only empty if all the initial segments of i_{seq} satisfy P, but none of the states gone through by m starting from s with inputs i_{seq} satisfy B – i.e. the transition fails to terminate.

The following points should be noted of the semantics of:

$$A \xrightarrow[Q]{P} B$$

(i) The predicate Q is required to hold of all initial segments of the sequence of states making up of the transition, not just of the complete transition.

(ii) The predicate P is required to hold of all initial segments of the input sequence i_{seq} during the transition, not just of the single sequence of inputs from start to finish.

(iii) The sequence of states making up a transition includes the final state, but not the initial state.

The reason for (i) is connected with rules for reasoning about NSAs. Suppose, for example, that:

$$m \models A \xrightarrow[Q]{P} B \qquad \text{and} \qquad B \Rightarrow B'$$

then it would be nice to be able to infer (by analogy with the consequence rule of Hoare logic) that:

$$m \models A \xrightarrow[Q]{P} B'$$

However, this would not be true if the semantics of NSAs only required the transition postcondition Q to hold of the complete transition. The reason for this is that the machine might reach a state satisfying B' before it reaches a state satisfying B, and there would in general be no guarantee that if $Q(s_1 s_2 \ldots s_m \ldots s_n)$ then $Q(s_1 s_2 \ldots s_m)$. As a concrete example, if Q is the predicate (written $=n$ above) that is defined to be true of a sequence if and only if it has length n, then it will not be true of any shorter sequence.

The reason for (ii) is symetry with (i). It is eventually hoped to be able to have some kind of 'rule of parallel composition' that combines a transition with output Q with another with input Q. This has not yet been explored, but it would seem to be desirable to make transition preconditions and postconditions be the same kind of thing. However, for the examples looked at so far, it would suffice to have transition preconditions apply just to the complete sequence of inputs of a transition, rather than to all initial subsequences.

The reason for (iii) is because of the interaction between (i) and the transition predicate $=\delta$. If one defines:

$$=\delta(s_1 s_2 \ldots s_n) \quad \equiv \quad (\delta = n)$$

then if $\delta > 1$ it will never be the case that:

$$A \xrightarrow[=\delta]{P} B$$

because, by (i), not only would the whole transition have to have length δ, but so would all initial subsequences, which is clearly impossible. This problem can be got around by defining:

$$=_B\delta(s_1 s_2 \ldots s_n) \quad \equiv \quad B(s_n) \Rightarrow (\delta = n)$$

then

$$A \xrightarrow[=_B\delta]{P} B$$

will be true if the transition (assuming it happens) has length δ. Note that $=_B B(s_1 s_2 \ldots\ s_m)$ holds vacuously for all proper initial subsequences of the complete transition $s_1 s_2 \ldots s_n$, since none of the states except the last one satisfy B (this is part of the definition of a transition). This trick only works if the destination state s_n is included in the sequence making up the transition.

5 Proof rules for NSAs

The semantics of NSAs given in the previous section can be used to justify various proof rules, which are analogues to aspects of Hoare logic [2] and Interval Temporal Logic [3]. These are expected to be a crucial part of the method for real-time programming described here — but the exact details are still in a state of flux. The example rules in this section have not been fully checked yet and I would expect there to be errors.

If p is a predicate on states, then the predicates $\lceil p \rceil$ and $\lceil p)$ on sequences of states are defined by:

$$\lceil p \rceil (s_1 s_2 \ldots s_n) \quad = \quad p(s_1) \wedge p(s_2) \wedge \ \ldots \ \wedge p(s_n)$$

$$\lceil p)(s_1 s_2 \ldots s_n) \quad = \quad p(s_1) \wedge p(s_2) \wedge \ \ldots \ \wedge p(s_{n-1})$$

The predicates $=_B\delta$ and $\leq\delta$, where $\delta \in \mathbf{N}$, are defined by:

$$=_B\delta(s_1 s_2 \ldots s_n) \quad = \quad B(s_n) \Rightarrow (\delta = n)$$

$$\leq\delta(s_1 s_2 \ldots s_n) \quad = \quad (n \leq \delta)$$

An NSA:

$$A \xrightarrow[=_B\delta]{P} B$$

will normally be written as:

$$A \xrightarrow[=\delta]{P} B$$

since the subscript B is clear from the context.

If P and Q are predicates on sequences of states, define $\neg P$, $P \wedge Q$ and $P \vee Q$, also predicates on states, by:

$$(\neg P)(s_1 s_2 \ldots s_n) \quad = \quad \neg(P(s_1 s_2 \ldots s_n))$$

$$(P \wedge Q)(s_1 s_2 \ldots s_n) \quad = \quad P(s_1 s_2 \ldots s_n) \wedge Q(s_1 s_2 \ldots s_n)$$

$$(P \vee Q)(s_1 s_2 \ldots s_n) \quad = \quad P(s_1 s_2 \ldots s_n) \vee Q(s_1 s_2 \ldots s_n)$$

The rules that follow are written in the standard 'natural deduction' inference-rule notation: hypotheses above a horizontal line and conclusion below it.

The first three rules chain together NSAs that happen in sequence.

$$\frac{A \xrightarrow[\leq\delta_1 \wedge [q_1]]{P_1} B \qquad B \xrightarrow[\leq\delta_2 \wedge [q_2]]{P_2} C}{A \xrightarrow[\leq(\delta_1+\delta_2) \wedge ([q_1] \vee [q_2])]{P_1 \wedge P_2} C}$$

Note that it is possible that C might be reached *en route* from A to B, so $\leq$ cannot be replaced by $=$. This is precluded in the following rule:

$$\frac{A \xrightarrow[=\delta_1 \wedge ([q_1] \wedge \neg[C])]{P_1} B \qquad B \xrightarrow[=\delta_2 \wedge [q_2]]{P_2} C}{A \xrightarrow[=(\delta_1+\delta_2) \wedge ([q_1] \vee [q_2])]{P_1 \wedge P_2} C}$$

The next rule is useful for inferring transitions satisfying conditions of the form $[p)$.

$$\frac{A \xrightarrow[\leq\delta \wedge [q]]{P_1} B \qquad B \xrightarrow[=1 \wedge \neg[q]]{P_2} C}{A \xrightarrow[\leq(\delta+1) \wedge [q)]{P_1 \wedge P_2} C}$$

The following rule enables alternatives to be combined.

$$\frac{A_1 \xrightarrow[Q_1]{P_1} B_1 \qquad A_2 \xrightarrow[Q_2]{P_2} B_2}{A_1 \vee A_2 \xrightarrow[Q_1 \vee Q_2]{P_1 \wedge P_2} B_1 \vee B_2}$$

Finally, the following is a rule like the rule of consequence in Hoare Logic:

$$\frac{A' \Rightarrow A \qquad P' \Rightarrow P \qquad A \xrightarrow[Q]{P} B \qquad B \Rightarrow B' \qquad Q \Rightarrow Q'}{A' \xrightarrow[Q']{P'} B'}$$

where, slightly overloading our notation, $A' \Rightarrow A$ and $B \Rightarrow B'$ are true if for all states s, $A'(s) \Rightarrow A(s)$ and $B(s) \Rightarrow B'(s)$ are true, respectively.

The manner in which it is planned to use rules like this is sketched in Section 11, however not enough work has been done yet to guarantee that the sketch there can be enlarged to a fully formal proof.

6 Specification of OP

The behaviour informally diagramed in Figure 5 can be represented by five NSAs. In the first of these, T is the predicate that is always true.

1. Holding $req = 0$ for at most δ_1 puts OP in state S_0 with $avail = 1$.

$$\mathsf{T} \xrightarrow[\le\delta_1]{[req = 0]} S_0 \land avail = 1$$

2. Holding $req = 0$ keeps OP in state S_0.

$$S_0 \land out = v \land avail = 1 \xrightarrow[=1]{[req = 0]} S_0 \land out = v \land avail = 1$$

3. Holding $req = 1$ in state S_0, with in_1 and in_2 kept stable with values m and n, results in a transition to state $S_1(m,n)$ in less then δ_2. The value of out is stable throughout the transition; the value of $avail$ changes from 1 to 0 at the end of the transition.

$$\begin{array}{l} S_0 \land \\ out = v \land \\ avail = 1 \end{array} \xrightarrow[\begin{array}{l} \le\delta_2 \land \\ [avail = 1) \land \\ [out = v] \end{array}]{\begin{array}{l} [req = 1] \land \\ [in_1 = m] \land \\ [in_2 = n] \end{array}} \begin{array}{l} S_1(m,n) \land \\ out = v \land \\ avail = 0 \end{array}$$

4. Holding $req = 1$ keeps OP in state $S_1(m,n)$.

$$\begin{array}{l} S_1(m,n) \land \\ out = v \land \\ avail = 0 \end{array} \xrightarrow[=1]{[req = 1]} \begin{array}{l} S_1(m,n) \land \\ out = v \land \\ avail = 0 \end{array}$$

5. Holding $req = 0$ in state $S_1(m,n)$ results in a transition to state S_0 in less then δ_3. The value of *out* changes to $m \otimes n$ at some unspecified time during the transition; the value of *avail* changes from 0 to 1 at the end of the transition.

$$\begin{array}{lcl} S_1(m,n) \wedge & [req = 0] & S_0 \wedge \\ out = v \wedge & \xrightarrow{\hspace{5em}} & out = m \otimes n \wedge \\ avail = 0 & \leq\delta_3 \wedge & avail = 1 \\ & [avail = 0) & \end{array}$$

To implement the specification in Figure 5, it is necessary to produce a machine whose behaviour has the properties asserted by the five NSAs above. Such a machine will need to have a state that assigns values to variables (e.g. *avail* and *out*) and a set of inputs that assigns values to input names (e.g. *req*, in_1 and in_2). To interpret the NSAs as assertions about the machine, it is necessary to define the predicates S_0 and $S_1(m,n)$ in terms of the state of the implementing machine. This is done in Secrion 11.

Before describing the processor that will be used to implement OP, the programming language used to program it will be given. The semantics of this language will be specified by a compiler in Section 9.

7 A real-time programming language

The programming language described in this section is about as simple as one can imagine. It has two syntactic classes: expressions and commands. The evaluation of an expression returns a value; the execution of a command changes the state, which is a mapping of variable names to values. Both the evaluation of expressions and the execution of commands takes time. The actual times taken are specified by a compiler (described in Section 9) that translates each expression or command to a sequence of machine instructions for a simple processor (specified in Section 8). It is assumed that one unit of time corresponds to one machine cycle.

The metavariables E and C (possibly with subscripts) will be used to range over expressions and commands, respectively. The metavariables X and V will be used to range over variables and constants (V for "value"); these are both kinds of expressions.

The input and output is assumed to be 'memory mapped', however input and output are in different name spaces. For each name X there is a variable, denoted by just X and an input, denoted by `INPUT` X. The outputs are just the variables. The reason for separating inputs from variables is to avoid having to specify what happens if a program assigns a value to an input: does an error result, is the resulting value always the one assigned by the program, is it the value input by the environment, or is it some non-deterministic choice between these last two possibilities? For simplicity, it is assumed that for each X there is a value set by the program and an unrelated value set by the environment.

The syntax of expressions and commands is specified by the following BNF:

E	::=	X	(Get value of variable X)
	|	`INPUT` X	(Get input at X)
	|	V	(A constant)
	|	$op_1\ E$	(Unary operation applied to E)
	|	$E_1\ op_2\ E_2$	(Binary operation applied to E_1 and E_2)

C	::=	`SKIP`	(Do nothing)
	|	X`:=`E	(Assign value of E to X)
	|	C_1`;`C_2	(Execute C_1 and C_2 in sequence)
	|	`IF` E `THEN` C_1 `ELSE` C_2	(Conditional)
	|	`WHILE` E `DO` C	(While-command)

The constants V are assumed to include the single bits `1` and `0`, which will be used as the truth-values (`1` = *true*) and (`0` = *false*). The unary operations are assumed to include `NOT` (negation) and the binary operations are assumed to include the operation $\otimes$ that the device OP computes.

The following abbreviations will be used later:

- `WHENEVER` E `DO` C $\equiv$ `WHILE 1 DO IF` E `THEN` C `ELSE SKIP`
- `AWAIT` E $\equiv$ `WHILE NOT` E `DO SKIP`

The implementation of OP is shown in Figure 6.

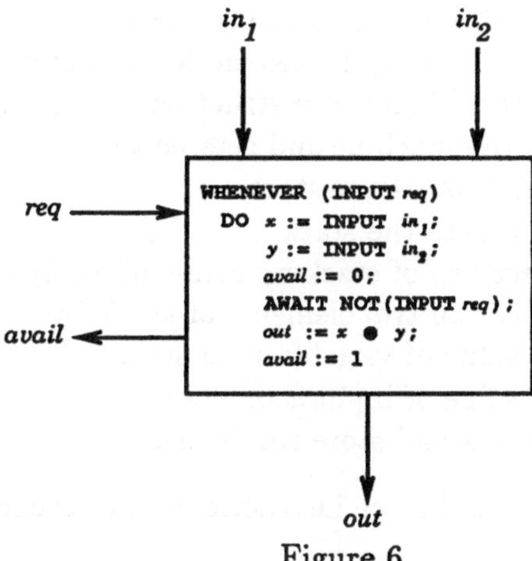

Figure 6

Notice that the requirement that in_1 and in_2 remain stable during Phase 2 (see Figure 2) ensures that the program reads the desired values m and n, even though the exact time when the inputs are sampled is unknown (though it could be determined by close examination of the compiled code).

The method of verifying the program in Figure 6 against the specification in the previous section, is to derive NSAs describing the behaviour of the program by examining the processor and compiler, and then to combine these, using laws, to obtain the specification. We repeat that this approach has not yet been tested on significant examples – the proof sketched in Section 11 is still to be completed.

8 A processor

The processor on which the program in Figure 6 will be run is presented here at a fairly abstract level of description. An implementation of it is planned using Xilinx user programmable gate arrays.

Each state $s \in \mathsf{S}$ of the processor is a triple (pc, stk, mem) where $pc \in \mathsf{N}$ is the program counter, $stk \in \mathsf{V}^*$ is a stack of values, and $mem : \mathsf{N} \rightarrow \mathsf{V}$ is a 'memory' that associates a value with each name.

Each input $i \in \mathsf{I}$ is a function $i : \mathsf{N} \rightarrow \mathsf{V}$, determining a value for each input name. The environment is assumed to provide an input at every time.

There are eleven instructions:

`JMP` n	Unconditional jump to instruction number n
`JMZ` n	Pop stack, jump to instruction number n if result 0
`JNZ` n	Pop stack, jump to instruction number n if result 1
`STP`	Stops the machine and sets pc to
`POP`	Pop the top of the stack
`OPO` v	Push v onto the stack
`OP1` op_1	Replace top of stack by result of applying op_1
`OP2` op_2	Replace top two elements of stack by result of applying op_2
`GET` x	Push value of variable x on stack
`INP` x	Push value of input x on stack
`PUT` x	Pop stack and store result in x

In specifying the meaning of instructions and programs, the following notation will be used.

- Instruction is the set of instructions.
- Len $v_1 v_2 \ldots v_n = n$
- Hd $v_1 v_2 \ldots v_n = v_1$
- Tl $v_1 v_2 \ldots v_n = v_2 \ldots v_n$
- $v_1 v_2 \ldots v_n \,\hat{}\, u_1 u_2 \ldots u_m = v_1 v_2 \ldots v_n u_1 u_2 \ldots u_m$
- Pc $(pc, stk, mem) = pc$
- Stk $(pc, stk, mem) = stk$
- Mem $(pc, stk, mem) = mem$
- $mem\ x$ is the values of variable named x in memory mem
- $i\ x$ is the values at input named x in input i
- Store $v\ x\ mem$ is the memory resulting from storing value v at x in mem. So if $x \neq x'$ then:

  (Store $v\ x\ mem)\ x = v$ and (Store $v\ x\ mem)\ x' = mem\ x'$

It is routine to formalize the semantics of the eleven instructions by defining a function:

$$\mathsf{Step} : \mathsf{Instruction} \to \mathsf{I} \to \mathsf{S} \to \mathsf{S}$$

satisfying the following equations:

$$
\begin{array}{lcl}
\mathsf{Step}\ (\texttt{JMP}\ n)\ i\ (pc, stk, mem) & = & (n, stk, mem) \\
\mathsf{Step}\ (\texttt{JMZ}\ n)\ i\ (pc, stk, mem) & = & (\textbf{if}\ (\mathsf{Hd}\ stk = 0)\ \textbf{then}\ n\ \textbf{else}\ pc{+}1), \\
 & & \mathsf{Tl}\ stk, \\
 & & mem) \\
\mathsf{Step}\ (\texttt{JMN}\ n)\ i\ (pc, stk, mem) & = & ((\textbf{if}\ (\mathsf{Hd}\ stk = 1)\ \textbf{then}\ n\ \textbf{else}\ pc{+}1), \\
 & & \mathsf{Tl}\ stk, \\
 & & mem) \\
\mathsf{Step}\ \texttt{STP}\ i\ (pc, stk, mem) & = & (0, stk, mem) \\
\mathsf{Step}\ \texttt{POP}\ i\ (pc, stk, mem) & = & (pc{+}1, \mathsf{Tl}\ stk, mem) \\
\mathsf{Step}\ (\texttt{OP0}\ v)\ i\ (pc, stk, mem) & = & (pc{+}1, v\hat{}\,stk, mem) \\
\mathsf{Step}\ (\texttt{OP1}\ op_1)\ i\ (pc, stk, mem) & = & (pc{+}1, (op_1(\mathsf{Hd}\ stk))\hat{}\,\mathsf{Tl}\ stk, mem) \\
\mathsf{Step}\ (\texttt{OP2}\ op_2)\ i\ (pc, stk, mem) & = & (pc{+}1, \\
 & & (op_2(\mathsf{Hd}(\mathsf{Tl}\ stk), \mathsf{Hd}\ stk))\hat{}\,\mathsf{Tl}(\mathsf{Tl}\ stk), \\
 & & mem) \\
\mathsf{Step}\ (\texttt{GET}\ x)\ i\ (pc, stk, mem) & = & (pc{+}1, (mem\ x)\hat{}\,stk, mem) \\
\mathsf{Step}\ (\texttt{INP}\ x)\ i\ (pc, stk, mem) & = & (pc{+}1, (i\ x)\hat{}\,stk, mem) \\
\mathsf{Step}\ (\texttt{PUT}\ x)\ i\ (pc, stk, mem) & = & (pc{+}1, \mathsf{Tl}\ stk, \mathsf{Store}\ (\mathsf{Hd}\ stk)\ x\ mem)
\end{array}
$$

A *program* is a sequence of instructions. Each program P determines a machine:

$$\mathsf{Machine}\ \mathsf{P} : \mathsf{I} \times \mathsf{S} \to \mathsf{S}$$

by:

$$\mathsf{Machine}\ \mathsf{P}\ (i, s) \ = \ \mathsf{Step}\ (\mathsf{Fetch}\ \mathsf{P}\ (\mathsf{Pc}\ s))\ i\ s$$

where:

$$
\begin{array}{l}
\mathsf{Fetch}\ ins_1 ins_2 \ldots ins_m \ldots ins_n\ m = \\
\quad \textbf{if}\ 1 \le m \le n\ \textbf{then}\ ins_m\ \textbf{else}\ \texttt{STP}
\end{array}
$$

Notice that the machine jumps to 'location 0' if it tries to execute an instruction not in the program.

9 A compiler

The compiler defined in this section maps expressions and commands to programs (i.e. sequences of instructions).

The expression compiler is a function CompileExp defined recursively by:

$$\begin{aligned}
\mathsf{CompileExp}\ X &= \mathtt{GET}\ X \\
\mathsf{CompileExp}\ (\mathtt{INPUT}\ X) &= \mathtt{INP}\ X \\
\mathsf{CompileExp}\ V &= \mathtt{OP0}\ V \\
\mathsf{CompileExp}\ (op_1\ E) &= (\mathsf{CompileExp}\ E)\hat{}\,\mathtt{OP1}\ op_1 \\
\mathsf{CompileExp}\ (E_1\ op_2\ E_2) &= (\mathsf{CompileExp}\ E_1)\hat{}\,(\mathsf{CompileExp}\ E_2)\hat{}\,\mathtt{OP2}\ op_2
\end{aligned}$$

The command compiler is a function CompileCom which is also defined recursively. It takes a command C and a number n as arguments and returns a sequence of instructions which are assumed to start at 'location n' – i.e. any labels in the generated code will be offset by n. Functional programming notation will be used: let $x = e_1$ in e_2 means the value of e_2 with x having the value of e_1.

CompileCom `SKIP` n = the empty string

CompileCom $(X\texttt{:=}E)$ n = (CompileExp E)^`PUT` X

CompileCom $(C_1\texttt{;}C_2)$ n =
  let l_1 = CompileCom C_1 n **in**
  let l_2 = CompileCom C_2 (n + Len l_1) **in**
  l_1^l_2

CompileCom (`IF` E `THEN` C_1 `ELSE` C_2) n =
  let l_1 = CompileExp E **in**
  let n_1 = n + Len l_1 **in**
  let l_2 = CompileCom C_1 (n_1+1) **in**
  let n_2 = (n_1+1) + Len l_2 **in**
  let l_3 = CompileCom C_2 (n_2+1) **in**
  let n_3 = (n_2+1) + Len l_3 **in**
  l_1^`JMZ` (n_2+1)^ l_2^ `JMP` n_3^ l_3

CompileCom (`WHILE` E `DO` C) n =
  let l_1 = CompileExp E **in**
  let n_1 = n + Len l_1 **in**
  let l_2 = CompileCom C (n_1+1) **in**
  let n_2 = (n_1+1) + Len l_2 **in**
  l_1^`JMZ` (n_2+1)^l_2^`JMP` n

Programs are assumed to start at location 1, hence the compiler function Compile is defined by:

Compile C = CompileCom C 1

If C_{OP} is the command in Figure 6, then:

Compile C_{OP} =

```
OPO 1          (instruction number 1)
PUT avail      (instruction number 2)
OPO 1          (instruction number 3)
JMZ 26         (instruction number 4)
INP req        (instruction number 5)
JMZ 25         (instruction number 6)
INP in1        (instruction number 7)
PUT x          (instruction number 8)
INP in2        (instruction number 9)
PUT y          (instruction number 10)
OPO 0          (instruction number 11)
PUT avail      (instruction number 12)
INP req        (instruction number 13)
OP1 NOT        (instruction number 14)
OP1 NOT        (instruction number 15)
JMZ 18         (instruction number 16)
JMP 13         (instruction number 17)
GET x          (instruction number 18)
GET y          (instruction number 19)
OP2 op         (instruction number 20)
PUT out        (instruction number 21)
OPO 1          (instruction number 22)
PUT avail      (instruction number 23)
JMP 25         (instruction number 24)
JMP 3          (instruction number 25)
```

It is this machine code program that ultimately defines the semantics for the 'high level' program in Figure 6. Our goal is eventually to characterize the semantics specified by the compiler and the machine abstractly, but until this has been done the verification will proceed directly from the machine code. First steps towards this are described in the next section.

Each command C determines a machine:

$$\mathsf{Machine}\ C : \mathbf{I} \times \mathbf{S} \rightarrow \mathbf{S}$$

by

$$\mathsf{Machine}\ C\ (i, s) \ = \ \mathsf{Step}\ (\mathsf{Fetch}\ (\mathsf{Compile}\ C)\ (\mathsf{Pc}\ s))\ i\ s$$

10 NSAs from machine instructions

Recall that each state $s \in \mathsf{S}$ of the processor is a triple (pc, stk, mem) where $pc \in \mathsf{N}$ is the program counter, $stk \in \mathsf{V}^*$ is a stack of values, and the function $mem : \mathsf{N} {\rightarrow} \mathsf{V}$ is a 'memory' that associates a value with each name. The following predicates are defined on such states:

- If $n \in \mathsf{N}$, then "$PC = n$" is true of a state if its program counter component is n.
- If $v^* \in \mathsf{V}^*$, then "$STK = v^*$" is true of a state if its stack component is v^*.
- If $v \in \mathsf{V}$, then "$TOP = v$" is true of a state if the head of its stack component is v.
- If $f : \mathsf{N} {\rightarrow} \mathsf{V}$, then "$MEM = f$" is true of a state if its memory component is f.
- If X is variable name and v a value then "$X = v$" is true of a state s if the value of X in the memory component of s is v.
- If $n \in \mathsf{N}$, $v^* \in \mathsf{V}^*$ and $f : \mathsf{N} {\rightarrow} \mathsf{V}$ then "$\langle n, v^*, f\rangle$" is the predicate that is true of the state (n, v^*, f) and false of all other states.

These may be summarized by:

$$
\begin{array}{lcl}
(PC = n)(s) & = & (\mathsf{Pc}\ s\ =\ n) \\
(STK = v^*)(s) & = & (\mathsf{Stk}\ s\ =\ v^*) \\
(TOP = v)(s) & = & (\mathsf{Hd}(\mathsf{Stk}\ s)\ =\ v) \\
(MEM = f)(s) & = & (\mathsf{Mem}\ s\ =\ f) \\
(X = v)(s) & = & (\mathsf{Mem}\ s\ X\ =\ v) \\
\langle m, v^*, f\rangle(s) & = & (\mathsf{Pc}\ s\ =\ n) \wedge (\mathsf{Stk}\ s\ =\ v^*) \wedge (\mathsf{Mem}\ s\ =\ f)
\end{array}
$$

These predicates on states can be converted to predicates on sequences of states by enclosing them in $[\cdots]$ and $[\cdots)$. For example, $[avail = 1]$ is true of a sequence of states if $avail = 1$ is true of each state in the sequence, i.e. if the value of $avail$ is 1 in the memory of each state in the sequence.

Each command C determines a machine Machine C, and from the specification of the processor, primitive NSAs can be determined for each instruction in Compile C. For example:

$$\text{Fetch (Compile } C\text{) } pc \ = \ \texttt{JMP } n \ \Rightarrow$$
$$\text{Machine } C \models \langle pc, stk, mem\rangle \xrightarrow[=1]{[\mathsf{T}]} \langle n, stk, mem\rangle$$

and

$$\text{Fetch (Compile } C\text{) } pc \ = \ \texttt{INP } X \ \Rightarrow$$
$$\text{Machine } C \models \langle pc, stk, mem\rangle \xrightarrow[=1]{[X = v]} \langle pc{+}1, v\hat{\ } stk, mem\rangle$$

To avoid notational clutter, if the only thing below an arrow in an NSA is $=1$, then this will be omitted, and if the only thing above a line is T, then this will be omitted. It is convenient to abbreviate Fetch (Compile C) n to Inst C n. With these conventions, the NSAs above become:

$$\text{Inst } C \ pc \ = \ \texttt{JMP } n \ \Rightarrow$$
$$\text{Machine } C \models \langle pc, stk, mem\rangle \longrightarrow \langle n, stk, mem\rangle$$

and

$$\text{Inst } C \ pc \ = \ \texttt{INP } X \ \Rightarrow$$
$$\text{Machine } C \models \langle pc, stk, mem\rangle \xrightarrow{[X = v]} \langle pc{+}1, v\hat{\ } stk, mem\rangle$$

If C_{OP} is the command in Figure 6, then Inst C_{OP} 25 $=$ **JMP 3** and Inst C_{OP} 5 $=$ **INP** *req*, hence the two NSAs above imply:

$$\text{Machine } C_{\mathsf{OP}} \models \langle 25, stk, mem\rangle \longrightarrow \langle 3, stk, mem\rangle$$

and

$$\text{Machine } C_{\mathsf{OP}} \models \langle 5, stk, mem\rangle \xrightarrow{[req = v]} \langle 6, v\hat{\ } stk, mem\rangle$$

Analogous NSAs for all the instructions in the compiled code can be mechanically generated. These give the real-time semantics of C_{OP}. The hope is that by combining these (using much mechanical assistance) the NSAs in Figure 5 can be deduced using the kind of rules described in Section 5. An outline of how this may proceed is given in the next section.

11 Verification of C_{OP}

To show that the program in Figure 6 implements the NSAs in Figure 5, it is first necessary to say what the predicates S_0 and $S_1(m,n)$ are. Examination of the compiled form of C_{OP} leads to S_0 being identified with the states in the loop waiting for $req = 1$. Hence:

$$S_0 \equiv \mathsf{Pc} = 3 \lor \mathsf{Pc} = 4 \lor \mathsf{Pc} = 5 \lor \mathsf{Pc} = 6 \lor \mathsf{Pc} = 25$$

and $S_1(m,n)$ can be identified with waiting for $req = 0$, togther with the invarient that the program variables x and y have values m and n respectively:

$$\begin{array}{l} S_1(m,n) \equiv \\ \quad (\mathsf{Pc} = 13 \lor \mathsf{Pc} = 14 \lor \mathsf{Pc} = 15 \lor \mathsf{Pc} = 16 \lor \mathsf{Pc} = 17) \\ \quad \land\ x = m \land y = n \end{array}$$

The third of the five NSAs formalizing Figure 5 is:

$$\begin{array}{c} S_0 \land \\ avail = 1 \land \\ out = v \end{array} \xrightarrow[\substack{\leq\delta_2 \land \\ [avail = 1) \land \\ [out = v]}]{\substack{[req = 1] \land \\ [in_1 = m] \land \\ [in_2 = n]}} \begin{array}{c} S_1(m,n) \land \\ avail = 1 \land \\ out = v \end{array}$$

A sketch of thederivation of this is now given. The first stage is to deduce a number of immediate consequences of the atomic NSAs from the instructions numbered 6 to 11. Let Q stand for the condition $avail = 1 \land out = v$, then:

$$PC = 6 \land TOP = 1 \land Q \xrightarrow[=1 \land [Q]]{} PC = 7 \land Q$$

$$PC=7 \wedge Q \xrightarrow[=1 \wedge [Q]]{in_1 = m} PC=8 \wedge Q \wedge TOP=m$$

$$PC=8 \wedge Q \wedge TOP=m \xrightarrow[=1 \wedge [Q]]{} \begin{array}{l} PC=9 \wedge Q \wedge \\ x=m \end{array}$$

$$\begin{array}{l} PC=9 \wedge Q \\ \wedge\, x=m \end{array} \xrightarrow[=1 \wedge [Q]]{in_2 = n} \begin{array}{l} PC=10 \wedge Q \wedge \\ x=m \wedge TOP=n \end{array}$$

$$\begin{array}{l} PC=10 \wedge Q \wedge \\ x=m \wedge TOP=n \end{array} \xrightarrow[=1 \wedge [Q]]{} \begin{array}{l} PC=11 \wedge Q \wedge \\ x=m \wedge y=n \end{array}$$

$$\begin{array}{l} PC=11 \wedge Q \wedge \\ x=m \wedge y=n \end{array} \xrightarrow[=1 \wedge [Q]]{} \begin{array}{l} PC=12 \wedge Q \wedge \\ x=m \wedge y=n \wedge TOP=0 \end{array}$$

These six NSAs can be chained together using the rule:

$$\frac{A \xrightarrow[\leq \delta_1 \wedge [q_1]]{P_1} B \qquad\qquad B \xrightarrow[\leq \delta_2 \wedge [q_2]]{P_2} C}{A \xrightarrow[\leq(\delta_1+\delta_2) \wedge ([q_1] \vee [q_2])]{P_1 \wedge P_2} C}$$

to deduce, using a little Boolean algebra, that:

$$\begin{array}{l} PC=6 \wedge \\ TOP=1 \wedge \\ Q \end{array} \xrightarrow[\leq 6 \wedge [Q]]{\begin{array}{l} in_1 = m \wedge \\ in_2 = n \end{array}} \begin{array}{l} PC=12 \wedge Q \wedge \\ x=m \wedge y=n \wedge \\ TOP=0 \end{array}$$

Using this, the rule:

$$\frac{A \xrightarrow[\leq \delta \wedge [q]]{P_1} B \qquad\qquad B \xrightarrow[=1 \wedge \neg[q]]{P_2} C}{A \xrightarrow[\leq(\delta+1) \wedge [q]]{P_1 \wedge P_2} C}$$

and the atomic NSA:

$$\begin{array}{l} PC = 12 \wedge Q \wedge \\ x = m \wedge y = n \wedge \\ TOP = 0 \end{array} \xrightarrow[\begin{array}{l} =1 \wedge \\ [avail = 0] \wedge \\ [out = v] \end{array}]{} \begin{array}{l} PC = 13 \wedge \\ x = m \wedge y = n \wedge \\ avail = 0 \wedge out = v \end{array}$$

yields:

$$\begin{array}{l} PC = 6 \wedge TOP = 1 \wedge \\ Q \end{array} \xrightarrow[\begin{array}{l} \leq 7 \wedge \\ [avail = 1) \wedge \\ [out = v] \end{array}]{\begin{array}{l} in_1 = m \wedge \\ in_2 = n \end{array}} \begin{array}{l} S_1(m,n) \wedge \\ avail = 0 \wedge out = v \end{array}$$

Next, NSAs starting from the instructions numbered 3, 4, 5, 6 and 25 (which define states in S_0) and ending with instruction 6 are derived by chaining (details of the derivations omitted).

$$PC = 3 \wedge Q \xrightarrow[\leq 3 \wedge [Q]]{req = 1} PC = 6 \wedge TOP = 1 \wedge Q$$

$$PC = 4 \wedge Q \xrightarrow[\leq 2 \wedge [Q]]{req = 1} PC = 6 \wedge TOP = 1 \wedge Q$$

$$PC = 5 \wedge Q \xrightarrow[\leq 1 \wedge [Q]]{req = 1} PC = 6 \wedge TOP = 1 \wedge Q$$

$$PC = 6 \wedge Q \xrightarrow[\leq 5 \wedge [Q]]{req = 1} PC = 6 \wedge TOP = 1 \wedge Q$$

$$PC = 25 \wedge Q \xrightarrow[\leq 4 \wedge [Q]]{req = 1} PC = 6 \wedge TOP = 1 \wedge Q$$

Now, since:

$$S_0 \;=\; \mathsf{Pc} = 3 \vee \mathsf{Pc} = 4 \vee \mathsf{Pc} = 5 \vee \mathsf{Pc} = 6 \vee \mathsf{Pc} = 25$$

the cases rule:

$$\frac{A_1 \xrightarrow[Q_1]{P_1} B_1 \qquad\qquad A_2 \xrightarrow[Q_2]{P_2} B_2}{A_1 \vee A_2 \xrightarrow[Q_1 \vee Q_2]{P_1 \wedge P_2} B_1 \vee B_2}$$

can be used to combine the NSAs for instructions numbered 3, 4, 5, 6 and 25 to obtain:

$$S_0 \wedge \mathcal{Q} \xrightarrow[\leq 5 \;\wedge\; [\mathcal{Q}]]{req = 1} PC = 6 \wedge TOP = 1 \wedge \mathcal{Q}$$

It has already been shown that:

$$\begin{array}{l} PC = 6 \;\wedge \\ TOP = 1 \;\wedge \\ \mathcal{Q} \end{array} \xrightarrow[\begin{array}{l} \leq 7 \;\wedge \\ [avail = 1) \;\wedge \\ [out = v] \end{array}]{\begin{array}{l} in_1 = m \;\wedge \\ in_2 = n \end{array}} \begin{array}{l} S_1(m,n) \;\wedge \\ avail = 0 \;\wedge \\ out = v \end{array}$$

hence by chaining:

$$S_0 \wedge \mathcal{Q} \xrightarrow[\leq 13 \;\wedge\; [\mathcal{Q}]]{\begin{array}{l} req = 1 \;\wedge \\ in_1 = m \;\wedge \\ in_2 = n \end{array}} S_1(m,n) \wedge avail = 0 \wedge out = v$$

which, after expanding out $\mathcal{Q}$, is the original goal with δ_2 refined to 13.

This 'proof' is not formal enough to be trusted, however it is clear that the details are pretty mechanical and closely follow a natural 'symbolic evaluation'. Because of this, there is a good chance that an interactive theorem proving tool can be used to manage and check the details, so that only high level strategies need be supplied by the human verifier. Experiments to test this are in progress.

12 Conclusions

It is hoped that this paper has given an impression of a possible formal method for developing hard real-time programs. In summary, this method is as follows:

(i) Write the specification using annotated state-transition diagrams and interpret them as sets of non-instantaneous state-transition assertions (NSAs).

(ii) Develop a program by identifying nodes in the diagram with sets of processor states.

(iii) Verify the program by showing that its transitions (which are mechanically derived from the compiler and processor specification) entail the required transitions using laws for combining NSAs.

Concerning (i), it is not yet clear whether NSAs will be a sufficient tool for expressing specifications. It may be necesary to also use 'raw logic', possibly to capture more abstract aspects of requirements.

No systematic method for (ii) has been given here. It is hoped to investigate tools that could automatically generate programs for certain classes of NSAs (of course, it is impossible in principle to do this for all NSAs, since these can contain arbitrary logical conditions in the nodes and on the arcs). Another possibility is to use the semantics given here to justify formal rules of refinement in the style developed by Ralph Back and others [1].

Concerning (iii), it is hoped to mechanize most of the routine details. In particular, the generation of NSAs for code segments generated by compiling straight-line high level commands should be fully automatable, and so the software engineer need not have to delve into the details of compiled code unless a very 'fine grain' analysis is required.

13 Acknowledgements

The work described here is jointly supported by the SERC/DTI project number IED/1036 ("SAFEMOS: Demonstration of the Possibility of Totally Verified Systems") lead by Inmos, the SERC project GR/E/53262 ("High Level Theorem-Proving Strategies with Applications to Hardware and Software Verification") and the SERC project GR/G 33837 ("HOL Verification of ELLA Designs").

I would like to thank Roger Hale for discussions on Interval Temporal Logic and models of input and output, Rachel-Cardell Oliver for help in formulating the notion of non-instantaneous state-transition assertions (she had thought up a somewhat similar idea earlier), David May for discussions on the role of temporally well-behaved processors for real-time programming and Jonathan Bowen for comments on the example.

This paper was typeset using LaTeX. The NSAs were typeset using macros from "Commutative Diagrams in TeX" available from Paul Taylor, Department of Computing, Imperial College of Science, Technology and Medicine, London (pt@doc.ic.ac.uk). The diagams were produced by John Van Tassel.

References

[1] R.J.R. Back, *Correctness Preserving Program Refinements: Proof Theory and Applications*, Mathematical Centre Tracts 131, Mathematical Centre, Amsterdam 1980.

[2] C.A.R. Hoare, 'An axiomatic basis for computer programming', *Communications of the ACM*, **12**, pp. 576-583, October 1969.

[3] J. Halpern, Z. Manna and B. Moszkowski., 'A Hardware Semantics based on Temporal Intervals', In the proceedings of the *10-th International Colloquium on Automata, Languages and Programming*, Barcelona, Spain, 1983.

Constructing and Refining Modules in a Type Theory

Shahad N. Ahmed
Joseph M. Morris

Department of Computing Science
University of Glasgow
Glasgow G12 8QQ
Scotland, U.K.

Abstract

The need to apply formal specification and development of programs to large problems has highlighted a need for methods to support the modular development of specifications and their implementations. Here we present a methodology, in the framework of a type theory, that supports both these activities. We show how modular specifications may be incrementally constructed by combining individual specification units or modules with the use of appropriately defined specification building operators. We show how such modular specifications may be systematically refined to calculate an implementation. Our approach is to use a rich type theory which allows us to specify modules purely by their type. The basic theoretical notion underlying our approach is then that a specification is a type, and that an implementation of such a specification is any element in the type.

1. Introduction

As formal specification and development of programs is applied to larger problems, so the size and complexity of specifications has increased. Consequently, the need has arisen for the development of facilities supporting the modular development of specifications and their implementations. We take the view that specifications should be built in a modular fashion from small and relatively independent specification units or *modules*. One advantage of such a methodology is that it allows large specification problems to be broken into a number of smaller, and more manageable tasks. Another advantage of encouraging the development of modular specifications is that it may allow us to build up a library of re-useable specifications.

The main body of work in the development of modular specifications has been carried out in the context of algebraic specification languages such as CLEAR [BuG86], OBJ [GoT86] etc. Of particular interest recently has been the development of Extended ML

[SaT87], a framework for the construction and implementation of modular algebraic specifications. The model-oriented view of specification has also recognised the need for modular development, with recent proposals for module facilities for both Z [SaM90] and VDM [Mid89].

In order to make modular specifications, appropriate language constructs must be developed, both to construct and manage modular specifications. These include specification combinators, as well as parametrisation of specifications; parametrisation is particularly important in the context of re-use as it allows us to make generic modules that can be instantiated as needed. Any formal study of these issues requires a formal semantics for the specification and programming languages concerned. The semantics used in specification languages such as CLEAR, OBJ and Extended ML are based on the interpretations of specifications as specifying algebras. These semantics are often very complex and require the combination of many different formalisms, such as predicate logic, set theory and the lambda calculus.

In the following, we introduce a formal framework, based on Martin-Löf's type theory [Mar82,Mar84,NPS90], for constructing and refining modular specifications. The use of Martin-Löf's type theory has the advantage that it unifies concepts such as first-order logic, set theory and the lambda calculus within one framework. In particular, the notion of a module as a collection of inter-dependent components can be readily specified within the type theory using the concept of dependent types. The semantics of the type theory also gives a much simpler notion of implementation and also provides a potential calculus to allow the implementation of modules from specifications.

In this paper we show how a rich type system can be used to specify modules. We will proceed mainly by example, and we use the minimum amount of type theory that is required to make our point. Our examples illustrate a style of specification that uses specification building constructs to make specifications. All such constructs have a formal mathematical definition within the type theory, but we omit many of the details of the mathematical underpinnings of our method for brevity. However, the reader should be aware that our specifications have a formal semantics in type theory so that we can give a mathematical definition of refinement and can hence derive formal laws concerning the construction and refinement of specifications.

2. Types as Specifications

Whenever we see an expression like x:T in a programming language we often read it as saying "x has type T". For example, the declaration $f:\mathbf{N}\rightarrow\mathbf{N}$ says that f is a function on the natural numbers. A more unusual way of reading x:T is to think of it as a requirement that says "implement a value x that has type T ": we think of the type T as a specification of x and any value in the type T is acceptable as a correct implementation of x. For example, $f:\mathbf{N}\rightarrow\mathbf{N}$ says let f be any function of type $\mathbf{N}\rightarrow\mathbf{N}$, so that both f = **fun**($x\in\mathbf{N}$).x+1 and f = **fun**($x\in\mathbf{N}$).x*x, to take two examples, are acceptable implementations for f. However, simple types such as we know from programming languages, are of little use as specifications since we cannot express the behaviour of objects, such as functions, purely using such types. Our approach is to use a very rich type system, namely Martin-Löf's type theory, which allows us to specify the detailed behaviour of objects purely by their type; objects include functions and – the main interest to us – modules. The task of implementation is then that of finding any value in this type.

Martin-Löf's type theory has the usual standard types such as **N** and Bool, together with the usual operations on them such as +, -, n^2 etc and $\wedge$, $\neg$, if_then_else_ etc, respectively. The type theory also includes the usual type constructors such as $\rightarrow$ and $\times$. Type constructor $\rightarrow$ is used for forming function types and type constructor $\times$ is used for forming pair types. For pair values we have the usual projection functions **fst** and **snd** to extract the individual elements. One of the features of the type theory is that functions and types can be treated as values. For example, both functions and types may be actual parameters to functions, and components in tuples. Another important feature of the type theory is that types themselves have types. In type theory, types of types are often called *kinds*. The kind U_1 (known as the *1st universe*) is the kind of simple types such as those introduced so far (although U_1 is not an element of itself); for example, $\mathbf{N} \in U_1$, $\mathbf{N} \rightarrow (\mathbf{N} \rightarrow \text{Bool}) \in U_1$ etc. One unusual type available in the type theory is the empty type $\emptyset$ which is the type that contains no values. Any specification that is equivalent to $\emptyset$ is treated as an inconsistent specification since to find a value $x{:}\emptyset$ is impossible; a requirement asking for $x{:}\emptyset$ is asking for a miracle.

One of the interesting features of Martin-Löf's type theory is the notion of dependent types. One example of such types are the *dependent function* types. The elements of a dependent function type are functions for which the *type* of any result is determined by the ***values*** of the arguments applied to them. The type $\prod x \in P.Q(x)$ is an example of a dependent function type, where P is a type and Q(x) is a type expression defined in terms of variable x of type P. The elements of $\prod x \in P.Q(x)$ are functions that take an element – p, say – of type P and return an element of type Q(p). For example, the elements of type $\prod x \in \mathbf{N}.(\underline{\text{if}}\ x \neq 0\ \underline{\text{then}}\ \mathbf{N}\ \underline{\text{else}}\ \text{String})$ are functions that take a value – n, say – of type **N** and if $n \neq 0$ they return a value of type **N**, otherwise if n=0 they return a value of type String. Another form of dependent types are the *dependent product* types. The type $\sum x \in P.Q(x)$ is a typical dependent product type where P is a type and Q(x) is a type expression defined in terms of variable x of type P. The elements of this type are pairs $\langle p,q \rangle$ where p has type P and q has type Q(p); observe that the type of q is dependent on the value p. As an example, the elements of type $\sum x \in U_1.x$ are all pairs where the first component is a type and the second component is an element of that type. The pairs $\langle \mathbf{N},6 \rangle$, $\langle \mathbf{N},0 \rangle$, $\langle \text{Bool},\text{true} \rangle$, $\langle \text{String},\text{"hello"} \rangle$ etc are all elements of type $\sum x \in U_1.x$. We note in passing that normal function types $P \rightarrow Q$ are a special case of the dependent function types and are equivalent to $\prod x \in P.Q$ where Q is not dependent on x. Similarly, types of the form $P \times Q$ are equivalent to $\sum x \in P.Q$ where Q is not defined in terms of variable x.

3. Module Specifications

We regard a module as a tuple with syntactic form ‹e_1, ...,e_n› where each e_i may be a type or value. We define the type of modules using dependent product types. The reason for using dependent product types, rather than the cross-product types, is that in general, there can be dependencies between components in a module and such dependencies cannot be expressed by the normal cross product type. For example, suppose we wish to define a type for mathematical groups. A group is module of the form ‹G,_*_,inv,i› where G is a type; _*_ is an associative infix binary operator of type (G×G)→G; inv is an inverse with type G→G; and i is a two sided identity for _*_ and has type G. We may capture the fact that the types of the components _*_, inv and i depend on the first component of the group by defining groups to have the following dependent product type:

$$\Sigma G \in U_1.(\Sigma \_*\_ \in G\times G \rightarrow G.(\Sigma inv \in G \rightarrow G.(G)))$$

A typical element in such a type is ‹int,‹+,‹-,0››› where int is the type of all integers, (+) is integer addition and (-) is unary integer minus. In the following we shall always flatten pairs such as ‹int,‹+,‹-,0››› to ‹int,+,-,0›.

Although dependent product types are more expressive than ordinary product types, they are still not expressive enough to specify modules fully. For example, if we wish to specify a module whose first component is a type and whose second component is an identity function on the first component, then the type $\Sigma X \in U_1.X \rightarrow X$ is too loose as a specification. This is because $\Sigma X \in U_1.X \rightarrow X$ allows the second component to be any arbitrary total function on the first component. What we require is the type whose elements are pairs ‹X,id› with type $\Sigma X \in U_1.X \rightarrow X$ and also satisfying the proposition $\forall a \in X.(id(a) = a)$. In short, we wish to introduce propositions as parts of types. It so happens – and this is one of the remarkable features of type theory that makes it attractive for program specification – that propositions can be expressed in the theory we have just been describing. There is no need for additional logical constructs. The essential idea underlying this trick is to equate propositions with types: a proposition (i.e. type) is true iff it is non-empty (or "inhabited"). Each of the familiar logical constructs then has its counterpart in the type theory; for example, $P \wedge Q$ corresponds to the type $P \times Q$ and $\exists x \in P.Q$ corresponds to $\Sigma x \in P.Q$. Figure 1 gives the correspondence between the operators of first order logic, and their corresponding type constructors in Martin-Löf's type theory. In the first column of Figure 1, P and Q denote propositions and in the second column P and Q denote types; R is a type and p and q are values of type R.

Of course one has to give an argument that this correspondence between propositions and types is a reasonable one, and that argument can be given [Mar82,Mar84,NPS90]. A logic in which types are used as propositions is called an *intuitionistic* or *constructive* logic. The actual values in a propositional type are not important, its truth is determined only by whether the type is inhabited. Any proposition true intuitionistically is true classically, but one limitation of constructive logic is that propositions that can be proved true classically cannot always be proved true constructively. The precedence for each type constructor is equivalent to the precedence of the logical connective it identifies, and grouping the logical connectives in decreasing precedence we get: $\neg$;$\wedge$,$\vee$; $\Rightarrow$. For $\exists$ and $\forall$ we also adopt the convention that quantified expressions of the form, $\forall x\in P.Q\wedge R$, are interpreted as $\forall x\in P.(Q\wedge R)$ and not $(\forall x\in P.Q)\wedge R$; and similarly for $\exists$.

Proposition	Type	Type Name
True	T	Top - the type that is always inhabited
False	$\emptyset$	Empty - the type with no values
$P\wedge Q$	$P\times Q$	Cartesian product
$P\vee Q$	$P+Q$	Disjoint sum
$P\Rightarrow Q$	$P\rightarrow Q$	Function space
$\neg P$	$P\rightarrow\emptyset$	
$\forall x\in P.Q$	$\prod x\in P.Q$	Dependent function space
$\exists x\in P.Q$	$\sum x\in P.Q$	Dependent product
$p=q$	$p=_R q$	Equality type on R - inhabited iff p=q

Figure 1: Identity between propositions and their corresponding type.

We have chosen to regard module specifications as nested dependent product types (i.e. types of the form $\sum x_1\in T_1.\sum x_2\in T_2...\sum x_{n-1}\in T_{n-1}.T_n$) and modules as being elements of such types. Using propositional types, we can define dependent product types that specify constraints on the behaviour of the components in modules. This may be done by extending a dependent product type by an extra final field that is a propositional type specifying the desired behaviour of the preceding components defined by the dependent product type. Only modules whose components satisfy the added propositional type – which we call the *restriction type* – are elements of such an extended dependent product type. For example, we may define the type of all modules that contain a type X and an identity function on type X, by:

$$SP = \sum X\in U_1.(\sum id\in X\rightarrow X.(\prod(a\in X).id(a) =_X a))$$

For specification SP, $\prod(a\in X).id(a) =_X a$ is the restriction type and corresponds to the classical proposition $\forall a\in X.(id(a)=a)$. To see how a restriction type specifies the behaviour of components in a module consider any module $\langle X,id,r\rangle\in SP$. Since we know that r is a member of $\prod(a\in X).id(a) =_X a$, we know that for the particular values of X and id in $\langle X,id,r\rangle$ the type $\prod(a\in X).id(a) =_X a$ is non-empty, i.e true. Therefore, we may conclude that the corresponding classical proposition $\forall a\in X.(id(a)=a)$ is true for X and id in module $\langle X,id,r\rangle$. Since the actual value of r is not important (only its existence) we shall omit the final field when writing modules that satisfy a specification. The following module m_1 satisfies SP,

$$m_1 = \langle \mathbf{N}, \textbf{fun } (x:\mathbf{N}).x, ...\rangle$$

We will also choose – rather loosely – to regard m_2, below, as satisfying SP.

$$m_2 = \langle \mathbf{N}, \mathbf{fun}\ (x{:}\mathbf{N}).x \rangle$$

Returning to our previous example concerning groups, we can now specify groups fully as the type:

$$\Sigma G \in U_1.(\Sigma\_*\_ \in G{\times}G \rightarrow G.(\Sigma inv \in G \rightarrow G.(\Sigma i \in G.$$
$$(\Pi a \in G.\Pi b \in G.\Pi c \in G.$$
$$a*(b*c) =_G (a*b)*c \times$$
$$i*a =_G a \times$$
$$a*i =_G a \times$$
$$inv(a)*a =_G i \times$$
$$a*inv(a) =_G i\ ))))$$

In what follows, we shall usually write module types in the form exemplified by the following rewriting of SP above:

Elements
$X \in U_1.$
$id \in X \rightarrow X$
Restrictions
$\forall a \in X.(id(a) = a)$

The list of declarations after **Elements** indicates the names and types of the components we require to be in any module implementing SP - we call this list the *signature* of the specification (and also of any module that implements the specification). Instead of writing the restriction type for a specification in the unfamiliar notation of propositional types we shall use the more familiar classical notation. Therefore, the proposition after **Restrictions** is the proposition that corresponds to the restriction type on the elements specified by the signature. In the following, we shall allow components in modules to be named. The names of components in modules will correspond to the names of the bound variables used in the dependent types that specified the module. For example, $\langle X{=}\mathbf{N}$, $id{=}\mathbf{fun}\ (x{:}X).x \rangle$ is a module of type SP; the names in the module correspond to the bound names used in SP. Since the variables in dependent types are bound variables, strictly speaking their names are not important; for example, SP is equivalent to $\Sigma Y \in U_1.(\Sigma any \in X \rightarrow X.(\Pi(a \in Y).any(a) =_Y a))$. Therefore we have attached more importance to the names in module types than we really should. We do this here to allow ease of reference to components in a module, and the reader should be aware that introducing names requires further technical justification which we must omit here for brevity. Components of modules may be extracted via their name using a Pascal record style dot notation, so that for, m = ‹X=**N**, id=**fun** (x:X).x›,

both m.X=**N** and m.id=**fun** (x:X).x are examples of use of the dot notation.

As a further example of a module specification, we define the type PointModule, given in Figure 2, which specifies a module that contains a type to represent points on a plane. PointModule also specifies an operation to make a point value from a cartesian representation, as well as operations to return the x- and y-coordinates for cartesian equivalents of a *Point* value.

PointModule =
  Elements
    Point∈ U_1.
    mkPoint∈ **N**×**N**→Point.
    X∈ Point→**N**.
    Y∈ Point→**N**
  Restrictions
    ∀x∈ **N**.∀y∈ **N**.
    X(mkPoint(x,y)) = x ∧
    Y(mkPoint(x,y)) = y

Fig. 2:Specification defining a Point type.

The module PointImp, defined in Figure 3, gives one possible implementation for PointModule, i.e. PointImp∈ PointModule. PointImp is made by choosing to represent *Point* values as pairs of natural numbers. Note that the final component has no particular computational relevance in PointImp, and by our convention it is omitted.

PointImp =
  ‹ Point = **N**×**N**,
    mkPoint = **fun**(x,y:**N**).‹x,y+100›,
    X = **fun**(p:Point).**fst**(p),
    Y = **fun**(p:Point).**snd**(p)-100,
    ...
  ›

Fig. 3: An implementation of PointModule.

To finish off this section we give some more examples of module specifications using the approach outlined above. Figure 4 gives a specification, SeqNat, for a module defining sequences of natural numbers. SeqNat defines some standard sequence operations: *empty* is the empty sequence; the infix operator ‹_› makes a unit sequence; the binary infix operator _ _ concatenates two sequences; *head* returns the first element in a sequence; and *tail* yields all but the first element in a sequence.

SeqNat =
  Elements
    Seq∈ U_1.
    empty∈ Seq.
    <_>∈ **N** → Seq.
    _•_∈ Seq → Seq → Seq.
    head∈ Seq → **N**.
    tail∈ Seq → Seq.
  Restrictions
    ∀x∈ **N**.∀s,s1,s2∈ Seq.
    empty•s = s ∧
    s•empty = s ∧
    s•(s1•s2) = (s•s1)•s2 ∧
    head(<x>•s) = x ∧
    tail(<x>•s) = s ∧
    tail(empty) = empty

Fig. 4:Specification defining sequences of natural numbers.

A list type is available as a standard type in Martin-Löf's type theory, such that the lists of elements of type P form a type denoted by the expression List(P). The elements of a type List(P) are the empty list, denoted by *nil*∈ List(P), and any expressions of the form a:l where a∈ P and l∈ List(P). In addition, primitive recursion is defined on lists using the operator *Listelim* as follows. We normally define a recursive list function f∈ List(P)→Q in clausal form by:

f (*nil*) = e_1
f (a:l) = e_2(a,l,h)

where

a∈ P, l∈ List(P), h=f(l), e_1∈ Q, e_2(a,l,h)∈ Q

Such a definition of f may be written using *Listelim* by:

f(x) = *Listelim*(x , e_1 , [a,l,h] e_2(a,l,h))

Consequently, one possible implementation of SeqNat may be made by defining *Seq* to be List(**N**) and using *Listelim* to define the operations. Such an implementation, named SeqImp, is given in Figure 5. Since the specification SeqNat did not specify what the value of *head*(*empty*) should be in any implementation, we have the freedom to decide; in SeqImp we define *head*(*empty*)=0. Of course there is a proof obligation to show that SeqImp is an implementation of SeqNat, but this is omitted here.

```
SeqImp =
  ‹Seq = List(N),
  empty = nil,
  ‹_› = fun (x:N).x:nil,
  _•_ = fun (s1, s2 : Seq).Listelim(s1 , s2 , [a,l,h] a:h),
  head = fun (s : Seq).Listelim(s , 0 , [a,l,h] a),
  tail = fun (s : Seq).Listelim(s , nil , [a,l,h] l) ›
```

Fig. 5:An implementation of SeqNat.

As a more substantial example, Figure 6 gives a specification, named Catalogue, for a module defining a catalogue of books for a library. The component *Book* is a type whose values denote individual books, and the component *Stock* is a type denoting collections of books. Catalogue also includes operations to add and remove books to and from a stock. The operation *catalogue* queries whether a book is in stock. The constant *empty* represents an empty stock, and an operation *isempty* queries whether a stock value is empty.

```
Catalogue =
  Elements
    Book∈U1.
    Stock∈U1.
    empty∈Stock.
    add∈Book×Stock → Stock.
    remove∈Book×Stock → Stock.
    catalogued∈Book×Stock → Bool.
    isempty∈Stock → Bool.
  Restrictions
    ∀s∈Stock.∀m,n∈Book.
    isempty(empty) = true ∧
    isempty(add(m,s)) = false ∧
    catalogued(m,empty) = false ∧
    catalogued(n,add(n,s)) = true ∧
    ¬(m=n) ⇒ catalogued(n,add(m,s)) = catalogued(n,s) ∧
    remove(n,empty) = empty ∧
    remove(n,add(n,s)) = remove(n,s) ∧
    ¬(m=n) ⇒ remove(n,add(m,s)) = add(m,remove(n,s))
```

Fig. 6:Specification of a book library catalogue.

In any implementation of Catalogue, *Book* might be implemented by N to denote a book number, and *Stock* might be implemented by List(*Book*) to denote a collection of books. Using the two implementation choices mentioned above for *Book* and *Stock*, the operations specified in Catalogue might be implemented via the standard list operations _•_, *head, tail* etc.

A fully developed library specification must also define operations on books, such as constructing a book value as a triple given a books number, author and title; querying the author and title of a book, etc. These operations might be specified by adding them directly as extra components of Catalogue. However, a more modular solution is to develop a separate book module specification, and then combine it with Catalogue. To allow such modular development of specifications requires the definition of specification building operations that allow the development and composition of specifications. We discuss such operations in the following.

4. Structured Specifications

For writing large specifications it is convenient to design specifications in a structured manner by combining and modifying smaller specifications. This supports a modular decomposition of specifications into manageable pieces, and also helps to control the complexity arising from large numbers of type, function and value symbols. In the following section we introduce several specification building operators which allow the combination and modification of module specifications. The operators can be viewed as part of a meta-language for manipulating module types. Semantically, these specification building operations are functions that take a list of arguments, including specifications, and give a specification as result. In the following we shall adopt the convention that the name SP (possibly primed or with a following integer) always denotes a specification. Similarly, S denote a signature, and E (possibly with a following integer) denotes restriction types. For any expression X we let $X[x_1/y_1,...,x_n/y_n]$ denote X with each occurrence of variable y_i replaced by x_i and we call expressions such as $[x_1/y_1,...,x_n/y_n]$ "renamings".

The specification building operations we define are similar to those available in many algebraic specification languages, and are given below.

1. The union of two specifications SP1 and SP2:
   SP1 + SP2

The union operator allows us to make individual module specifications in isolation and then combine them to make a new specification. The specification SP1 + SP2 contains the components defined in both SP1 and SP2, but duplicate components (those with the same name and type) appearing in both SP1 and SP2 only appear once. The restriction type on a specification SP1 + SP2 is the conjunct of the restriction type of SP1 and SP2. We have avoided some technical details concerning the union operator, in particular name clashes, and we mention these in the discussion latter.

2. Enriching a module specification SP by new components S and an extra constraint E
   Enrich SP by Elements S Restrictions E

The **Enrich** operator allows us to modify an existing specification by adding new components and restrictions. The new components, given by a signature S and the new restriction E, may both be defined in terms of the components specified in SP. Again names are important, and new components in S should not have names already defined in SP.

3.Hiding the components of SP given by the set of component identifiers ids:
Hide ids **in** SP

The **Hide** operator allows a specifier to modify an existing specification by removing components from its signature while still preserving the same behaviour for the remaining components in the specification. A general definition of **Hide** is not straightforward and we discuss issues concerning the **Hide** operation in the discussion at the end of this paper.

4. Hiding the components of SP other than those given by the set of identifiers ids:
Export ids **from** SP

The **Export** operator is similar to **Hide,** it simply allows the convenience of saying what components not to hide rather then what components to hide.

5. Renaming components in a specification SP by a renaming r:
Rename SP **by** r

The **Rename** operator allows a specifier to rename the components defined in the signature of a specification. For example, a specifier may find it convenient to rename specifications to avoid name clashes when using the union operator. Renaming is also useful if we wish to reuse an existing specification whose component names are not meaningful in the context in which it is being reused.

The above are not the only operators that are possible; however, we believe them to be a useful collection and they are sufficient for our purposes here. As mentioned, one of the difficulties that arises in combining specification operators is that of controlling the name space, and in particular that of name clashes. In this presentation we ignore these difficulties but the reader should be aware that they can arise. We illustrate how the specification building operators may be used to make specifications and we give some examples. Firstly, we consider extending the library specification, given in Figure 6, by adding operations on books. We can develop a separate book module specification - given by BookModule in Figure 7 - defining a type *Book* whose values give the author, title and book identifier of a book. In practice we would parameterise BookModule with respect to types *Author*, *Title* and *Id*, but for simplicity we shall assume that these types have been defined in some global context. For example, *Author* and *Title* could be defined as strings of characters, and book identifiers *Id* by natural numbers.

BookModule =
Elements
$Book \in U_1$
$mkBook \in Author \times Title \times Id \rightarrow Book.$
$author \in Book \rightarrow Author.$
$title \in Book \rightarrow Title.$
$bookId \in Book \rightarrow Id.$
Restrictions
$\forall a \in Author. \forall t \in Title. \forall i \in Id.$
$author(mkBook(a,t,i)) = a \wedge$
$title(mkBook(a,t,i)) = t \wedge$
$bookId(mkBook(a,t,i)) = i$

Fig. 7:Specification of a book module.

Using the union operator, we may define a new specification for the book catalogue by combining the old Catalogue specification with BookModule to give:

Catalogue2 = Catalogue + BookModule

The new specification Catalogue2 specifies modules that contain all the components specified by Catalogue and BookModule, such that these modules satisfy the original constraints on both Catalogue and BookModule. In more detail, Catalogue2 is obtained by merging the signatures of Catalogue and BookModule and by taking the cross-product (conjunction) of their restrictions. Note that the duplicate component, *Book*, that appears in Catalogue and BookModule is merged to a single component in Catalogue2, thus making all operations specified in Catalogue and BookModule defined over the same *Book* type. A full expansion of Catalogue2 is given in Figure 8.

Catalogue2 =
Elements
$Book \in U_1.$
$Stock \in U_1.$
$empty \in Stock.$
$add \in Book \times Stock \rightarrow Stock.$
$remove \in Book \times Stock \rightarrow Stock.$
$catalogued \in Book \times Stock \rightarrow Bool.$
$isempty \in Stock \rightarrow Bool.$
$mkBook \in Author \times Title \times Id \rightarrow Book.$
$author \in Book \rightarrow Author.$
$title \in Book \rightarrow Title.$
$bookId \in Book \rightarrow Id.$

Restrictions

(∀s∈ Stock.∀m,n∈ Book.
isempty(empty) = true ∧
isempty(add(m,s)) = false ∧
catalogued(m, empty) = false ∧
catalogued(n , add(n,s)) = true ∧
¬(m=n) ⇒ catalogued(n,add(m,s)) = catalogued(n,s) ∧
remove(n, empty) = empty ∧
remove(n , add(n,s)) = remove(n,s) ∧
¬(m=n) ⇒ remove(n,add(m,s)) = add(m,remove(n,s)))

∧

(∀a∈ Author.∀t∈ Title.∀i∈ Id.
author(mkBook(a,t,i)) = a ∧
title(mkBook(a,t,i)) = t ∧
bookId(mkBook(a,t,i)) = i)

Fig. 8:Expansion of Catalogue2.

We may regain a specification similar to Catalogue from Catalogue2 by use of the **Hide** operator; for example, consider the following specification,

Catalogue3 =
Hide {mkBook,author,title,bookId}
in Catalogue2

Catalogue3 specifies exactly those components specified in Catalogue, and this is done by hiding all the components in Catalogue2 not defined in Catalogue. However, Catalogue3 is not equal to Catalogue, since the restriction type for Catalogue3 is still the conjunction of the restriction types of Catalogue and BookModule. However, Catalogue3 and Catalogue are similar, in that every implementation of Catalogue3 is also an implementation of Catalogue; such a similarity is important, and will be made more concrete in section 5.

If we were to continue developing a library specification, then we might wish to specify a module for a register of library users. Such a specification would be very similar to Catalogue as we would require operations to add and remove users to and from a register; as well as operations to query the status of a register and individuals. One possible specification of a register module may be defined simply by renaming some of the components of Catalogue, giving the following specification:

Register =
Rename Catalogue **by**
[Person/Book, Users/Stock, addUser/add,
removeUser/remove, registered/catalogued]

In practice, when we reuse a specification such as Catalogue, it may contain components that we do not require and these may be hidden using the **Hide** or **Export** operator. Additionally, we may wish to add some new components defined in terms of existing components, and these may be added using the **Enrich** operator. For example, suppose we require an extra operation in a register module so that we may calculate the number of registered users. This may be specified as an enrichment of Register by,

Register2 =
  Enrich Register **by**
  Elements
    size∈ Users → **N**
  Restrictions
    ∀s∈ Users.∀m∈ Person.
    size(empty) = 0 ∧
    size(addUser(m,s)) = (if registered(m,s) then size(s) else size(s) + 1)

In any register, we might keep the name, address and personal identifier of each library user, such that we might define a type *Person* in terms of some types *Name*, *Address*, and *Pid* respectively. We may specify a module defining a person by reusing BookModule:

PersonModule =
  Rename BookModule **by**
    [Person/Book, Name/Author, Address/Title,
    Pid/Id, mkPerson/mkBook, name/author,
    address/title, personId/bookId]

Putting all the pieces together, we may specify a user register containing the personal details of each user by the combination:

LibraryRegister = Register2 + PersonModule

5. Refinement

Refining a specification may be regarded as the task of making concrete design decisions about properties of the specification that were left open by the specifier – the choice of data structures and error messages for example. The definition of refinement we use here is one where we add more detail to a specification to get a refinement. We regard refinement as being different from implementation. Specifications are *types*, and any refinement of a specification is a specification and hence a type. However, implementations are *values* in a type, and so implementation is the task of finding a value in a specification (type). We don't make implementations in one go, instead we proceed to an implementation by refining the specification. Implementations become easier the more we refine a specification, and so we keep refining a specification until we arrive at a specification that strongly suggests an implementation. Then we proceed by finding an implementation from the specification using a constructive proof. This last step is usually clerical, and so we shall omit its discussion here. We refer the reader interested in deriving programs via constructive proofs to [Bac89,NPS90].

One possible definition of refinement for types used as specifications – not just module specifications – is that of implementation inclusion. A specification SP' is a refinement of a specification SP (written SP≤SP') if all the implementations of SP' are also implementations of SP; SP' is said to be a subtype of SP. We can define this form of refinement for module specifications by comparing the "restrictions" on the components defined in SP and SP': the restrictions on a component include its type, as declared in the signature, together with any additional constraints specified on the component by the restriction type. Formally, we say that SP≤SP' iff the signature of SP' contains the same component names as the signature of SP, and for each named component in SP', the restrictions on the component imply the restrictions on the component with the same name in SP. The preceding definition is equivalent to saying that the type of each component in SP' is a subtype of the type of its equivalent in SP. In practice, such a definition of refinement is overly restrictive. For example, when we refine specifications we often wish to add extra components which only play an intermediary role in helping to make refinements. However, using the above definition of refinement, we cannot refine a module specification by adding extra components to its signature; even if all the components in the refinement, excluding extra components, imply their original restrictions.

Some type systems similar to Martin-Löf's, but without propositions as types, have a more flexible definition of subtyping defined on them. For example, the language Quest [Car89] – which has dependent types, and module types without restriction types – has such a subtype relation defined over its types. Subtyping here should not be confused with subset types as in [NPS90]. Informally, type P is a subtype of type Q if every expression of type P may be used in a context requiring an expression of type Q. For example, the Quest subtype relation allows a module type S to be a subtype of a module type T, if S has at least all the component declarations of T; and S may declare extra components not declared in T. Allowing S to define extra components does not conflict with the informal definition of subtyping. Any implementation of (module in) S can be used in any context where an implementation of T can: the extra components in an implementation of S are ignored by – and do not interfere in – any context requiring an implementation of T.

The subtype relation in Quest is defined formally as part of the type system by an inductive definition over all types. We adopt such a subtype relation as a refinement relation and extend it, inductively, over those types in Martin-Löf's type theory not available in a language such as Quest. The extensions to the subtype relation are defined in such a way as to ensure that if type P is a subtype of type Q then, when we consider P and Q as propositions, P implies Q. For module specifications, if SP' is a subtype of SP, then the restrictions on all the components in SP' imply the restrictions on the components in SP. For any specifications SP and SP', SP≤SP' iff SP' is a subtype of SP. The formal definition of subtyping is omitted here; readers interested in how subtyping is formally defined on types are referred to [Car89]. One of the advantages of using extended subtyping as a refinement relation is that refinement is defined over all types, not just module specifications. Therefore, subtyping can be viewed as a refinement relation for any type we choose to regard as a specification. A practical test for refinement of module specifications (though not the definition of refinement) is given by law 1.

Law 1: Given specifications SP1 and SP2 with restrictions E1 and E2 respectively, then SP1≤SP2 if SP2 contains, at least, all the component declarations (with matching names and types) that SP1 contains, and E2 implies E1.

Law 1 does not capture some the advantages of using subtyping as a definition of refinement. For example, although for every named component in SP there must be a component with the same name in SP', their types need not match exactly: using subtyping as a definition of refinement allows us to refine a module specification by refining the declared type of any component. For example, if SP declares a function $f \in \mathbb{N} \rightarrow int$, then a refinement of SP may declare f as having type $int \rightarrow \mathbb{N}$. Such a refinement is valid since $int \rightarrow \mathbb{N}$ is a subtype of $\mathbb{N} \rightarrow int$; it should be clear that we may use a function of type $int \rightarrow \mathbb{N}$ in a context requiring a function of type $\mathbb{N} \rightarrow int$. We should be aware that the type constraints given by the signature may not be the only constraints on a component. A naive refinement of a components declared type may cause any further constraints, given by the restriction type, to become inconsistent. For example, the restriction type of SP may imply that $\forall x \in \mathbb{N}.f(x)<0$. Such a requirement together with the refinement of f to $f \in int \rightarrow \mathbb{N}$ clearly leads to inconsistent requirements on f; such a refinement of SP is an inconsistent specification. However, refining any specification to an inconsistent specification is a valid – if somewhat useless – refinement step. A good example of when refinement of the declared type of a component may be needed, is the case where a component of a module is also a module.

To define the style of subtyping given in [Car89] we allow specifications to name the components in a module. Naming components in specifications allows us to define relationships between module specifications by pairing off and comparing components with the same name. For example, we have already defined refinement by comparing the types of components with the same name; our insistence that component names do not change under refinement always ensures that such comparisons are possible. Component names in specifications are also important in allowing us to define specification operations such as union, hide etc. We must recognise that using subtyping as a definition of refinement has its limitations. For example, we have stated that we allow extra components to be defined in refinements. However, we do not have a mechanism to remove these extra components since our definition of refinement does not allow any refinement of a specification to define less components than the specification it refines.

As an example of a refinement, consider the following specification of a module containing two functions f and g:

SP =
Elements
$f \in \mathbf{N} \rightarrow \mathbf{N}$.
$g \in \mathbf{N} \rightarrow \mathbf{N}$
Restrictions
$\forall\, a \in \mathbf{N}$.
$[f(a) > a = \text{true}] \wedge$ (1)
$[g(a) < f(a) = \text{true}]$ (2)

One possible refinement of SP is given by the specification SP'

SP' =
Elements
$f \in \mathbf{N} \rightarrow \mathbf{N}$.
$g \in \mathbf{N} \rightarrow \mathbf{N}$.
$h \in \mathbf{N}$
Restrictions
$\forall\, a \in \mathbf{N}$.
$[(f(a) = a + 27) = \text{true}\,] \wedge$ (3)
$[(g(a) = f(a) - h) = \text{true}\,] \wedge$ (4)
$[h = 3\,]$ (5)

To see why SP≤SP' we observe that for all f, g and h, the conjunction of (4) and (5) implies (2); and (3) implies (1), and hence the restrictions on SP' imply the restrictions on SP. Therefore, by Law 1, SP≤SP'. For an intuitive understanding, it is enough to observe that any implementation satisfying the restrictions on SP' must also satisfy the restrictions on SP, since the restrictions on SP' are stronger than those on SP. Therefore, every implementation of SP' (ignoring component h) is an implementation of SP.

The form of SP' above strongly suggests module m below as a possible implementation of SP'. It is easy to show, by constructive proof, that m is indeed an implementation of SP' (i.e. m∈ SP').

m =
‹ f = **fun** (a:**N**).a+27,
g = **fun** (a:**N**).f(a)-3,
h = 3 ›

We observe that module m is not quite an implementation of the original specification SP, above, since m contains the extra component h. This is sad and is a consequence of the problem mentioned earlier whereby extra components in a specification cannot be removed by refinement. However, m with component h hidden can be shown (constructively) to satisfy specification SP. We shall discuss this issue in the discussion later.

In general, for two arbitrary specifications SP1 and SP2, verifying that SP1≤SP2 is difficult. However, since we have a definition of refinement, we may prove a collection of useful laws, such as law 1 above, that can help make refinements. We shall give some laws here, but omit their proofs. It is important to be aware that refinement laws can and must be proved, otherwise there is no guarantee that refinement yields acceptable specifications and implementations. The laws given below are in no way a complete collection, and serve only to illustrate the style of laws that might be useful in practice. For example, useful laws include the facts that ≤ is reflexive and that the refinement relation is transitive:

Law 2: SP≤SP
Law 3: SP1≤SP2 and SP2≤SP3 implies that SP1≤SP3

The transitivity property of ≤ is particularly useful as it allows a specification, SP, to be refined to a specification, SP_n, via a series of intermediate refinements, such that SP ≤ $SP_1 \leq ... \leq SP_{n-1} \leq SP_n$. If a sufficient number of useful laws can be developed, they can be built up into a calculus. Rather than guess a refinement for a specification, and then verify it afterwards, the motivation behind a calculus is that we refine a specification by systematically applying the laws of the calculus to it until we arrive at an acceptable refinement. One useful property of refinement is that we may refine a structured specification by refining its individual parts in relative isolation, and then compose these individual refinements to get a refinement of the original specification; this property may be expressed by the following laws:

Law 4: if SP1≤SP1' and SP2≤SP2' then SP1+SP2 ≤ SP1'+SP2'
Law 5: if SP1≤SP2 then **Rename** SP1 **by** r ≤ **Rename** SP2 **by** r
Law 6: if SP1≤SP2 then **Hide** ids **in** SP1 ≤ **Hide** ids **in** SP2
Law 7: if SP1≤SP2 then **Enrich** SP1 **by Elements** S **Restrictions** E
≤**Enrich** SP2 **by Elements** S **Restrictions** E

where r is any renaming and ids is any set of identifier names. Laws 4 - 7 are sometimes summarised by saying that each of the structuring operations is *refinement preserving* in their specification arguments or, more formally, that they are monotonic with respect to ≤. Transitivity and monotonicity of ≤ are the two properties that make stepwise refinement an effective notion for structured specifications. In addition to the above properties, we may also define additional refinement rules for specifications. For example:

Law 8: SP ≤ **Enrich** SP **by Elements** S **Restrictions** E
Law 9: For any SP', SP ≤ SP + SP'

Law 10: If ids contain all the elements defined in SP and SP≤SP', then
SP ≤ Export ids **from** SP'

Law 11: If ids does not contain any elements defined in SP and SP≤SP', then
SP ≤ **Hide** ids **in** SP'

Law 8 states that any well-defined enrichment to a specification constitutes a refinement. Law 9 allows a specification to be refined by unioning it with any other specification. Law 10 allows additional components added to a specification during the refinement process to be hidden from the signature. Such a refinement is useful if we wish to redefine the constraints on a specification in terms of additional auxiliary operations without the additional operations appearing in the signature of the module.

As a more substantial example of refinement, we consider the refinement of PointModule defined previously in Figure 2. The refinement we aim for is a new specification defined in terms of specification SeqNat, defined previously in Figure 4, for a sequence of natural numbers. We refine PointModule by choosing to represent *Point* values as sequences of naturals, such that the the head of the sequence gives the x-coordinate and the second value in the sequence gives the y-coordinate. The refinement is given by the specification Point_by_Seq given in Figure 9.

```
Point_by_Seq =
  Export {Point,mkPoint,X,Y} from
    Rename SeqPoint  by [Point/Seq]
```

where

```
SeqPoint =
  Enrich  SeqNat by
    Elements
      mkPoint∈ N×N→Seq.
      X∈ Seq→N.
      Y∈ Seq→N.
    Restrictions
      ∀p∈ Seq.∀x,y∈ N.
      mkPoint(x,y) = ‹x›•‹y› ∧
      X(p) = head(p) ∧
      Y(p) = head(tail(p))
```

Fig. 9: A refinement of PointModule.

An energetic reader would not find it intellectually taxing to verify that the restrictions on Point_by_Seq imply the restrictions on PointModule, but it would be long and tedious work. In practice, Point_by_Seq is arrived at via a sequence of intermediate refinements. We give an outline of the refinement of PointModule but omit some details for reasons of space. The first move in the refinement is to combine SeqNat with PointModule, renaming type *Seq* in SeqNat to ***Point***. This makes all the usual sequence operations well-defined on *Point* values. The signature of the resultant specification now contains the extra operations supplied by SeqNat.

PointModule
≤ " Law 9 , SeqPoint' = **Rename** SeqNat **by** [Point/Seq] "
PointModule + SeqPoint'

Next, we refine the expression PointModule + SeqPoint'. We add our main design decision that Point values are to be defined as sequences of natural numbers.

≤ "Law 8 ie any restriction enrichment is a refinement"
Enrich (PointModule + SeqPoint') **by**
Restrictions
$\forall x,y \in \mathbb{N}$.
mkPoint(x,y) = ‹x›•‹y›

Omitting several steps, we may rewrite the above specification in the following form to reveal the operations and restrictions on PointModule:

≤
Enrich SeqPoint' **by**
Elements
mkPoint$\in \mathbb{N}\times\mathbb{N}\rightarrow$Point.
X$\in$Point$\rightarrow\mathbb{N}$.
Y$\in$Point $\rightarrow\mathbb{N}$.
Restrictions
$\forall x,y \in \mathbb{N}$.
mkPoint(x,y) = ‹x›•‹y› ∧ (a)
X(mkPoint(x,y)) = x ∧ (1)
Y(mkPoint(x,y)) = y (2)

The refinement of this specification involves using the relationship mkPoint(x,y) = ‹x›•‹y›, given by (a), to calculate new restrictions that subsume the old restrictions (1) and (2) on PointModule. We first consider (1) and (2) which define the X and Y operations. By substituting the definition of mkPoint(x,y), given by (a), into (1) and (2), together with straightforward logical manipulation and case analysis, we may calculate that the restrictions (b) and (c), below, imply (1) and (2).

X(p) = head(p) (b)
Y(p) = head(tail(p)) (c)

Hence, we may show that (a)∧(b)∧(c) implies (a)∧(1)∧(2). Using Law 1, we may deduce the following refinement for the above:

≤ "(a)∧(b)∧(c) implies (a)∧(1)∧(2), Law 1, definition of SeqPoint' "
Enrich (**Rename** SeqNat **by** [Point/Seq]) **by**
Elements
mkPoint∈ **N**×**N**→Point.
X∈ Point→**N**.
Y∈ Point →**N**.
Restrictions
∀p∈ Point.∀x,y∈ **N**.
mkPoint(x,y) = ‹x›•‹y› ∧
X(p) = head(p) ∧
Y(p) = head(tail(p))

The remainder of the refinement then proceeds by considering **Rename** SeqNat **by** [Point/Seq]. Bringing the above enrichment of **Rename** SeqNat **by** [Point/Seq] inside the **Rename** construct, and carefully renaming the enrichment by [Seq/Point] gives us **Rename** SeqPoint **by** [Point/Seq].

≤
Rename SeqPoint **by** [Point/Seq]

So far we have that PointModule ≤ **Rename** SeqPoint **by** [Point/Seq]. Since we know that the identifiers *Point*, *mkPoint*, *X* and *Y* are the names of all the components defined in PointModule, we may use Law 10 to get:

PointModule
≤ " Law 10, PointModule ≤ **Rename** SeqPoint **by** [Point/Seq] "
Export {Point,mkPoint,X,Y} **from**
Rename SeqPoint **by** [Point/Seq]

The form of the refinement Point_by_Seq is not accidental, it illustrates how we may reuse specifications such as SeqNat not only in the specification process, but also when refining specifications. There are further implications for this reuse when we come to make implementations, and we shall come back to this point in section 7.

6. Parametrisation

We have already shown how different forms of specification combinators may be defined to help structure specifications. Another important way specifications may be structured is by parametrisation. Parametrisation allows a specifier to make general purpose specifications that may be instantiated in different ways; parametrisation therefore provides a useful mechanism for the reuse of specifications. Semantically, we regard parametrised specifications as functions that, when applied to an appropriate list of argument specifications, return a specification as result. The body of a parametrised specification is simply a structured specification defined in terms of some formal parameter names. The result of applying a parametrised specification to an actual parameter is just that of replacing each formal parameter with the corresponding actual parameter in the body of the parametrised specification. As an example of parametrisation we define a parametrised specification, called *Triple*, that takes the union of three specifications:

Triple = **fun** (SP1∈ Spec, SP2∈ Spec, SP3∈ Spec).(SP1+SP2)+SP3

where the kind Spec is actually the type of all module specifications. Intuitively the kind Spec is the type of all dependent product types, and such a kind may be defined formally in Martin-Löf's type theory. Any specifications – between which the union operation is valid – may be used as actual parameters for Triple, since the only requirement on any actual parameters is that they be members of Spec. In practice, a specifier will want to put constraints on specifications that may be allowed as actual parameters to a parametrised specification. That is, the specifier may wish to constrain actual parameters to be specific subkinds of Spec. For example, we might wish to define a parametrised specification that may only be applied to specifications that specify a component *identity*$\in \mathbf{N}\rightarrow\mathbf{N}$, say; and so the argument to such a parametrised specification must be a member of the kind of all specifications that specify a component *identity*$\in \mathbf{N}\rightarrow\mathbf{N}$. Such a kind is a subkind of Spec.

One way a specifier may define useful subkinds on Spec is to define a sample specification, called the *requirements specification*, that defines the minimum components and behaviour that must be specified by each specification in the subkind required. From a requirements specification - SP_{Par}, say - we may define a suitable subkind of Spec as being one whose elements are all the specifications that are refinements of SP_{Par} : we denote such a kind by $|SP_{Par}|$. Intuitively, the elements the kind $|SP_{Par}|$ are the elements in the set $\{SP\in Spec \mid SP_{Par} \leq SP\}$. Thus, for parametrised specifications such as P below, only refinements of SP_{Par} may be used as actual parameters for P. Since refinement is subtyping, $|SP_{Par}|$ is the kind of all subtypes of SP_{Par}.

P = **fun**(x∈ $|SP_{Par}|$).SP

CirclePackage, defined in Figure 10, is an example of a parametrised specification that may be used to specify a module containing a type to represent circles and operations on circles. *Circle* values are made by giving the origin and radius of the circle required, the origin being defined using a type named *Point*. The specification for type *Point* and its related operations is supplied by the parameter P, where an actual parameter P for

CirclePackage may be any refinement of PointModule (defined previously in Figure 2).

```
CirclePackage =
  fun(P∈ |PointModule|).
    Enrich P by
    Elements
      Circle∈ U₁.
      mkCircle∈ Point × N → Circle.
      origin∈ Circle → Point.
      radius∈ Circle → N.
      intersect∈ Circle × Circle → Bool
    Restrictions
      ∀c₁,c₂∈ Circle.∀p₁, p₂∈ Point.∀r₁,r₂∈N.
      c₁ = mkCircle(p₁,r₁) ⇒ (origin(c₁) = p₁ ∧ radius(c₁) = r₁ ) ∧
      c₁ = mkCircle(p₁,r₁) ∧ c₂ = mkCircle(p₂,r₂) ⇒
      intersect(c₁,c₂) = (X(p₁)-X(p₂))² + (Y(p₁)-Y(p₂))² ≤ (r₁+r₂)²
```

Fig. 10: Parametrised specification for a circle module.

We may specify a module, which we call CircleModule1, that defines a *Circle* type using PointModule itself as an actual parameter to CirclePackage, since by Law 2 PointModule ≤ PointModule, giving

CircleModule1 = CirclePackage(PointModule)

Alternatively, we can also define another specification, which we call CircleModule2, defining a circle module similar to CircleModule1 by using Point_by_Seq, the refinement of PointModule defined in Figure 9. Since we have that PointModule ≤ Point_by_Seq we may define CircleModule2 as

CircleModule2 = CirclePackage(Point_by_Seq)

Now we consider refining specification expressions such as CirclePackage(PointModule). One way we can do this is by refining the parameter PointModule. In general, specifications of the form P(SP), where P is a parametrised specification, may be refined by refining the actual parameter SP (i.e. parametrised specifications are also refinement preserving with respect to their arguments):

Law 12: For any parametrised specification P, given two suitable actual parameters SP1 and SP2 for P, if SP1 ≤ SP2 then P(SP1) ≤ P(SP2).

Refinement law 12 should not come as to much of a surprise since the body of any parametrised specification will be defined in terms of the usual specification operators

Enrich, +, **Hide** etc, which we have already stated are also refinement preserving in their arguments. Law 12 can therefore be proved from laws 4-7 and structural induction on the body of P. As an example of the use of law 12, we may conclude that the specification CircleModule2 is a refinement of CircleModule1 from the fact that PointModule ≤ Point_by_Seq.

Another way we might consider refining specifications of the form P(SP) is by defining a separate notion of refinement for parametrised specifications. Such a notion of refinement can be defined so that if we use it to refine P to a parametrised specification P', say, then P(SP) ≤ P'(SP). In theory this allows a parametrised specification to be refined independently of any actual parameter applied to it. One definition we have considered is as follows. A parametrised specification P1 is refined by another parametrised specification P2, written as P1 $\leq_p$ P2, if all argument specifications applicable to P2 are applicable to P1, and for all argument specifications SP applicable to P2, P1(SP) ≤ P2(SP). The refinement relation, $\leq_p$, also has many of the properties of ≤; for example, its is both reflexive and transitive. However, in practice this definition is difficult to use : the requirement that we show that for all parameters SP for P2, P2(SP)$\leq_p$P1(SP) is not in general easy to prove. The practical use of $\leq_p$ requires the development of effective laws which have yet to be developed. One rule that would be useful is that analogous to the rule that allows us to refine Pascal functions (with value parameters) by refining the function body independently of any actual parameters.

7. Implementation

We noted when discussing refinement that refinement was different to implementation. Refinement is the task of transforming a specification (i.e type) to another specification (i.e type) with similar properties. Implementation is the task of finding a module (i.e value) defined by such a specification (i.e type). In this section we outline how the structure of a specification may sometimes be used to decompose the implementation task into that of implementing individual pieces of a specification, so that the implementations may be glued together to form an implementation of the specification. We ignore the implementation of flat specifications (i.e specification not constructed using specification operators). Flat specifications may be implemented by the constructive proof methodology. Alternatively, if we have a large flat specification it may first be structured and then implemented using the technique we describe below. In the following, where we require the implementation of a flat specification we simply state the implementation although the reader should be aware that work needs to be done to produce such implementations.

Let us consider specifications of the form F(SP) where F may be a parametrised specification or specification building operator and SP is an actual parameter for F: semantically specification building operators can be viewed as pre-defined parametrised specifications. If we have a specification of the form F(SP) and we develop an implementation m for SP then we would like to know if there is an operator - f, say -

similar to F, but at the implementation level, such that f(m) is an implementation for F(SP). In general there is not always such a function f; however, in some situations under suitable restrictions we can find such a function. For example, let us consider the specification **Rename** SeqPoint **by** [Point/Seq]. If we implement SeqPoint by a module, m say, then it is possible to show that m[Point/Seq] is an implementation of **Rename** SeqPoint **by** [Point/Seq]. In fact it is possible to prove that this generalises to the following law:

Law 13: For specifications of the form **Rename** SP **by** [x/y] where x and y are variable names, if we have an implementation m for SP, then for f = **fun** (s:SP).s[x/y], f(m) is an implementation of **Rename** SP **by** [x/y].

We can also show that any use of the **Hide** and **Export** operators has an equivalent at the implementation level. (We shall give an example for **Export** later). The situation is more complex with the + and **Enrich** operations. For example, consider the specification:

SP1 = **Enrich** SP **by Elements** S **Restrictions** E.

To implement SP1 we would like to develop an implementation m of SP independently of the enrichment of SP, and then add to m an implementation for the components declared in signature S. Our aim is to borrow our implementation of SP to make an implementation for the components of S. It is possible that some implementations of SP may make the restrictions E inconsistent: inconsistencies can arise since m is implemented without considering any extra restrictions on SP introduced by E. An unfortunate choice of implementation for SP may prevent an implementation for the components in S. It may be possible to show that for an implementation of SP there is no enrichment that satisfies E. However, showing that an implementation of SP avoids such 'dead-end' developments requires proving that the remaining implementation task is consistent. It can be shown – and this is one of the interesting features of using type theory to develop programs – that trying to prove that E is consistent, for an arbitrary implementation of SP, is equivalent to making an implementation for the components defined in S.

Given that we have an implementation of SP, the next stage in developing SP1 is to implement the components declared in S. The enrichment of SP in SP1, namely **Elements** S **Restrictions** E, can almost be viewed as a module specification; it is not a complete module specification since it is defined in terms of components declared in SP. However, we may make the enrichment a complete specification by replacing the free names of components from SP by actual implementations of such components taken from any implementation of SP. Given an implementation m∈SP, we may implement the components of S by finding an implementation – n, say – such that n∈(**Elements** S **Restrictions** E)[$m.x_1/x_1,\ldots, m.x_n/x_n$] where $x_1,\ldots,x_n$ are the names of the components in m (and SP). Given implementations m and n, as above, it can be shown that combining m and n by module concatenation (++ defined below) gives m++n as an implementation for SP1. Given two modules P = $\langle x_1 = p_1,\ldots,x_n = p_n\rangle$ and Q = $\langle y_1 = q_1,\ldots,y_m = q_m\rangle$, where the names in P and Q are distinct, P ++ Q denotes the module $\langle x_1 = p_1,\ldots, x_n = p_n, y_1 = q_1,\ldots, y_m = q_m\rangle$.

The components declared in S may also be implemented by a function that takes any implementation of SP and returns an implementation of the components of S. The type of such a function is a dependent product type F, say, where F = $\prod$m∈ SP.(**Elements** S **Restrictions** E)[$m.x_1/x_1,\ldots, m.x_n/x_n$]; and F may be regarded as the specification of a parametrised module. For any f∈ F and m∈ SP, we can show that m++f(m)∈ SP1. In practice, F is often inconsistent; since as above, some m∈ SP may make E inconsistent, and hence F becomes inconsistent. Therefore, it is often easier to borrow a specific m∈ SP – as discussed previously – to implement the enrichment.

As an example, let us consider how we might implement Point_by_Seq (the refinement of PointModule defined previously in Figure 9) i.e.

Point_by_Seq =
  Export {Point,mkPoint,X,Y} **from**
    Rename SeqPoint **by** [Point/Seq]

where

SeqPoint =
  Enrich SeqNat **by**
  Elements
    mkPoint∈ N×N→Seq.
    X∈ Seq→N.
    Y∈ Seq →N.
  Restrictions
    ∀p∈ Seq.∀x,y∈ N.
    mkPoint(x,y) = ‹x›•‹y› ∧ (1)
    X(p) = head(p) ∧ (2)
    Y(p) = head(tail(p)) (3)

We may begin by implementing SeqPoint which is expressed above as an enrichment of SeqNat. We already have an implementation for SeqNat, namely SeqImp defined earlier in Figure 5, and we shall use SeqImp as our implementation of SeqNat here. As a check against miraculous development, we may observe, informally, that SeqImp does not appear to make restrictions (1),(2) and (3) inconsistent. We now require to implement the enrichment as a module containing *mkPoint*, *X* and *Y*. The first step is to substitute the occurrences of the component names *Seq*, *head*, *tail* and _•_ in the enrichment by actual implementations of these components; for example, using SeqImp we may use the implementations SeqImp.*Seq*, SeqImp.*head*, SeqImp.*tail* and for the binary operator _•_ we shall write its implementation extracted from SeqImp as $\_\bullet_{SeqImp}\_$. Making such a substitution transforms the enrichment into a complete specification. We omit the details of making the implementation for the enrichment but give a possible implementation in the body of function f1 below, where f1 also concatenates this implementation with any implementation of SeqNat. Thus, f1(SeqImp)∈ SeqPoint where

f1 = **fun**(s : SeqNat).
    s ++ ‹mkPoint = **fun** (x,y : **N**).‹x›$\bullet_s$‹y›,
        X = **fun** (p:Seq).(s.head(p)),
        Y = **fun** (p:Seq).(s.head(s.tail(p))) ›

Next, we consider implementing the expression **Rename** SeqPoint **by** [Point/Seq]. By Law 13 if we implement a function f2 where

f2 = **fun** (x : SeqPoint).(x[Point/Seq])

then using the implementation f1(SeqImp) of SeqPoint calculated above, we can conclude

f2(f1(SeqImp)) ∈ **Rename** SeqPoint **by** [Point/Seq]

Finally, we consider implementing the expression:

Export {Point,mkPoint,X,Y} **from**
  Rename SeqPoint **by** [Point/Seq]

At the implementation level, the **Export** operator above may be defined as a function that takes an implementation of **Rename** SeqPoint **by** [Point/Seq], and extracts from this implementation the named components *Point*, *mkPoint*, *X* and *Y*. For example, a possible implementation of the above use of **Export** is the function f3 such that:

f3 = **fun** (x : **Rename** SeqPoint **by** [Point/Seq]).
    ‹Point = x.Point,
    mkPoint = x.mkPoint,
    X = x.X,
    Y = x.Y ›

Combining f3 with our implementation of **Rename** SeqPoint **by** [Point/Seq], we finally get an implementation of Point_by_Seq given by:

f3(f2(f1(SeqImp))) ∈ Point_by_Seq

Making implementations via functions has some interesting consequences. One of these is illustrated in the example above, which shows how reusing an existing specification such as SeqNat, to make a new specification like Point_by_Seq, also allows us to reuse an existing implementation of SeqNat, namely SeqImp, to make an implementation of Point_by_Seq. This is a consequence of being able to refine and sometimes implement the individual components of a structured specification in a relative degree of isolation. In general, it shows that if we reuse existing specifications to make new specifications, then it may also be possible to reuse their corresponding implementations when implementing the new specifications.

8. Discussion and Conclusion

The methodology presented in this paper is in no way complete and we recognise serious limitations that still have to be addressed. We look at only some of the issues here. One of the most important limitations of our approach is that we still have an unsatisfactory definition of refinement. This was highlighted by the problem of not being able to refine away intermediary components that sometimes arise during refinement. The observant reader may have realised that laws 10 and 11 do allow extra components to be removed from specifications, but these laws are only applicable by referring to be original specification that is being refined. Such laws cannot usually be applied as a step in a transitive sequence of refinements. One solution to this that we are pursuing is to allow the refinement relation to be defined with respect to a signature which tells us which components we can and cannot throw away; therefore, any components not defined in such a signature can be added or hidden as required. Such a solution would also solve the problem highlighted in section 5 where we found that the implementation of specification SP' where SP' was a refinement of SP, was not an implementation of SP because it contained an extra intermediary component.

Another important issue is that of names and name space. For example, one of the problems of defining the union operation is that of deciding how to resolve name clashes. In the case of a specification SP1+SP2 where SP1 and SP2 both define a component with the same name, we insist that such a component must also have the same type in SP1 and SP2, otherwise SP1+SP2 is undefined. Further constraints on names when composing specification operators still have to be looked at. In this paper we have used the convention that bound variables in specifications are used as names for components in implementations. In practice, we have looked at several ways of defining names for components in modules. For example one way this is done is by defining a type constructor that can be used to specify types containing singles names. Using this type constructor we specify components in a module as pairs consisting of a name and an actual computational component such as a type or value as before.

An issue still to be resolved is how best to define the **Hide** operator. Since both the restriction type and other components in the signature of a specification may depend on the components to be hidden, it is not clear whether such dependent components should be removed entirely or whether the components to be hidden should be made local to the specification in some way. By saying that a component is made local we mean that the component still appears in a specification, but may not be used in any way by other specifications. Of course, this then raises the issue of how such specifications should be refined; for example, should hidden components appear as local implementations or not? Perhaps, given a suitable definition of implementation, the implementer should have the freedom to decide.

So far in this section we have mentioned some of the limitations that still have to be overcome; however, there are also some interesting possibilities that we have not mentioned and still have to be explored. Many of the following possibilities arise because we use type theory for specification. One interesting possibility we are looking at is that of refining flat specifications by 'lifting' the restriction types into the signature so that the type of each component in a signature also becomes a specification. Another possibility that is worth exploring is that of defining partial function types to allow the development of operations in separate parts which are then combined at a later stage; for example, this may allow the separate development of error handling operations. Other areas include the use of higher order functions to describe restrictions, as well as specifying polymorphic components in modules.

When discussing implementing enrichments, in section 7, we showed how dependent function types may be used to decompose part of the task of implementing a module specification into that of implementing functions representing parametrised modules. Such a technique illustrates how, in general, types can be specifications of objects other than modules. Since in type theory all types, and hence specifications, are defined within the same framework, we can reason about the relationship between specifications for different objects such as modules and parametrised modules etc; and (as we saw in section 7) we can also use these relationships to help make implementations. For example, we have observed a useful relationship that allows us, by the use of dependent function types, to systematically transform parametrised specifications (as in section 6) into specifications for parametrised modules.

In summary, we have outlined how Martin-Löf's type theory may be used as a framework for the development of modular specifications and their implementations. The attraction of using type theory is that specifications and implementations can be expressed in the same framework, and this allows us to formally define the notions of specification refinement and implementation. In particular, we have shown how Martin Löf's type theory, can be used as a basis for a simple modular specification language. Such a language included specification building operations, as well as allowing parametrised specifications. We have also shown how specification building operators may be used to combine and modify structured specifications, and we have shown how these operations can be used to construct structured specifications piecewise. By defining a notion of specification refinement and implementation, we have shown how we may add design decisions to a specification by formally transforming the specification and indicated how we might proceed to an implementation.

Acknowledgements

The authors appreciate the critical comments of two anonymous referees.

References

[Bac89] R.C. Backhouse et al : Do-it-yourself type theory. Formal aspects of computing. Vol.1, No. 1, Jan-Mar 1989.

[BuG86] R.M. Burstall, J.A Goguen: An Informal Introduction to Specifications Using CLEAR, in N. Gehani,A.D. McGettrick (ed): Software Specification Techniques (Addison-Wesley, 1986).

[Car89] L. Cardelli: Typeful Programming. Technical Report 45, DEC Systems Research Center, 1989.

[GoT86] J.A. Goguen, J.J. Tardo: An Introduction to OBJ: A language for writing and testing formal algebraic program specifications, in N. Gehani, A.D. McGettrick (ed): Software Specification Techniques (Addison-Wesley, 1986)

[Mar82] P. Martin-Löf : Constructive mathematics and computer programming. in Logic, Methodology and philosophy of science, 6, Proc of the sixth international congress, 1979, North-Holland, Amsterdam, 1982.

[Mar84] P. Martin-Löf : Intuitionistic Type Theory : Bibliopolis, Naples 1984.

[Mid89] C.A. Middelburg : VVSL: A Language for Structured VDM Specifications. Formal aspects of computing. Vol.1, No. 1, Jan-Mar 1989.

[NPS90] B. Nordstrom, K. Petersson and J.M. Smith : Programming in Martin-Löf's type theory : Oxford Clarenden Press 1990.

[SaM90] A. Sampaio and S. Meira: Modular Extensions to Z. In D. Bjorner et al (eds): VDM '90, L.N.C.S 428. Berlin: Springer 1990.

[SaT87] D.T. Sannella and A. Tarlecki: Towards formal development of programs from algebraic specifications: implementations revisited. In H. Ehrig et al (eds): TAPSOFT '87, L.N.C.S 249. Berlin: Springer 1987.

The Varieties of Refinement

Jeremy Jacob

Oxford University Computing Laboratory
Programming Research Group
11 Keble Road, OXFORD, OX1 3QD, United Kingdom
Jeremy.Jacob@prg.oxford.ac.uk

Abstract

This paper explores what it means to be a refinement relation. After picking on one of the uses of the term, we consider the variety of relations which are fall into this definition. Each refinement relation defines a property. Each property represents the viewpoint of a different specifier role, allowing us to structure specifications in a proof oriented way.

1 Introduction

The word *refinement* has been used in technical contexts in several related but subtly different ways. Some use it as a relation on specifications and treat an implementation as a special case of a specification, while some use it as a relation on (models of) systems. To yet others it means the process of finding a product that implements a specification. All three uses will be found in the proceedings of the first and third workshops on refinement [14, 17]. One of the purposes of this paper is to clarify the differences between these ideas. The other, and main, purpose of this paper is to show how different refinement relations capture different kinds of properties of deliverable products.

In this paper we use the word *refinement* for relations between *deliverable products* (or just *products*). To say that one product refines another means that the former product is no worse *with respect to some property of interest* than the latter system. This accords with sense 4 in the definition of "refinement" given in the Concise Oxford Dictionary (COD) [1]; the definition is quoted in figure 1. A better product is obtained from a worse one by adding the ability to satisfy more specifications; the better product is certainly an improvement. The only difference between the definition in the COD and the technical one is that the technical does not imply *better*, only ***no worse***.

To refer to the relation between specifications we use the word *reification* (see Cliff Jones [13, page 84]).

The phrase "with respect to some property of interest" is an important one. In almost all work on reification and refinement the property of interest is non-determinism. That is, P is no worse than Q if in any situation where Q can terminate, then so can P, and whenever Q can terminate with a particular result, P

> **refinement** *n.* **1** the act of refining or the process of being refined. **2** fineness or feeling of taste. **3** polish or elegance in behaviour or manner. **4** an added development or improvement (*a car with several refinements*). **5** a piece of subtle reasoning. **6** a fine distinction. **7** a subtle or ingenious example or display (*all the refinements of reasoning*).

Figure 1: The definition of "refinement" from the COD

can terminate with the same result. The first of that pair of conditions is usually summed up as saying that P is at least as live as Q, and the second by saying P is as least as safe as Q. Concealed in the definition is the assumption that the environment is to be considered as a structureless, monolithic entity; when the assumption of structure in the environment is made it is possible to weaken the this notion of refinement (see example 9).

Other properties are also of interest. In [8, 12] I developed three refinement relations which encoded different assumptions about the environment. In [8, 10] I developed a refinement relation for the property of information-flow confidentiality across a system. There are many others. The various refinement relations actually *define* the different properties.

A pair of toy properties which illustrate many of the issues are *cheapness* and *prestige*. One product (system, implementation, or any other synonym) is a cheapness refinement of another if it costs no more. A product is a prestige refinement of another if it costs no less. When specifying a product an accountant fixes the cheapness specification ("It may cost no more than the amount in account X."), while the public relations officer fixes the prestige specification ("We must be able to say that we have the most expensive computerized facilities of all our competitors.").

There are several problems to be faced by an implementor. The first is consistency of specifications: there may not be a system which satisfies both these specifications (one of the competitors may have spent more on their product than the amount in account X). There is now the choice of having no system or of weakening one or both of the specifications so that they are no longer inconsistent (money can be added to account X, or it may only be necessary to be in the top five, not the top one.)

Another, more subtle problem, is in the development process. The two refinement relations generated by these two properties are inverses of each other. Satisfying both and then improving on *one* of the two properties does not guarantee that the other is preserved. Another way of looking at this to take the combined specification ("The system must cost between a and b") and then showing only that a system has the right cheapness property (it costs less than some number in the range a to b); it cannot be claimed that just because a system is cheap enough that it passes the prestige test. While such reasoning is trivial for these two properties, contrary refinement relations can arise in more subtle circumstances, for example between determinism and information-flow [11].

The rest of this paper formalises the viewpoint of this introduction. First we review the definition of pre-orders. Then the notion of a deliverable product is discussed. In section 4 we discuss what a specification is, and, in section 5 we show how specifications can be grouped together to form properties. This leads on to the notion of refinements. Finally we discuss the impact of this work on a design method.

Notation

The mathematics is presented using the *f*UZZ dialect of Z [20, 21]. The rest of this section reviews some of the notation of Z which may cause difficulty for those unfamiliar with it.

Set comprehension: The notation

$$\{ v : V \mid P(v) \bullet e(v) \}$$

means the set of all terms $e(v)$, where v is drawn from V and the predicate $P(v)$ is true. The usual mathematical notation would place the term $e(v)$ first. Z has a special construct for abstracting the pattern "$v : V \mid P(v)$", the *schema*. Schemas are usually defined in a vertical form, for example:

```
┌─ S ──────────────────────────────
│ v : V
├──────────
│ P(v)
└──────────────────────────────────
```

The schema S can then be used to define the above set:

$$\{ S \bullet e(v) \}$$

There is much more to Z and the use of schemas for structuring the presentation of mathematics than this, and the interested reader is referred to the growing literature (for example [18]).

Other specialised notations that may be unfamiliar to the reader are the various operators on relations and sequences. We briefly summarise them here:

The inverse of relation r	$r^{\sim}$
The image of relation r through set S	$r(\!\mid S \mid\!)$
The restriction, or filtering, of sequence t by set S	$t \upharpoonright S$

2 Pre-orders

Pre-orders are important in this paper. A pre-order is a reflexive and transitive relation. We restrict ourselves to pre-orders over a base type *Product*, which will be introduced formally in section 3. The set of all pre-orders over *Product* is introduced with the help of a schema.

```
┌─ PRE-ORDER ──────────────────────
│ order : Product ↔ Product
├──────────
│ id Product ⊆ order
│ order ; order ⊆ order
└──────────────────────────────────
```

The set of all pre-orders over *Product* is defined:

$$
\begin{array}{|l}
Pre\text{-}order : \mathbb{P}(Product \leftrightarrow Product) \\
\hline
Pre\text{-}order = \{ \ PRE\text{-}ORDER \bullet order \ \}
\end{array}
$$

3 Products

The basic objects in our modelling are ***products.*** We introduce the symbol *Product* to stand for the set of all such objects.

$[Product]$

A product (that is, a member of *Product*) is something that an implementor can deliver to a client.

Example 1 A deliverable product might be:

- a CMOS package;
- an unprogrammed PLA;
- a programmed PLA;
- a $3\frac{1}{2}$" high-density floppy disk with a particular magnetic pattern stored on it;
- a workstation with certain hardware configuration;
- a workstation running a given operating system;
- a network containing workstations and file-servers.

□

4 Specifications

A *specification* is a contract between a customer and an implementor.

The simplest form that the contract can take is the set of all products that would satisfy the customer.

$Specification == \mathbb{P}\ Product$

If $p \in Product$ and $S \in Specification$ then p is a valid implementation of S exactly when $p \in S$. We prefer to say that S allows p in fulfilment of the contract.

$$
\begin{array}{|l}
\_ \text{ allows } \_ : Specification \leftrightarrow Product \\
\hline
\forall S : Specification;\ p : Product \bullet \\
\qquad S \text{ allows } p \Leftrightarrow p \in S
\end{array}
$$

Some authors reverse this and say that p satisfies S:

$$\_\ \text{sat}\ \_ : \textit{Product} \leftrightarrow \textit{Specification}$$

$$(\_\ \text{sat}\ \_) = (\_\ \text{allows}\ \_)^{\sim}$$

In practice, specifications are described using a special notation, called a *specification notation.*

There is a natural ordering on specifications: set inclusion, $\_ \subseteq \_$. For specifications $S, T \in \textit{Specification}$ we say S is stronger than T exactly when $S \subseteq T$; any implementation which S allows is also an implementation which T allows. This ordering is a good candidate for the name *reification* as a (singleton set containing a) product materializes from out of a cloud of products. As we already have the term "subset" for this relationship, the term "reification" is perhaps best reserved for the activity of finding an implementation that meets a specification or as a synonym for the relation $(\_\ \text{allows}\ \_)^{\sim}$.

5 Properties

When constructing a specification a customer has many different concerns. The customer will have certain desires for the safety properties of a product, for the liveness properties, for information flow properties, for integrity properties, for cheapness properties, and so on. How does a customer specify, for example, a safety property? He or she defines a set of the form

$$\{\ p : \textit{Product} \mid p \text{ has the desired safety property}\ \}$$

Without any other notation for enunciating safety properties this set must be given by listing all of its elements. In this way we can regard the set as the safety property. The question now arises: which sets of products can we call safety properties? A suitable definition of the term "safety properties" would be to give a set of sets of products; different individuals might give different sets of sets and each would reflect their personal prejudices about the word "safety". All definitions would have to share four properties to be sensible, however. These four properties (of definitions of properties) are not specific to "safety", but to any property (of products). Let $P \in \mathbf{P}\,\textit{Specification}$ (that is, P is a set of sets of products). We call the members of P the *degrees* of P. For P to define a property we require:

1. $\varnothing \in P$. We must be able record the fact that we have inconsistent requirements.
2. $\textit{Product} \in P$. We must be able to say that we do not care to which degree a product enjoys a property.
3. P is closed under intersections. We must be able to say that a product must exceed both of two degrees of the property; if they are inconsistent then the intersection is empty, which is allowed by 1.
4. P is closed under unions. We must be able to say that we do not care which of two degrees of a property a product exceeds.

We summarise such a collection in the schema *PROPERTY*.

$$\begin{array}{|l}
\textit{PROPERTY} \\ \hline
degree : \mathbb{P}\ Specification \\ \hline
\varnothing \in degree \\
Product \in degree \\
\forall DS : \mathbb{P}\ degree \bullet \bigcap DS \in degree \\
\forall DS : \mathbb{P}\ degree \bullet \bigcup DS \in degree \\ \hline
\end{array}$$

The name "*degree*" in the signature of *PROPERTY* is chosen because each specification in *degree* represents the amount, or degree, of the property the customer wishes a product to enjoy. The set of all properties is defined:

$$\begin{array}{|l}
Property : \mathbb{P}(\mathbb{P}\ Specification) \\ \hline
Property = \{\ PROPERTY \bullet degree\ \} \\ \hline
\end{array}$$

Example 2 One set of sets that satisfies the above rules is

$$\begin{array}{|l}
Universal : Property \\ \hline
Universal = \{\varnothing, Product\} \\ \hline
\end{array}$$

(This definition may be read "*Universal* is a property that has two degrees: nothing and anything".) This property is the coarsest structure that satisfies *PROPERTY*. *Universal* considers all products to be the same, but different to no product at all.
□

Example 3 Another set of sets that satisfies *PROPERTY* is the one that allows the finest distinctions:

$$\begin{array}{|l}
Discrete : Property \\ \hline
Discrete = \mathbb{P}\ Product \\ \hline
\end{array}$$

(This may be read "*Discrete* is a property with as many degrees as possible".) This allows *any* collection of products as a specification. Every product is distinguishable from every other product. □

We will give other examples of properties, which fall between these two extremes, later.

6 Refinements

Every property, in the sense of *PROPERTY*, gives rise to a pre-order over *Product*. This order says product p is related to product q exactly when q appears in every degree that p appears in. We can capture this idea with a function *preorder*:

$$preorder : Property \rightarrowtail\!\!\!\!\twoheadrightarrow Pre\text{-}order$$

$$\forall P : Property;\ p, q : Product \bullet \\ p \mapsto q \in preorder\ P \Leftrightarrow (\forall D : P \bullet p \in D \Rightarrow q \in D)$$

Now we come to a key point of this paper: *Pre-order* is the set of all refinement relations. Think of each pre-order as listing, for each product, all those products which are at least as good *for the property captured by the pre-order.*

As *preorder* is a bijection it has a bijective inverse:

$$\_\text{-property} : Pre\text{-}order \rightarrowtail\!\!\!\!\twoheadrightarrow Property$$

$$(\_\text{-property}) = preorder^{\sim}$$

An equivalent way of defining _-property is

$$\forall r : Pre\text{-}order;\ S : Specification \bullet \\ S \in r\text{-property} \Leftrightarrow r(\!|S|\!) = S$$

This says that an r-property must be upward closed: if q is at least as good as p, relative to r, then q enjoys every r-property that p enjoys.

While properties and pre-orders convey the same information, pre-orders often convey their meaning more lucidly. We now consider several examples.

Example 4 The property *Universal* of example 2 generates the universal pre-order:

$$preorder\ Universal = Product \times Product$$

$$(Product \times Product)\text{-property} = Universal$$

This pre-order says that every product is considered to be the same as any other product. □

Example 5 The property *Discrete* of example 3 generates the identity pre-order:

$$preorder\ Discrete = \mathrm{id}\ Product$$

$$(\mathrm{id}\ Product)\text{-property} = Discrete$$

This explains the use of the name "discrete". No product may be replaced by another, in general. □

Example 6 Suppose that there is a function which gives the cost of a product.

| $cost : Product \rightarrow \mathbb{N}$

We define the pre-order _ no-costlier _:

$$\_\ \text{no-costlier}\ \_ : \mathit{Pre\text{-}order}$$

$$\forall p, q : Product \bullet$$
$$\quad p \ \text{no-costlier}\ q \Leftrightarrow cost\ p \leq cost\ q$$

Similarly, we define _ no-cheaper _ to be:

$$\_\ \text{no-cheaper}\ \_ : \mathit{Pre\text{-}order}$$

$$\forall p, q : Product \bullet$$
$$\quad p \ \text{no-cheaper}\ q \Leftrightarrow cost\ p \geq cost\ q$$

These two pre-orders are opposed to each other; if p is better than q in one order it is worse in the other. This has profound implications for trying to meet both a cheapness specification (that is, one based on _ no-costlier _) and a prestige specification (that is, one based on _ no-cheaper _). We discuss this in section 7. □

Note the way that the pre-orders were defined in example 6. A semantic function (in both cases *cost*) maps from *Product* to a suitable domain ($\mathbb{N}$), and a partial ordering is given in the domain (in one case $\leq$, in the other $\geq$, both of which happen to be total orders). This is a very useful pattern to copy.

Example 7 In the theory of Communicating Sequential Processes [7] several semantic functions are defined. They are all relative to a universe of synchronisation events.

[*Event*]

Three are:

$$traces : Product \rightarrow \mathbb{P}_1(\text{seq}\ Event)$$
$$failures : Product \rightarrow \text{seq}\ Event \leftrightarrow \mathbb{P}\ Event$$
$$divergences : Product \rightarrow \mathbb{P}(\text{seq}\ Event)$$

The axioms which define the relationship between these functions may be found in [7]. For a process p, *traces* p gives all sequences of actions which p might be observed to do. *failures* p gives, for each trace of p, all the offerings by the environment which p might refuse. *divergences* p gives all the traces of p after which it might behave chaotically. The traces model was first discussed in [6]; failures and divergences were first discussed in [3, 4].

Various orderings can be defined on *Product* using these functions.

$$\_\ \text{no-safer-than}\ \_ : \mathit{Pre\text{-}order}$$

$$\forall p, q : \mathit{Product} \bullet$$
$$p \text{ no-safer-than } q \Leftrightarrow \mathit{traces}\ q \subseteq \mathit{traces}\ p$$

One product is safer than another if it can do fewer things. In [7] this relation is written $\_ \sqsupseteq \_$.

$$\_\ \text{no-more-determined-than}\ \_ : \mathit{Pre\text{-}order}$$

$$\forall p, q : \mathit{Product} \bullet$$
$$p \text{ no-more-determined-than } q$$
$$\Leftrightarrow \mathit{failures}\ q \subseteq \mathit{failures}\ p$$
$$\wedge\ \mathit{divergences}\ q \subseteq \mathit{divergences}\ p$$

One product is better than another if it can fail less often and diverge less often. This ordering is often called the *determinism* ordering, as the better products are more deterministic than the poorer products. This order is written $\_ \sqsubseteq \_$ in [7].

Bill Roscoe has defined an order using these semantic functions which captures *definedness* of products; the reader is referred to [19] for details. □

Example 8 In [2] the notions of *conformance* is defined for Lotos processes; conformance is related to *inheritance* in object-oriented languages. product p conforms to q if, whenever p has behaved in a way that q can behave in, then p can continue to behave in a way that q can. p does not need to allow every behaviour of q, nor does every behaviour of p need to be a behaviour of q.

In [5] the concept is transferred from Lotos to Hoare's Communicating Sequential Processes [7] (see example 7). We take the definition from [5].

$$\_\ \text{conforms}\ \_ : \mathit{Pre\text{-}order}$$

$$\forall p, q : \mathit{Product} \bullet$$
$$\forall s : \mathit{traces}\ p \cap \mathit{traces}\ q;\ r : \mathbb{P}\ \mathit{Event} \bullet$$
$$p \text{ conforms } q \Leftrightarrow ((s, r) \in \mathit{failures}\ p \Rightarrow (s, r) \in \mathit{failures}\ q)$$

The relation $(\_\ \text{conforms}\ \_)^{\sim}$ is the desired refinement ordering in the sense of this paper.

Two other relations, restrictions of conformance, are of interest.

$$\_\ \text{extends}\ \_ : \mathit{Pre\text{-}order}$$
$$\_\ \text{reduces}\ \_ : \mathit{Pre\text{-}order}$$

$$(\_\ \text{extends}\ \_) = (\_\ \text{no-safer-than}\ \_) \cap (\_\ \text{conforms}\ \_)$$
$$(\_\ \text{reduces}\ \_) = (\_\ \text{no-safer-than}\ \_)^{\sim} \cap (\_\ \text{conforms}\ \_)$$

Again, it is $(\_\ \text{extends}\ \_)^{\sim}$ and $(\_\ \text{reduces}\ \_)^{\sim}$ which are the desired refinement relations. See [2, 5] for details of their use. □

Example 9 In example 7 all the orderings assume that the environment in which the product is to exist is one unstructured, monolithic entity—a single user. In [12] orderings are given where the environment is assumed to consist of several users. Two different orderings are presented, one assuming that the different users are *cooperating* on a task, and one assuming that they are engaged on *independent* tasks. Here we will just describe these refinement relations based on the semantic function *traces* of example 7; in [12] the theory is parameterised by the semantic function.

Note that the pre-order _ no-safer-than _ satisfies:

$$\forall p, q : \mathit{Product} \bullet \\ \quad p \text{ no-safer-than } q \Leftrightarrow (\forall s : \mathit{traces}\ q \bullet \exists t : \mathit{traces}\ p \bullet s = t)$$

To obtain the pre-order called co-operating refinement the equality between traces is replaced by a weaker equivalence relation that describes when two traces are equivalent as seen by the environment. Each (interesting) part of the environment is connected to the product through some subset of the interface, which we call *the windows of interest*, one window per user:

$$\mathit{Windows} : \mathbb{P}(\mathbb{P}\ \mathit{Event})$$

Note that we do not require that *Windows* is either disjoint or a cover of *Event*, so that the notion of user is quite a liberal one.

The desired equivalence does not distinguish two traces when both have the same appearance through each window.

$$\_ \cong \_ : \text{seq}\ \mathit{Event} \leftrightarrow \text{seq}\ \mathit{Event}$$

$$\forall s, t : \text{seq}\ \mathit{Event} \bullet \\ \quad s \cong t \Leftrightarrow (\forall W : \mathit{Windows} \bullet s \upharpoonright W = t \upharpoonright W)$$

In [12] the resulting pre-order is written $\_ \trianglelefteq \_$.

$$\_ \trianglelefteq \_ : \mathit{Pre\text{-}order}$$

$$\forall p, q : \mathit{Product} \bullet \\ \quad p \trianglelefteq q \Leftrightarrow (\forall s : \mathit{traces}\ q \bullet \exists t : \mathit{traces}\ p \bullet s \cong t)$$

The order called independent refinement is defined:

$$\_ \trianglelefteq \_ : \mathit{Pre\text{-}order}$$

$$\forall p, q : \mathit{Product} \bullet \\ \quad p \trianglelefteq q \Leftrightarrow (\forall W : \mathit{Windows};\ s : \mathit{traces}\ q \bullet \\ \qquad \exists t : \mathit{traces}\ p \bullet \\ \qquad\quad s \upharpoonright W = t \upharpoonright W)$$

A further refinement relation, ***transaction refinement***, which falls between co-operating and independent refinement, is described in [12], to which the reader is referred for details. □

Example 10 Another class of refinement relations is that whose members measure ***confidentiality*** in terms of information flow between users. These relations assume that one user is trying to gain information about another user ***without*** the second user's co-operation. A Shannon style treatment of information-flow, which assumes that the sender is co-operating, is not appropriate for this (see, for example, [22] for a discussion of Shannon's theory and [23] for its use in a security context).

In [10] a set of refinement relations based on the semantic function *traces* is given (see example 7); in [9] these relations are made generic on the semantic function. Here, as in example 9, we restrict ourselves to *traces*.

From all the users of a product in *Windows* (see example 9), pick two, H and L, say.

$$H, L : \mathit{Windows}$$

We are interested in information flow from H to L and a refinement relation which says that it is better to let *less* information flow. We need two subsidiary semantic functions, *view* and *infer*, which are defined in terms of traces. *view* tells us, given a product, which traces are possible at window L, and *infer* tells us, for a given product p, which traces at window H are consistent with a trace ℓ at window L. This captures the information that can be gained about H's use of p by observing ℓ at window L.

$$
\begin{array}{l}
\mathit{view} : \mathit{Product} \rightarrow \mathbb{P}(\mathrm{seq}\, \mathit{Event}) \\
\mathit{infer} : \mathit{Product} \rightarrow \mathrm{seq}\, L \rightarrow \mathbb{P}(\mathrm{seq}\, H) \\
\hline
\forall p : \mathit{Product} \bullet \\
\quad \mathit{view}\ p = \{\, t : \mathit{traces}\ p \bullet t \upharpoonright L \,\} \\
\forall p : \mathit{Product};\ \ell : \mathrm{seq}\, L \bullet \\
\quad \mathit{infer}\ p\ \ell \\
\quad = \{\, h : \mathrm{seq}\, H \mid \exists t : \mathit{traces}\ p \bullet t \upharpoonright H = h \wedge t \upharpoonright L = \ell \,\}
\end{array}
$$

The refinement relation which represents no greater information flow from H to L is:

$$
\begin{array}{l}
\_\ \text{no-greater-confidentiality-than}\ \_ : \mathit{Pre\text{-}order} \\
\hline
\forall p, q : \mathit{Product} \bullet \\
\quad p\ \text{no-greater-confidentiality-than}\ q \\
\quad \Leftrightarrow \mathit{view}\ q \subseteq \mathit{view}\ p \wedge (\forall \ell : \mathit{view}\ q \bullet \mathit{infer}\ p\ \ell \subseteq \mathit{infer}\ q\ \ell)
\end{array}
$$

This relation says that q is no worse than p at keeping confidences about H from L exactly when it offers L no more opportunities for discovering information about H, and for each of those opportunities gives no less uncertainty about H's behaviour. In [10, 9] the relation is written $\_ \preceq \_$ with appropriate sub- and superscripts.

There is no claim that _ no-greater-confidentiality-than _ is the *only* relation which captures confidentiality. The values of L and H may vary. Given any set of such relations their intersection also expresses confidentiality, but with respect to a set of ordered pairs of windows. There are other relations that represent conditional confidentiality properties. □

Example 11 For the last example we present the classical refinement relation for sequential systems. Here products are considered to be state transformers:

$[State]$

$Product == State \leftrightarrow State$

For a product p, $\operatorname{dom} p$ is the set of states for which the product terminates. The final state from a starting state x is a member of the set $p(\{x\})$.

The refinement relation is written $\_ \sqsubseteq \_$ and is defined:

$$\_ \sqsubseteq \_ : Pre\text{-}order$$

$$\forall p, q : Product \bullet \\ \quad p \sqsubseteq q \Leftrightarrow \operatorname{dom} p \subseteq \operatorname{dom} q \\ \qquad \wedge (\forall x : \operatorname{dom} p \bullet q(\{x\}) \subseteq p(\{x\}))$$

This refinement relation can be modelled in other ways, for example by basing its definition on the weakest precondition calculus (see, for example, [15, chapter 21]). □

Other properties of interest that we have not looked at in this section include: *integrity*, the degree to which local data may not be altered by another, *availability* (usually called *denial of service*), the degree to which one user cannot prevent another user gaining access to resources, and *safety-criticality*, the degree to which one system is less likely to cause severe damage in unconsidered circumstances. The reader may care to invent others and capture them as refinement relations.

7 A development method

The method we propose for developing a specification is as follows:

1. decide on the properties of interest (that is, those properties where the desired degree is not all of *Product*);

2. formalise each property by giving a refinement relation;

3. give a degree of each property; and

4. check for the mutual consistency of all degrees

If at step 4 the various degrees are found to be inconsistent then nothing further can be done, except to persuade the problem owners to change their desires and demands.

The development from specification to product is more difficult. Consider the development of a product which must satisfy both prestige and cheapness properties (see example 6). Suppose the prestige requirement is "cost at least P" and the cheapness requirement is "cost at most C". If we find a product X with the right cheapness property ($cost\ X \leq C$) but not the right prestige property we could just improve prestige and replace X by a Y for which Y no-cheaper X. However, there is no guarantee that *cost* $Y \leq C$; in general we would have to reprove the property was specified.

We may refine products according to a relation which respects both cheapness and prestige. The largest such relation is the intersection of the two relations:

(_ no-cheaper _) ∩ (_ no-costlier _)

This allows a product to be replaced by one which costs exactly the same amount.

Another pair of opposed properties, of more importance, are determinism (example 7) and confidentiality (example 10) [11]. The intersection of these two relations is very close to identity in the traces or failures model, although some room for manœuvre is gained by weakening determinism to one of the relations discussed in example 9.

Development by derivation (see, for example [15]) is going to be difficult when more than one property is involved, and when those properties act against one another. We are thrown back upon "guess-and-verify" as a method:

> Pick (with intelligence rather than randomly) a product and then verify it against the specification (usually against one component of the specification at a time); if the verification fails, pick another product and repeat.

8 Conclusion

Much work remains to be done. What are the implications for designing specification notations? It seems likely that each property must have a different specification notation, but is it possible to harmonise notations for radically different properties? How do methods such as data refinement techniques (for example, [16]) fit into the scheme of this paper?

Most importantly, heuristics for designing products are needed, especially when (non-trivial) degrees of opposed properties, such as determinism and confidentiality, are required. This is a rich and wide open research area.

Acknowledgements

Several people have made contributions to the ideas in this paper. From among my colleagues at the PRG and RSRE I must single out Ruaridh Macdonald for a careful and constructive reading through of an early version. Two anonymous referees also made constructive comments.

The work was funded through the Royal Signals and Radar Establishment.

References

[1] R. E. Allen, editor. *Concise Oxford Dictionary.* Oxford University Press, Oxford, UK, eighth edition, 1990.

[2] Ed. Brinksma and G Scollo. Formal notions of implementation and conformance in lotos. Memorandum INF-86-13, Universiteit Twente, The Netherlands, December 1986.

[3] S. D. Brookes, C. A. R. Hoare, and A. W. Roscoe. A theory of communicating sequential processes. *Journal ACM*, 31(7):560–599, 1984.

[4] S. D. Brookes and A. W. Roscoe. An improved failures model for communicating sequential processes. In *Proceedings NSF-SERC Seminar on Concurrency.* Springer Verlag, New York, NY, 1985.

[5] Elspeth Cusack, Steven Rudkin, and Christopher. Smith. Objective lotos: A first report on object oriented specification in lotos. British Telecom Internal Document, July 1989.

[6] C. A. R. Hoare. A model for communicating sequential processes. In R. M. McKeag and A. M. McNaughton, editors, *On the Construction of Programs.* Cambridge University Press, 1980.

[7] C. A. R. Hoare. *Communicating Sequential Processes.* Series in Computer Science. Prentice-Hall International, London, UK, 1985.

[8] Jeremy Jacob. *On Shared Systems.* PhD thesis, University of Oxford, 1987.

[9] Jeremy Jacob. A security framework. In *Proceedings The Computer Security Foundations Workshop*, pages 98–111, Bedford, MA, 1988. The MITRE Corporation.

[10] Jeremy Jacob. Security specifications. In *Proceedings 1988 IEEE Symposium on Security and Privacy*, pages 14–23, New York, NY, April 1988. IEEE Computer Society Press.

[11] Jeremy Jacob. On the derivation of secure components. In *Proceedings 1989 IEEE Symposium on Security and Privacy*, pages 242–247, New York, NY, May 1989. IEEE Computer Society Press.

[12] Jeremy Jacob. Refinement of shared systems. In John McDermid, editor, *The Theory and Practice of Refinement: Approaches to the Formal Development of Large-Scale Software Systems*, pages 27–36. Butterworths, London, UK, 1989.

[13] Cliff Jones. Data reification. In John McDermid, editor, *The Theory and Practice of Refinement: Approaches to the Formal Development of Large-Scale Software Systems*, pages 79–89. Butterworths, London, UK, 1989.

[14] John McDermid, editor. *The Theory and Practice of Refinement: Approaches to the Formal Development of Large-Scale Software Systems.* Butterworths, London, UK, 1989. Proceedings of the first workshop on refinement.

[15] C. Carroll Morgan. *Programming from Specifications.* Series in Computer Science. Prentice-Hall International, London, UK, 1990.

[16] C. Carroll Morgan and Paul H. B. Gardiner. Data refinement by calculation. *Acta Informatica*, 27:481–503, 1990.

[17] C. Carroll Morgan and James C. P. Woodcock, editors. *Third BCS-FACS Refinement Workshop.* Springer UK, 1990.

[18] John E. Nicholls, editor. *Z User Workshop: Proceedings of the Fourth Annual Z User Meeting.* Springer-Verlag, 1990.

[19] A. W. Roscoe. Two papers on CSP. Technical Monograph PRG-67, Oxford University Computing Laboratory, 1988.

[20] J. M. Spivey. *The fUZZ manual.*. Computing Science Consultancy, 2 Willow Close, OXFORD, OX9 9AN, UK, 1988.

[21] J. M. Spivey. *The Z Notation: A Reference Manual.* Series in Computer Science. Prentice-Hall International, London, UK, 1989.

[22] D. Welsh. *Codes and Cryptography.* Oxford University Press, Oxford, UK, 1988.

[23] T. J. Wittbold and D. M. Johnson. Information flow in nondeterministic systems. In *Proceedings 1990 IEEE Symposium on Security and Privacy,* pages 144–161, New York, NY, May 1990. IEEE Computer Society Press.

Timed Process Algebra, Petri Nets, and Event Refinement

David Murphy,
Department of Computing Science,
University of Glasgow,
Glasgow. G12 8QQ
dvjm@uk.ac.glasgow.cs

Abstract

This paper is concerned with an exploration of the relationship between the formalisations of the notions of concurrency and nondeterminism in Petri nets and in process algebras. A novel timed process algebra whose notions of nondeterminism and concurrency are particularly easy to represent in nets will be presented; it is intended as a tool for specifying and reasoning about the detailed behaviour of implementations of distributed systems. This process algebra, *interval process algebra*, is given a non-interleaving semantics using timed asynchronous transition systems.

The interpretation of interval process algebra terms in timed nets is discussed and contrasted with the usual net-theoretic interpretation of CCS terms. Some insight is thus obtained into the relationship between the formalisms used for 'concurrency' and 'nondeterminism' in conventional process algebras, nets, and interval process algebra.

The introduction of timing into a process algebra often permits a simple and powerful notion of event refinement. This is the case here, giving a useful perspective into event refinement in timed and untimed nets.

Several applications of interval process algebra, — to performance measurement of distributed systems, and to the design of self-timed VLSI, — are briefly discussed.

... Some craven scruple
Of thinking too precisely on the event.

Shakespeare

1 INTRODUCTION

Petri nets and process algebras such as CSP or CCS are both well known models of concurrency. The connection between the two has received extensive investigation. In this paper, rather than trying to find yet another necessarily *ad hoc* connection between these two kinds of concurrency theories, we rethink process algebra from a net–theoretic standpoint. Since nets are more implementational models than process algebras (as evinced by [Olderog 1988], [Pnueli 1985]), it makes sense to work this way round. Thus we seek to develop a process algebra with good compositionality properties that has a natural interpretation in nets, and in this way to come to a better understanding of the relationship between the formalisms used for 'nondeterminism' and 'concurrency' in nets and in process algebras. A byproduct will be the definition of a process algebra with a very clean non–interleaving semantics.

Our basic program, then, is to define a process algebra and give it a net–theoretic semantics. This will shed some light on the interpretation of standard process–algebraic constructions in nets. As an intermediate step in the translation, a timed non–interleaving operational semantics will be developed; this technique is of potentially widespread applicability.
Several features of this work are new:

- the process algebra developed here, *interval process algebra*, or IPA, is a *classical* process algebra; it is based on the notion of observing a process rather than interacting with it. We shall be thinking of concurrent systems as models of happenings in the world rather than as necessarily computational objects. This intuition accords with the basic intuition that a net is a description of the relationship between happenings;

- we shall deal with timed nets and a timed process algebra. This is because the introduction of time *simplifies* things, and because it offers greater verisimilitude of the model;

- we will offer a simple notion of event refinement both in our process algebra and in nets. In so doing we isolate *algebraically* a class of 1–safe nets with a simple notion of event refinement which may serve as descriptions of certain kinds of implementations.

The rest of this section is devoted to an examination of the current state of the connection between nets and process algebras, and a further discussion of the nature of classical concurrency theories.

There is only room in this paper to discuss some of the issues the definition of IPA has brought up; a more complete discussion, including a description of the connection between IPA and timed event structures, can be found in the work of [Murphy 1989].

1.1 Nets and Process Algebra

Petri nets are very well known models of concurrency. An extensive bibliography can be found in [Best & Fernandez 1988], while [Reisig 1985] is a good introduction. We will assume familiarity with the basic net model. Nets are essentially *implementational* models; they are excellent tools for describing the detailed behaviours of concurrent systems.

Process algebras are popular as tools for reasoning about and implementing systems with atomic events and concurrency; formalisms such as CSP [Brookes et al. 1984], COSY [Lauer 1984] and CCS [Milner 1989] have achieved some success. (We assume familiarity with CSP or CCS.) A process algebra expression can be viewed as a specification of how to construct a structure that behaves a certain way. Thus a net might be a good description of the behaviour of a concurrent system that was built as described by a process algebra expression. Most process algebras are not as descriptive as nets; they cannot specify systems with the perversities of behaviour that nets can describe. That, however, is no bad thing; a specification language should only allow one to write processes that 'should' be implemented, while an implementational language should allow the description of perversities, so that one can check that implementations are free of them. By building a process algebra from the tools available in nets we provide a compositional model of a subclass of nets and an easy translation from a specification-oriented to an implementational framework.

There is an extensive literature on the relationship between nets and process algebras; the reader is referred to the work of Degano, [Degano et al. 1987], [Degano et al. 1988]; Goltz, [Goltz & Mycroft 1984]; Olderog, [Olderog 1987], [Olderog 1988]; Shields, [Shields 1987], and van Glabbeek, [van Glabbeek & Vaandrager 1987]. A comprehensive survey, discussion and series of constructions is given in [Goltz 1990]. The thesis [Taubner 1989] is also of considerable relevance.

1.2 Classical Concurrency Theory

The ideas that there are many possible observers of a concurrent system, none of them privileged, and that the only way of finding out something about it is to interact with it, have been dominant in concurrency theory. But there is room, as shown in [Murphy 1990], for an approach where it is assumed that one observer can see everything in the system and time it, without having to interact with it.[1]

This is a *classical* notion of observation; classically, a process is an autonomous entity that evolves without reference to its environment, and nondeterminism is "completely unknowable choice" – a notion that would have been familiar to the church fathers. The idea that processes don't interact with their environment unless called upon to do so seems natural; concurrent systems in reality 'do their own thing' until their surroundings force their attention upon them.[2] Such systems are *live*; they do their events as soon as possible; we can only force them to pause by using a specific wait event.

In this sort of model the notion of *causality* is central; causality determines the sequence in which things happen. Two processes are concurrent if they are not completely causally related. Thus concurrent processes may be distributed. There is no necessary relationship between concurrency and simultaneity.

Classical models permit a very simple and intuitive introduction of *time*; events are compound objects with durations; the times they start and finish are observed. This posture also lets us allow a process to refine an event just when it lasts no more time than that event. This natural definition of event refinement can be used in both net-theory (which is unsurprising, as it is quite classical) or in a suitable classical process algebra such as IPA.

The main advantage of classical models is *verisimilitude*; the basic notions they have match

---

[1]Note that this is *not* necessarily a global clocks assumption, as the observer's clock is not influencing the behaviour of the system.

[2]This means that it makes little sense to build into a classical model a specific notion of synchronisation; a process just engages in its events; these are always visible to its surroundings, which can interact with them if they choose. More usual notions of synchronisation can be built in as the need arises. This is the notion called *non-participatory concurrency* in [Murphy 1990].

well with the fundamental behaviour of implementations of distributed systems, and with the way users think about them. The issues of time and liveness are particularly important; many models suffer from not being able to articulate the simple requirement 'this must happen now.'

It will not be claimed that classical models are any better than non-classical ones; they address different concerns and are both part of the broad sweep of concurrency theory.

The remainder of the paper is organised as follows; the next section is devoted to a description of the process algebra used in this paper, interval process algebra or IPA. A non-interleaving operational semantics for IPA in terms of timed asynchronous transitions systems follows. These transitions systems are then used to give a semantics for IPA in terms of timed nets. The compilation raises several questions about how to interpret process-theoretic notions in nets; various alternatives are discussed and compared, both for IPA and for a more conventional CSP-like process algebra. Finally some applications are briefly discussed.

2 INTERVAL PROCESS ALGEBRA

In this section interval process algebra will be introduced. As discussed in the introduction, IPA will be a 'classical' process algebra, based on a naïve-physics interpretation of the usual process algebraic combinators.

It will also be a *timed, non-interleaving* process algebra. There has been comparatively little work on timed process algebras (as distinct from real-time languages); the only mature approaches we know of in this direction are timed CSP [Davies & Schneider 1989] and timed ACP [Baeten & Bergstra 1990].[3] IPA is derived from both CCS and timed CSP, but is rather different semantically from either of those formalisms, because we intend it to have a natural model in the world of Petri nets. In contrast to the dearth of work in timed concurrency theory, there has been considerable work in the area of non-interleaving process algebras: IPA falls midway between the poset approach of [Boudol & Castellani 1987] & [Casley et al. 1989] and the interleaving algebras modelled in [Winskel 1984].

We begin by introducing the syntax of IPA and informally explaining the meaning of the combinators. Since IPA is timed, it will be necessary to explain how long processes last; this occupies another subsection. Timing gives several obvious notions of event refinement; these are discussed.

2.1 The Syntax of IPA

We shall adopt a syntax similar to that of timed CSP. Suppose that we have a finite set of (nonatomic) observable events E, with typical element e. A primitive action in the algebra will be an occurrence of an event or a wait. Actions are then combined to form processes:

$$\begin{array}{lll} \texttt{Action} ::= & e \mid \texttt{Wait}\, t & e \in \mathbf{E}, t \in \mathbb{R}^+ \\ \texttt{Proc} ::= & \texttt{Action} \mid \texttt{Proc} + \texttt{Proc} \mid \texttt{Proc} \,;\, \texttt{Proc} \mid \texttt{Proc}\ {}_S\|\ \texttt{Proc} & S \subset \prod_{i \in \omega} \mathbf{E} \cup \{*\} \end{array}$$

(Here $\mathbb{R}^+$ is the set of the non-negative reals plus ∞. The process Skip is an abbreviation for Wait 0, while Stop abbreviates Wait ∞, much as in CSP. The importance of the set S will become clear shortly.)

---

[3] Of some interest, too, is the timed CCS [Hennessy & Regan 1990] and the 'multiform time' model of [Roncken & Gerth 1990].

It will be helpful in the ensuing discussion to define the *alphabet* of an IPA process, P, written $\alpha(\text{P})$. Loosely, this is the set of events that the process can be seen to engage in.

$$
\begin{array}{rclrcl}
\alpha(e) & = & \{e, *\} & \alpha(\texttt{Wait}\ t) & = & \{*\} \\
\alpha(\text{P} + \text{Q}) & = & \alpha(\text{P}) \cup \alpha(\text{Q}) & \alpha(\text{P} \,;\, \text{Q}) & = & \alpha(\text{P}) \cup \alpha(\text{Q}) \\
\alpha(\text{P}\ {}_S\|\ \text{Q}) & = & \multicolumn{4}{l}{\{(p,*) \mid p \in \alpha(\text{P})\} \cup \{(*,q) \mid q \in \alpha(\text{Q})\} \cup} \\
 & & \multicolumn{4}{l}{\{(p,q) \mid p \in \alpha(\text{P}), q \in \alpha(\text{Q}), (p,q) \in S\}}
\end{array}
$$

The omnipresent $*$ can be thought of as an 'on-light' or silent event. The first thing a process does is to start, – $*$ begins, – and the last thing it does is to end, – $*$ ends. Thus the presence of $*$ in the alphabet of every process indicates that all processes are active sometime. It also has a technical role in the treatment of parallel composition. We assume $* \notin \text{E}$.

2.2 An Informal Introduction to IPA

The intended interpretation of the process combinators is as follows;

$+$ This is nondeterministic composition. In an execution of P+Q either P or Q will be executed; there is no means to influence or way of knowing which, much like CSP $\sqcap$.

; This is sequential composition. In an execution of P ; Q the process P will be executed, followed by Q.

${}_S\|$ This is a novel form of parallel composition with synchronisation. In an execution of P ${}_S\|$ Q the processes P and Q will execute together. When an event of P overlaps (in time) with an event of Q, and the pair of events is in S, then a synchronisation happens; otherwise events occur asynchronously.

S is the *synchronisation set*; it indicates which events we want to synchronise. Whenever a parallel composition is written, a synchronisation set must be provided as well, containing all the desired synchronisations; a synchronisation will only happen if it is desired and time permits. Read P ${}_S\|$ Q as "P par Q with the synchronisations S desired."

Note the form of the alphabet of P ${}_S\|$ Q; a parallel composition always displays pairs of events to the outside world; (a, b) indicates a synchronisation, ($*$, b) an asynchronous occurrence of b from the process on the right of the par, and (a, $*$) an asynchronous occurrence of a from the process on the left of the par. Thus asynchronous occurrences are synchronisations with $*$, as in [Winskel 1984]. Consider two events a and b in processes P and Q respectively. Suppose that a starts at t_1 & has duration $\Delta(\text{a})$, and b starts at t_2 & has duration $\Delta(\text{b})$. Then P ${}_S\|$ Q will display the synchronisation (a, b) just when a and b overlap in time and the synchronisation is desired, i.e.

$$[t_1, t_1 + \Delta(\text{a})) \cap [t_2, t_2 + \Delta(\text{b})) \neq \emptyset \quad \wedge \quad (\text{a},\text{b}) \in S$$

In this case we say a sync b. The form of the synchronisation set in BNF is

$$S \ ::= \ (\text{E} \cup \{*\}) \times (\text{E} \cup \{*\}) \ \mid \ (\text{E} \cup \{*\}) \times S$$

Synchronisation is not allowed on waits;

$$(\text{a},\text{b}) \in S \quad \Rightarrow \quad \text{a} \neq * \ \wedge \ \text{b} \neq *$$

Thus, the presence of $(\mathtt{a}, \mathtt{b})$ in S indicates that we want a and b to synchronise, while a four–fold parallel composition such as $(((\mathtt{P}\ {}_{\mathtt{S}_1}\|\ \mathtt{Q})\ {}_{\mathtt{S}_2}\|\ \mathtt{R})\ {}_{\mathtt{S}_3}\|\ \mathtt{S}$ would generate terms like $(((\mathtt{a}, *), \mathtt{b}), \mathtt{c})$ in S_3, indicating that we want a to occur asynchronously in the innermost par, but want it to synchonise with b in the next one out and with c in the outermost. This can only happen if the times of the occurrences of all three events allow, and the more tightly bound pars permit.

Notice too, that the order of parallel composition is important; consider

$$\mathtt{a}\ {}_{\{(\mathtt{a},(*,\mathtt{c}))\}}\|\ (\mathtt{b}\ {}_{\{(\mathtt{b},\mathtt{c})\}}\|\ \mathtt{c})$$

Here the synchronisation $(\mathtt{b}, \mathtt{c})$ will happen and $(\mathtt{a}, (*, \mathtt{c}))$ won't, as b and c are more tightly bound than a and c. Thus our form of parallel composition is *local* in the sense that the ordering of application of $\|$ is important. In particular, we have

$$\begin{aligned} \mathtt{P} \| \mathtt{Q} &\neq \mathtt{Q} \| \mathtt{P} \\ \mathtt{P} \| \mathtt{P} &\neq \mathtt{P} \end{aligned}$$

in contrast to the 'global' parallel composition of CSP or CCS. Our behavioural subtleties are bought at the cost of fewer laws; cf. [Baeten & Bergstra 1990].[4]

The synchronisation discipline outlined above is in sharp contrast to that of CCS or CSP; both of these languages allow us to require that a synchronisation happens or deadlock occurs. Here, we cannot; it will only happen if the times of the matching events allow, and the calculus has no notion of deadlock. This does not mean that IPA can't deal with a more conventional synchronisation paradigm; we can always prefix one event of a matching pair with a wait fixed to enforce the desired synchronisation.

2.3 The Timing and Refinement of Processes

IPA is a *timed* process algebra; each occurrences of an event takes a fixed given nonzero amount of time. Thus, in contrast to timed CSP, events are associated with *intervals of time*. The function $\Delta : \mathtt{Action} \rightarrow \mathbb{R}^+$ will be provided to return the durations of events.[5]

---

[4]The local nature of IPA parallel composition means that we also have

$$\mathtt{P} \| (\mathtt{Q} \| \mathtt{R}) \neq (\mathtt{P} \| \mathtt{Q}) \| \mathtt{R}$$

If fair synchronisation is required, the user must explicitly state how it is to be implemented. In practise more stringent requirements than fairness are usual (such as requiring not only that no synchronisation is always preferred to another, but also that no synchronisation is often preferred to another, for some suitable notion of often), so the user will often have to provide their own scheduler anyway. This seems reasonable since it is hard to see how to implement completely–fair synchronisation; our local form of parallel composition reflects the notion that multiple synchronisations can only be built from binary ones. [Lamport 1985] has an interesting perspective here.

[5]The assumption that the duration of an event is the same every time it occurs is not necessary; we could take $\Delta : \mathtt{Action} \rightarrow \mathbb{P}\mathbb{R}^+$ without much complication.

Our aim in making the proviso that durations should be nonzero is to ensure that only a finite computation can take place in a finite time on a finite machine. (It can be argued that infinite machines incorporating unbounded angelic nondeterminism or unbounded parallelism are capable of infinite computation in a finite time.) The requirement that only finite computation is possible in finite time is seen as basic to the well-foundedness of timed models in [Joseph & Goswami 1985]; we agree with this analysis, and forbid Zeno machines.

We will assume that actions have non-zero durations; this means that Skip is not strictly an action, as it lasts no time. This is of little real consequence provided we never deal with a recursion like $\mu x.\ \mathtt{Skip}\ ;\ x$.

This means that the set of times that a process P lasts, $\Lambda(\mathtt{P})$, where $\Lambda : \mathtt{Proc} \rightarrow \wp(\mathbb{R}^+)$ can be defined thus;

$$\begin{array}{rcll} \Lambda(e) & = & \{\Delta(e)\} & e \in \mathbf{E} \\ \Lambda(\mathtt{Wait}\ t) & = & \{t\} & t \in \mathbb{R}^+ \\ \Lambda(\mathtt{P}+\mathtt{Q}) & = & \Lambda(\mathtt{P}) \cup \Lambda(\mathtt{Q}) & \\ \Lambda(\mathtt{P}\ ;\ \mathtt{Q}) & = & \{\, t+t' \mid t \in \Lambda(\mathtt{P}),\ t' \in \Lambda(\mathtt{Q})\,\} & \\ \Lambda(\mathtt{P}\ {}_s\|\ \mathtt{Q}) & = & \{\, \max(t,t') \mid t \in \Lambda(\mathtt{P}),\ t' \in \Lambda(\mathtt{Q})\,\} & \end{array}$$

This definition means that events happen as soon as possible (so called 'maximal liveness') and that deadlock is not possible.

It is instructive to contemplate some more of the laws that are *not* true for IPA. For instance, one of the laws which is false is (a ; b) || (c ; d) = (a || c) ; (b || d). The reason we want this law to be false is that in (a || c) ; (b || d) both a and c must be over before b or d start. This is not true in (a ; b) || (c ; d). The second law above is proposed in [Meseguer & Montanari 1988] as "capturing a rather basic fact about concurrency," – this intuition does not extend to our framework, as we have a rather finer notion of behaviour. The introduction of timing makes this point clear; parallel composition is not functorial here.

There is one immediate advantage to giving events durations; two simple notions of event refinement. Loosely, a process can refine an event just when it lasts no longer than that event. Alternatively we can demand that a process can refine an event just when it lasts exactly the same time as the event. Thus, for a process Q (with $\alpha(\mathtt{P}) \cap \alpha(\mathtt{Q}) = \emptyset$) to refine an event a in a process P we might demand either the 'loose interpretation' or the 'tight interpretation':

$$\begin{array}{lcll} \mathtt{Q} \text{ refines } \mathtt{a} & \iff & \forall t \in \Lambda(\mathtt{Q}) \,.\, t \leq \Delta(\mathtt{a}) & (\textit{Loose interpretation}) \\ \mathtt{Q} \text{ refines } \mathtt{a} & \iff & \Lambda(\mathtt{Q}) = \{\Delta(\mathtt{a})\} & (\textit{Tight interpretation}) \end{array}$$

The 'correct' definition will be discussed latter. Some further discussion of event refinement in process algebra can in found in [Darondeau & Degano 1990i], [Darondeau & Degano 1990ii], [Hennessy 1988] and [Aceto & Hennessy 1988].

It should be mentioned that event refinement is, *pace* CCS & CSP, very useful, particularly in applications where there are many levels of detail, such as telecoms; it is in these systems too that observation–based models are often most appropriate.

It is perhaps appropriate at this point to mention Milner's 'two stage' program. The paradigm for giving semantics that we will follow in the next section will be first, to compile the syntax to an appropriate abstract machine (a transition system), and then to give a notion of equivalence of machines. The most important feature of the first stage is dealing with concurrency, either by compiling a || b as (a ; b) + (b ; a) as Milner does, or by subtler 'true concurrency' means, as we do. In either case, by the time we come to the second stage of the program, we need only consider the branching structure of the system. This means that it is easiest to separate consideration of notions of equivalences (which are defined over transitions systems), from consideration of how to deal with concurrency. Furthermore, following this program makes comparison with other work in this traditions, such as [Hennessy & Regan 1990], easier.

It would be fairly easy to alter IPA to fit the timed CSP paradigm where events are atomic and operations (like ; or +) take time; however that step won't be taken as the 'event have durations' approach is more atune with our classical intentions.

3 OPERATIONAL SEMANTICS

This section introduces a timed operational semantics for IPA. The framework used for this semantics, that of *asynchronous timed transition systems*, is new; an introduction to timed transition systems forms the first subsection of this section, followed by asynchronicity. The formalism is then applied, giving an operational semantics for interval process algebra.

The operational semantics of IPA will be in the structured operational semantics tradition of [Plotkin 1981]. There every expression, s, is associated with a transition system $(S, \mathrm{Ev}, \longrightarrow)$ where S is the set of subterms of s, Ev is the set of events that s can be observed to engage in (usually closely related to the alphabet of s), and $\longrightarrow$ is the transition relation, a relation in $S \times \mathrm{Ev} \times S$. In conventional transition system semantics [Milner 1989], [Keller 1974], we might write

$$s \xrightarrow{e} s'$$

to indicate that the term s could perform an e action and hence be transformed into the term s'. We, though, must have timing:

3.1 Timed transition systems

A timed transition system semantics is much like an untimed one; it is a triple $(S, A, \longrightarrow)$, where $\longrightarrow$ is relation on $(S \times \mathbb{R}^+) \times (A \times \mathbb{R}^+) \times (S \times \mathbb{R}^+)$. We shall adopt almost the same course as before, writing

$$s\,t \xrightarrow{e@t''} s'\,t'$$

to indicate that the term s, beginning at time t can be transformed into the term s' which is incapable of any action until time t'. This transformation is accompanied by an occurrence of the event e at time t''. As before we assume that the duration of events is predefined by $\Delta : \mathtt{Action} \rightarrow \mathbb{R}^+$. Since all events e must occupy some finite non–empty interval of time of length $\Delta(e)$, we shall require the temporal consistency property[6]

$$t \le t'' \le (t'' + \Delta(e)) \le t'$$

Timed transition systems (TTSs) will be used to give an operational semantics to IPA. Note, however, that they are not limited to this application. TTSs (and the ATTSs introduced below) are suitable for use in giving operational semantics to a wide variety of timed concurrency theories, particularly timed process algebras such as timed CSP or timed CCS. In the next two sections we relate transition systems labels to the events that IPA processes can display, and introduce a mechanism for dealing with parallel composition in IPA. This clears the way, after an example, for the operational semantics of IPA.

3.2 Transitions in IPA

The first question we must address is how the set A that labels transitions is related to the alphabet of the process we are dealing with. Given an underlying set of events of $\mathbf{E}$ say, the set

---

[6]This proviso is the weakest one that makes sense. Usually at least one of the $\le$s would be a $<$. For other languages much more restricting inequalities might hold; if we were dealing with timed CSP, for instance, would have $t = t'' = t' - \delta$, where δ is the timed CSP system delay constant. Note that our $e@t$ is the $e(t)$ of timed ACP.

of transition labels A is built up in quite a complex way. Clearly $\mathbf{E} \cup \{*\}$ will be contained in A to handle 'ordinary' happenings and waits. However, we also have to cope with the parallel composition. Events resulting from asynchronous occurrences will be of the form $(e, *)$ or the form $(*, e)$, while synchronisations will take the form (e_1, e_2). Thus, to deal with binary synchronisations we need $A = \mathbf{E} \cup \{*\} \cup ((\mathbf{E} \cup \{*\}) \times (\mathbf{E} \cup \{*\}))$. However, we have to cope with multiple parallel compositions like P || (Q || R), and we also need a reserved label τ for technical purposes, so

$$A = \{\tau\} \cup (\mathbf{E} \cup \{*\}) \cup (\mathbf{E} \cup \{*\})^2 \cup \ldots$$

(The union is only potentially infinite since the syntax can only generate a finite number of parallel processes without recourse to terms of infinite length.)

3.3 Asynchronous Timed Transition Systems

Thus far we merely have a timed generalisation of transition systems that can handle events with duration. This structure is not quite enough to allow us to describe non-interleaving concurrency,[7] so another transition relation, $\Longrightarrow$, will be introduced. We shall adopt the idea due to [Degano et al. 1987] of decomposing a parallel composition into a pair of subprocesses, known there as *grapes*. These subprocesses will be allowed to evolve independently. Once they have terminated, their behaviour will be combined to give the transitions of the parallel composition. This accords with the intuition that in the process P || Q the subprocesses P and Q proceed independently (except for synchronisations), and the composite is over once both P and Q have terminated. The grapes and the grape transition relation $\Longrightarrow$ give us a way of determining the behaviour of P || Q from the behaviours of P and Q. We have

$$\Longrightarrow \; :: \; (S \times \mathbb{R}^+)^2 \times (A \times \mathbb{R}^+) \times (S \times \mathbb{R}^+)^2$$

Parallel composition can then be modelled using transitions between tuples of term/time pairs. A transition system endowed with $\Longrightarrow$ will be called an *asynchronous timed transition system* (or ATTS).

An asynchronous timed transition system is a quadruple $(S, A, \longrightarrow, \Longrightarrow)$ where

(i) S is a set of states,

(ii) A is a set of transition labels,

(iii) $\longrightarrow$ is an ordinary timed transition relation, that is, a relation respecting timing over $(S \times \mathbb{R}^+) \times (A \times \mathbb{R}^+) \times (S \times \mathbb{R}^+)$ and

(iv) $\Longrightarrow$ is a grape transition relation, that is, a relation respecting timing over $(S \times \mathbb{R}^+)^2 \times (A \times \mathbb{R}^+) \times (S \times \mathbb{R}^+)^2$. We will write the grapes with continental quotes, « and » as the order of elements in it is (superficially) important.

---

[7]There have been many attempts at producing a non-interleaving (or truly concurrent) operational semantics for CCS–like languages; see, for instance [Boudol & Castellani 1989], [Degano et al. 1988], [Goltz 1990], [Olderog 1987]. All of this work is designed to eliminate the unfortunate feature of vanilla CCS, that a || b = (a ; b)+(b ; a). Also of some relevance to this discussion are the asynchronous transition systems of [Bednarczyk 1987] and [Shields 1990], and other variants on transition systems due to [Stark 1989] and [Gaifman 1989].

The grape transition relation, as we will see in the next section, will be used to derive the ordinary transition relation for parallel compositions. A typical asynchronous occurrence will be represented by

$$_{s}\langle\!\langle s_1\, t_1, s_2\, t_2\rangle\!\rangle \xrightarrow{(f_1,*)@t''} {}_{s}\langle\!\langle s_1'\, t_1', s_2\, t_2\rangle\!\rangle$$

while a synchronisation might be represented by

$$_{s}\langle\!\langle s_1\, t_1, s_2\, t_2\rangle\!\rangle \xrightarrow{(f_1,f_2)@t''} {}_{s}\langle\!\langle s_1'\, t_1', s_2'\, t_2'\rangle\!\rangle$$

We will write $\Longrightarrow^*$ for the transitive closure of $\Longrightarrow$.

3.4 Example

We will examine the transition system generated by a process with embedded choice and parallelism to give a rough idea of how the grape transition relation is used before going into the technicalities in the next section. Recall that synchronisations only happen if they are requested (i.e. are in the synchronisation set) and there is some temporal overlap between the events. Consider

$$\mathtt{a}\ {}_{\{(\mathtt{a},(\mathtt{b},*)),(\mathtt{a},(*,\mathtt{d}))\}}||\ ((\mathtt{b}+\mathtt{c})\ {}_{\{(\mathtt{c},\mathtt{d})\}}||\ \mathtt{d})$$

Take the innermost subprocess $(\mathtt{b}+\mathtt{c})$ first. There are two ways to resolve the nondeterminism, either;

$$(\mathtt{b}+\mathtt{c})\,t \xrightarrow{\tau@t} \mathtt{b}\,t \xrightarrow{\mathtt{b}@t} \mathtt{Skip}\,(t+\Delta(\mathtt{b}))$$

(Notice that τ, being just a technical transition, takes no time.) Alternatively;

$$(\mathtt{b}+\mathtt{c})\,t \xrightarrow{\tau@t} \mathtt{c}\,t \xrightarrow{\mathtt{c}@t} \mathtt{Skip}\,(t+\Delta(\mathtt{c}))$$

Furthermore $\mathtt{d}\,t \xrightarrow{\mathtt{d}@t} \mathtt{Skip}\,(t+\Delta(\mathtt{d}))$. Thus, ignoring the τ transitions, and writing S for $\{(\mathtt{c},\mathtt{d})\}$

$$
\begin{array}{rcl}
{}_{s}\langle\!\langle(\mathtt{b}+\mathtt{c})\,t,\mathtt{d}\,t\rangle\!\rangle & \overset{\mathtt{b}@t}{\Longrightarrow} & {}_{s}\langle\!\langle\mathtt{Skip}\,(t+\Delta(b)),\mathtt{d}\,t\rangle\!\rangle\\
{}_{s}\langle\!\langle(\mathtt{b}+\mathtt{c})\,t,\mathtt{d}\,t\rangle\!\rangle & \overset{\mathtt{c}@t}{\Longrightarrow} & {}_{s}\langle\!\langle\mathtt{Skip}\,(t+\Delta(c)),\mathtt{d}\,t\rangle\!\rangle\\
{}_{s}\langle\!\langle\mathtt{Skip}\,t',\mathtt{d}\,t\rangle\!\rangle & \overset{\mathtt{d}@t}{\Longrightarrow} & {}_{s}\langle\!\langle\mathtt{Skip}\,t',\mathtt{Skip}\,(t+\Delta(\mathtt{d}))\rangle\!\rangle\\
{}_{s}\langle\!\langle(\mathtt{b}+\mathtt{c})\,t,\mathtt{d}\,t\rangle\!\rangle & \overset{\mathtt{d}@t}{\Longrightarrow} & {}_{s}\langle\!\langle(\mathtt{b}+\mathtt{c})\,t,\mathtt{Skip}\,(t+\Delta(\mathtt{d}))\rangle\!\rangle\\
{}_{s}\langle\!\langle(\mathtt{b}+\mathtt{c})\,t,\mathtt{Skip}\,(t+\Delta(\mathtt{d}))\rangle\!\rangle & \overset{\mathtt{b}@t}{\Longrightarrow} & {}_{s}\langle\!\langle\mathtt{Skip}\,(t+\Delta(\mathtt{b})),\mathtt{Skip}\,(t+\Delta(\mathtt{d}))\rangle\!\rangle\\
{}_{s}\langle\!\langle(\mathtt{b}+\mathtt{c})\,t,\mathtt{Skip}\,(t+\Delta(\mathtt{d}))\rangle\!\rangle & \overset{\mathtt{c}@t}{\Longrightarrow} & {}_{s}\langle\!\langle\mathtt{Skip}\,(t+\Delta(\mathtt{c})),\mathtt{Skip}\,(t+\Delta(\mathtt{d}))\rangle\!\rangle
\end{array}
$$

Hence, again ignoring τs, simplifying a little and noticing that $\mathtt{c}$ sync $\mathtt{d}$, we have, writing $t_{e_1e_2}$ for $\max(t+\Delta(e_1),t+\Delta(e_2))$

$$
\begin{array}{c}
((\mathtt{b}+\mathtt{c})\ {}_{s}||\ \mathtt{d})\,t \xrightarrow{(\mathtt{b},*)@t} {}_{s}\langle\!\langle\mathtt{Skip}\,(t+\Delta(\mathtt{b})),\mathtt{d}\,t\rangle\!\rangle \xrightarrow{(*,\mathtt{d})@t} \mathtt{Skip}\,t_{bd}\\
((\mathtt{b}+\mathtt{c})\ {}_{s}||\ \mathtt{d})\,t \xrightarrow{(*,\mathtt{d})@t} {}_{s}\langle\!\langle\mathtt{b}\,t,\mathtt{Skip}\,(t+\Delta(\mathtt{d}))\rangle\!\rangle \xrightarrow{(\mathtt{b},*)@t} \mathtt{Skip}\,t_{bd}\\
((\mathtt{b}+\mathtt{c})\ {}_{s}||\ \mathtt{d})\,t \xrightarrow{(\mathtt{c},\mathtt{d})@t} \mathtt{Skip}\,t_{cd}
\end{array}
$$

For the whole term, on expanding the grapes we find that either b is chosen and a can synchronise with $(\mathtt{b},*)$ or c is chosen, $(\mathtt{c},\mathtt{d})$ happens and a must occur asynchronously; the synchronisation (a, (c, ∗)) can never happen, as if c occurs it always synchronises with d. Thus we have, given $S' = \{(\mathsf{a},(\mathsf{b},*)),(\mathsf{a},(*,\mathsf{d}))\}$ the complete behaviour

$$\mathsf{a}\ {}_{S'}\|\ ((\mathsf{b}+\mathsf{c})\ {}_S\|\ \mathsf{d})\ t \xrightarrow{(\mathsf{a},(\mathsf{b},*))@t} {}_{S'}\langle\!\langle \mathtt{Skip}\ t_{ab}), {}_S\langle\!\langle \mathtt{Skip}\ (t+\Delta(\mathsf{b}), \mathsf{d}\ t\rangle\!\rangle\rangle\!\rangle \xrightarrow{(*,(*,\mathsf{d}))@t} \mathtt{Skip}\ t_{abd}$$

$$\mathsf{a}\ {}_{S'}\|\ ((\mathsf{b}+\mathsf{c})\ {}_S\|\ \mathsf{d})\ t \xrightarrow{(*,\mathsf{d})@t} {}_{S'}\langle\!\langle \mathsf{a}\ t, {}_S\langle\!\langle \mathsf{b}\ t, \mathtt{Skip}\ (t+\Delta(\mathsf{d}))\rangle\!\rangle\rangle\!\rangle \xrightarrow{(\mathsf{a},(\mathsf{b},*))@t} \mathtt{Skip}\ t_{abd}$$

$$\mathsf{a}\ {}_{S'}\|\ ((\mathsf{b}+\mathsf{c})\ {}_S\|\ \mathsf{d})\ t \xrightarrow{(*,(\mathsf{c},\mathsf{d}))@t} {}_{S'}\langle\!\langle \mathsf{a}\ t, \mathtt{Skip}\ t_{cd}\rangle\!\rangle \xrightarrow{(\mathsf{a},*)@t} \mathtt{Skip}\ t_{acd}$$

$$\mathsf{a}\ {}_{S'}\|\ ((\mathsf{b}+\mathsf{c})\ {}_S\|\ \mathsf{d})\ t \xrightarrow{(\mathsf{a},*)@t} {}_{S'}\langle\!\langle \mathtt{Skip}\ (t+\Delta(a)), {}_S\langle\!\langle \mathsf{c}\ t, \mathsf{d}\ t\rangle\!\rangle\rangle\!\rangle \xrightarrow{(*,(\mathsf{c},\mathsf{d}))@t} \mathtt{Skip}\ t_{acd}$$

The net which we will associate with this example is given at the end of the next section.

It is clear from this example that in analysing the behaviour of P || Q we have to resolve *all* of the nondeterminism in P and in Q before we can determine *any* of the behaviour of the composite, because we need to know what the grapes are going to do in order to determine the behaviour of whole composition. This is what $\Longrightarrow$ is for.[8] Notice too that although we have a choice in which transition to fire, the transition labels preserve information about what the concurrency of the situation is, and the times tell us about simultaneity.

3.5 The asynchronous timed transition system of IPA

We can now go on to describe the operational semantics of IPA in terms of our asynchronous timed transition systems. The elements of S will be IPA terms, and a transition will hold between one term and another just when the first can perform the event in the label of the transition and be transformed into the second. The complete set of transitions is given at the end of the section; they are discussed below. In the following description f (and derived variables like f_1) will be assumed to range over transition labels, i.e. over the set A defined in section 3.2 above.

Actions. The transitions for the base level terms $e \in \mathbf{E}$ and `Wait` t are straightforward. These are the rules Event and Wait.

Notice that an implicit quantification over time has been assumed. If we had an event `fastidious` that could only begin at certain times, during some set *allowed*(`fastidious`) $\subseteq \mathbb{R}^+$ say, its introduction rule would be different;

$$\text{Fastidious}\quad \frac{t \in \mathit{allowed}(\mathtt{fastidious})}{\mathtt{fastidious}\ t \xrightarrow{\mathtt{fastidious}@t} \mathtt{Skip}\ t + \Delta(\mathtt{fastidious})}$$

By this means we can reason about events with limited firing times, or events whose starting times are otherwise constrained.

The interpretation of stop as a deadlocked process is usually reflected by the lack of a transition coming out of it. However, consider `Skip`; a moment's reflection will indicate that `Skip` cannot have any transitions, as the only sensible one would be

$$\text{Skip}\quad \frac{}{\mathtt{Skip}\ t \xrightarrow{\tau@t} \mathtt{Skip}\ t}$$

---

[8]In going from $\Longrightarrow$ transitions to $\longrightarrow$ ones we decide which synchronisations happen. In the world of [Winskel 1984], this is pruning the product of the synchronisation trees to leave only those synchronisations that are temporally valid and desired; everything else occurs asynchronously. Thus, each branch of the $\Longrightarrow$–transitions for P and for Q gives rise to a $\longrightarrow$ branch for P || Q, but synchronisation may amalgamate P $\Longrightarrow$–transitions with Q $\Longrightarrow$ ones.

which gives us the possibility of a process which does not progress in time (livelock). We impose $0 \notin \text{rng}(\Delta)$ as a *temporal progress* requirement; when things happen, time must go on.

Stop, on the other hand, is easy. The rule Stop indicates that the on light of stop is always on, but the condition $t' > \epsilon$ forbids an infinite number of observations of this fact in a finite time, and hence of introducing a form of livelock.[9] Since this transition is a technical one it carries the label τ rather than $*$.

Choice. Choice can be dealt with using a variant of the usual operational technique; either one thing is chosen, or the other is. Notice that using silent transitions to accomplish this rather than the first transitions of the respective processes means that Skip is not a zero of choice; we don't want it to be.

Sequential Composition. This too is straightforward; two transition rules suffice, one to deal with the first process in the combination, SeqI, and one to eliminate Skip, SeqE.

Parallel Composition. Parallel composition gives rise to the most complicated set of transition rules of all. As mentioned above, we shall decompose a parallel composition into a set of terms that will be allowed to proceed independently.

We have, then, a transition to get us into the grapes, ParI, the grape evolution rules, ParGL, ParGR, and a transition to eliminate grapes, ParE. (Notice that these two rules ensure that Wait t for $t \leq \min(\Lambda(\mathsf{P}))$ is a zero of $\mathsf{P} \parallel \_$.)

Once the whole transition behaviour of the components has been captured by $\Longrightarrow$, and any nondeterminism thus resolved, we can begin to analyse the behaviour of the whole. There are three separate things that can happen as a parallel composition evolves; either an asynchronous event from one component occurs, ParAsyncL, or an asynchronous event from the other, ParAsyncR, or a synchronisation, ParSync. We can only fire an occurrence asynchronously if there is nothing it should synchronise with, and we can only fire a synchronisation if the two events are in the synchronisation set and the times are supposed to match.

The duration of a compound event is the union of their durations. Without loss of generality, suppose $t_1'' < t_2''$. Then $\Delta(f_1, f_2) = \max(t_1'' + \Delta(f_1),\ t_2'' + \Delta(f_2)) - t_1''$, and $\Delta(f_1, *) = \Delta(f_1)$.

The order in which we are allowed to fire events in a parallel composition respects causality, but not, in contrast to timed ACP, time; we can allow one parallel stream of execution to evolve first and then deal with another. The choice we are allowed to make in deciding which transition to fire corresponds precisely to the different interleavings possible under an interleaving semantics.

(**Aside:** It should be mentioned that a main topic we shall not tackle is observational equivalence; we shall not give the 'second stage' of Milner's program mentioned at the end of the last section. While there does not seem to be any obvious problem in using our transition system to define an observational equivalence (in the style of bisimulation equivalence, or, better, [Bloom et al. 1990], ready simulation), it seems more natural in this setting to concentrate on equivalences of implementational structures. A topic of some interest in this setting is notions of equivalence that are congruences of refinement. Notice that this issue is independent of the treatment of concurrency. See [Vogler 1990] and [van Glabbeek & Goltz 1990] for a taste of work in this area.)

---

[9] Here ϵ is a constant real greater than zero; think of it as the time it takes to make an observation. In contrast to timed ACP, [Baeten & Bergstra 1990], we believe that it is important to allow only a finite number of observations of a process in a finite time.

It is slightly counterintuitive that Stop is the only wait that can be seen to be waiting (it is the assumption that one can 'see' deadlock); it is not clear, however, without this feature, how to distinguish between Skip and Stop.

$$\text{Event}\ \frac{}{e\,t \xrightarrow{e@t} \mathtt{Skip}\ t + \Delta(e)} \qquad \text{Wait}\ \frac{}{(\mathtt{Wait}\ t')\ t \xrightarrow{*@t} \mathtt{Skip}\ t + t'}$$

$$\text{Stop}\ \frac{}{\mathtt{Stop}\ t \xrightarrow{\tau@t} \mathtt{Stop}\ t + t'}\ t' > \epsilon$$

$$\text{SumEL}\ \frac{}{(s_1 + s_2)\,t \xrightarrow{\tau@t} s_1\,t} \qquad \text{SumER}\ \frac{}{(s_1 + s_2)\,t \xrightarrow{\tau@t} s_2\,t}$$

$$\text{SeqI}\ \frac{s_1\,t \xrightarrow{f@t''} s_1'\,t_1'}{(s_1\,;\,s_2)\,t \xrightarrow{f@t''} (s_1'\,;\,s_2)\,t_1'} \qquad \text{SeqE}\ \frac{}{(\mathtt{Skip}\,;\,s)\,t \xrightarrow{\tau@t''} s\,t}$$

$$\text{ParGL}\ \frac{s_1\,t_1 \xrightarrow{f_1@t_1''} s_1'\,t_1'}{\mathrm{s}\langle\!\langle s_1\,t_1, s_2\,t_2\rangle\!\rangle \xRightarrow{f_1@t_1''} \mathrm{s}\langle\!\langle s_1'\,t_1', s_2\,t_2\rangle\!\rangle} \qquad \text{ParGR}\ \frac{s_2\,t_2 \xrightarrow{f_2@t_2''} s_2'\,t_2'}{\mathrm{s}\langle\!\langle s_1\,t_1, s_2\,t_2\rangle\!\rangle \xRightarrow{f_2@t_2''} \mathrm{s}\langle\!\langle s_1\,t_1, s_2'\,t_2'\rangle\!\rangle}$$

$$\text{ParI}\ \frac{}{(s_1\ \mathrm{s}||\ s_2)\,t \xrightarrow{\tau@t} \mathrm{s}\langle\!\langle s_1\,t, s_2\,t\rangle\!\rangle}$$

$$\text{ParE}\ \frac{}{\mathrm{s}\langle\!\langle \mathtt{Skip}\,t_1, \mathtt{Skip}\,t_2\rangle\!\rangle \xrightarrow{\tau@t''} \mathtt{Skip}\ t''}\ t'' = \max(t_1, t_2)$$

$$\text{ParSync}\ \frac{\begin{array}{c}\mathrm{s}\langle\!\langle s_1\,t_1, s_2\,t_2\rangle\!\rangle \xRightarrow{f_1@t_1''} \mathrm{s}\langle\!\langle s_1'\,t_1', s_2\,t_2\rangle\!\rangle \\ f_1\ \mathrm{sync}\ f_2 \\ \mathrm{s}\langle\!\langle s_1\,t_1, s_2\,t_2\rangle\!\rangle \xRightarrow{f_2@t_2''} \mathrm{s}\langle\!\langle s_1\,t_1, s_2'\,t_2'\rangle\!\rangle\end{array}}{\mathrm{s}\langle\!\langle s_1\,t_1, s_2\,t_2\rangle\!\rangle \xrightarrow{(f_1,f_2)@t''} \mathrm{s}\langle\!\langle s_1'\,t_1', s_2'\,t_2'\rangle\!\rangle}\ t'' = \min(t_1'', t_2'')$$

$$\text{ParAsyncL}\ \frac{\begin{array}{c}\mathrm{s}\langle\!\langle s_1\,t_1, s_2\,t_2\rangle\!\rangle \xRightarrow{f_1@t_1''} \mathrm{s}\langle\!\langle s_1'\,t_1', s_2\,t_2\rangle\!\rangle \\ \neg\exists s_3\,.\,(s_2\,t_2 \Longrightarrow^* s_3\,t_3 \xRightarrow{f_3@t_3''} s_3'\,t_3' \ \wedge\ f_1\ \mathrm{sync}\ f_3)\end{array}}{\mathrm{s}\langle\!\langle s_1\,t_1, s_2\,t_2\rangle\!\rangle \xrightarrow{(f_1,*)@t_1''} \mathrm{s}\langle\!\langle s_1'\,t_1', s_2\,t_2\rangle\!\rangle}$$

$$\text{ParAsyncR}\ \frac{\begin{array}{c}\mathrm{s}\langle\!\langle s_1\,t_1, s_2\,t_2\rangle\!\rangle \xRightarrow{f_2@t_2''} \mathrm{s}\langle\!\langle s_1\,t_1, s_2'\,t_2'\rangle\!\rangle \\ \neg\exists s_3\,.\,(s_1\,t_1 \Longrightarrow^* s_3\,t_3 \xRightarrow{f_3@t_3''} s_3'\,t_3' \ \wedge\ f_2\ \mathrm{sync}\ f_3)\end{array}}{\mathrm{s}\langle\!\langle s_1\,t_1, s_2\,t_2\rangle\!\rangle \xrightarrow{(*,f_2)@t_2''} \mathrm{s}\langle\!\langle s_1\,t_1, s_2'\,t_2'\rangle\!\rangle}$$

The Asynchronous Timed Transition System for Interval Process Algebra

4 FROM PROCESS ALGEBRA TO PETRI NETS

The purpose of this section is to discuss the net–theoretic interpretation of various process–algebraic constructs, including those found in IPA. Given an IPA process P, a Petri net, $\mathcal{N}(\mathtt{P})$, will be defined in the first subsection.[10] This translation will then be contrasted with the more usual translation of a CSP–like language into nets. None of our constructions are new to the net community; the contribution of this paper is to define an algebra based on them.

4.1 IPA into Nets

Our translation will be *structure–oriented* in the sense that if $\mathcal{N}(\mathtt{P})$ is the net representing P, then there are net interpretations of the process–algebraic combinators *op* so that $\mathcal{N}(\mathtt{P}\ op\ \mathtt{Q}) = \mathcal{N}(\mathtt{P})\ op\ \mathcal{N}(\mathtt{Q})$. Furthermore we will only compile into a limited class of nets. Every IPA process will be represented by a finite 1–safe contact–free confusion–free net with one marked place and one home place.[11] Notice that we cannot construct a net with the causality of the N–poset; this is crucial to being able to decompose processes, – see [Boudol & Castellani 1989]. For each constructor considered, the ATTS transition and associated net are given. The time that the token leaves the place and the time the transition fire are also indicated.[12]

Actions

The interpretation of elementary actions and waits is straightforward:

$$e\,t \xrightarrow{e@t} \mathtt{Skip}\ t + \Delta(e)$$

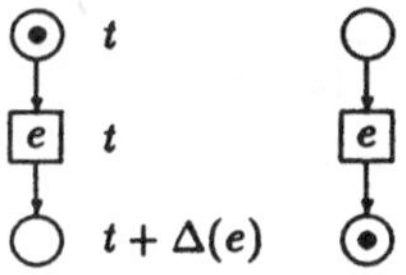

t

t

$t + \Delta(e)$

$$(\mathtt{Wait}\ t')\ t \xrightarrow{*@t} \mathtt{Skip}\ t + t'$$

t

t

$t + t'$

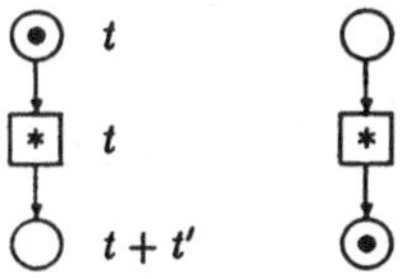

[10] We will not discuss here the precise connection between general ATTSs and nets. Eventually we hope to understand this connection more thoroughly, but as it will probably rely on the interpretation of nets as symmetric monoidal categories, [Meseguer & Montanari 1988], and an extension of the work of [Bednarczyk 1987], it will not be pursued here.

[11] *1–safe* means that there is at most one token at any place. The existence of a single marked place initial and a single home place means that there are defined non–distributed starting and finishing states, and hence a clean approach to hierarchical nets; every process can be abstracted by two places connected by a single transition.

[12] It might be argued from a net–theoretic standpoint that the most natural timed net is one where the time 'elapses' in the conditions rather than the events. Our approach, however, is more natural from the process algebraic viewpoint. Cf. [Ramchandan 1974].

Nondeterminism

This is a little more complicated as there is more than one 'obvious' way to compile $\mathcal{N}(\mathtt{P}+\mathtt{Q})$ given $\mathcal{N}(\mathtt{P})$ and $\mathcal{N}(\mathtt{Q})$. We will choose to resolve the nondeterminism by firing a 'silent' transition.

$$\text{SumEL}\ \frac{}{(s_1+s_2)\,t \xrightarrow{\tau @ t} s_1\,t}$$

$$\text{SumER}\ \frac{}{(s_1+s_2)\,t \xrightarrow{\tau @ t} s_2\,t}$$

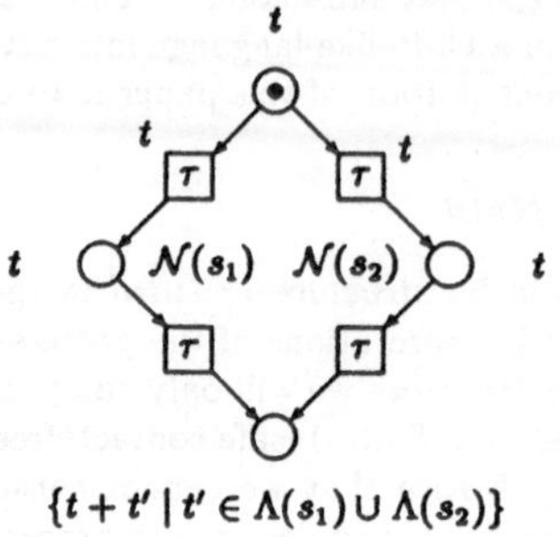

$\{t+t' \mid t' \in \Lambda(s_1) \cup \Lambda(s_2)\}$

Sequential Composition

This is completely straightforward;

$$\text{SeqI}\ \frac{s_1\,t \xrightarrow{f @ t''} s_1'\,t_1'}{(s_1\ ;\ s_2)\,t \xrightarrow{f @ t''} (s_1'\ ;\ s_2)\,t_1'}$$

$\mathcal{N}(s_1)$ $\mathcal{N}(s_2)$

$$\text{SeqE}\ \frac{}{(\mathtt{Skip}\ ;\ s)\,t \xrightarrow{\tau @ t''} s\,t}$$

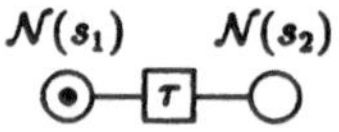

Parallelism

Here we give the net interpretation of each rule separately

$$\text{ParI}\ \frac{}{(s_1\ {}_{\mathrm{s}}\|\ s_2)\,t \xrightarrow{\tau @ t} {}_{\mathrm{s}}\langle\!\langle s_1\,t, s_2\,t\rangle\!\rangle}$$

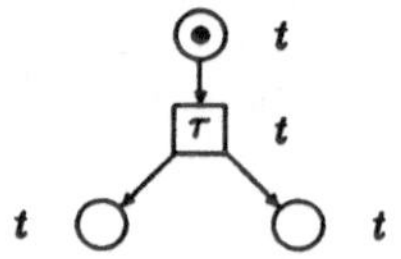

$$\text{ParE}\ \frac{}{{}_{\mathrm{s}}\langle\!\langle \mathtt{Skip}\,t_1, \mathtt{Skip}\,t_2\rangle\!\rangle \xrightarrow{\tau @ t''} \mathtt{Skip}\,t''}$$

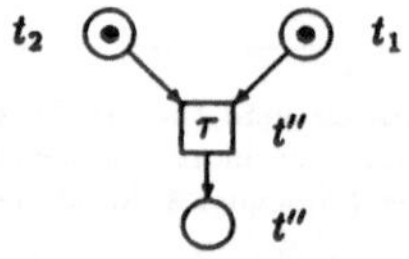

$$\text{ParSync}\ \frac{{}_{\mathrm{s}}\langle\!\langle s_1\,t_1, s_2\,t_2\rangle\!\rangle \xRightarrow{f_1 @ t_1''} {}_{\mathrm{s}}\langle\!\langle s_1'\,t_1', s_2\,t_2\rangle\!\rangle \quad f_1\ \mathrm{sync}\ f_2 \quad {}_{\mathrm{s}}\langle\!\langle s_1\,t_1, s_2\,t_2\rangle\!\rangle \xRightarrow{f_2 @ t_2''} {}_{\mathrm{s}}\langle\!\langle s_1\,t_1, s_2'\,t_2'\rangle\!\rangle}{{}_{\mathrm{s}}\langle\!\langle s_1\,t_1, s_2\,t_2\rangle\!\rangle \xrightarrow{(f_1,f_2) @ t''} {}_{\mathrm{s}}\langle\!\langle s_1'\,t_1', s_2'\,t_2'\rangle\!\rangle}$$

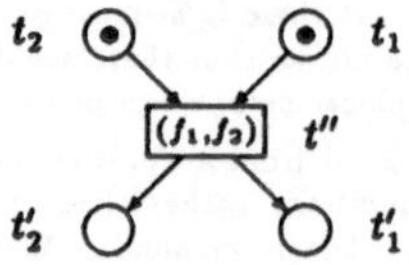

$$\text{ParAsyncL}\quad \frac{s\langle\!\langle s_1\, t_1, s_2\, t_2\rangle\!\rangle \xrightarrow{f_1 @ t_1''} s\langle\!\langle s_1'\, t_1', s_2\, t_2\rangle\!\rangle \quad s_1 \text{ should occur asynchronously}}{s\langle\!\langle s_1\, t_1, s_2\, t_2\rangle\!\rangle \xrightarrow{(f_1,*) @ t_1''} s\langle\!\langle s_1'\, t_1', s_2\, t_2\rangle\!\rangle}$$

The picture for ParAsyncL is t_1 t_2 $[(f_1,*)]$ t_1'' t_1' with the obvious change for ParAsyncR.

It can now been seen that we are not disrespecting causality or indulging in time travel in the definition of $\longrightarrow$ for P || Q; we only have to evaluate all of the behaviour of the components in order that we know what *labels* to put on transitions, not so as to let future transitions influence past ones. The net interpretation shows the causality of the situation clearly.

4.2 More usual compilations

There is very little choice in how to compile the firing of a single event or the sequential combination of two processes; things become more interesting when we consider how the other combinators are normally compiled:

Nondeterminism

Compare our approach with the more usual denotation;

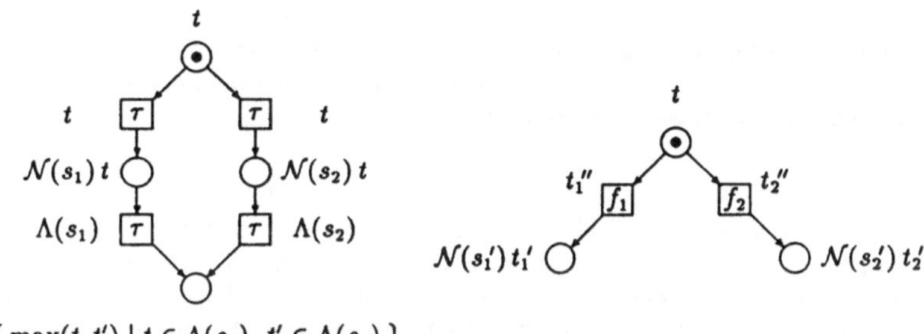

The denotation we chose had one home place rather than two, so we are not always forced to make two copies of $\mathcal{N}(\mathrm{R})$ in (P + Q) ; R. We only know which place is the home state, however, not when it will be occupied, even if P and Q are totally deterministic.

Notice that our choice would cause difficulties if we introduced recursion; it would be hard to see how to compile a process like $\mu x\,.\,\mathrm{P} + \mathrm{a}\,;\, x$ where $x \notin \alpha(\mathrm{P})$ without resorting to the more usual compilation. Our interpretation assumes that the process R in (P + Q) ; R has no way of 'knowing' whether P or Q was chosen; in [Winskel 1989] this kind of causality (called 'instability' there) is expressly forbidden. We, like [Boudol & Castellani 1987], having a different perspective (and in particular having no wish to investigate the order structure of the histories of processes), see no difficulty.

Parallel Composition

There is a fundamental difference between the parallelism evident in conventional process algebras and in nets. In a process algebra we write P || Q for a single process consisting of the processes P and Q running in parallel; we think of a single entity which starts both off, and which can be said to be over. In net terms, parallelism can mean complete independence; unconnected nets bear no relationship whatsoever to each other. Thus the usual compilation of a || b is

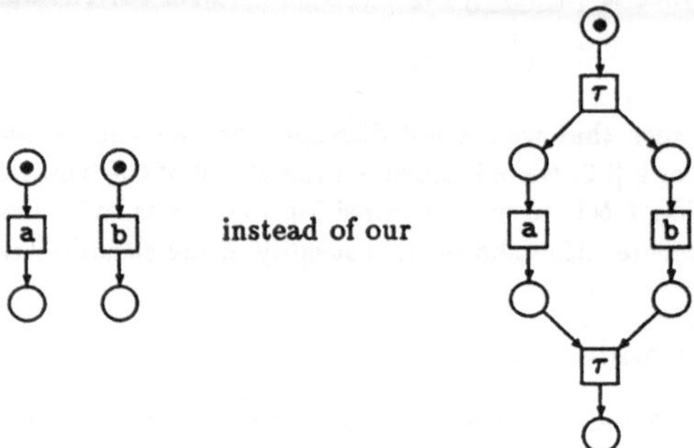

The difference is that we have unique starting and finishing places rather than a distributed starting and finishing state. We think of there being a single state before P || Q has started and a single state after it has finished. Again, our approach gives better compositionality.

Event refinement reconsidered

We can now indicate the form of event refinement we shall choose for IPA and why:

The 'loose' definition of event refinement goes with Λ as we have defined it; a set of possible run times is associated with a process, and we have maximal liveness, – things happen as soon as possible. The point is clearest if we consider

$$P\,;\,a\,;\,Q$$

with R refines a. Notice that a starts at one of the times $t \in \Lambda(P)$ and Q at one of $\{t + \Delta(a) \mid t \in \Lambda(P)\}$. If we perform the refinement, then Q will start at one of $\{t + t' \mid t \in \Lambda(P), t' \in \Lambda(R)\}$; this is maximal liveness. Notice that we have not preserved timing information in the refinement; it is possible for Q to start earlier after the refinement than before. This seems to be the most natural definition for IPA. However, another approach is possible:

If we wanted to preserve timing information then we would have to associate *one* time with a process, – the longest time it could possibly last, – defining

$$\begin{aligned}\Lambda(P+Q) &= \max(\Lambda(P), \Lambda(Q))\\ \Lambda(P\,;\,Q) &= \Lambda(P) + \Lambda(Q)\\ \Lambda(P \,||\, Q) &= \max(\Lambda(P), \Lambda(Q))\end{aligned}$$

This would fit with the 'tight' notion of event refinement; all operations would then preserve absolute timing information. With the definition of Λ above, and tight refinement, in the example P ; a ; Q, Q will start at the same time, $\Lambda(P) + \Delta(a)$, both before and after the refinement.

Notice that we have a duality between abstraction and refinement; a process can always be abstracted by a single transition, and a single transition can always be refined by a process. We never lose causal information in this process, only temporal, as indicated above.

The test of any notion of event refinement is its interaction with parallel composition. Consider $\mathtt{P} \stackrel{\text{def}}{=} \mathtt{a}\ _{\{(\mathtt{a},\mathtt{b})\}}\|\ \mathtt{b}$. And suppose that $\mathtt{Q} \stackrel{\text{def}}{=} \mathtt{c}\ ;\ \mathtt{d}\ ;\ \mathtt{e}$ refines a. When we refine a in P by Q, every occurrence of a in the synchronisation set of anything involving P must be replaced by every $\mathtt{c} \in \alpha(\mathtt{Q})$. We write $\mathtt{P}\left[\frac{\mathtt{Q}}{\mathtt{a}}\right]$ for P with Q refining a, so here

$$\mathtt{P}\left[\frac{\mathtt{Q}}{\mathtt{a}}\right] = (\mathtt{c}\ ;\ \mathtt{d}\ ;\ \mathtt{e})\ _{\{(\mathtt{c},\mathtt{b}),(\mathtt{d},\mathtt{b}),(\mathtt{e},\mathtt{b})\}}\|\ \mathtt{b}$$

Now, we may very well have

$$\mathtt{c}\ \mathtt{sync}\ \mathtt{b} \qquad\qquad \mathtt{d}\ \mathtt{sync}\ \mathtt{b}$$

so the synchronisation $(\mathtt{c},\mathtt{b})$ will happen and d will occur asynchronously. But this may not be what we want; c might be some kind of 'setup' and we want d to do the synchronising. This means that we have to allow the synchronisation set to be cut down in refinement, so for $(\mathtt{P}\ _S\|\ \mathtt{R})\left[\frac{\mathtt{Q}}{\mathtt{a}}\right]$ we allow (assuming $\alpha(\mathtt{P}) \ni \mathtt{a} \notin \alpha(\mathtt{Q}) \cup \alpha(\mathtt{R})$)

$$\left(\mathtt{P}\left[\frac{\mathtt{Q}}{\mathtt{a}}\right]\right)\ _{S'}\|\ \mathtt{R}$$

with not just

$$S' \ = \ \{\,(\mathtt{q},\mathtt{b}) \mid \mathtt{q} \in \alpha(\mathtt{Q}),\ (\mathtt{a},\mathtt{b}) \in S\,\} \ \cup\ \{\,(\mathtt{a}',\mathtt{b}) \mid \mathtt{a}' \neq \mathtt{a},\ (\mathtt{a}',\mathtt{b}) \in S\,\}$$

but also with

$$S' \ = \ \{\,(\mathtt{q},\mathtt{b}) \mid q \in \alpha(\mathtt{Q}),\ (\mathtt{a},\mathtt{b}) \in S,\ \mathtt{q} \in \mathit{desired}(\mathtt{Q})\,\} \ \cup\ \{\,(\mathtt{a}',\mathtt{b}) \mid \mathtt{a}' \neq \mathtt{a},\ (\mathtt{a}',\mathtt{b}) \in S\,\}$$

for some nonempty set $\mathit{desired}(\mathtt{Q})$.

In the example of this section, taking $\mathit{desired}(\mathtt{Q}) = \{\mathtt{d}\}$ we have

$$\mathtt{P}\left[\frac{\mathtt{Q}}{\mathtt{a}}\right] = (\mathtt{c}\ ;\ \mathtt{d}\ ;\ \mathtt{e})\ _{\{(\mathtt{d},\mathtt{b})\}}\|\ \mathtt{b}$$

and d sync b but not c sync b.

This gives us the flexibility to allow event refinement to interact with parallel composition in a useful way, without endangering the hierarchical aspects of the model.

Notice that there are no further conditions on valid refinements; refinement never introduces deadlock, for instance, or livelock, as neither are possible in the model. The only slightly tricky point is to check that refinement doesn't introduce extra synchronisations. For this reason it is easiest to demand that a refining process contains no events mentioned before, nor does it contain products of them. In other words, the events mentioned in the transition system of the refining process should be disjoint from those of the context in which it is used (as well as those of the process it refines).

4.3 Example revisited

The net generated by the last section's example is

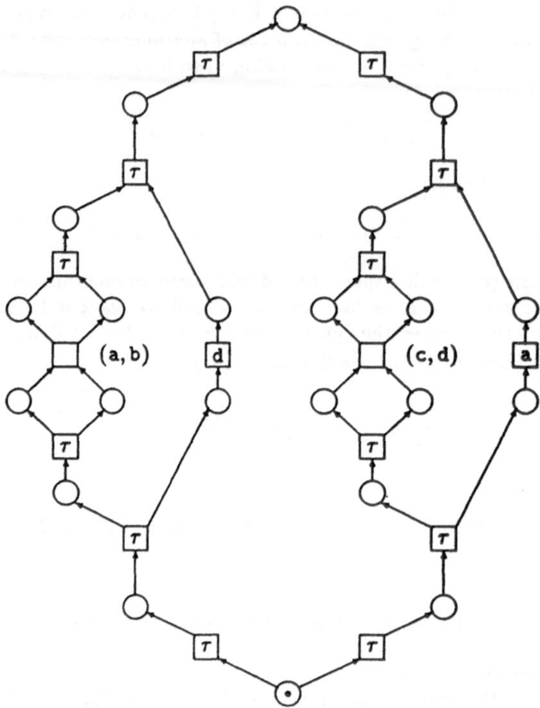

Note that since all are constructions are symmetric we could have drawn this net with all the arrows reversed and with the top rather than the bottom place marked without affecting its behaviour. Note too that we can affect some simplification by removing multiple τ transitions in the obvious way.

5 APPLICATIONS

Yet another concurrency theory, whatever its theoretical niceties, is little more than a burden to the literature without some thought for its usefulness. Here we briefly indicate several areas where IPA may be a useful tool.

Performance analysis. A widely used tool in the performance analysis of distributed systems are *series/parallel graphs* [Sahner & Trivedi 1987]. These are descriptions of implementations that are very similar to a subset of IPA; one starts with the descriptions of a system as a single node. Any node can be replaced by a sequence of two nodes, and any three nodes in sequence can be replaced by a diamond of four nodes (hence 'series/parallel'). This hierarchical decomposition is clearly very similar to that of IPA. Furthermore, IPA may offer a vehicle for algebraic reasoning about timed behaviours in this context.

The design of self–timed VLSI. Self–timed circuits depend for their operation on the explicit synchronisation of asynchronous, autonomous components, [Martin 1986]. As such, their design is clearly within the purview of concurrency theory. However, to date attempts to use process algebra to design self–timed VLSI, such as [Josephs & Udding 1990], have relied on models with participatory concurrency. IPA, in contrast, with its timing, maximal liveness, primitive notion of synchronisation, and event refinement is ideal here, as will be shown in a latter paper.

Extensions to LOTOS. IPA could form the basis of a timed specification–oriented calculus that could be of benefit to the LOTOS community. While timed LOTOS exists, [Quemada & Fernandez 1987], it does not yet incorporate either the classical intuitions of this paper, which seem appropriate to LOTOS, or the ineluctability of time. IPA offers an alternative.

6 CONCLUDING REMARKS

Conclusions. The conclusions of this work can be summarised thus:

- It is possible to develop a new non-interleaving timed process algebra which uses net–theoretic combinators and hence has a natural interpretation in nets.
- Thus, we can obtain some insight into the differences between the usual process–algebraic and net–theoretic constructions.
- The introduction of timing in this framework is natural, and gives a simple algebraic characterisation of event refinement.
- We have developed a new timed non–interleaving operational formalism of potentially widespread applicability.

We have identified an interesting class of hierarchical Petri nets and given them timing and an algebra. It remains to be seen whether this work can be extended by the addition of further operators from CCS or CSP.

Further work. It should be admitted that this is the first paper of two. There are many issues that we have not treated here. Some, such as the introduction of hiding, are easy. Details of others, such as a sensible notion of equivalence of transition systems (that is a congruence of event refinement), and an algebraic characterisation of it, will be given latter. We will also say more about compositionality in the second paper. Finally, we should admit that there are topics whose treatment is unclear in this world, such as recursion.

For the net theorist a little work is left. It would be nice to prove that the net we generate has the same step semantics as the transition system. The precise class of nets that we can generate should also be elucidated in more detail. It would be interesting too to see if the translation into nets could be automated.

Thanks. My thanks are due to Pierpaulo Degano, Ursula Goltz, Alan Jeffrey, Tim Regan and Mike Shields for insightful remarks. This work was partly supported by IED Grant 1759, and partly by the SERC of Great Britain.

BIBLIOGRAPHY

[Aceto & Hennessy 1988] L. Aceto, M. Hennessy, *Towards Action-Refinement in Process Algebra*. Technical Report 3/88, Department of Computer Science, University of Sussex.

[Baeten & Bergstra 1990] J. Baeten, J. Bergstra, *Real Time Process Algebra*. Technical Report P8916b, Programming Research Group, University of Amsterdam.

[de Bakker et al. 1989] J. de Bakker, W. de Roever, G. Rozenberg (Eds.), *Linear Time, Branching Time and Partial Order in Logics and Models for Concurrency*, Springer-Verlag LNCS 354.

[Bednarczyk 1987] M. Bednarczyk, *Categories of Asynchronous Systems*. Ph.D. Thesis, University of Sussex.

[Best & Fernandez 1988] E. Best, C. Fernandez, *Nonsequential Processes, A Petri Net view*. EATCS Monographs on theoretical computer science, Volume 13, Springer-Verlag.

[Bloom et al. 1990] B. Bloom, S. Istrail, A. Mayer, *Bisimulation can't be traced*. Technical Report TR 90–1150, Department of Computer Science, Cornell University.

[Boudol & Castellani 1987] G. Boudol, I. Castellani, On the Semantics of Concurrency: Partial orders and Transition systems. In the *Proceedings of TAPSOFT 1987*, Springer-Verlag LNCS 249.

[Boudol & Castellani 1989] G. Boudol, I. Castellani, Permutations of Transitions: An Event Structure Semantics for CCS and SCCS. In [de Bakker et al. 1989].

[Brookes et al. 1984] S. Brookes, C. Hoare, A. Roscoe, A Theory of Communicating Sequential Processes. In the *Journal of the ACM*, Volume 31.

[Casley et al. 1989] R. Casley, R. Crew, J. Meseguer, V. Pratt, Temporal Structures. In D. Pitt et al. (Eds.), *Proceedings of Category Theory and Computer Science 1989*, Springer-Verlag LNCS 389.

[Darondeau & Degano 1990i] P. Darondeau, P. Degano, Event structures, Causal trees, and Refinements. In B. Rovan (Ed.), *Mathematical Foundations of Computer Science*. Springer-Verlag LNCS 452.

[Darondeau & Degano 1990ii] P. Darondeau, P. Degano, *Atomic Refinement in Process Description Languages*. Manuscript, Dipartimento di Informatica, Università degli Studi di Pisa.

[Davies & Schneider 1989] J. Davies, S. Schneider, *An introduction to timed CSP*. Technical Monograph Number 75, Oxford University Computing Laboratory.

[Degano et al. 1987] P. Degano, R. de Nicola, U. Montanari, CCS is an (augmented) contact-free C/E system. In M. Venturini-Zilli (Ed.), *Mathematical Models for the Semantics of Parallelism*. Springer-Verlag LNCS 280.

[Degano et al. 1988] P. Degano, R. de Nicola, U. Montanari, On the consistency of truly concurrent operational and denotational semantics. In the *Proceedings of LICS 1988*, Pp. 133–141.

[Gaifman 1989] H. Gaifman, Modelling Concurrency by Partial Orders and Nonlinear Transition Systems. In [de Bakker et al. 1989].

[van Glabbeek & Goltz 1990] R. van Glabbeek, U. Goltz, *Refinement of Actions in Causality Based Models*. In J. de Bakker et al. (Eds.), *Stepwise Refinement of Distributed Systems*, (REX 1989), Springer-Verlag LNCS 430.

[van Glabbeek & Vaandrager 1987] R. van Glabbeek & F. Vaandrager, Petri Net models for algebraic theories of concurrency. In de Bakker, Nijman, Treleaven (Eds.), *Proceedings of the PARLE conference*, Springer-Verlag LNCS 259.

[Goltz 1990] U. Goltz, *CCS and Petri Nets*. Arbeitspapiere der GMD 467, Gesellschaft für Mathematik und Dataverarbeitung, St. Augustin.

[Goltz & Mycroft 1984] U. Goltz, A. Mycroft, On the relationship of CCS and Petri Nets. In the *Proceedings of the 11th ICALP*, Springer-Verlag LNCS 172.

[Hennessy 1988] M. Hennessy, Axiomatising Finite Concurrent Processes. In the *SIAM Journal of Computing*, Volume 17, Number 5, Pp. 997–1017.

[Hennessy & Regan 1990] M. Hennessy, T. Regan, *A Temporal Process Algebra*. Technical Report 2/90, Department of Computer Science, University of Sussex.

[Joseph & Goswami 1985] M. Joseph, A. Goswami, *Relating Computation and Time*. Report RR 138, Department of Computer Science, Warwick University.

[Josephs & Udding 1990] M. Josephs, J. Udding, Delay–insensitive circuits: an algebraic approach to their design. In J. Baeten, J. Klop (Eds.), *CONCUR '90*. Springer-Verlag LNCS 458.

[Keller 1974] R. Keller, The Formal Verification of Parallel Programs. In the *Communications of the ACM*, Volume 17, Number 7.

[Kwiatkowska et al. 1990] M. Kwiatkowska, M. Shields, R. Thomas (Eds.) *Semantics for Concurrency*, Springer-Verlag Workshops in Computing Series.

[Lamport 1985] L. Lamport, What it means for a concurrent program to satisfy a specification: why no one has specified priority. In the *Proceeding of the 12th ACM Symposium on the Principles of Programming Languages*, Pp. 78–83.

[Lauer 1984] P. Lauer, The COSY Approach to Distributed Computing Systems. In D. Duce (Ed.), *Distributed Computing Systems Program*, Peregrinus.

[Martin 1986] A. Martin, Compiling Communicating Processes into Delay Insensitive VLSI Circuits. In *Distributed Computing*, Volume 1, Pp. 226–234.

[Meseguer & Montanari 1988] J. Meseguer, U. Montanari, Petri Nets are Monoids: A new algebraic foundation for Net theory. In *Proceedings of LICS 1988*, Pp. 155–164.

[Milner 1989] R. Milner, *Communication and concurrency*. International series on computer science, Prentice Hall International.

[Murphy 1989] D. Murphy, *Time, causality, and concurrency*. Ph.D. Thesis, Department of Mathematics, University of Surrey, 1989.

[Murphy 1990] D. Murphy, Approaching a Real-Timed Concurrency Theory. In [Kwiatkowska et al. 1990].

[Olderog 1987] E-R. Olderog Operational Net Semantics for CCSP. In G. Rozenberg (Ed.), *Advances in Petri Nets 1987*, Springer-Verlag LNCS 266.

[Olderog 1988] E-R. Olderog, *Nets, terms and formulas*. Manuscript, Institut für Informatik und Praktische Mathematik, Christian-Albrechts-Universität, Kiel. To appear, M.I.T. Press. A preliminary version appears in [de Bakker et al. 1989].

[Pnueli 1985] A. Pnueli, Linear and Branching Structures in the Semantics and Logics of Reactive Systems. In W. Brauer (Ed.), *Proceedings of the 12th ICALP*. Springer-Verlag LNCS 194.

[Plotkin 1981] G. Plotkin, *A structural approach to operational semantics*. Report DAIMI FN-19, Computer Science Department, University of Aarhus.

[Quemada & Fernandez 1987] J. Quemada, A. Fernandez, Introduction of Quantitative Relative Time into LOTOS. In H. Rudin, C. Wood (Eds.), *Protocol Specification, Verification and Testing VII*. North Holland.

[Ramchandan 1974] C. Ramchandan, *Analysis of asynchronous concurrent systems by timed Petri nets*. Ph.D. Thesis, M.I.T., Project MAC TRI20.

[Reisig 1985] W. Reisig, *Petri Nets: An Introduction*. EATCS Monographs on theoretical computer science, Springer-Verlag, 1985.

[Roncken & Gerth 1990] M. Roncken, R. Gerth, A Denotational Semantics for Synchronous and Asynchronous Behaviour with Multiform Time. In [Kwiatkowska et al. 1990].

[Sahner & Trivedi 1987] R. Sahner, K. Trivedi, Performance Analysis and Reliability Analysis using Directed Acyclic Graphs. In the *IEEE Transactions on Software Engineering*, Volume SE-13, Number 10.

[Shields 1987] M. Shields, Algebraic models of parallelism and net theory. In Voss et al. (Eds.), *Concurrency and Nets*, Springer-Verlag.

[Shields 1990] M. Shields, *Elements of a theory of parallelism*. Manuscript, Electrical Engineering Laboratory, University of Kent. To appear, M.I.T. Press.

[Stark 1989] E. Stark, Concurrent Transition Systems. In *Theoretical Computer Science*, Volume 64, Pp. 221-269.

[Taubner 1989] D. Taubner, *Finite representations of CCS and TCSP programs by automata and nets*. Springer-Verlag LNCS 369.

[Vogler 1990] W. Vogler, Bisimulation and Action Refinement. Technical Report 342/10/90A, Institut für Informatik, Technische Universität München.

[Winskel 1989] G. Winskel, An introduction to Event Structures. In [de Bakker et al. 1989].

[Winskel 1984] G. Winskel, Synchronisation Trees. In *Theoretical Computer Science*, Volume 34, Pp. 33-84.

Author Index

Also in this series

AI and Cognitive Science '89, Dublin City University, Eire, 14–15 September 1989
A. F. Smeaton and G. McDermott (Eds.)

Specification and Verification of Concurrent Systems, University of Stirling, Scotland, 6–8 July 1988
C. Rattray (Ed.)

Semantics for Concurrency, Proceedings of the International BCS-FACS Workshop, Sponsored by Logic for IT (S.E.R.C.), University of Leicester, UK, 23–25 July 1990
M. Z. Kwiatkowska, M. W. Shields and R. M. Thomas (Eds.)

Functional Programming, Glasgow 1989, Proceedings of the 1989 Glasgow Workshop, Fraserburgh, Scotland, 21–23 August 1989
K. Davis and J. Hughes (Eds.)

Persistent Object Systems, Proceedings of the Third International Workshop, Newcastle, Australia, 10–13 January 1989
J. Rosenberg and D. Koch (Eds.)

Z User Workshop, 1989, Proceedings of the Fourth Annual Z User Meeting, Oxford, 15 December 1989
J. E. Nicholls (Ed.)

Formal Methods for Trustworthy Computer Systems (FM89), Halifax, Canada, 23–27 July 1989
Dan Craigen (Editor) and Karen Summerskill (Assistant Editor)

Security and Persistence, Proceedings of the International Workshop on Computer Architecture to Support Security and Persistence of Information, Bremen, West Germany, 8–11 May 1990
John Rosenberg and J. Leslie Keedy (Eds.)

Women into Computing: Selected Papers 1988–1990
Gillian Lovegrove and Barbara Segal (Eds.)

3rd Refinement Workshop (organised by BCS-FACS, and sponsored by IBM UK Laboratories, Hursley Park and the Programming Research Group, University of Oxford), 9–11 January 1990, Hursley Park
Caroll Morgan and J. C. P. Woodcock (Eds.)

Designing Correct Circuits, Workshop jointly organised by the Universities of Oxford and Glasgow, 26–28 September 1990, Oxford
Geraint Jones and Mary Sheeran (Eds.)

Functional Programming, Glasgow 1990, Proceedings of the 1990 Glasgow Workshop on Functional Programming, Ullapool, Scotland, 13–15 August 1990
Simon L. Peyton Jones, Graham Hutton and Carsten Kehler Holst (Eds.)

Software Re-use, Utrecht 1989, Proceedings of the Software Re-use Workshop, Utrecht, The Netherlands, 23–24 November 1989
Liesbeth Dusink and Patrick Hall (Eds.)

AI and Cognitive Science '90, University of Ulster at Jordanstown, 20–21 September 1990
Michael F. McTear and Norman Creaney (Eds.)